Financial Management

SECOND EDITION

Stephen H. Archer
Atkinson Graduate School of Management
Willamette University

G. Marc Choate
Atkinson Graduate School of Management
Willamette University

George Racette
University of Oregon

John Wiley & Sons

New York   Chichester   Brisbane   Toronto   Singapore

Cover design by Kevin J. Murphy

Library of Congress Cataloging in Publication Data

Archer, Stephen Hunt.
   Financial management.

   Includes bibliographies and index.
   1. Business enterprises—Finance. 2. Corporations—
Finance. I. Choate, G. Marc. II. Racette, George.
III. Title. IV. Series.

HG4026.A745 1983   658.1'5   82-23890
ISBN 0-471-09001-8

Printed in the United States of America

10 9 8 7 6 5 4 3 2

To Lana, Conch, and Susan

About the Authors

Steve Archer is the Guy F. Atkinson Professor of finance at Willamette University's Atkinson Graduate School of Administration at Salem, Oregon. He also taught at the University of Washington for a number of years, where he was also Chairman of the Department of Finance, Business Economics and Quantitative Methods. He has taught graduate and undergraduate courses in corporation finance, investments, and international finance. He has served as consultant to financial and industrial firms as well as government and educational institutions in the Northwest.

A native of Minnesota, where he earned his Ph.D., he is now active in the Financial Management Association, Western Finance Association, and the American Institute of Decision Sciences. He was a recent President of the Financial Management Association and recently Treasurer of the American Institute of Decision Sciences. He was founder and editor of the *Journal of Financial and Quantitative Analysis*. He has served on the Editorial Board of the *Journal of Finance and Economic Perspectives*. Many articles have appeared in professional journals. He has written *Introduction to Mathematics for Business Analysis* (with Robert Meier) in 1960, *Business Finance: Theory and Management* (with Charles D'Ambrosio) in 1966 (revised 1972), *The Theory of Finance* (with Charles D'Ambrosio) in 1967 (revised in 1976 and 1983) and *Portfolio Analysis* (with Jack Francis) in 1971 and revised for 1979.

G. Marc Choate is a professor of finance at the Atkinson School of Administration, Willamette University at Salem, Oregon. He has also taught at the University of Massachusetts at Amherst and the University of Washington at Seattle. Dr. Choate has taught graduate and undergraduate courses in corporate finance, monetary theory, macroeconomics and microeconomics.

Raised in Seattle, Professor Choate earned his Ph.D. in Finance from the University of Washington. He is a member of the American Finance Association, Financial Management Association and Western Finance

Association. He has authored articles for professional journals and has actively engaged in educational activity in hospital financial management. He also acts as a consultant to the health care industry.

George Racette is an associate professor of finance at the University of Oregon. He received his Ph.D. from the University of Washington at Seattle. He has taught at the University of Washington, Purdue University, and Ohio State University. Professor Racette has instructed graduate and undergraduate courses in business finance, financial theory, investments, and valuation of firms. Special research interests include the theory of financing and investment policy and valuation of closely-held firms. Papers he has written have appeared in major academic journals.

Preface

In this second edition we have made significant changes in organization and mode of presentation. However, even though we completely rewrote about three-fourths of the book, we maintained the view of the first edition that a survey text should expose the student to the fundamental tools and concepts that comprise the heart of the subject. We continue to believe that students should be viewed as intelligent individuals who are quite capable of grasping the logic underlying the fundamental principles of finance if that logic is presented in a coherent manner.

No instructor expects to have all of his or her students become experts in finance; on the contrary, most will not. Yet a student understanding the logic, structure, and orientation of the subject at a basic level will be in a better position to build upon that beginning either in more advanced courses or through work experience once the classroom is left behind. For this reason, this book emphasizes key concepts and tools within a framework of reasoning—with the understanding that future application will require *practice* in using the tools and, more important, *imagination* in knowing when and how the tools should be applied.

This emphasis on concepts, tools, and reasoning carries some clear pedagogical advantages. Generally we have found that when students understand concepts and the framework of reasoning in which they are linked, such knowledge is retained longer than when purely descriptive material has been committed, rather temporarily, to memory. Second, the necessity of avoiding more ethereal levels of abstraction means that a problem orientation is necessary in a basic course both to hold the interest of the student and to convey the essential concepts, tools, and reasoning.

Accordingly, a major difference between this and other textbooks is the extensive inclusion, integration, and application of the conceptual foundations of finance. Yet, we avoid as much as possible the inclusion of theory without showing appropriate applications. While quickly involving the student in the problems facing the financial decision-maker, the first two chapters are a much smaller hurdle for both students and instructor than were the General Introduction and Chapters 1 to 3 in the first edition. We have sacrificed some of the completeness of these chapters of the first edition for a more streamlined presentation that quickly leads the student to Chapters 3 to 5 where discussions of financial markets, risk and required return, and compound rate of return appear. This discussion leads directly into five chapters (Chapters 6 to 10), which deal with the investment decision rather than the more demanding and time-consuming material on firm valuation and capital structure that followed in the first edition. We have found that this revised sequence allows students to become more comfortable with discounting and present value analysis before they face the more demanding logic of firm valuation, financing policy, and cost of capital that appear in Chapters 11 to 16. Within this topic area Chapter 13 presents an up-to-date discussion of personal taxes, bankruptcy, and adverse incentives, which we tried to make intelligible to introductory students. The special topics of leasing, growth by acquisition, and inflation are treated in Chapters 17, 18, and 19, respectively. Chapters 20 to 24 consider noncapital expenditure decisions—the level, mix, and financing of current assets. Although this organization deviates from that of many textbooks because it delays consideration of noncapital expenditure decisions until the latter part of the text, we feel that such decisions will make more sense and therefore be more readily understood *after* the student has been exposed to the basic financial tools and objectives. Finally, Chapter 25 concludes the book with a discussion of the special problems arising in international transactions.

Within the limits of practicality, we have tried to make this text an integrated whole. Still, some material can be omitted from a course plan depending on the time available, the preparation of the audience, and the objective of the course. For example, Chapters 17 on leasing, 18 on growth through acquisition, 19 on inflation, and 25 on international finance could be omitted with no integrative loss. Also, the last half of Chapter 9 on the economic life of an asset could be withheld from the course plan. An instructor who wishes to place more emphasis on short-term financing and investment decisions might wish to use Chapters 1 to 8, 11, and 16, then turn to Chapters 20 to 24, which develop the concepts underlying those decisions. As an example of additional flexibility, Chapters 20 to 25 could be dropped to make the course shorter or to emphasize the capital expenditure and financing decision sections while postponing discussion of short-term financing and investment decisions until a second course. Also, Chapters 4 to 10 could form the core of a capital budgeting oriented course.

Our presentation of purely descriptive material is also rather different from many other books in that we place this material in appendices to some chapters. This organization is not a downgrading of the importance of descriptive material. Rather, it is designed to let the analysis, the line of reasoning, proceed without distracting, but interesting, digressions. It is our view that not all introductory students need to cover elements of the descriptive material since they often encounter them in other courses in the typical undergraduate or graduate curriculum. For such students, the appendices are a useful resource to refresh their knowledge. For students unfamiliar with some definitions and descriptions, the appendices are an efficient way of providing that information. Consequently, the book can be used without appendices or with selected appendices, depending on instructor preferences.

The book is relatively comprehensive and (including the appendices) encyclopedic. Although prerequisite courses are not a must, most students in a business or public administration program who have been exposed to introductory economics, accounting, and statistics will find the opportunity to build on this knowledge. The text is not mathematically rigorous and needless technical apparatus has been purged. Only elementary algebra is used. Glossaries and summaries have been provided at the end of each chapter to reinforce the learning process. For the same reason, questions and problems have been included. An Instructor's Guide is available.

In preparing this revision we received suggestions from many individuals. Reviewers Fred Kaen and Robert Jennings offered both encouragement and criticism. Galen Hite provided forceful advice. He had a clear point of view and was willing to take the time and effort to put that view on paper. Because he grew impatient with many books that botched analysis of leasing decisions, Mike Hopewell provided forceful impetus for us to try to get it right. We hope that our efforts are not far off the mark. To those anonymous individuals who answered a questionnaire from our publisher we offer thanks. We studied the responses carefully and tried to incorporate many good suggestions that were given to us. In addition to preparing many creative, new questions and problems that appear in this edition, Dorothy Koehl offered numerous suggestions for revision and clarity. In offering advice she always kept student needs foremost in mind. Our editor, Richard Esposito, was patient, refrained from harassment, and kept his cool when we lagged behind schedule. Finally, we thank several typists who suffered through our sometimes illegible drafts—Lana Jo Archer, Nola Ventura, and Cora Snow.

Even with the help of all of the above people, writing and revising are lonely jobs. We could not satisfy everyone and knew that it would be foolish to try to do so in an area where preferences are so diverse. Our goal was to offer an improvement over the first edition. Users of the text can judge whether we were successful.

Stephen H. Archer
G. Marc Choate
George Racette

Contents

SECTION I   **Some Essentials**   **1**

1. An Introduction   **3**

Elements of Finance   4
Investment and Financing Decisions   9
Financial Markets and Investor Wealth   10
The Goal of Financial Decisions: Maximization of
    Owners' Wealth   11
An Overview of the Rest of the Book   13
Glossary of Key Terms   14
Questions and Problems   15

2. An Introduction to Financial Decisions   **18**

Harris Company: The Initial Condition   18
Expected Rate of Return and Risk   22
Wealth Consequences of the Initial Investment and
    Financing Decisions   26
Financial Leverage   26
Business and Financial Risk   30
Summary   36
Glossary of Key Terms   38
Questions and Problems   39
Appendix 2A Forms of Business Organization   45
Appendix 2B The Structure of the Larger Firm   49
Appendix 2C Income Tax Rates   54

SECTION II   **Markets, Risk and Rates of Return**   **57**

3. Financial Markets   **59**

Types of Markets   60
Perfect Markets   64

The Equal Rate of Return Principle		65
Market Imperfections		67
Efficient Markets		72
Summary		73
Glossary of Key Terms		74
Selected References		75
Questions and Problems		75
Appendix 3A Types of Financial Securities		77
Appendix 3B Investment Banking		83

4.   Markets, Diversification, and Required Rates of Return   **91**

Single Period Expected Rate of Return and Standard Deviation	92
The Dominance Principle	92
Effect of Diversification on Risk: A Two-Security Portfolio	94
Diversification with Many Risky Securities	101
Diversification Including a Risk-Free Security	102
Risk of a Single Security	104
Required Rate of Return and Risk	111
Summary	117
Glossary of Key Terms	118
Selected References	119
Questions and Problems	119

5.   Time and Compound Returns   **124**

Compound Rate of Return and Future Value	126
Present Value	132
Internal Rate of Return	140
Some Special Uses of Compounding Tables	144
Capital Budgeting: Net Present Value and Internal Rate of Return Methods	146
Summary	149
Glossary of Key Terms	152
Selected References	152
Questions and Problems	153

SECTION III   Investment Decisions   **159**

6.   The Capital Budgeting Process   **161**

An Overview	162
Planning Phase	164

Evaluation Phase   169
Selection Phase   178
Implementation Phase   179
Control Phase   180
Auditing Phase   181
Summary   181
Glossary of Key Terms   182
Selected References   183
Questions and Problems   184

7.   Selection of Investment Projects   188

Net Present Value   189
Internal Rate of Return   197
Comparing NPV and IRR Methods   199
Payback Method   210
Accounting Rate of Return   213
Investment Criteria in Use   214
Summary   215
Glossary of Key Terms   216
Selected References   217
Questions and Problems   217

8.   Cash Flow Analysis for Investments   222

The Incremental After-tax Cash Flows   222
Constructing Cash Flows for Cost-Saving Investment
   Projects   224
Constructing Cash Flows for Revenue-Expanding Projects   231
Some Important Errors   236
Summary   244
Glossary of Key Terms   246
Selected References   247
Questions and Problems   247
Appendix 8A   The Impact of Depreciation Methods on
   Present Value   251
Appendix 8B   The Investment Tax Credit   253

9.   Unequal and Economic Life Investment Problems   255

The Problem of Unequal Lives   255
Determining the Economic Life of an Investment   265
Summary   273
Glossary of Key Terms   274
Selected References   275
Questions and Problems   275

10. Determining the Capital Budget   278

The Capital Budget: No Constraints on the Availability of
    Capital   279
The Capital Budget: A Constraint on the Availability of
    Capital   282
The Causes of Capital Constraints   288
Other Managerial Practices that Create Problems   291
Summary   294
Glossary of Key Terms   294
Selected References   295
Questions and Problems   295

SECTION IV **Valuation and Financing Decisions**   299

11. Valuation   301

The J. C. Layton Valuation Problem   302
Value   303
Valuation of Securities   308
The Value of the Firm   322
Summary   324
Glossary of Key Terms   325
Selected References   326
Questions and Problems   326
Appendix 11A   Failure, Bankruptcy, and Reorganization   331
Appendix 11B   Valuing an Option   336

12. Capital Structure and the Cost of Capital   342

Capital Structure: Perfect Markets and No Income Taxes   343
Capital Structure: Perfect Markets with Income Taxes   355
Summary   361
Glossary of Key Terms   363
Selected References   364
Questions and Problems   364

**13. Additional Influences on the Capital Structure
       Decision**   369

Perfect Markets with Corporate and Personal Taxes   370
Financial Distress and Bankruptcy   380
Bondholder–Shareholder Conflicts of Interest   384
Finding an Optimal Capital Structure   391
Summary   392

Glossary of Key Terms 394
Selected References 395
Questions and Problems 396

14. Dividend Policy 399

The Barfield Case 399
The Argument That Dividend Policy Is Irrelevant 402
Personal Taxes, Market Imperfections, and Dividend Policy 406
The Barfield Problem 415
Dividend Mechanics 421
Inflation and Dividend Policy 421
Stock Dividends and Stock Splits 422
Stock Repurchase as a Method of Distributing Cash and
   Information 424
Summary 427
Glossary of Key Terms 428
Selected References 429
Questions and Problems 429

15. Steps for Estimating the Cost of Capital of the Firm 434

Introduction to the Issues: Zuber Milling Case 435
Step 1: Capital Structure and the Cost of Capital 437
Step 2: Estimating the Cost of Each Source of Funds 441
Step 3: Computing the Cost of Capital of the Firm 441
Zuber Milling's Revised Cost of Capital Procedures 442
Summary 443
Glossary of Key Terms 444
Selected References 445
Questions and Problems 445

16. Estimating the Marginal Cost of Capital 447

Valuation and Risk-Return Methods for Estimating Costs of
   Individual Financing Sources 448
Cost of Debt Financing 448
Cost of Preferred Stock Financing 451
Cost of Common Stock Financing 451
Cost of Retained Earnings 459
Estimating the Marginal Cost of Capital for the Firm 460
Estimating the Marginal Cost of Capital for Investment
   Proposals of Differing Business Risk 464
Summary 468
Glossary of Key Terms 469

Selected References   469
Questions and Problems   470
Appendix 16A   Computing Beta and k_e for a Firm   472
Appendix 16B   Estimating k_e from a Comparable Firm   475

SECTION V   **Leasing, Combining Firms, and Inflation**   479

17.   Leasing   481

Types of Lease Arrangements   482
Alleged Advantages of Leasing or Buying   483
Leasing, Borrowing, and Corporate Capital Structure   487
The Choice Between Lease and Purchase Alternatives   490
Summary   500
Glossary of Key Terms   501
Selected References   502
Questions and Problems   503
Appendix 17A   Derivation of the Leasing Model   505
Appendix 17B   Verification of the Equivalent Loan   508

18.   Combining Firms and Internal Expansion   510

Types of External Expansion   511
Comparison of Internal and External Expansion: Jorgenson
    Company   511
An Analysis of Reasons for Acquisition   517
Price of an Acquisition   526
Summary   529
Glossary of Key Terms   531
Selected References   531
Questions and Problems   532
Appendix 18A   Business Combinations: Legal and
    Accounting   535

19.   Inflation and Financial Decisions   538

Nominal Dollars, Real Dollars, and Purchasing Power
    Losses   538
Investment Returns, Inflation, and Purchasing Power Risk   540
Expected Inflation and Required Rates of Return   541
Purchasing Power Risk and Market Value   548
Implications for Financial Decisions   549
Expected Inflation and the Cost of Capital   549

Capital Budgeting Decisions and Expected Inflation   552
Summary   558
Glossary of Key Terms   559
Selected References   560
Questions and Problems   561

SECTION VI   **Financial Analysis and Working Capital**   563

20.   Financial Analysis and Planning   565

Financial Analysis and Planning   565
The Ambiguity of Financial Ratios   568
Financial Ratios for Winn Company and the Calculator
  Industry   568
Liquidity Analysis by Ratios: Winn Company Compared to
  the Industry   570
Leverage Analysis by Ratios: Winn Company Compared to
  the Industry   575
Profitability Analysis by Ratios: Winn Company Compared
  to the Industry   577
Ratio Analysis of Winn Company Compared to the
  Industry: A Recapitulation   585
Ratio Analysis of Winn Company Over Time   586
Financial Planning of Operating Performance and Condition
  by Use of Ratios   588
Distorting Effects of Accounting Practice and Inflation on
  Financial Ratios   591
Sources of Financial Ratios   593
Summary   594
Glossary of Key Terms   595
Selected References   596
Questions and Problems   596

21.   Working Capital Management   600

Some Terminology   603
Why Firms Invest in Current Assets   604
Variation in the Level of Current Asset Investment   609
Current Asset Financing Sources   611
Working Capital Management and Shareholder Wealth
  Maximization   614
Summary   618
Glossary of Key Terms   619

Selected References   620
Questions and Problems   621

22. Management of Liquid Assets   625

Total, Seasonal, Intramonthly, and Random Variation of Net
    Cash Flow   626
The Cash Budget   628
Minimum Liquid Asset Balances   633
Nonoperating Liquid Asset Balance Management   640
The Borrowing Alternative   642
The Mix of Liquid Asset Holdings   643
Cash Flow Management   646
Summary   650
Glossary of Key Terms   651
Selected References   652
Questions and Problems   653

23. Receivables and Inventory Management   657

Receivables Management   658
Inventory Management   671
Summary   676
Glossary of Key Terms   677
Selected References   678
Questions and Problems   678

24. Financing Current Assets   683

The Proportion of Short- and Long-Term Financing   683
Unsecured Forms of Short-Term Financing   693
Secured Forms of Short-Term Financing   704
Choosing Among Short-Term Financing Sources   710
Summary   713
Glossary of Key Terms   715
Selected References   716
Questions and Problems   716

SECTION VII   **International**   721

25. International Finance   723

Some Basics of Exchange Rates   723
Equilibrium Exchange Rates   727
Causes of Interest Rate Differentials Between Countries   733

Equilibrium Exchange Rates: Some Final Comments   **736**
International Financial Management   **736**
Summary   **745**
Glossary of Key Terms   **746**
Selected References   **747**
Questions and Problems   **748**

Appendices   751

Index   761

SECTION I

Some Essentials

CHAPTER 1

An Introduction

This book is about **finance** and financial management. No brief definition of any field of study can ever fully capture the scope of that field. Our definition of finance should be seen as an aid to *beginning* an inquiry into the field: finance is the study of how a present, known amount of cash is converted into a future, perhaps unknown amount of cash. Financial management concerns decisions made within this field—such decisions are defined in this chapter and more thoroughly investigated in later chapters.

To provide the flavor of the range of financial decisions without stopping to define terms or explain matters in detail, consider the following press announcements concerning Calray Corporation.

1. Calray announces plans to build new chemical plant in Springfield.

2. Calray to raise $30 million through sale of 10-year bonds; Fleet and Fleet to act as underwriter.

3. Calray to repurchase its own outstanding preferred stock.

4. Calray to close Redfield plant for 6 months (renovation and modernization program).

5. Calray completes lease financing arrangements with group of New York banks.

6. Wiggin Industries to be acquired by Calray for an undisclosed amount of cash.

7. Dividend increase to 12 cents per share announced by Calray.

Although perhaps not obvious in all cases, these announcements reflect financial decisions encompassed by our definition of finance.

We begin our study on a more basic level by introducing the elements of finance: *cash, time, risk,* and *expected return.* With these elements in hand, we can introduce investment and financing decisions made by business firms, the focal point for decision making in this book. We will then see how financial markets act to *value* investment and financing decisions and to identify the subsequent effect of those decisions on the wealth of the owners of the firm. The underlying goal of financial decisions—to maximize the wealth of owners—is defined and discussed. That discussion is followed by an overview of what is covered in subsequent chapters.

ELEMENTS OF FINANCE

The elements of finance are cash, time, risk, and expected return. These will be illustrated in the context of an investment and an individual investor. An investment is the sacrifice of *present cash* with the prospect of receiving higher amounts of *future cash.* A person making that current sacrifice is an investor. The following investments are used to illustrate elements of finance.

1. Purchasing a $1000 insured savings certificate from a bank with the prospect of redeeming it for a larger total amount 1 year later.

2. Loaning $1000 to a friend who promises to repay a higher total amount 1 year later. This constitutes purchase of an IOU from the friend. Every loan, of course, involves not only a lender but a **borrower.**[1]

3. Purchasing a small coal mine for $3 million, with the intent of working it over a 3 year span of time until it is uneconomic to operate the mine. Total cash proceeds from sale of coal are expected to exceed the $3 million originally invested.

Cash

Individuals and investors usually own **assets,** things perceived to have value by the owner and others. Your pencil sharpener and stereo system are assets. And once undertaken, the investments described above—a savings certificate, an IOU from a friend, or a coal mine—all involve owning assets. Cash too is an asset having its own unique characteristics.

Cash is the medium of exchange, an asset generally acceptable as

---

[1]Terms in boldface type are defined in the glossary at the end of the chapter in which they appear.

means of payment for goods and services. It is also generally accepted as the means of settling debts. For example, it is necessary to pay for a market basket of groceries with cash, not a used but valuable fishing rod. And it happens that repayment of $20 borrowed from a friend will usually take the form of $20 cash, not a sweater coveted by that friend.

Examples of cash include coin, currency, and account balances at financial institutions that can be directly transferred to another party by means of a check or draft. Deposits in a checking account represent such balances. Note that the three investments are assets but they are not cash. This is obvious for the loan to a friend and the coal mine, but it remains true for the savings certificate. The certificate is *near* cash in that it can be redeemed before the year is up and the proceeds can be used for payments to others. But the certificate itself cannot be transferred as means of payment.

Investment involves initial *conversion* of present cash into another asset form (a savings certificate, an IOU from a friend, or a coal mine) with subsequent *reconversion* to cash (redemption of the certificate, repayment by the friend, operation of the coal mine and sale of coal). This process of conversion and reconversion is fundamental to all investments.

Time

The element of time is also common to investment. There is a delay between the present time at which an investment is undertaken and the date at which future cash is received upon reconversion. Although time is continuous, it is often convenient to work with discrete **intervals of time**: minutes, hours, days, months, or years. Figure 1-1 represents a time line showing how continuous time is broken into three intervals. The intervals of time are represented by T and the **points in time** separating them by t. For example, T_1 describes the interval between points in time $t = 0$ and $t = 1$; T_2 is the interval between points in time $t = 1$ and $t = 2$. When an investment is being considered by an investor, time $t = 0$ is always the *present* point in time.

Using the three investments as examples, suppose that the present time, $t = 0$, is October 3, 1983. The designated interval of time is 1 year, or, an annual interval. The savings certificate investment is a **single**

Figure 1-1   *A Time Line*

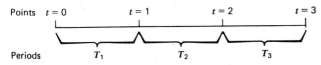

period investment, since the certificate will be redeemed 1 year hence on October 3, 1984. The loan to a friend is also a single period investment, whereas the coal mine is a **multiperiod investment;** the loan will be repaid with cash 1 year hence, whereas the mined coal will be sold for cash each year for 3 years. The distinction between single and multiperiod investments is important to keep in mind.

Of what significance is time to investment? Simply this: when an investment is made, the investor must *sacrifice* present consumption of goods and services that could have been enjoyed if the investment had not been undertaken. The $1000 needed to purchase either the savings certificate or the IOU of a friend *could* have been used to purchase food, clothing, or transportation. As it is, the investor must wait until the investment has been reconverted to cash before these additional comforts can be enjoyed. Investors *as a group* dislike having to defer present consumption plans. They will do so but, as we will see, they must be compensated for such a postponement.

Risk Many investments are risky. At the time such investments are made, the total amount to be received upon reconversion is unknown. The investor may have an estimate, a best guess, of total cash to be received, but he or she cannot be certain of that amount. In contrast, some investments are **risk-free investments.** At the time of investment, the investor *knows* the total amount of cash to be received; there is no chance that the total amount to be received will differ from this known amount.

The savings certificate is a risk-free investment because it is insured. Therefore, if the certificate states that it may be redeemed 1 year hence for $1100, the U.S. Government guarantees that $1100 will be paid. There is no chance that an amount greater or less than $1100 will be repaid.

In contrast, both the loan to a friend and coal mine investments are subject to risk. Suppose that the friend *promises* to repay you $1400 1 year hence. But knowing the friend, the investor recognizes that *less* than this promised total may be received. The investor's best guess is that the friend will repay $1300 in 1 year. But it is possible that the friend will repay the $1400 promised, or only $500.

Possible Total Repayment from Loan to a Friend

$1400

$1300

$500

The investor cannot know which of these outcomes will occur at the time of investment; the loan to a friend is risky.

Before investing in the coal mine, the individual *expects* to receive $5 million in cash proceeds from sale of coal over 3 years. However, he also recognizes that only $2 million, or as much as $8 million, might be received.

Possible Total Cash Received from Coal Mine

$8 million

$5 million

$2 million

The investor cannot, at time of investment, know which total cash receipt will occur; the coal mine investment is risky.

Risk is of significance to investors because it is an unattractive aspect of investing. Other things equal, investors prefer less risk to more risk. Investors *will* bear risk by undertaking risky investments, but they must expect **compensation** for bearing that risk. Otherwise a risky investment will be rejected.

The difference between the total cash expected to be received from investment and the cash originally invested is the **expected return** from investment. For the three investments, the expected returns are:

Expected Return

	Expected Cash Receipts	Less	Cash Investment	Equals	Expected Return
Savings Certificate	$1100		$1000		$100
Loan to Friend	$1300		$1000		$300
Coal Mine	$5 million		$3 million		$2 million

These expected returns reflect compensation for deferred consumption *and*, with the risky loan and coal mine investments, for risk bearing.

The differences in expected return between the savings certificate and the loan to a friend illustrate additional compensation for bearing risk. Both require a $1000 investment, but the risky loan to a friend provides an expected return of $300 rather than $100. Of that $300, a $100 portion is therefore compensation for delayed consumption and the remaining $200 is expected compensation for risk bearing. Since investors dislike risk, they will not undertake risky investments without sufficient expected return as compensation for that risk. For example, the investor would not make the loan to a friend for a total expected payment of

$1100 and an expected return of $100. The return would compensate only for delayed consumption, not for risk bearing.

Generally speaking, the longer consumption is delayed, the greater must be the expected compensation for delayed consumption. For example, a 2-year risk-free savings certificate might promise a total of $1210 2 years hence for an expected and risk-free return of $210 to compensate for a consumption delay of 2 years. Similarly, the greater the risk associated with an investment, the greater must be expected return to compensate for the additional risk borne. If the loan to a friend could result in *no* repayment instead of $500 as a lower limit, the friend might be required to *promise* repayment of a *greater* amount, to provide additional compensation for the higher risk perceived.

It is important to distinguish expected returns from promised returns. A **promised return** is a formal commitment to pay a fixed return, no more and no less. The savings certificate promises a return of $100. The loan to a friend investment *promises* a return of $400 in the form of a signed IOU. If an investment is risk free, then promised and expected returns are always equal; the amount promised will always be paid (e.g., $100 for the savings certificate). With a risky investment, promised returns always exceed expected returns. The promised return represents an upper limit on returns. With some chance that less than the promised return will be paid, the expected return must be less than the promised return. Thus the promised return for the loan to a friend was $400 but the expected return was $300. Not all investments have specific promised returns. By its nature, the coal mine investment provides no promise of a cash receipt. Upper and lower limits on returns are unknown because the exact amount of coal, the price of coal, and the costs of mining are unknown.

It is also important to distinguish expected returns from realized returns. An expected return is an estimate of future returns. A **realized return** is the return actually received from investment. For risk-free investments, expected and realized returns are always the same. The insured savings certificate will pay a return of $100, no more or less, with certainty. The realized return will be $100 and equal to the expected return. With risky investments, the realized return may differ from that which was expected. For example, the loan to a friend investment had three possible repayments in 1 year: $1400, $1300, and $500. For a $1000 investment the possible returns are:

Possible Returns for the Loan to a Friend Investment

$$1400 - \$1000 = \$400$$
$$1300 - \$1000 = \$300$$
$$500 - \$1000 = -\$500$$

Only one of these returns will be realized: $400, $300, or a loss (negative return) of −$500. The investor might realize a $300 return but could also realize greater and smaller returns of $400 and −$500. The reader can verify that the risky coal mine investment, though having an expected return of $5 − $3 = $2 million, could result in *realized* returns of $5, $2, *or* −$1 million.

This new terminology allows us to offer a narrower definition of risk: it is the possibility that realized return may differ from expected return.

The elements of finance contained in these simple examples are present in more complex situations confronted by business firms. It is useful to categorize decisions having these elements as **investment** or **financing decisions;** together they constitute financial decisions made by business firms. The same categorization can apply to financial decisions made by individuals or not-for-profit organizations, but the business firm is our principal area of inquiry.

INVESTMENT AND FINANCING DECISIONS

Investment decisions involve the selection of assets to be used by the firm in generating future cash receipts. Among the types of decisions belonging to this category are: (1) Should the firm acquire a new plant to produce a new product? (2) Which competing types of equipment should be used in the new plant? (3) What is the optimal size of the new plant? Results of such decisions determine the assets owned and used by the firm in generating future cash receipts. Consistent with our initial definition of finance, investment decisions are concerned with present *expenditures* of cash being converted into future *receipts* of cash, all conducted in a risky environment.

Financing decisions involve the question of how to obtain cash to undertake investments. Firms can sell *claims* to the income stream generated by investments. Broadly viewed at this point, those claims can take one of two forms. Firms can either borrow funds from an external lender or solicit funds from owners of the firm (or owners to be!).

Borrowing of funds gives rise to **debt claims,** promises by the firm to repay the lender the amount borrowed plus a fixed promised return, known in this case as **interest.** Holders of debt have first claim on the firm's income stream. Realized returns on those claims may differ from expected returns but cannot exceed the upper limit posed by the fixed promised return.

Obtaining funds from owners gives rise to an **equity claim.** No promises to repay amounts obtained are given the owners. Rather, they are entitled to cash receipts left over after paying promised amounts to lenders. For owners, realized returns may differ from expected returns, but there is no upper limit on realized returns.

Firms can select alternative proportions of debt and equity financing to finance investments; the choice of a proportion, along with other yet unspecified characteristics, constitutes a financing decision. Financing decisions are also consistent with our definition of finance in that a present known amount of cash received will be converted into future cash, all in the context of risk.

Financial decisions made by firms must have some objective or goal. To understand that goal, we need to understand financial markets and their link to investor wealth.

FINANCIAL MARKETS AND INVESTOR WEALTH

We often think of a *market* as a place (or places) where assets are exchanged, especially cash for noncash assets by buyers and noncash assets for cash by sellers. However, a market is not so much a place as it is a system for facilitating transactions—a system of physical, moral, institutional, and legal relationships. A market incorporates buyers and sellers (but may also include middlemen who help arrange transactions between buyers and sellers), explicit and implicit rules governing the behavior of market participants, and communication devices to facilitate transactions and transmit information.

A **financial market** facilitates transactions in debt and equity claims on firms as well as debt claims on government. Some financial markets are better than others in that transactions there can be made quickly, easily, and at low cost. For example, commercial banks offer a market for debt claims on themselves; you purchase such a debt claim by depositing cash with the banks. Large organized markets such as the New York Stock Exchange offer market participants facilities to buy and sell equity claims on business firms. Other well-organized markets facilitate transactions in debt and equity claims. In contrast, the market for a loan to a friend, cited earlier, may be very poor. If you did not want to wait a year for repayment, you could attempt to sell the IOU, the debt claim on your friend, to another party. Such a buyer would receive the right to the risky promise of a $400 return. Your friend is not well known to others, and not all IOUs are the same. There may be few potential buyers of the IOU, thus limiting opportunities for a transaction.

Whether elaborate or primitive, financial markets place current **market values** on debt and equity claims. These values are indicated by the prices at which debt and equity claims to future cash receipts of firms are traded between buyers and sellers. (In the discussion of Chapter 3, market prices are consensus views on the current value of these future cash receipts.) Therefore, we can envision the market as sitting in judgment on financial decisions taken by firms and reflected in the expected

Figure 1-2   *Wealth, Markets, and Financial Decisions*

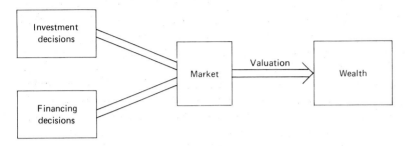

return and risk of debt and equity claims. A financial decision perceived by market participants as increasing the expected return or reducing risk of a debt or equity claim will cause an *increase* in market value of the claim. A decision seen as reducing expected return or increasing risk will provide a *reduction* in market value.

How are financial decisions and financial markets related to investor wealth? **Wealth** is defined as the *current* market value of assets. Financial decisions that cause markets to place a given market value on debt and equity claims also result in particular levels of wealth for investors owning assets in these forms. Financial decisions leading to a reduction in market value of debt and equity claims cause a reduction in wealth of investors. Decisions resulting in an increased market value produce an increase in investor wealth. The relation between financial decisions, markets, and investor wealth is represented in Figure 1-2.

THE GOAL OF FINANCIAL DECISIONS: MAXIMIZATION OF OWNERS' WEALTH

Investor wealth is a stockpile for present and future consumption expenditures. Like most people, investors prefer more present and future consumption expenditures to fewer. Therefore, they prefer more wealth to less wealth, a larger stockpile to a smaller one.

If individual investors want to maximize their wealth, it follows that business firms organized *by* and *for* the benefit of owners exist as means of maximizing wealth of the owners. And this is the goal of financial decision making in business firms: maximization of owners' wealth.

Objections to this goal may arise in the reader's mind. You may object strongly to the goal, perhaps to the extreme point of believing that firms should not receive the returns on investment giving rise to an increase in owner's wealth. If so, you are probably enrolled in the wrong course; you are certainly reading the wrong book. But you may well object on grounds of "realism." You may assert (rightly) that owners may have

other goals they wish to serve with their wealth, ranging from investment only in firms producing "socially desirable" products (e.g., no
tobacco or alcoholic beverages), using "socially desirable" (nonpollut-
ing) production methods to giving away some wealth to charity. Wealth
maximization is not inconsistent with these "realities." The "socially
conscious" owner can select socially conscious equity investments; once
selected, the wealth maximization goal can be served. And charitably
inclined owners should embrace wealth maximization because it will
permit giving more rather than less wealth to charity. Furthermore,
given diversity in owner preferences, wealth maximization is the *only*
financial goal common to owners.

A more serious objection may be lodged. Ownership of equity claims
in larger firms may involve loss of meaningful ownership control, such
control being effectively in the hands of the firm's chief officers. Uncon-
trolled decision makers may serve other goals such as making charitable
contributions demonstrating good corporate "citizenship" to customers
and employees. But such actions may actually be *indirect* means of
owner wealth maximization. They may preserve and expand the firm's
customer clientele and preserve a stable work force, reducing costly
employee turnover. As for actions by decision makers that blatantly *are*
inconsistent with owner wealth maximization, remember that the financial market and the market for managers sit in judgment on **financial
decisions.** Poor decisions lead to reduced market values of claims and
make it more difficult and (as we shall see) more expensive for firms to
obtain and maintain financing for conduct of operations. Periodic reading of *The Wall Street Journal* will show that executive tenure in business
firms experiencing financial difficulty is often remarkably short. The link
to financial markets and the market for managers may not always be
precise, and judgments may be delayed, but ultimately, these markets
will have their way if organizations are to prosper.

It can be argued that financial models based on owner wealth maximization lead to logical, internally consistent decision rules—rules and
implications that can be tested to see whether they explain behavior of
the market value of debt and equity claims. In fact, the empirical evidence supports the wealth maximization goal as a *positive* goal. If other
goals are sought, they do not appear to alter the results achieved by
assuming that wealth maximization is the goal of financial decision making. We are entitled to act *as if* firms sought solely to maximize shareholder wealth, even if a variety of other diverse goals are also sought
from time to time. Whatever these other goals may be, they are of little
help in explaining market evaluation of financial decisions.

We will see that for corporations, equity claims are divided into
shares of common stock. Therefore, we often refer to the shareholder

rather than owner wealth maximization goal. They are, of course, the same goal.

Finally, the person making financial decisions often is referred to as a **financial manager.** In smaller firms, this person may be either the owner or an employee hired to make these decisions. Larger firms have many individuals making the decisions of financial managers. We do not confront the task of coordinating many different individuals to act as if they were one person operating under logical decision rules to maximize owner's wealth. It is easier to talk of one person, "the" financial manager, who makes all financial decisions.

Future chapters develop investment and financing decisions in much greater detail. The next chapter, which completes the first section of the book, illustrates investment and financing decisions in a simplified form for a small firm. It also serves to introduce further issues, such as risk measurement and risk concepts relevant to market valuation of investment and financing decisions.

AN OVERVIEW OF THE REST OF THE BOOK

In Section II, three chapters focus on the role of markets in determining the relationships between risk and the rates of return required by investors to compensate them for delayed consumption and risk bearing. Notions of compound rate of return and present value are introduced at the end of the section.

With the onset of Section III, we are ready to begin making investment decisions as described by the term "capital budgeting decisions." These investments primarily concern longer lived assets such as plant and equipment. The five chapters in this section deal with investment decision rules, identifying appropriate cash expenditures and receipts for investments, finding and making adjustments to economic lives of investments, and determining the total expenditures to be made on investments.

Investments undertaken by the firm must be financed. Section IV contains one chapter on valuation and five chapters centered on the financing decision. Valuation of the firm's outstanding financial claims is illustrated in Chapter 11. Then the impact of the *mix* of debt and equity claims is discussed. Of central interest are the factors that affect the value-maximizing mix of these sources of funds. Dividend decisions and their implications for financing decisions are considered next. That analysis is followed by two chapters that focus on the problem of estimating required rates of returns to be used in evaluating specific investments.

Section V, which is somewhat briefer, addresses more specialized topics of leasing, growth by acquisition, and inflation.

In Section VI, five chapters take up the area of financial analysis and working capital management. Analytical tools for evaluating firms from their financial statements are introduced. There is a detailed discussion of investment in current assets and financing these assets using a variety of borrowing arrangements.

The last section consists of a single chapter on international finance. This treatment is essentially an introduction to the special aspects of financial decision making in an international setting.

Especially in the earlier chapters, the end-of-chapter glossaries are very important because of the large number of new terms being introduced. We suggest that the reader not move on to a new chapter without using the glossary in the preceding chapter to help organize definitions and concepts. Needless to say, the glossaries are also helpful for review purposes.

GLOSSARY OF KEY TERMS

Asset	Something owned and having value to the owner and others.
Borrower	A person, firm, or government selling a debt claim to a lender and promising to repay the loan plus a fixed return, called interest.
Cash	An asset having unique characteristics as generally accepted means of payment for goods and services and for settlement of debts.
Compensation	As used here, expected returns to investors in payment for delaying consumption of goods and services and for bearing risk.
Debt Claim	A promise to repay a loan plus a fixed return, called interest, by the borrower to the lender.
Equity Claim	A claim on a firm's cash receipts by the owner(s) of the firm. Equity claims are entitled to cash receipts after payment of promised amounts to holders of debt claims.
Expected Return	The excess of cash receipts over cash expenditures an investor expects to receive from investment.
Finance	The study of how a present, known amount of cash is converted into a future, perhaps unknown, amount of cash.
Financial Decisions	Investment and financing decisions taking account of elements of cash, time, risk, and expected return.
Financial Manager	The "person" making financial decisions.

Financial Market	A system for facilitating transactions between buyers and sellers of debt and equity claims.
Financing Decisions	Decisions concerning the sources of financing to be used in financing investments.
Interest	The fixed return promised by borrowers to lenders, holders of debt claims on borrowers.
Interval in Time	The span between two points in time (e.g., an interval of 1 year).
Investment Decisions	Decisions to acquire or not to acquire assets by purchase to generate future cash receipts.
Market Value	The value for debt and equity claims established in financial markets by prices at which claims are traded.
Multiperiod Investment	An investment requiring more than one time interval for receipt of all expected future cash.
Point in Time	A point separating intervals of time.
Promised Return	The fixed return promised for some types of investments; it represents an upper limit on realized returns.
Realized Return	The actual return received by the investor from an investment.
Risk	The case of total cash receipts from investments being unknown at the time of investment. Equivalently, the possibility that realized returns may differ from expected returns.
Risk-Free Investment	An investment on which the actual return cannot vary from expected return.
Single Period Investment	An investment requiring a single interval of time to generate all future cash receipts.
Wealth	The current market value of assets.

QUESTIONS AND PROBLEMS

1. How is cash related to the concept of investment?

2. What determines whether an investment is a single period or a multiperiod investment?

3. Distinguish between expected return, promised return, and realized return for (a) a riskless investment and (b) a risky investment.

4. Classify the following financial decisions into investment decisions or financing decisions.

(a)   The decision to acquire a plant to produce a new product.

(b)   The decision to repurchase some outstanding stock using proceeds from sale of debt.

(c)   The decision to carry more in inventory.

(d)   The decision to replace an old machine with a new one.

(e)   The decision to raise funds by issuing new debt.

(f)   The decision to increase cash dividends to shareholders (instead of retaining earnings to finance the equity portion of financing needs).

5.   Consider the following investments.

Amount	Investment	Expected Cash Receipts	Time to Receipt of Expected Cash
$1,000	Riskfree Savings account	$1,060	1 year
$1,000	Rare violin	$1,300	1 year
$1,000	Real estate lot	$1,200	1 year

(a)   Find the expected dollar return of each investment.

(b)   Answer the following questions.

   (i)   How much of the return is compensation to the investor for delayed consumption?

   (ii)   How much is compensation for risk-bearing services?

   (iii)   Which of these are promised returns?

   (iv)   Use these investments to explain how time and risk affect the compensation investors require for these investments.

6.   Identify some institutions that facilitate financial market transactions.

7.   Identify some institutions that facilitate the transmission of information to financial market participants.

8.   How can a firm's contribution to the Metropolitan Opera be consistent with the goal of owner wealth maximization?

9.   Estimate your current wealth. How do markets affect your wealth?

Should you include your education in the calculation of your wealth?

10. Phil and Drew plan to paint houses during the summer to earn money for their college expenses. What kinds of investment and financing decisions must they make?

CHAPTER 2

An Introduction
to Financial Decisions

In Chapter 1, financial managers were presumed to make financial decisions (investment and financing decisions) to maximize the wealth of the owners of a business. In this chapter, we cover some important aspects of financial decisions in a simplified form. Instead of having financial managers making decisions for the benefit of owners of the firm, we have a single entrepreneur making decisions regarding a new firm, to be owned by that individual. By following the decision-making processes portrayed, the reader will learn more about investment and financing decisions, the expected returns and rates of return from investment, how investment decisions can increase the wealth of the owner, and the effects of using borrowed funds—that is, debt—to provide part of the financing for the firm. But simplicity has its costs. The analysis that follows is not the last word. Some details are modified later.

HARRIS COMPANY: THE INITIAL CONDITION

Frank Harris, a man of entrepreneurial spirit, invented a prefabricated aluminum shed. He considered establishing a firm to manufacture the new shed. He had available $8000 of his own capital and was willing to invest it all if the decision to proceed were favorable.

To evaluate the prospects for the business, Frank made several preliminary choices. Provisionally, he decided to form a corporation. Alternative *legal forms of organization* he might have selected include a proprietorship or a partnership with some other individual(s). (Details on legal forms of business organization are contained in Appendix 2A to this chapter.) He also had to decide on the *internal management structure* of his company. The small size and simple character of Harris Company made this decision relatively easy. Frank, who was in his final year of college, would initially manage the firm himself on a part-time basis. Labor would be hired to manufacture the sheds, with Frank supplementing that labor as necessary.

But these decisions would not have been so easily made if Harris Company were to be a much larger firm. In that event, the internal organization would have involved *many* individuals carrying out various tasks, including financial decision making, and organizing and coordinating financial decision making would have been matters for careful study. (Appendix 2B deals with problems of internal organization.)

Provisional decisions still to be made included those pertaining to investment and financing. To assist in such decisions, Frank made preliminary estimates of total investment and resulting annual sales. He regarded the minimum investment necessary to manufacture sheds to be $10,000, an initially worrisome result because it exceeded the available $8000. Frank estimated that a $10,000 investment would generate $60,000 of annual sales. Based on these initial estimates, he developed the **pro forma** (i.e., projected or estimated) annual cash flow statement shown in Table 2-1 and the balance sheet shown in Table 2-2, below. A **cash flow** is receipt or expenditure of cash during an interval of time. Frank's cash flows are assumed for simplicity to occur at the *end* of each annual interval (e.g., at points in time $t = 1, t = 2, \ldots$). These statements reflected Frank's belief that the $60,000 of sales would be a constant amount each year, forever. The $10,000 total investment would also be forever maintained.

Preliminary Cash Flow Estimates

Table 2–1 *Pro Forma Annual Cash Flow Statement: Harris Company*

Expected Collections on Sales		$60,000
Expected Cash Expenditures		
Material Purchases	$30,000	
Labor Services	15,000	
Salary—Frank Harris	9,000	
Replacement of Tools and Equipment	500	
Utilities	1,500	56,000
Expected Net Operating Cash Flow (taxable income)		+$ 4,000
Expected Income Taxes (17% of taxable income)		− 680
Expected Net Cash Flow (net income)		$ 3,320

Frank's pro forma cash flow statement was identical in this case to the pro forma income statement.[1] Based on $60,000 of expected sales, he anticipated receiving $60,000 of annual cash collections. To produce that level of sales, certain estimated cash expenditures would be required: these included material purchases, labor services, Frank's salary, and utilities. The remaining expenditure, replacement of tools and equipment, was the cash outlay required to replace worn-out items. It was analogous to the depreciation charge (an accounting accrual, *not* a cash flow!) of the typical income statement. Expected total cash expenditures of $56,000, when deducted from the $60,000 cash inflow, left $4000 in expected *net* operating cash flow, analogous to net operating income of the income statement.

A **net cash flow** is the difference between a cash inflow and cash outflow. Cash inflows are positive cash flows; cash outflows are negative cash flows. Since Frank initially contemplated no borrowing, there was no interest expense. Consequently, the $4000 of net operating cash flow was *also* equal to taxable income. Net operating cash flow is before payment of income taxes and interest charges on debt, the latter not yet applicable because Harris is debt free. Since federal corporate income taxes applicable to this firm would be 17 percent of the first $25,000 of taxable income, taxes of $680 must be paid on $4000 of income. The remaining $3320 of expected net cash flow would be paid to the owner of the firm (Frank) as an annual return to his equity investment.

| **Preliminary Investment and Financing Decisions** | Now what of the assets used to generate the sales and net cash flow Frank estimated in Table 2-1? Those assets are shown in Table 2-2, the balance sheet. They reflect both preliminary investment and financing decisions. |

The $10,000 total investment was allocated between fixed and current assets. Frank estimated that $2000 must be invested in tools and equipment. No investment in land or buildings would be required. (Fortuitously, Frank's parents had made available free of charge a barn and surrounding land for Frank's use.) In addition, Frank estimated that $8000 would have to be invested in current assets or **working capital.** Of

---

[1] The income statement contains accounting accruals and does not necessarily measure cash flows. Sales reflected in an income statement are not necessarily cash collections on sales because sales made on credit may not be collected during the period of sale. In this case, however, it is assumed that collections equal sales. Income statements use depreciation charges to measure the using up of capital. But in Harris's case, depreciation is replaced by cash outlays of identical amounts to replace worn out capital. Therefore, the net cash flow in Table 2-1 happens to equal net income as would be reported in an income statement. This is not always the case.

Table 2–2   *Pro Forma Balance Sheet: Harris Company*

Current Assets		Current Liabilities	
Cash	$ 1,000	Accounts Payable	$ 2,000
Receivables	2,000	Total	*$ 2,000
Inventories	5,000		
Total	$ 8,000		
Fixed Assets		Equity	
Tools and Equipment	2,000	Ownership	8,000
		Total Liabilities and Capital	$10,000
Total Assets	$10,000		

this sum, $1000 was needed to maintain a cash reserve for unanticipated cash payments. Since Frank planned to extend credit to his customers as a means of stimulating sales, it would be necessary to maintain an investment of $2000 in receivables. This investment equaled the average level of unpaid amounts that would be owed to the firm by customers. Finally, inventories of finished sheds and manufacturing materials combined were estimated to be $5000. Finished shed inventory would accommodate unanticipated increases in customer demand; manufacturing materials inventory would help avoid interference with the flow of production due to temporary material shortages.

To finance the $10,000 total investment, Frank distinguished between current liability and long-term financing sources. He realized that the firm would be purchasing various materials on short-term credit and without an explicit interest charge. The average amount to be owed to suppliers was given by the $2000 accounts payable entry on the balance sheet. The remaining $8000 of financing would have to be from long-term sources. Frank first decided to be an all-equity firm and to provide the entire $8000 himself. Such a decision would result in an **unlevered firm.** Unlevered firms make no use of borrowing (i.e., debt financing) to meet part of the long-term financing needs. (The word "unlevered" comes from the practice of referring to debt financing as **financial leverage.** A levered firm uses some debt financing; an unlevered firm does not.)

The combined preliminary investment and financing decisions Frank made can also be described in this way: Frank's $10,000 total investment is financed by $2000 of current liabilities and $8000 of **equity.** The $8000 investment in working capital (current assets) is financed by $2000 in current liabilities and $6000 of long-term capital. The difference between $8000 of current assets and $2000 of current liabilities is $6000, the amount of the firm's **net working capital.** Net working capital is financed by long-term capital, in this case Frank's equity. The $2000 investment in fixed assets is financed by the remaining portion of Frank's equity. (Decisions on working capital investment and its financing are covered in Chapters 20 to 24. Decisions on fixed assets and capital budgeting decisions are dealt with in Chapters 6 to 10.)

The decisions reflected in Tables 2-1 and 2-2, are Frank's preliminary, not his *final*, investment and financing decisions. These would be made only when the effect on his wealth of establishing the business had been estimated and found to be favorable. To make this assessment, Frank first evaluated the expected rate of return and the risk associated with the proposed investment. (Additional steps beyond this point are dealt with as we come to them.)

EXPECTED RATE OF RETURN AND RISK

From the preliminary information of Tables 2-1 and 2-2, Frank expected to receive the constant amount of $3320 per year *in perpetuity* for an initial and maintained equity investment of $8000. In this special case, the annual expected return was the $3320 annual expected net cash flow. He then proceeded to compute the **expected rate of return.**

Expected Rate of Return

The expected annual rate of return, also in this special case, is the constant expected annual return $3320, divided by the $8000 maintained investment. Letting r^* be the expected annual rate of return, Frank computed the expected annual rate of return on his $8000 equity investment to be $r^* = 41.5$ percent.

$$r^* = \frac{\text{Expected return}}{\text{Equity investment}} = \frac{\$3320}{\$8000} = 0.415, \quad \text{or } 41.5\%$$

Thinking of the 5 percent his $8000 was presently earning in a savings account, Frank was enthusiastic at the prospect of investing to earn such a high rate of return. But the timely arrival of his friend, Mary Brown, soon restrained his joy. Mary examined Frank's pro forma statements and the 41.5 percent expected rate of return. Turning to Frank, Mary asked whether the $3320 annual return Frank expected to receive was a "sure thing." Was it not possible that bad times in some years could result in Frank's receiving *less* than this amount? If so, the investment was a *risky* one.

Risk

Mary defined "risk" to be the possibility that the realized return from investment will differ from the expected return. The realized return is the actual return received from investment. Only in the case of risk-free investments are realized returns *always* equal to expected returns. Mary cited Frank's $8000 insured savings account as an example of a riskless investment. That investment had an expected rate of return of 5.0 percent, the interest rate to be paid by the bank. The expected return was $(0.05) \times \$8000 = \$400$ for 1 year. One year hence, Frank would also *realize* a $400 return. There was no chance of the realized return being higher or lower than the $400 expected return.

Turning to the proposed Harris Company, Mary pointed out that the $3320 expected return was predicated on $60,000 of expected sales and the expected costs associated with generating that level of sales. Asked if he admitted the possibility that actual sales might be higher or lower than $60,000, Frank acknowledged that he did. This meant, declared Mary, that he must acknowledge that the realized returns from his investment might also be higher or lower than the $3320 expected amount. The Harris Company would entail a risky investment.

Frank asked if the now-exposed presence of risk meant that his proposed investment in Harris was undesirable. Mary responded that the world was full of risky investments held by people who were **risk averse,** people who regarded risk as undesirable. Such people would not select risky investments unless the expected return were high enough to compensate them for the risk being borne. In the case of Harris Company, the degree of risk had to be measured before it was possible to determine whether the expected return would be high enough to justify the investment.

Mary helped Frank rethink his estimates in an attempt to measure the risk of the proposed investment. The first results of that effort are shown in Table 2-3.

Table 2–3   *Possible Cash Inflows, Outflows, and Investment Returns: Harris Company*

(1)	(2)	(3)	(4)	(5)	(6)	(7)	(8)
Probability P_i	Annual Collections on Sales	Fixed Expenditures	Variable Expenditures	Total Expenditures	Net Operating Cash Flow	Taxes	Net Cash Flow (Return)
0.10	$ 20,000	$2000	$18,000	$20,000	$ 0	$ 0	$ 0
0.20	40,000	2000	36,000	38,000	2000	340	1660
0.40	60,000	2000	54,000	56,000	4000	680	3320
0.20	80,000	2000	72,000	74,000	6000	1020	4980
0.10	100,000	2000	90,000	92,000	8000	1360	6640

Figure 2-1   *Probability Distribution of Rates of Return for Harris Company*

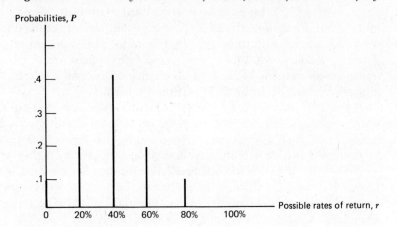

Frank considered that there would be five possible outcomes for sales levels, ranging from $20,000 to $100,000, shown in column 2. He also expressed his assessment of the chances of each sales level occurring by a **probability distribution.**

These probabilities are shown in column 1. Frank's probability distribution is also shown in Figure 2-1, where the probability of the first outcome ($20,000 of sales) is $P_1 = 10$ percent, the probability of the second ($40,000 of sales) is $P_2 = 20$ percent, and so on. (In general, the *i*th outcome has a probability, a chance of occurring, of P_i.) To find the corresponding five possible levels of net cash flow for Frank's investment, it was necessary to estimate fixed and variable cash expenditures. Fixed expenditures do *not* vary with the level of sales. For Frank's firm, the only fixed expenditure was the $2000 for replacement of tools and equipment. Remaining expenditures would vary proportionately with the level of sales. The sum of **fixed expenditures** and **variable expenditures** in columns 3 and 4 equaled total expenditures in column 5. When these amounts were subtracted from collections in column 2, the alternative net operating cash flows of column 6 were found. Application of the 17 percent corporate income tax rate to net operating cash flow gave the income taxes shown in column 7. The alternative levels of net cash flow (returns) shown in column were net of these taxes.

From these computations, Frank obtained five possible outcomes for net cash flow (return) and their probabilities of occurrence. Table 2-4 converts these outcomes to rates of return. For each annual sales level and net cash flow, there was a corresponding rate of return, r_i, on Frank's $8000 equity investment. For example, if sales are $80,000, then a $4980 net cash flow (return) and a rate of return of $r_i = 62.3$ percent would be realized.

$$r_i = \frac{\$4980}{\$8000} = 0.623, \quad \text{or } 62.3\%$$

The *range* of rates of return lies between 0 and 83 percent. If each rate of return outcome were weighted by its probability of occurrence as done in Table 2-4, the expected rate of return would be $r^* = 41.5$ percent. Expected rate of return was computed based on alternative outcomes given in Table 2-4 as follows.

$$r^* = \sum_{i=1}^{n} r_i P_i \tag{2-1}$$

Although Frank *expected* a rate of return of $r^* = 41.5$ percent, he now recognized that it was possible to earn either more *or* less than this rate. The 41.5 percent rate of return was *not certain*. He enjoyed the possiblity of earning more than 41.5 percent, but was not pleased with the possibility of earning less. But Frank found the array of outcomes and probabilities a cumbersome way to reflect risk. Mary suggested that the **standard deviation of the rate of return** be computed, as a more compact measure of variability of possible rates of return *around* the expected rate of return.

Using σ to denote standard deviation, the expression for computing this measure is:

$$\sigma = \sqrt{(r_i - r^*)^2 P_i} = \sqrt{\sigma^2} \tag{2-2}$$

The subscript i indicates the ith possible rate of return. From each possible rate of return, the expected rate of return is subtracted, to form the deviation from the expected rate $r_i - r^*$. These deviations are squared, multiplied by their respective probabilities of occurrence, and summed over each possible rate of return, to estimate the **variance of the rate of return, σ^2.** The standard deviation is the square root of the variance.

Table 2–4   *Expected Rate of Return: Harris Company*

Annual Collections on Sales	Net Cash Flows (Returns)	Rates of Return on $8000 Equity	Probability	Rate of Return (times) Probability
$ 20,000	$ 0	0.0%	0.1	0 (0.1) = 0.0%
40,000	1660	20.7	0.2	20.7 (0.2) = 4.1
60,000	3320	41.5	0.4	41.4 (0.4) = 16.6
80,000	4980	62.3	0.2	62.3 (0.2) = 12.5
100,000	6640	83.0	0.1	83 (0.1) = 8.3
				$r^* = 41.5\%$

Based on the information in Table 2-4, Frank computed the standard deviation of the rate of return and found $\sigma = 22.75$ percent.

Variance: $\sigma^2 = (0.0 - 0.415)^2 (0.10) + (0.207 - 0.415)^2 (0.20)$

$$+ (0.415 - 0.415)^2 (0.40) + (0.623 - 0.415)^2 (0.20)$$

$$+ (0.83 - 0.415)^2 (0.10)$$

$$= 0.05175$$

Standard deviation: $\sigma = \sqrt{0.05175} = 0.2275, \quad \text{or } 22.75\%$

Mary told Frank that the greater the variability of rate of return about the expected rate of return, the greater the standard deviation. Furthermore, Mary indicated that standard deviation of the rate of return would, provisionally, be the measure of risk to be employed. (Other measures of risk are evaluated in Chapter 4.) Frank still didn't know how to evaluate the proposed investment. The expected rate of return was $r^* = 41.5$ percent and the risk, as measured by standard deviation, was $\sigma = 22.75$ percent. But how was this information to be used?

THE WEALTH CONSEQUENCES OF THE INITIAL INVESTMENT AND FINANCING DECISIONS

Mary asked Frank what objective he wanted to serve by making the investment. Frank indicated that he wanted to increase his wealth. (By how much? The maximum!) Mary then noted that to find the wealth consequences of undertaking the investment, Frank would have to estimate what value the market would place on the equity in the firm. (Remember! Wealth is the current market value of assets—in this case, Frank's equity investment in the proposed firm.) Market value depends on the required rate of return the market establishes for investments having a degree of risk like Frank's investment.

Required Rate of Return and Risk

Mary informed Frank that the expected rate of return of the proposed investment had to be compared to the required rate of return established in the marketplace for investments of the *same* risk as the shed business. The relationship between required rate of return and risk was described in a general way by Mary as:

$$k = r_f + \phi \tag{2-3}$$

The term k is the **required rate of return**; r_f is the **risk-free rate** (also called the riskless or default-free rate of return); and ϕ is the **risk premium**—the compensation risk-averse investors in the market require before they will consent to bear the risk of the investment. The risk-free rate compensates investors for the present consumption of goods and services they must give up (defer) to make investments. It is a reward only for waiting and applies solely to investments on which there is *no chance* that the realized rate of return will differ from the expected rate. When risk is also to be borne, the risk premium adds the necessary compensation for bearing that risk. Thus, risky investments provide compensation both for delayed consumption *and* for risk.

Frank stated that the relationship portrayed in Equation (2-3) was interesting but did not help unless one could estimate the risk-free rate r_f and the risk premium ϕ. Mary responded that riskless investments from which the risk-free rate can be estimated do exist. One example, a 90-day U.S. Treasury bill involves no default risk and so provides a riskless rate of return. The risk premium, Mary said, depended on the standard deviation of the rate of return (implying at the same time that this was not the last word on risk measures). In fact, the risk premium was recently estimated by Mary to be $\phi = 1.5\sigma$, or 1.5 times the standard deviation. Therefore, Mary wrote down the more specific relationship between required rate of return and risk, as the risk–return line.

$$k = r_f + 1.5\sigma \qquad (2\text{-}4)$$

A check of recent trading prices for U.S. Treasury bills allowed Mary to estimate the current risk-free rate to be $r_f = 5$ percent. Incorporating this in Equation (2-4) yielded Mary's current estimate of the risk–return line.

Figure 2-2   *Required Rate of Return and Risk*

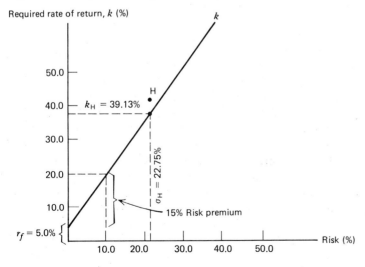

$$k = 5\% + 1.5\sigma \tag{2-5}$$

She drew this relationship in Figure 2-2.

A risk-free investment had a standard deviation of $\sigma = 0.0$ and the required risk-free rate was $r_f = 5$ percent. Therefore, the risk–return line intersected the vertical return axis at 5 percent. The presence of risk added the risk premium to this risk-free rate. For example, if the standard deviation was $\sigma = 10$ percent, the risk premium would be:

$$1.5\sigma = 1.5(10\%) = 15\%$$

When added to the $r_f = 5$ percent risk-free rate, the required rate of return was $k = 5 + 15 = 20$ percent. Investments having greater risk would have greater risk premiums and higher required rates of return.

Examining Figure 2-2, Frank realized immediately that he could find the required rate of return for Harris Company—if it were established. The standard deviation of the rate of return was already known ($\sigma = 22.75$ percent). Substituting this into Equation (2-5), he found the required rate of return to be $k = 39.13$ percent:

Required Rate of Return for Harris Company

$$k_H = 5\% + 1.5(22.75\%)$$
$$= 5\% + 34.13\%$$
$$= 39.13\%$$

The risk premium appropriate for the risk of the sheds was 34.13 percent. Frank himself drew the $k = 39.13$ percent rate of return (k_H for Harris) in Figure 2-2 for the corresponding standard deviation of $\sigma_H = 22.75$ percent.

Market Value and Frank's Wealth

Given the required rate of return for Harris, it was time to assess the wealth consequences of the proposed investment. The expected rate of return for the investment (calculated earlier to be $r^* = 41.5$ percent) exceeded the required rate of return for investments of such risk, which was $k_H = 39.13$ percent. If expected rate of return exceeded required rate of return ($r^* > k$), someone investing \$8000 in the equity of the shed business would be *more* than compensated for risk and delayed consumption. Such an investment was a desirable investment. Mary reinforced her point by making a dot next to the letter H *above* the risk–return line in Figure 2-2 to indicate the expected rate of return for the Harris Company equity investment.

Frank commented that finding an investment with an expected rate of return greater than the required rate (given the risk) sounded like a good thing. In fact, it seemed as though the investment should be made. But he recalled that Mary had emphasized the wealth consequences of investment, and he saw no reference to wealth. Mary asserted that before undertaking the investment, Frank's wealth would be $8000, but once the $8000 had been invested in the firm, Frank's wealth would be whatever the market would *pay* Frank for that equity if he sold it; that is, wealth would equal current market value of the equity. Mary wrote down an expression for market value, being careful to note that it applied *only* to this special case where net cash flow (return) was of constant perpetual amount.

$$V = \frac{\text{Expected return}}{k} \qquad (2\text{-}6)$$

The market value V equaled the expected return (net after-tax cash flow) divided by the appropriate required rate of return. Substituting the expected return of $3320 and $k = 39.13$ percent required rate into Equation (2-6), Mary showed that the market value of Frank's equity in the proposed firm would be $8485.

$$V = \frac{\$3320}{0.3913} = \$8485$$

Frank's wealth would be expected to increase by $8485 - $8000 = $485 if he entered the shed business. Frank asked why the market would pay a sum for the equity investment *greater* than his own $8000 initial investment. Mary responded with a two-part answer. First, others did not *yet* know that an investment in the shed business would yield an expected rate of return greater than that required for the amount of risk being borne. Second, if Frank got his business established and *then* made known its prospects, investors would rush to purchase a risky investment offering an expected rate of return of $r^* = 41.5$ percent when the required rate was only $k = 39.13$ percent. (This statement assumes that investors agree with Frank on the prospects for the firm.) Investors would *bid up* the value of the equity until the higher prices *reduced* the expected rate of return to the point that it equaled the required rate of return. Offer prices would go no higher than this upper limit; otherwise the expected rate of return would be less than that required. That upper limit on market value was V, as computed in Equation (2-6). If the firm's equity were purchased at a price equal to $8485, the expected rate of return would equal the required rate (i.e., $r^* = k = 39.13$ percent). Mary demonstrated the point by use of the formula:

$$\begin{array}{l}\text{Expected rate of} \\ \text{return if purchased} \\ \text{at market value}\end{array} = \frac{\text{Expected return}}{V} = \frac{\$3320}{\$8485} = 0.3913, \quad \text{or } 39.13\%$$

Frank was initially astonished that the buyer of the equity would not enjoy the extra rate of return he himself would receive for his initial $8000 investment (i.e., $r^* - k = 41.5 - 39.13 = 2.37$ percent). Mary explained that *only* Frank, being in possession of the opportunity and able to pay only $8000 for the equity, could enjoy that extra benefit. Another investor would not be able to pay $8000 for the equity, but would have to pay the higher market value of $8485. At that price, there was no extra return to be earned.

Frank concluded that his proposed investment in the shed business was desirable. It would be expected to increase his wealth. He was on the verge of leaving for his bank to withdraw the $8000, but Mary suggested that he consider altering his financing decision before making a final commitment. She pointed out that, save only the modest $2000 of current liability financing, the provisional plan was for an all-equity, unlevered firm. Mary thought it wise to explain the effects of utilizing financial leverage to make Harris a **levered firm.**

FINANCIAL LEVERAGE

Mary suggested that Frank examine the effect on the proposed firm of borrowing $4000 from an outside party at the current interest rate of 10 percent. If this were done, Frank's equity investment in the firm would be only $4000 rather than $8000. Frank could retain $4000 in his bank account. The particular type of borrowing Frank would make use of was again to be a special case, *perpetual* debt. The $4000 amount borrowed (the principal) would never be repaid. But annual interest payments on that perpetual debt would be met (Chapter 11 introduces debt with principal and interest payments). These annual interest payments would be 10 percent of $4000, or $400.

To show the effects of financial leverage, Mary helped Frank to construct the revised pro forma balance sheet and cash flow statement shown in Table 2-5. Compared to Table 2-2, when Harris was an unlevered firm in its initial condition, the only difference lay in the mix of *claims* on the proposed firm. Instead of Frank's $8000 equity claim in the unlevered condition, there is a $4000 debt claim owned by the lender to the firm (the firm's liability to that lender) plus Frank's (now smaller) $4000 equity claim. As for the cash flow statement, the statement in Table 2-5 for a levered version of Harris was identical to the unlevered situation in Table 2-1 from collections on sales down to net operating cash flow. But with the levered version, the $400 interest payment to the lender would be deducted from net operating cash flow before computation of taxable income. Mary pointed out that interest payments are deductible from taxable income, whereas payments to equity invest-

Table 2–5 *Pro Forma Annual Cash Flow Statement: Harris Company*

Expected Collections on Sales		$60,000
Expected Cash Expenditures		
Materials Purchased	$30,000	
Labor Services	15,000	
Salary—Frank Harris	9,000	
Replacement of Tools and Equipment	500	
Utilities	1,500	56,000
Expected Net Operating Cash Flow		$ 4,000
Interest Payments		400
Expected Taxable Income		$ 3,600
Expected Income Taxes (17% of taxable income)		612
Expected Net Cash Flow (net income)		$ 2,988

Pro Forma Balance Sheet: Harris Company

Current Assets		Current Liabilities	
Cash	$ 1,000	Accounts Payable	$ 2,000
		Total	$ 2,000
Receivables	2,000		
Inventories	8,000		
Total	$ 8,000		
Fixed Assets		Debt (10%)	4,000
Tools and Equipment	2,000	Equity	4,000
Total Assets	$10,000	Total Liabilities and Capital	$10,000

ment are not. Income taxes that resulted were deducted from taxable income to determine the expected net cash flow to be received by Frank. This flow, $2988, was *smaller* than the $3320 for the unlevered version. As Mary explained, Frank's equity investment was no longer $8000 but the smaller amount—$4000.

Frank noted that whereas his expected net cash flow from equity investment would fall from $3320 in the unlevered case to $2988 in the levered case, the amount of the decrease was only $2988 − $3320 = −$332. Yet the interest payments deducted from net operating cash flow equaled $400. How could the use of financial leverage cause the firm to pay out $400 in interest while sustaining only a $332 reduction in net cash flow payable to equity?

The Interest Tax Subsidy

Mary explained that this result was caused by the tax deductibility of interest payments. That is, the government was bearing part of the cost of financing the firm. The government's share of that cost was called the **interest tax subsidy.** Its role was demonstrated by Mary with the following tabulation.

Effect of Interest Tax Deductibility on Net Cash Flow to Equity

Reduction in taxable income due to interest tax deductibility	$400	(Interest Payment)
Reduction in income taxes due to interest tax deductibility: (0.17)$400	− 68	(Interest Tax Subsidy)
Reduction in net cash flow available to equity	$332	(After-tax Interest Payment)

Comparing the levered and unlevered annual cash flow statements in Tables 2-5 and 2-1, interest payments would reduce taxable income by $400. The comparative reduction in income taxes would be $68, the unlevered tax bill being $680 in Table 2-1 and the levered tax bill in Table 2-5 is $612. After taxes, the Harris firm would pay not $400 of interest, but only $332. The reduction would equal the $68 interest tax subsidy.

Understandably impressed by the benefits of the interest tax subsidy, Frank asked why more debt and less equity financing should not be employed (e.g., $7000 of debt and only $1000 of equity). Mary's reply emphasized that the favorable interest tax subsidy was not the only result of using financial leverage. There were other effects to be explored.

Expected Rate of Return and Risk Under Financial Leverage

Using the information in the pro forma statements for the levered firm in Table 2-5, Mary noted that the expected return to equity of $2988 for a smaller equity investment of $4000 resulted in an expected rate of return of $r^* = 74.7$ percent.

$$r^* = \frac{\text{Expected return}}{\text{Equity investment}} = \frac{\$2988}{\$4000} = 0.747, \quad \text{or } 74.7\%$$

This result greatly impressed Frank, since the expected rate of return for the *unlevered* firm had been found to be much lower ($r^* = 41.5$ percent). But Mary cautioned that increases in the *expected* rate of return to equity do not always follow when financial leverage is employed. It would happen only if *pre-tax* expected rate of return on long-term capital (debt and equity combined) exceeded the interest rate. Mary computed this pre-tax expected rate in the following way.

$$\text{Pre-tax expected rate of return} = \frac{\text{Net operating cash flow}}{\text{Debt + equity}}$$

$$= \frac{\$4000}{\$4000 + \$4000} = 0.50, \quad \text{or } 50\%$$

This was well in excess of the 10 percent interest rate in the case of the proposed Harris firm; therefore, the expected rate of return or equity *would* rise with financial leverage. Had this not been the case, expected rate of return would have fallen with the use of financial leverage. Mary demonstrated the latter assertion by assuming that the pre-tax expected rate of return for Harris was only 8 percent. On $8000 of long-term capital, the expected net operating cash flow would be only $640 for the firm instead of $4000 as in Tables 2-1 and 2-5. Mary proceeded to compute taxable income, taxes, net cash flow, and expected rate of return for equity in both the levered and unlevered cases for this much less favorable situation.

Expected Rate of Return Falls with Financial Leverage

	Unlevered Firm ($8000 Equity)	Levered Firm ($4000 Debt, $4000 Equity)
Net Operating Cash Flow	$ 640.00	$ 640.00
Interest	—	− 400.00
Taxable Income	$ 640.00	$ 240.00
Income Tax (17% ratio)	108.80	40.80
Net Cash Flow	$ 531.20	$ 199.20
Expected Rate of Return	$r^* = \dfrac{\$531.20}{\$8000} = 0.0664,$ or 6.64%	$r^* = \dfrac{\$199.20}{\$4000} = 0.0498,$ or 4.98%

In this situation, an unlevered version of Harris would generate an expected rate of return on equity of $r^* = 6.64$ percent; a levered version would generate only $r^* = 4.98$ percent. The 8 percent pre-tax expected rate of return on long-term capital would be too low compared to the 10 percent rate to make the employment of financial leverage a desirable action for equity owners.

Satisfied that Harris's use of leverage was expected to be profitable, Frank was prepared to borrow $7999 and invest $1 of equity in the proposed firm. He added that the term leverage took on real meaning to him. Obviously, the fixed interest charge was a *lever* for returns to equity. Once the fixed charge for interest had been paid, any net operating flows above that amount were received by equity; the higher the net cash flow, the greater the increase of cash flow available to equity. Thus, the pre-tax expected rate of return on long-term capital of 50 percent meant that once the 10 percent interest rate was paid, the excess 40 percent, pre-tax, was "gravy" for equity. On an after-tax basis, Harris's proposed use of financial leverage with only $4000 of debt resulted in the levering of an $r^* = 41.5$ percent expected rate of return to equity for an unlevered firm into an $r^* = 74.7$ percent expected rate for the levered version.

Mary agreed with Frank's description of how leverage worked, but because of the effects of financial leverage on *risk* for equity owners, she strongly disagreed with the idea of borrowing of $7999 to finance the proposed firm. She demonstrated the point using Table 2-6, an analysis based on the use of $4000 of debt as in Table 2-5. Columns 1 and 2 show the five possible outcomes for collection on sales and net operating cash flow described in Table 2-3, as well as the same probabilities of occurrence in column 7. Column 3 contains the $400 interest expense, which is fixed for all five levels of sales. Column 4, net operating cash flow less interest expense, reveals alternative levels of taxable income. Column 5 lists net cash flow (return) outcomes after payment of taxes assessed at the 17 percent rate. (Column 5 is $1 - 0.17 = 0.83$, or 83 percent, of column 4.) Column 6 lists the alternative rates of return on equity. Weighted by their probability of occurrence in column 8, using Equation (2-1), the expected rate of return of $r^* = 74.7$ percent is again obtained.

The critical issue in Table 2-6 is the increased range of rate of return outcomes compared to the range prevailing in the unlevered situation. Back in Table 2-4, the range in rate of return outcomes was 0.0–83

Table 2–6   *Expected Rate of Return and Risk with Financial Leverage: Harris Company*

(1) Annual Collections on Sales	(2) Net Operating Cash Flow	(3) Interest	(4) Taxable Income	(5) Net Cash Flow (Return)	(6) Rate of Return	(7) Probability	(8) Rate of Return (times) Probability
$ 20,000	$ 0	$400	−$ 400	−$ 332	−8.3%	0.1	0.83
40,000	2000	400	1600	1328	33.2	0.2	6.64
60,000	4000	400	3600	2988	74.7	0.4	29.88
80,000	6000	400	5600	4648	116.2	0.2	23.24
100,000	8000	400	7600	6308	157.7	0.1	15.77
							$r^* = 74.7\%$

percent for the unlevered situation. But in Table 2-6, the effect of financial leverage was to broaden the range to −8.3 to +157.7 percent. Risk had been increased because of financial leverage. Further verification was provided for the existence of increased risk by Mary's calculation of the new standard deviation using Equation (2-2).

Variance: $\sigma^2 = (-0.083 - 0.747)^2 (0.1) + (0.332 - 0.747)^2 (0.2)$

$$+ (0.747 - 0.747)^2 (0.4) + (1.162 - 0.747)^2 (0.2)$$

$$+ (1.577 - 0.747)^2 (0.1)$$

$$= 0.20667$$

Standard deviation: $\sigma = \sqrt{0.20667}$

$$= 0.45461, \quad \text{or } 45.46\%$$

With financial leverage, the standard deviation is increased to $\sigma = 45.46$ percent from the lower level of $\sigma = 22.75$ percent in the unlevered situation.

It is obvious from Table 2-6 that financial leverage can be either beneficial or harmful. Rate of return consequences for alternative sales levels are *augmented* by financial leverage. Whereas the worst outcome in the unlevered situation of Table 2-4 is to earn zero net cash flow and a zero rate of return, with $20,000 annual sales, the same sales level results in a net cash *outflow* of $400 before taxes and a negative rate of return of −8.3 percent. In that event, the firm could not meet its $400 interest payment with cash generated from operations.[2] At the same time, the best unlevered outcome is a rate of return of 83.3 percent, whereas the best levered rate is 157.7 percent. And although Table 2-6 does not show this effect, use of even greater financial leverage would further augment the range of rate of return outcomes.

Confronted with increased risk and expected rate of return produced by financial leverage, Frank was unsure whether to lever his proposed firm or let it remain in the unlevered state. He decided to estimate the required rate of return for the higher risk resulting from financial leverage.

----

[2]If the firm has $20,000 of sales and zero net operating cash flow in some year, there will be no funds generated by the firm to meet the $400 interest payment. Frank is constrained to maintain a $4000 equity investment and must therefore invest an extra $400 in the firm to maintain his equity investment by paying the interest due. He still enjoys a $68 interest tax subsidy, which reduces his net extra payment to $332 (we ignore the fact that the interest tax subsidy cannot be applied until later years when the tax loss can be carried forward to offset future taxable income).

Required Rate of Return and Wealth Consequences of Financial Leverage

Frank reasoned that if financial leverage increases risk as measured by the standard deviation, it must increase required rate of return as well. For the higher the risk, the greater the compensation required for risk bearing by the market. Using the risk–return line in Equation (2-5) with the higher standard deviation of $\sigma = 45.46$ percent, Frank found the required rate of return with $4000 of financial leverage:

$$k = 5.0\% + 1.5(45.46\%)$$
$$= 5.0\% + 68.19\%$$
$$= 73.19\%$$

This exceeds the required rate of $k = 39.125$ percent earlier found for the unlevered situation because of the increased risk caused by financial leverage.

Frank proceeded immediately to evaluate the wealth consequences of using financial leverage. He compared the expected rate of return of $r^* = 74.7$ percent to the $k = 73.19$ percent required rate of return. Since the expected rate *exceeded* the required rate, $(r^* > k)$, he knew (from Mary's earlier discussion on wealth consequences) that use of financial leverage would be expected to *increase* his wealth. Still, this comparison did not tell Frank which course of action—levered or unlevered—would maximize his expected wealth increase. He was about to employ Equation (2-6) to find out, but Mary suggested that this would not be appropriate. Equation (2-6) could not be used to help find out which financing plan would maximize the expected increase in Frank's wealth. Although acceptable for an unlevered firm with perpetual net cash flows, the expression does not adequately account for the influences of the interest tax subsidy and several yet undiscussed variables related to financial leverage on the firm. (These more complex matters are dealt with in Chapters 12 and 13.) Mary said that it was enough for the present to know that financial leverage provides an interest tax subsidy, increased expected rate of return and risk, and increased required rate of return.

Frank asked what decision on financial leverage he should make for the firm to maximize his wealth. Mary suggested that lacking more complete knowledge of the effects of financial leverage on wealth, Harris should remain unlevered. However, she pointed out the distinction between business risk and financial risk.

BUSINESS AND FINANCIAL RISK

Mary had Frank recall that the word "risk" describes the possibility that realized returns (or rates of return) will differ from expected returns (or rates of return) from investment. The variability of possible realized rates of return about the expected rate of return is measured by the standard deviation of the rate of return.

But there are two types of risk: business and financial. **Business risk** is the variability of realized about expected rate of return for an *unlevered* firm. In the initial and unlevered state of Harris Company, the standard deviation of rate of return of $\sigma = 22.75$ percent was a measurement of business risk. The only sources of that variability were variations in cash inflows from sales and operating cash outflows of the business. No additional variability was produced by the use of financial leverage. But when the use of financial leverage was investigated, the standard deviation rose to $\sigma = 45.46$ percent. The additional variability was caused by the levering effect of financial leverage and is called **financial risk.** Thus, for levered firms, the *total* risk for the equity invested consists of business *and* financial risk. For unlevered firms, total risk equals business risk only.

Distinction between total, business, and financial risk carries through to the risk premiums incorporated in the required rate of return. Mary demonstrated this by restating the general risk–return relationship of Equation (2-3) and breaking the total risk premium ϕ into separate components for business risk ϕ_B, and financial risk ϕ_F.

$$k = r_f + \phi = r_f + \phi_B + \phi_F \qquad (2\text{-}7)$$

In evaluating unlevered firms, only the business risk premium is relevant; the financial risk premium is $\phi_F = 0.0$ in such cases. The total risk premium equals the business risk premium; that is, $\phi = \phi_B$. For levered firms, both business and financial risk premiums are of concern.

For example, the business risk for Harris Company in the unlevered state is based on a standard deviation of $\sigma = 22.75$ percent. Mary's estimate of the risk–return line indicates that the risk premium is $\phi = 1.5\sigma$. Therefore, the business *and* total risk premium is:

$$\phi = \phi_B = 1.5(22.75\%) = 34.125\%$$

But for the levered version of Harris, the higher standard deviation due to financial risk is $\sigma = 45.46$ percent. This results in a *total* risk premium of:

$$\phi = \phi_B + \phi_F = 1.5(45.46\%) = 68.19\%$$

The change in total risk premium due to use of financial leverage is:

Change in Total
Risk Premium due
to Financial Leverage $= \phi_B + \phi_F - \phi_B = 68.19\% - 34.13\% = 34.06\%$

In this case, use of financial leverage *doubles* the total risk premium.

The distinction between business and financial risk is ímportant when otherwise identical levered and unlevered firms are being compared. Other things equal, equity investments in levered firms will *always* have higher required rates because of the addition of financial risk premiums to business risk premiums.

SUMMARY   In establishing a business enterprise, the entrepreneur must choose a legal form of business organization and settle on the internal management structure. Then, preliminary investment and financing decisions must be made. Pro forma cash flow statements and balance sheets are useful ways to summarize some of the expected consequences of preliminary investment and financing decisions. But it still remains to evaluate the consequences of alternative investment and financing decisions for the entrepreneur's wealth. A first step in this process is to find the wealth consequences for a prospective firm using only equity as a source of long-term capital. Such a firm is an unlevered firm, since it makes no use of debt financing, or financial leverage, to help finance long-term capital requirements.

For an unlevered firm, the entrepreneur must decide on the total investment in fixed and current assets (working capital). Given this investment decision, the level of current liabilities is estimated. Current liabilities provide part of the financing for current assets. Remaining financing for these plus financing for fixed assets poses the long-term capital requirement, which is to be met entirely by equity financing in the unlevered case. To evaluate this decision, the entrepreneur must estimate the expected return, the expected rate of return, and the risk for the equity investment. Risk is measured (on a preliminary basis only) by the standard deviation of the rate of return. It reflects the variability of rate of return, the possibility that the realized rate of return will differ from the expected rate of return. Once risk has been measured, the required rate of return can be estimated. This rate consists of the risk-free rate plus a risk premium. The risk-free rate is required by investors to compensate them for the delayed consumption opportunities they forego by investing rather than spending wealth for consumption. The risk premium compensates risk-averse investors for bearing risk. The higher the level of risk, the greater the risk premium and the higher the required rate of return. To increase an entrepreneur's wealth, the expected rate of return on the equity investment must *exceed* the required rate of return for the given level of risk. In that circumstance, the market value of the equity will exceed the initial investment made by the entrepreneur.

Once the wealth consequences of investment in an unlevered firm have been assessed, the effects of using financial leverage in the firm can be evaluated. Financial leverage involves the use of borrowed funds, with the obligation to repay, in place of some of the equity financing used in an unlevered firm. Interest payments on debt are tax deductible. Consequently, government bears part of the cost of financing levered firms, and the portion borne is referred to as the interest tax subsidy. The fixed interest payments also act as a lever. When profitably employed, so that the firms earns more than enough to cover fixed interest payments, financial leverage increases the expected rate of return for equity investment. But it also augments the range of rate of return outcomes and so increases risk. Consequently, financial leverage also increases the required rate of return for equity investment. Still, if the expected rate of return exceeds the required rate, the entrepreneur's wealth will be increased through equity investment in a levered firm. Whether the increase in the entrepreneur's wealth from equity investment is greater with levered or unlevered firms is an issue deferred until later.

The risk premium included in required rate of return may comprise both a business and a financial risk premium. Business risk pertains to the risk of unlevered firms. Financial risk is the additional risk produced by financial leverage. The total risk premium for an unlevered firm equals just the business risk premium. For a levered firm, the total risk premium is the sum of risk premiums for business *and* financial risks.

GLOSSARY OF KEY TERMS

Business Risk	The variability of realized returns about expected returns for owners' equity in an unlevered firm. Reflects variation in cash inflows and outflows in the employment of the firm's assets.
Cash Flow	A receipt (cash inflow) or expenditure (cash outflow) in an interval of time.
Expected Rate of Return	The periodic expected return to be earned per dollar of investment.
Equity	Ownership financing.
Financial Leverage	Using a fixed-cost source of funds such as debt to finance investments.
Financial Risk	Additional variability of realized returns about expected returns for owners equity in levered firms. Results from fixed interest payments on

debt being deducted from variable returns on the firm's assets. Financial risk is over and above business risk.

Fixed Expenditures	Cash expenditures that do not vary with the level of sales.
Interest Tax Subsidy	That portion of interest payments paid by government in the form of reduced taxes, which stems from the tax deductibility of interest.
Levered Firm	A firm using at least some debt to provide long-term financing of its assets.
Net Cash Flow	Cash receipts less cash expenditures.
Net Working Capital	Current assets minus current liabilities.
Probability Distribution of Rates of Return	A distribution showing possible rates of returns and their probabilities of occurrence.
Pro Forma	Projected or prospective (e.g., pro forma cash flow statements).
Required Rate of Return	The minimum rate of return investors must expect to receive to be compensated for bearing risk and for delaying present consumption.
Risk Averse	The characteristic of disliking to bear risk.
Risk-Free Rate	The required rate of return for risk–free investments at which there is no chance that expected and realized rates of return will differ.
Risk Premium	The additional return investors require if they are to bear a given level of risk.
Standard Deviation of the Rate of Return	The square root of the variance of the rate of return and a measure of risk.
Unlevered Firm	A firm using no debt but only equity to provide long-term financing of the firm's assets.
Variable Expenditures	Cash expenditures that vary proportionately with the level of sales.
Variance of the Rate of Return	The weighted average of squared deviations of possible from expected rates of return.
Working Capital	Current assets.

QUESTIONS   1.   How would a cash flow statement be expected to differ from an income statement?

2. If the required rate on an investment in a sugar cane plantation is 15 percent and the expected rate of return is 10 percent, would your wealth be increased or decreased by undertaking the investment? Would you decide to accept or reject?

3. In what sense are the terms "claim" and "investment" interchangeable?

4. Suppose Frank failed to consider working capital needs. Why would this be a serious oversight?

5. What is business risk? How might it be measured?

6. Explain each term in the formula $k = r_f + \phi$. What is the rationale for using such a formula?

7. How does financial risk arise?

8. Why is a tax subsidy received when a firm finances with debt?

9. The variability of rates of return on equity increases with leverage. Explain why this occurs and develop a simple numerical example of your own.

10. Explain how the fixed interest charge is a *lever* for returns to equity.

11. Explain why Frank Harris would be the only investor to enjoy the increase of $485 in the value of his firm.

1. Calculate the rate of return if an investment of $100 now, yields **PROBLEMS** $120 a year from now.

2. Calculate the dollar return and the rate of return on an investment of $40 now, which returns $45 in 1 year.

3. Find the wealth of Alice, whose only asset is a claim to receive $325 a year from now. The required rate of return is 8 percent.

4. A loan to the Choice Tobacco Company has the following prospects of returns during the coming year: 8 percent with 0.8 probability, 9 percent with 0.1 probability, and 7 percent with 0.1 probability. Calculate its expected rate of return and standard deviation.

5. Find the risk of a loan from Mike to Pat if the possible returns are 0 and 20 percent, with a 50:50 chance of each occurring.

6. If the market required rate of return for different levels of risk is

given by $k = 6$ percent $+ (2)\sigma$, calculate k when $\sigma = 5$ percent and $\sigma = 10$ percent.

7. Find the present value of a $1250 cash flow in perpetuity if k equals 10 percent.

8. A firm that expects level, perpetual operating earnings of $32,050 per year has made an equity investment of $125,000. Assuming tax rates of 15 percent on the first $25,000 of taxable income and 18 percent on the remaining amount, compute the expected rate of return on equity.

9. Three firms, A, B, and C, have standard deviations and expected rates of return as shown below. If the relationship between risk and required return is $k = 8$ percent $+ 1.4(\sigma)$, which of the firms earns an expected rate of return greater than the required rate?

Firm	$\sigma(\%)$	$r^*(\%)$
A	18	30
B	5	18
C	12	26

10. Compute the risk premium for each firm shown in Problem 9.

11. Hendricks Metals is an all-equity firm with a total equity investment of $30,000. The probability distribution of level, perpetual sales, and net operating cash flows is given below. Assume that all income is taxed at 15 percent and that the cash flows are expected to be level through the perpetual life of the firm.

Sales	Net Operating Income	Probability
$100,000	$ 4,400	0.3
150,000	10,400	0.4
200,000	16,400	0.3

(a) Compute the expected rate of return and standard deviation of the rate of return on equity.

(b) Find the market value of the unlevered firm.

(c) Now assume that the firm replaces $10,000 of equity with $10,000 of 10 percent debt. Compute the expected rate of return and standard deviation for equity.

(d) How much of the risk of the levered firm is business risk? Financial risk?

(e) If the relationship between risk and required rate of return is $k = 10$ percent $+ 1.4(\sigma)$, what is the required return on both levered and unlevered equity?

12. Diana is considering investing $5000 of her savings in a single period project that has the following prospects.

Possible Conditions	Dollar Outcome	Probability
Boom	$6500	0.65
Normal	5500	0.25
Disaster	3000	0.10

(a) Compute a rate of return for each dollar outcome; then find the expected rate of return and the standard deviation of those rates of return. Graph the probability distribution of the rates of return.

(b) Suppose that the market required rate of return for different levels of risk is given by $k = 5$ percent $+ 1.5(\sigma)$. Draw the market risk–return relationship and plot Diana's investment.

(c) Should Diana go ahead with this investment?

13. The probability distribution of sales and net operating cash flow of Murray Manufacturing is shown below. Murray is an all-equity firm with a total equity investment of $50,000. Earnings are expected to be level throughout the perpetual life of the firm, and a flat tax rate of 25 percent is assumed to apply to all earnings.

Annual Sales	Net Operating Cash Flow	Probability
$250,000	$15,000	0.2
300,000	20,000	0.6
350,000	25,000	0.2

(a) Compute the expected rate of return and standard deviation of rates of return on equity.

(b) If $k = 6$ percent $+ 1.2(\sigma)$, compute the market value of Murray Manufacturing.

14. Doug Smith decided to invest $13,000 in an unlevered firm to manufacture sleds. Expected annual sales are $100,000 in perpetuity. To support this level of sales, Doug estimated that he would need $8500 on average invested in inventory, $1500 in cash,

$3000 in each of receivables and payables. His estimates for cash expenditures were: labor, $35,000; materials, $50,000; replacement of tools, $800; utilities, $2200. He planned to invest $3000 in tools and equipment. He set his own salary at $15,000. Use a tax rate of 17 percent.

(a)   Prepare a pro forma annual cash flow statement and a pro forma balance sheet based on Doug's estimate of $100,000 sales per year. Assume an all-equity firm.

(b)   What is the level of net working capital?

(c)   Find the expected annual rate of return on equity for the business firm.

15.   (Based on information and calculations done in Problem 14.) Doug decided to estimate a probability distribution for sales. His projections were as follows.

Probability	Annual Collection on Sales
0.1	$ 60,000
0.2	80,000
0.4	100,000
0.2	120,000
0.1	140,000

(a)   Calculate the probability distribution of rates of return. (Assume that utilities and replacement of tools are fixed expenses and that the remaining cash expenditures vary proportionately with the level of sales.)

(b)   Compute the standard deviation of the rate of return.

(c)   Determine the required rate of return for the firm if the market risk–return relationship is given by $k = 5$ percent $+ 1.5\sigma$.

(d)   What is the market value of equity? What assumptions are you making when you project this change in wealth as a result of the investment?

16.   (Based on information and calculations done in Problems 14 and 15.) Doug decided to explore the benefits of leverage. He found that he could borrow $1000 at 10 percent interest and so reduce his equity investment to $12,000. Assume that this was to be perpetual debt to prepare a pro forma annual cash flow statement and balance sheet.

(a) What is the expected rate of return on equity for the levered firm?

(b) What is the dollar amount of the interest tax subsidy?

(c) Use the probability distribution of sales given in Problem 15 to compute the probability distribution of rate of return outcomes for equity in the levered firm.

(d) Calculate the standard deviation of the rate of return.

(e) Compute the required rate of return if the market risk–return relationship is given by $k = 5$ percent $+ 1.5\sigma$.

(f) How much of the risk is business risk? How much is financial risk?

APPENDIX 2A

FORMS OF BUSINESS ORGANIZATION

We are basically interested in three kinds of modern business organization: individual proprietorships, general partnerships, and corporations. Our discussion of these three forms is brief, however, for we wish to consider only the more important characteristics of each that are pertinent to a study of business finance.

The Proprietorship

The proprietorship is the simplest form of business organization. The ownership consists of one individual: the proprietor. In general, he or she needs no formal documents or special licenses to operate. Inasmuch as the proprietor assumes all the risk of the enterprise, if it prospers he receives all the benefits; if it fails he personally absorbs all the losses. The life of this form of organization is coincidental with the tenure of the proprietor or the occurrence of bankruptcy. Dissolution would take place concurrently with the proprietor's decision (or the court's in the case of a court-ordered dissolution) to quit business.

Under this form of organization, there are no bylaws, charters, or other legal documents attesting to the firm's existence, and there are no certificates of ownership. The proprietor is the complete authority in all decisions unless he decides to delegate authority to some of his employees.

In case of legal failure, the creditors of the business may look to all the assets of the business for satisfaction of their claims. If their debts are not completely satisfied, however, they may also look to the personal assets of the individual; the proprietor's personal bank account, his securities, and his other personal assets may be attached for satisfaction of his business debts. This liability relationship is described as *unlimited liability* for business debts.

The earnings of the business are merged with the personal income of the individual and are taxed as such.

The Partnership

The *general partnership* is a form of business organization in which two or more individuals act as co-owners of an enterprise. No papers attesting to its existence need to be drawn up. Each partner has an unlimited liability for the debts of the partnership and, in the absence of any other specified arrangement to the contrary, the business income is allocated equally without regard to the respective capital contributions of the partners. A partner's portion of the earnings of the partnership, whether or not distributed, is merged with his personal income for income tax purposes.

For the legal protection of the several partners, it is desirable to draw up a partnership contract that sets forth, among other things, the contributions of each partner, the method and extent of distributing earnings, and the responsibilities and salaries of each partner who assumes a managerial position. Rules relating to general partnerships have been established by common law; however, most states have adopted the Uniform Partnership Act, which sets forth specific rules.

It is particularly noteworthy that each partner is a general agent for the business. Each one is able to make or enter into a contract that binds the whole partnership. For example, if one partner agrees to purchase a machine, all partners are responsible for payment of the bill. Because of this liability and responsibility, one cannot be too cautious in the selection of partners.

The partnership is terminated when one of the partners withdraws, goes personally bankrupt, or dies—any one of which, in effect, forces a change in the firm. For example, if one of several partners dies, a new organization must be created to perpetuate the business. Perhaps it will be formed by the remaining partners, by new partners, or by some combination of both. In any event, existing partners cannot be forced to accept any newcomer into the partnership. Incidentally, the claim against the partnership of a withdrawing partner extends only to the value of his investment in the venture.

The liability of the members of a partnership is joint and several. Any creditors that are not completely satisfied out of a partnership's assets can look to the personal assets of the various partners for payment. Firm assets, however, must be completely extinguished before creditors can look to the personal property of partners. Even when unsatisfied creditors seek payment from partners' personal assets, their claims are subordinated to those of the various partners' personal creditors.

To avoid the unlimited liability of a general partnership, the *limited partnership* form of organization is sometimes used. A business becomes a limited partnership if one or more of the partners possesses limited liability for the activities of the firm and its partners and one or more of the partners is a general partner with unlimited liability. A limited partnership does not ordinarily come into being until a statement expressing the intention of the various partners is filed with the appropriate state official and, of course, in accordance with the governing state laws. Customarily, limited partners may not participate in the management of the business, and their liability is limited to the amount of capital they have invested. The limited partner is a silent partner and his name does not appear in the name of the organization.

The Corporation

The corporation, as distinguished from the partnership or proprietorship, is viewed as a separate entity, as if it were an imaginary being. Indeed, it is treated in the eyes of the law as if it were a person capable of entering into a contract in its own name, not in the names of individuals who own or control it. The various states authorize its existence and, depending on the charter provisions, its legal life continues indefinitely regardless of changes in ownership. It has only the powers given to it by the state in which it is incorporated. These powers are set forth in its *charter*, which evidences state sanction for its existence.

The cost of incorporating is customarily not excessive and usually is as low as a few hundred dollars. Each year thereafter the state of incorporation requires payment of *franchise taxes*, which are typically based on the par value of securities authorized under the corporate charter.

The granting of a charter customarily requires the name and address of the corporation, a minimum number (usually very small) of incorporators, the creation of certain officer positions, the submission of a purpose for which the corporation is created (which may be very general), and the securities authorized for issues. The number of shares of common stock of the corporation must also be authorized at this time.

The corporation form of business enterprise vests its ownership shares with certain characteristics that render them very popular with many investors. Not only do common and preferred stock certificates possess limited liability, they are also legally transferable from one owner to another without affecting the corporate existence. The common stockholder's liability (the amount he can lose) extends only to the limit of the investment by the stockholder—his personal assets being insulated from creditors for mistakes, errors, and/or debts of the corporation. Consequently, many investors (stockholders) who do not wish to participate in the management of the firm but would like to be somewhat akin to limited partners, entitled to participate in the profits and losses, may so participate without assuming any additional personal liability beyond the individual's investment. This provision of limited liability gives the corporate form a distinct advantage over the partnership and the proprietorship.

Ordinarily, if more capital is needed, additional shares can be sold. (The sale of additional shares is not accomplished as easily as this statement implies, of course.) If enough shares have not been authorized originally, it is not difficult for the corporation to obtain an amendment of the corporate charter to provide for the issuance of more shares. Usually not all the authorized shares are issued initially by the corporation, and shares authorized but not outstanding remain available for later issue by the corporation as the need arises.

Each corporation establishes a set of *bylaws* that contain rules binding the directors, officers, and stockholders with respect to the operations of the business. The major difference between the charter and the bylaws is that the latter are more detailed, although bylaws cannot expand the powers contained in the charter. A common feature of bylaws are rules governing the issuance and transfer of stocks. Also, they invariably contain the time and place for stockholder meetings, methods for calling stockholder meetings, provisions for directors' meetings, and payment of and provision for special committees.

The subjects of dividends and corporate finance are generally covered in the bylaws, the charter, and statutes of the state of incorporation. Obviously the corporation has the power to deal in business related to the purpose for which it was created. It has the power to borrow money, to make ordinary contracts, to execute notes, to write checks, and to engage in other financial acts involving the corporation.

A corporation that becomes bankrupt is governed by the bankruptcy laws which set down the principles for the corporation's liquidation or reorganization. Because the owners have limited liability, the creditors of the corporation may not look to any personal assets of the stockholders for the payment of the debt claims. Hence the stockholders are protected from any additional liability.

According to corporate law the stockholders of the firm are its legal owners, and two primary ownership characteristics are found in most common stocks. First, the holders usually have the right to vote on matters that may materially affect their interests. Second, they are entitled to share in the corporate earnings. This is accomplished by declarations of dividends, which are made at the discretion of the board of directors chosen by the stockholders. Undistributed profits are reinvested in the corporation. The earnings of the corporation are subject to federal income tax. Remaining earnings distributed to stockholders as dividends are subject to the individual's personal income tax.

APPENDIX 2B

THE STRUCTURE OF THE LARGER FIRM

Presumably larger business firms are organized to facilitate the pursuit of their goals. Achievement of goals requires a decision-making process, which in turn implies the responsibility for making choices and the authority to effect them. Making the proper decisions requires information about alternatives and their expected results. To secure this information, the decision maker may seek the aid of staff experts. The staff performs an advisory or supportive function and usually does not make any actual operating decisions. The judgment and support of the staff is required, however, to enable "line" personnel to make decisions. Personnel performing in line capacities are engaged directly in the profit-generating activities of the firm: production and distribution. Many firms have an extensive staff of experts whose competence is especially adapted to areas in which decisions of far-reaching importance are frequently made; outside consultants may be engaged when the problem is so specialized that the firm's staff advisers are not able to handle it. A typical organization chart is shown in Figure 2B-1.

The large firm is organized so that broad policy decisions concerning matters such as goals, products, expansion, election of officers, security flotations, and dividend policies are usually made by the board of directors or by a committee of the board that follows the advice of a group of experienced personnel whose judgment is well acknowledged. The authority for these decisions resides in the board of directors, which is elected by the shareholders, and the members of the board of directors may or may not be salaried. The board meets periodically to review the overall strategy of the firm in the pursuit of its goals and to make new decisions for the future in light of current developments.

Figure 2B-1   *Company Organization Chart*

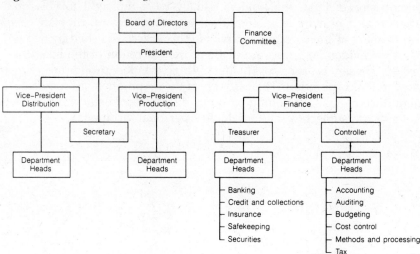

The actual execution of these policy decisions is delegated to the firm's executives. The president or executive vice-president customarily is delegated the chief responsibility for carrying out the overall policy objectives and coordinating the activities of subordinate officers who head the functional divisions. These officers are often designated vice-presidents or some equivalent term. Below each of the departments or divisions are various levels of managers with different degrees of authority and responsibility. Each level is empowered to make decisions up to a given point. Decisions beyond that point usually are referred to and decided by a higher authority. For example, the regional manager in charge of sales may be empowered to make individual capital expenditures (noncurrent expenditures) over a given period of time up to $10,000 (decided by higher authority as the amount sufficient to handle routine requirements). Any expenditure decisions in excess of that amount must be made by, say, the vice-president in charge of soap sales. In turn, the vice-president may be empowered to make decisions concerning capital expenditures that do not require a sum in excess of $50,000. Any expenditure proposed beyond that amount must go to the president, who himself may be limited to decisions involving $100,000 or less. All the decisions involving over $100,000 are made by the board of directors.

In addition to these officers, two others should be briefly discussed at this point: the treasurer and the secretary.

The treasurer is usually responsible for the receipts and disbursements of the firm as well as for its securities and list of stockholders. Closely associated with this position is that of controller (comptroller). The controller normally has the responsibility of keeping the accounting records. The making of financial plans for future periods may be the responsibility of the controller, the treasurer, or the financial vice-president. These plans for the future are called cash and capital budgets and represent a systematic analysis of anticipated financial needs and resources.

The secretary is responsible for recording the minutes of the board of directors' meetings. The secretary might also send out proxy statements, annual and periodic reports to shareholders, and notifications of special meetings.

Below the so-called top management group, there is the middle management group, which consists primarily of persons heading various sections under each of the major divisions or subdivisions of the firm. The scope of middle managers' authority and responsibility is even more constrained than that of their superiors.

Although the structure of large firms may appear to be different from that of smaller firms, the same basic functions are performed in each. The titles vary and the number of persons involved is quite different among business firms. Indeed, the actual operations of a business—the lines of authority—whether the firm be large or small, a corporation, partnership, or proprietorship, a manufacturing or merchandising firm, or whatever, are not actually as clear as this discussion implies. On the contrary, lines of authority and methods of operations are as diverse as are the persons who operate enterprises.

Financial control is the utilization of a firm's financial resources to achieve the goals of the firm. Financial control, especially in the larger firms, is a most difficult, and at times seemingly impossible, task. It must be constantly exercised because of the dynamic state of the financial world in which the firm operates. Continuous measurement and feedback of information from the firm's activities necessitates changes in the planned activities of the firm in pursuit of its goals. Usually these data cannot be processed immediately, so that some time lag inevitably is involved in adjusting the firm to new circumstances. Data must be processed, summarized, and analyzed before valuable information is made available to management for control purposes. Elaborate summary forms and reports may be prepared periodically; these reports serve as the basis for controlling a firm's financial operations. They should contain the information necessary for higher management to evaluate

Financial Control

the performance of the section reporting. Thus, closely allied with controlling the enterprise is the method of reporting information and the comparison of the measured results with the goals of the enterprise.

The chief tools of financial control are the cash budget and the capital budget, although other techniques such as pro forma income and balance sheet statements and breakeven analysis are also employed. Cash budgets refer to the forecast of cash disbursements and receipts for a specified period of time, one year being typical. Capital budgets are forecasts of cash disbursements for and receipts from investments in long-lived assets. In each case budgets serve as control mechanisms insofar as actual performance is compared with projected performance. As feedback continues to accumulate, modification of each of the budgets is often necessary. So important is the capital budget as a control mechanism that much of the analytical effort of modern business finance is devoted to this complex problem.

Communication of Financial Information

Since budgets and other statements of control are also methods of communicating financial information, it is important to discuss them. Most communication of financial data relies heavily on the use of certain accounting techniques and records.

To communicate with the general public, and with stockholders in particular, the annual report is used extensively. In the annual report there is generally a breakdown of the assets, liabilities, and net worth of the business enterprise, and a summary statement of the accounting profit picture for the recent period (usually 1 year). In addition, there is usually a message from the chairman of the board or the president (or both), a breakdown of the products of the firm, information concerning the prospects of the firm, and a summary of financial data for perhaps 5 or 10 years past. Unfortunately, some reports fail to convey enough financial data for present and prospective suppliers of capital (investors) to make adequate decisions regarding the financial integrity of the firm. This can be a serious handicap, since lack of adequate financial information may influence a firm's cost of capital adversely. In short, the firm may have to pay more for its capital funds than might have been the case, had it divulged more financial information.

Others means of communicating financial data to the public are quarterly (and/or semiannual) reports of financial condition similar to, but more abbreviated than, annual reports; prospectuses and registration statements filed with the Securities and Exchange Commission; and listing statements filed with the various national and regional securities exchanges. Obviously, these methods of communication are used by national or large business enterprises whose equity securities are held by the public. For smaller firms, the only effective means of communicating such data to the public may be newspaper advertisements similar to those used by banks. On the other hand, there may be no desire to communicate such information, as is the case with large, closely held firms.

For purposes of securing credit, either from trade sources, banks, or other financial institutions, small, nonpublicly held firms as well as publicly owned firms may be required to provide such items as internal statements of control, detailed income statements and balance sheets for several years past, projected income statements, and sales, cash, and other budgets. Personal interviews by potential creditors are often required as well.

Within the firm, the means of communicating financial data are varied and there seems to be no clear-cut way that can be considered "best." Obviously, the more information a business enterprise has with respect to its overall internal operations, the more capable it is of being controlled. The question to be asked is, Will the additional information result in additional benefits exceeding the additional cost necessary to derive such information? Usually, no precise statement can be made regarding the acquisition of additional information. The problem is one of trying to balance the additional benefits derived from having more information against the additional cost of securing it. Presumably the additional benefit will exceed the additional cost.

Internal statements of control—such as cash budgets, projected income statements, breakeven data, and capital budgets—often terminate on specific dates, as, for example, during seasonal lows of business activity. They are the basic means of communicating financial information within the firm. Usually these statements are of varying quality. Except for capital budgets, they often involve very short periods of time and are designed as a means of planning for the future. Moreover, they may be expressed in either physical or monetary terms. Production, purchase, and cash budgets, and their accompanying analyses, are often the sole means of communicating the short-term financial status of the firm, for they are rarely cast for periods longer than 6 to 12 months. Their contribution lies in comparing the actual results with projections in order to analyze changes that are taking place; this allows management to adjust its cash expectations and other requirements.

Projected income statements and balance sheets, as well as financial analyses, are also frequently employed. Projects requiring large expenditures, the benefits of which are not to be realized except over long periods of time, are typically described by means of a capital budget. These, as well as the shorter term budgets already mentioned, are designed, of course, to keep tabs on the financial health of the enterprise. Usually, it is not until many of them have been taken together that the financial integrity of the firm can be evaluated. Short-run budgets usually facilitate the long-run goal of the firm, which, as we have seen, is to maximize the wealth of shareholders. Because of the uncertainty surrounding all business decisions, the planning horizon of most firms is often short, even for capital expenditures.

The role of the financial manager in communicating financial data is not precise. In many firms he or she reports directly to the president. In others, the financial manager may report to the finance committee, which may consist of, say, the president, the chairman of the board, a few other directors, and the financial vice-president.

APPENDIX 2C

CORPORATE AND PERSONAL INCOME TAXES

Income taxes are an important influence on financial decisions. This appendix describes tax rates assessed by the federal government against corporate and personal income.

Corporate Income Taxes

For corporations, tax rates applicable to operating earnings after deducting interest charges (corporate taxable income) have a *progressive* structure. The effects of progressive taxes can best be seen by distinguishing between marginal and average corporate tax rates. The marginal tax rate is the rate applicable to an *additional* dollar of taxable income. The average tax rate is the effective rate applicable to the *entire* amount of taxable income. For 1983, the marginal tax rate structure for various income levels is shown below.

1983 Marginal Tax Rates on Corporate Taxable Income

Taxable Income Range	Increments of Taxable Income	Marginal Corporate Tax Rate
$0– $25,000	$25,000	15%
25,000– $50,000	25,000	18
50,000– $75,000	25,000	30
75,000–$100,000	25,000	40
Over $100,000	Any	46

Successive increments of taxable income are taxed at higher rates to a maximum of 46 percent for increments for income levels above $100,000. Thus, the average corporate tax rate is below the marginal tax rate as the ensuing example illustrates.

Casey Corporation has a taxable income of $150,000. Starting from $0 of income, successive increments of taxable income are taxed at the marginal rates indicated.

Increments of Income	×	Marginal Tax Rate	=	Corporate Tax
25,000	×	0.15	=	$ 3,750
25,000	×	0.18	=	4,500
25,000	×	0.30	=	7,500
25,000	×	0.40	=	10,000
50,000	×	0.46	=	23,000
		Total Tax		$48,750

The average tax rate applicable to the entire $150,000 of taxable income is:

$$\frac{\$48,750}{\$150,000} = 0.325, \quad \text{or } 32.5\%$$

This is below the 46 percent marginal rate for Casey's last $50,000 increment of income.

A further presentation of average tax rates computed for alternative levels of taxable income is provided below.

Corporate Taxable Income	Average Tax Rate
$ 25,000	15.0%
50,000	16.50
75,000	21.00
100,000	25.75
150,000	32.50
.	.
.	.
.	.
1,000,000	43.98

At even higher levels of taxable income, the average tax rate approaches the maximum 46 percent marginal rate.

Long-term capital gains earned by corporations through purchase and resale of assets are typically taxed at *lower* rates than those applicable to corporate income. Long-term capital gains apply to assets owned 1 year or more. Short-term capital gains for assets owned for less than 1 year are taxed as corporate income. For example, if land is purchased and ultimately sold by a firm at a higher price, the difference between sale price and purchase price is a capital gain. There are alternative methods for computing taxes on capital gains, the firm being able to choose the method that minimizes the tax. Consideration of these complexities is beyond the scope of this book. The important point to remember is that capital gains are taxed at lower rates than corporate income.

Personal Income   Individuals are also subject to different tax rates on ordinary income (from salaries, and interest and dividend payments) and capital gains (from sale of assets). Tax rates on ordinary income are, as with corporations, progressive. Marginal personal tax rates on ordinary income increase with the level of taxable income.

Treatment of capital gains for individuals depends on how long the asset was held by the individual. Long-term capital gains are taxed at rates lower than ordinary income. For 1983 the approximate tax rate on capital gains is 40 percent of the tax rate on ordinary income. Thus, a person in the 45 percent marginal tax bracket for ordinary income would pay a tax rate of $(0.40)(45.0)\% = 18.0$ percent on a long-term capital gain.

Personal income taxes are a complex matter. Tax rates vary with marital status and other characteristics of the tax payer. A host of exclusions and deductions make effective tax rates for individuals vary widely. Only tax attorneys and consultants benefit from this state of affairs. At this point we need to remember simply that personal tax rates on ordinary income are progressive and that long-term capital gains are taxed at lower rates than ordinary income.

SECTION II

Markets, Risk
and Rates of Return

CHAPTER 3

Financial Markets

Investor wealth was defined in Chapter 1 as the market value of assets. Many assets held by investors are financial claims to future cash flows. Their market value (and the investor wealth attributable to holding these claims) is determined in financial markets, which are systems for facilitating transactions in claims.

It is difficult to overstate the importance of financial markets in financial decision making. Recall from Chapter 2 that business decisions were evaluated on the basis of their impact on Frank Harris's wealth as determined by prospective valuation of his investment and financing decisions in the marketplace. Throughout ensuing chapters, too, financial decisions made by firms are evaluated on the basis of their impact on owner wealth. Wealth is not a function solely of expected return. Risk associated with cash flows generated by the firm and the required rate of return established in markets for the particular level of risk are key determinants of wealth.

The debt and equity claims traded in financial markets are called **financial securities.** This chapter explores how these instruments are traded in financial markets. We begin with a description of two important types of markets: primary and secondary. Then we define a particular market setting, a **perfect market.** Perfect markets establish conditions enabling us to understand how financial securities are valued. An important consequence of perfect markets can then be developed: **the equal rate of return principle.** This principle of valuation proves to be of great use in helping understand market valuation, not only under conditions of perfect markets but in the broader context of imperfect markets. **Market imperfections** also are introduced in this chapter. Such imperfections exist in financial markets, and awareness of them is necessary to understand how they may affect valuation of financial securities and the wealth of owners of the firm. Finally, we discuss the concept of **efficient markets,** wherein information regarding the future cash flows and risks of financial securities is quickly processed by financial markets and reflected in security prices.

Two appendixes to this chapter provide additional information. Appendix 3A describes the myriad of financial securities existing in the market. Appendix 3B describes the activities of an important market participant—the investment banker.

TYPES OF MARKETS

The market in which the effects of financial decisions on the equity positions of owners are valued can be divided into two categories: primary and secondary. Newly issued financial securities are sold in a **primary market,** whereas existing securities issued at some previous time are traded in **secondary markets.** Primary and secondary markets are interdependent and, as we shall see, involve **direct** and **indirect transactions** in securities.

Securities Traded in Primary and Secondary Markets

The financial securities bought and sold in primary and secondary markets come in many varieties and forms (see Appendix 3A for details). All the security forms have one thing in common: they depend for their worth on future streams of expected dollar returns. This holds true even for U.S. government debt; it consists intrinsically only of pieces of paper, but that paper bears a promise to pay future dollars secured by the taxing power of the government. We are concerned, within very broad categories, with the following principal classes of financial securities.

1. *Debt*. A claim on the firm that provides a promise of fixed periodic interest payments as well as future principal payments over a defined period of time to the debtholders.

2. *Preferred Stock*. A type of equity claim in which the owners of the preferred stock are promised a periodic fixed dividend.

3. *Common Stock*. The residual claim on the earnings of the firm after all debt claims and preferred stock claims have been satisfied. As with preferred stock, this claim receives dividends only if declared by directors of the corporation.

Any of these classes of securities would serve equally well in our discussion of primary and secondary markets. However, **common stock** is used in most of the examples that follow. **Preferred stock** and various forms of debt are discussed in Appendix 3A.

Let us suppose that Frank Harris did incorporate a shed business, as discussed in Chapter 2, and that, happily, it has prospered and grown. Frank and many other investors own shares of Harris Company common stock. Once Frank and other investors have purchased these shares (invested in the firms), the shares are considered to be *previously issued.* Any further purchases and sales of these previously issued shares will take place in a *secondary market.* We describe both direct and indirect transactions in secondary markets.

A Direct Transaction in a Secondary Market   If Frank wants to sell his own shares of Harris stock to an outside party, he could undertake a direct transaction with a buyer and the *transaction function* of the market would thereby be accomplished. For example, Frank could have lunch at McDonald's, and if he happened to meet there a willing buyer for the shares at an agreed price, the restaurant would have served as a marketplace for this risky asset. Alternatively, if Frank learned that Monroe Gilmour in Durham, North Carolina, was an interested buyer, a long-distance telephone call would constitute the market for a transaction with Gilmour.

Direct transactions in secondary markets are not uncommon, but the cost of transacting is relatively high. For example, Frank might have to eat several McDonald's lunches before finding a buyer for his shares. This is expensive in terms of time and resources. Alternatively, Frank might have to seek long and hard to locate Gilmour in North Carolina. In either case, the cost of information concerning the existence of willing buyers may be very high.

An Indirect Transaction in a Secondary Market   Instead of seeking a direct transaction, Frank could utilize the services of an intermediary in selling the shares of Harris Company in the secondary market. One form of intermediary, a **dealer,** "makes a market" by owning an inventory of each financial security in which he or she deals. If a dealer, Sam Pace, happens to make a market in previously issued Harris stock, an indirect transaction might well occur in the following way.

1. Frank contacts Pace indicating his desire to sell shares at the prevailing market price.

2. Gilmour contacts Pace indicating his desire to purchase shares at the prevailing market price.

3. Pace, the dealer, buys Frank's shares and sells them to Gilmour. (If Gilmour had not been ready to buy, Pace might have purchased from Frank anyway, adding the shares to his inventory for later sale.)

A market's function of facilitating a transaction has been accomplished indirectly through the services of an intermediary. Because neither Frank nor Monroe Gilmour has to spend time and resources to learn of the other's desire to transact, Pace has made the cost of the transaction lower than it would otherwise be. These cost savings enable the dealer Pace to mark up the cost of the stock (in effect, to charge a transaction fee) for his valuable service.

If Harris stock were *listed* on an organized stock exchange, such as the New York Stock Exchange, Frank and Gilmour could have undertaken another type of indirect transaction through **brokers.** Brokers do not own quantities of the financial securities in which they deal; that is, they do not "make markets." Rather, they simply arrange transactions between buyers and sellers. For example, the following sequence describes a transaction facilitated by brokers.

1.   Frank tells his broker that he wants to sell shares of Harris Company.

2.   Gilmour tells his broker that he wants to buy shares of Harris Company.

3.   The brokers "meet" on the floor of the New York Stock Exchange and, as agents for Frank and Gilmour, exchange shares for cash at the prevailing market price of the shares.[1]

Each broker charges a commission, or transaction fee, for the valuable service performed. Neither Frank nor Gilmour has had to spend time and resources locating the other.

The examples used so far to illustrate the function of markets in assisting direct and indirect transaction dealt with previously issued common stock; however precisely the same kinds of transactions can take place with previously issued *debt.* For instance, assume in the examples above that Harris Company has previously issued marketable debt outstanding and that Frank, besides owning shares, also owns some of this debt and wishes to sell a quantity of it. Gilmour is then a buyer of debt and Pace can be a dealer in debt. If, alternatively, the debt is listed

---

[1]This is a much oversimplified view of transactions in listed stocks. In practice, the brokers representing Harris and Gilmour would instruct their own representatives on the floor of the exchange. The representatives would go to the place on the floor of the exchange where Harris shares are traded and agree on a share price at which the transaction will be made. Cash does not actually change hands until the settlement date which is four business days after the date of the transaction. If they did not meet simultaneously, other participants representing other buyers and sellers could be involved in the transaction. Failing that, a specialist is available at the exchange who acts as a dealer, ready to buy and sell. A specialist, in acting for his own account, facilitates transactions and may reduce share price fluctuations.

on, say, the New York Bond Exchange, the brokers in the transaction are acting as brokers in debt securities.

Primary markets are markets where *new issues* of financial securities are sold to buyers. As in secondary markets, transactions can be either direct or indirect. When new securities have been sold in the primary market, they become part of the secondary market.

Transactions in Primary Markets

A Direct Transaction in Primary Markets   If Harris Company wished to raise additional funds by selling *newly issued* common stock or debt, management could deal directly with buyers. Representing the firm in this sale of newly issued securities, Frank could again have eaten lunch at McDonald's or searched the country for Gilmour. In direct transactions, costs of information needed to locate buyers are often high.

An Indirect Transaction in Primary Markets   Harris Company could also sell new issues of stock or debt through an indirect transaction by use of an intermediary. For new issues of securities, the intermediary is an **investment banker**—a firm acting to purchase new securities from Harris Company and resell them to buyers—Gilmour being, presumably, among them. Characteristics and operations of investment bankers are detailed in Appendix 3B. Investment bankers charge various fees to issuers of new securities. Such fees are known as **flotation costs** because to issue a new security is, in the vernacular, to "float" an issue.

A special case of indirect transactions in primary markets occurs through *financial intermediaries* such as banks and insurance companies. These firms can purchase newly issued debt securities from firms like Harris Company (or debt from the secondary market). Technically, such financial intermediaries loan funds to firms issuing new debt. But to loan funds is to purchase a financial security. The *indirect* purchasers of such newly issued securities are then, in fact, the individuals who add to their bank deposits or buy new insurance policies. The financial intermediary transfers the funds obtained from new bank deposits or insurance policies to the sellers of the new issues of debt. Once again, costs of producing and collecting information needed to locate transactors are saved for the issuers of new securities as well as for those buying them— albeit indirectly.[2]

---

[2]Financial intermediaries serve many other functions as well. Also, this explanation was couched in terms of a debt issue; however, mutual savings banks and all insurance companies are permitted by law to purchase newly issued and previously issued common stock as well as debt. Commercial banks are prohibited from such activity.

The Role of Secondary Markets

Secondary markets greatly assist firms in issuing new securities in the primary market. If no active secondary market existed, purchasers of newly issued securities would have to hold acquisitions with restricted resale possibilities. This would be disadvantageous to the purchaser because a change in future consumption plans requiring the availability of more cash could not be easily met by selling the security. For example, an investor may need $100 of a $1000 investment right away to finance an unanticipated expenditure. With no active secondary market for his securities investment, he will have difficulty quickly disposing of it (or part of it) at full value. Thus, the absence of a secondary market means the purchaser would require a higher rate of return to purchase a security. Stated alternatively, the purchaser would not pay as high a price for a security having limited marketability as he would for a security capable of being immediately resold at the prevailing market price. Generally, the more marketable a security, the higher the price purchasers are willing to pay.

The secondary market for a firm's securities improves as the number of investors in those securities, the quantity of the securities outstanding, and the number of transactions taking place, all increase. Enhanced marketability reduces the rate of return investors will require to purchase newly issued securities of the firm. Firms having poor markets for their securities, characterized by small numbers of transactions and investors, and a low quantity of securities traded, will pay higher rates of return because investors will require them.

PERFECT MARKETS

We have seen how primary and secondary markets act to facilitate transactions between buyers and sellers of financial securities. From the market-determined prices at which financial securities are traded, the wealth of their owners can be determined. These market values reflect the expected future streams of cash returns, the risks of those streams, and the market-determined required rates of return for these securities.

Because the market value of securities is allied to the concept of wealth, it is very important to know why market values of securities are what they are. Such explanations require the use of valuation models. In its more abstract sense, a **valuation model** is a functional relationship between the value of a security and a set of variables determining that value. (See Appendix 3A for a more complete set of definitions of various types of securities and Chapter 11 for valuation models.)

The model builder's lot is not a happy one! Because of the difficulties of construction, many valuation models are built upon the assumption of hypothetical perfect markets. This assumption greatly simplifies the difficulties of construction and testing of valuation models and is thus very useful. The requirements for perfect markets are:

1. There are no transactions costs to buy or sell existing securities and no flotation costs to issue new financial securities.

2. Information concerning the future expected returns and risks of securities is freely available to all participants in the market.

3. No single buyer or seller of securities is large enough to affect the market price of any security when that person (or entity) transacts.

4. If necessary, financial securities are divisible into infinitely small portions—that is, a security having a price of $1000 can be divided into 1000 portions with each portion having a price of $1.

The requirements of item 1 rule out the fees charged by brokers and dealers (transaction costs) for security trades in secondary markets, and investment banking fees (flotation costs) for issuing securities in primary markets.

The absence of transaction and flotation costs, together with the other requirements, means that perfect markets are hypothetical marketplaces that do not conform to real-world conditions. Compared to perfect markets, real-world markets have market imperfections of various types. We discuss such imperfections after demonstrating the equal rate of return principle—a consequence of perfect markets.

THE EQUAL RATE OF RETURN PRINCIPLE

The equal rate of return principle is among the most important ideas, if not the most important idea, in finance. That principle states that *all securities of equal risk must be priced to yield identical expected rates of return.*

To illustrate this fundamental idea, consider the common stock of two firms, A and B. Investors believe that these common stocks are equally risky. The shares sell for $15 and $25 each, respectively.

Firm	Share Price	Expected Annual Dollar Return	Expected Rate of Return
A	$15	$4.50	30%
B	25	5.00	20

In addition, investors expect to receive a perpetual annual cash flow of $4.50 per share for firm A and $5 per share for firm B.

Given this information, the expected rates of return on A and B may be written:

$$r_A^* = \frac{\$4.50}{\$15} = 0.30, \quad \text{or } 30\%$$

and

$$r_B^* = \frac{\$5}{\$25} = 0.20, \quad \text{or } 20\%$$

Can such a situation continue to exist? Clearly, it cannot. No rational investor would want to own the shares of B when the expected rate of return is 20 percent as long as it is possible to purchase the shares of A and expect to earn 30 percent while bearing the *same* level of risk. Investors would want to sell shares of B and purchase those of A. In that process, the price of B should fall and that of A should increase until both shares have the same expected rate of return and investors are willing to hold both shares. When, as with A and B, two securities of identical risk are priced to provide different expected rates of return, an **arbitrage** opportunity is said to exist. In this case A and B are the "same" in that they have identical risk. Arbitrage involves buying and selling of the same commodity or security at the same time for a gain. The arbitrage gain from selling 3 shares of B for $75 and buying 5 shares of A for $75 is the expected, perpetual cash flow or $(0.30 - 0.20)\$75 = \$7.50$ per year. Note that for the same cost ($75) and for the same risk the investor expects to receive an *extra* $7.50 per year forever.

Suppose that the required rate of return for investments with the same level of risk is, as established in the market, 24 percent. Assuming that investors expect to receive a perpetual annual dollar return of $4.50 for A and $5 for B, Equation (2-6) may be used to compute the appropriate prices for both A and B. Those prices are denoted P_A and P_B, respectively.

$$P_A = \frac{\text{Expected dollar return}}{k} = \frac{\$4.50}{0.24} = \$18.75$$

$$P_B = \frac{\text{Expected dollar return}}{k} = \frac{\$5.00}{.24} = \$20.83$$

Note that P_A should increase to $18.75, while P_B should fall to $20.83. At those prices, both shares have the same expected rate of return, which is equal to the required rate in the market. No arbitrage gains are then possible.

As an additional illustration, consider the problem of valuing the shares of a new firm which have yet to be traded in the market. How might such a valuation proceed? First, investors must form expectations of future cash flows. Assume that they expect a perpetual cash flow of $2.50 per share. Second, they need to assess the appropriate required rate of return and to apply the equal rate of return principle. To do this they need to find firms whose shares are already traded in the market and have a degree of risk identical to that of shares of the new firm. Such firms must operate in the same industry and have financing policies identical to those of the new firm. Thus, they and the new firm would be affected in the same way by the same economic forces. If a 20 percent required rate of return is appropriate for the risk of these comparable shares, it should also be appropriate for the shares of the new firm. The appropriate price per share for the new firm, P_N, is therefore

$$P_N = \frac{\$2.50}{0.20} = \$12.50$$

When the price of the new firm is $12.50, investors expect to earn 20 percent, the same rate expected by investors who own other securities of identical risk.

We cannot overemphasize the importance of the equal rate of return principle. It must be retained as a central concept in market valuation.

The idealized conditions of perfect markets are not met in reality. Trading in securities *does* involve transactions costs. Issuing new securities *does* mean that flotation costs will be sustained. Information for investors is *not* freely available and, under certain conditions, single buyers and sellers of securities *can* affect the price of securities. Finally, securities are *not* divisible into infinitely small portions. Yet in the face of these conditions, known as market imperfections, many useful valuation models for securities and portfolios of securities continue to assume that perfect markets exist—that is, that there are no market imperfections present.

MARKET IMPERFECTIONS

However, in spite of possible temptation, the reader should not dismiss valuation models based on perfect markets on the grounds that they are "unrealistic" and therefore useless. Models in many fields are often declared to be unrealistic because they ignore some factor observed to exist in the "real world." But this criticism *by itself* is not valid because by its very nature, a model always *abstracts* from reality (assuming that one can even define reality!) by eliminating factors or influences thought to have little or no importance. The real issue is whether the omitted factors have effects so important that they cannot be safely ignored by the user of the model.[3]

---

[3]For example, managers make decisions by forming a model of the decision problem, even if it is casually constructed in the mind and not committed to paper. That model will include what are viewed as useful factors or variables and exclude those that are viewed as not useful. For example, it is well known that a price increase in any commodity tends to affect demand for other commodities as consumers realign their spending plans. Thus a rise in the price of bananas may cause consumers to buy fewer bananas, more apples and, perhaps, more garden fertilizer. A farmer planning apple production *should* take into account the price of bananas. A manufacturer planning fertilizer output, however, will take into account many factors but will probably *ignore* the price of bananas. The fertilizer manufacturer is "unrealistic" because the price of bananas does affect the demand for

A valuation model based on perfect markets enables us to reach some important equilibrium results—such as the equal rate of return principle. Once such results have been obtained, market imperfections should be introduced into the model to see whether they systematically and materially alter the results obtained from the model. If a particular market imperfection that is introduced fails to change the results of a valuation model based on perfect markets, that market imperfection can be ignored. Some observers may still view the perfect market model as unrealistic, but the ability of the model to explain the real world would not be enhanced by incorporating the imperfection. On the other hand, if the introduction of a given imperfection would importantly alter the results of a perfect market model, the perfect market model is inadequate and may be correctly and usefully termed unrealistic.

Often it is not easy to bring market imperfections into perfect market valuation models, but the effort is necessary. For some financial decisions, certain imperfections are material and cannot safely be ignored if shareholders are to be well served by financial managers. We cannot describe here all the efforts made to introduce market imperfections, but we comment on them as imperfections are confronted in subsequent chapters. For now, we simply describe the nature and potential importance of some of these imperfections.

Transactions and Flotation Costs in Trading and Issuing Securities

Perfect markets require that there be no transaction costs for trading in existing securities or flotation costs for issuing new securities. In fact, however, brokers charge a fee, and dealers a markup, to facilitate transactions in existing securities. Investment bankers impose flotation costs to market newly issued securities.

Transaction Cost Structure   **Transaction costs** to buy and sell existing securities can be very high if the money value of the transaction is small. Table 3-1 shows the range of stock transaction costs as a percentage of the total money value of a transaction.[4]

Clearly, as the dollar size of the transaction increases, transaction costs decline as a percentage of the total dollar value of the transaction.

Transaction costs make it more expensive for investors making only small dollar investments to profitably invest in securities. For example, an investor seeing an arbitrage gain to be made between two securities will not undertake the transaction to exploit the gain if, say, the gain is

---

fertilizer. However, the influence of banana prices is so small that he may safely ignore (abstract from) the price of bananas in his decision model.

[4]Brokerage fees may now be negotiated between broker and client. The transaction rates shown in Table 3-1 are "suggested" rates taken from information given by a brokerage house.

Table 3–1   *Typical Stock Transaction Rates*

Money Value of Transaction	Approximate Charge
$ 100	25.00%
1,000	3.6
5,000	2.2
10,000	2.1
50,000	1.9
100,000	1.5

worth $25 but the transaction costs to buy and sell total $50. Lacking the incentive to exploit arbitrage gains, small investors will tend not to produce the price adjustments in shares that wipe out arbitrage gains and insure that the equal rate of return principle holds. Transaction costs also make it expensive for small investors to *diversify* by holding many securities. As we discuss in Chapter 4, diversification is of great benefit to investors and has important implications for the development of the required rate of return for securities established in the market.

Fortunately, there are ways for small investors to band together to increase the dollar size of their transactions and so reduce the cost of transactions per dollar invested. Mutual funds (see Appendix 3A) are an example of a device for reducing transaction costs and providing lower cost diversification. Mutual funds, together with individuals and institutions investing large quantities of funds, help reduce the potential disturbance posed by transaction costs to the establishment of equilibrium prices and required rates of return for securities.

Transaction costs may also have an important role in influencing the dividend policy of firms. We discuss that issue more fully in Chapter 14.

Flotation Cost Structure   As in the case of transaction costs, flotation costs of issuing new debt and equity securities can be relatively high for small issues. This state of affairs makes the cost of financing much higher for small firms than for large firms. In a study of common stock issues newly registered with the Securities and Exchange Commission, the size of the issue accounted for about one half the variation in flotation costs among security issues.[5] Furthermore, as the firm's size of

---

[5]U.S. Securities and Exchange Commission, *Cost of Flotation of Corporate Securities, 1971–1972* (Washington, DC: Government Printing Office, December 1974).

Table 3–2   *Average Costs of Flotation (Percent of Issue Price)*

Size of Issue ($000,000)	Bonds	Preferred Stock	Common Stock
Under 0.5	14.1		23.6
0.5 to 0.9	8.9		20.7
5.0 to 9.9	3.1	2.5	8.7
20.0 to 49.9	1.4	1.7	5.0
50.0 and over	1.2	1.6	4.2

Source: U.S. Securities and Exchange Commission, *Cost of Flotation of Corporate Securities, 1971–1972* (U.S.G.P.O., 1974).

security issue increases, flotation costs decrease (as a percentage of the size of the issue). This suggests that there are fixed costs of issue regardless of the size of the issue. Table 3-2 provides data from a study covering flotation costs of bonds, preferred stock, and common stock.[6]

The services provided by investment bankers to earn flotation costs are presented in detail in Appendix 3B, but we point out here that flotation costs, by imposing greater proportionate costs on small firms than on large, restrict the opportunities of small firms to grow through additional capital investment. Such problems may be severe enough, some argue, to lead to strict capital constraints on the firm (discussed in Chapter 10). In addition, flotation costs may have an effect on the dividend policy of the firm (see Chapter 14).

Availability of Information to Investors

Perfect markets require that all information concerning future returns and risks of securities be available to all investors. This requirement cannot be met in reality. For one thing, gathering information is costly in terms of time and resources. Investors having smaller wealth positions find it *relatively* more expensive to acquire a given quantity and quality of information from which to form expectations of future returns and risks than investors having large wealth positions. Second, some individuals have access to special knowledge of a given security's prospects that is not available to other investors, although the U.S. Securities and Ex-

---

[6]S. H. Archer and L. G. Faerber, "Firm Size and the Cost of Equity Capital," *Journal of Finance* (March 1966), pp. 69–84.

change Commission does not permit "insiders" to benefit from trading based on private information. For either reason, investors can be expected to hold different sets of information about the prospects for risky securities and, as a result, to have diverse expectations about future expected returns and risks.

That information is costly to investors can hardly be doubted. Even readily available accounting data about firms has defects (see Chapter 20). For example, differences in allowable accounting practices make the validity of comparisons of operating results between firms questionable without further investigation and sometimes modification of the data.

Fortunately, diverse expectations among investors about the future returns and risks of securities do not necessarily disturb the conclusions drawn from perfect market models. For example, some investors, particularly larger institutional traders like mutual funds and pension fund managers, may have better information (because it is cheaper for them to obtain relative to the size of their transactions) than small investors. When these large traders receive a change in information about a security's prospects, this information is quickly processed into a change in share price as traders act to obtain profits or avoid losses. Thus the new market price reflects the new information even though not all investors were aware of it at the same time.

The discussion later in this chapter concerning efficient markets elaborates on this issue. Costs of information may also have implications for the dividend policy of firms (see Chapter 14).

Size of Buyer or Seller Transaction

By offering a large quantity of a given security for sale within a short period of time, it is sometimes possible to depress the price of that security. Such behavior of security prices is more pronounced when the particular securities have poor, inactive markets. Nevertheless, for the large quantity of securities traded in active markets, the ability of any seller (or buyer) to *systematically* affect a security's price when the market's perception of the value of a security is unchanged is strictly limited in duration and degree. This particular market imperfection is not a major concern in this text.

Divisibility

Finally, perfect markets imply that securities are infinitely divisible. This assumption avoids the problem of "lumpiness" brought about by indivisible securities having high unit cost. For example, a person with only $100 to invest cannot use that sum to purchase 10 percent of one share of a common stock selling for $1000.

Lack of divisibility makes it more difficult for investors to diversify.

However, as mentioned in the discussion of transaction costs, mutual funds help overcome problems of divisibility for small investors and, for large investors, lack of divisibility does not pose a severe problem.

Lack of divisibility is one of the arguments used in favor of stock splits or stock dividends, as discussed in Chapter 14.

EFFICIENT MARKETS

With costly information, investors hold different expectations about the prospects for firms. Changes in information may cause changes in expectations and revisions in security prices. The revised security price may then be thought of as reflecting a new consensus of expectations among investors. (Anyone disagreeing with the consensus would buy or sell at the consensus price, causing a further revision of price until all were content to hold the security at its consensus price.)

But whether markets are perfect or have significant imperfections, they can still be termed **efficient markets.** In an efficient market, changes in information about the prospects for a given security are quickly reflected in that security's price. Favorable information about a security will cause an immediate price increase, and unfavorable information will produce an immediate price decline.

In an efficient market, quick penalties and rewards in the form of share price changes result from managerial decisions in a firm once the information about these decisions has flowed into the market. For example, suppose that a firm decides to build a new manufacturing plant. The market believes that as a result, the cash dividends stream in *perpetuity* for the firm's common stock will rise from $1 to $1.50 per share. If the market's required rate of return for that firm's common stock remains at $k = 10$ percent, the old and new common stock prices can be found by dividing cash dividends per share by the required rate of return.

Old Price	New Price
$P = \dfrac{\$1}{0.10} = \$10$	$P = \dfrac{\$1.50}{0.10} = \$15$

Even though the new plant has not yet been built, once the information about new higher returns becomes available to investors, the market will efficiently process it into an *immediate* price increase from $10 to $15 per share. There will be no delay. The same result extends to unfavorable news. If the market recognizes the increased returns but views the *risk* of the common stock as also increasing, it may raise the required rate of return on the stock to $k = 20$ percent. Then even with higher earnings the new stock price will immediately decline to $7.50, since

$$P = \frac{\$1.50}{0.20} = \$7.50$$

An important consequence of efficient markets is the equality of security price and the value the market places on a security. Given the information making up consensus expectations about the prospects for a security, the market perceives a value for that security. If market price should differ from that value, buying or selling transactions will take place, causing market price to rise or fall to the value placed on that security by the market. Thus at any point in time, security price is a good estimate of the value placed on the security by the market under efficient markets.

SUMMARY

The market value of any financial security represents part of the current wealth of the owner of that security. Firms seeking to maximize the wealth of the owners of the firm must therefore look to the effects of their decisions on their securities' market value, and thus the wealth of the owners of the firm.

The principal classes of corporate securities valued in markets are debt, preferred stock, and common stock. Primary security markets aid transactions in newly issued securities. Secondary security markets facilitate transactions in previously issued securities. Both types of markets make use of direct and indirect transactions. Direct transactions are made between the ultimate seller of the security and the ultimate buyer, whereas indirect transactions make use of an intermediary such as a broker, dealer, or investment banker. The existence of security markets greatly reduces the costs of time and other resources used to find buyers or sellers for securities. Securities enjoying good marketability tend to sell at higher prices than securities having poor, inactive markets.

Perfect markets are characterized by (1) no transaction or flotation costs, (2) information freely available to all investors, (3) many buyers and sellers, any one of which cannot affect market prices by trading securities, and (4) perfect divisibility. Valuation models for financial securities constructed under perfect market assumptions provide insight into factors affecting the value of a security. Underlying such valuation models is the equal rate of return principle, which states that all investments having identical risk must sell at prices to yield identical expected rates of return. If this condition is not met, arbitrage gains are possible. Exploitation of these gains will revise security prices. Market imperfections remain important if they systematically and materially alter the results of valuation models constructed under the assumptions of perfect markets.

Efficient markets very rapidly incorporate new information concerning the prospects of securities into changes in security prices. Efficient markets quickly produce a price change once new information on a security is made known. The rapid price changes brought about by efficient markets create swift penalties or rewards for decisions made by the managers of the firm. With efficient markets, security prices represent the value the market places on them.

GLOSSARY OF KEY TERMS

Arbitrage	The simultaneous purchase and sale of identical risk securities priced to have different expected rates of return.
Broker	An intermediary acting as an agent in facilitating the trading of stocks between buyer and seller.
Common Stock	A financial security representing the residual claim on the earnings of the firm.
Dealer	An intermediary who maintains an inventory of securities from which he sells to buyers of securities and to which he adds by buying from sellers of securities.
Direct Transaction	A sale of a financial security by a seller to a buyer without the services of an intermediary.
Equal Rate of Return Principle	The important principle stating that all securities of equal risk must be priced to yield identical expected rates of return.
Efficient Markets	Markets in which information concerning changes in the prospects for securities is immediately reflected in changes in security prices.
Financial Securities	Claims on future cash flows of business firms, or perhaps governments.
Flotation Costs	Fees charged by investment bankers to market newly issued securities.
Indirect Transaction	A sale of a financial security by a seller to a buyer using the services of an intermediary.
Investment Banker	An intermediary facilitating the sale of newly issued securities.
Market Imperfection	Any violation of the conditions characterizing perfect markets.
Perfect Markets	Markets having the following conditions: (1) no transaction or flotation costs for securities, (2) information concerning future expected returns

and risk freely available to all investors, (3) no single buyer or seller of securities large enough to affect market price, and (4) financial securities divisible into infinitely small portions.

Preferred Stock   An ownership claim promising to pay a fixed cash dividend in perpetuity.

Primary Market   The market for new securities to be issued.

Secondary Market   The market for previously issued securities.

Transaction Costs   Fees charged by brokers and dealers to facilitate trade in previously issued securities.

Valuation Model   A functional relationship between the value of a security and a set of variables determining that value.

SELECTED REFERENCES

Baumol, William J. *The Stock Market and Economic Efficiency.* New York: Fordham University Press, 1965.

Friend, Irwin, James R. Longstreet, Morris Mendelson, Ervin Miller, and Arleigh R. Hess, Jr. *Investment Banking and the New Issues Market.* Cleveland: World Publishing Co., 1967.

Furst, Richard W. "Does Listing Increase the Market Price of Common Stocks?" *Journal of Business* (April 1970), pp. 174–180.

Hayes, Samuel L., III. "Investment Banking Power Structure in Flux," *Harvard Business Review* (March–April, 1971), pp. 135–152.

Reilly, Frank K. "A Three Tier Stock Market in Corporate Financing," *Financial Management* (Autumn 1975), pp. 7–16.

Sears, Gerald A. "Public Offerings for Smaller Companies," *Harvard Business Review* (September–October, 1968), pp. 112–120.

Stoll, Hans R., and Anthony J. Curley. "Small Business and the New Issues Market for Equities," *Journal of Financial and Quantitative Analysis* (September 1970), pp. 309–322.

QUESTIONS

1. Financial markets were not created by legislation but arose as private institutions that survive because people are willing to pay for their existence. Comment.

2. Why are financial markets important in financial decision making?

3. Identify the market, primary or secondary, in which each of the following transactions would take place.

   (a) Purchase of 50,000 shares of Apple Computer stock when Apple first went public in December 1980.

   (b) Sale of 1000 shares of Apple Computer in 1981 through your broker, trading on the over the counter market.

   (c) A local bank purchases U.S. Treasury bills at the Monday auction.

   (d) Three friends form a corporation and pool their savings to purchase shares in the new business.

   (e) You lend $5000 to a friend to provide funds for expanding his business.

4. Distinguish between a direct and indirect transaction. Which of the transactions in Problem 3 would most likely be direct?

5. How does the existence of active secondary markets benefit firms issuing new securities in primary markets?

6. What are the characteristics of a good secondary market?

7. Distinguish between a perfect market and an efficient market. Is a perfect market likely to be efficient?

8. When is a market imperfection important? How should a financial manager determine whether a market imperfection should be included in a decision model?

9. Explain the equal rate of return principle and how arbitrage ensures that it will hold under perfect markets.

10. In an efficient securities market, how is a small investor with little access to information likely to find out about changes affecting a security's prospects?

PROBLEMS 1. Goodier Financial Advisory Services, Inc., is for sale. The sole owner, Goodier, offers to sell it to you for the book value of the equity, which is $100,000. The expected annual earnings, all to be paid out as cash dividends to the owner, are $15,000 per year in perpetuity. You carefully consult information available in the market and find that equities of identical risk are priced so that the market requires rates of return of (a) $k = 12\frac{1}{2}$ percent, (b) $k = 15$ percent, (c) $k = 17\frac{1}{2}$ percent. In each alternative case, what will your response to the offer be? Why? What is owner Goodier's wealth in each of the cases—the offer to sell notwithstanding?

2. Mead Amusement Company and Ajax Novelty, Inc., have common shares that bear identical risks. Mead shares are expected to pay a $0.60 dividend per share in perpetuity. Ajax shares are expected to pay $1.50 per share in perpetuity. Mead shares sell for $10 per share, and Ajax shares are currently priced at $15 per share. You own 30 Mead shares. What arbitrage opportunity exists here? If the equilibrium required rate of return is $k = 8$ percent, at what price for each of the two securities will opportunities for arbitrage gains cease? Assume that there are no transaction costs.

3. A new Portland General Electric preferred stock issue is priced at $27.50 per share with a $4.40 annual dividend. (Preferred stock pays a fixed dividend in perpetuity to the holder.) What is the required market rate of return for securities with identical risk characteristics? Assume perfect markets.

4. Two preferred stocks have identical risk characteristics. The market requires a 12 percent rate of return for securities with this level of risk. Preferred stock A pays an annual dividend of $4.40 and preferred stock B pays a $2.60 dividend each year. Find the prices of the two stocks such that no arbitrage opportunities exist. Suppose that the market prices of A and B are $36 and $22 per share, respectively. What action will investors take to achieve the equilibrium rate of return?

5. A share of Ajax sells at $10 and pays a dividend (perpetual) of $1 per year. New information results in a consensus view that the dividend will increase to $1.50 and that the added risk increases the required rate of return by 2 percent. In an efficient market, what will be the new price? When will this price change occur?

APPENDIX 3A

In a very general sense, a financial security is a claim signifying either ownership or a debtor–creditor relationship. Some kinds of ownership, **FINANCIAL SECURITIES** such as proprietorships and partnerships, may lack such formal documentation, but they are claims well defined by law and we include them under the general category of *financial securities* for reasons of simplicity.

The variety of financial securities representing claims on firms, individuals, and governments is extremely large. The type of security used varies to some extent with the nature of the issuer. Individuals and governments issue only debt securities, whereas corporations issue both debt and equity securities. Some securities cannot be transferred from one party to another and are called *nonnegotiable*. Securities that can be bought and sold are *negotiable* securities.

The list of securities presented below is not exhaustive but represents the more common types issued.

Debt Securities   Debt securities have a prior claim on the assets of the firm over equity securities in the event that the firm is liquidated, dissolved, or reorganized. Most debt is interest bearing in that the issuing firm, the borrower, is obliged to make fixed interest payment(s) to the owner of the debt. All debt, with one rare exception (perpetual debt), obliges the issuer to repay the amount borrowed, the *principal,* to the owner of the debt. Debt securities normally have a fixed *maturity* date by which time all principal and interest must be fully paid by the issuer. The possible terms to maturity are referred to as *short term, intermediate term,* and *long term.* Short-term debt has a maturity of less than 1 year; intermediate-term debt has a maturity of 1 to 5 years; and long-term debt covers debt maturities exceeding 5 years. Failure to make contractual payments gives the lender the right to proceed legally against the issuer to satisfy claims. This action may force liquidation of the firm, bankruptcy, or reorganization.

Short-Term, Interest-Bearing Debt   Firms, governments, and individuals may avail themselves of the use of short-term, interest-bearing debt as a way of borrowing funds. Some examples follow.

Notes Payable   *Notes payable,* often called simply *notes,* require the borrower, or issuer of the note, to repay principal plus interest by a designated time—usually within 1 year. Commercial banks play a large role in lending money on notes. Notes represent promises to pay that are sometimes negotiable (marketable) but usually are not.

Notes may be *secured* or *unsecured.* A secured note gives the lender a claim on specific assets of the issuer called *collateral* (such assets include inventory, accounts receivable, the cash value of life insurance, bonds, or stocks owned by the issuer). Some notes are secured by a *cosigner*—a third party guaranteeing payment of the note if the issuer fails to repay the debt. In the special case of a note that is secured by real estate, the note is a *mortgage*. If secured by equipment or portable goods, the note is called a *chattel mortgage*. Both types of mortgage often have maturities of intermediate or longer terms.

Commerical Paper   Firms can issue marketable short-term debt called *commercial paper*. It is frequently issued through a small number of dealers. The minimum size issue of commercial paper and the high standard of creditworthiness required restrict this market to very large, well-established firms. Some commercial paper is sold directly to buyers; such a transaction is called a *private placement*.

Tax Anticipation Notes   Municipal, county, and state governments issue marketable *tax anticipation notes* to facilitate spending of major inflows in advance of tax revenues from sources such as property taxes. Interest payments are not taxable by the U.S. government for the purchaser of the note (lender).

U.S. Treasury Bills   The U.S. government issues large quantities of a type of short-term debt called a *Treasury bill*. Treasury bills are auctioned weekly and sold at a price less than the face value (i.e., at a discount), the interest return being the difference between that price and the face value. They have varying maturities, usually 90 or 180 days, but can extend up to 1 year. Treasury bills are marketable and the interest is taxable. Other short-term debt is issued by U.S. Government *agencies* with the implied backing of the Treasury. Agency obligations are not legal obligations of the Treasury; however, most analysts believe the government would support an agency to prevent default.

Certificates of Deposit   A certificate of deposit is a short-term obligation of a commercial bank.

Intermediate-term debt is always interest bearing. Maturities range from 1 to 5 years. Some examples follow.

Intermediate-Term, Interest-Bearing Debt

Installment Loans   Sometimes referred to as *term loans, installment loans* require the borrower (the issuer) to repay debt over time in periodic payments of principal and interest. These loans may be secured or unsecured and are issued by firms and individuals. They are usually not marketable.

U.S. Treasury and Federal Agency Notes   The U.S. Treasury and some government agencies issue securities called *notes* that have a maturity of 1 to 10 years. These are not installment notes; they pay interest periodically, but principal is paid in a lump sum at maturity.

Long-Term,
Interest-Bearing
Debt

Individuals, firms, and governments may all issue at least some form of long-term, interest-bearing debt—normally called *bonds*. Typically, only interest is paid over the life of the debt, with a lump sum principal payment at maturity. There are exceptions, however. Some types of long-term, interest-bearing debt are described below.

Debentures   Firms may issue unsecured bonds called *debentures*. In some cases, debentures are *subordinated* to earlier debentures issued by a firm. All debentures have a claim junior to *secured* bonds on the security pledged.

Secured Bonds   Bonds may be secured by various kinds of assets owned by the issuer. If secured by other financial securities owned by the issuer, the bonds are called *collateral trust bonds*. *First mortgage bonds* are secured by a first (prior claim) mortgage on property of the issuing firm.

Convertible Bonds   Some bonds, usually debentures, are *convertible* at the option of the holder into common stock of the issuing firm on specified terms.

Income Bonds   *Income bonds* are usually issued during the reorganization of firms in financial difficulty. Interest is required to be paid only if the firm earns it. No legal action can be taken by the bondholders if interest is not earned and not paid.

Other Features of
Corporate Bonds

Bonds may be sold initially either to the public at large through the market, or through a *private placement* with a single lender or small group of lenders (purchasers). Some mortgage bonds have an *after-acquired* clause whereby property acquired by the issuing firm after the bonds are issued is included in the assets securing the bonds. The terms *open end* and *closed end* refer to whether the firm is permitted to issue more of the same bonds at a later date. Open-end bonds permit such issues, but closed-end bonds prohibit them. Many bonds have a *call feature* permitting the issuing firm to redeem (call) part or all of the issue. Bonds typically are *noncallable* for a minimum period of time after issue and then, for some subsequent interval, callable only if a *call premium* is paid to holders of the bonds. The call premium diminishes over time to zero. Corporate bonds, especially debentures, may require that the issuer maintain a minimum amount of cash and securities as assets and limit its cash dividend payments to owners of common shares. *Sinking fund* bonds require that the issuer retire some portion of an issue periodically or set aside funds to retire the bond issue at maturity. *Serial* bonds have maturities staggered over time to enable gradual retirement of the issue.

Tax-exempt Bonds   Municipal, county, and state governments issue long-term debt wherein the interest payments are exempt from federal income taxes for the lender (buyer). Sometimes just referred to as "municipals," *tax-exempt issues* may be either *general obligation* or *revenue* bonds. General obligation bonds are secured by the tax revenues of the governmental body issuing the debt. Revenue bonds are secured only by revenues obtained from specific revenue-generating assets such as toll bridges or college dormitories constructed with the proceeds of the sale of the bonds.

U.S. Treasury and Federal Agency Bonds   The U.S. Treasury is a major issuer of long-term, interest-bearing debt. Interest payments are taxable to the lender (purchaser). Agencies of the U.S. government such as the Federal National Mortgage Association (FNMA), issue long-term debt with the implied backing, in the event of prospective default, of the U.S. Treasury.

Equity Securities

Equity securities are residual claims on the earnings and assets of the firm after all debt claims are satisfied. Shown in the net worth section of a balance sheet, equity claims represent ownership of the firm.

Proprietors and Partnerships

For proprietors, the equity claim is simply the owner's equity or net worth. For partnerships, it is the partners' equity or net worth as allocated among the partners according to the partnership agreement.

Preferred Stock

Preferred stock is a financial security representing ownership, but it has a prior claim over common stock against earnings and assets of the firm.
   Preferred stock pays a fixed dividend in perpetuity to the holder. If the firm fails to pay a dividend, the holder of preferred stock cannot proceed legally against the firm, but firms failing to pay a preferred stock dividend cannot pay dividends on common stock. Typically, preferred

stock is *cumulative* in that any unpaid dividends accumulate and must be fully paid before any common stock dividends can be paid. Most preferred stock is *nonvoting* unless dividends are skipped by the firm.

Common Stock   *Common stock* is the last, or most junior, claim on the earnings and assets of the firm. Since all debt (except income bonds) and preferred stock claims on the firm are fixed, the returns to holders of common stock can be very good if the firm fares well but very poor if things go badly.

Holders of common stock have a *voting right* to select the board of directors of the firm and to receive common stock cash dividends if they are declared by the board of directors. Common stockholders have the right to inspect the books of the corporation but, to avoid nuisance inspections, courts of law have limited this right.

If the corporate charter, or superseding state law, requires it, shareholders have a *preemptive right* to purchase a *pro rata share* of any new common stock to be issued by the firm. The authorization to purchase a pro rata share of new stock issues, called a *right,* is marketable, and can be sold (if there are buyers) when the shareholder does not wish to exercise the right. Rights usually have a life of less than 1 year.

Some Miscellaneous Securities   A few types of security do not fit the standard classifications. We list some of them here.

Warrants   A warrant gives the holder the right (option) to purchase common stock of the firm at specific prices over an often long interval of time—sometimes in perpetuity. Warrants are often attached to bond sales because they act as "sweeteners" to make the bond issue more attractive. They represent marketable opportunities to buy common stock. Once issued, warrants may be bought and sold like other securities, separately from the bonds, if they are *detachable*. Nondetachable warrants can be sold only with their accompanying bonds.

Options   An *option* is a contract between two parties external to a business firm. The holder of the option is given the right to sell or purchase a security of a business firm by another party at a specific price over a specified period of time, usually not to exceed 1 year. Depending on the behavior of the price of the security in question, option values can be highly volatile. Options are negotiable; that is, they are bought and sold. Options differ from warrants in that warrants are issued by the firm itself and involve newly issued securities. Options are issued by external parties and involve, in the case of common stock options, previously issued and outstanding stock.

Investment Company (Mutual Fund) Shares   Investment companies purchase a portfolio of stocks and/or bonds and finance these purchases by selling shares in their funds to investors. The shares are not negotiable if the fund is an *open-end fund* (mutual fund), but may be redeemed with the fund by the owner of the shares. Shares in *closed-end funds* are bought and sold in the market. Mutual (open-end) funds appeal to the smaller investor because they provide diversification without the proportionately higher transaction costs that would be sustained if the individual investor sought to buy small amounts of several stocks. A money market fund is a type of mutual fund that invests its funds in short-term securities such as Treasury bills, commercial paper, and certificates of deposit.

Appendix 3B

Investment bankers, like other bankers, are *intermediaries*. They channel funds from investors to those who have profitable uses for funds. Whereas commercial bankers channel funds largely into short-term and intermediate-term loans and savings bankers channel relatively more funds into longer term loans, investment bankers channel funds from investors into permanent and long-term securities. Investment bankers tend to serve firms that must raise large amounts of permanent capital. Investments in bonds, preferred stock, and common stock are generally riskier and yield a greater return than the short-term loans of commercial banks or the long-term loans, secured by real estate, made by savings banks. Although bond issues of corporations may be placed in public hands by investment bankers, the high quality, low risk corporate bonds tend to be placed in institutional hands directly by the operating firm, frequently bypassing the investment banker.

INVESTMENT BANKING

The primary functions of an investment banker are underwriting and selling. Other functions include investigation, analysis, and advising. Various clients of investment bankers may use all or only some of these services.

Functions of an Investment Banker

Underwriting and Selling

Underwriting provides an insurance function (risk-bearing function), because the banker provides the client firm with certainty that the desired capital at the agreed price will be made available; this is possible because the underwriter (investment banker) buys the entire new issue from the firm at the agreed price and undertakes the risk of not being able to sell the issue at all. Not all marketing efforts are underwritten, however. The bankers may refuse to buy an issue at any feasible price because it is simply too risky. More than one investment banker has seen poor times or gone under as a result of an error in underwriting judgment. Investment bankers have also, on occasion, bought overpriced issues that could not be resold without cutting the selling price and have thus suffered losses; in some cases enough losses to destroy the underwriter financially have been sustained. Selling the new issue means placing the securities in the hands of investors. If the issue is not underwritten, the banker may still be hired to market it, even though the banker bears no risk. Such an effort is called a *best efforts distribution*.

Advising

Advice may be desired and purchased from the investment banker because of his or her intimate knowledge of the market. Such advice may eventually lead to a marketing effort, underwritten or not.

Analysis

Investigation and analysis are done by the banker in preparation for a marketing effort or for the sale of advice to clients.

Description of Activity

Any organization in which the foregoing functions play a dominant role may legitimately regard itself as an investment banker. Firms seemingly involved in carrying out other functions occasionally act as investment bankers. For example, firms such as Merrill, Lynch, Pierce, Fenner and Smith are known as brokerage firms because a substantial part of their business is brokerage (buying and selling as agents for a commission), but they are also well-known investment bankers. Perhaps most securities firms in the country that employ salespeople and are registered with the National Association of Securities Dealers (NASD) have participated in one securities distribution or another—some rather frequently. Various security firms may create a risk-sharing or a marketing network that can be harnessed into temporary groups, called *syndicates*, at different times to underwrite and/or sell a large issue of securities.

Investment banker distributions may or may not involve new money for the corporation. Those that involve new money are called *primary distributions*. They may be:

1. Issues of a company going public for the first time.

2. Issues of a company that already is publicly held.

Distributions may also involve securities previously issued and outstanding but not publicly distributed. Occasionally, though rarely today, a special selling effort is required to distribute a portion of an issue already publicly held but so large in size that it requires a syndicated, underwritten effort by the securities industry equivalent to the other cases above.[1]

The buyers of the securities sold through these various marketing efforts vary depending on the issue. An issue of common stock may be bought by an individual investor, a pension fund, an insurance company, a mutual fund, and so forth. Bonds and preferred stock are more likely to be sold to institutions.

In a security distribution, three groups of investment bankers may be involved. The *originator* (1) provides advice to the seller, (2) investigates and analyzes both the issue to be sold and the issuing firm, (3) negotiates the price and the terms of purchase and sale, and (4) organizes the efforts of the underwriters and, if involved, the investment banker selling group. Because the originator may not wish to assume all the risk-bearing functions of an underwriting, he may form an *underwriting syndicate* of bankers who will share the risk. Under an agreement with the issuer of the securities, each member of the syndicate underwrites a portion of the distribution. A *divided account* limits the liability of each banker to his share of the total, whereas in an *undivided account*, each member of the syndicate is liable for a pro rata portion of the total unsold amount. The *selling group* of investment bankers agrees to attempt to sell a certain amount of the securities, but they are not involved in the risk-bearing activity of the underwriting syndicate and are not legally liable to the issuer for unsold securities (though the pride and reputation of each selling group member rests on his ability to sell the agreed-upon number of shares). The originator and organizer of the marketing effort negotiates the purchase price terms for most security offerings from security-issuing industrial firms, but competitive bids may be common for public utilities, rails, and others.

In *negotiated* sales, the firm issuing securities selects an investment banking firm and works with it in setting up the sale. Jointly, the price, features, and terms of the issue are agreed upon. The selected invest- *Negotiated and Competitive Sales*

[1]Sometimes these issues are handled by brokers in what is called a "secondary offering." However, today these are more often handled as "block trades" or most often by "third" or "fourth" market trading, that is, purchase and sale of large blocks of previously registered securities.

ment banker is the originator. If the issue is large enough this person will invite other investment bankers to form an underwriting syndicate to share the risk and perhaps to form a selling group to aid in the distribution. Negotiated sales involve most issues in the nongovernmental area except railroads and public utilities.

Railroads are required by the Interstate Commerce Commission (ICC) to sell their issues through competitive bidding, as are public utility holding companies required by the Securities and Exchange Commission (SEC). Issues of states, cities, counties, and various other governmental subdivisions of the states use the competitive bidding process by law, custom, or choice. Under this bidding process, *competitive* syndicates *bid* for the securities and the highest bidder buys. However, sellers usually reserve the right to refuse all bids.

Under competitive bidding, the firm or government could hire an investment banker to advise on the terms of the offering and prepare registration statements and the prospectus for the SEC, however this is not required for state and local governments. Then the issue is advertised for sale. Syndicates are formed to prepare bids, the prices bid being heavily influenced by ratings of investment advisers such as Moody's or Standard and Poor's and technical market conditions. At the proper date and time the bids are opened and the securities may be awarded to the highest bidder or not at all. All bidders are required to provide a "good faith" deposit with their bid, usually amounting to a small percent of the total security value.

Regulation   Both state (except Delaware) and federal governments regulate the sale of new securities. The SEC is the regulatory agency primarily involved at the federal level. (The ICC regulates railroad issues.) The Securities Act of 1933 requires the full disclosure of information to investors in new securities, and the Securities Exchange Act of 1934 introduced regulation into the sale of issues already outstanding. Both acts are implemented by the SEC. The SEC has no jurisdiction over securities sold entirely within one state, over real estate (except interstate), or over government debt issues and certain other offerings. Most companies wishing to go public find it desirable to register with the SEC even though initial sales may be intrastate. This is because stockholders will not wish to be restricted to intrastate buyers when, in the future, they wish to sell their holdings.

The SEC in recent years has relaxed certain requirements, to enable smaller businesses to raise money, usually equity capital. Issues involving no more than $2 million can be sold at relatively low flotation costs under Rule 242, which limits the number of "outsiders" to which the firm may sell its securities. Regulation A public offerings are limited currently to $1.5 million, but registration requirements are simplified compared to large public issues.

A nonexempt (not exempt from SEC registration) public offering of securities in excess of $1.5 million requires not only the registration statement and prospectus on the issues but also periodic financial reports thereafter; moreover, it subjects the company and its principals to other reporting regulations. The *prospectus* is a publication prepared for distribution to buyers and prospective buyers. It is essentially a condensed version of the registration statement. Prior to SEC approval it carries a red ink disclaimer of SEC approval and is called a "red herring" by the securities industry. The prospectus *must* be given to all prospective buyers of publicly issued new securities. The SEC has 20 days after filing in which to delay or stop the sale. The agency frequently requires alterations in the prospectus, but the SEC is not responsible for assessing the value or attractiveness of the issue. The SEC emphasis is on full and complete *disclosure*. Many investors fail to read the prospectus in any case. SEC regulations do not prevent the sale of speculative (very high risk) issues.

To protect their citizens from fraudulent offerings, states (except Delaware) have laws that are designed to regulate the sale and promotion of securities. These laws are called *blue sky* laws. In Colorado, for example, the Securities Commissioner administers the state's Uniform Securities Act; in New York, the Attorney General enforces the Martin Act.

INVESTMENT BANKING EFFORTS TO MARKET SECURITIES

Regular Underwritings

Larger stock issues require a very large underwriting and selling group to break down the quantities offered into the smaller portions necessary to reach a geographically dispersed market of smaller investors. For example, when Ford Motor Company went public in the 1950s a huge underwriting and selling group had to be created, involving nearly every securities firm in the country.

Sales of bond issues are somewhat different in that prospective buyers are generally institutions, and sales to each institution typically occur in much larger dollar amounts. A $100 million issue might be taken in minimum size amounts of $100,000, with many sales involving several million dollars. The buyers are thus professional and sophisticated, and costs of selling to this smaller number of buyers are correspondingly much lower. Because of lower selling costs, some firms bypass the investment banker, finding it cheaper to place their issue privately with a limited number of institutions. Preferred stock sales are handled similarly but occur less frequently.

Best Efforts   Often investment bankers do not want to guarantee the underwriting of a small new public issue, and the company must settle for a *best efforts* distribution. The investment banker or bankers only promise to do their best to sell the issue. Customarily the time involved with the sale is considerably longer. The banker is not in as much of a hurry during a best efforts sale because no underwriting risk of changing market conditions is being borne. Best efforts sales do not usually generate the same enthusiasm as an underwriting on the part of the banker.

Often, because of the absence of urgency and enthusiasm among investment bankers, a best efforts sale is undertaken by the issuing firm itself. Some member(s) of the issuing firm becomes legally qualified to sell securities and seeks to sell the stock to the firm's customers, suppliers, friends, the public, or whoever comes along.

Privileged   In a privileged subscription, the firm decides to offer new common stock
Subscription   for sale to their present security holders in the same proportion as their existing holdings. In the majority of cases, privileged subscription is associated with the offering of new common stock to existing shareholders. Some companies may even be required to offer new shares to their stockholders because of a preemptive right. A preemptive right is a right of stockholders to maintain a pro rata equity interest in the company. This means that no new shareholders may be brought into the company without first giving the existing shareholders an opportunity to maintain their proportionate interest in the firm. Some states require this provision in corporate charters; in other states, some firms include it voluntarily.

If a privileged subscription is planned, the firm must sell shares at a price that stimulates buying interest on the part of their shareholders. Customarily, they offer stock at a discount from the current market price. If the publicly traded price were $20, for example, the company might offer the new stock at $18. Many shareholders, however, may not be able to invest additional funds, or may not wish to. However their *rights* to purchase new shares are negotiable and can be sold.

Suppose the Solarsky Corporation, whose stock is selling at $20, decides to raise $3.6 million through privileged subscription. It has 1 million shares outstanding and decides to sell 200,000 new shares. To stimulate its present shareholders to buy the new shares, the company settles on an $18 per share price. It will offer to its shareholders the right to buy one new share for each five shares presently held, at a price of $18 per share. Holders of 100 shares can buy 20 new shares at $18 per share, for a total outlay of $360 for the new shares. Customarily, stockholders have several weeks to decide whether to invest more in the company. If the shareholder does not "exercise" the rights and buy new stock, he or she should sell the rights to buy at the preferred price. For a period after the announcement, the shares trade in the market with the rights "attached." Buyers of shares with rights attached receive the privilege of buying new shares at the lower price. Just before actual rights are distributed, the old shares sell *ex rights* (without such rights) because the rights themselves are negotiable and detached from the stock.[2]

During the period of the rights offering, the publicly traded price of Solarsky stock could fall below $18; then no shareholders would choose to exercise their rights and the company would fail in its effort to raise new equity capital. In such an eventuality, an investment banker could be hired to eliminate the risk by making a standby commitment. That is, the investment banker would agree to take to the public any shares not purchased by the privileged shareholders.

Private Placement

If the value of underwriting or selling as performed by the investment banker is judged to be not worth the cost involved, the issue will not be sold publicly and the banker may be bypassed. *Private placement* refers to the sale of large blocks of securities by the issuer directly to a small number of major investors without the use of an investment banker. If the buyers are few enough, it need not be a public issue, saving the costs of registration and the issuance of a prospectus and greatly speeding up the issuing process. Most private placements involve corporate bonds. If an investment banker is used, it is for market advice only. Institutional

---

[2]The value of a right per share in the absence of any transaction costs can be calculated easily. If the market price of the stock with rights is M_1, the value of one right should be:

$$V_1 = \frac{M_1 - P}{N + 1}$$

where N = the number of shares required to buy one new share

In the case of Solarsky, $V_1 = (\$20 - \$18)/(5 + 1) = \$0.33$. For the 100 shares, the value of the rights is $33. However, since transaction costs do exist, the rights will sell at a discount from such a theoretical value.

buyers do not easily let the issuer capture all if any of the savings of a private placement—they will negotiate a tough price.

Venture Capital   The Small Business Administration (SBA), a federal government agency, facilitated creation of the Small Business Investment Corporation (SBIC) to provide equity capital (venture capital) to small businesses. Regional SBICs financed jointly by local equity sources and the SBA supply venture capital to smaller firms that have promise.

Raising equity funds for smaller companies is a problem in many respects. To the potential investor, the lack of a good market for the stock poses a most serious problem. This problem might be overcome in some cases by offering participation in the management of the firm to new shareholders. Yet the original owners are usually loath to introduce new managing owners. Rule 242 sales (allowed since 1980) improve the prospects for small business to secure equity capital, but active public markets for these securities do not exist.

CHAPTER 4

Markets, Diversification of Investments, and Required Rates of Return

In Chapter 2, it was established that the required rate of return the market uses in valuing an investment depends on the level of risk associated with the investment; the higher the risk, the higher the required rate of return. In Chapter 3, the discussion of markets contained the important equal rate of return principle, under which all securities having the same level of risk are priced in perfect markets to yield the same expected rate of return. The notion of required rate of return and the equal rate of return principle are important in this chapter. Here we examine the appropriate concept and measurement of risk underlying required rates of return for securities when investors hold diversified *collections* of securities.

We will find that when investors efficiently diversify their investments under perfect markets, market risk is the relevant concept for establishing the required rate of return for securities. By holding a diverse collection of securities rather than a single security, some risk is diversified away, leaving market risk of the security as the only remaining relevant risk. Market risk supplants standard deviation, the provisional risk measure adopted in Chapter 2. Standard deviation remains important here as a step on the way to showing the risk-reduction benefits of diversification.

We begin by defining the single period rate of return and standard deviation underlying the analysis that follows. The important dominance principle is introduced, after which the effects of diversification of risky securities on risk of investment are examined. Broadening this discussion to include investment in a risk-free security leads us to the notion of market risk for a single security. The required rate of return for a security depends on market risk. The implications of this relationship for investment decisions by the firm are then indicated.

SINGLE PERIOD EXPECTED RATE OF RETURN AND STANDARD DEVIATION

The analysis that follows relies on a single period framework for return and risk. The expected single period rate of return for a security is expressed as:

$$r^* = \frac{C_1 + \Delta P_1}{P_0} \qquad (4\text{-}1)$$

The term r^* is the single period expected rate of return from investing in a security at time $t = 0$ by purchasing it at the current price P_0. The expected returns include C_1, the expected cash payment (a dividend on equity, an interest payment on debt) to be obtained during the single period and ΔP_1, the change in price of the asset between time $t = 0$ and the end of the interval, $t = 1$. The standard deviation of the single period rate of return is denoted as σ. Together, the expected rate r^* and standard deviation, σ, are assumed to describe the relevant characteristics of a security for an investor.

For example, suppose that McCrae Company's common stock has a present price of $P_0 = \$50$. An investor expects the price 1 year hence to be $P_1 = \$52$, so the expected price change is $\Delta P = P_1 - P_0 = \$52 - \$50 = \$2$. A cash dividend payment of $C_1 = \$0.50$ is also expected to be paid. For that investor, the expected rate of return, using Equation (4-1), is:

$$r^* = \frac{\$0.50 + \$2}{\$50} = \frac{\$2.50}{\$50} = 0.05, \quad \text{or } 5.0\%$$

Without formally estimating the standard deviation, we suppose it to be $\sigma = 8$ percent. For the single security, $r^* = 5$ percent and $\sigma = 8$ percent completely describe the characteristics of McCrae common stock.

The single period expected rate and standard deviation may be defined for any period we wish: a day, a month, a year, . . . , even 20 years. For easy familiarity, assume that it is 1 year.

THE DOMINANCE PRINCIPLE

Suppose that an investor must choose among single securities, including McCrae common stock. The expected return and risks of three common stocks are as follows.

Company	Expected Rate of Return, r^*	Standard Deviation, σ
Amherst	10%	8%
Beloit	5	4
McCrae	5	8

These expected returns and risks are plotted in Figure 4-1, with standard deviation on the horizontal axis and expected rate of return on the vertical axis.

In choosing among these securities, the **dominance principle** applies. For risk-averse investors, this principle states that one investment dominates another if it offers more expected return for the same risk, less risk for the same expected return, or more expected return *and* less risk. Clearly, McCrae common shares are dominated by both Amherst and Beloit shares. Amherst's 10 percent expected rate of return exceeds McCrae's 5 percent return while having the same 8 percent standard deviation. Beloit's 5 percent expected return equals McCrae's, but Beloit's standard deviation is a lesser 4 percent. In fact, any *other* security having an expected rate of return of 5 percent or more and a standard deviation

Figure 4-1   *The Dominance Principle*

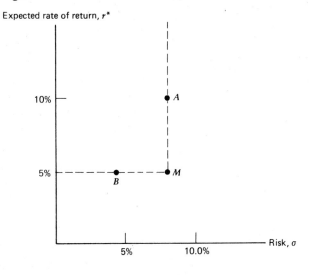

of 8 percent or less will dominate McCrae shares. Expected return and risk for such securities will lie in the sector inside the dashed lines through points *A*, *M*, and *B*.

The dominance principle cannot be applied to make a choice between Amherst and Beloit shares. Amherst shares offer more risk but also provide a higher expected return. Such a choice could be made only by reference to the risk–return preferences of the investor. Amherst shares might be selected by an investor having a lower degree of risk aversion, one willing to take on higher risk in exchange for a relatively smaller increase in expected rate of return, than a highly risk-averse investor. A highly risk-averse investor might choose the lower risk and return of Beloit shares.

But such choices are not very interesting once we recognize that investors could form a portfolio of Amherst and Beloit shares. We will see that any such portfolio would also dominate McCrae shares. More important, it may be possible to reduce risk of investment through such diversification.

EFFECT OF DIVERSIFICATION ON RISK: A TWO-SECURITY PORTFOLIO

Few people invest solely in a single security. They own several different common stocks as well as debt issues and other securities. Extending beyond financial securities, **diversification** continues through holding assets of other types such as real estate, paintings, and old coins. For the present, we consider only financial securities. Risky financial securities, when combined in various proportions, allow investors to achieve superior combinations of risk and expected return not attainable with a single security. To see how this happens, we begin by defining the terms "portfolio" and "expected rate of return and risk" (for a two-security portfolio).

Portfolios

A **portfolio** consists of one or more investments. For now, we deal only with portfolios containing risky securities. (Later on, portfolios will contain risk-free securities as well.) A risky security portfolio is specified by designating each risky security held in the portfolio and the proportion of total dollars invested in each risky security. Such proportions are referred to as weights.

Suppose an investor forms a two-security portfolio of Amherst and Beloit shares by purchasing them at their current market price. Of the $1000 total amount invested, suppose that $333.33 is invested in Amherst shares and $666.67 in Beloit shares. The proportion invested in Amherst is the weight W_A and the proportion for Beloit is W_B. Since the total $1000 is invested in both securities, the weights W_A and W_B must sum to 1.0. In this case, the weights are:

$$W_A = \frac{\$333.33}{\$1000} = \frac{1}{3} \quad \text{and} \quad W_B = \frac{\$666.67}{\$1000} = \frac{2}{3}$$

This is a unique portfolio, one of many alternative portfolios of Amherst and Beloit shares that could be found by varying the proportions invested in the two securities.

Any two-security portfolio has an expected rate of return r_p^* of:

$$r_p^* = W_A r_A^* + W_B r_B^* \tag{4-2}$$

The expected rate of return is simply a weighted average of the expected rates for the individual securities, the weights for each security in the portfolio being used to compute the average. Investors can change the expected rate of the portfolio by altering the proportions invested in the two securities.

In the initial portfolio of Amherst and Beloit shares, the weights were $W_A = \frac{1}{3}$, $W_B = \frac{2}{3}$. The expected rates of return for the two securities were $r_A^* = 10$ percent and $r_B^* = 5$ percent. Using Equation (4-2), we can compute the expected rate of return for that portfolio.

$$r_p^* = (\tfrac{1}{3})\ 10\% + (\tfrac{2}{3})\ 5\% = 6\tfrac{2}{3}\%$$

But we could increase the expected rate for a portfolio of Amherst and Beloit shares by increasing the proportion of funds invested in Amherst shares (and reducing the proportion for Beloit shares). An alternative portfolio of the two securities with weights $W_A = \frac{1}{2}$, $W_B = \frac{1}{2}$ will have a higher expected rate of:

$$r_p^* = (\tfrac{1}{2})10\% + (\tfrac{1}{2})5\% = 7.5\%$$

Looking ahead to Table 4-1, columns I and II show weights for alternative portfolios of Amherst and Beloit shares. Column III shows the expected rates of return on the alternative portfolios. The highest possible expected return, $r_p^* = 10$ percent, is obtained by investing *solely* in Amherst shares (i.e., $W_A = 1.0$, $W_B = 0.0$). The lowest possible expected return, $r_p^* = 5$ percent, occurs if all funds are invested in Beloit shares (i.e., $W_A = 0.0$, $W_B = 1.0$). All alternative portfolios containing *both* Amherst and Beloit shares have expected rates of return between 5 and 10 percent.

As to portfolio risk, intuition might suggest that portfolio risk would, analogous to expected return, be a weighted average of the standard deviation of each security—for example, $\sigma_p = W_A \sigma_A + W_B \sigma_B$, where σ_p

Expected Rate of Return and Risk: Two-Security Portfolios

Table 4–1   *The Effect of Changing Weights W and Correlation Coefficients ρ_{AB} on the Risk σ_p of a Two-Security Portfolio: Amherst and Beloit Shares*

I	II	III	IV	V	VI	VII	VIII
Weights for Portfolios		Expected Rate of Return	Portfolio Risk (σ_p) *if* Correlation Coefficient Is:				
W_A	W_B	r_p^*	$\rho_{AB} = +1$	$\rho_{AB} = 0.5$	$\rho_{AB} = 0$	$\rho_{AB} = -0.5$	$\rho_{AB} = -1$
1 1	0	10%	8.0	8.0	8.0	8.0	8.0
2 3/4	1/4	8.75	7.0	6.56	6.08	5.56	5.0
3 2/3	1/3	8.33	6.67	6.11	5.50	4.81	4.0
4 1/2	1/2	7.50	6.0	5.29	4.47	3.46	2.0
5 1/3	2/3	6.67	5.33	4.62	3.77	2.67	0
6 1/4	3/4	6.25	5.0	4.36	3.61	2.65	1.0
7 0	1	5.0	4.0	4.0	4.0	4.0	4.0

is the standard deviation of rate of return for the portfolio. But as we shall see, this is true only in a very special case. In general, the standard deviation of rate of return for a two-security portfolio is expressed as:

$$\sigma_p = \sqrt{\sigma_p^2} = \sqrt{W_A^2\sigma_A^2 + W_B^2\sigma_B^2 + 2W_A W_B\, \rho_{AB}\sigma_A\sigma_B} \qquad (4\text{-}3)$$

Although Equation (4-3) is slightly formidable in appearance, we are already familiar with most of the terms in it. The terms summed under the square root sign are σ_p^2, the *variance* of portfolio rate of return. This variance equals the sum of the weighted variances of rate of return for each security, $W_A^2\sigma_A^2$ and $W_B^2\sigma_B^2$ plus two times the respective weights, W_A and W_B, times the terms $\rho_{AB}\sigma_A\sigma_B$. The latter represents the **covariance** of the rates of return for the two securities. In this application, covariance is a measure of the relation between rates of return on the two securities. If covariance is positive, the rates of return on the two securities tend to move up and down *together*. If they tend to move up and down in opposite directions, covariance is negative. If the rates of return on two securities move independently, covariance is zero.

Covariance is expressed in Equation (4-3) as the product of the two standard deviations σ_A and σ_B and ρ_{AB}, the **correlation coefficient,** which is also a measure of how returns from two investments vary together. It is useful to talk of comovements of security returns in terms of the correlation coefficient since, given that standard deviation terms σ_A and σ_B are positive, the sign of the correlation coefficient determines the sign of the covariance portion of portfolio risk in Equation (4-3). The correlation coefficient may have a value ranging from -1.0 to $+1.0$. When rates of return on two securities have a perfect negative relationship, the coefficient is $\rho_{AB} = -1.0$. With a perfect positive relationship, $\rho_{AB} = +1.0$. If security returns are independent, $\rho_{AB} = 0.0$ and security returns are said to be *uncorrelated*. Of course, the correlation coefficients are not confined to values of $\rho_{AB} = +1.0$, 0.0, and -1.0. A coefficient between 0.0 and $+1.0$ is positive and the security returns are then positively correlated. But the relationship is not perfect. Returns do not *always* move together. A negative coefficient between 0.0 and -1.0 indicates negative correlation but not perfectly so. Returns do not always move in opposite directions.

If we suppose that rates of returns on Amherst and Beloit shares are positively correlated with a correlation coefficient of $\rho_{AB} = 0.6$, we can compute the standard deviation of a portfolio with weights $W_A = \frac{1}{4}$, $W_B = \frac{3}{4}$. Substituting these values plus the standard deviations $\sigma_A = 8.0$ and $\sigma_B = 4.0$ percent into Equation (4-3), the portfolio standard deviation is:

$$\sigma_p = \sqrt{(\tfrac{1}{4})^2 (8.0)^2 + (\tfrac{3}{4})^2 (4.0)^2 + 2(\tfrac{1}{4})\,(\tfrac{3}{4})\,(0.6)\,(8.0)\,(4.0)}$$

$$= \sqrt{4.0 + 9.0 + 2(\tfrac{1}{4})\,(\tfrac{3}{4})\,(19.2)} \qquad \text{Cov}$$

$$= \sqrt{20.2}$$

$$= 4.494\%$$

The weighted variance is 4.0 for Amherst and 9.0 for Beloit shares. The covariance is 19.2 (positive because the correlation coefficient is positive). The sum of all three terms is the variance of the portfolio rate of return of $\sigma_p^2 = 20.2$ and the standard deviation is $\sigma_p = 4.494$ percent.

Knowing the components of portfolio risk and how to compute portfolio standard deviation, we can explore the risk-reduction benefits of diversification by looking at the effects of the correlation coefficient on portfolio risk with alternative portfolios.[1]

Diversification Benefits Under Alternative Correlation Coefficients

Correlations between security returns are rarely, if ever, perfectly positive. Consequently, combining securities to form a portfolio usually reduces risk to some degree. Variations in the rate of return for one security partially offset variations in the return of another. This is the benefit of diversification, as illustrated in Table 4-1.

Columns I and II of Table 4-1 contain different portfolio combinations

---

[1]Risk for portfolios with more than two securities follows the same concept. See J. C. Francis and S. H. Archer, *Portfolio Analysis*, 2nd ed. (Englewood Cliffs, NJ: Prentice-Hall, 1979).

of Amherst and Beloit shares. Column III, as earlier indicated, shows the expected return for each of these different portfolios as obtained by using Equation (4-2). Columns IV to VIII contain portfolio standard deviations (portfolio risks) computed using Equation (4-3) for various correlation coefficients ranging from $\rho_{AB} = +1.0$ to $\rho_{AB} = -1.0$. If we examine the rows for portfolios containing *both* securities (rows 2–6), the effect on portfolio risk of smaller correlation coefficients is obvious:portfolio risk declines. Diversification is of greatest benefit in risk reduction when the correlation between two securities is negative. However, as long as returns from two securities are not perfectly positively correlated, *some* benefit from diversification exists. (Naturally, the portfolios in rows 1 and 7 show *no* risk reduction as the correlation coefficient declines because these portfolios consist of only *one* security and no diversification benefit can exist.)

An example to show the benefits of diversification when the correlation coefficient declines can be quickly given. For a given portfolio, say $W_A = \frac{1}{3}$, $W_B = \frac{2}{3}$, the formula in Equation (4-3) becomes, with $\sigma_A = 8$ percent and $\sigma_B = 4$ percent:

$$\sigma_p = \sqrt{(\tfrac{1}{3})^2(8.0)^2 + (\tfrac{2}{3})^2(4.0)^2 + 2(\tfrac{1}{3})(\tfrac{2}{3})(8.0)(4.0)\rho_{AB}}$$

$$= \sqrt{(\tfrac{1}{9})(64.0) + (\tfrac{4}{9})(16.0) + 2(\tfrac{1}{3})(\tfrac{2}{3})(8.0)(4.0)\rho_{AB}}$$

$$= \sqrt{14.2222 + 14.2222\rho_{AB}}$$

If Amherst and Beloit share. returns are perfectly positively correlated, $\rho_{AB} = +1.0$, then:

$$\sigma_p = \sqrt{28.4444} = 5.33$$

However, if they are positively correlated with $\rho_{AB} = +0.5$, then:

$$\sigma_p = \sqrt{21.3333} = 4.62$$

If lower correlation coefficients are inserted in the equation, portfolio risk will continue to decline. For any portfolio, the lowest possible risk occurs when perfect negative correlation ($\rho_{AB} = -1.0$) between security returns exists. For the portfolio of one third Amherst and two thirds Beloit shares, the portfolio risk becomes zero when $\rho_{AB} = -1.0$, since

$$\sigma_p = \sqrt{14.2222 - 14.2222} = 0$$

However, not *any* portfolio can produce zero risk when security returns are perfectly negatively correlated. For Amherst and Beloit shares, the portfolio having the composition $W_A = \frac{1}{3}$, $W_B = \frac{2}{3}$ is the *only* portfolio of the two securities to produce a zero risk when $\rho_{AB} = -1.0$. As Table 4-1 shows, all other portfolios have positive risks, even with perfect negative correlation.

Just as an investor can alter portfolio return by changing its composition, so the same action can change portfolio risk. To see this, refer again to Table 4-1. For a given correlation coefficient, say $\rho_{AB} = +0.5$, the risk of the portfolio declines as, moving from row 1 to row 7, the composition of the portfolio is altered in favor of lower risk Beloit shares and fewer higher risk Amherst shares. This also holds true for the perfect positive correlation case, $\rho_{AB} = +1.0$. Only in this special case, is the relation between portfolio risk, portfolio composition, and risk of individual securities a simple weighted average of σ_A and σ_B [Equation (4-3) simplifies to $\sigma_p = W_A\sigma_A + W_B\sigma_B$ if $\rho_{AB} = +1.0$].

But for the uncorrelated and negatively correlated cases in Table 4-1 (columns VI–VIII), risk declines and then *increases* as portfolios are altered in favor of more lower risk Beloit shares. For example, for $\rho_{AB} = 0.0$, portfolio risk with the composition $W_A = \frac{1}{4}$, $W_B = \frac{3}{4}$, is only $\sigma_p = 3.61$, compared to $\sigma_p = 4.0$ if only Beloit shares are held. This result occurs because offsetting variation between the two securities is so great that very large degrees of risk reduction are possible for some combinations of securities.

The Effect of Portfolio Composition on Portfolio Risk

If Table 4-1 were expanded to include all possible portfolio combinations of Amherst and Beloit shares, the resulting portfolio risk and return combinations could be graphed as in Figure 4-2. As the proportion of Beloit common stock, with its lower expected return and standard devia-

Portfolio Composition and Correlation of Security Returns Considered Together

Figure 4-2 *Risk Reduction Through Portfolio Formation: Amherst and Beloit Shares*

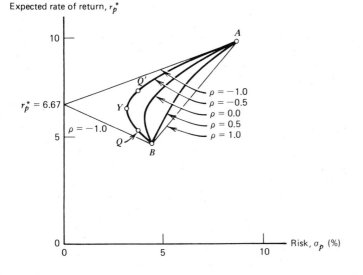

tion, increases, expected rate of return r_p^* always declines. Portfolio risk σ_p does not behave so consistently. In all cases it initially declines; however, the decline is faster for lower correlation coefficients. When ρ_{AB} is zero or below, σ_p reaches a minimum below 4 percent and actually begins to increase as a larger proportion of funds is invested in Beloit shares.

Some risk and expected return combinations for lower correlation combinations of Amherst and Beloit will always *dominate* those with higher correlation. Applying the dominance principle, a risk-averse investor would prefer to be able to choose a portfolio from the set represented by $\rho_{AB} = -1.0$ than from any other sets shown. (This is only a matter of preference, since the type of correlation between returns of Amherst and Beloit shares is what it is. An investor cannot choose which correlation coefficient he wants to exist between these two securities.)

Also note that not all combinations of Amherst and Beloit shares for a given correlation coefficient are viable choices for a risk-averse investor. For example, when $\rho_{AB} = -0.5$, portfolio risk reaches a minimum at point Y in Figure 4-2 and begins to increase as more Beloit shares are included in the portfolio (W_B increases). Yet the expected rate of return continues to decrease. A rational, risk-averse investor would not choose a portfolio on the curve segment YB. That segment is *dominated* by combinations on segment YA having a *lower* proportion of B *and* a higher expected return for the same level of risk. An example of such a situation is illustrated by points Q and Q'. Both have the same risk, but an investor would always choose Q' over Q because the former has a higher expected rate of return.

Implications of Portfolio Formation

Diversification benefits obtained through forming portfolios have several implications for financial management. First, as long as investors can diversify their investments, it may not be necessary for *firms* to diversify their internal investments to achieve diversification benefits for shareholders. Shareholders can achieve their own diversification in financial securities. Internal diversification efforts by firms provide no unique benefits for shareholders. (Chapters 6 and 18 deal further with this issue.) Second, the risk of any particular security must reflect its contribution to the risk of the investor's portfolio. Standard deviation is still a relevant measure of the risk of an investor's *portfolio*, but since some of the variability of an individual asset can be diversified away when it is combined with another asset (assuming $\rho_{AB} \neq +1.0$), standard deviation is not an appropriate measure of risk for an *individual* security. As we soon demonstrate, the correlation coefficient plays an important role in determining the risk of an individual security.

Further implications of the ability to diversify can be seen if we extend the analysis to allow for diversification with many securities and, ultimately, a risk-free asset.

When there are many risky securities from which to choose, opportunities for diversification abound. Individuals may hold, directly, hundreds of different risky securities. By combining them, some risk will be eliminated or diversified away, as long as security returns are not perfectly positively correlated ($\rho \neq +1.0$). As the investor adds more nonperfectly positively correlated securities, risk will continue to decline for the portfolio. At some point, however, so many securities are involved that no further risk reduction in the portfolio will take place, without giving up some return. Such a portfolio is an **efficient portfolio;** it cannot be *dominated* by another portfolio.

There exist many efficient portfolios. Though computations of expected rate of return and standard deviation of all efficient portfolios would be lengthy with a large number of securities, the resulting risk–return combinations offered by efficient portfolios could be plotted to form the *efficient frontier* in Figure 4-3. The frontier could be obtained by selecting the portfolios with the highest expected rate of return for *each* level of standard deviation or portfolios with the lowest standard deviation for *each* expected rate of return. In other words, the group of

DIVERSI-FICATION WITH MANY RISKY SECURITIES

Figure 4-3   *The Efficient Frontier*

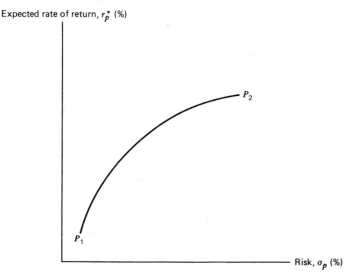

Expected rate of return, r_p^* (%)

P_2

P_1

Risk, σ_p (%)

these efficient portfolios would *dominate* all other possible (nonefficient) portfolios. After completing the selection process (the mechanics are not important here), an investor would face the group of efficient portfolios on the efficient frontier described by curve P_1P_2, shown in Figure 4-3. That curve represents all nondominated portfolios of *risky* securities from which investors may choose.

DIVERSIFICATION INCLUDING A RISK-FREE SECURITY

Until now, portfolio construction has been limited to risky securities. Under that restriction, investor opportunities for selection of a portfolio would be confined to the efficient frontier in Figure 4-3. But important consequences follow if we realistically broaden investment opportunities to include a risk-free security. This changes investor opportunities dramatically. A person with $20,000 to invest can invest some portion of it in a risky (but efficient!) portfolio and the remainder in the risk-free security. For example, suppose a person invests $10,000 in a risk-free security (perhaps a U.S. Treasury bill) and $10,000 in an efficient portfolio. The expected (and certain) rate of return on the risk-free security is $r_f = 10$ percent and its risk is zero, $\sigma_{rf} = 0.0$. The efficient portfolio has an expected rate of $r_p^* = 15$ percent and standard deviation of $\sigma_p = 8$ percent. Looking back at Equation (4-2), we can treat the risk-free security as security A and the efficient risky portfolio as security B. The expected rate of return on this combination ($W_A = W_B = 0.50$) of risk-free security and efficient portfolio is:

$$r_p^* = (\tfrac{1}{2})10\% + (\tfrac{1}{2})15\% = 12.5\%$$

The risk can be similarly found using Equation (4-3) for the risk of a two-security portfolio.

$$\sigma_p = \sqrt{(\tfrac{1}{2})^2(0)^2 + (\tfrac{1}{2})^2(8.0)^2 + 2(\tfrac{1}{2})\,(\tfrac{1}{2})\,(0)\,(0)\,(8.0)}$$

Since the risk-free security has a standard deviation of $\sigma_r = 0.0$, the portfolio risk of a combination of risk-free security and the efficient portfolio reduces to:

$$\sigma_p = \sqrt{(\tfrac{1}{2})^2(8.0)^2} = \sqrt{16.0} = 4.0\%$$

This combination of expected return and risk ($r_p^* = 12.5$ and $\sigma_p = 4$ percent) is one point on an entirely *new* set of investment opportunities shown by line *CPX* in Figure 4-4. The expected rate of return and zero risk of the risk-free security are shown by point *C* on the vertical axis. The expected rate of return and risk of the efficient portfolio are denoted by point *P*, where line *CPX* is tangent to the efficient frontier. The combination of equal portions of risk-free security and efficient portfolio is represented by point *J*, between points *C* and *P*. Note that the new

Figure 4-4 *Original (P_1P_2) and Revised (CPX) Efficient Frontiers*

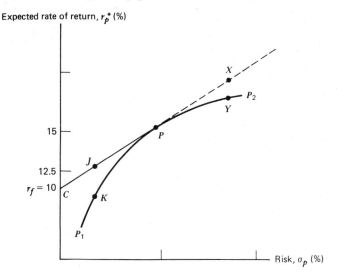

portfolio at *J dominates* the efficient portfolio *K* on the frontier by offering more expected return for the same level of risk. Other combinations of the risk-free security and efficient portfolio *P* represent a *new* series of efficient portfolios all along the line segment *CP*. All of those portfolios dominate those on the original efficient frontier below point *P*.

Above *P*, line segment *PX* shows new efficient portfolios dominating original efficient portfolios above point P_2 on the original frontier. Such dominant positions are reached by use of *financial leverage*. To illustrate, suppose the investor can *borrow* at the risk-free rate. If an additional $20,000 is borrowed to accompany the investors own $20,000, it would be possible to invest $40,000 in efficient portfolio *P*. The investor would earn a r_p^* = 15 percent expected rate on the $40,000 investment and pay r_f = 10 percent on the $20,000 of borrowed funds. The expected rate of return on the investor's $20,000 *equity* investment is:

$$r_p^* = \frac{(\$40,000 \times 0.15) - (\$20,000 \times 0.10)}{\$20,000} = 0.20, \quad \text{or } 20\%$$

However, the new risk position is also higher—σ_p = 16 percent in this case.[2] Such an investment is represented by point *X* in Figure 4-4, which

---

[2]This can be determined by using, again, Equation (4-3) and designating security A as the risk-free security and security B as efficient portfolio *P*. The weights for this case become W_A = −1.0 for the risk-free security and W_B = 2.0 for efficient portfolio *P*. As required, these weights sum to 1.0, the negative weight for W_A, indicating that funds have been borrowed at the risk-free rate.

dominates the original efficient portfolio indicated by point *Y*. Varying degrees of financial leverage permit attaining any point along line segment *PX*. The higher the degree of leverage, the greater are expected rate of return and risk.

We conclude that if our investor can borrow or invest at the risk-free rate, the *new* efficient frontier for that investor is line *CPX*. That line represents that investor's *investment opportunity set* given the investor's expectations concerning risk and returns.

RISK OF A SINGLE SECURITY

To get at the concept and measurement of the risk of a single security in the context of portfolio formation by investors, we introduce three assumptions. First, *all* investors can borrow or invest at the risk-free rate. Second, perfect markets exist, so that costless information is available to all investors. Finally, all investors have *identical* expectations concerning the risk and expected rate of return of each security and all possible portfolios of risky assets.

The Capital Market Line and the Market Portfolio

Under these foregoing conditions, the investment opportunity set available from combining the riskless security with an efficient portfolio of risky securities is *identical* for all investors. That set has a special name: the **capital market line** (CML). Note in Figure 4-5 that the CML is upward sloping—to obtain a higher expected rate of return, the investor must accept higher risk. The slope of the CML reflects compensation in term of expected rate of return investors require *per unit of risk*. That slope is called the *price of risk*, whereas the risk-free rate would be called the *price of time*—the price of waiting, of postponing consumption expenditures required by the act of investment.

The risk of an individual investment should reflect its *contribution* to the risk of the portfolio *M* in Figure 4-5. Why portfolio *M*? Portfolio *M* is the only portfolio of risky securities that remains—all others are dominated by using financial leverage to buy more *M* or by combining *M* with investing in a risk-free security. *M* is the portfolio of all risky securities, the **market portfolio.** Since it is the *only* risky security portfolio held by investors in combination with the risk-free security, it must contain *all* risky securities in the market. In that portfolio, all risk that possibly can be eliminated by diversification of risky securities is diversified away.

At first, it may appear that the assumption that all investors hold every security in the market as a portion of their portfolios is ludicrous. Yet in reality *every* investor does not have to be so well diversified. It need only be true that financial markets are *dominated* by investors who

Figure 4-5 *The Capital Market Line*

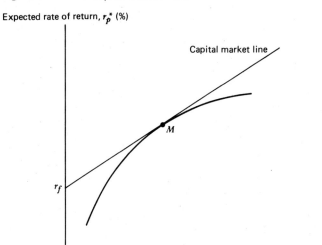

Expected rate of return, r_p^* (%)

Capital market line

M

r_f

Risk, σ_p (%)

are well diversified for our concept to be a reasonable description of reality.

That the market portfolio *M* has nondiversifiable risk can be noted by the location of *M* relative to the risk axis in Figure 4-5. We often hear about "the market," "the Dow," or some index of market security prices being "up" or "down." When "the market" is down, the average stock is down; when "the market" is up, the average of security prices is up, reflecting adjustments in the outlook for returns. The index may be up or down as a result of some fundamental factor such as the outlook for profits, inflation, or an international scare. Individual security prices also change because of these fundamental factors and are therefore sensitive to changes in price of the market portfolio. This degree of sensitivity to changes in the market represents a security's prime contribution to the risk of the market portfolio *M*. It is this sensitivity we seek to capture as our new measure of risk of a single security.

Since all the benefits of diversification have been exhausted when the market portfolio is held, the risk of the market portfolio cannot be further reduced. Consequently, for any individual security, the only risk that is relevant is the portion of the variability of the individual security's return that is attributable to variation in returns (the risk) of the market portfolio *M*.

We can think of total risk (all variability) of an individual security as

Market and Nonmarket Risk of a Single Security

being composed of two parts: **market risk** and **nonmarket risk.** Market
risk refers to the part of the individual security's total risk that is related
to the risk of the market portfolio. The nonmarket risk is the part of an
individual security's total risk that is unique to the security and not
related to the risk of the market portfolio. All nonmarket risk of an

Table 4–2   *Variability in Returns: Crinis Corporation and the Market*

(1) Year	(2) Rate of Return, Crinis Corporation r_c	(3) Market Rate of Return, r_m	(4) Crinis Deviation from Mean, $r_i - \bar{r}_c$	(5) Crinis Squared Deviation $(r_i - \bar{r}_c)^2$	(6) Market Deviation, $r_m - \bar{r}_m$	(7) Market Squared Deviation $(r_m - \bar{r}_m)^2$	(8) Crinis Deviation from Projected, $r - \hat{r}_c$	(9) Crinis Squared Deviation $(r_c - \hat{r}_c)^2$
1	−1	0	−6	36	−4	16	0	0
2	5	4	0	0	0	0	0	0
3	8	6	3	9	2	4	0	0
4	12	8	7	49	4	16	1	1
5	16	10	11	121	6	36	2	4
6	12	9	7	49	5	25	0.5	0.25
7	6	7	1	1	3	9	3.5	12.25
8	2	4	−3	9	0	0	3	9
9	−3	0	−8	64	−4	16	−2	4
10	−10	−4	−15	225	−8	64	−3	9
11	−3	−1	−8	64	−5	25	0.5	0.25
12	4	2	−1	1	−2	4	2	4
13	14	8	9	81	4	16	3	9
14	10	6	5	25	2	4	2	4
15	18	14	13	169	10	100	−2	4
16	3	2	−2	4	−2	4	1	1
17	8	6	3	9	2	4	0	0
18	6	4	1	1	0	0	1	1
19	−2	0	−7	49	−4	16	−1	1
20	−5	−5	−10	100	−9	81	3.5	12.25
	100	80		1066		440		76

$$\bar{r}_c = \frac{100}{20} = 5 \qquad \bar{r}_m = \frac{80}{20} = 4 \qquad \sigma_c^2 = \frac{1066}{20} = 53.3 \qquad \sigma_m^2 = \frac{440}{20} = 22 \qquad \sigma_{nc}^2 = \frac{76}{20} = 3.8$$

individual security can be diversified away by holding the market port-folio. Market risk cannot be diversified away because the market port-folio containing the individual security already represents the limit of efficient diversification. The relationship between total, market, and nonmarket risk is:

Total security risk = Market risk + Nonmarket risk

To give an example demonstrating these risk concepts and their mea-surement, consider the historical data for Crinis Corporation in Table 4-2. The annual rates of return, r_c, for Crinis common shares over the past 20 years have been computed and are shown in column 2. The corresponding annual rates of return, r_m, for the market portfolio are shown in column 3. At the bottom of these columns, the average annual rate of return over the 20 years is shown to be higher for Crinis than for the market portfolio, since $\bar{r}_c = 5$ percent, whereas for the market, $\bar{r}_m = 4$ percent. We can also observe that the total risk of Crinis stock is greater than the total risk of the market portfolio. Total risk is measured by the variance of rate of return. For Crinis, that variance is computed using columns 4 and 5. The sum of the squared deviation of Crinis's rate of return from average rate of return in column 5 is averaged over 20 years to obtain a variance of $\sigma_c^2 = 53.3$. This compares to the variance for the market portfolio, obtained using columns 6 and 7, of $\sigma_m^2 = 22$. The greater total risk of Crinis stock compared to the market portfolio is pictured in Figure 4-6.

But since Crinis Corporation is held in the market portfolio, total risk is not the relevant risk concept. We want to find market risk. On a historical basis, market risk is computed by finding the relation between rate of return of an individual security and of the market portfolio, as in Figure 4-6, which plots historical rates of return for Crinis against histor-ical rates of return for the market portfolio. A line of best fit for these plotted points is estimated. This line of best fit is called a *characteristic line*. It measures the average response of rates of return of Crinis com-mon stock to changes in rates of return of the market portfolio. The estimated equation of the characteristic line for Crinis is[3]:

$$\hat{r}_c = -1.0 + 1.5r_m$$

We are interested in the slope of this line because it represents the historical sensitivity of Crinis's rate of return to the rate of return of the market portfolio. This measure of sensitivity is called the **beta** coeffi-

[3]The characteristic line is a line that minimizes the squared deviations from that line, the least squares solution. It happens to intercept the vertical axis at -1.0 and has a slope of 1.5.

Figure 4-6   *Historical Annual Rates of Distributions of Returns, Crinis Common Stock and the Market Portfolio*

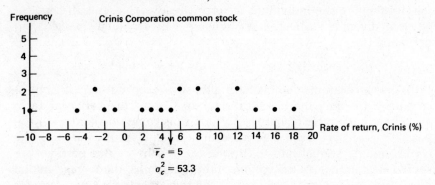

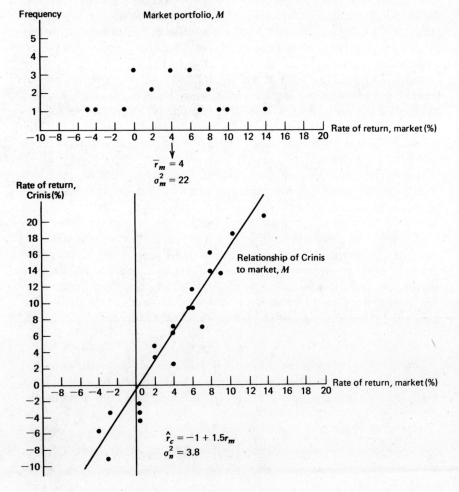

cient, or β. In the Crinis case, $\beta_c = 1.5$, indicating that a 1.0 percent change in the rate of return on the market portfolio is associated with a 1.5 percent change in the rate of return of Crinis common stock.

Now market risk itself for some security i can be measured by:

$$\text{Market risk} = \beta_i^2 \sigma_m^2 \qquad (4\text{-}4)$$

Since the variance of rate of return of the market portfolio was estimated in Table 4-2 as $\sigma_m^2 = 22$, the market risk for Crinis common stock, given its beta of $\beta_c = 1.5$, is:

$$\text{Crinis market risk} = \beta_c^2 \sigma_m^2 = (1.5)^2\, 22 = 49.5$$

For Crinis, we know from Table 4-2 the total risk is $\sigma_c^2 = 53.3$ and market risk is $\beta_c^2 \sigma_m^2 = 49.5$. What of nonmarket risk? This is denoted as σ_n^2 and is computed using columns 8 and 9 of Table 4-2. Column 7 contains the deviations of historical rates of return from the values given by the characteristic line, or $r_c - \hat{r}_c$. For example, the year 1 actual rate of return in column 2 is -1.0 percent. That same year, the rate of return of the market portfolio in column 3 was 0.0 percent. Substituting these values into the estimated characteristic line gives a value of

$$r_c = -1.0 + 1.5(0.0) = -1.0$$

for that year. And the deviation of actual from characteristic line value for year 1 is $r_c - \hat{r}_c = -1.0 - (-1.0) = 0.0$ percent, as shown in column 8. All such deviations are squared and summed in column 9 to produce a variance of $\sigma_n^2 = 3.8$, a measure of nonmarket risk.

We have now measured total, market and nonmarket risk for Crinis Corporation common stock on *a historical basis*. **Total risk** is divided between market and nonmarket risk as follows.

$$\text{Total risk} = \text{Market risk} + \text{Nonmarket risk}$$

$$\sigma_c^2 \quad = \quad \beta_c^2 \sigma_m^2 \quad + \quad \sigma_n^2$$

$$53.3 \quad = \quad 49.5 \quad + \quad 3.8$$

Of the total market risk, $\sigma_c^2 = 53.3$, $\beta_c^2 \sigma_m^2 = 49.5$ is *market risk*, and $\sigma_n^2 = 3.8$ is *nonmarket risk*. Approximately 93 percent of the total risk of Crinis stock is market risk, and 7 percent is nonmarket risk.[4] Held in the market portfolio, the nonmarket risk of Crinis is diversified away. Only the market risk is relevant for Crinis—risk that contributes to the risk of the market portfolio and cannot be diversified away.

---

[4]For the typical stock, the market risk component has historically been closer to 30 percent of the total. For a more elaborate discussion of the breakdown between market and nonmarket risk of the typical stock, see W. F. Sharpe, *Investments*, 2nd ed. (Englewood Cliffs, NJ: Prentice-Hall, 1981), pp. 353–354.

Finding the slope of the characteristic line is one way to estimate historical beta. It may also be calculated by using the correlation coefficient introduced earlier, for it too measures the relation between rates of return on individual securities and on the market portfolio. Given the correlation coefficient ρ_{im}, the beta for security i is:

$$\beta_i = \frac{\rho_{im}\sigma_i\sigma_m}{\sigma_m^2} \qquad (4\text{-}5)$$

Viewed in this way, we see that beta is a *relative* measure of market risk, since it is the ratio of the covariance of the rates of return, $\rho_{im}\sigma_i\sigma_m$, to the variance of the market portfolio return.

For Crinis, the historical correlation coefficient is $\rho_{cm} = 0.96$. Based on the total risk, measured by variance $\sigma_c^2 = 53.3$, the standard deviation is

$$\sigma_c = \sqrt{\sigma_c^2} = \sqrt{53.3} = 7.3$$

for Crinis. The variance of the market portfolio was $\sigma_m^2 = 22.0$, corresponding to a standard deviation of

$$\sigma_m = \sqrt{\sigma_m^2} = \sqrt{22.0} = 4.7$$

for the market portfolio. Using Equation (4-5), the beta value for Crinis is, as before,

$$\beta_c = \frac{(0.96)(7.3)(4.7)}{22.0} = 1.5$$

The market risk component of Crinis Corporation stock is a much higher percentage of total risk than nonmarket risk. This suggests that Crinis stock is relatively sensitive to variations in the rate of return on the market portfolio. We can further appreciate the sensitivity by noting that the beta for the market portfolio is always $\beta_m = 1.0$. Using Equation (4-5),

$$\beta_m = \frac{\rho_{mm}\sigma_m\sigma_m}{\sigma_m^2} = \frac{\rho_{mm}\sigma_m^2}{\sigma_m^2} = \rho_{mm} = 1.0$$

This must be so because the correlation coefficient of the rate of return on the market portfolio with itself must be positive and perfect (i.e., $\rho_{mm} = +1.0$). The beta for the *average* security is also $\beta = 1.0$. This is true because the beta for the market portfolio is simply the weighted average of all securities held in the market portfolio. This means that Crinis common stock, with a beta of 1.5, is one and a half times as risky as the average risky security in the market.

In general, betas may be greater or smaller than the 1.5 value found for Crinis. Securities having returns less sensitive to the market would have beta values below 1.0. If a security's returns are negatively correlated with returns on the market portfolio, its beta will be negative. Holding other factors constant, the lower the correlation coefficient, the lower the beta. Values for beta assuming different values of the correlation coefficient for Crinis and computed using Equation (4-5) are as follows.

ρ_{cm}	β_c
0.96	1.5
0.70	1.1
0.50	0.8
0.25	0.4
0.00	0.0
−0.50	−0.8

As the correlation coefficient approaches zero, so do beta *and* market risk relative to nonmarket risk. With a beta close to zero, most of the total risk of a security can be diversified away.

We have used hypothetical rate of return data to estimate a *historical* beta. Such a procedure can be employed with an actual security and a broadly based price index of securities to estimate historical betas. But required rates of return for securities rest on the beta to prevail in the future. Analysts may assume that future beta will be similar to the historical beta and use a historical beta to estimate required rate of return. Or they may use other approaches to estimating the future beta. Whatever approach is used, we now assume that we have an estimate of the appropriate beta for a security, one that applies to the future.[5]

REQUIRED RATE OF RETURN AND RISK

With beta as the proper measure of risk for a security held as part of the market portfolio, how is that risk measure related to the required rate of return? That question is answered graphically in Figure 4-7.

The Security Market Line

Any security having a beta of zero, when included in the market portfolio, should be priced as a risk-free security. Its required rate of return should equal the risk-free rate. This rate, denoted as r_f, appears on the vertical axis in Figure 4-7. Any security with a $\beta = 1.0$ must have a required rate equal to the required rate on the entire market because its

[5]Our historical approach was employed for illustrative purposes. Many analysts estimate historical beta based on *excess* rates of return of the security and market portfolio over the risk-free rate. See W. F. Sharpe, *Investments*, 2nd ed. (Englewood Cliffs, NJ: Prentice-Hall, 1981).

Figure 4-7   *Relation Between Required Rates of Return and Beta*

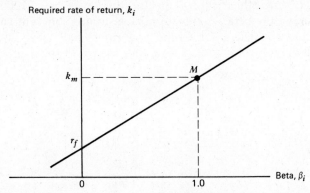

*While we continue to recognize that beta may be negative and that the required rate for such securities is less than the risk-free rate as indicated by the extension of the line to the left of the vertical axis, we do not focus on such cases in the remainder of this text.

market risk is identical to that of the market. That point is plotted as (1.0, k_m) between the vertical and horizontal axes. Note that k_m is used to denote the required return on the market for $\beta_m = 1.0$.

Since the relation between beta and required return can be shown to be a straight line, the two points plotted in Figure 4-7 are sufficient to obtain an equation for that relationship. The vertical intercept is r_f, the risk-free rate of interest. The slope of the straight line is simply "rise over run." The "rise" can be written as $k_m - r_f$ and the "run" is the market beta, $\beta_m = 1.0$, minus the beta of the risk-free rate, which is zero. Thus:

$$\text{Slope} = \frac{k_m - r_f}{\beta_m - 0} = (k_m - r_f)$$

since $\beta_m = 1.0$. With that information, the required rate of return for any security when the market is in equilibrium can be written[6]:

---

[6]Any security can be viewed as a combination of borrowing or lending at the risk-free rate and investing in the market portfolio. Therefore, the required return on that security, k_i, may be written

$$k_i = (W_{rf} \cdot r_f) + (W_{k_m} \cdot k_m) \tag{i}$$

where W_{rf} and W_{k_m} represent the proportions of an investor's funds in the riskless security and in the market portfolio, respectively. Furthermore, we know that $W_{rf} + W_{k_m} = 1$ and, therefore, $W_{rf} = 1 - W_{k_m}$. Consequently, k_i in Equation (i) can be rewritten as:

$$k_i = r_f + W_{k_m}(k_m - r_f) \tag{ii}$$

Also, the market risk of any security may be written as a weighted average of the market risk of a risk-free asset (zero) and the beta of the market ($\beta_m = 1.0$).

$$\beta_i = W_{rf} \cdot 0 + W_{k_m}\beta_m$$

$$k_i = r_f + (k_m - r_f)\beta_i \qquad (4\text{-}6)$$

In Equation (4-7), k_i is the required rate of return and β_i is a measure of relative market risk for any security; the market risk *premium* is represented by the terms $(k_m - r_f)\beta_i$. A security with $\beta_i = 0$ would have a required rate of $k_i = r_f$. But if risk is present, a risk premium is added to r_f to compensate for market risk. This equation is called the **security market line** (SML). The SML may be used to estimate required rate of return for any security, given estimated values of r_f, k_m, and β_i.

The required rate of return k_i for an individual security on the SML is calculated for a single period of time. The framework of portfolio selection on which the SML rests specifically assumes such a single period. We would like to use the SML, however, to determine the required rates in a world where cash flows from investments extend over many periods of time. The extension of a single period model to a multiperiod framework is a complex process and we will not pursue the details here.[7] Rather, we assume that the SML yields the best estimate possible within a risk–return framework—at least as good as other estimation techniques to be introduced in Chapter 16.

Estimating the Required Rate of Return for a Single Security from the Security Market Line

Consider again the case of Crinis common stock. Suppose that one wanted to estimate the rate that investors should require if $\beta_c = 1.5$. Suppose that short-term Treasury bills will earn investors 8 percent. We might use this rate as our best estimate of the risk-free rate, since there can be no default on Treasury bills (the government has the taxing power). Suppose further that the required return on the market portfolio is estimated to be $k_m = 16$ percent. Using these estimates, the equation for the required rate of return, the SML, becomes:

$$k_i = 8\% + (16\% - 8\%)\beta_i$$

The required rate of return on Crinis common stock would then be:

$$k_c = 8\% + (16\% - 8\%)1.5$$

$$= 8\% + 12\%$$

$$= 20\%$$

Because the market risk of the risk-free asset is zero and because the beta of the market is $\beta_m = 1.0$, one can write $\beta_i = W_{k_m}$ for the expression above. Substituting $W_{k_m} = \beta_i$ into Equation (ii), we can write

$$k_i = r_f + (k_m - r_f)\beta_i \qquad (iii)$$

which is Equation (4-6).

[7]See Eugene F. Fama, "Risk Adjusted Discount Rates and Capital Budgeting Under Uncertainty," *Journal of Financial Economics* (August 1977), pp. 3–24.

Figure 4-8   *The Security Market Line*

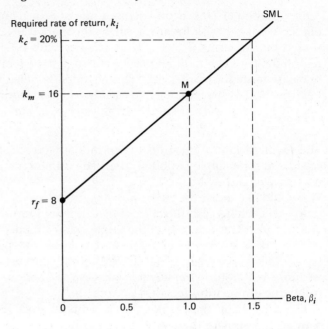

That rate reflects a risk-free rate of interest of 8 percent plus a risk premium associated with market risk of 12 percent. These results appear graphically in Figure 4-8. In addition to the total risk premium for Crinis shares, notice the difference between the risk premium on the market portfolio and on Crinis shares. The latter is 4 percent (20 percent − 16 percent) greater than the market. An additional 4 percent is necessary to compensate investors for the greater market sensitivity of Crinis.

The Security Market Line and Portfolio Required Rates of Return

Required rates for individual securities may be found along the SML. This also holds true for portfolios. For the beta of a portfolio is the weighted average of the betas of individual securities in the portfolio. We can show this using Figure 4-9.

These required rates for two securities, A and B, are plotted on the SML. The estimated line is:

$$k_i = 8\% + (16\% - 8\%)\beta_i$$

Security A has a beta of $\beta_A = 0.5$ and a required rate of return of:

$$k_A = 8\% + (16\% - 8\%)\,(0.5) = 12\%$$

Security B has a beta of 2.0 and a required rate of:

Figure 4-9 *Portfolio Required Rates on the Security Market Line*

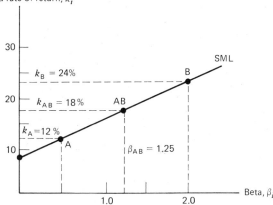

$$k_B = 8\% + (16\% - 8\%)(2) = 24\%$$

Now consider a portfolio AB consisting of equal portions of each security (i.e., $W_A = W_B = 0.5$). Its required rate of return should be the weighted average of required rates of each security.

$$k_{AB} = W_A k_A + W_B k_B = (0.5)(12\%) + (0.5)(24\%) = 18\%$$

But what of the portfolio beta? It is the weighted average of the individual security betas or,

$$\beta_{AB} = W_A \beta_A + W_A \beta_B + (0.5)(0.5) + (0.5)(2.0) = 1.25$$

This beta should, when used with the SML line, result in the same required rate as achieved with the weighted average of the security required rates of return. And it does, as can be readily seen:

$$k_{AB} = 8\% + (16\% - 8\%)(1.25) = 18\%$$

Not only securities but portfolios lie along the security market line.

Security Pricing on the Security Market Line

Under perfect markets, all securities must be priced so that their expected rates of return equal required rates for a given level of risk (Figure 4-10). Point I on the SML shows the required rate of return for all securities priced so that their expected and required rates of return are equal to k_I for the common level of risk β_I. Point I^* is for another security priced so that its expected rate of return r_I^* exceeds the required rate k_I for the identical level of risk β_I. This situation could not persist under the

Figure 4-10   *Asset Pricing and the Security Market Line*

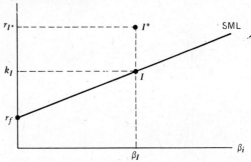

Expected and required rates of return

equal rate of return principle. Investors would *hurry*, in efficient markets, to purchase security I^*, bidding up its price and lowering its expected rate of return to $r_{I^*} = k_I$. They would do so because security I^* offers a greater expected rate of return for the same level of risk than other securities with risk β_I. Once the expected rate on I^* equaled that for I, no further extraordinary returns would be possible and the equal rate of return principle would hold: all securities having the same risk must be priced to yield the same expected return.

Implications of the Security Market Line for Investment Decisions by the Firm

The SML has been based on diversification of investments in securities. How does this line apply to investment decisions to plant, equipment, and other assets made by the firm on behalf of shareholders? We cannot fully answer this question in this chapter. But we can make two points, assuming that the firm in question is an unlevered firm such that β represents only the *business risk* of the firm's shares when held in an efficient portfolio. (Recall from Chapter 2 that there is no financial risk premium in required rates when a firm does not use financial leverage.)

First, because the firm has special opportunities and knowledge, it wants to find investment opportunities offering more than the rate of return required by the market for the level of risk of the investment. Referring again to Figure 4-10, assume that I^* is the expected rate of return on one of the firm's investment opportunities having a level of risk characterized by β_I. The expected rate of return on the investment would exceed the required rate. The investment would be expected to increase shareholder wealth because of the excess return. The equal rate of return principle dictates that the value of the investment must increase, in order to lower its expected rate to equal the required rate of return. The firm must identify the risk of investment opportunities, find the appropriate required rate of return, and select investments offering expected rates of return in excess of required rates.

Second, a firm may have several investment opportunities of *differing* business risks. Consider once again Figure 4-9. Suppose a new firm is forming and plans to undertake one investment having a business risk of β_A and another with a business risk of β_B. According to the SML, the firm should use *two different* required rates to assess these investment opportunities: k_A for investments having risk β_A and k_B for investments having risk β_B. Failure to do this, such as using k_A to evaluate an investment with risk β_B might result in the acceptance of an undesirable investment.

SUMMARY

Using a single period framework for expected rate of return and risk for individual securities, we wanted to find the appropriate concept of risk and its measurement that underlies required rates of return for individual securities when investors hold diversified portfolios of securities. We began by illustrating the dominance principle with choices among individual securities. We saw that an investment is dominated by another when it offers a lower expected rate of return for the same risk, more risk for the same expected rate of return, or a lower expected rate of return *and* more risk than the other investment. We then went on to see the effects of diversifying investments in securities.

Diversification among investments in securities is valuable and can eliminate some risk when the correlation coefficients between pairs of securities are less than one. The correlation between rates of return on two securities is a measure of association between those returns. If movements in the rate of return of one security tend to be in the same direction as movements of returns on another security, those rates are said to be positively correlated. If they tend to move in opposite directions, the correlation is said to be negative. In general, the lower the correlation between returns on two securities, the greater the risk reduction associated with combining them in a portfolio.

The benefits from diversification in portfolios suggest that the proper measure of risk for any security should reflect how much risk it contributes to an investor's portfolio, or in other words, the risk of an individual security that is not diversified away within a portfolio. To obtain such a risk measure, we need to know which portfolio an investor will hold.

Under certain assumptions, all investors will choose the same portfolio of risky securities. This portfolio, consisting of all *risky* securities in the market, is held with some combination (either borrowing or lending) of the risk-free security. Different investors will choose different combinations of the market portfolio and the riskless security along the capital market line (CML), but each will hold the market portfolio with all or part of his wealth.

When investors behave in this manner, the measure of risk for any single security must reflect its contribution to the risk of the *market portfolio*, since that is the risky security portfolio each investor holds. That is, it must reflect the security's *market risk*. That risk cannot be diversified away. Nonmarket risk reflects variability that is unique to the specific security and can be eliminated through diversification.

Market risk is measured by the relation between the returns of an individual security to the returns on the market. That relationship is captured in a measure of market risk, beta. Using beta as the risk measure, the required rate of return may be written:

$$k_i = r_f + (k_m - r_f)\beta_i$$

which is an expression for the security market line (SML). The first term of this equilibrium relationship between risk and return is the risk-free rate, and the second term is the risk premium necessary if investors are to be willing to bear market risk. The SML relates market risk and required return for all investments. In perfect markets, all securities must be priced to yield an expected rate of return equal to the required rate of return indicated by the SML for a given level of beta, market risk.

A financial manager can draw two important conclusions from our discussion.

1.   The relevant measure of risk for any investment is beta, a measure of the relative market risk of that investment.

2.   Investments with different risks (betas) should be evaluated using different required rates of return.

These points appear again in several of the chapters that follow.

GLOSSARY OF KEY TERMS

Beta	A measure of relative market risk.
Capital Market Line	The set of investment opportunities available from combining a risk-free security with the market portfolio.
Correlation Coefficient	A standardized measure of the relation between rates of return on two different investments (in this application).

Covariance	A measure of relationship between two variables, in this case returns on securities.
Diversification	Holding two or more investments rather than one investment alone.
Dominance Principle	States that one investment dominates another if it offers more expected return for the same risk, less risk for the same expected return, or less risk and more expected return.
Efficient Portfolio	A portfolio that is not dominated by another portfolio.
Market Portfolio	A portfolio consisting of all risky securities held in proportion to their respective market values.
Market Risk	The portion of the total risk of an individual security that cannot be diversified away.
Nonmarket Risk	The portion of the total risk that is unique to the individual security. It can be eliminated by efficient diversification.
Portfolio	A collection of investments in one or more assets.
Security Market Line	A market-determined relationship between the required rate of return for an individual security or portfolio and beta (a measure of market risk).
Total Risk	The total variation of the rate of return for an individual security as measured by the standard deviation or variance of the rate of return.

SELECTED REFERENCES

Modigliani, Franco, and Gerald Pogue. "An Introduction to Risk and Return: Concepts and Evidence, Part I," *Financial Analysts Journal* (March–April, 1974), pp. 68–80.

Sharpe, William F. "Capital Asset Prices: A Theory of Market Equilibrium Under Conditions of Risk," *Journal of Finance* (September 1964), pp. 425–442.

Sharpe, William F. *Portfolio Theory and Capital Markets.* New York: McGraw-Hill Book Co., 1970.

QUESTIONS

1. Why is the standard deviation of rates of return on an individual investment unlikely to be the proper measure of risk for computing a required rate of return?

2. What information does the correlation coefficient between rates of return on two securities provide?

3. Why might investors decide to diversify their investment portfolios among many different securities?

4. What is the relationship between the dominance principle and the concept of an efficient portfolio?

5. Referring to Figure 4-2, identify nondominated combinations of Amherst and Beloit shares when the correlation coefficient, ρ_{AB} is -1.0.

6. What is beta? Why is it employed as a measure of risk of an individual asset or security?

7. Under what special conditions is portfolio risk the weighted average of the standard deviations of the two securities?

8. Explain why an asset with a high beta will have a larger required rate of return than one with a low beta.

9. Distinguish between the capital market line and the security market line. Which should be used to determine the required rate of return on an investment?

10. Why was Crinis described as having high market risk?

11. Why might the required rate of return on an individual investment differ from the required rate of return for the firm considering that investment?

PROBLEMS

1. The expected rates of return and standard deviation for two investments, A and B, are shown below.

Investment	r^*	σ
A	25%	12%
B	18	9

If both investments require equal outlays and their returns are independent (have zero correlation) of each other, give the risk and expected return of a firm that combines these investments. Compare the risk of each individual investment with that of the combined investments. Explain what you observe.

2. Montrose Investment Advisors, Inc., is investigating combinations of two securities to offer as portfolios to clients. Firm A's common

shares are priced so that the expected rate of return is $r_A^* = 5$ percent with a standard deviation of $\sigma_A = 20$ percent. Firm B's common shares have an $r_B^* = 20$ percent expected return with a standard deviation of $\sigma_B = 80$ percent. Assuming the following alternative correlation coefficients, calculate the portfolio risks for a portfolio consisting of $W_A = 20$ percent of firm A and $W_B = 80$ percent of firm B.

(a) $\rho_{AB} = +1.0$

(b) $\rho_{AB} = +0.6$

(c) $\rho_{AB} = 0$

(d) $\rho_{AB} = -0.4$

(e) $\rho_{AB} = -1.0$

3. Consider firm B's shares in Problem 2. Suppose that you borrow $1000 at the risk-free rate of 4 percent and use $1000 of your own funds to invest a total of $2000 in firm B's shares. Find the expected rate of return and the risk of your levered investment.

4. Show that the risk of a portfolio with one risky security, R, combined with the risk-free asset is $W_R(\sigma_R)$.

5. For Montrose Investment Advisors in Problem 2, assume that the correlation coefficient is $+0.6$ between the two returns. Trace out the risk and return combinations achieved with the following portfolio compositions.

(a) $W_A = 10\%, W_B = 90\%$

(b) $W_A = 30\%, W_B = 70\%$

(c) $W_A = 50\%, W_B = 50\%$

(d) $W_A = 70\%, W_B = 30\%$

(e) $W_A = 90\%, W_B = 10\%$

6. For Montrose Investment Advisors in Problem 2, assume that the correlation coefficient is -1.0 between the two returns. Find W_A and W_B such that the portfolio risk is zero. (Hint: Zero risk weight for Security A in this situation is $W_A = \dfrac{\sigma_B}{\sigma_A + \sigma_B}$)

7. Two friends meeting in a park exchange the following information.

Jack: "I bought W_A = 50 percent of August Moon shares and W_B = 50 percent of Blue Bottle shares: r_A^* = 10 percent, r_B^* = 20 percent, σ_A = 10 percent, and σ_B = 20 percent. The correlation coefficient is ρ = 0.0."

Jill: "I bought W_C = 50 percent of Cowbell shares and W_D = 50 percent of Doghouse shares: r_C^* = 10 percent, r_D^* = 20 percent, σ_C = 8 percent, and σ_D = 18 percent. The correlation coefficient is ρ = 0.9."

Which friend has made the best decision?

8. You observe the following history of the 1-year rates of return for the market portfolio—and individual securities A, B, and C.

	r_M	r_A	r_B	r_C
1973	7%	3%	9%	5%
1974	10	−1	14	4
1975	8	2	12	6
1976	15	−3	17	5
1977	5	8	8	6
1978	11	0	15	7

Using market return on the horizontal axis and individual security returns on the vertical axis, plot the return on each security with returns on the market. Draw a freehand line of best fit through the data points plotted. Then judge which security has the most and which the least market risk. (The slope of the line of best fit reflects the correlation between the returns: e.g., a positive slope indicates positive correlation; a negative slope indicates negative correlation.)

9. You estimate that the security market line can be best estimated by letting the risk-free rate of r_f = 6 percent and the required rate of return on the market portfolio be k_m = 10 percent. Compute the required rates of return for the following firms with their respective betas.

(a)   Firm A, β_A = 0.5

(b)   Firm B, β_B = 1.5

(c)   Firm C, β_C = 2.4

Then find the value of these unlevered firms if the perpetual annual cash flow for common shareholders is $8000 for each firm.

10. Assume that the beta of Crinis shares is 2.6 instead of 1.5. Using the security market line shown in Figure 4-8, compute the required rate of return on Crinis shares. Would you expect such a dramatic change in beta to have an impact on the market price of those shares? Explain.

11. Suppose that Crinis uses the historical firm beta of 1.5 to designate a 20 percent return as the cutoff rate for acceptance of firm projects. Use the security market line in Figure 4-8 to demonstrate the errors that might be made when the firm considers the following projects:

	Expected Return	Beta
Project A	22%	2
Project B	16	1.2

12. We indicated that the beta of a firm is simply the weighted average of the betas of its individual investments. Using the data from Problem 9, we wish to compute these weights, and the beta, for a diversified firm that is a combination of A, B, and C. First, sum the values of A, B, and C. That total should be $217,949. Now divide the individual values of A, B, and C by that total. The resulting numbers will be the weights for each beta. Multiply each weight by its respective beta and add to obtain the beta of a firm of A, B, and C together. That beta should be approximately 1.25. Now estimate the required rate of return on the diversified firm. Is that rate necessarily appropriate for making investment decisions? Explain.

CHAPTER 5

Time and
Compound Returns

Throughout the preceding four chapters, we have used either single period or multiperiod perpetual cash flows in demonstrating basic financial concepts. But many financial decisions involve multiperiod cash flows that are not perpetual: for example, a firm making an investment decision to acquire an asset spends cash *now* in exchange for future expected cash inflows to be received over 3, 6, 10 or some other number of periods. Such cash inflows are not perpetual, but they extend beyond a single period of 1 year. Furthermore, the same firm makes a *financing decision* concerning the combination of debt and equity funds to be used in financing the investment. Payments to the owners of debt and equity claims can be expected to occur over many years as well. Therefore, it is essential to extend the wealth, share price, and rate of return structure used earlier to a more general multiperiod framework.

We want to be able to find a value for all types of future cash flows. We know from earlier chapters that the value of any future cash flow depends on the required rate of return appropriate for the risk associated with that flow. That required rate of return is, in general, $k = r_f + \phi$, where r, is the *riskless rate of return* and ϕ is the *risk premium*. Thus, the required rate of return compensates investors both for the factor of time (deferred consumption of goods and services) and for bearing risk. The required rate of return is also known as the *risk-adjusted discount rate* and the *capitalization rate*. Throughout this chapter, the required rate of return k is assumed to be appropriate for the risk of the cash flows being evaluated.

We begin with an introduction of the **compound rate of return,** and of the **future value** of cash flows invested at the compound rate of return.

Then, the time sequence is reversed and we examine the **present value** of future cash flows. Following that, the determination of the **internal rate of return** for investment proposals is described; then we discuss some special applications of the present value concept, the determination of growth rates, and the **uniform annual equivalent cash flow.** Finally, the *net present* value and *internal rate of return methods* of evaluating investment proposals are introduced. This chapter centers on the mechanics of compound rate of return calculations as well as on their meaning.

The notion of compound rate of return is not complex. Any reader having invested funds in a savings account has experienced the benefit of compound rate of return, as an example will quickly demonstrate. Suppose that a college student, Susan Cook, invests $1000 in a savings account at her bank. The bank promises to pay her a 5 percent rate of return (interest) per annum (per year). At the end of the first year, Susan's savings account balance will be $1050, consisting of the $1000 amount she invested plus the 5 percent return on that amount, or

COMPOUND RATE OF RETURN AND FUTURE VALUE

$$\$1000 \times 0.05 = \$50$$

Susan decides to leave her entire savings account balance, now consisting of $1050, in the account for another year (a total of 2 years). At the end of the second year, her savings account balance is $1102.50. The $52.50 return received for the second year consists of two parts: a $50 return on the original $1000 Susan invested($0.05 \times \$1000 = \$50$); plus a $2.50 return on the $50 earned during the *first* year and reinvested at the end of that year ($0.05 \times \$50 = \$2.50$). This is the **compounding** notion. When returns earned in one time period are reinvested for one or more additional time periods, returns are earned *on* returns. In contrast, a *simple rate of return* involves no compounding of return upon return but pays returns only on the original amount invested. For example, a 5 percent simple return (simple interest) paid on Susan's savings account would amount to $50 per year, for each year. At the end of the second year her account balance would be only $1100. Normally, compound, not simple, rates are used in rate of return computations.

Some people talk about the "miracle" of compound rates of return. The amounts of future dollars capable of being generated when an investment is left to earn a compound return can be impressive. Even at the compound rate of return of 5 percent earned on Susan's savings account, the account balance will grow rather rapidly over time (Table 5-1). From the time Susan deposited her original $1000, her account

Table 5–1   *Susan's Passbook:*
5% Rate of Return

Years from Date of Deposit	Deposit Credited	Returns Credited	Balance
0	$100		$1000.00
1		$ 50.00	1050.00
2		52.50	1102.50
3		55.12	1157.62
4		57.88	1215.50
5		60.78	1276.27
30		205.81	4321.94

balance grew to $1050 in 1 year and $1102.50 in 2 years. The compounding effect of return being earned on return is evidenced by the larger returns earned by the account each year. The last year shown in Table 5-1 is 30 years after the original investment; by that time the original investment of $1000 has more than quadrupled! Higher rates of return would, of course, generate even larger balances.

Future Value   The *future value* of any present amount, now invested, is the total sum generated when that investment earns a compound return at some specified rate for some specified number of periods. The future value of an invested present dollar amount is precisely what we have viewed as Susan's bank balance in Table 5-1. The expression for future value FV is[1]:

$$FV = A(1 + k)^n \qquad (5\text{-}1)$$

where A is the present number of dollars invested, k is the rate of return earned per time period, and n is the total number of time periods for which the dollars are invested.

To use the expression in Equation (5-1), we can generate some of the

---

[1]To establish (5-1), we need note only that the future value after one period is $FV = A + kA = A(1 + k)$. After two periods:

$$FV = A(1 + k) + kA(1 + k) = A(1 + k)(1 + k) = A(1 + k)^2$$

For n periods, future value must be:

$$FV = A(1 + k)^n$$

balances shown in Susan's bank account. These balances are future values for $A = \$1000$ and $k = 5$ percent.

Years Invested, n	$A(1 + r)^n$	FV
1	$\$1000(1 + 0.05)^1$	$\$1050.00$
2	$1000(1 + 0.05)^2$	1102.50
3	$1000(1 + 0.05)^3$	1157.62

The future value equation can be used to find *any* future value, provided we know:

1. The number of dollars to be invested (A).

2. The required rate of return to be earned per period (k).

3. The number of time periods funds are to be invested (n).

The calculation of future values is greatly aided by the use of a future value table such as Table A in the Appendix to this book. The factors in Appendix Table A are *future value factors* for an investment of $A = \$1$ for n years at k percent, or simply, $(1 + k)^n$. Appendix Table A shows, under a rate of return of 5 percent, that the first three values are as follows.

Years Invested, n	Future Value Factor
1	$(1 + 0.05)^1 = 1.05$
2	$(1 + 0.05)^2 = 1.10250$
3	$(1 + 0.05)^3 = 1.15762$

To compute the values for Susan's bank balance, we can multiply the factor for each year by $1000. The future value of $1 at 5 percent in 3 years is $1.15762, so for $1000, the future value would be $1000(1.15762), or $1157.62.

A somewhat more formal, but useful, way of viewing future value and all other compound rate of return concepts is to construct a time line like that presented in Chapter 1, Figure 1-1.

Future Value on a Time Line

$t = 0$	$t = 1$	$t = 2$	$t = 3$	$t = 4$	$t = 5 \ldots t = n$
A	$A(1 + k)^1$	$A(1 + k)^2$	$A(1 + k)^3$	$A(1 + k)^4$	$A(1 + k)^5$ $A(1 + k)^n$
$\$1000$	$\$1050$	$\$1102.50$	$\$1157.62$	$\$1215.50$	$\$1276.27$?

At the end of each year on the time line, the future value expression for that year is shown as well as Susan's bank balance from Table 5-1. The initial amount invested, $A = \$1000$, is the investment occurring at the point in time $t = 0$.

Frequency of Compounding   In computing future value, it is possible to consider frequencies of compounding other than the annual (yearly) compounding used in Equation (5-1). For example, most banks pay a stated annual rate of return of, say, $k = 6$ percent, but will provide for compounding of returns more frequently than once a year. To demonstrate this, suppose that the Matthew D. Savings Bank pays a 6 percent annual rate of return—compounded *quarterly*. This amounts to paying a 1.5 percent rate of return per quarter, arrived at by dividing the 6 percent per annum rate by the four compounding periods (quarters) per year. The appropriate future value factor for each quarter is $(1 + 0.015)$ and the future value factor for 1 year is now $(1 + 0.015)^4$. For a 6 percent savings account, compounded quarterly, an initial investment of $1000 develops the *quarterly* savings account balances shown in Table 5-2. Clearly, the future value after 1 year is higher with quarterly compounding than with annual compounding, which at 6 percent would generate, using Equation (5-1), only $1060. This is always the case.[2]

---

[2]The more general future value expression for any frequency of compounding is

$$FV = A \left(1 + \frac{k}{m} \right)^{mn}$$

where m is the frequency of compounding per year. Thus, for 6 percent compounded quarterly, the future value factors for $A = \$1$ after one quarter ($m = 1$), two quarters ($m = 2$), three quarters ($m = 3$), and four quarters ($m = 4$) are:

$$\left(1 + \frac{0.06}{4} \right)^1 = (1 + 0.015)^1 = 1.0150$$

$$\left(1 + \frac{0.06}{4} \right)^2 = (1 + 0.015)^2 = 1.0302$$

$$\left(1 + \frac{0.06}{4} \right)^3 = (1 + 0.015)^3 = 1.0457$$

$$\left(1 + \frac{0.06}{4} \right)^4 = (1 + 0.015)^4 = 1.0614$$

Sometimes daily compounding is used, but it is easier computationally to use *continuous compounding*, which provides a very close approximation.

To compound *continuously*, the future value expression is

$$FV = e^{kn}$$

where $e = 2.7183$. The future value factor for 1 year at 6 percent is:

$$FV = e^{(0.060)1} = 1.0618$$

for an effective annual rate of return of 6.18 percent—the limit to the increase in the effective rate as the frequency of compounding is increased. Continuous compounding is used primarily for more abstract aspects of financial analysis. For a more thorough discussion, see Richard E. Beckwith, "Continuous Financial Processes," *Journal of Financial and Quantitative Analysis* (June 1968), pp. 113–133.

Table 5–2   *Matthew D Savings Bank*

Date	Deposit Credited	Returns Credited	Quarterly Balance
12/31/78	$1000		$1000.00
3/31/79		$15.00	1015.00
6/30/79		15.22	1030.22
9/30/79		15.46	1045.68
12/31/79		15.68	1061.36

The higher the frequency of compounding, the greater the **effective annual rate of return** becomes. For the quarterly compounding shown in Table 5-2, the effective annual rate of return is 6.14 percent. For monthly compounding the effective annual rate would be 6.17 percent.

Except for certain specialized cases, annual compounding provides sufficient accuracy for most financial decisions. For example, a new factory generates cash flow every hour it is operating. Yet, we usually assume that a year's cash flow actually occurs at the *end* of the year and employ annual compounding to evaluate the cash flow.

Future Value of an Uneven Stream of Cash Flows   We need not confine ourselves to future values generated by investing a *single* amount now. Instead, we can find future values resulting from investing a *stream* of dollars over time at a compound rate of return. For example, suppose that Mindy Gray has three future payments to be received from her grandmother. The first payment is $A_1 = \$900$ to be received in 1 year; the second payment is $A_2 = \$1500$ to be received in 2 years; and the final payment is $A_3 = \$1000$ to be received in 3 years. On a time line, this stream of payments appears as follows.

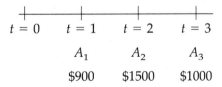

Mindy would like to invest these sums, when they are received, at 6 percent per year, compounded annually, with the aim of spending the accumulated funds 3 years from now, at $t = 3$. How much will be accumulated by time $t = 3$? The first payment, to be received at $t = 1$, can be invested at 6 percent for 2 years, the second payment at 6 percent for 1 year. The final payment will not be invested, since it will be received exactly when Mindy wishes to spend it. Using the future value formula in Equation (5-1), the final amount accumulated will be $3601.24 as follows.

	Future Value
First Payment Invested	$ 900(1 + 0.06)^2 = $1011.24
Second Payment Invested	1500(1 + 0.06)^1 = 1590.00
Third Payment (not invested)	1000 = 1000.00
Total Accumulated	$3601.24

Mindy will accumulate $3601.24 by $t = 3$. (Verify this by using Appendix Table A.) Total payments to her will be $900 + $1500 + $1000 = $3400, so that at 6 percent compounded annually, the total return earned is $3601.24 − $3400 = $201.24.

A more formal way of expressing the future value of an uneven stream of cash flows received at the end of each period is:

$$FV = A_1(1 + k)^{n-1} + A_2(1 + k)^{n-2} + \cdots + A_{n-1}(1 + k)^1 + A_n \quad (5\text{-}2)$$

$$= \sum_{t=1}^{n} A_t(1 + k)^{n-t}$$

The future value of an uneven stream is found by finding the future value of each payment in the stream using the formula in Equation (5-1) and summing them as shown in Equation (5-2).

As a second demonstration, suppose that Barbara Dixon will receive the following payments from her next four summer jobs: $2500, $2750, $3000, and $3250. The first payment will be received in 1 year. If she invests each of these payments when received at $k = 7$ percent, how much will she accumulate by $t = 4$? Recognizing that $A_1 = 2500, $A_2 = 2750, $A_3 = 3000, $A_4 = 3250, $k = 7$ percent and $n = 4$, we substitute these values into Equation (5-2). Appendix Table A is then used to find the appropriate present value factors:

$$FV = $2500(1 + 0.07)^3 + $2750(1 + 0.07)^2 + $3000(1 + 0.07)^1 + $3250$$

$$= $2500(1.2250) + $2750(1.1449) + $3000(1.0700) + $3250$$

$$= $3062.50 + $3148.48 + $3210 + $3250$$

$$= $12,670.08$$

Future Value of a Uniform Stream of Payments   When payments in the series of payments to be invested happen to be equal in amount, the future value problem becomes computationally more simple. The formula for this case is called the *future value of a uniform stream* (or, often, the *future value of an annuity*), and is given as[3]:

$$FV = A \left[\frac{(1 + k)^n - 1}{k} \right] \tag{5-3}$$

The expression in brackets is the future value of $1 invested at the end of each year beginning at the end of year 1 for n years to earn the rate of return of k. That expression can be calculated directly, but it is often easier to use a table like Appendix Table B, which contains the future value of a stream of $1 payments for different numbers of years and for different rates of return. Given the appropriate future value factor, we need only multiply the constant cash payment A to find, with Equation (5-3), the future value of any given stream of payments. The following examples show how Appendix Table B is used to solve uniform stream problems.

1. Frank Amato invests $5000 at the end of each year for 20 years at $k = 9$ percent ($A = \$5000$, $k = 9$ percent, $n = 20$):

    $$FV = \$5000(51.16011) = \$255,800.55$$

2. King Deets invests $3250 at the end of each year for 17 years at $k = 3$ percent ($A = \$3250$, $k = 3$ percent, $n = 17$):

    $$FV = \$3250(21.76158) = \$70,725.14$$

The future value of a uniform stream formula, Equation (5-3), can be used to solve **sinking fund problems.** A sinking fund problem exists when a known future sum is to be accumulated by investing a constant dollar amount, which must be calculated, per year. This situation often occurs when a firm has borrowed, and must accumulate funds with which to pay back a *lump sum* at a future time. In many cases, the firm

Sinking Fund Problems

---

[3]To derive Equation (5-3), we need only note that in Equation (5-2) all payments are constant, which means that $A_1 = A_2 = \ldots = A_n = A$, a constant. Therefore, Equation (5-2) can be written as:

$$FV = A[(1 + k)^{n-1} + (1 + k)^{n-2} + \cdots + (1 + k)^1 + 1] \tag{i}$$

Multiplying both sides of Equation (i) by $(1 + k)$, we obtain:

$$(1 + k)FV = A[(1 + k)^n + (1 + k)^{n-1} + \cdots + (1 + k)^2 + (1 + k)^1] \tag{ii}$$

Subtracting Equation (i) from Equation (ii), the result is Equation (5-3):

$$(1 + k)FV - FV = A[(1 + k)^n - 1]$$

$$FV = A \left[\frac{(1 + k)^n - 1}{k} \right]$$

may have agreed to a sinking fund provision to pay the principal amount borrowed in an indenture (legal agreement with bondholders) established when long-term bonds were initially sold. Sometimes, a firm voluntarily chooses to establish a sinking fund to meet such a future lump sum payment.

To solve a sinking fund problem and determine the constant annual payment, we simply rearrange Equation (5-3) in the following way.

$$A = FV \div \left[\frac{(1 + k)^n - 1}{k} \right] \qquad (5\text{-}4)$$

This rearrangement asks the following question. Given the future sum to be accumulated FV, the rate of return to be earned k, and the number of yearly payments into the sinking fund n, what constant payment per year (A) into the sinking fund will generate the desired future sum in the fund?

As an example of how Equation (5-4) is used, suppose that Balkins, Inc., has just issued $10 million worth of bonds due in 20 years. Balkins wants to find the annual amount that must be set aside each year for 20 years into a sinking fund so that, 20 years hence, $10 million will have been accumulated. The rate of return earned on funds set aside will be k = 8 percent. With FV = $10 million, k = 8 percent, and n = 20, Appendix Table B can be used to find the uniform annual payment, A, with Equation (5-4).

$$A = \frac{\$10,000,000}{45.76195} = \$218,522.15$$

In other words, if Balkins invests approximately $218,522 each year, beginning at the end of the first year, and earns 8 percent on the funds invested, the necessary $10 million to pay the principal amount owed on the bonds will have been accumulated by t = 20.

PRESENT VALUE

Present value involves the same concepts as future value except that the valuation is at the present time, t = 0, rather than at some future time, t = n. The process of finding present value is also known as *discounting* or *capitalizing*. Future cash flows are discounted or capitalized to find the *present value* at t = 0 of those future cash flows. If the *discount rate* used to find present value properly reflects the risk of these cash flows, present value measures the contribution of the cash flows owned to the total wealth of the owner.

Single Payment

At the beginning of this chapter, Susan Cook put $1000 in the bank at 5 percent interest per year, compounded annually, and had $1050 available at the end of the first year. Therefore, if the discount rate is 5 percent, the present value of $1050 to be received in 1 year should be $1000. We can compute this value by solving the future value formula of Equation (5-1) for the present amount A.

$$FV = A(1 + k)^n$$

Dividing both sides of the formula by $(1 + k)^n$, we obtain present value (PV) in Equation (5-5).

$$A = \frac{FV}{(1 + k)^n} = \frac{C}{(1 + k)^n} = PV \tag{5-5}$$

where A is relabeled PV, for present value, and FV is relabeled C, for cash flow. For Susan the present value of her $1050 discounted at 5 percent for 1 year is:

$$PV = \frac{C}{(1 + k)^n} = \frac{\$1050}{(1 + 0.05)^1} = \frac{\$1050}{1.05} = \$1000$$

One thousand dollars invested at 5 percent for 1 year produced $1050 future value; when that future value of $1050 is discounted back to the present at a 5 percent discount rate for one year, the present value is $1000.

An important point is that Susan will be *indifferent* between a future value of FV = $1050, and a present value of PV = $1000, as long as $k = 5$ percent represents a rate at which she may invest funds or obtain funds in the "market."[4] If we offered to give Susan $1050 a year from now, or $1000 right away, it would make no difference to her which gift she received, for both gifts have the same *present value* of $1000. If she were to receive the $1050 gift at $t = 1$ but wanted to spend as much as she could now, at $t = 0$, she could obtain funds in the market at 5 percent and receive $1000 to spend right away. One year hence, she would repay this amount plus a 5 percent return, or $1050. Alternatively, if she received $1000 right away but wanted to maximize next year's cash for spending, she could invest $1000 at 5 percent to produce $1050 next year. Thus, no matter what Susan's preferences are for present compared to future spending on goods and services, she will be indifferent in choosing between dissimilar cash flows having the same present value—even though these cash flows occur at different points in time and may not coincide with the timing of her spending plans—*as long as* she can invest or obtain funds in the market to readjust cash flows over time to suit her plans. Only the present values of the cash flows matter, not their distribution through time.

---

[4]The term *market* is used in the broadest sense here to represent any place where funds may be invested or obtained.

Finding the present value of a single future payment using Equation (5-5) is made easier by Appendix Table C, which gives present value factors for $1 received n years hence when the rate of discount is k. In other words, Appendix Table C gives the term

$$\frac{1}{(1 + k)^n}$$

from Equation (5-5). To find the present value of any single future payment, we need only find the appropriate present value factor from Appendix Table C and multiply it times C, the future cash payment.

The following examples demonstrate how present values of single future payments are calculated using Equation (5-5) and Appendix Table C.

1. Kent Hickam will receive a legacy of $150,000 in 10 years. Assuming that he could borrow some amount now, at a rate of $k = 8$ percent, and repay the loan 10 years hence with the $150,000 legacy, what is the maximum amount he can borrow? ($C = $150,000$, $k = 8$ percent, $n = 10$)

$$PV = \$150,000 \times 0.46319 = \$69,478.50$$

2. Karen Kemper is considering the purchase of an antique fan. She estimates that in 15 years the fan can be sold for $1200. If Karen could invest funds elsewhere at the rate of $k = 7$ percent, what is the fan worth to her now? ($C = 1200, $k = 7$ percent, $n = 15$)

$$PV = \$1200 \times 0.36245 = \$434.94$$

Present Value and Future Value

It should be obvious now that a dollar in hand today is worth more than the same dollar, if it were to be received in the future, is worth today. This is true because the market opportunity to invest funds at the rate of return k ensures that present dollars can be invested to generate higher future dollars. Similarly, a given amount of *future* dollars is worth less *today* than would the same dollars if available now. Some examples of the greater worth of present dollars were shown above. The person from whom Kent Hickam will borrow funds at $k = 8$ percent will receive $150,000 in future dollars at $t = 10$, but that lender will not give Hickam $150,000 today. If he did, and he were to be repaid with Hickam's legacy, he would receive only $150,000 in 10 years and would have earned no return. Since the lender *can* earn in the market a return of $k = 8$ percent, he will loan Hickam a lesser amount $69,478.50 so that the lender will earn the rate of 8 percent on the loan. The future dollars are worth less than today's dollars because of that opportunity to invest at 8

Table 5–3 *Present Value and Time*
(k = 5%)

n	Present Value of $10,000
5	$7835.30
10	6139.10
15	4810.20
20	3768.90
25	2953.00

percent, and the smaller present value of the loan amount reflects this state of affairs. Similarly, Karen Kemper's fan is worth $1200 in 15 years but only $434.94 today. Kemper can earn 7 percent in the market by investing funds. If she invested $434.94 today at 7 percent, it would be worth $1200 in fifteen years. The fan is worth no more than $434.94 to Kemper if it will yield only $1200 in 15 years.

It should also be clear from Equation (5-5) that the farther away in

Figure 5-1 *Time and Present Value (k = 5%)*

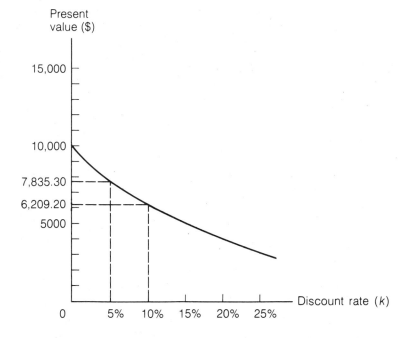

time a cash payment occurs, the less it is worth today. This is because the number of compounding periods over which the rate of return is earned is increased. Thus, $10,000 received in 5 years has a present value at $k = 5$ percent of $10,000 × 0.78353 = $7835.30, as shown in Table 5-3 and Figure 5-1. However, $10,000 to be received in 10 years has the smaller present value at $k = 5$ percent of $10,000 × 0.61391 = $6139.10.

Similarly, the higher the rate of discount k, the smaller the present value. This result occurs because any future cash payment becomes worth less today as the rate at which funds may be invested today becomes larger. For example, $10,000 received in 5 years had a present value of $7835.30 in the example above. In other words, a person could invest $7835.30 today at $k = 5$ percent and generate $10,000 by the end of the fifth year. However, if the rate of discount were higher, say $k = 10$ percent, the present value of $10,000 in 5 years would be only $6209.20. *The higher the discount rate, the smaller the present value*, as shown in Figure 5-2, because a smaller amount can be invested at $k = 10$ percent to generate $10,000 in 5 years than if the discount rate were only $k = 5$ percent.

Another aspect of the relationship of present value to future value should be clearly understood. Equation (5-1) for the future value of $1 is:

$$FV = (1 + k)^n$$

Figure 5-2   *Present Value and the Discount Rate (n = 5)*

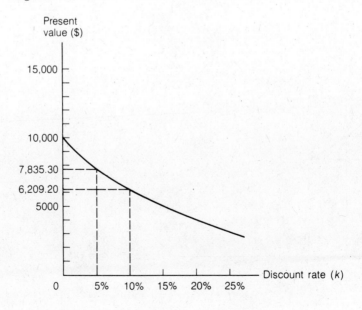

and Equation (5-5) for present value is:

$$PV = \frac{1}{(1 + k)^n}$$

Clearly, present value is the *reciprocal* of future value and alternatively, future value is the reciprocal of present value. The factors in Appendix Table C, therefore, are simply the reciprocals of the values in Appendix Table A. For example, the future value of a dollar in 10 years at 8 percent in Appendix Table A is 2.15892. The reciprocal

$$\frac{1}{2.15892} = 0.46319$$

is found in Appendix Table C for 10 years at 8 percent.

The present value of an uneven stream of payments over time is found by determining the present value of each future payment using Equation (5-5), and then summing these. Formally stated:

Present Value of an Uneven Stream of Payments

$$PV = \frac{C_1}{(1 + k)^1} + \frac{C_2}{(1 + k)^2} + \cdots + \frac{C_{n-1}}{(1 + k)^{n-1}} + \frac{C_n}{(1 + k)^n} \qquad (5\text{-}6)$$

$$= \sum_{t=1}^{n} \frac{C_t}{(1 + k)^t}$$

To show how Equation (5-6) is used, we suppose that Joe Kincaid will receive the following cash flows over the next 3 years.

Kincaid's Time Line

$t = 0$	$t = 1$	$t = 2$	$t = 3$
	$C_1 = 1500$	$C_2 = 1000$	$C_3 = 1750$

Assuming that Kincaid's discount rate is $k = 9$ percent, what are these flows worth to him? Using Equation (5-6) and Appendix Table C, the present value of these cash flows is:

$$PV = \$1500 \times \frac{1}{(1 + 0.09)^1} + \$1000 \times \frac{1}{(1 + 0.09)^2}$$

$$+ \$1750 \times \frac{1}{(1 + 0.09)^3}$$

$$= (\$1500 \times 0.91743) + (\$1000 \times 0.84168) + (\$1750 \times 0.77218)$$

$$= \$1376.15 + \$841.68 + \$1351.32$$

$$= \$3569.15$$

Thus the stream of payments is worth approximately $3569 to Kincaid. Stated another way, he would be indifferent between receiving $3569.15 as a lump sum now or receiving the future stream of payments over 3 years' time.

Present Value of a Uniform Stream of Payments

In the special case of all future payments being identical in amount, the present value computation is considerably simplified. Often called the present value of an annuity, the present value formula for this is[5]:

$$PV = C\left[\frac{(1 + k)^n - 1}{k(1 + k)^n}\right] \tag{5-7}$$

The expression in brackets is called a *present value of uniform stream factor* (or, often, a *present value of an annuity factor*) for $1 received each year for n years when the rate of discount is k. Appendix Table D contains these present value factors for various discount rates and time periods. When the number of time periods and the rate of discount are specified, the present value of any stream of payments having a constant value C can be found directly from Equation (5-7). The present value factor is multiplied times the periodic cash payment C.

Illustrating this class of problems, suppose that Damon McCauley is just finishing 2 years in graduate school. He estimates the additional annual salary that will result from his graduate studies as $3000. McCauley's rate of discount is $k = 4$ percent. If he works for 25 years and then retires, what is his graduate training worth? To answer this question, McCauley need only find the present value of the additional $3000 per year, received for 25 years, at a discount rate of $k = 4$ percent. Using Equation (5-7) and Appendix Table D,

$$PV = \$3000 \times 15.6220 = \$46,866$$

---

[5] To derive Equation (5-7), let $C_1 = C_2 = \cdots = C_n = C$, a constant, in Equation (5-6).

$$PV = C\left[\frac{1}{(1 + k)^1} + \frac{1}{(1 + k)^2} + \cdots + \frac{1}{(1 + k)^n}\right] \tag{i}$$

Multiplying both sides of Equation (i) by $(1 + k)$, we obtain

$$(1 + k)PV = C\left[1 + \frac{1}{(1 + k)^1} + \cdots + \frac{1}{(1 + k)^{n-1}}\right] \tag{ii}$$

Subtracting Equation (i) from Equation (ii) and solving for PV,

$$(1 + k)PV - PV = C\left[1 - \frac{1}{(1 + k)^n}\right] = C\left[\frac{(1 + k)^n - 1}{(1 + k)^n}\right]$$

$$PV = C\left[\frac{(1 + k)^n - 1}{k(1 + k)^n}\right] \tag{iii}$$

which is Equation (5-7).

If McCauley had to pay *now* for his graduate studies, he should be willing to pay *up to* $46,866. That is what graduate school is worth to him in present dollars, for McCauley could invest $46,866 now and generate a stream of payments of $3000 per year for 25 years—exactly what his graduate education will provide him.

Present Value of a Perpetuity

For some purposes, it is useful to assume that a constant stream of payments continues forever—that is, perpetually. This is a special case of the present value of a uniform series of payments and is called the *present value of a perpetuity*. The formula is quite simple.[6]

$$PV = \frac{C}{k} \tag{5-8}$$

No tables are required to calculate the present value of a perpetuity. For example, if someone promises to pay Rick Mockler $1000 each year in perpetuity, what is that promise worth if Mockler's discount rate is $k = 8$ percent? Substituting into Equation (5-8), the present value of the promise is:

$$PV = \frac{\$1000}{0.08} = \$12,500$$

Capital Recovery Problems

When our concern is not with the present value of the stream of payments but with the size of the periodic payments C, we encounter the class of problems called **capital recovery problems.**

A typical capital recovery problem is to find the amount of the constant annual payment over time needed to repay the principal plus interest on a loan. *Capital recovery* is an apt term for such a situation because the lender is recovering his capital (the amount of the loan), plus interest.

To solve capital recovery problems, it is necessary only to rearrange Equation (5-7) to solve for the constant payment C:

$$C = PV \div \left[\frac{(1 + k)^n - 1}{k(1 + k)^n} \right] \tag{5-9}$$

---

[6]To show how Equation (5-8) is derived, the present value of a uniform stream shown in Equation (5-7) can be written as follows.

$$PV = \frac{C}{k}\left[1 - \frac{1}{(1 + k)^n} \right]$$

If we let n approach infinity as the perpetual cash flow notion requires, the term in brackets goes to 1 and we are left with Equation (5-8).

Given any PV, k and n values, the constant annual payment C necessary to recover an initial amount, PV, plus returns generated at the rate k can be found. For example, suppose that Kosesan Perfume Company wants to borrow $25,000 at 7 percent and repay the loan in equal annual install-ments over 5 years. What must the equal annual payments be so that the lender recovers his $25,000 of capital plus a 7 percent return? Noting that PV = $25,000, k = 7 percent, and n = 5, Kosesan can use Appendix Table D to find the uniform annual payment C:

$$C = \frac{\$25,000}{4.1002} = \$6,097.26$$

If Kosesan pays five annual payments of $6097.26 to the lender, the lender will recover the principal amount loaned plus a 7 percent return.

INTERNAL RATE OF RETURN

In many cases, the cash flows C and the present value PV, representing the outlay made to acquire those cash flows, are known. In such cases the *internal rate of return*, the rate earned by making the outlay and receiving the cash flows, can be determined. The internal rate of return, like present value, is a discounted cash flow concept.

Single Payment Internal Rate of Return

An investment involving an outlay I will generate, after n periods, a cash flow C. The internal rate of return r^* is the discount rate that makes the present value of the future cash flow C just *equal* to the outlay I. In other words, an investment of I dollars, if it generates C dollars over n periods, will earn the *internal rate of return r^**. We express this relationship in Equation (5-10).

$$I = \frac{C}{(1 + r^*)^n} \tag{5-10}$$

The right-hand side of Equation (5-10) is the present value of the future cash inflow discounted at the internal rate of return r^*. By setting that present value equal to the outlay I, the unknown internal rate of return (r^*) can be found.

If the investment is for a single period, n = 1, the solution for the internal rate of return is direct. Rearranging Equation (5-10) and letting n = 1,

$$r^* = \frac{C}{I} - 1$$

This is the rate of return expression used in Chapter 2 and it is easily found. If an investment requires an outlay of $I = \$1700$ and the cash inflow next period is $C = \$2100$, then the internal rate of return is:

$$r^* = \frac{\$2100}{\$1700} - 1 = 0.2353, \text{ or } 23.53\%$$

When the single cash inflow is several periods away, it is possible to solve the expression in Equation (5-10) by taking roots, but it is easier to use Appendix Table C.[7] Again, Equation (5-10) is rearranged—this time by dividing both sides by C.

$$\frac{I}{C} = \frac{1}{(1 + r^*)^n} \qquad (5\text{-}11)$$

The expression on the right-hand side of Equation (5-11) is the present value factor for n periods and r^*. Since I and C are known, we need only compute the *ratio I/C* and find r^* from Appendix Table C for the appropriate number of time periods n. To see how this procedure in Equation (5-11) is carried out, consider the following examples:

1. An investment requires an outlay of $I = \$2000$ and returns $C = \$2438$ in $n = 10$ years:

$$\frac{I}{C} = \frac{\$2000}{\$2438} = 0.82034$$

Examining Appendix Table C for $n = 10$, we find the computed present value factor in the column for $r^* = 2$ percent.

2. If \$5000 invested now will return \$5961 in 4 years, what is the internal rate of return?

$$\frac{I}{C} = \frac{\$5000}{\$5961} = 0.83879$$

Referring to Appendix Table C for $n = 4$, the computed present value factor is very close to that shown for 4.5 percent. Therefore, the internal rate of return is approximately $r^* = 4.5$ percent.

Uneven Streams of Payments and Internal Rate of Return

In the absence of a suitable electronic calculator with an internal rate of return algorithm, calculation of the internal rate of return for a stream of uneven cash flows is tedious because it requires a trial-and-error procedure. We must first restate Equation (5-6) in terms of the outlay I (instead of PV) and the unknown internal rate of return r^* (in place of k).

---

[7]Appendix Table A, working in terms of future value, could also be used if desired, since the factors are the reciprocals of the factors in Appendix Table C.

$$I = \frac{C_1}{(1 + r^*)^1} + \frac{C_2}{(1 + r^*)^2} + \cdots + \frac{C_n}{(1 + r^*)^n} \qquad (5\text{-}12)$$

We must find the rate of discount r^* such that the present value of the future cash flow is equal to the investment outlay I.

Suppose that an investment opportunity for Farmer Company requires an outlay of $I = \$100,000$ and generates two succeeding cash inflows of $C_1 = \$80,000$ and $C_2 = \$33,000$. What is the internal rate of return? The time line for the cash flows is:

$t = 0$	$t = 1$	$t = 2$
I	C_1	C_2
$-\$100,000$	$+80,000$	$+\$33,000$

Using Equation (5-12), the internal rate of return must satisfy the following relationship.

$$\$100,000 = \frac{\$80,000}{(1 + r^*)^1} + \frac{\$33,000}{(1 + r^*)^2}$$

To find r^*, we first *try* a discount rate of 8 percent, using single payment present value factors from Appendix Table C:

$$PV = \frac{\$80,000}{(1 + 0.08)^1} + \frac{\$33,000}{(1 + 0.08)^2}$$

$$= (\$80,000 \times 0.92593) + (\$33,000 \times 0.85734)$$

$$= \$74,074.40 + \$28,292.22$$

$$= \$102,366.62$$

At 8 percent, \$102,366.62 is required to generate the future cash flows specified. However, since the Farmer Company's investment opportunity generates the same future cash flows with only a \$100,000 outlay, the internal rate of return must *exceed* 8 percent. Trying now a discount rate of 12 percent and repeating the solution process, the present value of the cash inflows is:

$$PV = \frac{\cdot\,\$80,000}{(1 + 0.12)^1} + \frac{\$33,000}{(1 + 0.12)^2}$$

$$= (\$80,000 \times 0.89286) + (\$33,000 \times 0.79719)$$

$$= \$71,428.80 + \$26,307.27$$

$$= \$97,736.07$$

Clearly, 12 percent is too high, since only $97,736.07 would be required to generate the future cash flows but the investment opportunity requires a $100,000 outlay. Trying once again with 10 percent, we find that the internal rate of return is $r^* = 10$ percent, for at that rate:

$$PV = \frac{\$80,000}{(1 + 0.10)^1} + \frac{\$33,000}{(1 + 0.10)^2}$$

$$= (\$80,000 \times 0.90909) + (\$33,000 \times 0.82645)$$

$$= \$72,727.20 + \$27,272.85$$

$$= \$100,000.05 \sim \$100,000$$

The present value of the future cash flows at $r^* = 10$ percent equals (except for rounding error) the outlay of $100,000, as required.

When an investment outlay generates a uniform stream of payments (an annuity), the internal rate of return is quite easy to calculate using Appendix Table D. In such a case, we need only restate Equation (5-7) in the following way.

Uniform Stream of Payments and Internal Rate of Return

$$I = C \left[\frac{(1 + r^*)^n - 1}{r^*(1 + r^*)^n} \right] \qquad (5\text{-}13)$$

The right-hand side of Equation (5-13) is the present value of the uniform cash flow stream discounted at the internal rate of return r^*. This present value expression must equal the investment outlay I shown on the left-hand side of Equation (5-13).

To solve for r^*, we must first divide both sides of Equation (5-13) by the uniform cash flow term C.

$$\frac{I}{C} = \left[\frac{(1 + r^*)^n - 1}{r^*(1 + r^*)^n} \right] \qquad (5\text{-}14)$$

Then, by computing the ratio of I to C, both of which are known, we find the present value factor for a uniform stream. From Appendix Table D, we can then find, for the appropriate number of periods n, the discount rate yielding the same present value factor as computed in Equation (5-14).

Illustrating the procedure laid out in Equation (5-14), we consider two examples.

1. Charlie Peck has an investment that requires an outlay of $I = \$100,000$ and returns a constant cash flow of $C = \$15,400$ per year for $n = 12$ years. What is the internal rate of return on the investment?

$$\frac{I}{C} = \frac{\$100,000}{\$15,400} = 6.4935$$

From Appendix Table D for $n = 12$ periods, the approximate internal rate of return is $r^* = 11$ percent. (The value in the table for 11 percent is 6.4925. This is sufficiently close for most purposes.)

2. A Chandler Company investment requiring a $40,000 outlay returns $5814 per year for 8 years. What is the internal rate of return?

$$\frac{I}{C} = \frac{\$40,000}{\$5,814} = 6.8799$$

Appendix Table D shows, for $n = 8$ periods, that the return is approximately $r^* = 3.5$ percent.

Perpetual Cash Flows and the Internal Rate of Return

The internal rate of return is especially easy to calculate if the investment outlay produces constant cash flows in perpetuity. We can restate Equation (5-8) in modified form.

$$I = \frac{C}{r^*} \tag{5-15}$$

The right-hand side of Equation (5-15) is the present value of the perpetual cash flow C discounted at the internal rate of return r^*. At the true internal rate of return, the present value of future cash flows must equal the outlay I. Solving Equation (5-15) for r^*, the internal rate of return is:

$$r^* = \frac{C}{I} \tag{5-16}$$

To demonstrate the use of Equation (5-16), suppose that an investment opportunity requires an outlay of $I = \$450,000$ and returns $21,000 per period in perpetuity. The internal rate of return is:

$$r^* = \frac{\$21,000}{\$450,000} = 0.046, \quad \text{or } 4.6\%$$

SOME SPECIAL USES OF COMPOUND-ING TABLES

Occasionally, some variations on the usual usage of the compounding tables assist in solving certain kinds of problems. We demonstrate two of these variations: calculation of compound growth rates and **uniform annual equivalent** (UAE) **cash flow** calculations.

Sometimes we wish to find out how rapidly some variable such as sales, earnings, or value has grown over time. The factors for the future value of a single payment, shown in Appendix Table A, assist the calculation of such growth rates. For example, suppose that the sales of a firm over time have the following pattern.

Calculation of Compound Growth Rates

Sales ($000)					
1970	1971	1972	1973	1974	1975
$40.00	$42.40	$44.94	$47.64	$50.50	$53.53

We can use Equation (5-1) to solve for the compound growth rate g of the firm's sales. Equation (5-1) was stated as:

$$FV = A(1 + k)^n$$

Modifying (5-1), let FV equal the most recent (1982) sales level and let A equal the oldest (1977) sales level. Then substitute the compound growth rate g for k, to produce Equation (5-17).

$$1982 \text{ sales} = 1977 \text{ sales}(1 + g)^5 \tag{5-17}$$

We can rearrange Equation (5-17) by dividing both sides by 1977 sales. The resulting equation is:

$$\frac{1982 \text{ sales}}{1977 \text{ sales}} = (1 + g)^5$$

By substituting the sales data for 1977 and 1982, a future value factor is calculated:

$$\frac{\$53.53}{\$40.00} = (1 + g)^5$$

$$1.3385 = (1 + g)^5$$

We can now search Appendix Table A in row 5 ($n = 5$) for the factor 1.33825. This factor is under the 6% column. Thus, the annual growth rate in sales from 1977 to 1982 was 6 percent.

For certain types of capital expenditure analysis problems (see Chapter 10), it is often useful to convert an uneven stream of cash flows to an *equivalent uniform stream*—equivalent in the sense of having the *same present value* as the actual, uneven stream of cash flows. Such an equivalent stream is called the *uniform annual equivalent (UAE)*.

Uniform Annual Equivalent Cash Flow

To show how uniform annual equivalents are calculated, suppose that an investment produces the following stream of uneven cash inflows:

$$\begin{array}{c|c|c|}
 & & \\
t = 1 & t = 2 & t = 3 \\
C_1 = \$1000 & C_2 = \$2000 & C_3 = \$2500
\end{array}$$

Using Equation (5-6) and Appendix Table C, the present value of this stream at $k = 8$ percent is:

$$PV = \$1000 \times 0.92593 + \$2000 \times 0.85734 + \$2500 \times 0.79383$$

$$= 925.93 + \$1,714.68 + \$1984.58$$

$$= \$4625.19$$

Now, what uniform annual equivalent (UAE) cash flow, received each year for three years, will have the *same* present value? To find out, we use the capital recovery Equation (5-9) and let UAE replace C.

$$UAE = \$4625.19 \div \left[\frac{(1 + 0.08)^3 - 1}{0.08(1 + 0.08)^3} \right]$$

Using Appendix Table D for the present value of a uniform series of payments factor with $n = 3$ and $k = 8$ percent, we find:

$$UAE = \frac{\$4625.19}{2.5771}$$

$$= \$1794.73$$

This means that a *constant* cash inflow of $1794.73 per year (the UAE) for 3 years will have the same present value as the present value of the original *uneven* stream.

CAPITAL BUDGETING: NET PRESENT VALUE AND INTERNAL RATE OF RETURN METHODS

Our final step in this chapter is the specification of two methods of evaluating capital investment proposals; the *net present value method* and the *internal rate of return method*. Both approaches rely on compounding and are considered to be **discounted cash flow methods.** Discounted cash flow methods are ways of using the compound return notion to adjust for differences in the timing of cash flows by converting them to a common equivalent measure. Our present purpose in dealing with these methods remains introductory. Chapter 7 discusses in greater detail the advantages of both these methods of evaluating investment proposals as well as the characteristics of other methods. For now, the mechanics and rationale for each method are briefly described.

Given that the firm has an appropriate discount rate k to evaluate cash flows, the net present value method is quite direct. The **net present value** (NPV) of an investment proposal is the present value of all future cash flows minus the investment outlay, I, or

The Net Present Value Methods

$$NPV = PV - I \qquad (5\text{-}18)$$

The decision rule for acceptance or rejection of an investment proposal is the following.

NPV Value	Decision
Positive	Accept
Negative	Reject
Zero	Indifferent

The rationale for the decision rule is clear. If the future cash flows of a proposal are worth *more*, in present value terms, than the proposed present cash outlay that would be required to obtain them, it pays to accept the proposal—net present value will be positive in this case. If the investment proposal is worth *less* today than the outlay required to undertake it, the net present value will be negative and the proposal should be rejected. If the proposal is just equal in worth to the outlay, so that net present value is zero, it makes no difference whether the proposal is undertaken.

To illustrate use of the net present value method, we evaluate the purchase of an office building requiring an initial outlay of $100,000 and returning a uniform rental cash flow (net of expenses) of $16,275 per year for 10 years. Three different discount rates will be used to calculate net present value: $k = 8$ percent, $k = 10$ percent, and $k = 12$ percent. Using Equation (5-18) and calculating present value from Equation (5-7) and Appendix Table D, the resulting net present values are:

1. $k = 8$ percent

$$
\begin{aligned}
NPV &= PV - I \\
&= \$16,275 \times 6.7101 - \$100,000 \\
&= \$109,206.87 - \$100,000 = \$9,206.87 > 0
\end{aligned}
$$

Accept, because NPV > 0.

2. $k = 10$ percent

$$
\begin{aligned}
NPV &= PV - I \\
&= \$16,275 \times 6.1446 - \$100,000 \\
&= \$100,000 - \$100,000 = 0
\end{aligned}
$$

Indifferent, because NPV = 0.

3. $k = 12$ percent

$$NPV = PV - I$$
$$= \$16,275 \times 5.6502 - \$100,000$$
$$= \$91,957.00 - \$100,000 = -\$8043 < 0$$

Reject, because NPV < 0.

Of the three discount rates, only $k = 8$ percent is low enough, in compensating investors for time and risk, to make the project worth more than the outlay. At $k = 12$ percent, NPV < 0 occurs and the project is not worthwhile. If $k = 10$ percent, NPV $= 0$ and the choice is a matter of indifference.

The Internal Rate of Return Method

The **internal rate of return** (IRR) method requires that the firm calculate the internal rate of return r^*, on the investment proposal and compare that return with the required rate of return, k. The decision rule for accepting or rejecting a proposal is:

**Internal Rate of Return
Compared to Required
Rate of Return**

Rate of Return	Decision
$r^* > k$	Accept
$r^* < k$	Reject
$r^* = k$	Indifferent

The rationale for the decision rule is obvious; no project will be undertaken unless the internal rate of return exceeds the rate of return required by investors to compensate them for time and risk.

Demonstrating the IRR method with the office building project evaluated under the NPV method, we use Equation (5-14) and Appendix Table D to find the internal rate of return r^*.

$$\frac{I}{C} = \frac{\$100,000}{\$16,275} = 6.1444$$

For $r = 10$, Appendix Table D shows that the internal rate of return is approximately $r^* = 10$ percent. Again assuming the three alternative required rates of return of $k = 8$ percent, $k = 10$ percent, and $k = 12$ percent, the following decisions would be made.

1. $k = 8$ percent
Accept, because $r^* = 10$ percent $> k = 8$ percent.

2. $k = 10$ percent
Indifferent, because $r^* = 10$ percent $= k = 10$ percent.

3. $k = 12$ percent

Reject, because $r^* = 10$ percent $< k = 12$ percent.

Comparing the NPV and IRR methods, we see that both techniques signal accept the proposal if $k = 8$ percent, reject if $k = 12$ percent, and be indifferent to the proposal if $k = 10$ percent. This agreement, between the two methods will often, but not always, occur. Chapter 7 confronts the circumstances where lack of agreement exists.

Until this chapter, examples of financial problems dealt with single peri-   **SUMMARY**
od or perpetual multiperiod problems. To provide for the analysis of financial investment problems, most of which are of the multiperiod, nonperpetual type, we needed to expand our computational tools. In the financial world returns are usually expressed periodically (frequently yearly), requiring us to introduce the concept of *compounding*.

Under compounding, a periodic rate of return is earned for each time period on the amount invested at the beginning of that time period. The amount invested may include accumulated returns from prior compounding periods if two or more compounding periods are involved. Consequently, returns are earned on prior returns as well as on the initial investments of dollars.

Future value (FV), present value (PV), and the internal rate of return (IRR) are only a few of the useful figures that can be derived using the concept of compound returns.

Future values involve computing the future worth of an amount, after a specified number of periods, that has been invested at the rate k and periodically compounded. A table of future value factors (Appendix Table A) facilitates the computation of such amounts. The more frequent the compounding, the greater the effective annual returns. Except for special types of problems, however, annual compounding is sufficiently accurate for most uses. Both uneven and uniform periodic streams of payments can be converted into future values of the streams of payments. Where the periodic payment in the stream is of uniform size, an "annuity" factor from Appendix Table B simplifies the computation. The future value computations can be used to solve a special type of problem: that of the sinking fund. In such a problem, a future sum must be accumulated by investing a constant periodic dollar amount at the rate k. The future amount is known but the periodic payment must be found from the computation.

Present values of future cash flows are found by discounting (capitalizing) the flows at the rate k. Present values of future dollars are always less than the future dollars when k is > 0—reflecting the idea that a dollar today is worth more than one to be received tomorrow. The farther in the future a dollar is expected to be received, the less its present value. For any future dollar, the higher the discount rate applied to that dollar, the lower its present value. Present values for single payments or an uneven stream of payments can be calculated using present value factors from a table like Appendix Table C. When the stream of payments is uniform, the "annuity" table, Appendix Table D, can be used for ease of computation. A capital recovery problem, which asks for the uniform stream of payments having a given present value, can be solved using Appendix Table D and the present value concept. Uniform annual equivalent (UAE) cash flows are simply uniform cash flows having the same present value as an uneven stream of cash flows. These UAE cash flows can be found using present value computations.

The net present value and internal rate of return methods for evaluating investments are both discounted cash flow methods. The net present value decision rule accepts investments when the discounted stream of cash inflows, using the rate k, exceeds the outlay required to undertake the investment. If the discounted value of inflows is less than the outlay, the net present value method rejects the investment. The internal rate of return method computes the rate of return to be earned by making the outlay for the investment and receiving the subsequent cash inflows. If this internal rate exceeds the required rate k, the investment is accepted. If the internal rate is less than k, the investment is rejected.

For future use, the more important compound rate of return formulas presented in this chapter are summarized here.

Future Value of a Single Payment

$$FV = A(1 + k)^n \tag{5-1}$$

Future Value of an Uneven Series of Payments

$$FV = \sum_{t=1}^{n} A_t(1 + k)^{n-t} \tag{5-2}$$

Future Value of a Uniform Series of Payments

$$FV = A\left[\frac{(1 + k)^n - 1}{k} \right] \tag{5-3}$$

Sinking Fund

$$A = FV \div \left[\frac{(1 + k)^n - 1}{k} \right]$$

(5-4)

Present Value of a Single Payment

$$PV = \frac{C}{(1 + k)^n}$$

(5-5)

Present Value of an Uneven Stream of Payments

$$PV = \sum_{t=1}^{n} \frac{C_t}{(1 + k)^t}$$

(5-6)

Present Value of a Uniform Stream of Payments (Annuity)

$$PV = C \left[\frac{(1 + k)^n - 1}{k(1 + k)^n} \right]$$

(5-7)

Present Value of a Perpetuity

$$PV = \frac{C}{k}$$

(5-8)

Capital Recovery

$$C = PV \div \left[\frac{(1 + k)^n - 1}{k(1 + k)^n} \right]$$

(5-9)

Internal Rate of Return, Single Payment

$$\frac{I}{C} = \frac{1}{(1 + r^*)^n} \text{ or } r^* = \frac{C}{I} - 1 \quad \text{for} \quad n = 1$$

(5-11)

Internal Rate of Return, Uneven Stream of Payments

$$I = \frac{C_1}{(1 + r^*)^1} + \frac{C_2}{(1 + r^*)^2} + \cdots + \frac{C_n}{(1 + r^*)^n}$$

(5-12)

Internal Rate of Return, Uniform Stream of Payments

$$\frac{I}{C} = \left[\frac{(1 + r^*)^n - 1}{r^*(1 + r^*)^n} \right]$$

(5-14)

Internal Rate of Return of a Perpetuity

$$r^* = \frac{C}{I}$$

(5-16)

GLOSSARY OF
KEY TERMS

Capital Recovery Problem	Finding the constant periodic payment required to repay the initial capital investment, plus a return, when the number of periods and the rate of return are known.
Compound Rate of Return	The periodic rate of return earned on amounts invested, where such amounts include accumulated returns plus an initial investment. Thus a return is earned *on* returns.
Discounted Cash Flow Methods	Methods of adjusting for differences in timing among cash flows by converting them to a common point in time.
Effective Annual Rate of Return	The annual rate of return earned when the frequency of compounding occurs more often than once a year.
Future Value (FV)	The accumulated value at some future point in time of dollars to be received from a present investment.
Internal Rate of Return (IRR)	The rate of return that equates the present value of both the cash inflows and cash outflows of an investment.
Net Present Value (NPV)	Present value of future cash flows minus the initial capital outlay or investment.
Present Value (PV)	The value today (discounted value) of future cash flows.
Required Rate of Return (k)	The return required by investors to compensate them for risk and time. It is also known as the *risk-adjusted discount rate* and the *capitalization rate*.
Sinking Fund	A future lump sum accumulated by constant periodic payments invested at a compound rate of interest.
Uniform Annual Equivalent (UAE) Cash Flow	A periodic even cash flow, equivalent in present value to an uneven cash flow stream.

SELECTED REFERENCES

Cissell, R., and H. Cissell. *Mathematics of Finance*, 4th ed. Boston: Houghton Mifflin Co., 1973.

Grant, Eugene L., et al. *Principles of Engineering Economy*, 6th ed. New York: Ronald Press, 1976.

Lutz, F., and V. Lutz. *The Theory of Investment of the Firm*. Princeton, NJ: Princeton University Press, 1951.

Osborn, R. *The Mathematics of Investment*. New York: Harper & Row, 1957.

Taylor, G. A. *Managerial and Engineering Economy*. Princeton, NJ: Van Nostrand, 1969.

QUESTIONS

1. In the future value formula, Equation (5-1), define A, k, and n.

2. One Los Angeles bank advertises interest compounded daily on passbook savings accounts while a nearby bank compounds interest quarterly. What competitive advantage does one have over the other if both banks pay a 7 percent annual interest rate?

3. What is the sinking fund problem? How is its solution related to finding future values?

4. How is discounting related to (a) capitalizing, and (b) finding a present value?

5. Can a person be indifferent to whether he receives $1 now or, instead, $1 a year from now? Explain.

6. How are the present value of a single payment, and the future value of a single payment, related to each other?

7. If $PV = \dfrac{FV}{(1 + k)^n}$ what is $\dfrac{PV}{FV} = \dfrac{1}{(1 + k)^n}$?

8. If you have an uneven projected cash inflow stream and an investment outlay I, can you solve directly for the internal rate of return from an annuity table like Appendix Table D? Why?

9. How would you compute the rate of growth in your annual wages over the past 4 years?

10. What method would you use to find your monthly car payments if you must repay a loan balance and interest with 24 equal monthly payments?

11. If John needs $5000 in 4 years, how would he compute his end-of-month payments over the 4 year period, at 8 percent annual interest, to generate the $5000?

12. The price of a Stroganoff painted during the old master's Polka Dot Period has doubled in the past 50 years. Since you could have earned 3 percent per year in a savings account over the same 50

years that you have owned the painting, your investment in art was (a) a resounding success, (b) ho hum, (c) terrible. Support your answer.

PROBLEMS

1. Alf lent Jean $5000 to help establish her in the lawn service business. Jean agreed to pay 10 percent interest compounded annually and to return the $5000 plus interest in one lump sum in five years. How much will Jean have to pay Alf?

2. Barney frequently refers to his "rule of 72" which says that an amount at x percent interest compounded annually will *double* in n years, where $n = 72 \div x$. How soon then will Gracie's $100 investment double if she is paid 4 percent? 8 percent? 12 percent? Verify this "rule" from Appendix Table A.

3. If you invest $50,000 in a business, how much should you have when you retire in 20 years if you expect to earn 15 percent per year, compounded annually, on that investment?

4. If Ida and Dick buy a home for $40,000 and expect it to appreciate at 7 percent per year, how much should it be worth in 10 years?

5. You have $10,000 to invest for 5 years. Compute the amount you will have accumulated at the end of the fifth year under both quarterly and annual compounding if the annual interest rate is 12 percent.

6. Compute the *effective annual rate of return* when an annual rate of 12 percent is compounded (a) yearly, (b) quarterly, and (c) monthly.

7. Sally invests $500 a year from now, $700 at the end of the second year, and $900 at the end of the third year.

    (a) How much will she have at the end of year 3 if the return is 6 percent per annum, compounded annually?

    (b) How much would she have at the end of a fourth year at 6 percent, compounded annually, if she has added no more money beyond the third year?

8. How much money will Curly have in 5 years if he is able to invest $1000 at 6 percent for four years at $t = 1$, $1500 at 5 percent for 3 years at $t = 2$, $1500 at 4 percent for 2 years at $t = 3$ and $2000 at 3 percent for 1 year at $t = 4$, compounded annually?

9. Alice signs up for a payroll savings plan at work that will deduct

$50 from her salary per month. How much will she have in a year and a half if her account is credited at 12 percent annual interest compounded monthly? The first deduction will be 1 month from now.

10. Starting next year, Mr. Piker plans to put away $2000 a year for 15 years at 6 percent per year interest, compounded annually. How much will he have when he retires in 15 years?

11. Suppose that Ann wants to have the sum of $100,000 when she retires in 20 years. How much will she have to invest at the end of each year to accumulate that amount if she can earn 7 percent per year, compounded annually? Investment will start next year.

12. Suppose that you need to accumulate $75,000 5 years from now.

    (a) If you can earn 6 percent per year, compounded annually, how much would you have to invest at the end of each year, beginning next year, to achieve your goal?

    (b) If you preferred to deposit a lump sum right now to achieve your goal, how much would you need to invest?

13. A rich uncle has promised Esther $10,000 when she finishes college in 4 years. If Esther's required rate of return is 8 percent, what is the present value of the payment?

14. Joe was asked to renew a magazine subscription and either pay $40 immediately to obtain the magazine for the next 3 years or pay $15 at the *beginning* of each of the 3 years. If the appropriate discount rate is 5 percent, what is the present value of the cost of the subscription under each plan?

15. (a) What is the maximum Barbara should pay for an annuity issued by Total Insurance Company that would provide $100 a year for the first 10 years and $200 a year for the remaining 5 years of its life, if the appropriate discount rate is 10 percent?

    (b) Also calculate the worth if $200 a year were received for the first 5 years and $100 a year for the last 10 years.

    (c) Which option, (a) or (b), should Barbara choose?

16. What is the present value of $1000 received each year for 14 years when the discount rate is (a) 15 percent, (b) 25 percent, (c) 40 percent?

17. What is the present value of

    (a) $2000 received each year for 15 years when the discount rate is 40 percent?

(b)   What is the present value if the $2000 were paid each year for only 14 years?

(c)   What is the difference in present value between (a) and (b)?

18.   Using a 10 percent required rate of return:

(a)   What is the present value of $6000 received yearly for 5 years?

(b)   What is the present value (k = 10 percent) of $1500 received each quarter for 5 years?

(c)   What is the difference in present value between (a) and (b)?

19.   What is the present value (when k = 10 percent) of an investment paying $12,345 a year in perpetuity?

20.   What is the present value of an investment in a machine that is expected to yield cost savings as follows: year 1, $2000; year 2, $2000; year 3, $2000; year 4, $5000; year 5, $4000, if the required rate of return for this type of investment is 5 percent per year?

21.   A new car costs Ginny $8000. She can pay 20 percent down, and the rest monthly at a 12 percent annual interest rate over 24 months. What are her equal monthly payments?

22.   A house costs $50,000. The purchaser must pay 25 percent down, then pay the remaining amount in equal monthly installments over the next 20 years. How would you determine the monthly payment, if the mortgage interest rate is 6 percent annually?

23.   If Carrie has $50,000 in a savings account that earns 6 percent per year interest compounded annually, what is the maximum amount she can withdraw per year "forever"?

24.   Leslie was promised $10,000 as a present upon graduation in 4 years. However, she has requested instead to receive $6800 now. What rate of interest is she paying for the use of the money if she receives $6800 now?

25.   What is the internal rate of return on an investment that costs $10,000 and returns $3000 a year for 5 years?

26.   Henry received a bill for fire insurance on his house. He could pay the total bill of $56 now, or he could pay it in quarterly payments of $18, $14, $14, and $14. Payments occur at the beginning of each quarter. Find the percentage cost to Henry if he selects the latter plan.

27.   Jack the "Con" promises Ferdinand that Ferdinand will *double* his

money in 3 years by making a certain land purchase. What compounded or internal rate of return is the "Con" promising?

28. Felix White can buy a boat for $10,000 and rent it out, returning to him $5000, $4000, $3000, $2000, and $1000 at the end of each of 5 successive years. What would be his internal rate of return on the purchase and rental of the boat?

29. The Unreal Casino in Nevada has been put up for sale, for $3.6 million cash; alternatively, it can be purchased by paying nothing down and $1.2 million per year for 5 years. What is the interest cost for not buying the casino on a cash basis?

30. What is the rate of growth in Podolak County over the past 10 year period if the population went from 120,000 in 1970 to 400,000 in 1980?

31. A close relative gave Ida $100,000. How much could she withdraw at the end of every year for 10 years and not use the gift up until the end of the tenth year, if she invested it at 8 percent per year compounded annually?

32. Net cash inflows associated with an investment in a small apple-coring machine are $50, $100, and $150, respectively, for the next 3 years. If the discount rate is 15 percent and the cost of the machine is $200, should the machine be purchased, using the NPV decision rule?

33. If purchase of an efficient machine at a price of $100 resulted in net cash inflows from cost savings of $25, $37.50, and $75, respectively, for each of 3 years, should the machine be purchased if the required rate of return is 15 percent? Use the IRR decision rule.

34. For how many years must Cynthia invest $1000 in an account that pays 10 percent annually to be able to stop payments and then draw $1000 each year forever?

35. Dr. Des Ert, a geology professor, is planning his sabbatical starting 3 years hence. Since he will be on half-salary during his sabbatical year he figures he will need to withdraw $500 each month from his savings account starting at the end of his first month (12 withdrawals during the year). The savings account pays a 12 percent annual interest rate, compounded monthly. In addition, he will need $5000 to purchase a truck and equipment. He plans to purchase the truck at the beginning of his sabbatical. His last full paycheck will arrive at that time. How much must he save each month for the next 3 years starting next month to manage to just meet his needs for this sabbatical?

36. Janie's grandmother has given Janie a savings account that had been started several years ago with a deposit of $1000. The current balance is $1372.79. The bank has paid interest at an annual rate of 8 percent compounded quarterly. How long ago was this account opened?

37. On January 1, 1978, Laura opened a bank account with a $100 deposit. She made a deposit of $100 every 6 months. The bank paid interest at an annual rate of 6 percent, compounded quarterly. On January 1, 1981, Laura transferred her account to a bank that pays 8 percent compounded semiannually. She has continued making her semiannual deposits. How much will Laura have in her account after making the most recent deposit of $100 on January 1, 1983?

38. Five years ago John took out a $50,000 mortgage on his house at 9 percent amortized over 30 years. After 5 full years of monthly payments, John sold the house. The bank allowed the new owners to "assume" John's mortgage at a new interest rate of 14%. What is the amount of the new owners' monthly mortgage payment?

SECTION III

Investment Decisions

CHAPTER 6

The Capital
Budgeting Process

At the end of Chapter 5 we used compound rate of return techniques to evaluate a simple investment in an office building. That investment required an outlay of $100,000 in exchange for expected cash inflows of $16,275 per year over a 10-year period. Every day millions of firms face such investment opportunities. Always, the basic question is whether funds should be committed to the opportunity, given that financial managers wish to maximize the wealth of shareholders.

In the chapters of Section III, we discuss the investment or capital budgeting decision in much greater detail and show how a wide range of investment opportunities can be identified and evaluated in a manner consistent with wealth maximization. In connection with this goal, the firm must answer three basic questions: (1) Which assets *should* be acquired? (2) What is the desirable scale of outlay for each asset? (3) What is the desirable scale of the total outlay for all assets to be acquired? The significance of each of these questions is illustrated as we proceed through our discussion of capital budgeting.

This chapter provides an overview of the capital budgeting decision process. Chapter 7 examines the decision criteria by which capital investment proposals are accepted or rejected. The problem of specifying expected cash flows for investment opportunities is discussed in Chapter 8. Chapter 9 undertakes the analysis of investments having unequal lives and of the determination of the optimal economic life of an investment proposal. Limitations on the total cash outlay in the capital budget are reviewed in Chapter 10. In a later section we evaluate the special problems raised by leasing assets and by acquiring assets through acquisition of existing firms. However, the latter topics are delayed until students have studied corporate valuation, capital structure decisions and cost of capital in Chapters 11 to 16.

Throughout Chapters 6 to 10 the required rate of return or cost of capital for an investment is assumed to reflect the *market* risk associated with cash flows generated by the investment, a concept earlier discussed in Chapter 4. A detailed study of the steps necessary to estimate that rate follows the capital budgeting discussion. For now, our goal is to understand the capital budgeting process, to develop confidence in our ability to identify and calculate appropriate cash flows, and to apply investment criteria properly.

AN OVERVIEW

Defined for some set interval of time such as a year, a **capital budget** shows all longer lived assets that a firm plans to acquire during that year, together with the scale of the cash outlay for each asset and for the total assets to be acquired.

The entire **capital budgeting process** can be divided into six phases: planning, evaluation, selection, implementation, control, and auditing. These phases are shown schematically in Figure 6-1. The decision process begins with an investment opportunity, perhaps sketchily framed at first, that requires an outflow of cash in the near future in exchange for subsequent cash inflows. The opportunity then enters the **planning phase** where the potential effect on the firm's fortunes is assessed and the ability of the management of the firm to exploit the opportunity is determined. Opportunities having little merit and considered to be unworthy of further time and effort for analysis may be rejected during this early phase. Promising opportunities are advanced in the form of a proposal to enter the **evaluation phase.** During the latter phase, proposals are considerably more refined and estimates of a proposal's cash inflows and outflows are obtained. Relationships of one proposal with other proposals may result in some proposals being grouped together into *projects* during the evaluation phase. Other proposals may turn out to be so obviously disadvantageous that they are rejected during this phase. Proposals surviving evaluation become, singly or with other proposals, projects that enter the **selection phase,** where capital budgeting decision criteria are applied to determine which projects can be expected to increase shareholder wealth. Projects not expected to meet this criterion are rejected, while acceptable projects enter the **implementation phase.** Here, funds are acquired and disbursed to obtain the assets required by the project, and projects are placed in operation. Once the projects have been placed in operation, they are in the **control phase,** wherein the firm tries to see to it that the assets, labor, and materials

Figure 6-1   *The Capital Budgeting Decision Process*

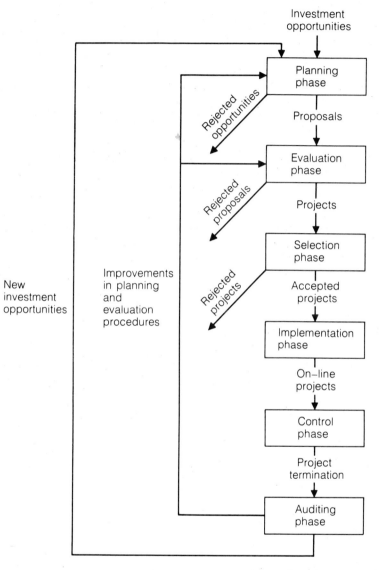

used in the project are efficiently managed. Finally, the original project comes to the end of its life and is terminated. At that time, and often before, the project enters the **auditing phase,** where the performance of the entire project is subjected to review. Whether the project was successful or unsuccessful, ideas for new investment opportunities, including replacement of the terminated project, are generated in the auditing phase. These ideas, along with other new ideas extraneous to the auditing phase, reenter the decision process at the planning phase as new investment opportunities for consideration by the firm.

Financial managers are involved in all phases of the capital budgeting process. However, because of the difficulties of reversing decisions involving fixed assets once the decisions have been made, special attention is paid to the first three phases, when funds have yet to be committed to assets. It is in these areas that mistakes can still be avoided relatively cheaply. This fact accounts for the emphasis given in later chapters to these three initial phases of the decision process. However, all the phases are further illustrated in this chapter using a specific firm: Curly's Chicks, Inc.

PLANNING PHASE

Frank Feather is financial manager of Curly's Chicks, Inc. Curly's Chicks raises chicks for resale to ranchers and egg producers. Formed as a corporation by several families some years back, Curly's now has gross revenues of some $5 million annually and the common stock is publicly traded. Many of the original family members and their descendants

Table 6–1   *Investment Opportunities: Curly's Chicks, Inc.*

	Idea	Proposer	Estimated Expenditure
A	Raise chicken broilers for slaughter	Tim (President)	$ 75,000
B	Purchase a new truck	Bill	5,000
C	Produce chicken eggs	George (Treasurer)	85,000
D	Establish a poultry slaughterhouse	Doug (Vice-President)	150,000
E	Overhaul truck	Jason	1,000
F	Grow apples	Sabrina	25,000
G	Replace manually operated chicken feeders	Carrie	3,000
H	Expand chick production	Dave	60,000
I	Go into dog food business	Charlie	500,000
J	Go into chicken fertilizer business	Micah	25,000
K	Raise turkey chicks	Kathy (Secretary)	85,000
L	Install automatic chicken feeders	Casey	7,000
M	Buy in-house computer system	Frank	80,000
			$1,101,000

serve on the board of directors and also work for the company on a salaried basis.

The directors are concerned that growth in the chick production industry is slowing down and that further growth in profits will require more profitable ways of producing chicks or some changes in the type of product being produced. Consequently, directors and a few employees have produced a number of ideas for capital investment opportunities (Table 6-1). Frank Feather has the important task of analyzing them, and he immediately begins the *planning phase* for these opportunities, a phase consisting of three parts: identification of opportunities, preliminary analysis, and initial screening.

Obviously, opportunities for capital expenditures must exist before they can be analyzed. Frank is fortunate to have so many ideas already available from various contributors. In other circumstances, opportunities, especially good ones, might not be readily available and Frank would have to try rather hard to generate them.

Identification of Opportunities

In examining the available opportunities for capital expenditure, Frank sees some similarities among them and decides to group them according to their potential impact on the revenues and/or costs of Curly's Chicks. Specifically, he groups together all opportunities that appear to reduce operating costs under the category of **cost reduction investment opportunities.** Thus, the overhauling of a truck or purchase of a new truck are ways of reducing costs caused by mechanical breakdowns. Replacing old, manually operated chicken feeders with new feeders of the same type will also reduce costs when compared to the *present* manually operated feeders. Finally, a computer system is suggested as a means to reduce various paperwork processing costs.

Preliminary Analysis

Opportunities tending to increase revenues have the effect of increasing output. The latter can be broken into three categories of **revenue-expanding investment opportunities.** First, the *revenue expansion—same product line* category refers to opportunities such as expansion of chick production. Second, the *revenue expansion—new line (related)* category applies to opportunities for expanding output of products having either a similar marketing distribution system or using production methods similar to those of the existing chick product line. Opportunities to produce chicken broilers, chicken eggs, dressed chickens (as processed by the slaughterhouse), dog food (produced from chickens), fertilizer, and turkey chicks all fall in this category. Finally, the *revenue expansion—new line (unrelated)* category applies to opportunities such as growing apples.

By categorizing each **investment opportunity** in this way, the manner in which investment opportunities would change the nature of Curly's Chicks' *existing* operations can be more clearly identified. The strengths and weaknesses of Curly's management compared to the talents required to exploit particular opportunities can be assessed. Significant changes in the skills possessed by Curly's existing management may be required by some opportunities—changes that may or may not be immediately feasible. The extent to which Curly's *existing* stock of capital and its technology is related to investment opportunities can also be evaluated. Some opportunities may be quite compatible with Curly's existing capital investment and technology. Little additional outlay or risks with new technology are posed by such opportunities. Other opportunities may require substantial changes—both in the size of Curly's stock of capital and in the sophistication of its technology. By assessing the changes in Curly's existing management and the capital and technology required by investment opportunities, the future revenue and costs associated with opportunities can be more clearly identified.

When Frank Feather has classified available investment opportunities

Table 6–2   *Grouping of Opportunities for Capital Expenditures: Curly's Chicks, Inc.*

I.	Cost Reduction Opportunities	
	B Purchase a new truck	$ 5,000
	E Overhaul truck	1,000
	G Replace manually operated chicken feeders	3,000
	L Install automatic chicken feeders	7,000
	M Buy in-house computer system	80,000
II.	Revenue Expansion—Same Product Line	
	H Expand chick production	60,000
III.	Revenue Expansion—New Line (Related)	
	A Raise chicken broilers	75,000
	C Produce chicken eggs	80,000
	D Establish poultry slaughterhouse	150,000
	I Go into dog food business	500,000
	J Go into chicken fertilizer business	25,000
	K Raise turkey chicks	85,000
IV.	Revenue Expansion—New Line (Unrelated)	
	F Grow apples	25,000

as shown in Table 6-2, he realizes that further analysis will require much more precise information than the sketchy ideas initially submitted. He recognizes that in the case of cost reduction opportunities, it is not enough to know that costs may be reduced if an opportunity is exploited. He must know the manner of cost reduction as well as the length of time over which cost savings will be produced. For example, the opportunity to replace an old truck with a new truck must be made much more specific. What kind of new truck should be purchased— large or small? How long will the new truck be operated? Two years? Ten years? These questions must be answered before formal investment proposals may be specified for subsequent evaluation. Moreover, there may exist several alternative and apparently plausible answers to such questions. Consequently, several proposals may result from one investment opportunity—buy a small truck and operate it for 3 years, buy a large truck and operate it for 5 years, and so forth.

Opportunities for expanding revenue have even more detailed information requirements to show how revenues and costs of the firm will be affected. For example, the opportunity to raise turkey chicks raises several important questions. What pattern of output will be produced over time? What will be total output? When will turkey chick production begin? When will it end? What manner of production technology will be used to produce turkey chicks? Frank must answer these questions to frame proposals for evaluation. Table 6-3 shows a set of possible answers Frank might obtain in pursuing such questions.

Frank has found two alternative patterns of output for turkey chicks. Pattern A is a "bold entry" strategy obtainable only if Curly's can ac-

Table 6–3   *Alternative Output Patterns*
and Production Technologies
(Output in Thousands of Turkey Chicks)

Output Patterns	Year					
	1	2	3	4	5	Total
A	400	500	600	600	600	2700
B	200	300	400	500	600	2000

Production Technologies

Type 1:   Capital Intensive/Low Annual Operating Cost

Type 2:   Labor Intensive/High Annual Operating Cost

quire an existing turkey chick producer. Pattern B is more cautious and requires that Curly's purchase physical plant and equipment and hire additional labor to produce turkey chicks. Each pattern assumes that production starts next year. However, either one or both patterns could be delayed as an option subject to evaluation. Both patterns extend over 5 years, but shorter or longer production periods are possible and could be analyzed. To obtain these output patterns, Frank must make a forecast based on pricing policies for turkey chicks and on competitive conditions. Ultimately projections of future revenue depend heavily on the quality of these forecasts. On the cost side, the capital outlay and expected future operating costs of producing turkey chicks will depend on the type of production technology employed. Frank has identified two types of technology: type 1—capital intensive, and type 2—labor intensive. Type 1 requires a larger scale of initial cash outlay but features lower expected future operating costs. Type 2 permits a lower initial scale of capital outlay but results in higher expected future operating costs. Obviously, other technologies capable of use might be analyzed as well.

The number of separate proposals stemming from a given revenue-expanding opportunity might be large. For example, the two output patterns and two production technologies for producing turkey chicks in Table 6-3 provide *four* possible proposals to produce turkey chicks, all of which may be worthy of subsequent evaluation.

Initial Screening

The large number of options associated with any given opportunity make it necessary and desirable that an *initial screening* be undertaken to reduce their number. For the manager, this screening process is a matter of judgment exercised without complete data and especially without the cash flow estimates made in the subsequent evaluation plan for formal proposals. This means that managers rejecting opportunities at this early stage without complete information incur the risk of rejecting opportunities that appear to be undesirable at first but would prove to be desirable if more analysis were given to the opportunity. Consequently, only very unlikely, perhaps outlandish, proposals can safely be eliminated in the initial screening.

As an example of the process of reducing the number of proposals in the initial screening process, suppose that Frank Feather reevaluates the turkey chick production opportunity. Four potential output pattern–production technology proposals were identified on preliminary evaluation. However, Frank may find that output pattern A is probably not feasible because no existing turkey chick producer is willing to sell at a reasonable price. In addition, the type 1 production technology, though available, is subject to an alarming rate of breakdowns; costs of production will probably be far too high to make this a serious option. Consequently, only the output pattern B–type 2 production technology option is worthy of framing into a formal proposal for more detailed evaluation. The output pattern A–type 1 production technology option is eliminated in the initial screening.

Sometimes, the initial screening process can discard *all* possible proposals stemming from any given opportunity. For example, the idea of going into the dog food business might involve a type of managerial experience and marketing channels that Curly's lacks and cannot obtain for a reasonable price. Thus that opportunity will be discarded and no formal proposal will result from the initial screening.

In the *evaluation phase*, all investment opportunities surviving the planning phase in the form of **investment proposals** are further refined by estimating all cash flows associated with the proposals. (Chapter 8 considers at length the problem of proper cash flow determination for proposals.) Then, by noting the nature of economic relationships between proposals, they are grouped into **investment projects.** Finally, there is a secondary screening of projects and some projects may be eliminated. All projects surviving the evaluation phase go on to the selection phase.

EVALUATION PHASE

Using the output and other estimates developed in the planning phase, cash flow estimates for proposals are made. These estimates include not only the initial outlay required to purchase the assets but also the resulting cash inflows.

Cash Flow Estimation

For Curly's Chicks, all surviving proposals will require cash flow estimates, and Frank Feather must meet this need. In the case of the original turkey chick production opportunity, the only surviving proposal was output pattern B–type 2 production technology. Using the information developed about this proposal in the earlier planning phase as well as additional estimates of product selling price and costs of production, cash flow estimates for the proposal can be established. Frank's estimates for that proposal are shown in Table 6-4.

Notice that not only are each year's cash flows estimated but that the initial outlay is now $100,000 rather than the $85,000 shown for the original opportunity in Table 6-1. This kind of change is to be expected in the evaluation phase as more study is given to a proposal and, as better information is obtained, estimates of cash flow are refined.

At this point in the evaluation phase, Feather has generated cash flow

Table 6–4   *Proposal for Turkey Chick Production*

Proposal	Raise Turkey Chicks by Producing Output Pattern B and Using Type 2 Production Technology	
Cash Flows	Inital Outlay	$100,000
	Year 1 Cash Inflow	$20,000
	Year 2 Cash Inflow	30,000
	Year 3 Cash Inflow	40,000
	Year 4 Cash Inflow	50,000
	Year 5 Cash Inflow	60,000

estimates for all surviving proposals and is ready to group these proposals, when necessary, into projects.

Grouping of Proposals Into Projects

Many of the proposals considered by a firm may be related in that the cash flow magnitudes for one proposal depend on whether another proposal is undertaken. Such relationships are described by the term **economic dependence** and include both complementary and substitute proposals. The nature of economic dependence between proposals is a question of degree and can be described by the continuum in Figure 6-2.

In **complementary proposals** (complements) the selection of one proposal increases the cash inflow associated with some other proposal(s). That is, the cash inflows received when both proposals are undertaken *exceed* the sum of the separate proposal cash inflows. In **substitute proposals** (substitutes) the selection of one proposal *reduces* the cash inflows of the other proposal(s). In this case, the cash inflows received when both proposals are undertaken are less than the sum of the separate cash inflows for each proposal. In **independent proposals** the cash inflows of one proposal are completely *unaffected* when the other proposal(s) is undertaken. The cash inflows received when both independent proposals are taken equal the sum of the separate proposal cash inflows.

Curly's Chicks has a number of proposals needing to be characterized by the nature of their economic dependence. Examples of each type of

Figure 6-2   *Continuum of Economic Dependence*

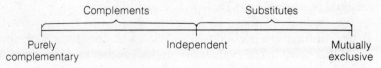

Table 6–5   *Complementary Proposals*
                  ($000)

Proposal	Cash Inflows by Year			
	1	2	3	4
Broilers	$10	$11	$12	$14
Slaughterhouse	10	15	18	20
Both	22	30	35	40

dependence relationship can be found in Curly's Chicks' proposals and some grouping of proposals into projects must be undertaken if correct choices among proposals are to be made.

Complementary Proposals   Among the proposals available to Curly's Chicks are the proposals to raise chicken broilers and to establish a chicken slaughterhouse. Although each of these proposals can be undertaken separately, it happens that selecting both the broiler proposal *and* the slaughterhouse proposal *raises* the combined cash inflow of both these projects above the sum of the separate cash flows for each proposal. Consequently, these two proposals are economically dependent and complementary. If only the broiler proposal were taken, broilers would be sold to a slaughterhouse. In turn, if only the slaughterhouse proposal were taken, broilers would have to be purchased elsewhere. By taking both proposals, Curly's can enjoy the cost saving from cutting out "middlemen." These issues are demonstrated in Table 6-5. Note that if both proposals are undertaken, the resulting cash inflows exceed the sum of the separate proposal cash inflows.

In the extreme case of purely complementary proposals, one proposal

Table 6–6   *The Extreme Case of Purely*
                  Complementary Proposals
                  ($000)

Proposal	Cash Inflows by Year			
	1	2	3	4
Broilers	$10	$11	$12	$14
Slaughterhouse	0	0	0	0
Both	22	30	35	40

Table 6–7   *Substitute Proposals ($000)*

Proposal	Cash Inflow by Year			
	1	2	3	4
Overhaul Truck	$2	$2	$2	$1
New Truck	2	2	2.5	2.5
Both	2.1	2.1	2.6	2.6

can be undertaken *only* if another proposal is also undertaken. For Curly's, a case of such extreme complements exists if it is assumed that the chicken slaughterhouse cannot be undertaken *unless* the broiler proposal is also accepted. For this situation, the resulting cash inflows are described in Table 6-6. By itself, the slaughterhouse proposal generates zero cash inflow. However, when combined with the broiler proposal, the combined proposal generates greater cash inflow than the latter proposal taken separately.

Substitute Proposals

Some of the Curly's Chicks proposals are substitutes in that undertaking two proposals causes the resulting cash inflow to be *less* than the sum of the separate proposal cash inflows. The proposals to overhaul a truck and purchase a new truck are examples of substitute proposals. If both proposals are undertaken, the firm will own two trucks: an old (but overhauled) vehicle plus a new one. The firm may not be able to use two trucks efficiently in its operation, and at least one truck will have substantial idle time. Table 6-7 shows the cash inflow for this situation.

When both proposals are undertaken, the total cash inflow received is less than the sum of the separate proposal cash inflows and very little

Table 6–8   *Mutually Exclusive Proposals ($000)*

Proposal	Cash Inflows by Year			
	1	2	3	4
Overhaul Truck	$2	$2	$2	$1
New Truck	2	2	2.5	2.5
Both	2	2	2.5	2.5

more than either of the separate proposals. These proposals are substitutes.

The extreme case of substitutes consists of **mutually exclusive investment proposals:** not only is the total cash inflow received when both proposals are undertaken less than the sum of the separate proposals' cash inflows, but it will not exceed the cash inflow of the best one of the two proposals. When the overhaul proposal is compared to the new truck proposal, the situation is a mutually exclusive case if, when both proposals are undertaken, the overhauled truck is *never* used. Under such circumstances, the cash flows for the proposals behave as shown in Table 6-8. Note there that the combined cash inflow is simply the cash inflow attributable to the new truck—the only vehicle being used.

Independent Proposals

Some of the Curly's Chicks proposals are independent of each other. For example, the proposals to overhaul a truck and to raise broilers can both be undertaken without affecting their respective cash inflows. This result can be seen in Table 6-9. There the cash inflows obtained when both projects are undertaken exactly equal the sum of the separate proposal cash inflows. This result is quite different from the situation presented in Tables 6-5 to 6-8, where proposals are dependent.

Creating Projects From Proposals

It should now be clear that because of dependence relationships, Frank Feather cannot simply evaluate proposals separately, for this might result in purchasing a new truck *and* overhauling an old one when only one of these substitute proposals is worthy of consideration. Or, Frank might erroneously decide to evaluate separately the broiler and slaughterhouse proposals, consequently overlooking the potentially valuable benefit of taking both these complementary proposals. Frank must combine proposals into *projects* that are **economically independent** of each

Table 6-9   *Independent Proposals ($000)*

Proposal	Cash Inflows by Year			
	1	2	3	4
Overhaul Truck	$ 2	$ 2	$ 2	$ 1
Broilers	10	11	12	14
Both	12	13	14	15

Table 6–10   *Capital Projects*

Independent Projects from Independent Proposals (Table 6–2)

1. Produce chicken eggs (C)

2. Expand chick production (H)

3. Go into chicken fertilizer business (J)

4. Raise turkey chicks (K)

5. Grow apples (F)

6. Buy in-house computer system (M)

Independent Projects from Grouped Dependent Proposals (Table 6–2)

7. Overhaul truck (E) *or* Purchase new truck (B)—(substitutes)

8. Replace manually operated feeders (G) *or* Install automatic chicken feeders (L)—(substitutes)

9. Raise chicken broilers (A) *and* Establish poultry slaughterhouse (D)—(complements)
   OR
   Raise chicken broilers (A)
   OR
   Establish poultry slaughterhouse (D)

other. Only then can projects be separately evaluated. Accordingly, each project must ultimately consist of either a *group* of dependent proposals that, together, are independent of other projects, or of a *single* economically independent proposal. Table 6-10 shows how Frank has performed this grouping for the proposals facing Curly's Chicks.

Frank has decided that the chicken egg, increased chick production, chicken fertilizer, turkey chick, and computer system proposals are all economically independent. Consequently, each of these proposals forms an individual independent project.[1] Frank has also identified substitute proposals and grouped these into independent projects. Thus,

---

[1]The reader might anticipate some dependencies among the proposals Frank has classed as independent. This particular classification is done for simplicity. However, this goal should hold, as much as possible, in actual applications. If we were to consider every possible dependency between proposals, however trivial, just 20 proposals would yield 1,048,575 projects for evaluation. In general, the number of such projects is given by $2^N - 1$, where N is the number of proposals.

the proposals to overhaul the old truck or to purchase a new truck are substitutes that together form *one* project—a project independent from all others. Similarly, the proposals to replace manually operated chicken feeders or install automatic chicken feeders are viewed as substitutes and are grouped into one project. Finally, the complementary proposals for producing broilers and establishing a slaughterhouse are grouped as one project independent of all others. Within that project, three mutually exclusive proposals exist: Curly's Chicks may undertake *both* the broiler and slaughterhouse proposals *or* only the broiler proposal *or* only the slaughterhouse proposed.

For selection purposes, Frank has thus been able to group proposals such that all resulting projects are economically independent.[2] However, Frank may also wish to consider another type of relationship, *statistical correlation,* in evaluating proposals.

Statistical Correlation

Even though two projects may be deemed economically independent, there may remain a statistical relation between annual cash flows of the two projects. Rather like the discussion in Chapter 4, where rates of return on two securities could have positive, negative, or zero correlation, cash inflows from two projects may also be correlated. The significance of this correlation is that combining projects may allow the firm to reduce risk associated with cash inflows from projects if the cash inflows are not perfectly positively correlated.

The effect of the degree of correlation on the risk associated with the combined cash flows of two projects can be seen in Table 6-11.

In panel A, the annual cash inflows of each project are seen as uncertain. In each project, two possible outcomes exist and, again in each project, these outcomes are given equal probabilities of occurrence. With this information, the expected annual cash inflows, and the variance and standard deviation of annual cash inflows, can be calculated as shown in the table. For example, egg production has an expected annual cash inflow of $E = \$10,000$, variance of $\sigma_E^2 = 25,000,000$, and standard deviation of $\sigma_E = \$5000$. Now the risk of the cash inflow of the *combined* projects is the standard deviation of the sum of two random variables (here, the respective annual cash inflows from each project) as expressed by Equation (*i*) in Table 6-11. Calculation of that risk can be completed as soon as ρ, the correlation coefficient for the two projects' cash inflows, is known. In this example, three alternative correlation

---

[2]The scheme of grouping proposals into projects has been taken from C. W. Haley and L. D. Schall, *The Theory of Financial Decisions,* 2nd Ed. (New York: McGraw-Hill Book Co., 1979), pp. 47–62.

Table 6–11   *Correlated and Uncorrelated Project Cash Flows*

A.   Egg Production Project and Fertilizer Production Project Considered Separately

Egg Production Project:

Annual Cash Flow Outcomes and Probability of Occurrences

$$E_1 = \quad \$5000 \qquad\qquad P_1 = 0.50$$
$$E_2 = \$15,000 \qquad\qquad P_2 = 0.50$$

Expected Annual Cash Inflow

$$\bar{E} = E_1P_1 + E_2P_2$$
$$= \$5000(0.50) + \$15,000(0.50) = \$10,000$$

Variance and Standard Deviation of Annual Cash Inflow

$$\sigma_E^2 = \sum_{j=1}^{2} (E_j - \bar{E})^2 P_j$$

$$= (\$5000 - \$10,000)^2(0.50) + (\$15,000 - \$10,000)^2(0.50)$$

$$= 25,000,000$$

$$\sigma = \sqrt{\sigma_E^2} = \$5000$$

Fertilizer Production Project:

Annual Cash Flow Outcomes and Probability of Occurrence

$$F_1 = \$10,000 \qquad\qquad P_1 = 0.50$$
$$F_2 = \$30,000 \qquad\qquad P_2 = 0.50$$

Expected Annual Cash Inflow

$$\bar{F} = F_1P_1 + F_2P_2$$
$$= \$10,000(0.50) + \$30,000(0.50) = \$20,000$$

Variance and Standard Deviation of Annual Cash Inflow

$$\sigma_F^2 = \sum_{j=1}^{2} (F_j - \bar{F})^2 P_j$$

$$= (\$10,000 - \$20,000)^2(0.50) + (\$30,000 - \$20,000)^2(0.50)$$

$$= 100,000,000$$

$$\sigma_F = \sqrt{\sigma_F^2} = \$10,000$$

B.   Both Projects Considered Together

Combined Expected Annual Cash Inflow

$$\bar{E} + \bar{F} = \$10,000 + \$20,000$$

Combined Cash Flow Standard Deviation $\sigma_{E+F} = \sqrt{\sigma_{E+F}^2}$

$$\sigma_{E+F} = \sqrt{\sigma_E^2 + \sigma_F^2 + 2\rho_{EF}\sigma_E\sigma_F}$$

$$\sigma_{E+F} = \sqrt{25,000,000 + 100,000,000 + 2\rho_{EF}(\$5000)(\$10,000)}$$

If $\rho = +1.0$ (Perfect Positive Correlation), then

$$\sigma_{E+F} = \$15,000$$

Table 6–11   (*Continued*)

If $\rho = 0$ (Uncorrelated), then

$\sigma_{E+F} = \$11,180$

If $\rho = -1.0$ (Perfect Negative Correlation), then

$\sigma_{E+F} = \$5000$

coefficients are assumed: perfect positive correlation ($\rho = 1.0$), zero correlation ($\rho = 0.0$), and perfect negative correlation ($\rho = -1.0$). When these coefficients are used to help calculate the risk of the combined cash inflows, it can be seen that anything less than perfect positive correlation reduces the risk of the cash flow. In the case of perfect negative correlation ($\rho = -1.0$), the *risk* of both projects' cash inflow happens to equal that of only egg production, alone—even though the combined projects' cash inflow is much larger!

The question is whether this apparent risk reduction is relevant to investors. Does it affect their wealth? If investors can efficiently diversify, attempts to reduce risk through diversification by the firm cannot benefit shareholders. With efficient diversification, only market risk reflecting movements between individual security and market returns is relevant, not the correlation between returns on individual assets. Shareholders will not pay firms to internally diversify when they can achieve the same benefits by purchasing appropriate combinations of securities to obtain the same risk reduction.

If there are serious impediments to diversification, correlations among cash flows of a firm's existing assets, current capital budget, and even future capital budgets are relevant. Firm diversification is relevant because, by diversifying, firms offer a service that investors cannot provide for themselves. An asset does not have a unique "risk" because risk depends on the pattern of cash flows of other assets in a specific firm. Under such circumstances capital budgeting becomes *extremely* complex. Required rates of return on specific investments, *if they could somehow be estimated,* would depend on the pattern of cash flows of other investments in the firm's capital budget. In short, capital budgeting would be reduced to an almost ad hoc procedure in which a manager could make an investment look good or bad by including it in next year's capital budget rather than this year's.

Given the great breadth and depth of U.S. capital markets and the ready availability of instant sources of diversification such as mutual funds, it seems neither necessary nor "realistic" to let capital budgeting fall into such disarray. Although not all investors will be efficiently diversified, they can achieve adequate diversification at low cost. We would argue that in all but the most aberrant instances, the assumption that investors can adequately diversify is both realistic and necessary for meaningful capital budgeting analysis.

For Frank Feather and Curly's Chicks, the *assumption* that shareholders can efficiently diversify and hold *other* risky securities enables the projects in Table 6-10 to be considered without reference to the correlation of cash flows among projects. If Curly's Chicks shareholders are not efficiently diversified, two courses of action are open to Frank. He can ignore their seeming irrationality (holding nondiversified portfolios) in his decisions, or he can attempt the difficult task of specifying statistical relationships among possible projects *and* the firm's existing investments. If the latter action is taken, it is difficult to envision where the task will lead.

Secondary Screening   Once economically independent projects have been established, as in Table 6-10, the firm can make a secondary screening of them and, possibly, discard some projects without further analysis. Projects surviving the secondary screening then move to the selection phase of the capital budgeting process. Discarding projects at this stage normally occurs because the expected cash inflow of a project is insufficient to allow the firm to recover its initial outlay. Such a project would yield a negative return.

For Frank Feather, the secondary screening of projects in Table 6-10 might reveal the following estimated cash flows for project 6, the computer system.

Initial cash outlay	$80,000
Annual expected cash inflow	$10,000
Duration of cash inflow	7 years

Obviously, project 6 is not acceptable because expected annual cash inflows are insufficient to recover the initial cash outlay. Frank would eliminate project 6. Suppose, also, that Frank eliminates project 5, growing apples, and project 7, overhauling a truck *or* purchasing a new truck, on the same grounds. The surviving projects making the transition to the selection phase, then, are projects 1, 2, 3, 4, 8, and 9.

SELECTION PHASE   The firm may now apply more formal selection criteria to the surviving projects. We have seen in Chapter 5 that the net present value and internal rate of return methods are important formal project selection

Table 6–12   *Curly's Chicks Capital Budget*

Project	Outlay
3. Chicken Fertilizer	$ 25,000
4. Turkey Chicks	100,000
9. Chicken Broilers and Poultry Slaughterhouse	75,000
	150,000
	$350,000

criteria. These, together with other criteria, are discussed in detail in Chapter 7. At this point, it need only be said that in choosing a project from among several, the firm will attempt to maximize shareholder wealth with its chosen criterion of selection—taking account of the returns and risks of individual projects as well as the cost of capital for financing each project.

For Curly's Chicks, Frank applies the formal criterion used by the firm and takes the following actions: reject projects 1, 2, and 8; accept projects 3, 4, and 9. In the case of project 9, evaluation of the alternatives within that project led to the decision to both raise chicken broilers *and* establish a poultry slaughterhouse.

Table 6-12 shows the firm's capital budget for the next year, which consists of the accepted projects 3, 4, and 9.

Curly's Chicks plans to expend $350,000 in its capital budget—down considerably from $1,101,000, the original total in Table 6-1. In reaching that budget, Curly's Chicks had to decide which projects would be included and which would be discarded (selection phase, secondary screening, initial screening). It also had to determine, in the planning and evaluation phase, just what the outlays on each project would be. Frank has thus answered the first two important questions raised at the outset of this chapter, Which projects and on what scale should a project be included in the capital budget?

IMPLEMENTATION PHASE

To implement the decision to accept projects in the capital budget, the firm must acquire the necessary funds, purchase the assets, and begin operating the projects. This phase may concern financial managers relatively little if all prior phases in the capital budgeting process have been correctly performed. For the formal selection procedures should give adequate account of the cost and availability of capital for the project—given the particular financing mix of debt and equity to be employed by the firm. However, the necessary funds may not be available at the specified cost. This contingency means either that all projects must be reevaluated at a higher cost of capital than initially used or that some way of selecting projects under a capital constraint must be used to determine the size of the capital budget! In either case, higher than expected costs of capital will lead to a shrinkage of the total capital budget, with the result either that fewer projects will be taken than originally planned or that projects will be scaled down in size. Chapter 10 discusses this problem in more detail.

We assume Curly's Chicks was able to obtain $350,000 from desired capital sources on terms consistent with the costs of capital used by the firm in selecting projects. The assets were acquired and the projects, by being placed in operation, became part of the total investments of the firm. Thus, Frank Feather has answered the third important question raised at the beginning of this chapter, What is the scale of total outlay in the capital budget?

CONTROL PHASE

Once the projects have been implemented, the firm attempts to manage them to ensure that assets, labor, and material are efficiently employed. The control phase involves the comparison of actual and expected cash flows and the explanation of differences between actual and expected flows. The attempt to explain such differences has implications for the firm's planning and evaluation procedures.

For example, if cash inflows from an implemented project are larger than expected, the deviation may be due to defects in forecasting procedures or improper determination of economic dependence relationships among projects. Curly's Chicks may find that it underestimated the demand for chicken fertilizer by failing to account for the growth in home gardening in its forecasts. At the same time, it may have failed to notice that the decision to raise chicken broilers would greatly increase its own supply of chicken fertilizer to meet demand. Results for the chicken fertilizer project were much better than expected because the firm's forecasts of fertilizer demand were too pessimistic and, fortuitously, its failure to see the economic dependence of the fertilizer and broiler projects gave it supplies of fertilizer to exploit the unexpected higher level of fertilizer demand. Frank Feather should apply these lessons to Curly's Chicks' future planning and evaluation procedures.

When a project terminates, or even before, the firm should perform an
audit on the entire project to explain its success or failure. Like the
control phase, the auditing phase may have implications for the firm's
planning and evaluation procedures. In addition, the audit may produce
ideas for new improved proposals gained from the operation of projects
that have been terminated. This advantage of audits may be even more
important for projects judged to be relative failures insofar as it helps the
firm to avoid repeating mistakes.

From the auditing phase, Curly's Chicks might find that the poultry
slaughterhouse project, which turned out to be a "bomb," was a victim
of poorly designed machinery. Knowing this, the firm might well consider a proposal for a new slaughterhouse utilizing much improved
machinery. If the sole response of Curly's Chicks to the failure of the
original slaughterhouse proposal were to fire Doug (the original pro-
poser) and Frank Feather (and then try to forget about the entire un-
pleasant experience!), a valuable idea for a future project might be lost.
Audits are constructive in purpose.

AUDITING PHASE

The capital budgeting decision seeks to acquire for the firm the assets
that will, taking account of returns, risks, and the costs of capital, maximize increases in shareholder wealth. The process of making capital
budgeting decisions consists of six phases: planning, evaluation, selection, implementation, control, and auditing. The *planning phase* involves
identification, preliminary analysis, and initial screening of investment
opportunities to produce formal investment proposals. In the *evaluation
phase*, cash flow projections for proposals are made and proposals are
grouped into economically independent projects. If shareholders are not
efficiently diversified, the firm may have to group projects by the nature
of the statistical correlation of their cash inflows. Secondary screening
during this phase may remove some projects from consideration. Formal capital budgeting procedures, such as the net present value method, are applied to accept or reject proposals in the *selection phase*. The
firm's capital budget is established at this point. Funds are obtained and
necessary assets acquired and placed into operation during the *implementation phase*. The cash flow operating results of active projects are
analyzed to detect and explain variations between actual and expected
performance during the *control phase*. Lessons then learned are applied
to improve procedures in future planning and evaluation phases. Finally, an *auditing phase* is carried out to evaluate the performance of terminated projects. This phase may help improve the planning and evalua-

SUMMARY

tion phases as well as provide new investment opportunities for the firm.

GLOSSARY OF KEY TERMS

Auditing Phase

That part of the capital budgeting process in which previously undertaken investment projects are evaluated to explain their success or failure.

Capital Budget

The schedule of investment projects selected to be undertaken over some interval of time.

Capital Budgeting Process

The sequence of decisions leading to the acceptance or rejection of investment projects and the subsequent management of accepted projects.

Complementary Proposals

Investment proposals in which the combined cash inflows of two such proposals is greater than the sums of the individual proposals' cash flows.

Control Phase

The phase of the capital budgeting process in which the operating results of investment projects undertaken are managed to produce desirable results.

Cost Reduction Investment Opportunities

Investment opportunities producing cash inflows resulting from expected future cost savings.

Economic Dependence

The condition that exists when the combined cash inflows of two projects differ from the sum of the respective separate projects' cash inflows.

Economic Independence

The condition that exists when the combined cash inflows of two investment proposals equal the sum of the respective projects' cash inflows.

Evaluation Phase

The step in the capital budgeting process in which investment proposals are refined, given cash flow estimates, and subjected to a secondary screening.

Implementation Phase

The period of time over which the capital budget is carried out by acquiring and disbursing necessary funds and commencing operations with the projects.

Independent Proposals

Investment proposals are those in which cash flows of one are unaffected when other proposals are undertaken.

Investment Opportunity	The initial, often sketchy, form of ideas for capital expenditures.
Investment Project	Either a group of dependent proposals that, together, are independent of other projects *or* a single economically independent proposal.
Investment Proposal	An investment opportunity containing cash flow estimates.
Mutually Exclusive Investment Proposals	The extreme case of substitute proposals: the combined cash inflows of two proposals do not exceed the cash inflow of one proposal.
Planning Phase	The step in the capital budgeting process in which investment opportunities are given initial analysis and an initial screening before their formation as formal investment proposals in the capital budgeting process.
Revenue-Expanding Investment Opportunities	Investment opportunities producing cash inflows because of the production of additional salable units of output. These may arise in the same line of activity as the existing business or in new lines.
Selection Phase	The step in the capital budgeting process in which investment projects are accepted or rejected.
Substitute Proposals	Investment proposals in which the combined cash inflows of two projects are less than the sum of the respective cash inflows from the two separate projects.

SELECTED REFERENCES

Bierman, Harold, Jr., and Seymour Smidt. *The Capital Budgeting Decision*, 4th ed. New York: Macmillan Co., 1975.

Brigham, Eugene F., and Richard H. Pettway. "Capital Budgeting by Utilities," *Financial Management* (August 1973), pp. 11–22.

Grant, Eugene L., et al. *Principles of Engineering Economy*, 6th ed. New York: Ronald Press, 1976.

Hastie, K. Larry. "One Businessman's View of Capital Budgeting," *Financial Management* (Winter 1974), pp. 36–44.

Johnson, Robert W. *Capital Budgeting*. Dubuque, IA: Kendall/Hunt Publishing Co., 1977.

Lee, Sang M., and A. J. Lerro. "Capital Budgeting for Multiple Objectives," *Financial Management* (Spring 1974), pp. 59–66.

Lewellen, Wilbur G., Howard P. Lanser, and John J. McConnell.

"Payback Substitutes for Discounted Cash Flow," *Financial Management* (Summer 1973), pp. 17–23.

Myers, Stewart. "Procedures for Capital Budgeting Under Uncertainty," *Industrial Management Review* (Spring 1968), pp. 1–20.

Myers, Stewart. "Interactions of Corporate Financing and Investment Decisions—Implications for Capital Budgeting," *Journal of Finance* (March 1974), pp. 1–25.

Reinhardt, V. E. "Break-Even Analysis for Lockheed's Tri-Star: An Application of Financial Theory," *Journal of Finance* (September 1973), pp. 821–838.

Robichek, Alexander A., and James C. Van Horne, "Abandonment Value and Capital Budgeting," *Journal of Finance* (December 1967), pp. 577–590.

Weingartner, H. Martin. "Some New Views on the Payback Period and Capital Budgeting Decisions," *Management Science* (August 1969), pp. 594–607.

Weston, J. Fred. "Investment Decisions Using the Capital Asset Pricing Models," *Financial Management* (Spring 1973), pp. 25–33.

Williams, John D., and Jonathan S. Rakich. "Investment Evaluation in Hospitals," *Financial Management* (Summer 1973), pp. 30–35.

QUESTIONS

1. What important questions must be answered by the financial manager in establishing a capital budget?

2. What is achieved by grouping available opportunities into cost reduction and revenue expansion categories?

3. List some separate proposals that might stem from the opportunity for Curly's Chicks of growing apples.

4. How should one determine whether two proposals are complementary, independent, or substitutes?

5. Is it possible for the cash flows of economically independent proposals to be statistically correlated? Use an example to explain your answer.

6. How do availability and cost of funds enter the selection phase?

7. What are the implications for a firm's future capital budgeting

decisions of carrying the capital budgeting process only as far as the implementation phase?

8. Initial and secondary screening, respectively, of investment opportunities and investment projects can lead to rejection of the projects before formal capital budgeting criteria have been applied. What valid grounds exist for such rejection?

9. What kinds of decision error can occur if a financial manager fails to distinguish between investment proposals and investment projects?

10. Should a small firm having a small number of investors view statistical correlation among cash inflows of projects as important in choosing projects? Why or why not?

PROBLEMS

1. The Floor Drug Company in Floor, North Dakota, a small town just off the Interstate, does not sell drugs but sells a wide variety of merchandise within its four walls. Steve ("Flash") Gordon runs the place to bring in maximum tourist traffic. He and his immediate staff have come up with several exciting ideas requiring significant capital outlays. These include:

1.	Install a new security system that will cut insurance costs and theft losses	$100,000
2.	Remodel the Wild West Soda Fountain to increase labor efficiency	50,000
3.	Add ponies and a riding ring outside the store for kids	125,000
4.	Expand the Western Leather Goods Shop	75,000
5.	Install a western-type roller coaster outside the store	250,000
6.	Add 250 spaces to the parking lot	100,000
7.	Put in a shoe repair shop	50,000

(a) Classify these opportunities into the cost reduction category or into one of the revenue expansion categories listed in Table 12-2.

(b) How many *projects* do you estimate these opportunities would provide?

2.   Short-Haul Truck Rental Company owns, and rents out for hire, 100 ten-ton trucks. The company is located in a rural town in Missouri and rents primarily to families and college students making short-distance moves. Thomas Topshape, president of Short-Haul, has come up with the following investment opportunities.

Investment Opportunities	Estimated Outlay
A. Overhaul 40 old trucks	$ 200,000
B. Replace 40 old trucks with 40 new trucks	1,000,000
C. Purchase 25 new trucks	750,000
D. Purchase 50 farm tractors and rent them to local farmers	1,000,000
E. Purchase 100 new automobiles and rent them to businessmen at airport locations	1,000,000
F. Automate the reservation process for automobile rental business and reduce the number of clerks needed at airport location	1,000,000
G. Purchase 20 long-haul trucks and rent to trucking firms	1,500,000
	$6,450,000

Topshape regards the short-haul truck rental business as having considerable growth potential, and Short-Haul's existing fleet of 100 trucks will be insufficient to meet future demands.

Classify the investment opportunities given into the cost reduction category or into one of the categories of revenue-expanding opportunities.

3.   Subsequent assessment of opportunity C, the purchase of 25 new trucks, in Problem 2 reveals the following information.

(a)   The new trucks can be run very hard, with minimum maintenance, over 3 years and then sold. If this happens, cash inflows will be as follows.

Year 1	Year 2	Year 3
$500,000	$400,000	$600,000

Alternatively, trucks can be taken out of service for careful maintenance more frequently. Less revenue will be generated each year, but more will be obtained from buyers when the trucks are sold. The cash inflow pattern will then be as follows.

Year 1	Year 2	Year 3
$450,000	$350,000	$900,000

(b)   Trucks could be run for 3 additional years if an additional $300,000 were spent on major overhauls at the end of the first 3 years.

(c)   Trucks could be purchased from more than one manufacturer. These different trucks have somewhat different initial outlays and operating costs.

How many specific proposals can you see coming out of the single investment opportunity?

4.   From the description given in Problem 2, group the opportunities, which you may now view as proposals, into investment projects.

5.   University Music House sells sheet music. They have just signed a 20-year lease for an adjoining building. The owner has come up with the following opportunities for use of this space.

1.   Build in 10 soundproof rooms to rent to teachers as places to give lessons $10,000

2.   Buy musical instruments to rent to beginning music students $20,000

3.   Outfit an area as a shop for minor repairs and maintenance of musical instruments $5,000

4.   Purchase display racks for sale of musical instrument accessories such as rosin, strings, reeds, and mutes $2000

5.   Furnish an area with a piano and seating to rent to teachers for student recitals $2500

6.   Buy more display racks and augment the storage system for a larger inventory of sheet music $2000

7.   Build in an area to house a record shop $3000

8.   Purchase a computer for inventory control $5000

   Classify these opportunities as cost-reducing or revenue-expanding opportunities.

CHAPTER 7

Selection of
Investment Projects

As we saw in Chapter 6, investment projects consist of either single economically independent investment proposals or groups of economically dependent proposals. We also saw that in the selection phase of the capital budgeting process, formal selection criteria are applied to accept or reject projects consisting of single independent proposals and to choose among, or to reject all, dependent proposals grouped within a project. In this chapter, the formal criteria used to select investment projects in the selection phase are introduced and evaluated.

Four criteria presently in use by business organizations are discussed: the **net present value method** (NPV), the **internal rate of return method** (IRR), the **payback method,** and the **accounting rate of return method** (ARR). Of the four criteria, only the NPV method is generally consistent with the goal of shareholder wealth maximization. The remaining three methods may lead to selections of investment proposals that fail to maximize the expected increase in shareholder wealth. It is important to understand why this happens. Happily, the IRR method can be modified to produce correct solutions among investment proposals.

Most of the analysis in this chapter is devoted to understanding the NPV and IRR methods—as befits their importance. These two methods were introduced in Chapter 5, so the reader is already somewhat familiar with them. Both methods require that cash flows for investment projects be estimated, and we assume that this task, which is examined in Chapter 8, has been done.

Both the NPV and IRR methods require that an appropriate cost of capital or required rate of return be estimated. To simplify notation, that rate employed in this chapter is always denoted as K. (As distinguished from the generalized discount rate k used for simplicity to value any kind of cash flow in earlier chapters.) It is of great importance that the proper required rate be applied to each investment proposal; the risk premium contained in that rate must reflect the risk of the specific proposal. It is assumed that K always includes the appropriate risk premium for the investment proposal under evaluation. When the investment proposal has a degree of risk equal to that of the entire firm, K is the cost of capital for the firm. When the investment proposal has risk greater or less than that of the entire firm, K is assumed to be higher or lower than the cost of capital of the firm.

We begin with the NPV method and demonstrate its application, assumptions, and meaning with a very simple project—a barrel of wine. Then the method is applied to the more complex decisions facing Edwards Tool and Die Works, Inc.

Suppose that a firm has an investment project consisting of the following economically independent proposal: invest $1000 at time $t = 0$ in a barrel of red wine to be sold 1 year later at $t = 1$ at an expected price of $1200. To demonstrate the evaluation of this project using the NPV method, three alternative costs of capital are assumed: $K = 10$ percent, $K = 20$ percent, and $K = 30$ percent.

NET PRESENT VALUE

By the NPV method, the firm should compute the present value of the stream of future cash flows using the appropriate cost of capital and subtract, from the sum, the investment outlay. The resulting number is the net present value or, simply, the NPV of the project. The firm disposes of the project in the following way.

Application of the Method

Accept if   NPV > 0

Reject if   NPV < 0

Indifferent to if   NPV $= 0$

Applying this framework to the wine project, we first view the cash flows within the perspective of a time line, as in Figure 7-1:

Figure 7–1   *Cash Flows for the Wine Project*

t = 0   t = 1

−$1000   +$1200

Next the expected cash inflow at $t = 1$ is discounted at the appropriate cost of capital and the outlay is subtracted from this present value to find the NPV. For each of the three costs of capital alternatively assumed, the computations of NPV are shown below (using appropriate present value factors from Appendix Table C):

If the appropriate cost of capital is 10 percent, the firm should clearly *accept* the wine project. The NPV of $90.91 is positive—indicating that the expected future cash inflow is worth more *now* than the investment outlay required to "buy" that cash inflow. A positive NPV for this project is a clear signal for acceptance. However, if the appropriate cost of capital happens to be 20 percent, the firm is *indifferent* to the project. The NPV is then zero—indicating that the expected future cash inflow is *just* worth the investment outlay required to purchase that inflow. Finally, if the cost of capital is 30 percent, the firm should *reject* the project, for the NPV of—$76.92 is negative. The cash outflow necessary to purchase the barrel of wine exceeds the present value of the expected future cash inflows.

$$\textbf{NPV} = \textbf{Present Value} - \textbf{Investment Outlay}$$

$$
\begin{aligned}
\text{At } K = 10\% \quad \text{NPV} &= \$1200(0.90909) - \$1000 \\
&= \$1090.91 - \$1000 \\
&= \$90.91
\end{aligned}
$$

$$
\begin{aligned}
\text{At } K = 20\% \quad \text{NPV} &= \$1200(0.83333) - \$1000 \\
&= \$1000 - \$1000 \\
&= 0
\end{aligned}
$$

$$
\begin{aligned}
\text{At } K = 30\% \quad \text{NPV} &= \$1200(0.76923) - \$1000 \\
&= \$923.08 - \$1000 \\
&= -\$76.92
\end{aligned}
$$

The Effect of Cost of Capital on Net Present Value

It is obvious from Chapter 5 and from the wine project just evaluated that the present value of a future cash flow declines as the cost of capital (discount rate) increases. In most cases (an exception is discussed in note 3), higher costs of capital also reduce the NPV of investment projects. This happened for the wine project just evaluated, as the cost of capital increased from $K = 10$ percent to $K = 30$ percent.

The relationship between NPV and the cost of capital is graphically described by a NPV curve. Such a curve is shown in Figure 7-2 for the wine project. The NPV curve shows the NPV for an investment project at different costs of capital. Two points on that curve are worth special attention: the intercepts of the curve with the vertical and horizontal

Figure 7-2   *NPV Curve for the Wine Project*

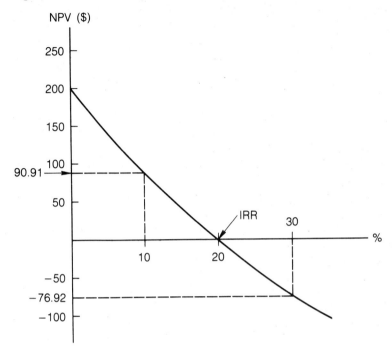

axes of the graph. On the vertical axis, the intercept of the NPV curve is the NPV of the project at a discount rate of $K = 0$ percent. At that rate, future cash flows of a project are not reduced in value when discounted. Thus, when $K = 0$ percent, the NPV is simply the sum of all future cash flows minus the outlay. For the wine project, NPV at $K = 0$ percent is just NPV $= \$1200 - \$1000 = \$200$ as indicated in Figure 7-2 on the vertical axis. On the horizontal axis, the intercept of the NPV curve occurs at the discount rate where NPV is zero. For the wine project, NPV $= 0$ at $K = 20$ percent, as marked in Figure 7-2 on the horizontal axis.

Studying Figure 7-2, we can identify a *range* of costs of capital over which a project may be accepted or rejected. For any cost of capital between $K = 0$ percent and $K = 20$ percent, the NPV of the wine project is positive—indicating a region of acceptance. At $K = 20$ percent, the firm is indifferent to the project since NPV $= 0$. For costs of capital higher than 20 percent, the NPV of the project is negative and this denotes a region of rejection.

Net Present Value: Assumptions and Meaning

Discussion of issues later in this chapter makes it worthwhile to examine the assumptions underlying the NPV method and to show what meaning is attached to the NPV for a project.

Assumptions   In the NPV method, it is assumed that the firm can obtain funds from, and invest funds in, the market at a rate equal to the cost of capital, K. Moreover, the cost of capital K is assumed to be constant over the life of the project under evaluation. Thus, any cash outflows required by a project may be financed from the market by raising funds having the cost K. Any cash inflow from a project may be invested in the market to earn the rate K. Finally, transaction and flotation costs in capital market transactions are assumed away in making subsequent comparisons of project selection criteria. Therefore, the cost of capital K and the required rate of return, after taxes, are the same thing here.

Meaning of NPV Calculated for Any Project   Acceptance or rejection of a single project because the computed NPV is positive or negative is an objective decision criterion but it is not sufficient for all types of decisions. When we compare NPVs for different investment proposals, the *magnitude* of NPV becomes important.

What meaning can be given to the NPV calculated for a project? It represents a measure of the *expected immediate change in shareholder wealth* occurring *if* a project is undertaken. The wine project is used to demonstrate this notion. Based on the risk of the project, investors require a rate of return of 10 percent. If they are not to be made worse off by taking the project rather than by investing $1000 in the market at 10 percent (in an identical-risk investment), the required project *dollar* cash inflow at $t = 1$ is (1.10)$1000 = $1100. By comparing the required cash inflow with the expected cash inflow of the project, we can see how much better or worse off shareholders are made by undertaking the project. Table 7-1 makes such a comparison.

Panel A of Table 7-1 shows cash flows for the wine project, reflecting the outlay of $1000 at $t = 0$ to purchase the barrel of wine and the $1200 expected cash inflow at $t = 1$. The next line gives the financing cash flows. Investors make an outlay of $1000 at $t = 0$ to finance the project and, at $t = 1$ require, given $K = 10$ percent, a cash inflow of $1100 to return the $1000 investment plus pay a $100 required return to compensate for the risk of the project. The *net* cash inflow at $t = 1$ is expected to be $100—the excess of the $1200 *expected* cash inflow from the project over the $1100 *required* inflow. In other words, shareholders expect to receive $100 more at $t = 1$ than is required to compensate them for the risk of the project. Shareholder *wealth*, at $t = 1$, increases by the $100

Table 7–1   *NPV and Shareholder Wealth*

	Cash Flows	Time	
		$t = 0$	$t = 1$
A.	If $K = 10\%$		
	Wine Project	−$1000	+$1200
	Financing	− 1000	+ 1100
	Net Cash Flow	$ 0	+$ 100
	Present Value at $K = 10\%$	0	+ 90.91
B.	If $K = 20\%$		
	Wine Project	−$1000	+$1200
	Financing	− 1000	+ 1200
	Net Cash Flow	$ 0	$ 0
	Present Value at $K = 20\%$	0	0
C.	If $K = 30\%$		
	Wine Project	−$1000	+1200
	Financing	− 1000	+ 1300
	Net Cash Flow	$ 0	−$ 100
	Present Value at $K = 30\%$	0	− 76.92

excess cash inflow. However, to find how much their wealth increases *now*, at $t = 0$, the future $100 cash inflow is discounted one period at $K = 10$ percent to obtain the present value of $90.91 shown in Table 7-1. That amount is the *immediate* (at $t = 0$) increase in wealth occurring if the wine project is undertaken (assuming that shareholders know of the project returns). It reflects the expected $100 excess of expected project cash inflow over the required cash inflow needed to compensate share-holders for risk and deferred consumption. But the $90.91 present value of excess cash flow is identical to the *net* present value of the project at $K = 10$ percent initially calculated for the wine project. [Remember NPV = $1200(0.90909) − $1000 = $90.91.]

Panels B and C of Table 7-1 are constructed for higher costs of capital but demonstrate the same points as panel A. When $K = 20$ percent, the required cash inflow is now $1200—equaling the expected cash inflow from the project. No excess cash flow exists at $t = 1$. Shareholders are made no better or worse off compared to the required return if the project is undertaken. The present value of a zero excess cash inflow remains zero—exactly equal to the NPV of the project at $K = 20$ percent. Shareholder wealth is not expected to be increased by taking the project if $K = 20$ percent. In panel C, $K = 30$ percent, and the required cash inflow of $1300 exceeds the expected $1200 cash inflows. Since share-holders expect to be $100 worse off compared to their required cash inflow, their wealth immediately declines (at $t = 0$) by the present value (at $K = 30$ percent) of that $100 loss, or, $76.92. This amount, again, equals the NPV of the project at $K = 30$ percent, for NPV = $1200(0.76923) - $1000 = - $76.92.

Summarizing to this point, we now know that a project, when evaluated by the NPV method, should be accepted if NPV exceeds zero and rejected if NPV is less than zero. The method rests on the assumption that firms can obtain funds from, or invest funds in, the market at the cost of capital K, used as a discount rate. As the cost of capital increases, the NPV of most projects declines. The magnitude of NPV for a project measures the expected change in shareholder wealth occurring *if* a project is undertaken.

Establishing a Capital Budget with the Net Present Value Method

Now that we know the assumptions underlying the NPV method and the meaning of NPV, we can apply the method to a set of investment projects for Edwards Tool and Die Works, Inc. Projects accepted by the NPV method will form the firm's capital budget. The projects under consideration by Edwards are shown in the following list.

Project	Investment Outlay	Life
1. Install a Heat Pump	$2,000	3 years
2. Purchase an Alpha Lathe	9,000	4 years
or	*or*	
Purchase an Omega Lathe	9,000	4 years
3. Produce Aircraft Dies	10,000	1 year
or	*or*	
Produce Aircraft Parts	15,000	1 year
or	*or*	
Produce Both	25,000	1 year

Project 1, the heat pump, consists of an economically independent proposal expected to produce cash inflows through energy savings. Project 2 consists of two mutually exclusive proposals for alternative types of lathe. Project 3 consists of three proposals, one of which combines two complementary proposals. Under a 1-year contract, Edwards can produce for an aircraft manufacturer either aircraft dies or aircraft parts, or can produce both dies and parts. Cash flows for each project have been estimated, and Edwards has determined that the appropriate required

Table 7–2   *The Heat Pump Project (K = 10%)*

Investment Outlay (t = 0)	Cash Inflows in Year *t*		
	t = 1	t = 2	t = 3
−$2000	+$1000	+$1000	+$2000

PV = $1000(0.90909) + $1000(0.82645) + $2000(0.75131)

$\quad$ = $909.09 $\quad\quad$ + $826.45 $\quad\quad$ + $1502.62

$\quad$ = $3238.16

NPV = 3238.16 − $2000 = $1238.16 > 0

rate of return for all projects is $K = 10$ percent. All investments are equally risky.

Dealing first with the heat pump project, the cash flows must be specified. These cash flows and computations of present values are shown in Table 7-2.

The heat pump project consists of an independent proposal, and it may be either accepted or rejected. Calculating the NPV as shown in Table 7-2, it is clear that the resulting decision is to accept the project. The NPV is positive, indicating that shareholder wealth is expected to increase by $1238.16 if the project is accepted. Accordingly, the heat pump will be included in the capital budget.

The lathe project consists of two mutually exclusive proposals for different types of lathe. Cash flows for these proposals are contained in Table 7-3. The Alpha lathe is a simple machine but tends to wear out relatively quickly. As a result, cash inflows are initially high but decline rapidly as repair costs increase. The Omega lathe is relatively durable but initially produces many defective items of output that must be discarded. Consequently, the first year cash inflow is low compared to later years because

Table 7–3   *The Lathe Project (K = 10%)*

Proposal	Investment Outlay (t = 0)	Cash Flows at Year *t*				PV	NPV
		t = 1	t = 2	t = 3	t = 4		
Alpha Lathe	−$9000	+$6000	+$3000	+$2000	+$1575	$10,512.25	$1512.25
Omega Lathe	− 9000	+ 500	+ 3500	+ 6500	+ 3670	10,737.30	1737.30

Table 7–4　*The Aircraft Project (K = 10%)*

Proposal	Investment Outlay (t = 0)	Cash Inflow at t = 1	PV	NPV
Aircraft Dies	$10,000	$12,000	$10,909.09	$ 909.09
Aircraft Parts	15,000	17,700	16,090.91	1090.91
Aircraft Dies and Parts	25,000	29,750	27,045.45	2045.45

it takes time to adjust the lathe to create improved performance. Since the lathe proposals are mutually exclusive, Edwards can accept the Alpha proposal and reject the Omega proposal, *or* accept the Omega proposal and reject Alpha, *or* reject *both* proposals and, consequently, the lathe project itself. Application of the NPV method at $K = 10$ percent results in acceptance of the Omega lathe because it has the highest NPV. Its acceptance is expected to increase shareholder wealth by $1737.30. If the Alpha lathe had been accepted, shareholder wealth would be expected to increase by only $1512.25. Consequently, the Omega lathe goes into the capital budget to join the heat pump, as accepted projects.

For the aircraft projects, the cash flows are displayed in Table 7-4. The dies and parts proposals are complementary. If both proposals are taken, the resulting cash inflow exceeds the sum of cash inflows from the separate proposals. Naturally, the *scale* of investment outlay is larger when both proposals are undertaken than it would be if either separate proposal were chosen. Edwards may take either separate proposal *or* the combined proposals but cannot take *both* a separate proposal *and* the combined proposals. However, all proposals, and thus the project, may be rejected. After calculating net present value, Edwards chooses the combined dies and parts proposals. All proposals have positive NPVs, but the combined proposal yields the largest increase in shareholder wealth.

Combining the accepted projects into one list, Edwards Tool and Die establishes the following capital budget.

Capital Budget: Edwards Tool and Die Works, Inc.

Project	Investment Outlay	NPV
Heat Pump	$ 2,000	$1238.16
Omega Lathe	9,000	1737.30
Aircraft Dies and Parts	25,000	2045.45
	$36,000	$5020.91

On a total investment outlay of $36,000, Edwards expects to *increase* shareholder wealth by $5020.91, the amount shown for the total NPV of all projects.

The IRR method, introduced in Chapter 5, is an alternative method for selecting capital projects. It requires the computation of the internal rate of return r^* on a project's cash flows. The internal rate of return is defined as *the rate of discount making the present value of the future cash flows equal to the investment outlay.* In other words, the *net* present value of a project's cash flows is zero when future cash flows are discounted at the internal rate. Projects are accepted or rejected by comparing the internal rate of return r^* to the cost of capital K under the following decision rule. **INTERNAL RATE OF RETURN**

$$
\begin{array}{ll}
\text{Accept if} & r^* > K \\
\text{Reject if} & r^* < K \\
\text{Indifferent to if} & r^* = K
\end{array}
$$

Thus, projects earning an internal rate in excess of the cost of capital are accepted, and those earning less than the cost of capital are rejected.

The wine project (Figure 7-1) provides a simple example to show how the IRR method can be applied. To find r^*, the internal rate of return, the future $1200 cash inflow is discounted at the unknown rate r^* and set equal to the $1000 outlay. By setting the discounted cash flow equal to the outlay, we are requiring that net present value equal zero at the discount rate r^*. Performing the calculation, the internal rate is found to be $r^* = 20$ percent for the wine project.

Present Value = Outlay

$$\$1200 \times \frac{1}{1 + r^*} = \$1000$$

$$1 + r^* = \frac{\$1200}{\$1000}$$

$$r^* = 20\%$$

Comparing the internal rate to the cost of capital, we find that the project is acceptable if $K = 10$ percent for, then, r^* exceeds K. If $K = 20$ percent, we are indifferent to the project for $r^* = K$. However, if $K = 30$ percent, then r^* is less than K and the project is rejected.

The decisions reached by the IRR method are exactly the same for the wine project as those reached by the NPV method at each alternative cost of capital. We may compare these choices graphically by referring back to the NPV curve in Figure 7-2. Whereas the net present value method examined the magnitude of the NPV on the curve at the 10 percent cost of capital to see if NPV was positive, the IRR method looks at the *intercept* of the NPV curve on the horizontal axis. At that point, the discount rate brings the NPV to zero. Since the internal rate of return, by definition, make NPV = 0, that intercept value of the NPV curve *is* the internal rate of return. Thus, the NPV curve intersects the horizontal axis of Figure 7-2 at the internal rate of return of $r^* = 20$ percent for the wine project. The accept/reject decision by the IRR method is made by looking *along* the horizontal axis at the cost of capital *K*. If *K* is less than r^*, the project is acceptable. For the wine project, the range of acceptance is any cost of capital less than *K* = 20 percent. Any cost of capital *beyond* the intercept at $r^* = 20$ percent lies in the range of rejection for the project.

Establishing a Capital Budget with the Internal Rate of Return Method

To further demonstrate the IRR method, let us assume that Edwards Tool and Die uses it, instead of the NPV method, to make up a capital budget from the list of available proposals.

Given the choice of accepting or rejecting the independent proposal represented in the heat pump project, Edwards would accept the project. Using the trial-and-error method described in Chapter 5 for the heat pump cash flows exhibited in Table 7-2, the internal rate of return is calculated to be approximately $r^* = 38.4$ percent.

Present Value Outlay of Cash Inflows

$$\$1000 \times \frac{1}{(1 + 0.384)^1} + \$1000 \times \frac{1}{(1 + 0.384)^2}$$

$$+ \$2000 \times \frac{1}{(1 + 0.384)^3} = \$1999.04$$

$$\$1999.04 \sim \$2000$$

The internal rate of return on the project exceeds the 10 percent cost of capital, and the heat pump project is incorporated into the capital budget.

Evaluating the lathe project with the IRR method, if either of the proposals (Alpha and Omega) had an internal rate of return less than the cost of capital, Edwards would reject it. If both proposals' rates of return exceeded the cost of capital, *the proposal having the higher internal rate would be accepted*. Using the trial-and-error method for the cash flows in Table 7-3, it turns out that the Alpha proposal has an approximate internal rate of return of $r^* = 20$ percent, whereas the Omega proposal yields a rate of $r^* = 17$ percent.

Alpha Proposal for $r^* = 20\%$	$\dfrac{\$6000}{(1 + 0.20)^1} + \dfrac{\$3000}{(1 + 0.20)^2} + \dfrac{\$2000}{(1 + 0.20)^3} + \dfrac{\$1575}{(1 + 0.20)^4}$	$= \$9000$

$$\$6000(0.83333) + \$3000(0.69444) + \$2000(0.57870) + \$1575(0.48225) = \$9000$$

$$\$4999.98 \quad + \quad \$2083.32 \quad + \quad \$1157.40 \quad + \quad \$759.54 \quad = \$9000$$

$$\$8999.34 \quad \sim \$9000$$

Omega Proposal for $r^* = 17\%$	$\dfrac{\$500}{(1 + 0.17)^1} + \dfrac{\$3500}{(1 + 0.17)^2} + \dfrac{\$6500}{(1 + 0.17)^3} + \dfrac{\$3670}{(1 + 0.17)^4}$	$= \$9000$

$$\$500(0.85470) + \$3500(0.7305) + \$6500(0.62437) + \$3670(0.53365) = \$9000$$

$$\$427.35 \quad + \quad \$2556.79 \quad + \quad \$4058.41 \quad + \quad \$1958.50 \quad =$$

$$\$9001.05 \quad \sim \$9000$$

Both internal rates exceed the cost of capital but, because the Alpha proposal has the higher internal rate, it is accepted and the Omega proposal is rejected.

The internal rates of return for each proposal in the aircraft project can be computed directly from the cash flows in Table 7-4 without the trial and error method because of the short (1 year) life of these proposals.

Proposal	Present Value = Outlay
Aircraft Dies	$\$12,000 \times \dfrac{1}{1 + r^*} = \$10,000$
	$r^* = 20\%$
Aircraft Parts	$\$17,700 \times \dfrac{1}{1 + r^*} = \$15,000$
	$r^* = 18\%$
Both Proposals	$\$29,750 \times \dfrac{1}{1 + r^*} = \$25,000$
	$r^* = 19\%$

Edwards must choose the dies *or* the parts proposal *or* the combined proposals. The firm cannot choose *both* a single proposal *and* the combined proposals. Each proposal has a rate of return in excess of the cost of capital, but the proposal to produce dies has the higher rate of return. Therefore, Edwards will choose the dies proposal and reject the parts *and* combined parts and dies proposals.

The reader will have been, perhaps, surprised to notice that application of the NPV and IRR methods to the same set of investment projects has produced two different capital budgets for Edwards Tool and Die

COMPARING NPV AND IRR METHODS

Table 7–5   *Comparative Capital Budgets by NPV and IRR Methods*
Edwards Tool and Die Works, Inc.
(K = 10%)

NPV Capital Budget				IRR Capital Budget			
Project	Outlay	NPV	IRR	Project	Outlay	NPV	IRR
Heat Pump	−$ 2,000	+1238.16	38.4%	Heat Pump	−$ 2,000	+$1238.16	38.4%
Omega Lathe	− 9,000	+ 1737.30	17.0%	Alpha Lathe	− 9,000	+ 1512.25	20.0%
Aircraft Dies and Parts	− 25,000	+ 2045.45	19.0%	Aircraft Dies	− 10,000	+ 909.09	20.0%
	−$36,000	+$5020.91			−$21,000	+$3659.50	

Works. The two budgets, together with the respective net present values and internal rates of return for projects contained in them, are summarized in Table 7-5.

The heat pump project was accepted by both methods but different accept/reject signals were given for the other projects. The NPV method accepted the Omega lathe, whereas the IRR method accepted the Alpha lathe.

Furthermore, the NPV method indicated that both aircraft parts and dies should be produced, but the IRR method signaled that only aircraft dies should be produced.

The disagreement in project selection raises three questions: Which method is consistent with the shareholder wealth maximization goal? Why do the methods sometimes lead to conflicting selections? Can anything be done to reconcile the two methods?

Consistency of Methods with Shareholder Wealth Maximization

The NPV method is fully consistent, under its assumptions, with the goal of maximizing shareholder wealth. To see this, recall that the NPV calculated for any investment proposal measures the expected change in shareholder wealth resulting from undertaking the proposal. Any investment project consisting of an economically independent investment proposal having a positive NPV will be accepted by the method and, consistent with the goal, shareholder wealth will be expected to increase because the project is selected. Investment projects consisting of economically dependent investment proposals may confront the firm with mutually exclusive alternatives. The NPV method will select that proposal having the highest NPV and thus contribute to the largest expected increase in shareholder wealth.

The IRR method does not always make the same selection of proposals as the NPV method. Since the NPV method makes choices consistent with the goal of shareholder wealth maximization and the IRR
method can conflict with these choices, the IRR method may be inconsistent with the goal of shareholder wealth maximization. Evidence of this is
available in Table 7-5. The proposals selected by the NPV method lead to
an expected increase in shareholder wealth of $5020.91, whereas pro-
posals selected by the IRR method are expected to increase shareholder
wealth by only $3659.50. Shareholders appear to be worse off if the IRR
method, rather than NPV method, is employed on their behalf.

**Why the NPV and IRR Methods Sometimes Produce Different Selec-
tions**   The NPV and IRR methods sometimes make conflicting selections for two reasons. First, in the case of an investment project consisting of a group of economically dependent investment proposals,
conflicting accept/reject decisions can arise because the IRR method *fails*
to properly evaluate what will be called the **differential cash flow** obtained by comparing mutually exclusive proposals. Second, for an investment project containing a single economically independent investment proposal, the two methods may disagree because the IRR method
has no single, unique solution—that is, there may be more than one
internal rate of return for a given proposal.

Differential Cash Flows   When mutually exclusive investment proposals within a project are considered, there exists a *differential* cash flow
between the proposals. Differential cash flows are computed by subtracting the cash flows of one proposal from those of another.
   Differential cash flows can have important effects on shareholder
wealth. This possibility arises either when the scale of investment outlay
differs between proposals or when one proposal's cash inflows produce a
faster rate of capital recovery than those of another proposal or
proposals.

Differences in Scale of Investment Outlay   Table 7-6 summarizes the
cash flows and earlier evaluations of the competing aircraft dies–aircraft
dies and parts proposals. The dies proposal has the higher internal rate
but the dies and parts proposal has the higher NPV at $K = 10$ percent—
producing the different selections made by the two methods. In explaining this difference in selection between the methods it is useful to compute the differential cash flows between the two proposals. In this case,
the differential flow arises because the dies and parts proposal requires a
larger initial outlay at $t = 0$ than does the smaller dies proposal. Under
this circumstance, the *rule* is to *subtract* the cash flows of the smaller

Table 7–6   *Analysis of Differential Cash Flows: Aircraft Project (K = 10%)*

Proposal	Investment Outlay ($t = 0$)	Cash Inflow ($t = 1$)	NPV	IRR
Aircraft Dies	−$10,000	+$12,000	+$ 909.09	20%
Aircraft Parts and Dies	− 25,000	+ 29,750	+ 2045.45	19
Differential Cash Flow	−$15,000	+$17,750	+$1136.36	18⅓

Net Present Value of Differential Cash Flow:

$17,750(0.90909) − $15,000 = $1136.36

outlay proposal (dies only) from those of the larger outlay proposal (dies and parts). This computation is performed in Table 7-6, and the result is identified as the differential cash flow. That differential flow is associated with the larger dies and parts proposal and is interpreted in the following way: *if* the larger proposal is undertaken, a differential outlay of $15,000 is required for which, at $t = 1$, a differential inflow of $17,750 is received.

In comparing the two proposals, shareholders will be concerned with the *value* of the differential cash flows obtained if the larger dies and parts proposal is undertaken. The question is, Is it *worth* spending $15,000 more on the larger proposal to receive $17,750 more at $t = 1$? Whether the expenditure is worthwhile depends on the required rate of return. We can see this by noting in Table 7-6 that the rate of return on the differential cash flow is 18⅓ percent. This return, called the *differential rate of return*, exceeds the 10 percent cost of capital, and thus the differential cash flows are worthwhile. This attractiveness is confirmed if we compute the present value of the differential flows at a 10 percent cost of capital—as is done in the table. This present value is $1136.36 and is positive; that is, the discounted differential inflow exceeds the differential outflow.

Now the NPV method, as applied to *both* proposals, *automatically* evaluates the differential cash flows of the larger dies and parts proposal. The NPV of the smaller dies proposal is $909.09 in Table 7-6, whereas that of the larger dies and parts proposal is $2045.45. The difference between these NPVs is $1136.36—exactly equal to the present value of the *differential* cash flow. In fact, the NPV of the dies and parts proposal exceeds the NPV of the dies proposal *because* of the value of the differential flows. Naturally, the NPV method can evaluate differential cash flows over a *range* of costs of capital. Figure 7-3 displays this versatility. There, the NPV curves of the dies and parts proposals are drawn. The two curves intersect at a discount rate of 18⅓ percent, or, at the differential rate of return. For any cost of capital less than 18⅓ percent, the NPV of the dies and parts proposal exceeds the NPV of the dies proposal (as it did for $K = 10$ percent in Table 7-6). Within that *range* of the cost of capital, the NPV method automatically evaluates the differential cash flow of the larger proposal and finds it worthwhile, since the *differential* rate of return exceeds the cost of capital. For costs of capital between 18⅓ and 20 percent, the NPV of the smaller dies proposal exceeds the NPV of the larger dies and parts proposal. The differential rate of return is less than costs of capital within that range, and the NPV method would select the smaller dies proposal.

In contrast, the IRR method makes the incorrect selection of the smaller dies proposal when $K = 10$ percent because the method is insensitive to the differential cash flows between the two proposals. The internal rate of return is a percentage, whereas NPV, the expected increase in shareholder wealth, is in dollars. The important differences in dollar scale of outlay and subsequent cash inflow between the proposals are eliminated when the percentage internal rate of return is separately computed for *each* of the proposals. This may be verified by noting that if the smaller dies proposal required an outlay of $1 (instead of $10,000) and produced an inflow of $1.20 (instead of $12,000), the internal rate of return of that proposal would remain at 20 percent. By the IRR method, the smaller dies proposal would still be preferred even though the differential cash flows of the larger dies and parts proposal are now even larger and will produce an even greater expected increase in shareholder wealth.[1]

The insensitivity of the IRR method to differential cash flows over a wider range of discount rates can be graphically seen in Figure 7-3. The IRR method makes the correct selection of the dies proposal *only* when the cost of capital is greater than 18⅓ percent. When the cost of capital is less than 18⅓ percent, the IRR method still selects the smaller dies proposal—ignoring the valuable differential cash flow associated with the larger proposal.

Differences in the Rate of Capital Recovery   Differential cash flows, and a possible decision error by the IRR method, can also occur if two mutually exclusive investment proposals have different rates of recovery of the initial capital outlay. Such was the case for the Alpha and Omega

---

[1]The differential cash flows for the parts and dies proposal under this modification are:

$t = 0$ $t = 0$
−$24,999 +$29,748.80

with a differential rate of return of nearly 19 percent.

Figure 7-3   *NPV Curves for the Aircraft Die/Aircraft Dies and Parts Proposals*

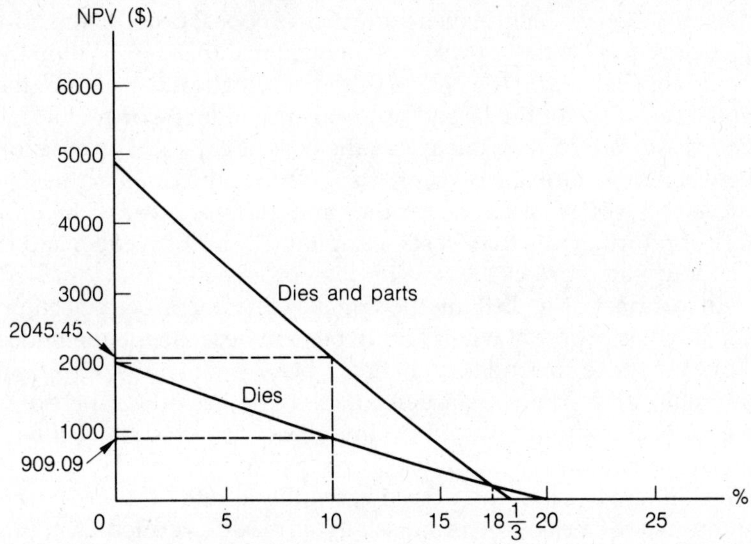

lathes evaluated earlier. Table 7-7 summarizes the cash flows and evaluations of the two proposals. The initial outlays for these two proposals happen to be equal in this example.[2] However, the Alpha proposal has the faster rate of recovery of initial outlay. The initial outlay is recovered in 2 years for the Alpha proposal, but 3 years is required for the Omega proposal. Consequently, the Alpha lathe has relatively higher cash inflows in early years compared to the Omega lathe.

In this case, the rule for computing differential cash flows is to subtract the cash flows for the proposal having the largest early cash inflow (fastest rate of capital recovery) from the proposal having the smallest early cash inflow (slowest rate of capital recovery). In Table 7-7, this means that we subtract cash flows for the Alpha proposal from those of the Omega proposal. The resulting differential cash flow stream is interpreted in the following way: *if* the slower capital recovery Omega proposal is selected, a $6000 − $500 = $5500 differential cash inflow is *forgone.* This sacrifice is rewarded by subsequent differential cash inflows.

As with all differential cash inflows, the question is, Are they worthwhile? As Table 7-7 reveals, the *differential* rate of return is 12.2 percent. At a cost of capital of 10 percent, these differential flows are worthwhile

---

[2]Initial outlays may be unequal, but the example is clearer if they are not.

Table 7-7   *Analysis of Differential Cash Flows: The Lathe Project (K = 10%)*

Proposal	Investment Outlay (t = 0)	Cash Flows at Year t				NPV	IRR
		t = 1	t = 2	t = 3	t = 4		
Alpha Lathe	−$9000	$6000	$3000	$2000	$1575	$1512.25	20%
Omega Lathe	− 9000	500	3500	6500	3670	1737.30	17
Differential Cash Flow	0	−$5500	+$ 500	+$4500	+$2095	$ 225.05	12.2

Present Value of Differential Cash Flow:

= −$5500(0.90909) + $500(0.82645) + $4500(0.75131) + $2095(0.68301)

= $225.05

and their positive present value of $225.05 confirms this. Again, the NPV method automatically evaluates the differential flows. The difference in the NPVs of the two proposals is $1737.30 − $1512.25 = $225.05 and is equal to the present value of the differential cash flows. The NPV method selects the Omega lathe, with its slower rate of capital recovery, *because* of the attractive differential flows when $K = 10$ percent.

Again, the IRR method is insensitive to the differential cash flows and incorrectly chooses the faster capital recovery Alpha proposal when $K =$

Figure 7-4   *NPV Curves for Alpha and Omega Lathe Proposals*

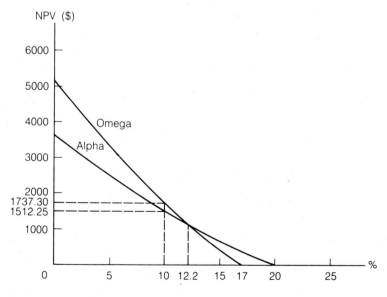

10 percent. This is seen in Figure 7-4. The NPV curves for the two proposals intersect at the differential rate of return of 12.2 percent. For any cost of capital less than 12.2 percent, the NPV method correctly chooses the Omega proposal, but it selects the Alpha proposal for any cost of capital greater than 12.2 percent. The IRR method chooses the Alpha proposal but will be correct in this choice only if the cost of capital is between 12.2 and 20 percent.[3]

The Absence of a Unique Internal Rate of Return

The NPV and IRR methods might yield conflicting selections if the IRR method produced more than one internal rate of return when applied to the cash flows of a proposal. No unique internal rate of return then would exist. The decision maker would not know which internal rate to utilize and, in selecting any one of the rates found to compare to the cost of capital, might make a decision inconsistent with maximizing shareholder wealth.

The possibility that more than one internal rate of return exists arises whenever the sequence of cash flows of a proposal has more than one reversal of sign. When more than one reversal of sign exists, the cash flow pattern is called a **broken cash flow series.** Table 7-8 illustrates broken cash flow series for proposals B and D. For proposal B the outlay

---

[3]We have not stated a position taken by some, namely, that the validity of the IRR method (compared to the NPV) depends on the rate earned on the reinvestment of cash inflows generated by a project. For example, two competing proposals A and B have the following cash flows, internal rates of return, and net present values:

	Cash Flows at Time t				NPV
Proposal	$t = 0$	$t = 1$	$t = 2$	IRR	(8%)
A	−$1000	$1000	$ 240	20%	$132
B	− 1000	0	1346	16	154

Some would argue that if the cash proceeds of proposal A could be invested at the internal rate of return of 20 percent, proposal A would be superior to proposal B even though B has the higher NPV. That is, the $1000 cash inflow for A at $t = 1$ could be reinvested at the internal rate of 20 percent to generate $1000(1.20) = $1200 at $t = 2$. This amount, combined with the $240 directly generated by the proposal in that year, would produce a *total* cash inflow for A of $1200 + $240 = $1440—superior to the $1346 generated by proposal B. This argument may be flawed because it implicitly assumes that the 20 percent rate of return, in excess of the 8 percent cost of capital, obtained by investing the $1000 cash inflow at $t = 1$ could not be received *without* the receipt of that cash inflow. It implicitly introduces what will be termed, in Chapter 10, a *capital constraint*—a constraint against obtaining funds of $1000 at a rate of 8 percent in the market at $t = 1$. This kind of constraint is inconsistent with the assumption underlying the NPV method (i.e., that funds may be obtained in the market at the prevailing cost of capital); the IRR method, when the market-determined 8 percent cost of capital is employed, makes the same assumption. If funds are assumed to be available at the rate K, that assumption must apply with equal force to both methods. We cannot legitimately use it for one and not the other.

Table 7–8 *Standard and Broken Cash Flow Series[a]*

	Year					
Proposal	0	1	2	3	4	5
A	−	−	−	+	+	+
B	−	+	+	+	−	+
C	−	+	+	+	+	+
D	−	+	−	+	−	+

[a]Symbols: + = cash inflow; − = cash outflow.

at $t = 0$ is followed by a cash inflow at $t = 1$ (one reversal of sign). Cash inflows continue until $t = 4$ when an outflow (reversal of sign) again occurs. At $t = 5$ an inflow (another reversal of sign) again appears. Altogether, three reversals of sign occur, and therefore proposal B may have as many as three internal rates of return. Proposal D may have as many as five, since, with alternate outflows and inflows, there are five reversals of sign. In general, a broken cash flow series may, as an upper limit, have as many different internal rates of return as there are reversals of sign.[4]

---

[4]As an example of a proposal having more than one internal rate of return, consider the following proposal. A firm has a cost of capital of $K = 25$ percent and is evaluating a project having the following cash flows:

$t = 0$	$t = 1$	$t = 2$
−$1000	+$2500	−$1540

Two reversals of sign are present and the cash flow series is broken.

The NPV of the proposal at $K = 25$ percent is $14.40 and the proposal should be accepted. Yet, the reader may verify that there are two internal rates of return that will bring the NPV of the cash flows to zero, 10 percent and 40 percent. If the 10 percent internal rate is used within the IRR method, the proposal will be erroneously rejected. If the 40 percent internal rate is used, the proposal will be properly accepted. The possibility for error exists.

The NPV of the proposal is *positive* and *negative* within the following ranges:

Cost of Capital	NPV
$0\% \leq K < 10\%$	Negative
$10\% < K < 40\%$	Positive
$40\% < K$	Negative

The NPV of the project rises between $K = 0$ percent and (it is asserted) begins to fall at $K = 25$ percent. This behavior is an exception to the usual case (true except for broken cash flow series), in which NPV always falls with higher discount rates. Only the NPV method can unambiguously and correctly select or reject this kind of proposal.

Proposals A and C in Table 7-8 are examples of **standard cash flow series.** In such series an unbroken stream of cash inflows follows one or more cash outflows. Only one reversal of sign occurs. Consequently, a unique internal rate of return exists for a standard cash flow series. The proposals confronting Edwards Tool and Die and evaluated earlier all had standard cash flow series.

Reconciliation of the NPV and IRR Methods

There is no way to reconcile the NPV and IRR methods if the proposals, either economically dependent or independent, have broken cash flow series. The NPV method should be used under such circumstances to render decisions consistent with the goal of shareholder wealth maximization. For evaluating dependent and mutually exclusive investment proposals where differential cash flows may be important, the conflict of the two methods must be resolved in one of two ways: abandon the IRR method and rely solely on the NPV method, or modify the IRR method so that it gives the same selections produced by the NPV method.

The obvious solution to the problems with the IRR method is simply not to use the method at all and confine project selection to the NPV method. However, the measurement of a *rate of return* is often more readily understood, intuitively, by members of a firm than is the NPV magnitude. Fortunately, if a firm insists on using an internal rate to measure the desirability of projects, it is possible to modify the IRR method so that, in the case of mutually exclusive proposals, it will give the correct choices made by the NPV method. The modification, called the *differential rate of return test*, requires an additional step in the IRR method.

The modified IRR method requires that the internal rate of return on *each* proposal be calculated in the usual fashion. If the internal rates exceed the cost of capital for both proposals, then *both* proposals are acceptable and the differential rate of return test must be applied to choose between the proposals. To make this test, determine the differential cash flows between the proposals. The rate of return on the differential cash flows, or **differential rate of return,** is then computed. If that rate exceeds the cost of capital, accept the proposal producing the differential cash flows and reject the remaining proposal. If the differential rate of return is less than the cost of capital, reject the proposal producing the differential cash flows and accept the remaining proposal.

Restudying Tables 7-6 and 7-7, it can be seen that the differential rate of return test will allow the IRR method to make selections consistent with the goal of maximizing shareholder wealth. In Table 7-6, the internal rates of return for both the aircraft dies and aircraft parts and dies proposals are positive and exceed the 10 percent cost of capital. This finding satisfies the first part of the procedure for use of the modified IRR method—that competing proposals *both* be acceptable at the prevailing cost of capital. Then the differential cash flows for the larger scale dies and parts proposal are found and the differential rate of return of 18⅓ percent determined. Since that differential rate of return exceeds the 10 percent cost of capital, the dies and parts proposal is accepted and the dies proposal rejected. Even though the dies proposal has the higher internal rate of return, the modified IRR method, by applying the differential rate of return test, has correctly evaluated the importance to shareholders of the differential cash flows obtained if the larger dies and parts proposal is undertaken.

The Alpha and Omega lathe problem in Table 7-7 can also be correctly evaluated by the modified IRR method. First, both proposals have internal rates of return in excess of the 10 percent cost of capital. Proceeding to the second part of the process, the differential cash flows for the Omega lathe have a differential rate of return of 12.2 percent. This return exceeds the 10 percent cost of capital and, by the modified IRR method, the Omega lathe is correctly selected.[5]

Summary

Either the NPV method or the IRR method, as modified by the differential rate of return test, gives correct choices among competing economically dependent investment proposals. Both methods are consistent with maximization of shareholder wealth as the goal of investment proposal selection decisions. The IRR method, when not modified by the differential rate of return test, breaks down because it is insensitive

---

[5]There are situations where, with dependent investments, no differential cash flows of a meaningful form exist—in which case the NPV and IRR methods give identical choices. In the following simple example, proposal B has a larger outlay than proposal A, leading to a differential cash outlay at $t = 0$ if proposal B is selected. However, proposal A is so much more profitable that taking proposal B leads to a differential *outflow* rather than inflow at $t = 1$. Since the NPV magnitude is higher for proposal A than for B, and the internal rate of return is also greater for A than for B, both methods select proposal A. This agreement between the methods will *always* occur with two dependent proposals if the differential cash flows are uniformly negative or if differential cash inflows do not exceed the initial cash outlay. In that case, one proposal completely dominates the other.

Proposal	Investment Outlay ($t = 0$)	Cash Inflow ($t = 1$)	NPV	IRR
A	−$10,000	+$14,000	$2727.26	40%
B	− 12,000	+ 13,800	545.44	15
Differential Cash Flow	−$ 2,000	−$ 200	−$2181.83	

to the differential cash flows and their significance for shareholder wealth.

For economically independent investment proposals, both the NPV and IRR methods usually lead to selections of proposals consistent with shareholder wealth maximization. The sole exception to this rule occurs when the proposal has a broken cash flow series. Then the NPV method makes a correct evaluation, but the IRR method may produce more than one internal rate of return. The NPV method should be used to evaluate projects with broken cash flow series.

Two remaining ways of selecting among investment proposals must now be evaluated. These methods, the payback and accounting rate of return methods, can also make selections inconsistent with results from the NPV method.

PAYBACK METHOD   The payback method was widely used prior to the development of present value techniques and continues to be an important decision-making tool for many firms. The method is quite simple to employ. First, the firm specifies a *maximum* payback period within which it will allow an investment proposal to recover (pay back) the initial cash outlay. Second, the firm calculates the payback period of an investment proposal to find the number of periods required by the proposal to recover the initial investment. Third, the payback period for the proposal is compared to the maximum payback period. If the payback period is less than the maximum, the proposal is accepted. If the payback period is greater than the maximum, the proposal is rejected. Choices between two competing proposals, each having payback periods less than the maximum, are made by the typical firm on the basis of which proposal has the shortest payback period.

This method can be illustrated with the example shown in Table 7-9. Two proposals, Able and Baker, require identical outlays of $800. However, the anticipated cash inflows differ considerably. The Able proposal

Table 7–9   *Able and Baker Proposals (K = 10%)*

		Cash Inflows for Years			
	Outlay	1	2	3	4
Able	$800	$400	$400	$400	$ 400
Baker	800	200	200	400	1300

has a level flow of $400 per year for 4 years, whereas Baker has level flows of $200 for each of the first 2 years, $400 the third year, and $1300 the fourth. The payback period for each proposal is easily calculated by adding the cash flows for each year until they equal the $800 outlay and then noting the number of years required for that sum to accumulate. The Able proposal has a 2-year payback period, but the Baker proposal has a 3-year payback period. The firm evaluating the Able and Baker proposals has set a maximum payback period of 2 years. Accordingly, the Able proposal is accepted and the Baker proposal is rejected. Is this a correct decision?

Application of the NPV method to the Able and Baker proposals, using a cost of capital of $K = 10$ percent, produces the following result: Able proposal, NPV = $1267.95 − $800 = $467.95; Baker proposal, NPV = $1535.56 − $800 = $735.56. Now if Able and Baker are *independent* proposals, *both* should be accepted by the NPV method. If the proposals are mutually exclusive, only Baker should be selected. By *this standard*, the payback method has given wrong choices. In the independent proposal case, a desirable investment proposal that would increase shareholder wealth was not undertaken. For the dependent proposal case, the method did not maximize increases in shareholder wealth.

An additional example of problems with the payback method can be found in the lathe project for Edwards Tool and Die Works, shown earlier in Table 7-7. As we know, the correct choice at $K = 10$ percent by the NPV method is the Omega proposal. However, if the firm had established a *maximum* payback period of 4 years, the Alpha lathe would have been (incorrectly) chosen. For the Alpha lathe has a *shorter* payback period (2 years) than the Omega lathe (about 2.75 years). Again, the payback method fails to maximize the increase in shareholder wealth.

Why does the payback method produce decisions inconsistent with the NPV method in some cases? To answer this question, we first indicate the method's more obvious faults. Then, we identify arguments in favor of the payback method.

First, the payback method ignores cash flows beyond the payback period. For example, the Able proposal generated flows of $400 per year for 2 years beyond the payback period and Baker generated $400 and $1300 after the payback period. Yet, these flows do not enter into the evaluation of the investments. *Second,* payback ignores the time value of money. All the computation tells us is that the amount of the investment is returned in some number of periods. The size and timing of the flows *within* that period are ignored. For example, an investment proposal that requires an outlay of $800 and returns $700 the first year and $50 in each of the next two years is equivalent to the Baker proposal if the payback method is the only criterion of choice. Yet, by the NPV method, the

Baker proposal is not as attractive. *Third,* there is no simple general rule that allows us to relate payback to shareholder wealth. Our concern is that a criterion of choice tell us whether we are selecting investments that are consistent with maximizing shareholder wealth. Unfortunately, payback standards tend to be arbitrarily determined and difficult to reconcile with shareholder wealth maximization.

In spite of these obvious faults, the payback method continues to be used in business decision making, though it appears to play a secondary or supplementary role in most larger corporations. Use of the method has been defended on a number of grounds.[6] Some argue that the future is so uncertain that flows beyond 3 or 4 years should, for practical purposes, be ignored. The response to this argument is that uncertainty in itself does not justify assuming that there is no chance (zero probability) of cash flows beyond the payback period occurring. To the extent that the uncertainty surrounding the cash inflows of a new investment is large relative to that of other investments of the firm, a higher cost of capital than that employed for other investments could be applied to that proposal. If this is done, the higher discount rate will discount returns far in the future by proportionately larger amounts than would lower costs of capital.

A second argument is that payback focuses on quick return and liquidity that may be extremely important to the firm. Again, if the discount rate is properly derived, this focus should be redundant, provided the firm has access to capital markets at the rate K and can obtain the capital it wants.

A third argument notes that firms emphasizing investments with short payback periods tend to create favorable short-term effects on earnings per share and these short-term effects then have a greater effect on share price than do projects that will not affect earnings until later years. This type of argument presumes that capital market participants are naive and easily fooled in the short run and that they will continue to be fooled by such practices in the longer run. Given the presumed high level of expertise among financial analysts and intense competition among market participants to discover new information about firms, the supposition that market participants can be continually fooled may, itself, be naive.[7]

---

[6]For a detailed discussion that includes an in-depth analysis of most of the supporting arguments, see H. Martin Weingartner, "Some New Views on Payback Period and Capital Budgeting Decisions," *Management Science* (August 1969), pp. 594–607.

[7]A large body of literature in finance has been directed toward the question of whether there is likely to be a systematic over- or undervaluation of a security. The preponderance of evidence in tests of efficient markets suggests that systematic and prolonged valuation errors of the sort necessary for the earnings argument to be valid are rare.

Finally, some argue that payback is easier to apply and less costly than other methods of evaluating investments. However, even if one examined only the explicit costs of gathering data and making the calculations, it is not clear that costs will be less. The basic information necessary to implement other criteria is also necessary to implement payback. Furthermore, if we include the opportunity cost to shareholders that is likely to stem from selecting a less than optimal capital budget when only the payback criterion is used, the cost is likely to be substantially higher than the discounted cash flow methods.

Another evaluation technique that has found some acceptance among managers is the accounting rate of return method. The accounting rate of return (ARR) is the ratio of average annual net income after taxes to the level of investment. Thus, in general terms, we can write **ACCOUNTING RATE OF RETURN**

$$\text{ARR} = \frac{\text{Average annual net income}}{\text{Investment level}}$$

The precise measures of income and investment incorporated in ARR will vary from firm to firm depending on the preferences of managers. The most common measure of average net income is the simple average of yearly income projections for the proposal being evaluated. To illustrate the calculation we assume an investment proposal requiring a $9000 outlay and generating the following net income stream.

$t = 0$	$t = 1$	$t = 2$	$t = 3$
	$300	$500	$700

Given the projected net income stream, the *average* annual net income is:

$$\frac{\$300 + \$500 + \$700}{3} = \$500$$

The investment level used in this method varies in practice. Some managers use the initial outlay, $9000 in this case, whereas others use the average dollar investment over the life of the proposal. Assuming that the assets purchased under this proposal have no value at the end of 3 years, the average investment is:

$$\frac{\$9000 + \$0}{2} = \$4500$$

The ARR, using average dollars invested as the measure of investment level, is:

$$\frac{\$500}{\$4500} = 0.111, \text{ or } 11.1\%$$

The ARR magnitude is then compared to the firm's cost of capital K (or perhaps an arbitrarily determined cutoff rate). If ARR exceeds K, the proposal is accepted. If ARR is less than K, the proposal is rejected. This particular proposal would be accepted, since ARR is greater than K.

Now if we evaluate the same proposal using the NPV method, we must convert the net income projections to cash flows. As Chapter 8 will show, depreciation is a noncash allocation of cost, *not* a cash flow. Since net income reflects the deduction of such noncash allocations from cash flow, depreciation charges must be added back to net income to obtain cash flows. Assuming that a straight line depreciation charge of $3000 per year is used, the cash flows for this proposal appear as follows.

Cash Flow in Year t

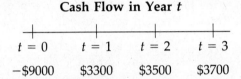

$t = 0$	$t = 1$	$t = 2$	$t = 3$
−$9000	$3300	$3500	$3700

Finding the net present value of these flows at $K = 10$ percent, the proposal is rejected because NPV = −$327.58. This correct decision is in conflict with the decision to accept given by the ARR method.

The ARR method fails because it emphasizes net income, not cash flow, and because it ignores the time value of money. Note, for example, that if the net income sequence in the proposal just evaluated were *reversed* in time so that the sequence was $700, $500, $300, rather than $300, $500, $700, that *average* net income would be unchanged. The average return, ARR = 11.1 percent, would also be unchanged. However, the NPV method would value the resulting cash flow sequence, $3700, $3500, $3300, quite differently from the sequence $3300, $3500, $3700, laid out above. The NPV magnitude would increase and the proposal would become more attractive. The ARR method is insensitive to this improvement because the method fails to account for the time value of money.

INVESTMENT CRITERIA IN USE

At this point, the NPV method has clear advantages over other selection techniques. But there may remain a question in the minds of many readers: How do business firms *really* make their decisions? Do they actually use net present value, or at least account for the time value of money in some way?

A number of surveys of capital budgeting practices have been pub-

Table 7–10   *Utilization of Evaluation Methods*

	1970	1964	1959
Discounting (IRR or NPV)	57%	38%	19%
Accounting Rate of Return	26	30	34
Payback	12	24	34
Urgency[a]	5	8	13
Total	100%	100%	100%

Source: Klammer (note 8), p. 393.

lished in recent years. For simplicity, we focus on an article by Thomas Klammer.[8] The results presented represent the responses of 184 out of 364 firms that were requested to fill out a questionnaire asking a wide range of questions about capital budgeting practices. Those responding were among the more technologically advanced firms, so one must be quite careful about generalizing the results to all firms. The respondents were asked to give their most sophisticated primary evaluation technique in 1959, 1964, and 1970. Their responses are shown in Table 7-10. Though the actual numbers are likely to have changed over the years between 1970 and the current date, the *trends* are quite important. They give some indication of the speed with which the discounted cash flow methods are being implemented.

The trend away from the payback and accounting rate of return methods toward discounted cash flow techniques is unmistakable. In 1959, 68 percent of the firms that responded to the questionnaire used either payback or accounting rate of return, whereas only 19 percent used some form of discounted cash flow technique. However, by 1970, only 38 percent of the firms used the former techniques as their primary standard and 57 percent of the firms used net present value or internal rate of return.

Selection among investment projects available to the firm requires a method general enough to make choices that are always consistent with the goal of maximizing shareholder wealth. Of the four methods considered in this chapter, only the net present value method made such **SUMMARY**

[8]Thomas Klammer, "Empirical Evidence of the Adoption of Sophisticated Capital Budgeting Techniques," *Journal of Business* (July 1972), pp. 387–397.

consistent choices—given the assumptions underlying the method. The calculated NPV, for any proposal contained in an investment project, measures the expected increase in shareholder wealth occurring if the proposal is selected. Where the problem is to choose between mutually exclusive proposals contained in a project, the NPV method correctly evaluates the differential cash flows between the two proposals.

The internal rate of return method does not always make choices consistent with those of the NPV method. In the case of economically independent proposals, the IRR method may yield more than one internal rate if cash flows are of the broken series type. The NPV method must be used in this situation. For dependent, and mutually exclusive, proposals, the IRR method may fail to make the same choice produced by the NPV method because the former approach is insensitive to the differential cash flows between the proposals. Use of the differential rate of return test to evaluate differential cash flows is a useful modification to the IRR method. This modification will cause the IRR method to yield the same decisions as the NPV method. However, this conclusion holds only where standard cash flow patterns rather than the broken series type [where reversal(s) of sign occur] are found.

The payback method and accounting rate of return method are less satisfactory for selecting investment projects. By ignoring the time value of money, and cash flows beyond the maximum payback period used by the firm, the payback method will make choices failing to maximize expected increases in shareholder wealth. The accounting rate of return method also ignores the time value of money and, in addition, fails to evaluate cash flows. It, too, often fails to maximize expected increases in shareholder wealth.

GLOSSARY OF KEY TERMS

Accounting Rate of Return Method

A selection method using average net income and investment outlay to compute a rate of return for a project. The method ignores the time value of money and cash flows.

Broken Cash Flow Series

A cash flow pattern characterized by more than one reversal of sign of the cash flows.

Differential Cash Flow

Differences in cash flow between two investment proposals (as distinguished from incremental cash flow described in Chapter 8).

Differential Rate of Return

The internal rate of return computed on the differential cash flows between two proposals.

Internal Rate of Return Method	A selection method using the compound rate of return on the cash flows of a project. This method is insensitive to the differential cash flows between proposals.
Net Present Value Method	A selection method using the difference between the present value of the cash inflows of a project and the investment outlay. This method evaluates differential cash flows between proposals.
Payback Method	A selection method in which a firm sets a maximum payback period during which cash inflow must be sufficient to recover the initial outlay. This method ignores the time value of money and cash flows beyond the payback period.
Standard Cash Flow Series	A series of cash flows having only one reversal of sign.

See Chapter 6.

SELECTED REFERENCES

QUESTIONS

1. What does the net present value magnitude measure?
2. Describe the relationship between NPV and the cost of capital.
3. What are the assumptions about the cost of capital used in the NPV method?
4. Under what circumstances can the net present value and internal rate of return methods disagree in selecting investment projects? Why do they disagree?
5. How does the differential rate of return test improve the selection of investment projects by the IRR method?
6. Why are the accounting rate of return and payback methods likely to prove unsatisfactory in selecting investment projects?

PROBLEMS

1. A firm is considering a project consisting of an independent proposal to purchase a coal mine. The mine costs $100,000 and would return $115,000 next year. After that the mine would be exhausted. The firm can invest in the market at a rate of return of $K = 12$ percent and can obtain funds at the same rate.

Find the differences in cash flows between the project and a 1-year investment of $100,000 in the market. Show that the present value of the differential cash flows equals the net present value of the project.

2. The Arzt Coffee Importing Company is evaluating the replacement of three old coffee bean roasters with two new, more efficient, roasters. The outlay on the new roasters is $50,000. The cash inflows, resulting from cost savings, over 5 years are as follows.

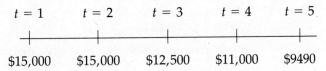

$t = 1$	$t = 2$	$t = 3$	$t = 4$	$t = 5$
$15,000	$15,000	$12,500	$11,000	$9490

The firm's cost of capital is $K = 10$ percent.

Compute the net present value and internal rate of return of the project. Should it be accepted?

3. Witt Marketing Services, Inc., is analyzing a project to establish a national service for exchanging customer mailing lists among companies. The project involves an outlay of $65,000. The cash flows for the project are as follows.

$t = 1$	$t = 2$	$t = 3$
$30,000	$25,000	$22,700

Find the IRR; should it be accepted if $K = 20$ percent?

4. The Erb Optical Company is reviewing three proposals for ways to reduce costs of grinding lenses for binoculars. The firm may select only one of the proposals: A, B, or C. The cash flows for each proposal are as follows.

Cash Flow at Time *t*

Proposal	$t = 0$	$t = 1$	$t = 2$	$t = 3$	$t = 4$
A	−$10,000	$4000	$6000	$3000	$3000
B	− 12,000	6000	4000	3000	3000
C	− 16,000	5000	6000	6000	8000

The firm uses the payback method to evaluate investment projects. The maximum payback period allowed is 2 years. Which proposal will the firm choose by the payback method? Which proposal would be accepted by the NPV method if $K = 8$ percent? Explain why the two methods yield different selections.

5. A small machine for harvesting salsify, a little-known root vegetable, is available for $6000. Lasting 3 years and having no value at the end of its life, the machine will have straight line depreciation charges of $2000 annually. Two alternative streams of net income to be considered for purposes of the problem are:

	$t = 1$	$t = 2$	$t = 3$
Stream A	$800	$300	$100
Stream B	100	300	800

The average amount invested in the project over 3 years is $3000. Assuming that the cost of capital is $K = 10$ percent, should the project be accepted by the ARR method for either stream of net income? What decision would the NPV method make? Explain any difference in decisions between the two methods.

6. Two mutually exclusive proposals to reduce the costs of producing drinking straws are under evaluation by a firm. Proposal 1 uses larger quantities of labor relative to capital, whereas proposal 2 uses more capital than labor. Cash flows for the two proposals are as follows.

	$t = 0$	$t = 1$	$t = 2$	$t = 3$
Proposal 1	−$20,000	$10,000	$10,000	$ 8,160
Proposal 2	− 40,000	20,000•	20,000	11,385

Which proposal should be taken if $K = 8$ percent? $K = 16$ percent? Use the NPV and IRR methods. Explain any differences in selection made by the two methods.

7. Twinkle Toy Company is considering two models of a machine to make a robot dog. Model A is fully automated and requires little supervision. However, management estimates it will need a thorough overhaul in the second year of operation and will have little salvage value at the end of the third year. Model B requires several operators but is known to be extremely dependable and is expected to have a good resale value at the end of the 3-year project.
    Cash flows for the two machines are as follows.

	t = 0	t = 1	t = 2	t = 3
Model A	-$1000	$ 50	$100	$1536
Model B	-$1000	$1000	$100	$ 377

(a) Calculate the IRR of each model's cash flows.

(b) Sketch the NPV curves for each model on a single graph as in Figure 7-3.

(c) Check the point of intersection of NPV curves by calculating the IRR of the differential cash flows.

8. A firm is evaluating two market strategies for introducing a new product. Product production and sales life are 3 years for either strategy, but strategy 1 involves heavy advertising expenses in the first year. Cash inflow will therefore be smaller in the first year compared to later years. Strategy 2 involves less advertising expense, with these outlays distributed more evenly over time. However, total cash inflow from strategy 2 is less than from strategy 1. Initial outlays for production facilities for the product are the same for both strategies.

	Outlay (t = 0)	Cash Inflow t = 1	t = 2	t = 3
Strategy 1	-$10,000	$4000	$5045	$4705
Strategy 2	- 10,000	5000	4500	4160

Which strategy should be chosen if $K = 4$ percent? If $K = 10$ percent? Use the NPV and IRR methods.

9. Apply the differential rate of return test to Problem 6.

10. The Thuringer Ranch is considering the purchase of a new hay baler. It can be purchased for $8000, and savings are expected in labor and storage costs. In addition, a larger amount of usable hay is expected because of the greater efficiency of the new machine. The project cash flows are as follows.

t = 0	-$8000	t = 3	+$2000
t = 1	+$2000	t = 4	+$2000
t = 2	+$2000	t = 5	+$4000

The fifth-year cash flow of $4000 reflects the desire of Thuringer to sell the machine at the end of 5 years for the expected salvage value of $2000. Find (a) the payback period, (b) the internal rate of return, and (c) the net present value when $K = 10$ percent.

11. The Doolittle Company is considering an investment in a bottling machine costing $150,000. It is expected to provide cash inflows of $17,000 per year for 10 years and to be valueless at the end of 10 years.

   (a) Compute the internal rate of return. (*Hint.* The internal rate of return can be computed using Appendix Table D.)

   (b) Find net present value ($K = 12$ percent).

   (c) Is the investment desirable if $K = 12$ percent?

12. A lawyer is considering a master's degree in business administration (MBA). He feels that he must have a 12 percent return on his investment to properly compensate him for the capital and risk. His outlays over the 2-year program are expected to be $2500 each at $t = 1$ and $t = 2$. His best estimates of take-home pay over his remaining working career with and without the degree are as follows.

	Without MBA	With MBA
$t = 1$ and 2	$10,000 per year	$ 0 per year
$t = 3$	10,000	15,000
$t = 4$	11,000	16,000
$t = 5$	12,000	17,000
$t = 6$	13,000	18,000
$t = 7$	14,000	19,000
$t = 8$	15,000	20,000
$t = 9$	16,000	21,000
$t = 10$	17,000	22,000
$t = 11–15$	18,000 per year	25,000 per year
$t = 16–20$	20,000 per year	30,000 per year

What should he do and why?

CHAPTER 8

Cash Flow Analysis for Investments

Chapter 7 treated cash flows for investment projects as given magnitudes. But we know from Chapter 6 that the magnitude and timing of all cash flows associated with investment projects must be determined by the firm as a prelude to final acceptance or rejection of projects. This chapter provides guidance on cash flow determination and registers some cautions concerning important errors to be avoided. The effect of inflation on cash flow analysis is, for simplicity, not included in the chapter (see Chapter 19). We begin by showing the appropriate concept used to view cash flows for investment projects.

THE INCRE-MENTAL AFTER-TAX CASH FLOWS

For any investment project generating either expanded revenues or cost savings for the firm, the appropriate cash flows used in evaluating the project must be **incremental after-tax cash flows.** By the term incremental cash flows we mean cash inflows and outflows occurring *because* a project is undertaken. In other words, incremental cash flows are *changes* in the firm's overall cash flow caused by undertaking a project. All other cash flows of the firm that are unaffected by an investment project are properly ignored in specifying project cash flows.

Figure 8–1 *Time Line for Cash Flows of New Truck Project*

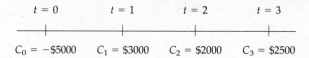

$t = 0$	$t = 1$	$t = 2$	$t = 3$
$C_0 = -\$5000$	$C_1 = \$3000$	$C_2 = \$2000$	$C_3 = \$2500$

Figure 8–2   *Time Line for Cash Flows of Powerplant Project ($000,000)*

$t = 0$	$t = 1$	$t = 2$	$\cdots\cdots\cdots\cdots$	$t = 10$	$t = 11$	$t = 12$

$C_0 = -\$3.2$ $C_1 = -\$6.8$ $C_2 = \$2.0 \cdots\cdots\cdots\cdots C_{10} = \$2.0$ $C_{11} = \$2.2$ $C_{12} = -\$1.0$

The incremental after-tax cash flows at time t for a project are denoted by C_t. These flows may be either positive, to indicate a cash inflow, or negative, to represent a cash outflow. Incremental cash flows extend at least from the present time $t = 0$ to $t = n$ when a project is terminated. But occasionally, cash flows occur after a project is terminated. Examples of incremental cash flows for two projects are shown on time lines in Figures 8-1 and 8-2. In Figure 8-1, incremental after-tax cash flows for a project to replace an old truck with a new truck are displayed. A cash outflow occurs at $t = 0$, followed by 3 years of cash inflows. Figure 8-2 describes the incremental after-tax cash flows for a project to build a powerplant. Cash outflows occur at $t = 0$ and at $t = 1$; cash inflows are indicated from $t = 2$ to $t = 11$. Another cash outflow appears at $t = 12$.

What we really want to know is how the incremental cash flows C_t were constructed for the new truck and powerplant projects. To accomplish this objective, it is useful to break up the incremental cash flows into three separate categories: initial investment outlays I_t, after-tax operating cash flows c_t, and terminal cash flows TC_t. Incremental after-tax cash flows for projects are constructed by first determining cash flows in these separate categories and then *combining* them to form the incremental flows C_t, as Tables 8-1 and 8-2 describe.

Having seen how incremental after-tax cash flows consist of initial investment outlays, after-tax operating cash flows, and terminal cash flows, we must now find out how to construct cash flows in each of these categories. The new truck project (Figure 8-1 and Table 8-1) serves

Table 8–1   *Incremental After-Tax Cash Flows: The New Truck Project*

Incremental Cash Flow Categories	Cash Flows at Time t			
	$t = 0$	$t = 1$	$t = 2$	$t = 3$
Initial Outlay, I_t	$I_0 = -\$5000$			
After-tax Operating Cash Flow, c_t		$c_1 = \$3000$	$c_2 = \$2000$	$c_3 = \$1000$
Terminal Cash Flow, TC_t				$TC_3 = \$1500$
Incremental After-tax Cash Flow, C_t	$C_0 = -\$5000$	$C_1 = \$3000$	$C_2 = \$2000$	$C_3 = \$2500$

Table 8–2   *Incremental After-tax Cash Flows: The Auxiliary Powerplant Project ($000,000)*

Incremental Cash Flow Categories	Cash Flow at Time t					
	$t = 0$	$t = 1$	$t = 2$	$\cdots$	$t = 11$	$t = 12$
Initial Outlay, I_t	$I_0 = -\$3.2$	$I_1 = -\$6.8$				
After-tax Operating Cash Flow, c_t			$c_2 = \$2.0$	$\cdots$	$c_{11} = \$2.0$	
Terminal Cash Flow, TC_t					$TC_{11} = \$0.2$	$TC_{12} = -\$1.0$
Incremental After-tax Cash Flow, C_t	$C_0 = -\$3.2$	$C_1 = -\$6.8$	$C_2 = \$2.0$		$C_{11} = \$2.2$	$C_{12} = -\$1.0$

as our example for the problem of constructing cash flows for a *cost-saving* project. The powerplant project (Figure 8-2 and Table 8-2) is used to demonstrate cash flow construction for a *revenue-expanding* project.

CONSTRUCTING CASH FLOWS FOR COST SAVING INVESTMENT PROJECTS

The new truck project is representative of a class of projects in which operating costs are expected to be reduced by purchasing new equipment or by installing new technology. The cash flows for cost-saving projects consist of *differences* in cash flows between two mutually exclusive proposals: (1) retain and use existing equipment, or (2) purchase and use new equipment. Therefore, the cost-saving project must express cash flows occurring *if* new equipment is purchased *and* old equipment is disposed of by the firm. Such cash flows are consistent with the incremental cash flow concept because the purchase of new equipment and the disposal of old equipment will change the cash flows of the firm.

Initial Investment Outlays

Initial investment outlays comprise incremental cash expenditures to acquire and prepare assets for operational use. Such outlays consist of the total outlay necessary to acquire and prepare the new truck for use *less* cash inflows received from the disposal of the old truck—all cash flows being adjusted to an after-tax basis. As summarized below, the

Initial Investment Outlay for Project to Purchase New Truck and Dispose of Old Truck

Total outlay for new truck	−$6300
Cash inflow from disposal of old truck	+ 1300
Initial investment outlay	−$5000

total outlay for the new truck is $6300 after taxes. However, the old truck can be disposed of for $1300 after taxes, to produce an incremental initial investment outlay of $5000.

We now need to see how the $6300 total outlay and $1300 cash inflow from disposal of the old truck are determined.

Total Outlay

The **total outlay** for the new truck consists of cash outlays depreciable for tax purposes and cash outlays immediately expensed for tax purposes. **Depreciable cash outlays** consist of expenditures to acquire, construct, or modify assets to be depreciated over future years. These outlays may include costs of labor, materials, equipment, and transportation charges necessary to acquire and prepare assets for operating purposes.

Panel A of Table 8-3 lists the depreciable cash outlays for acquiring and preparing the new truck for operation. To the truck's $4550 purchase price, the dealer preparation charge of $125 must be added as well as a $125 transportation charge to move the truck from the dealer to the firm. Depreciable outlays also include $1200 to modify the truck for the particular uses of the firm. Thus, depreciable outlays total $6000. To obtain the total outlay, the firm must add the after-tax cost of an outlay for driver training. This $500 outlay can be immediately expensed for tax purposes. The firm's tax rate is $\tau = 40$ percent. Therefore, the driver training outlay will reduce taxable income by $500 and produce a tax saving of $(0.40)\$500 = \$200$. The after-tax value of this cash outlay is only

Table 8–3   *Initial Investment Outlay for the New Truck Project*

	Cash Flow
A. Total Outlay on New Truck Proposal	
Depreciable Cash Outlays	
Purchase Price	−$4550
Dealer Preparation Charge	− 125
Transportation Charge	− 125
Modification Costs	− 1200
Total Depreciable Outlays	−$6000
Cash Outlays Expensed for Tax Purposes	
Driver Training ($500 pre-tax)	− 300
Total Outlay	−$6300
B. Cash Inflows from Disposal of Old Truck	
Market Value of Old Truck	+$ 500
Income Tax Adjustment	+ 800
Total	+$1300

$500 - $200 = $300. Taking into account the depreciable cash outlay and the after-tax outlay for driver training, the total outlay for the new truck is $6000 + $300 = $6300.

Cash Inflow on Disposal of an Old Asset   We have already seen that the firm will receive $1300, after taxes, upon disposal of the old truck. This cash inflow is obtained by determining the market value of the old truck and adjusting this market value for any income taxes resulting from disposal of the old truck.

Panel B of Table 8-3 indicates that the market value of the old truck is $500. This cash inflow, occurring if the old truck is sold, must be adjusted by any additional income taxes, or perhaps tax savings, resulting from the disposal of the old truck. In this instance, a tax saving of $800 happens to occur—bringing the total after-tax cash inflow to $1300.

The income tax consequences of disposing of an old asset depend on whether there are differences between market and book values of the old asset at time of disposal. In the case of the old truck, book value is $2500 at $t = 0$, $2000 in excess of market value. This excess of book over market value means that insufficient depreciation was charged against taxable income in the prior years of the old truck's life. Consequently, a correction for prior years' depreciation is made by charging the $2000 excess of book value over market value against taxable income in the current year. This $2000 is *not* a cash outlay, but at a tax rate of $\tau = 40$ percent, it will reduce taxable income by $2000 and income tax payments by (0.40)2000 = $800. The resulting $800 tax saving is added, as shown in Table 8-3, panel B, to the $500 market price received, to obtain the $1300 cash inflow obtained by disposing of the old truck.[1]

---

[1]If the market value of the old truck had been *greater* than the $2500 undepreciated book value, taxable income and income taxes at $t = 0$ would have been increased by the sale of the old truck. For example, had the old truck been worth $3500 in the market at $t = 0$, the firm would have taken excess depreciation in prior years in the amount of $3500 - $2500 = $1000. Sale of the truck would have led to a $1000 increase in taxable income at $t = 0$ to reflect a correction for excessive prior depreciation. At $\tau = 40$ percent, income taxes would rise by $(0.40)($1000) = $400. Consequently, the after-tax cash inflow received would be the $3500 sale price less the increased income tax payment, or $3100.

Other types of tax adjustment are possible when old assets are sold. If the old truck had been worth $6000 in the market at $t = 0$ but had originally cost only $5500, then the firm should never have charged depreciation in prior years, for the market value exceeds the original depreciable outlay of $5500. Sale of the old truck would mean that the $5500 original depreciable outlay less the $2500 undepreciated book value, or $3000, is excess depreciation. Taxes at $t = 0$ would *increase* by $(0.40)($3000) = $1200. In addition, the $500 excess of the $6000 market value of the truck over the $5500 original depreciable outlay would be treated as a capital gain and would be taxed at the capital gains rate τ_g. If $\tau_g = 20$ percent, the capital gains tax would be $(0.20)($500) = $100. The after-tax cash inflow at $t = 0$ would be $6000 - $1200 - $100 = $4700.

Tax treatment of disposal of old assets also depends on whether the asset is sold or traded in and upon the depreciation method employed. Federal tax law must be consulted to determine appropriate tax adjustments if any doubt exists.

In general, replacement of old assets with new may provide a re-duced need for some kinds of working capital, such as inventories, because of greater efficiency and reliability of the new assets. To the extent that this occurs, a cash inflow from the disposal of excess working capital results and is added to other cash flows received from disposal of the old asset. This did *not* happen for the truck project. Working capital cash flows are discussed when the powerplant project is dealt with later in the chapter.

Summary of Initial Investment Outlay   The incremental after-tax cash flow described by the term *initial outlay* was $I_0 = -\$5000$ at $t = 0$ for the new truck project. This magnitude resulted from finding the cash flows occurring if the new truck is purchased and the old truck is disposed of by the firm. Acquisition of the new truck involved a total outlay of $6300 resulting from a depreciable cash outlay of $6000 and a $300 after-tax expenditure to train drivers. Disposal of the old truck yielded an after-tax cash inflow of $1300. The new truck project (i.e., new truck pur-chased and old truck sold) resulted in an initial outlay of $-\$6300 - (-\$1300) = -\$5000$.

The second major category of incremental cash flows for a project con-sists of the periodic incremental after-tax operating cash flows c_t, gener-ated by the project over its life. These cash flows may be described by the following formula.

Incremental After-tax Operating Cash Flows

$$c_t = CF_t - \tau(CF_t - d_t)$$

where CF_t is the pre-tax incremental operating cash flow generated by the project and d_t is the incremental depreciation of the project. (The pre-tax incremental operating cash flow CF_t and the after-tax operating cash flow c_t are not to be confused with C_t, the after-tax incremental cash flow. Tables 8-1 and 8-2 should be used as a guide to help distinguish this notation.) Because incremental taxable income for the project is found by subtracting depreciation from pre-tax operating cash flow, the term $\tau(CF_t - d_t)$ represents the incremental income tax payment. Thus, in the formula, **incremental after-tax operating cash flow** is simply in-cremental operating cash flow before taxes minus incremental income taxes.

For our purposes, it is more convenient to rearrange the cash flow formula into the following forms.

$$c_t = (1 - \tau)CF_t + \tau d_t \qquad (8\text{-}1)$$

Viewed in this way, incremental after-tax operating cash flow consists of the after-tax proceeds from operating cash flow $(1 - \tau)CF_t$, plus a de-

Table 8-4 *Incremental After-tax Operating Cash Flows for New Truck Project*

	Cash Flows at Time t		
	$t = 1$	$t = 2$	$t = 3$
A. Incremental Operating Cash Flow: Truck Project			
Operating Cost of the New Truck	−$1000	−$4000	−$6000
Operating Cost of the Old Truck	− 6000	− 6667	− 7000
Incremental Operating Cash Flow (cost savings), CF_t	$5000	$2667	$1000
B. Incremental Depreciation: Truck Project			
Annual Depreciation Charges *if* New Truck Purchased	$1500	$1500	$1500
Annual Depreciation Charges *if* Old Truck Retained	1500	500	500
Incremental Depreciation Charge, d_t	$ 0	$1000	$1000
C. Incremental After-tax Operating Cash Flow: Truck Project			
Incremental After-tax Cost Savings $(1 - \tau) CF_t$	$3000	$1600	$ 600
Incremental Tax Subsidy, τd_t	0	400	400
Incremental After-tax Operating Cash Flow, c_t	$3000	$2000	$1000

preciation tax subsidy τd_t. This subsidy exists because depreciation is a tax-deductible expense but not a cash flow. Note that if depreciation were not tax deductible, the tax subsidy term τd_t would disappear entirely from the formula. It is useful to work with Equation (8-1) rather than the earlier version of the formula because it facilitates evaluation of the use of different depreciation methods. (See Appendix 8-A.)

For the truck project, use of Equation (8-1) requires that the pre-tax incremental operating cash flow CF_t and incremental depreciation charge d_t be estimated. Such estimates are contained in Table 8-4.

In panel A, the pre-tax incremental operating cash flow for the truck project represents pre-tax operating cost savings obtained by purchasing the new truck and disposing of the old one. Over the 3-year life of the new truck, its future operating costs, consisting of labor and material (all *cash* outlays), are estimated. These costs are expected to rise as the truck ages and repair costs increase. They are compared to the expected operating costs that would occur if the old truck were retained for that long. Naturally, these costs are higher than those of the more efficient and reliable new truck. By subtracting cash outlays for operating costs of the old truck from those for the new truck, the pre-tax incremental operating cash flow of the project is obtained.

Incremental depreciation charges for the truck project represent differences between depreciation charges on the new truck and on the old truck. Several depreciation methods could be utilized. In most cases, firms are benefited by using an accelerated depreciation method for tax purposes. This issue is discussed in Appendix 8A. To the extent that firms use the investment tax credit, as discussed in Appendix 8B, firms are also usually benefited. We assume that the firm uses the simpler straight line depreciation method. For this method the annual depreciation charge is given by:

$$\text{Depreciation charge} = \frac{\text{Depreciable outlay for asset} - \text{salvage value}}{\text{Depreciable life of asset}}$$

The new truck has a depreciable outlay of $6000 and will be depreciated over a life of three years. The expected **salvage value** is the cash flow the firm expects to receive when the asset is disposed of 3 years hence. The new truck is expected to be worth $1500 at that future time. Therefore, annual depreciation for the new truck will be:

$$\text{Depreciation charge} = \frac{\$6000 - \$1500}{3} = \$1500$$

This annual charge is shown in panel B of Table 8-4.[2]

The future depreciation charges for the old truck depend in part on the depreciation schedule originally established for the old truck at time of purchase. We assume that the old truck was acquired 2 years ago ($t = -2$) for a depreciable outlay of $5500. It was to be depreciated on a straight line basis for a 3-year life, to a salvage value of $1000. Annual depreciation charges have therefore been $1500.

$$\text{Depreciation charge} = \frac{\$5500 - \$1000}{3} = \$1500$$

At this point the past and future depreciation charges for the old truck can be described on the accompanying time line. If the old truck is retained for 3 more years until $t = 3$, the remaining $1500 depreciation charge from the original depreciation schedule would be taken at $t = 1$. At that point, the book value of the old truck will be $5500 - 3(\$1500) = \$1000$. Retention of the old truck for 2 additional years beyond its original depreciable life will require further depreciation of the $1000 book value remaining at $t = 1$.[3] We assume that the old truck, if retained, would be worthless at $t = 3$ and that the remaining $1000 of book value

---

[2]This computation of straight line depreciation is not necessarily the most advantageous from the standpoint of income tax minimization. In most circumstances, firms can depreciate to a zero salvage value even though a positive market value is likely to exist at the end of **depreciable life.** We ignore these details.

[3]There is no reason for the firm owning the old truck to be bound by its original plan to keep the old truck for 3 years, until $t = 1$. Plans of this type can always be changed if a change would be profitable. Replacement of the old truck with a new one is one such potential change in plan.

will be charged off in equal amounts of \$500 on a new straight line depreciation schedule over 2 years. Thus, from the time line above, the depreciation charges for $t = 1$, $t = 2$, and $t = 3$ for the old truck are given in panel B of Table 8-4.

Depreciation on Old Truck

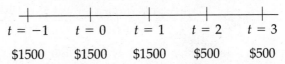

$t = -1$	$t = 0$	$t = 1$	$t = 2$	$t = 3$
\$1500	\$1500	\$1500	\$500	\$500

Subtracting, in panel B, the future depreciation charges for the old truck from those of the new truck, the incremental depreciation charges for the truck project are obtained. As it happens, no incremental depreciation occurs at $t = 1$ but, in later years, the truck project provides incremental depreciation.

The ultimate goal of this section, the determination of the incremental after-tax operating cash flows, is achieved in panel C of Table 8-4. Using Equation (8-1), the incremental pre-tax operating cash flows CF_t from panel A are reduced to the after-tax amount $(1 - \tau)CF_t$, using a tax rate of $\tau = 40$ percent. The incremental depreciation charges from panel B are multiplied by the tax rate to obtain the incremental **depreciation tax subsidy** term τd_t in each year. Finally, as required by Equation (8-1), the terms $(1 - \tau)CF_t$ and τd_t are added together to produce c_t—the incremental after-tax operating cash flows generated by the truck project when the new truck is acquired—and the old truck is disposed of by the firm. These flows are identical, of course, with those originally stated in Table 8-1.

Terminal Cash Flows

At the end of the life of the new truck, cash flows associated with its disposal may occur. We assume that the new truck could be sold at $t = 3$ for \$1500 on an after-tax basis.[4] This cash flow occurs if the new truck is purchased. However, to find the incremental after-tax terminal cash flow of the new truck project, we must compare that \$1500 cash inflow with the value of the old truck, if retained, at $t = 3$. If, as we assume, the old truck will be worthless at $t = 3$ if it is retained, the incremental after-tax **terminal cash flow** is \$1500 − \$0 = \$1500. Stated alternatively, the incremental terminal cash flow results from comparing the alternative after-tax *salvage values* of the two proposals—the after-tax salvage value

---

[4]This amount exactly equals book value of the new truck at the end of $t = 3$. If the firm expects book and market values of the new truck to differ at $t = 3$, tax adjustments similar to those carried out earlier for disposal of the old truck must be made.

being defined as the expected after-tax market value (possibly zero) of the new and old trucks at $t = 3$. If the old truck had an expected after-tax salvage value of $200 at $t = 3$, the incremental terminal cash flow would be only $1500 − $200 = $1300.

By comparing cash flows between two proposals (buy the new truck and keep the old truck), the incremental after-tax cash flows C_t initially described in Figure 8-1 were constructed. The construction process proceeded by finding incremental after-tax cash flows in three categories: initial outlay, after-tax operating cash flows, and terminal cash flow.

When the incremental after-tax cash flows for the new truck project have been determined, it remains only to evaluate them by the net present value method to decide whether the new truck should be purchased and the old truck sold. We assume that the appropriate cost of capital is $K = 10$ percent to compute a resulting net present value of $1258.45.

Summary and Evaluation of Cash Flows for the Cost-Saving, New Truck Project

$$NPV = \sum_{t=1}^{3} \frac{C_t}{(1 + K)^t} + C_0$$

$$= \$3000(0.90909) + \$2000(0.82645) + \$2500(0.75131) - \$5000$$

$$= \$1258.45 > 0$$

The new truck project is acceptable because NPV is positive. In other words, the incremental after-tax operating cash flows (after-tax cost savings) plus incremental terminal cash flow are worth more than the initial outlay. Shareholder wealth is expected to increase by $1258.45 if the new truck is purchased and the old truck is sold.

When a project consists of a proposal to expand revenue by the sale of additional output and no cost savings for the production of existing levels of output are envisaged, all cash flows identified with that project are, by definition, incremental.[5] Initial outlays, additional sales revenue, additional operating labor and material costs, additional depreciation, and additional terminal cash flow will not occur unless the revenue-expanding project is undertaken.

CONSTRUCT- ING CASH FLOWS FOR REVENUE- EXPANDING PROJECTS

---

[5] A project might both expand revenue *and* reduce costs of producing existing output levels. In such situations, techniques for constructing cash flows for *both* cost-saving *and* revenue-expanding projects must be combined. We ignore this more detailed kind of problem.

We illustrate cash flow construction for the revenue-expanding type of project with the powerplant project, using the after-tax incremental cash flows C_t in Figure 8-2 and Table 8-2. As in the case of the truck project, the construction process is demonstrated by breaking the cash flows C_t into three separate categories: initial outlays I_t, after-tax operating cash flows c_t, and terminal cash flows TC_t.

Initial Outlay   Because the $10 million outlay for the powerplant does not replace an existing powerplant, no cash flows resulting from disposal of an existing plant will occur if the new plant is built. Consequently, there is no need, as there was in the case of the new truck project, to determine the cash value of existing assets to be replaced. Instead, the total outlays on the powerplant directly express incremental cash flows required to construct the plant and prepare it for operation. However, the components of the initial outlay are spread over 2 years, as Table 8-5 indicates.

Depreciable Cash Outlays   The 2-year construction period for the powerplant requires depreciable outlays for construction labor and materials, construction site preparation, transportation of materials to the site, and for power-generating equipment to be installed at the plant. Depreciable outlays are $3 million at $t = 0$ and $6 million at $t = 1$ for the total depreciable outlay for the project of $9 million indicated in Table 8-5.

Net Working Capital Requirement   Revenue-expanding projects lead to the sale of additional physical output. Chapters 22 to 24 indicate that sale of additional output with consequent higher revenues may require increases in the level of current assets held by the firm. Depending on the working capital policies of the firm, some portion of the required increase in current assets will be financed by increases in current liabilities (i.e., from short-term sources). The remaining portion of the increase in current assets must be financed from long-term or perma-

Table 8–5   *Initial Outlays for Powerplant Project ($000,000)*

	$t = 0$	$t = 1$	Total
Depreciable Outlays	−$3.0	−$6.0	−$ 9.0
Net Working Capital Requirement	—	− 0.2	− 0.2
Expensed Cash Outlays	− 0.2	− 0.6	− 0.8
	−$3.2	−$6.8	−$10.0

Figure 8–3   *Time Line for Net Working Capital Requirement, Cash Flows of the Powerplant Project*

$t = 1$ $t = 11$

|——————————————————————————————|

$-\$0.2$ $+\$0.2$

nent financing sources and is called the **net working capital require-ment.** (Remember from Chapter 2 that net working capital is defined as the difference between current assets and current liabilities.)

Now when long-term capital sources are used to finance net working capital requirements, funds are tied up in just the way that investment in long-term fixed assets ties up funds. Since the cost of capital K reflects long-term capital costs of financing fixed assets and is used in net present value analysis of cash flows associated with these fixed assets, it is appropriate to evaluate cash flows associated with long-term net working capital requirements at the same rate K. Therefore, cash flows associated with net working capital requirements must be incorporated into the cash flows of the project.

The behavior of cash flows associated with the net working capital requirement of the powerplant project is described in Figure 8-3, which shows an outlay of $0.2 million occurring at $t = 1$ when the powerplant begins operation. This outlay might result, say, from a $0.5 million increase in required current assets and a $0.3 million increase in current liabilities. The remaining $0.2 million, the net working capital requirement, must be financed from long-term sources and is therefore an *outlay* at $t = 1$. Ultimately, at the end of the life of the powerplant project, the required amount of net working capital will be *released* because the original need for increased current assets will no longer exist. Consequently, at $t = 11$ when the powerplant has ceased operations, the original $0.2 million will be *released* and is shown in Figure 8-3 as a cash *inflow*.[6]

For the immediate purpose of determining the initial outlay, only the net working capital requirement outlay at $t = 1$ is considered. The release of working capital at $t = 11$ when the powerplant is terminated is

---

[6]The timing of cash inflows and outflows described in Figure 8-3 is an approximation. Increases in, say, accounts receivable financed by long-term capital sources, will be required because of a lag between the billing of energy sold to customers and the time that customers pay their bills. The increased accounts receivable levels to be financed will not instantaneously occur at $t = 1$, when the plant begins producing energy, as Figure 8-3 implies, but only with a time lag of, say, 1 to 2 months. Similarly, when the plant ceases operation at $t = 11$, it will take 1 to 2 months to collect the last bills sent out. The differences in timing between the actual cash inflows and outflows and the flows shown in Figure 8-3 are usually small enough that they may be safely ignored.

evaluated in our discussion of terminal cash flows. Accordingly, Table 8-5 shows the $0.2 million net working capital outlay at $t = 1$ as part of the initial outlay.

Cash Outlays Expensed for Tax Purposes   The powerplant project requires that on a pre-tax basis, the firm expend $0.33 million at $t = 0$ and $1.0 million at $t = 1$ to hire, relocate, and train workers to operate the plant. These outlays are tax deductible when they occur and, at a tax rate of $\tau = 40$ percent, they result in after-tax outlays of $(1 - 0.40)\$0.33 = \$0.2$ million at $t = 0$ and $(1 - 0.40)\$1.00 = \$0.6$ million at $t = 1$. (This adjustment assumes that other taxable income exists against which the $0.33 million can be deducted. If this did not hold, then other types of tax adjustment for prior and future years would be required.)

As Table 8-5 demonstrates, by summing all components of cash outflow in each year, the initial outlays of $I_0 = \$3.2$ million and $I_1 = \$6.8$ million are obtained. **Total initial outlay** over 2 years is $10 million, of which $9.0 million is depreciable, $0.2 million is a net working capital outlay, and $0.8 million is for after-tax cash outlays expensed for tax purposes.

Incremental After-tax Operating Cash Flows	Incremental after-tax operating cash flows consist of sales revenue less cash outlays on labor and materials—adjusted for income taxes and depreciation. We can view these components in Table 8-6. Since all operating cash flows are constant over time in the powerplant case, we need only look at operating cash flow for a single year. The pre-tax operating cash flow of $CF = \$2.73$ million is made up of annual sales revenue less outlays for annual labor and material expenses. Annual depreciation is $d = \$0.9$ million. Using Equation (8-1), the annual after-tax proceeds on the operating cash flow are $(1 - 0.40)\$2.73 = \$1.64$ million. The annual depreciation tax subsidy is $(0.40)(\$0.90) = \$0.36$ million. Summing these two values gives the annual after-tax operating cash flow of $c = \$2$ million. This corresponds exactly to the magnitude shown in Table 8-2.

Terminal Cash Flow   At $t = 11$ and $t = 12$, the powerplant proposal had terminal cash flows as exhibited earlier in Table 8-2. At $t = 11$ a terminal cash inflow of $TC_{11} = \$0.2$ million reflects the release of the $0.2 million initially committed at $t = 1$ to meet net working capital requirements. At $t = 12$, a cash outflow of $TC_{12} = -\$1$ million occurs. This outflow happens because, before taxes, a $1.67 million outlay to dismantle the powerplant will be incurred. Since this outlay is a tax-deductible expense and only after-tax

Table 8–6 *After-tax Operating Cash Flows for the Powerplant Project ($000,000)*

Pre-tax Annual Operating Cash Flow
  Annual Sales Revenue $4.00
  Labor and Materials   1.27
                                      $CF =$ $2.73

Depreciation[a]
  Annual Straight Line Depreciation Charge
                                      $d =$ $0.9

Incremental After-tax Operating Cash Flow
  $C = (1 - \tau)CF + \tau d$
    $= (1 - 0.40)\$2.73 + (0.40)(\$0.9)$
    $= \$2.0$

[a] The power plant is depreciated straight line over 10 years with no salvage value:

$$d = \frac{\$9.0 - 0}{10 \text{ years}} = \$0.9 \text{ million}$$

cash flows are desired for the analysis, we must reduce it by the amount of tax saving associated with that expenditure. That tax saving is $(0.40)(\$1.67) = \$0.67$ million. Therefore, the after-tax cash flow for dismantling costs is $TC_{12} = -\$1.67 + 0.67 = -\$1.0$ million.

Each category of incremental cash flows C_t, demonstrated in Table 8-2, has now been constructed. By summing these categories of cash flows for each year as in that table, the incremental after-tax cash flows generated for the powerplant project are found.

To evaluate the project, we suppose that the appropriate required rate of return is $K = 8$ percent. Computing the net present value of the cash flows C_t, the project is found to be acceptable.[7]

Evaluation of the Powerplant Project

---

[7] The NPV calculation is made using Appendix Tables C and D. The cash flows at $t = 1$, $t = 11$, and $t = 12$ are all single, unequal payments and are stated separately as $PV(C_1)$, $PV(C_{11})$, and $PV(C_{12})$ to indicate that Appendix Table C must be used to calculate the present value of these particular cash flows. However, the cash flows from $t = 2$ to $t = 10$ are constant payments and denoted, in present value terms, as $PV(C_2, \ldots, C_{10})$. The annuity table, Appendix Table D, can be used to find their present value *as of $t = 1$*. The annuity factor for 8 percent and 9 years is 6.2469 in Appendix Table D. At $t = 1$, their present value is $(6.2469)\$2.0 = \$12.494$. However, we want to find the present value *as of t $= 0$* of that annuity. To do that, we need only discount the magnitude $(6.2469)\$2.0 = \$12.494$ one more period by multiplying it times the present value factor from Appendix Table C for $K = 8$ percent and for 1 year, 0.92593. Thus, $(6.2469)\$2.0(0.92593) = \$11.568$ *as of $t = 0$.*

Net Present Value of Powerplant Project ($000,000)

$$NPV = PV(C_2, \ldots, C_{10}) + PV(C_{11}) + PV(C_{12}) + PV(C_1) + C_0$$

$$= 0.92593(6.2469)\$2.0 + 0.42888(\$2.2) + 0.39711(\$-1.0)$$

$$+ 0.92593(-\$6.8) - \$3.2$$

$$= \$2.62 > 0$$

SOME IMPORTANT ERRORS

By using the new truck and powerplant projects as examples, the proper way to construct incremental after-tax cash flows has been demonstrated. Yet it is easy enough to find cases of decision-makers either failing to correctly specify cash flows or misinterpreting components of these cash flows. These errors can be quite significant in that they may lead to the acceptance of projects that should be rejected and the rejection of projects that should be accepted. The most important of these errors is discussed next.

Confusing the Timing of Net Income with the Timing of Cash Flow

Net income as established from accounting procedures may have a quite different pattern through time for a project than the cash flows of that project. Discrepancies between the timing of net income and the timing of cash flows occur because accounting practices emphasize an accrual rather than a cash basis. The central emphasis of accrual accounting is the allocation of revenues and expenses to appropriate time periods to reflect when sales occur and when the costs of generating these sales are recognized. But the period of time when a revenue or expense is recognized may be very different from the period of time when the associated cash inflow or outflow occurs. If the timing of net income of a project is used to determine the timing of cash flows, serious biases in the net present value magnitude of the project may occur. Some examples demonstrate this point.

Panel A in Table 8-7 shows the projected net income statements for 2 years for a new manufacturing plant being evaluated by a fireworks company. The plant costs $1200 to build and will last 2 years. Apart from labor and materials and the straight line depreciation charge, the major expense of operating the plant is liability insurance to compensate the surrounding neighborhood in the event of an unfortunate manufacturing error. Net income, as projected, is $240 per year. But we now show that a number of different cash flow patterns may be associated with the same projected net income pattern. For example, panel B of Table 8-7 shows the initial outlay and after-tax operating cash flows for the fire-

Table 8–7 *Cash Flow Compared to Net Income for the Fireworks Plant Project*

		Years	
	$t = 0$	$t = 1$	$t = 2$
A. Net Income			
Sales	—	$2000	$2000
Labor and Materials	—	500	500
Liability Insurance Expense	—	500	500
Depreciation	—	600	600
Operating Income	—	$ 400	$ 400
Income Taxes ($\tau = 40\%$)	—	160	160
Net Income	—	$ 240	$ 240
B. Operating Cash Flow Synchronized with Net Income			
Collections on Sales		$2000	$2000
Labor and Materials Payments		500	500
Liability Insurance Payments		500	500
Cash Flow Before Taxes		$1000	$1000
Income Taxes (as computed in panel A)		160	160
After-tax Operating Cash Flow		$ 840	$ 840
Initial Outlay	−$1200		
After-tax Cash Flows	−$1200	$ 840	$ 840
C. After-tax Cash Flow if Insurance Paid at $t = 0$	−$2200	$1340	$1340

works plant under the assumption that all operating cash flows are perfectly synchronized with the timing of their respective components of net income. Specifically, collections from sales and cash outlays for labor, materials, and liability insurance premiums are made in the same year that the corresponding expenses are recognized for the purpose of determining net income and income taxes. Under this circumstance, the after-tax operating cash flow is $840 per year. These cash flows would be evaluated relative to an outlay of $1200 at $t = 0$ when the NPV method is applied to the cash flows.

A quite different cash flow pattern from that shown in panel B of Table 8-7 would be obtained if it were assumed that the firm pays in advance $1000 at $t = 0$ for 2 years of insurance coverage. By accounting practice, the expense for this insurance payment will be recognized at the same time as it was in panel A—in equal amounts of $500 at $t = 1$ and $t = 2$. But this is clearly not the pattern for the cash flows associated with liability insurance premiums. To adjust the cash flows shown in panel B, when it was assumed that cash flows were synchronized in time with net income, we must first increase the initial outlay at $t = 0$ by $1000 to reflect the advance payment of the premium for 2 years. We must also increase the panel B cash inflow by $500 in each year because it is no longer true that cash outlays for insurance occur at those times.[8] Cash inflows at $t = 1$ and $t = 2$ are thus increased to \$1340 per year. The net effect on cash flow timing of these adjustments is shown in panel C. Insurance cash outlays now occur early rather than later. Nevertheless, the timing of net income as portrayed in panel A remains the same in panel B.

Now the interesting thing about Table 8-7 is that panels B and C portray quite different cash flow patterns, which are yet consistent with the same net income statements in panel A. However, although net income is the same, the desirability of the fireworks project differs markedly as evaluated by the net present value method using an assumed cost of capital of $K = 20$ percent:

Panel B: Operating Cash Flow Synchronized with Net Income

$$\text{NPV} = \$840(1.52778) - \$1200 = \$83.33 > 0$$

Panel C: Insurance Paid in Advance at $t = 0$

$$\text{NPV} = \$1340(1.52778) - \$2200 = -\$152.78 < 0$$

The present value calculations, using Appendix Table D, show that only if operating cash flows are synchronized with the timing of net income will the fireworks plant project be acceptable. If insurance is paid in advance at $t = 0$, the project is not acceptable.

The only way to avoid the problem of improper timing of cash flows is to center attention on when the cash flows actually will occur, not on the timing of associated revenues or expenses. In this perspective, the observant reader may note that Equation (8-1) assumes that after-tax operating cash inflows and outflows are synchronized in time with net income based on accrual accounting. Use of this formula is reasonable if collections on receivables lag (in time) sales, and payments for expenses lead or lag the initial receipt by the firm of a bill from a supplier, by a relatively short time—say 1 or 2 months. In perhaps the majority of cases, Equation (8-1) is an adequate approximation for the timing of cash flows. However, significant differences in timing between cash flow and income must always be appreciated.

Confusing Depreciation Expense with Cash Flow   Depreciation expense is an accounting accrual designed to reflect the using up of the services of fixed assets in a particular time period. In the case of the fireworks plant in Table 8-7, panel A indicates that the annual depreciation charge is \$600 per year. This depreciation charge is definite-

---

[8]Tax payments need not be adjusted because taxes are based on net income established by accrual accounting practices. Net income is unchanged, although insurance coverage for 2 years is purchased at $t = 0$.

ly not a cash flow but it does affect the cash flow represented by income taxes, since depreciation charges are tax deductible.

Although it is difficult to know how the notion originated, the idea that depreciation is a cash flow nevertheless persists here and there in practice. One could say that depreciation is an allocation against cash inflow and, if such cash inflows exist, the depreciation charge may serve as a proxy for funds available for reinvestment. For example, panel B in Table 8-7 indicated that $840 in after-tax operating cash flow would be generated if cash flows were synchronized with net income. If this were true, we could allocate $600 of depreciation against the $840 cash inflow and call $600 of annual depreciation a proxy for $600 available annually for reinvestment. However, the same statement would be meaningless if annual operating cash inflows were zero before taxes rather than $1000 as indicated. For then, the fireworks company could make any allocation it cared to for depreciation but no pre-tax cash flow would exist. Depreciation is not a cash flow!

Failure to Identify Proper Investment Alternatives

Unless alternative investment proposals are completely identified, it is possible to reach erroneous conclusions in selecting investment projects, thus failing to maximize shareholder wealth. The following example illustrates this point.

Suppose that a soap company is considering plans A and B to modernize an existing plant. Not only will each modernization plan lower costs but each will also allow increased soap production and higher sales revenues over a life of 1 year. The computed after-tax cash flows C_t for each plan are as follows.

	Cash Flows at Year t	
	$t = 0$	$t = 1$
Modernization Plan A	−$500,000	$580,000
Modernization Plan B	−1,000,000	1,150,000

Application of the net present value method at $K = 12$ percent yields the following net present values for the two plans.

$$\text{NPV}_A = \$580,000(0.89286) - \$500,000 = \$17,857.11$$

$$\text{NPV}_B = \$1,150,000(0.89286) - \$1,000,000 = \$26,785.60$$

Apparently, plan B is superior to plan A because it yields the largest expected increase in shareholder wealth as measured by the respective NPV magnitudes. However, this conclusion is correct only if plans A and B reflect all feasible investment alternatives. Another alternative may exist that is far superior to both plans A and B. Suppose, for example, that the firm can cease producing soap and sell the existing plant to a party wanting to manufacture door locks. The firm estimates that taking into account the present value of lost future cash inflows without modernization and the cash inflow received from the buyer of the plant, the NPV of the liquidation alternative is $100,000. Thus liquidation is a third alternative to plans A and B, which require the plant to be both retained and modernized.

The proper comparison of the three alternatives is given below:

Net Present Value

$$NPV_A = \$17,857.11$$

$$NPV_B = 26,785.60$$

$$NPV_L = 100,000.00$$

The immediate after-tax proceeds from liquidating the plant and stopping production of soap have a net present value of $100,000. This alternative is superior to either modernization plan and should be undertaken for the benefit of shareholders. Modernization plan B was attractive in the earlier analysis only because it was compared to plan A, not to the alternative of liquidation.

What this example demonstrates is a simple but often overlooked point: any alternative (e.g., B) can be made to look good when compared to sufficiently inferior alternatives (e.g., A). Only when an acceptable alternative has been compared to and has survived competition with the next best alternative can we say that it is *the* best alternative and should be undertaken.

Failure to Distinguish Between Incremental and Nonincremental Cash Flows

Let us suppose that the soap company's plant is worthless and that modernization plan B with a net present value of $26,785.60 is the best investment alternative. Before deciding to undertake the modernization plan, the top management of the soap company indicates that overhead for general administrative services from the head office will be charged to the project at $t = 1$. This overhead totals $58,333. On an after-tax basis, with $\tau = 40$ percent, the overhead cost is $(1 - 0.40)\$58,333 = \$35,000$. The effect on the cash flows of the project is tabulated as follows.

At $K = 12$ percent, the project is now unacceptable because the net present value is negative.

Revised Cash Flow of Modernization Plan B

	$t = 0$	$t = 1$
Initial Outlay	$-\$1,000,000$	
Original After-tax Cash Flow		$+\$1,150,000$
Overhead Allocation from General Headquarters		$-\quad 35,000$
Revised Cash Flow	$-\$1,000,000$	$\$1,115,000$

$$NPV_B = \$1,115,000(0.89286) - \$1,000,000$$

$$= \$985,535.71 - \$1,000,000$$

$$= -\$4464.30 < 0$$

Whether the apparent decision to now reject the modernization plan is correct depends on whether the overhead allocation from general headquarters is a true incremental cash outflow. If in fact top management will find it necessary to increase staffing and to incur other incremental cash outlays at the general headquarters *because* of the modernization plan, then the allocation of these costs to the modernization plan is a perfectly correct procedure. Incremental cash flows are defined as those flows occurring *because* a project is undertaken. However, if no increase in cash outlays for overhead will be caused by the project then the inclusion of overhead in the cash flows for the modernization plan is incorrect. No incremental cash outlay is *caused* by the project. All that is happening is that *existing* cash outlays for overhead are being reallocated—with the modernization plan picking up a share.

Overhead allocations to cash flows of projects are also improper to the extent that the overhead represents **sunk costs.** Sunk costs are prior expenditures being allocated to the current time period. Prior plant and equipment expenditures or past research and development outlays are examples of such costs. These costs cannot be affected by current activity and are irrelevant to the decision affecting future cash flows.

Failure to Incorporate Net Working Capital Requirements

We assume that the soap company discovers that its allocation of overhead to the modernization plan is improper and rescinds the action. Net present value remains $26,785.60 and the project is acceptable. Now, however, it is realized that the company failed to include net working capital required to finance increases in current assets caused by the project. (Remember, the modernization plan permitted increases in output leading to higher levels of cash, receivables, and inventories.) We suppose that the net working capital requirement for the modernization plan is $300,000. The revised cash flows for the project are as follows.

Modernization Plan Cash Flows Revised to Include Net Working Capital Requirements

	$t = 0$	$t = 1$
Initial Outlay	−$1,300,000	
After-tax Operating Cash Flow		$1,150,000
Working Capital Release		300,000
Revised Cash Flow	−$1,300,000	$1,450,000

The initial outlay at $t = 0$ has been increased by $300,000 while the cash flow at $t = 1$ has also increased by the same amount to show the release of working capital. The effect of this modification on net present value is such that the project will be rejected.

$$NPV = \$1,450,000(0.89286) - \$1,300,000 = \$5,357.20 < 0$$

Failure to include net working capital requirements in project cash flows always biases the selection decision in favor of the project, because there can be no more **net working capital released** than is initially invested. Since the release of net working capital always follows the investment in net working capital, the time value of money must always make the present value of working capital released less than the initial investment of working capital. In the example at hand, the present value of working capital released at $t = 1$ is $300,000(0.89286) = $267,857.14. Since the net working capital invested at $t = 0$ is $300,000, the net present value of the net working capital cash flows alone is $267,857.14 − $300,000 = −$32,142.86. Because the cash flows of the net working capital investment and subsequent release always have a negative net present value, failure to include that requirement in project cash flows always overstates resulting calculations of NPV.

How serious the bias injected into evaluation of investment projects is when net working capital requirements are ignored depends on the situation. For many firms, the major portion of initial outlay on a project is for working capital—not land, buildings, and equipment. This is especially true for wholesalers and retailers. For other firms, the investment in net working capital is more modest. Regardless, no firm can afford to ignore this element of initial investment outlay.

Failure to Identify the Proper Project Time Horizon   As revised to include net working capital requirements, the soap company's modernization plan is not acceptable. However, one member of the company's project evaluation team now suggests that the project would have an operating life of 2 years rather than 1 year. His revised cash flows for a 2-year life are as follows.

Revised Modernization Plan for 2-Year Life

	t = 0	t = 1	t = 2
Initial Outlay	−$1,300,000		
After-tax Operating Cash Flow		$1,150,000	$350,000
Working Capital Release			300,000
Revised Cash Flow	−$1,300,000	$1,150,000	$650,000

The team member suggests that the modernized plant can be operated an additional year to generate $350,000 in after-tax operating cash flow. The release of $300,000 of working capital will be postponed 1 year if the life of the project is extended. At a cost of capital of $K = 12$ percent, the net present value of the project is now positive.

$$NPV = \$1,150,000(0.89286) + \$650,000(0.79719) - \$1,300,000$$

$$= \$244,962.50 > 0$$

The team member argues that the project should now be accepted.

The example above shows that if project life, or the **project time horizon,** is extended, the net present value of the project will increase as long as each additional year's cash flow is positive. This example also raises the problem of determining just what the proper time horizon for a project happens to be. What criteria control the proper discounting period to use?

A possible criterion for project time horizon is the maximum **physical life** of the assets contained in the project. A horizon constructed on this basis is very long indeed for many assets, since continued repair can keep many assets functioning nearly indefinitely if the costs of repair can be borne. The latter point is crucial in suggesting a more important criterion—the **economic life** of assets. Because technological advance causes assets to become obsolete and because repair and maintenance costs rise with age, the economic life of an asset is shorter than its physical life. For example, a firm producing some product may find it desirable to purchase new productive assets to replace old assets even though the old productive assets are not physically worn out. The economic life of the new assets will determine the project time horizon of cash flows. However, a project involving the production of an additional or new product will have an economic life based not on equipment used to produce the product but on the number of years the *product* will be produced. Products, like productive assets, become obsolete and have their own economic lives. Product life may equal, exceed, or be less than asset life. In either case, determination of the economic life of a project is a problem of optimization. As a definition, we may regard economic life as the time horizon maximizing the increase in shareholder wealth caused by the project. Finally, the concept of depreciable life of assets is sometimes used to define the time horizon for project cash flows. Depreciable life is the length of time over which an asset may be depreciated for tax purposes. Only by coincidence are depreciable and economic life the same thing (although for simplicity, examples in this chapter have made use of this coincidence).

In general, economic life is the proper concept to use in defining the project time horizon of cash flows. Physical life has relatively little meaning for defining time horizons, nor, except for computing depreciation charges and income taxes, does depreciable life. Yet, although economic life is significant for cash flow determination purposes, it is sometimes difficult to estimate with any precision. The consequences of this lack of precision are varied. Given the time value of money, it is evident that errors made in estimating the economic life of short-lived assets will be more costly than errors made with long-lived assets. For example, the extension of the life of the modernization plan for the soap company from 1 to 2 years made a substantial difference in net present value. This result occurs because additional years of cash flows in the near term are not discounted to a high degree. In contrast, an error made by treating a 26-year-life project as a 25-year-life project may be of little consequence because the twenty-sixth year's cash flow will be heavily discounted. Fortunately, short-lived assets, such as fleets of trucks or automobiles, often have project time horizons more easily estimated than horizons for long-lived assets.

The next chapter deals with the problem of estimating economic life to determine the time horizon of project cash flows. It is enough to point out now that the time horizon for project cash flows is an economic issue and is not defined in terms of either the physical or the depreciable life of assets.

SUMMARY   Cash flows for investment projects must adhere to the incremental after-tax cash flow concept. Incremental cash flows are the cash flows occurring *because* an investment project is undertaken. Adjustment of incremental cash flows for incremental income taxes caused by the project completes the specification of incremental after-tax cash flows.

Both cost-saving and revenue-expanding projects are best envisioned in terms of three categories of incremental after-tax cash flows: initial investment outlays, after-tax operating cash flows, and terminal cash flows. Initial investment outlays are all incremental cash outflows required to acquire, construct, or otherwise prepare project assets for operational use. After-tax operating cash flows stem from operating the project and are generated either by cost savings or by expanded revenue through the production and sale of additional output. Terminal cash flows, either inflows or outflows, occur at or after the point in time when the project is terminated and ceases to operate. Terminal cash flow is positive when assets can be disposed of for some incremental salvage value at the end of their lives. However, terminal cash flows may be negative if the firm must expend funds to dispose of the assets.

Although both cost-saving and revenue-expanding projects are viewed in terms of incremental after-tax cash flows, their respective cash flow construction processes differ somewhat. For cost-saving projects, incremental cash flows are found by comparing cash flows associated with acquiring, operating, and finally disposing of a new machine or technology with the cash flows given up by immediate disposal of an existing machine or technology. Differences between these alternative cash flow streams are, when adjusted for income taxes, the incremental after-tax cash flows occurring if the new machine or technology is acquired *and* the old machine or technology disposed of by the firm. Revenue-expanding investments are approached more directly, since, by definition, the cash outflows for initial outlay and subsequent after-tax operating cash inflows from the sale of expanded output will not occur unless the project is undertaken.

Some cautions are in order when cash flows for projects are being constructed. If project cash flows are not properly determined, then undesirable projects may be accepted and desirable projects rejected. Among the important cautions to be observed, it is desirable that the timing of cash flows be considered independently from the timing of associated revenues and expenses used in the accrual method of accounting to determine net income. Timing of cash flows and revenue and expense may often be close enough to use revenue and expense timing to determine cash flow timing; however, significant differences may exist. In such cases, the timing of cash flow, rather than revenue and expense, is controlling. It is also necessary to avoid confusing depreciation under accrual accounting with cash inflows. Depreciation is not a cash inflow. If cash inflow from operations does not exist, depreciation charges cannot create cash inflows.

Of additional importance in constructing cash flows is the caution against omitting favorable investment alternatives. If all alternatives being evaluated are relatively inferior to an omitted alternative, it is small satisfaction to successfully choose the best of a bad lot. Nor should we improperly include nonincremental cash expenditures or noncash sunk costs in project cash flows. These items are not incremental and will erroneously depress the net present value of projects. However, failure to include net working capital requirements in project cash flows will make projects look too desirable. For net working capital cash flows, though necessary, will always reduce the net present value of any proposal because of the time value of money. Such cash flows cannot be ignored. Finally, it is important to specify the appropriate time horizon over which the project will be operated. The appropriate concept in specifying project time horizon is the economic life of the project. For cost-saving projects, the economic life of the productive assets defines project time horizons. Revenue-expanding projects have their time horizons defined by the productive life span of the products being produced. The physical and depreciable lives of assets are not proper concepts for determining their time horizons.

GLOSSARY OF KEY TERMS

Depreciable Life
The allowable life over which an asset may be depreciated for tax purposes.

Depreciable Outlay
That portion of the total outlay for a project that is depreciated over the depreciable life of the project.

Depreciation Tax Subsidy
The income tax saving produced by the deductibility of allowed depreciation. It is computed as the product of the tax rate and the year's depreciation.

Economic Life
The economically optimal life of an investment project.

Incremental After-Tax Cash Flow
All changes in the firm's after-tax cash flows caused by the undertaking of a project composed of initial outlays, operating cash flows, and terminal cash flows.

Incremental After-Tax Operating Cash Flow
Cash flow generated by operating a project—either through cost savings or expanded revenue, excluding initial and terminal flows.

Initial Investment Outlay
The incremental after-tax cash flow required to acquire, construct, and prepare project assets for operations.

Net Working Capital Released
The cash inflows resulting from net working capital requirements freed up by the termination of the project.

Net Working Capital Requirement
The cash outflow required to finance the portion of desired increases in current assets caused by the project and not financed by current liabilities.

Physical Life	The life of assets as determined by the point where assets are worn out and cannot be repaired.
Project Time Horizon	The life of a project as determined by economic life.
Salvage Value	The market value of assets at the end of their economic life.
Sunk Cost	Past expenditures not affecting current decisions to undertake projects.
Terminal Cash Flows	Incremental cash inflows or outflows associated with the termination of a project.
Total Outlay	Total cash outlays, consisting of depreciable outlays, net working capital requirements, and cash outlays expensed for tax purposes, necessary to acquire new assets.

See Chapter 12. **SELECTED REFERENCES**

QUESTIONS

1. A university is evaluating a project to establish a graduate school of business administration. The university administration expects that the enrollment at the graduate school would be 10 percent of total university enrollment and thus assigns 10 percent of central administrative salaries and expenses to the cash flows of the project. Evaluate this decision.

2. Differentiate between the initial investment outlay and the total outlay for a cost-saving project to replace an old drill press with a new one. Is such a distinction necessary for a revenue-expanding project to produce more machined parts?

3. If depreciation is not a cash flow, why does the computation of after-tax operating cash flow frequently involve the use of depreciation charges?

4. Explain why the omission of cash flows associated with net working capital increases makes investment projects look too desirable.

5. Using the concept of economic life, explain why a wise investor probably chooses not to drive a 1968 automobile.

6. A firm spends $1 million on research and development as part of a project to produce and sell transport aircraft. The project has a 10-

year time horizon and the research and development expenditures occur at $t = 0$. The firm's accountants plan to charge off the research and development expenditures at a rate of $100,000 per year. Comment from the standpoint of cash flow determination for future investment projects.

PROBLEMS 1. Management of Hanawa Company, a food processor, is trying to decide whether it should replace an old air-conditioning system with a new one that will cost $300,000 plus a $15,000 installation charge. The old system is worthless and is fully depreciated. Retention of the old system over the next 15 years would result in $150,000 annual food spoilage expenses and labor turnover costs of $30,000 annually. The new system would produce only $90,000 of annual spoilage expenses, and labor turnover costs would be $10,000. The old system uses $50,000 of electricity per year and the new system, because of greater cooling coverage of the plant, would use $65,000 of electricity per year. The new system would have no salvage value at the end of its 15-year economic life. Use straight line depreciation over 10 years and assume that the firm's cost of capital is 10 percent. The tax rate is $\tau = 40$ percent. Should Hanawa purchase the new system?

2. The Johnson Corporation is trying to decide whether it should replace a manually operated machine with a fully automatic version of the same machine. The existing machine, purchased 10 years ago, originally cost $600,000. It is being depreciated over 20 years on a straight line basis. It has a current market value of $20,000 but will have no salvage value in 10 years. The proposed machine would cost $520,000 (including freight and installation). It is expected to have a 10-year life and a salvage value of $20,000 at the end of its life. This machine would require general servicing at the end of the fifth year. Estimated costs of servicing are $100,000—all of which must be expensed. Sales are not expected to increase as a result of using the new machine. However, annual operating costs are expected to be $75,000 lower over each of the next 10 years. Johnson has a current tax rate of 40 percent and will continue to use straight line depreciation. Its cost of capital is 12 percent. Should Johnson purchase the automatic machine?

3. Big Fir Company wishes to fence its log pond. Given the growth of Mineral City, the town in which Big Fir is situated, the firm will be

forced to move its plant in 10 years, hence will not need the fence past that time. A heavy chain-link fence would cost $10,000 now, but would require no upkeep. Snowfencing would cost only $4000 now, but annual costs (which would be expensed) of $1000 for each of the next 10 years would be incurred to keep the fence in repair. One alternative would do the job as well as the other. The cost of capital is 10 percent, the initial outlay of both alternatives would be depreciated to zero in 10 years, and the firm faces a 45 percent tax rate. Which alternative should it choose?

4. John Chinworth, inventor of the Chinworth orthopedic chair, is contemplating expansion of his product into a new territory. The sales manager has informed him that he can expect to capture 20 percent of the market in each of the first 2 years, expand to 30 percent of the market in the third year, and peak at 40 percent thereafter. The total market for the region is expected to be stable at 100,000 units, and Chinworth expects operating profits of $10 per unit before additional distribution costs, which are estimated to be $14,000 per year. The expansion of the current production facilities will cost $450,000, of which $50,000 represents an increase in net working capital. The facilities have an expected life of 8 years. Chinworth Chairs, Inc., is in the 50 percent tax bracket and has a current cost of capital of 8 percent. What is the net present value of the proposed expansion if straight line (no salvage value) depreciation is used?

5. Marmot Processing Company catches and processes wild marmots to produce pet food and hides for fur coats. It is considering the building of a new plant in unexploited marmot territory. The plant will require 2 years to build. Depreciable outlays are $300,000 at $t = 0$ and $700,000 at $t = 1$. Net working capital requirements are $100,000 at the end of the second year. Marmots are caught by using beaters and netters and, in the second year of construction, $50,000 must be spent to train new personnel for these tasks. In each year it is expected that the plant will process 3 million marmots. Each marmot hide sells for $0.10, and the value of the pet food per marmot is $0.05. Operating labor and materials will cost $300,000 per year. The plant will have no salvage value and will be depreciated over a 10-year life on a straight line basis. All operations would halt at $t = 11$ to comply with anticipated environmental regulations. The cost of capital is $K = 8$ percent and the company's tax rate is $r = 40$ percent. Should Marmot Processing build the plant? (*Note:* Depreciation does not start until $t = 2$, when revenues begin.)

6. Rubenstein Pulp and Paper Company owns a paper mill in Dennis City. The plant is fully depreciated but could be sold for $2 million after taxes. If held and operated for 10 more years, the plant could also be sold at that time for $2 million after taxes. Annual sales revenue for the plant is $500,000, and annual labor and material expense is $100,000. The firm's tax rate is $r = 40$ percent. The Dennis City Council has just passed a law to reduce pollution, requiring firms like Rubenstein to install pollution-reduction equipment. This equipment will not expand output, will cost $500,000, and will be depreciated for tax purposes over 10 years by the straight line method. Failure to purchase the equipment will result in the assessment of an annual fine of $50,000. The fine is not tax deductible. The firm's cost of capital is 10 percent. Considering the alternatives, what should the firm do?

7. The Seufert Fuel Company owns two chain saws, which were purchased a year ago at $225 each. A third saw is being rented at $5 per month. The Loring Sales and Service Company suggested that Seufert sell the two saws it owns to Loring for a total of $270 and rent two more saws (i.e., two in addition to the one already rented) at $5 each per month. Loring buys saws wholesale and services all rented saws and thus will assume responsibility for Seufert's service and repair costs. Seufert was depreciating the old saws over 5 years (straight line) at $40 a year each and estimated a salvage value of $25 at the end of 5 years for each saw. Seufert's annual costs of owning and maintaining each old saw are estimated at $30 per year repair, $40 per year depreciation, and $10 per year maintenance. What would you recommend to Seufert if its tax rate is 20 percent and its cost of capital is 10 percent? Do you recommend that Seufert continue to own the two saws, or rent them?

8. Five years ago the Vangelos Nursery installed a furnace for $9600. A salesman for the O'Brien Heating Company recently recommended that the furnace be replaced with a new heat pump. The O'Brien salesman estimated an annual saving in fuel cost of $2000 with no other differences in cost or service. The cost of the heat pump is $12,000, installed, but $2000 is allowed on the trade-in of the old furnace. The old furnace has a book value of $6400 and was being depreciated on a straight line basis at the rate of $640 per year over its expected 15-year depreciable life. It could operate another 10 years. The heat pump would be depreciated over a 10-year economic life and its salvage value is expected to be $2000. The effective corporate income tax rate is 30 percent, and the Van-

gelos Nursery has a 12 percent annual cost of capital. What should Vangelos do?

APPENDIX 8A

The speed with which a firm can depreciate assets is constrained by the Internal Revenue Service. In general, taxpayers have had less latitude in selecting a depreciation method since the passage of the 1981 Tax Reform Act, which states that:

"For most tangible depreciable property placed in service after 1980, capital costs must be recovered using the Accelerated Cost Recovery System (ACRS), which applies accelerated methods of cost recovery over statuatory periods."[1]

Those statutory periods are 3, 5, 10, and 15 years. Following is an example of the 5-year ACRS.

THE IMPACT OF DEPRE- CIATION METHODS ON PRESENT VALUE

ACRS Percentages by Year Placed in Service

	Property Placed in Service in:		
	1981–1984	1985	1986 and Thereafter
Year 1	15	18	20
Year 2	22	33	32
Year 3	21	25	24
Year 4	21	16	16
Year 5	21	8	8

The numbers tabulated reflect the percentage of cost that can be written off in any one year. For instance, to find depreciation in the second year for machinery costing $10,000 and placed into service in 1983, we multiply the proportion of depreciation allowed in year 2—namely, 0.22—by $10,000. That procedure yields depreciation of 0.22 × $10,000 = $2200.

---

[1]*1982 U.S. Master Tax Guide* (Chicago, Ill.: Commerce Clearing House, Inc.), paragraph 1165.

Two aspects of the 5-year ACRS are worth noting. First, in comparison to the 1981–1984 pe:iod, the rate of depreciation accelerates for assets placed in service in 1985, then accelerates further for assets placed in service in 1986 and beyond. Second, since the percentages add to 100, salvage value is ignored in calculating depreciation using this method.

Since straight line depreciation may also be elected under most circumstances, the purposes of this brief note are to show how the ACRS affects present value and to identify the conditions under which shareholders will benefit when management chooses ACRS rather than straight line depreciation. The central point of this comparison is that *even though the total amount of depreciation over the life of the asset is the same regardless of which method is chosen, some methods create larger depreciation tax subsidies earlier and as a result create larger net present values for assets.*

Assume that an investment requires an outlay of $15,000 and that this total amount is depreciated over a 5-year period. The corporate tax rate is 40 percent, and a 10 percent discount rate is used to evaluate the investment. Yearly depreciation amounts, depreciation tax subsidies, and present values for straight line depreciation and ACRS are shown in Table 8A-1. ACRS depreciation is shown for property put in service both during the 1981–1984 period and in 1985. The total amount depreciated is the same in all cases, as is the total amount of the depreciation subsidy. Neither of these totals reflects the time value of money, assumed here to be 10 percent per year.

When payments are adjusted for the time value of money, the present value of straight line depreciation is $4550, whereas the present value of ACRS for property put into service from 1981 to 1984 is $4499

Table 8A–1   *Impact of Depreciation Method on Present Value*

| | Method of Depreciation | | | | | | | | |
| | Straight Line | | | ACRS 1981–1984 | | | ACRS 1985 | | |
Year	Depreciation	Tax Subsidy	Present Value	Depreciation	Tax Subsidy	Present Value	Depreciation	Tax Subsidy	Present Value
1	$ 3,000	$1200	$1091	$ 2,250	$ 900	$ 818	$ 2,700	$1080	$ 982
2	3,000	1200	992	3,300	1320	1091	4,950	1980	1636
3	3,000	1200	902	3,150	1260	947	3,750	1500	1127
4	3,000	1200	820	3,150	1260	861	2,400	960	656
5	3,000	1200	745	3,150	1260	782	1,200	480	298
	$15,000	$6000	$4550	$15,000	$6000	$4499	$15,000	$6000	$4699

and the present value for property put into service in 1985 is $4699. These results are very interesting in that they indicate that until 1985 the ACRS is not really accelerated relative to straight line. That conclusion presumes that property that qualifies for 5-year ACRS will also qualify for 5-year straight line depreciation. Thus, it appears that management with sufficient earnings to obtain the depreciation tax subsidy would prefer the straight line method to the ACRS method for property put into service during 1981–1984. After 1984, the ACRS method will yield a faster writeoff and higher present values.

Higher discount rates, with their associated smaller weights attaching to future dollars, would increase the difference in the discounted depreciation tax subsidies; smaller rates would reduce it. Regardless of the magnitude of the required rate of return, firms selecting methods that allow faster depreciation will benefit shareholders only as long as earnings are sufficiently large to permit the firm to qualify for the tax subsidy.

APPENDIX 8B

THE INVESTMENT TAX CREDIT

From time to time federal tax law has permitted firms investing in assets to avail themselves of an investment tax credit. This credit can be deducted against income taxes (not taxable income!). The credit reduces the effective purchase price of assets and makes their acquisition more desirable. The allowable credit is expressed as a percentage of asset purchase price. Periodic changes in tax law have altered the allowable percentage, which also varies with the class of assets and their life. Under the Tax Reform Act of 1981, the allowable credit is 10 percent. Whether the total amount of the credit may be taken in the first year depends on the size of the firm's tax liability.

The favorable effect of the investment tax credit on incentives to purchase depreciable assets can be demonstrated by the following example. A company considers the purchase of a depreciable asset having a 10-year depreciable and economic life. The depreciable, and initial, outlay is $C_0 = \$65,000$. Annual after-tax operating cash flows are $C = \$10,000$ and the asset will have no salvage value or other terminal cash flows. At the firm's cost of capital of $K = 10$ percent, the net present value of the asset is negative.

$$NPV = \sum_{t=1}^{10} \frac{\$10,000}{(1 + 0.10)^t} - \$65,000$$

$$= \$10,000(6.1446) - \$65,000$$

$$= -\$3554 < 0$$

The firm would choose not to acquire the asset, but the existence of a 10 percent investment tax credit would allow it to reduce its income taxes at $t = 0$ by $0.10(\$65,000) = \$6500$. The after-tax initial outlay is thus reduced from \$65,000 to \$58,500. Recomputing the NPV of the asset yields a positive NPV.

$$NPV = \$10,000(6.1446) - \$58,500$$

$$= \$61,446 - \$58,500$$

$$= \$2946$$

The asset should now be purchased.

It is important to emphasize that tax credits make investment more desirable only if the firm has a sufficient taxable income and prospective tax bill to make use of them. Firms with substantial losses and a zero tax bill will be unable to use the tax credits to enhance the desirability of acquiring assets. (However, see Chapter 17 for a discussion of tax credit leases, under which such firms can acquire assets and sell tax benefits to other firms.)

C H A P T E R   9

Unequal and Economic Life Investment Problems

Given properly determined incremental after-tax cash flows and discount rates, the net present value method should produce correct accept/reject decisions. However, there remains one kind of project selection problem in which a misapplication of the NPV method to mutually exclusive investment proposals contained in a project *may* produce faulty decisions. This difficulty, the *unequal lives* problem, is the first of two major topics discussed in this chapter. The second topic is the determination of the *economic*, or optimal, life of a project. Chapter 8 first raised the issue, and it is dealt with more thoroughly here. Heretofore, the time horizon of project cash flows has been a given. Now, we need to find out why a project's cash flows extend, say, 5 years, not 4 or 6 years. Both the unequal lives and economic life problems use the *uniform annual equivalent* (UAE) calculation introduced in Chapter 5.

Mutually exclusive investment proposals may have different economic lives. The decision problem faced by the Victor Fabricating Company represents just such a situation. The firm is attempting to choose between two different types of plastic molding equipment systems. The first system, manufactured by Wolf Brothers, is a semiautomatic system. The second system is sold by the Pylon Company and is fully automatic. Cash flows for the two systems appear in Table 9-1A. The semiautomatic Wolf system requires a total outlay at $t = 0$ of \$180,000 and has an

THE PROBLEM OF UNEQUAL LIVES

Table 9–1A *Cash Flows for Wolf and Pylon Systems: Victor Fabricating Company*

Item	Time	Before Tax	After Tax	Annual Cash Flow
		The Wolf System		
Total Outlay	0	−$180,000	−$180,000	
Labor Cost	1–3	− 100,000	− 60,000	−$60,000
Depreciation Tax Subsidy	1–3	60,000	24,000	24,000
				−$36,000
		The Pylon System		
Total Outlay	0	−$400,000	−$400,000	
Labor Cost	1–5	− 8,000	− 4,800	−$ 4,800
Depreciation Tax Subsidy	1–5	80,000	32,000	32,000
				$27,200

expected economic life of 3 years. Annual labor costs are $100,000, but at the firm's 40 percent tax rate they are $(1 − 0.40)\$100,000 = \$60,000$ after taxes. Using the straight line depreciation method over a 3-year life, annual depreciation charges of $60,000 result in an annual depreciation tax subsidy of $(0.40)\$60,000 = \$24,000$. The annual *after-tax* operating cash outflow is only $36,000, since the depreciation tax subsidy partially offsets after-tax labor costs. A much larger outlay of $400,000 is required to purchase the fully automatic Pylon system. This system's expected economic life is 5 years, and annual labor costs are only $8000 before taxes and $(1 − 0.40)\$8000 = \$4800$ after taxes. The annual depreciation tax subsidy is $32,000, as determined by an $80,000 annual depreciation charge based on the straight line method over a 5-year economic life and a 40 percent tax rate. The annual after-tax operating cash flow is an inflow of $27,200, because the $32,000 depreciation tax subsidy outweighs the after-tax labor cost of $4800.

The apparent tradeoff between the two systems is expressed in the following way. Is it better to purchase the Wolf system for the relatively small outlay of $180,000, but pay higher operating costs over its short life of 3 years? Or is it better to pay $400,000 for the Pylon system and enjoy lower operating costs and a more favorable depreciation tax subsidy over the longer 5-year life of this system? To answer these questions, we first perform an *incorrect* analysis by applying the NPV method to the cash flows of these unequal-lived but mutually exclusive proposals. Subsequently, more correct methods are introduced and utilized to solve the decision problem.

Table 9–1B   *Differential Cash Flows: Victor Fabricating Company*

	$t = 0$	$t = 1$	$t = 2$	$t = 3$	$t = 4$	$t = 5$
Pylon System	−$400,000	$27,200	$27,200	$27,200	$27,200	$27,200
Wolf System	− 180,000	− 36,000	− 36,000	− 36,000	—	—
Differential Cash Flow	−$220,000	$63,200	$63,200	$63,200	$27,200	$27,200

As an initial solution to the decision problem, we specify the differential cash flows between the competing proposals and find the NPV of these differential flows.[1] The cost of capital deemed appropriate for the risk of these proposals is $K = 10$ percent. The differential cash flows are specified in Table 9-1B from the information given in Table 9-1A.

If the higher outlay Pylon system is purchased, an extra $220,000 of outlay is required for which differential cash inflows representing lower operating costs and a higher depreciation tax subsidy for the Pylon system are received (all Wolf system cash flows are subtracted from those of the larger outlay Pylon system). Taking the net present value of these differential cash flows requires the following computation.

$$\text{NPV} = \$63,200(2.4868) + \$27,200(0.68301) + \$27,200(0.62092) -$$
$$\$220,000 = - \$27,367 < 0$$

Clearly, the negative net present value indicates that it is not worthwhile to spend the extra $220,000 on the Pylon system and that the Wolf system should be purchased.

But is it so clear? We have, in a sense, been comparing apples and oranges. The Wolf system lasts only 3 years, whereas the admittedly more expensive (initially) Pylon system lasts 5 years. The lives of these two systems are unequal and we must somehow find a way to equalize them to permit valid comparisons between the systems. Our failure to equalize lives may seriously bias the decision concerning the Wolf and Pylon systems.

The problem of unequal lives, assumed away in earlier chapters, is not uncommon. The economic lives of competing assets to produce the

Comparisons of Unequal-Lived Investment Proposals

---

[1]Because neither alternative is being compared to existing equipment, differences in cash flows between these alternatives are *differential* cash flows as defined in Chapter 7. Incremental cash flows would be determined by comparing each system to cash flows associated with an existing system. Nevertheless, evaluation of differential cash flows is perfectly valid as long as our only concern is to find the lower cost system.

same output are likely to differ in many cases. A firm must often choose between assets that must be replaced frequently and those that are replaced less frequently. Proper procedure to equalize the lives of proposals requires that the replacement cycle for each proposal and a common life for both (or all) proposals be defined before the proposals are evaluated.

Replacement Cycles and a Common Life

The economic life of an investment proposal identifies the **replacement cycle** for that proposal. The replacement cycle concept assumes that the assets required by the proposal will be replaced at the end of their economic life (and repetitively so) with identical assets over the common life of the proposals. The **common life** of a proposal, in turn, has an upper limit described by the economic life of the overall project to produce, in the case of Victor Fabricating, molded plastic assemblies. We assume that the economic life of the project to produce plastic assemblies is 30 years. Thus, we can view the replacement cycles of the Wolf and Pylon systems over a time interval of *up to* 30 years. Within that 30-year period, the Wolf system will be replaced every 3 years, since that time interval describes the economic life and replacement cycle for the Wolf system. The Pylon system will be replaced every 5 years over the 30-year period because it has a 5-year economic life.

Although the upper limit on the common life of the two proposals is defined by the economic life of the project of which they are a part, it is often possible to find a shorter common life over which to compare proposals. In general, if the economic life of the longer lived proposal can be divided by the life of the shorter lived proposal to yield a whole number, the common life of both proposals is the life of the longer lived proposal. Thus, two proposals, having lives of 2 and 6 years, respectively, have a common life of 6 years, since $6 \div 2 = 3$, which is a whole number. Alternatively, the common life of the proposals may be found by multiplying the economic lives of the two proposals. Thus, proposals having economic lives of 4 and 6 years have a common life of $4 \times 6 = 24$ years. Sometimes, further simplification is possible at this point if the economic lives of each proposal and the resulting common life are all divisible by the same whole number and yield, respectively, whole numbers. Thus, 4, 6, and 24 years are all divisible by 2 and yield whole numbers of 2, 3, and 12 years. In such a case, 12 years is the shortest common life of the proposals.

The shortest common life for the Wolf and Pylon system is 15 years, that is, the product of the 3-year and 5-year economic life of each system. (The number 5 does not yield a whole number when it is divided by 3. The product $5 \times 3 = 15$ cannot be simplified by dividing each term by a whole number to yield whole numbers.) This means that we compare an initial purchase at $t = 0$ of the Wolf system, plus *four* successive replacements, with an initial purchase of the Pylon system plus *two* subsequent replacements.

One way of equalizing lives is to lay out all the cash flows for several replacement cycles over the common life of the proposal. Table 9-2 shows this procedure for the Wolf and Pylon systems. Using the cash flow information given earlier in Table 9-1A, the initial outlay of $180,000 at $t = 0$ is shown for the Wolf system. After-tax operating cash outflows of $36,000 are indicated at $t = 1$ and $t = 2$. At $t = 3$, the $216,000 outlay consists of the after-tax operating cash outflows of $36,000 plus a $180,000 outlay to replace the Wolf system at $t = 3$. From $t = 3$ onward, a cash flow pattern repeating in 3-year replacement cycles exists as equip-

Equalizing Lives by Specifying Cash Flows Over the Common Life

Table 9–2   *Specification of Cash Flows Over a Common Life: Victor Fabricating Company*

Years	Wolf System	Pylon System	Differential Cash Flows	PV Factor	Present Value
$t = 0$	$-$180,000	$-$400,000	$-$220,000		$-$220,000
$t = 1$	$-$ 36,000	$+$ 27,200	$+$ 63,200	0.90909	$+$ 57,454
$t = 2$	$-$ 36,000	$+$ 27,200	$+$ 63,200	0.82645	$+$ 52,232
$t = 3$	$-$ 216,000	$+$ 27,200	$+$ 243,200	0.75131	$+$ 182,719
$t = 4$	$-$ 36,000	$+$ 27,200	$+$ 63,200	0.68301	$+$ 43,166
$t = 5$	$-$ 36,000	$-$ 372,800	$-$ 336,800	0.62092	$-$ 209,126
$t = 6$	$-$ 216,000	$+$ 27,200	$+$ 243,200	0.56447	$+$ 137,279
$t = 7$	$-$ 36,000	$+$ 27,200	$+$ 63,200	0.51316	$+$ 32,432
$t = 8$	$-$ 36,000	$+$ 27,200	$+$ 63,200	0.46651	$+$ 29,483
$t = 9$	$-$ 216,000	$+$ 27,200	$+$ 243,200	0.42410	$+$ 103,141
$t = 10$	$-$ 36,000	$-$ 372,800	$-$ 336,800	0.38554	$-$ 129,850
$t = 11$	$-$ 36,000	$+$ 27,200	$+$ 63,200	0.35049	$+$ 22,151
$t = 12$	$-$ 216,000	$+$ 27,200	$+$ 243,200	0.31863	$+$ 77,491
$t = 13$	$-$ 36,000	$+$ 27,200	$+$ 63,200	0.28966	$+$ 18,307
$t = 14$	$-$ 36,000	$+$ 27,200	$+$ 63,200	0.26333	$+$ 16,642
$t = 15$	$-$ 36,000	$+$ 27,200	$+$ 63,200	0.23939	$+$ 15,129
				NPV =	$+$228,650

ment is replaced at $t = 3$, $t = 6$, $t = 9$, and $t = 12$. The last year, $t = 15$, has no outlay for replacement because the end of the 15-year common life has been reached. (It is possible, but unnecessary, to extend the repetitive cash flows through to the 30-year economic life of the project.) Similarly, the Pylon proposal requires an initial outlay of $400,000 at $t = 0$ followed by after-tax operating cash inflows of $27,200 at $t = 1$, $t = 2$, $t = 3$, and $t = 4$. At $t = 5$, the $27,200 operating cash inflow is more than offset by the $400,000 outlay to replace the original Pylon system—the net cash outlay being $372,800 at $t = 5$. From $t = 5$ onward, the cash flows repeat in 5-year replacement cycles as the Pylon system is replaced at $t = 5$ and $t = 10$. At $t = 15$, the end of the common life, no outlay for replacement is required.

By specifying the cash flows for the Wolf and Pylon systems for a 15-year common life, we assumed that the respective systems will be replaced with identical systems requiring the same outlays and producing the same operating costs. This assumption is discussed critically later. Under this assumption, we can evaluate the two proposals by the NPV method. The differential cash flows obtained by subtracting the Wolf system cash flows from those of the larger outlay Pylon system are shown over the 15-year common life in Table 9-2. These differential cash flows show the results of expending $220,000 *more* on the larger scale Pylon proposal in exchange for the ensuing pattern of differential cash inflows and outflows. At $K = 10$ percent, the NPV of the differential cash flows is $228,650.

Clearly, application of the NPV method to the differential cash flows of the Wolf and Pylon proposals over a 15-year common life results in the selection of the larger outlay Pylon system; the NPV of the differential flows is positive. This decision contrasts with the earlier, and erroneous, conclusion reached when the cash flows for unequal lives from Table 9-1B were used in applying the NPV method. There, the smaller outlay Wolf system was selected. Failure to use cash flows equalized over a common life yielded an incorrect decision. In effect, the cash outflows for the shorter lived Wolf system occurring at and after $t = 3$ were ignored. (Implicitly, in Table 9-1B, they were given a value of zero.) Since these outflows were ignored, the Wolf system tended to appear more favorable than it really was. Proper equalization of lives of proposals permits a valid comparison of the two proposals by the NPV method.

Equalizing Lives by the Use of Uniform Annual Equivalents   It is frequently much easier to use uniform annual equivalents to equalize lives of investment proposals than it is to specify cash flows over a common life. The procedure is relatively simple: the cash flows for each investment proposal are converted to a **uniform annual equivalent cash**

flow for the proposal using the separate *economic* life of each proposal. That is, we derive annualized cash flows over the economic life of a proposal. Then, the uniform annual equivalent cash flows of each proposal may be compared directly to make selections between proposals.

Dealing first with the mechanics of computing uniform annual equivalent (UAE) cash flows, we refer again to Table 9-1A for Victor Fabricating Company. We want to find the UAE cash flow for both the Wolf and the Pylon systems. The after-tax operating cash flows for the Wolf system happen to be of the annuity form since, over 3 years, they are constant cash *outflows* of $36,000 annually.[2] Consequently, those flows are *already* in UAE form. All that remains is to convert the initial outlay of $180,000 to a UAE flow over the proposal's 3-year economic life. Using the annuity factor for $K = 10$ percent and 3 years from Appendix Table D, the UAE (recall, from Chapter 5, how UAEs are calculated) for the outlay is:

$$UAE = \frac{-\$180,000}{2.4868} = -\$72,382$$

Table 9-3 summarizes the UAE cash flows for the Wolf system over its three-year life. The total UAE for all cash flows of the Wolf system is −$108,382.

The UAE flows for the Pylon system are also readily obtained. The constant annual after-tax operating cash inflow of $27,200 is already in UAE form. The $400,000 outlay for the Pylon system is converted to a UAE cash flow over the 5-year economic life of the system for $K = 10$ percent.

$$UAE = \frac{-\$400,000}{3.7908} = -\$105,519$$

The UAE cash flows for the Pylon system are also summarized in Table 9-3. The total UAE for all cash flows of the Pylon system is − $78,319.

Once the UAE cash flow for each system has been determined, the proposals can be immediately compared on the basis of their respective UAE cash flows. This comparison can be made even though no explicit equalization of proposal cash flows has been carried out over the 15-year common life. No such cash flow specification is necessary because the UAE cash flows for each proposal are the *same* for every replacement cycle. For example, the Wolf system will require a UAE cash outflow of $108,382 each year over its 3-year life. If the system is replaced at $t = 3$,

---

[2]If the after-tax operating cash flows were not constant over time, each future flow would have to be separately discounted using present value factors from Appendix Table C. Then, the sum of those discounted flows would be converted to a UAE flow using Appendix Table D.

Table 9–3   *Uniform Annual Equvalent Cash Flows: Victor Fabricating Company*

	$t = 1$	$t = 2$	$t = 3$	$t = 4$	$t = 5$
Wolf System					
UAE—After-tax Operating Cash Flow	−$ 36,000	−$ 36,000	−$ 36,000	—	—
UAE—Initial Outlay	− 72,382	− 72,382	− 72,382	—	—
(1) Total UAE	−$108,382	−$108,382	−$108,382		
Pylon System					
UAE—After-tax Operating Cash Flow	+$ 27,200	+$ 27,200	+$ 27,200	+$ 27,200	+$ 27,200
UAE—Initial Outlay	− 105,519	− 105,519	− 105,519	− 105,519	− 105,519
(2) Total UAE	−$ 78,319	−$ 78,319	−$ 78,319	−$ 78,319	−$ 78,319

the UAE cash outflow for periods $t = 4$, $t = 5$, and $t = 6$ is also $108,382. In fact, for either the 15-year common life used earlier to compare the two proposals or the 30-year upper limit on that common life, the UAE cash outflow of the Wolf system is − $108,382. For the same reason, we may regard the UAE cash outflow for the Pylon system as $78,319 per year over the 5-year economic life of that system, the 15-year common life, and up to the 30-year upper limit on the common life of both proposals.

Comparing the UAE cash flows for the two proposals, we can find the differential UAE cash flow for the Pylon system from the following relationship.

$$\text{Differential UAE} = \text{Pylon system UAE} - \text{Wolf system UAE}$$

$$= -\$78,319 - (-\$108,382)$$

$$= +\$30,063$$

The differential UAE is positive—indicating that the differential cash inflows, on a UAE basis, are positive. The Pylon system should be selected and the Wolf system rejected. This is the same decision as reached in Table 9-2, where the cash flows for each proposal were specified over a 15-year common life. In fact, the differential UAE of $30,063 calculated above is nothing more than the 15-year UAE of the NPV calculated in Table 9-2. To see this, we use the annuity factor for 15 years and $K = 10$ percent from Appendix Table D to find the present value of the $30,063 UAE cash flow.

$$\text{PV(UAE)} = \$30,063(7.6061) = \$228,662$$

Except for a small difference due to rounding error, the $228,662 is identical with the NPV of the differential cash flows of the Pylon system computed over a 15-year common life in Table 9-2.

The UAE approach to equalizing lives of investment proposals operates under the same assumptions as the other procedure of specifically equalizing cash flows over a common life as in Table 9-2. Frequently, the UAE approach is more advantageous in that fewer computations are required to make the comparison. It is especially advantageous when the economic lives of competing proposals are long. However, either specific equalization of cash flows or the UAE approach may be used to compare proposals with unequal lives.

Unfortunately, not all unequal-lived mutually exclusive proposals can be evaluated by the UAE method because the assumptions required do not apply—namely, the use of the same equipment with the same cash inflows and outflows over the assumed common life. For example, technological change may provide future opportunities to purchase superior plastic molding systems. Moreover, future inflation makes outlays and operating cash flows, constructed in *present* dollars, outdated if future replacement of an existing system is' assumed.

Problems with the Uniform Annual Equivalent Analysis

Dealing with the problem of technological change first, let us suppose that in 8 years, vastly superior plastic molding technology will be available to Victor Fabricating. This means that 8 rather than 15 years is the *imposed* common life. (This shortened common life also would be produced if plastic molding were expected to become so unprofitable that the firm would cease to produce such molding after 8 years.) Under these circumstances, the following four modified investment alternatives are possible over the next eight years.

1. Wolf semiautomatic for 8 years. The second replacement would be used for only 2 years of its 3-year life.

2. Wolf semiautomatic for the first 3 years and the Pylon automatic for the remaining 5 years.

3. Pylon automatic for the first 5 years and the Wolf semiautomatic for the remaining 3 years.

4. Pylon automatic for 8 years. The replacement at the end of the first 5 years could be used for only 60 percent of its useful life.[3]

---

[3]We must be a bit careful here because the economic life of any investment is dependent to some extent on replacement technology. It may be more economical to extend the life of the original automatic machine to 8 years through frequent repairs and careful maintenance than to use a replacement machine for only 3 years. Similarly, the life of a semiautomatic machine could be extended for 1 year so that two could last over 8 years. Management should always look for the cheapest combination and the possibility of additional repairs, given the imposed 8 year horizon, would also have to be investigated. We ignore this possibility in our examples.

If we accept a time horizon of 8 years, the choice among the mutually exclusive alternatives must be based on minimum discounted cash outflow over 8 years. Additional information about the scrap value of the assets when retired short of their economic lives would be required for proper comparison, but the criterion of choice is not affected by the inclusion of these flows. Although it is possible to compare these modified alternatives on the basis of UAE, it is not necessarily more efficient to do so. The manager would have to identify all flows for each technological sequence over 8 years. These flows could then be converted to present values and annualized. However, it makes little sense to undertake the annualization process because once we have the present value of cash outflows over the project time horizon we can simply choose the sequence with the lowest present value of cash outflows. In effect, imposition of an 8-year life due to technological change has equalized lives among the modified alternatives.

The complexity introduced by future *technological change* varies from situation to situation. If the price of future technology were known and reasonable estimates could be made of the time in the future when implementation might take place, the firm could analyze the impact of future technology on the optimal economic life of current alternatives. If radical improvements are expected every 8 years or so, the firm might select that period as a time horizon for all *present* technology being evaluated and select alternatives having the lowest UAE cash outflow over that period regardless of the apparent economic life of the present technology. On the other hand, if improvements were ill defined and potentially many years away from incorporation into production processes, the firm might treat the choice among current alternatives as if identical replacements were going to be the rule for some time in the future. In short, we can never set up unerring optimization models in a world of uncertainty. Yet, for a significant number of decisions, the assumption that identical replacement will occur is likely to be adequate and UAE analysis will be applicable. However, where technological change is rampant, the strategy of minimizing annual cost over some prespecified and imposed number of years is probably the best that the firm can hope for.

The problem of incorporating inflation into the analysis so that the UAE will reflect this phenomenon is one of simple mathematical adjustment. Conceptually, a single rate of inflation might be incorporated in the same manner that growth rates are incorporated into a present value equation. As will become clear when inflation is discussed in detail in Chapter 19 this comparatively easy solution to the problem of inflation breaks down when various components of proposals' cash flows change at different inflation rates. Perhaps different types of labor are required for implementation of each alternative and the costs of that labor change at different rates through time. At that point, we can still use UAE analysis but it will be no more efficient than other methods of analysis, for one can only compute the UAE after specifying flows for each replacement sequence.

We must now deal with the problem of determining the optimum (or simply *economic*) life of assets. We know from Chapter 8 that the economic and physical lives of assets are unlikely to be the same. The physical life of assets refers to the number of years an asset *can* produce a given level of output by continued maintenance and repair without reference to the *costs* of maintenance and repair. Economic life refers to the number of years an asset *should* be used to produce a given level of output and thereby to maximize shareholder wealth. Economic life must take into account two kinds of cost: operating and maintenance costs, and capital costs. **Operating and maintenance costs** cover all labor and material expenditures to maintain, repair, and operate the asset. **Capital costs** are costs of ownership; they are incurred because of the decline in value of the asset over time as it both ages and is used up in producing output. In other words, operating and maintenance costs are not independent of capital costs. To the extent that more funds are expended to repair and maintain an asset, the smaller is the decline in the value of the asset and the smaller are the capital costs.

DETER-MINING THE ECONOMIC LIFE OF AN INVESTMENT

Uniform annual equivalents are very useful in finding the economic life of an asset in that they allow us to annualize a given cost, or stream of costs, into a constant annual cost having the same present value as the original cost or stream of costs. Specification of the economic life of an asset requires that we find the replacement cycle that minimizes the uniform annual equivalent total cost [UAE(TC)] of owning and operating the asset. Thus UAE(TC) is the sum of the uniform annual equivalent operating and maintenance cost UAE(OM), and the uniform annual equivalent capital cost UAE(CC), or

$$UAE(TC) = UAE(OM) + UAE(CC) \qquad (9\text{-}1)$$

Figure 9-1 illustrates the behavior of uniform annual equivalent total, operating and maintenance, and capital costs as the replacement cycle for an asset is lengthened—that is, as the asset is used over a longer period. Uniform annual equivalent capital costs decline when the replacement cycle is lengthened, as the curve UAE(CC) reveals. This behavior is readily understood when it is recognized that if the replacement cycle is made long enough, the value of the asset will reach some lower limit—perhaps zero, or a small positive value as junk. Conse-

Figure 9-1   *Costs Over the Life of Equipment*

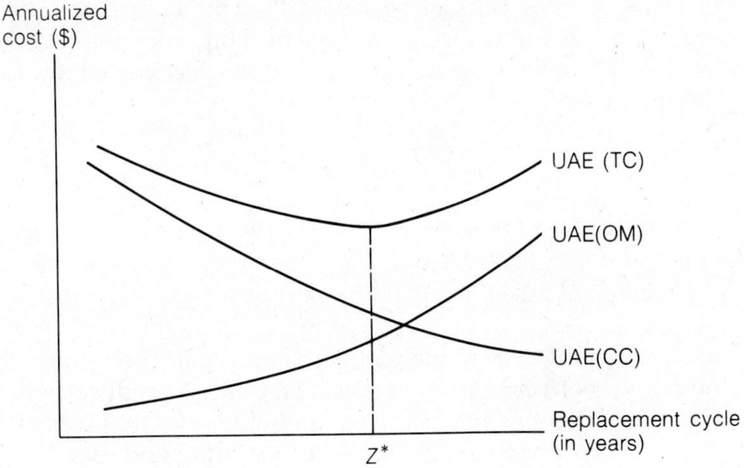

quently, as the replacement cycle is lengthened, the annual capital cost (in UAE form) must decline as the given initial outlay is spread over a greater number of years. Moving in the opposite direction, uniform annual equivalent operating and maintenance costs must increase when the replacement cycle is lengthened, as the curve UAE(OM) shows in Figure 9-1. The longer an asset is used, the more it will cost to maintain, repair, and operate to produce a *given* quality and level of output. The asset is more likely to break down as it ages as more and more parts wear out and must be replaced.

Since lengthening the replacement cycle will cause uniform annual equivalent capital costs to fall and uniform annual equivalent operating and maintenance costs to rise it is possible that their *sum*, the uniform annual equivalent total costs, will reach a *minimum* for some replacement cycle. The curve UAE(TC) in Figure 9-1 portrays such a minimum at the replacement cycle having the length Z*.

In summary, the problem of finding the economic life of an asset becomes the problem of finding the replacement cycle that minimizes the cost of owning and operating the asset.

The problem of finding the economic life of an asset can be easily enough set forth, but the required calculations can be quite tedious. In the specific economic life problem used to demonstrate the solution process below, the reader may be guided by the recognition that nearly all the calculations either result from various adjustments for income taxes or from the necessity of converting every cash flow to UAE form.

Table 9–4   *Operating and Maintenance Cash Outflows and Salvage Value of the Machine: Viscount Balloon Company*

	t = 1	t = 2	t = 3	t = 4	t = 5
Operating and Maintenance	−$ 300	−$500	−$900	−$1400	−$2000
Salvage Value at Time *t*	$1470	$910	$700	$ 610	$ 200

Viscount Balloon Company is considering the purchase of a machine designed to produce rubber balloons. However, the firm is unsure of the economic life of the machine. It has assembled the information given in Table 9-4 regarding expected future operating and maintenance costs and salvage (market) values of the machine as it grows older. This information assumes a given repair and maintenance policy to be applied to the machine in future years. The machine requires an initial, and depreciable, outlay of $3500 at $t = 0$. Operating and maintenance cash outflows grow larger the longer the machine is retained while, at the same time, the salvage value of the machine falls. The appropriate cost of capital for the machine is $K = 10$ percent and the machine will be depreciated for tax purposes over the minimum period of 4 years allowed by tax regulations. The firm will utilize the straight line depreciation method and a salvage value of zero in computing depreciation. The firm's tax rate is $\tau = 40$ percent.

The Economic Life Problem

Finding the economic life of Viscount Balloon's machine is best approached by considering operating and maintenance costs separately from capital costs. When these costs have been adjusted for income taxes and converted to UAE form, the total costs of owning and operating the machine can be evaluated over different replacement cycles.

Table 9–5   *Tax Adjustments and Discounting of Operating and Maintenance Cash Flows: Viscount Balloon Company*

	t = 1	t = 2	t = 3	t = 4	t = 5
Operating and Maintenance Cash Flows	−$300	−$500	−$900	−$1400	−$2000
Tax Saving	+ 120	+ 200	+ 360	+ 560	+ 800
After-tax Operating and Maintenance Cash Flows	−$180	−$300	−$540	−$ 840	−$1200
PV Factor for K = 10%	0.90909	0.82645	0.75131	0.68301	0.62092
Present Value	−$164	−$248	−$406	−$ 574	−$ 745
Cumulative Total of Present Values	−$164	−$412	−$818	−$1392	−$2137

Operating and Maintenance Costs

The operating and maintenance costs in Table 9-4 must be adjusted for income taxes and discounted at the 10 percent cost of capital as a preliminary step to conversion to the uniform annual equivalent form. This is done in Table 9-5. The operating and maintenance cash flows in the first row of Table 9-5 are taken from Table 9-4. These flows are tax deductible, and the after-tax values of these flows are given in the third row. The after-tax flows are obtained by deducting from the operating and maintenance cash flow the tax saving in the second row. Thus, at $t = 1$, $300 of cash outlay will reduce taxable income by that amount. At a tax rate of 40 percent, corporate income taxes will be reduced by $(0.40)\$300 = \$120$. Once the cash flows have been adjusted to an after-tax basis, they are discounted by the present value factors for $K = 10$ percent in the fourth row to obtain the present values shown in the fifth row. The sixth row consists of the total, accumulated present value of the after-tax cash outflow for operating and maintenance costs. This row is to be interpreted in the following way. If the machine is operated for 1 year, the total present value of after-tax operating and maintenance cash outlays will be $164. If operated for 2 years, the total outlay will be $412, and so on.

Having established the total present value of after-tax outlays for operating and maintenance expenses, the uniform annual equivalent of these outlays for replacement cycles of 1, 2, 3, 4, and 5 years can be found. This is done in Table 9-6. There the total present value of after-tax cash outlays for operating and maintenance expenses from Table 9-5 are restated as applicable for each alternative replacement cycle. Naturally, these outlays grow as costs increase for each added year in the replacement cycle. To convert these outlays to UAE form, the appropriate annuity factors for 10 percent from Appendix Table D are divided into the total present values. The resulting values are uniform annual equivalent

Table 9–6 *Uniform Annual Equivalent Operating and Maintenance Cash Outlays After Taxes: Viscount Balloon Company*

Replacement Cycle	Total Present Value of O and M Flows	Annuity Factor for $K = 10\%$	UAE(OM)
1 year	−$164	0.9091	−$180
2	− 412	1.7355	− 237
3	− 818	2.4868	− 329
4	−1392	3.1699	− 439
5	−2137	3.7908	− 564

cash outlays for each alternative replacement cycle. These cash outlays for operating and maintenance grow, in UAE form, as the replacement cycle lengthens, just as in Figure 9-1 the curve UAE(OM) rose for longer replacement cycles.

We have now established part of the uniform annual equivalent total cost formula, Equation (9-1). It remains to determine uniform annual equivalent capital costs.

Capital costs consist of three components: the depreciable outlay, the depreciation tax subsidy gained from the machine, and the salvage value received when the machine is sold at the end of a replacement cycle. Where appropriate, each of these components must be adjusted to an after-tax basis.

Capital Costs

Depreciable Outlay   The depreciable outlay of $3500 must be converted to UAE form for each alternative replacement cycle. This is done in Table 9-7. As the $3500 depreciable outlay is spread out over longer replacement cycles, the uniform annual equivalent flow necessarily falls.

Depreciation Tax Subsidy   The ability to enjoy an annual depreciation tax subsidy will, to some extent, affect the depreciable outlay. Depreciated over 4 years to a salvage value of zero, the annual depreciation charge will be $875 for years 1 through 4. No depreciation charge for the fifth year will be made, as the first row of Table 9-8 reveals. At a 40 percent tax rate, the annual depreciation tax subsidy over the first 4 years is (0.40)$875 = $350, as the second row shows. Using the appropriate annuity factor for $K = 10$ percent from Appendix Table D, the total present value of the depreciation tax subsidy accumulated over the years, in the fourth row, can be directly obtained. Thus if the machine is

Table 9–7   *Uniform Equivalent of Depreciable Outlay: Viscount Balloon Company*

Replacement Cycle	Depreciable Outlay	Annuity Factor for $K = 10\%$	Uniform Annual Equivalent of Depreciable Outlay
1 year	−$3500	0.9091	−$3850
2	− 3500	1.7355	− 2017
3	− 3500	2.4868	− 1407
4	− 3500	3.1699	− 1104
5	3500	3.7908	− 923

Table 9–8   *Discounting the Depreciation Tax Subsidy: Viscount Balloon Company*

	$t = 1$	$t = 2$	$t = 3$	$t = 4$
Depreciation Charge	$875	$875	$875	$875
Depreciation Tax Subsidy ($\tau = 40\%$)	$350	$350	$350	$350
Present Value Factor for Annuity	0.9091	1.7355	2.4868	3.1699
Cumulative Total of Present Values	$318	$607	$870	$1109

owned 1 year, the discounted depreciation tax subsidy will be $318; if owned 2 years, the discounted subsidy will be $607, with the amount increasing each year through the fourth year of ownership as additional depreciation is taken.

Table 9-9 converts the total discounted depreciation tax subsidy, applicable to each replacement cycle, to UAE form. For the 5-year replacement cycle, the total present value of the subsidy is $1109, the same as for the 4-year cycle, because no depreciation charge exists in the fifth year. Conversion to UAE form by dividing with the appropriate annuity factors yields a $350 UAE in the first 4 years—the same as the original annual depreciation tax subsidy. (This equivalence would not hold if an accelerated depreciation method were used.) The UAE declines to $293 in the fifth year as the depreciation taken over 4 years is spread over a longer period.

Salvage Value   The final component of capital costs, salvage value, also acts to partially offset the depreciable outlay. Because salvage value and the undepreciated book value of the machine differ for different replacement cycles, it will be necessary to make tax adjustments to cor-

Table 9–9   *Uniform Annual Equivalent Depreciation Tax Subsidy:*
                 Viscount Balloon Company

Replacement Cycle	Total Present Value of Depreciation Subsidy	Annuity Factor for $K = 10\%$	Uniform Annual Equivalent Tax Subsidy
1 year	$ 318	0.9091	$350
2	607	1.7355	350
3	870	2.4868	350
4	1109	3.1699	350
5	1109	3.7908	293

Table 9-10 *After-tax Salvage Value and Uniform Annual Equivalent of Salvage Value: Viscount Balloon Company*

	1	2	3	4	5	6	7	8	9
Replacement Cycle	Undepreciated Book Value	Salvage Value	Depreciation Error	Tax Adjustment	After-tax Salvage Value	PV Factor for $K = 10\%$	Present Value of Salvage	Annuity Factor for $K = 10\%$	Uniform Annual Equivalent Cash Flow
1 year	$2625	$1470	+$1155	+462	$1932	0.90909	$1756	0.9091	$1932
2	1750	910	+ 840	+ 336	1246	0.82645	1030	1.7355	593
3	875	700	+ 175	+ 70	770	0.75131	579	2.4868	233
4	0	610	– 610	– 244	366	0.68301	250	3.1699	79
5	0	200	– 200	– 80	120	0.62092	75	3.7908	20

rect for prior depreciation before converting to UAE form. Table 9-10 contains all the required computations. For each replacement cycle, the salvage value to be received at the end of the cycle is shown in column 2. (These values are taken from Table 9-4.) Column 1 lists the end-of-cycle undepreciated book values of the machine. These values are obtained by subtracting the $875 depreciation charge from the $3500 depreciable outlay and from each successive undepreciated book value until fully depreciated at the end of year 4. In column 3, the depreciation error made in prior years is found by subtracting the salvage value from the undepreciated book value. For a 1-year replacement cycle, the salvage value is less than book value, meaning that insufficient depreciation was taken in the first year. The depreciation error, +$1155, can be deducted against other taxable income at the end of the replacement cycle to produce a favorable tax reduction of (0.40)$1155 = $462 in column 1. For a 4-year cycle, salvage value exceeds undepreciated book value by $610, indicating that too much depreciation was taken in prior years. Taxable income will be increased by $610 to produce an unfavorable tax increase of (0.40)$610 = $244 in column 4. Favorable and unfavorable tax adjustments in column 4 are added to the salvage value in column 2 to obtain the after-tax salvage values in column 5. The present value factors for $K = 10$ percent (Appendix Table C) column 6 are used to find, in column 7, the present value of the after-tax salvage values for each replacement cycle. These present values are, in turn, converted to UAE form in column 9 by the use of the annuity factors (from Appendix Table D) for $K = 10$ percent. The UAE salvage values finally obtained naturally decline as the replacement cycle lengthens, since the underlying salvage values are also declining.

Determining Economic Life

All the information needed to determine economic life for Viscount Balloon Company's machine has now been obtained. That information is summarized in Table 9-11.

For each replacement cycle, column 1 shows the uniform annual equivalent after-tax operating and maintenance cash outlays UAE(OM), determined earlier in Table 9-6. Columns 2, 3, and 4 show, respectively, UAE cash flows for the three components of capital cost: depreciable outlay (from Table 9-7), depreciation tax subsidy (from Table 9-9), and after-tax salvage value (from Table 9-10). Summing the UAE for the three components of capital cost in columns 2, 3, and 4, yields the uniform annual equivalent cash flows for capital costs, UAE(CC), for each replacement cycle, in column 5. These costs fall as the replacement cycle lengthens—consistent with the behavior of the curve UAE(CC) in Figure 9-1. Following the logic of Equation (9-1), the UAE cash flows for

Table 9–11 *Uniform Annual Equivalent Cash Flows for Operating and Maintenance, Capital Costs and Total Costs: Viscount Balloon Company*

	1	2	3	4	5	6
Replacement Cycle	UAE(OM)	UAE Depreciable Outlay	UAE Depreciation Tax Subsidy	UAE After-tax Salvage Value	UAE(CC)	UAE(TC)
1 year	−$180	−$3850	+$350	+$1932	−$1568	−$1748
2	− 237	− 2017	350	593	− 1074	− 1311
3	− 329	− 1407	350	233	− 824	− 1153
4	− 439	− 1104	350	79	− 675	− 1114 [a]
5	− 564	− 963	293	20	− 610	− 1174

[a]Minimum UAE (TC).

total cost UAE(TC) are obtained in column 6 by summing UAE(OM) and UAE(CC) from columns 1 and 5.

Determination of the economic life (optimal replacement cycle) for the machine is now straightforward. The UAE cash outflow for total cost in column 6 initially declines and then increases as the replacement cycle lengthens [as was the case for the curve UAE(TC) in Figure 9-1]. The minimum UAE cash outlay for total cost is $1114, as indicated by the footnote in Table 9-11, for a replacement cycle of 4 years. We conclude that the economic life the machine is, therefore, also 4 years.

SUMMARY

When mutually exclusive investment proposals have unequal economic lives, it is usually invalid to apply the NPV method to their respective cash flows. The lives of the proposals must be equalized before valid comparisons can be made. A common life, over which each proposal will have one or more replacement cycles (equal to the economic life of each proposal), must be established. When this is done, valid comparisons between proposals can be made in one of two ways. The cash flows for repetitive replacement cycles can be identified over the common life and the NPV of the resulting differential cash flows determined. Alternatively, all cash flows over the replacement cycles for each proposal can be converted to uniform annual equivalent form. The resulting differential uniform annual equivalent cash flow for the proposals may then be determined and the selection made. The UAE approach is often comparatively easier.

For purposes of comparing investment proposals with unequal lives, the UAE analysis is not always appropriate because of its underlying assumptions. If the future introduction of new technology can be timed with reasonable certainty, an implied life for alternative proposals containing existing technology may have to be imposed. That imposed life may be longer or shorter than the economic life of individual proposals containing existing technology and established with UAE analysis under the assumption of continuing replacement of assets representing existing technology. However, the assumption of repeated replacement over time of old assets with new assets of the same technological type (implicit in the UAE analysis) is appropriate when the timing of new technology is highly uncertain.

The problem of determining the optimal economic life of an investment proposal or project can be solved by finding the uniform annual equivalent cash flow for different replacement cycles. Generally, longer replacement cycles produce higher annual operating and maintenance costs, but lower capital costs. At the point of optimal economic life, the increase in annualized operating and maintenance costs just offsets the decline in annualized capital costs and total annualized costs are minimized. In short, when the uniform annual equivalent total cost is minimized, the optimal economic life and replacement cycles of an investment proposal have been reached.

GLOSSARY OF KEY TERMS

Capital Costs

The difference between *annualized* values of the initial outlay *and* the combined depreciation tax subsidy and after-tax salvage value of assets contained in a proposal.

Common Life

The number of years over which, assuming a sufficient number of replacements with identical assets of the same technology, the lives of competing proposals will be rendered equal.

Operating and Maintenance Costs

All labor and material expenditures to maintain, repair, and operate an asset.

Replacement Cycle

The frequency with which assets in an investment proposal are replaced.

Uniform Annual Equivalent Cash Flow for the Proposal

The constant yearly cash flow (uniform annual equivalent cash flow) for a defined period of years having the same present value as the cash flows for the investment proposal.

Fleischer, Gerald A. *Capital Allocation Theory: The Study of Investment Decisions.* New York: Appleton-Century-Crofts, 1969.

Grant, Eugene L., et al. *Principles of Engineering Economy,* 6th ed. New York: Ronald Press, 1976.

SELECTED REFERENCES

QUESTIONS

1. What assumptions are required to utilize uniform annual equivalent (UAE) analysis to deal with the problem of unequal lives?

2. Why does the net present value (NPV) method, when improperly applied, tend to give incorrect choices among unequal-lived competing proposals?

3. In dealing with the problem of economic lives, UAE analysis requires that the uniform annual equivalent magnitude be computed for a *different* economic life for *each* competing proposal. What additional assumption is necessary to complete the evaluation on an equal-lived basis?

4. Why does fairly precise knowledge of the timing of future improved technology make uniform annual equivalent analysis less useful?

5. Why do uniform annual equivalent capital costs decline as the replacement cycle lengthens? Why do uniform annual equivalent operating and maintenance costs tend to increase as replacement cycle lengthens?

PROBLEMS

1. A tanker costing $2.6 million has an expected life of 25 years and an expected salvage value of $100,000. It is expected that it will cost $100,000 annually to operate and maintain the tanker. What is the estimated annual cost of the tanker to the owner? The cost of capital is $K = 8$ percent. (Assume that taxes are zero.)

2. The City of Arcadia is considering two different snowplows. The Gunning plow has a projected economic life of 10 years, and the Coulter plow has a projected economic life of 8 years. The Gunning plow costs $75,000 and is expected to have a salvage value of $5000 at the end of 10 years. The Coulter plow costs $60,000 and is projected to have a salvage value of $4000 at the end of 8 years. Arcadia pays no income taxes but uses a 6 percent cost of capital. Operating and maintenance costs of the Gunning plow are projected at $8000 a year, and the same costs for the Coulter plow are projected at $9000 a year. The plows have equal capacity, and whichever one is se-

lected, the city would likely continue to replace it with essentially the same machine indefinitely. Which plow should be selected?

3. Mockler Media Systems is evaluating a proposal to replace old transmitting equipment with new equipment. The new equipment has an optimal economic life of 5 years and, compared to the old equipment, produces annual pre-tax cost savings of $20,000 annually. The old equipment is fully depreciated and has no market value, but it could be used for another 5 years. The new equipment requires an outlay of $65,000 and will have a salvage value in 5 years of $5000. Mockler's tax rate is 40 percent and the firm customarily uses a cost of capital of $K = 6$ percent. Mockler depreciates assets by the straight line method. Using both the uniform annual equivalent and net present value forms of analysis, decide whether Mockler should replace the old equipment.

4. Hildebrand Housewrecking Company is comparing two alternative housewrecking machines. One, the Flattener, requires an initial outlay of $34,000, has an economic life of 3 years, will have a salvage value of $4000 at the end of its life, and will cost $30,000 per year to operate. The alternative machine, the Obliterator, requires an initial outlay of $100,000, will have no salvage value at the end of its 10-year economic life, and will cost $20,000 per year to operate. Hildebrand uses the straight line depreciation method, has a cost of capital of $K = 8$ percent, and a tax rate of 40 percent. Using uniform annual equivalent analysis, determine which housewrecking machine Hildebrand should purchase. What common life is being assumed for the two machines under the UAE analysis?

5. Using the information on the Hildebrand decision in Problem 4, find the choice that would be made by the net present value method if the lives of the Flattener and Obliterator machines are not equalized. Explain why NPV and UAE methods of analysis give different answers.

6. Amy Drake Company sews garments for fabric stores. The firm is evaluating a new sewing machine which costs $500. The machine will be depreciated to zero salvage value over 3 years using the straight line method. Drake's cost of capital is 12 percent. The tax rate is 30 percent. Estimates of operating and maintenance costs and salvage values are as follows.

	$t = 1$	$t = 2$	$t = 3$
Operating and Maintenance Costs	$150	$150	$300
Salvage Values	300	150	50

Use the method illustrated in this chapter (Viscount Balloon Company) to find the economic life of the sewing machine. Use your results to draw a graph similar to Figure 9-1 to illustrate your solution.

7. Gallagher Well Drillers is evaluating a new well-drilling machine requiring an outlay of $100,000. The following information concerning future operating and maintenance costs and salvage values is available: Gallagher is allowed under tax law to depreciate the machine to a zero salvage value over 5 years by the straight line method; Gallagher has a tax rate of 40 percent and a cost of capital of $K = 6$ percent.

	$t = 1$	$t = 2$	$t = 3$	$t = 4$	$t = 5$
Operating and Maintenance Costs	−$30,000	−$36,667	−$50,000	−$70,000	−$96,667
Salvage Values	70,000	50,000	35,000	25,000	17,500

Find the economic life for the well-drilling machine that minimizes the uniform annual equivalent cash flow of buying and operating the machine.

8. Using your solution to Problem 7, construct a graph similar to Figure 9-1 showing operating and maintenance costs on an annualized basis. Verify that total costs are minimized at the replacement cycle found to be optimal in your answer to Problem 6.

CHAPTER 10

Determining the
Capital Budget

We can now consider, in some detail, how the firm selects the investment projects to be incorporated into a capital budget. The capital budget, as Chapter 6 explained, is the enumeration of accepted investment projects to be undertaken by the firm. The background effort that precedes the creation of the capital budget includes the specification of incremental after-tax cash flows for investment proposals (Chapter 8), the determination of the economic lives of proposals and adjustments to permit comparison of unequal-lived mutually exclusive investment proposals (Chapter 9), the evaluation of each proposal at the appropriate risk-adjusted cost of capital, and the selection of proposals by capital budgeting selection criteria (Chapter 7).

Primarily, we are concerned with the determination of capital budgets under two alternative conditions: the absence of constraints on the availability of capital to the firm, and a constraint on the availability of capital to the firm. In addition, problems raised for the firm by the use of multiple investment selection criteria and artificially high discount rates are examined.

Throughout the chapter it is assumed that all projects being evaluated have the *same* risk and, therefore, that the same risk-adjusted cost of capital is applicable to them. This assumption is made because the area of concern is the *scale* of total investment outlay along with the composition of the capital budget, not differences in the risk of projects.

To demonstrate many of the concepts in this chapter, we use the budget of a single firm, Ross Concrete Products, a small producer of precast concrete items. The firm has generated the investment proposals listed in Table 10-1. Many of these proposals—A, C, and E in particular—are economically independent and can stand by themselves as independent investment projects. Other economically dependent pro-

Table 10–1   *Available Investment Projects: Ross Concrete Products*

Economic Dependence of Underlying Proposals	Proposal or Project	Description	Initial Outlay	NPV
Independent	A	Produce More Paving Blocks	$ 60,000	$ 33,620
Complementary	B:			
	B_1	Expand Concrete Block Output	75,000	40,000
		or		
	B_2	Expand Concrete Footing Output	150,000	55,000
		or		
	B_{12}	Expand Concrete Block & Footing Production	225,000	100,000
Independent	C	Replace Gravel Conveyor	25,000	5,000
Mutually Exclusive	D:			
	D_1	Produce Granite Facing: Automatic System	65,000	10,000
		or		
	D_2	Produce Granite Facing: Manual System	50,000	9,000
Independent	E	Reopen Old Sandhill	20,000	−909

posals are grouped, as required, into independent investment projects. (The reader may wish to review Chapter 6 on the subject of grouping dependent proposals into independent projects.) For example, proposals B_1 and B_2 are complementary. The possibility of undertaking both proposals creates a third proposal, B_{12}, to do just that. The complementary nature of B_1 and B_2 means that the net present value of B_{12} *exceeds* the sum of the net present values of B_1 and B_2. All three proposals, B_1, B_2, and B_{12} are grouped under investment project B. Proposals D_1 and D_2 are mutually exclusive and are grouped under project D. Either D_1 or D_2 may be taken, but not both. All net present values have been computed with the appropriate risk-adjusted cost of capital of $K = 10$ percent.

The decision problem faced by Ross Concrete is to choose from among the projects and proposals in Table 10-1 to establish its capital budget. The objective of this decision is to maximize expected increases in shareholder wealth as measured by net present value.

THE CAPITAL BUDGET: NO CONSTRAINTS ON THE AVAILABILITY OF CAPITAL

All the investment *projects* in Table 10-1 are, by definition, economically independent of one another. Ross Concrete is free to accept any or all of these projects by considering them separately from each other. On the assumption that sufficient capital may be obtained at the cost of capital of $K = 10$ percent to finance, if desired, *all* these projects, the rules for determining the capital budget are simple.

1. Accept all projects containing economically independent investment proposals and having positive net present values.

2. For projects containing complementary proposals, select the alternative proposal having the highest positive net present value. Reject proposals having negative net present values.

3. For projects containing mutually exclusive proposals, select the proposal having the highest positive net present value. Reject proposals having negative net present values.

Application of these rules to the available projects in Table 10-1 yields the following decisions.

1. Accept projects A and C and reject project E. These three projects contain economically independent proposals, and A and C have positive net present values. Project E has a negative NPV.

2. Accept proposal B_{12} in investment project B. Although all proposals in project B have positive net present values, the complementary relationship between B_1 and B_2 makes the combined proposal B_{12} have the highest NPV. Therefore, accept project B as represented by B_{12}.

3. Accept proposal D_1 in investment project D. Compared to the mutually exclusive proposal D_2, proposal D_1 has the highest (and positive) NPV. Therefore, accept project D as represented by D_1.

The capital budget consisting of accepted projects is described in Table 10-2. Total outlay is $375,000, with an expected increase in shareholder wealth, as measured by the total net present value of all accepted projects, of $148,620.

We can also illustrate graphically the determination of Ross Concrete's capital budget. For the purpose of graphical illustration, the respective internal rates of return (IRRs) for each independent project are also indicated in Table 10-2.[1] The same internal rates are drawn, beginning with the highest return project, in a step diagram in Figure 10-1. As more independent projects are undertaken (A, then B_{12}, then C, . . .), the internal rate or return falls.[2] The last project shown in the step

---

[1]These internal rates are computed *after* projects B and D, which contain multiple economically dependent proposals, have been reduced to single proposals by the NPV method. Remember from Chapter 7 that the internal rate of return method may make errors in evaluating proposals like B_1, B_2, B_{12}, D_1, and D_2 and can only properly evaluate independent projects containing single proposals.

[2]Figure 10-1 makes sense only in this very special case when all investments have the *same* level of risk and therefore the same required rate of return. Ordering investments that have different required rates according to their internal rates of return is not logical.

Table 10–2 *The Capital Budget:*
No Capital Constraints
Ross Concrete Products

Project	Outlay	NPV	IRR
A	$ 60,000	$ 33,620	72%
B_{12}	225,000	100,000	63
C	25,000	5,000	32
D_1	65,000	10,000	27
	$375,000	$148,620	

diagram is project E with an internal rate of return of 5 percent. This project, shown as available in Table 10-1, was rejected in determining the capital budget in Table 10-2.

Viewing the independent projects in terms of their respective internal rates, we can graphically compare these rates with Ross Concrete's cost of capital. The cost of capital is described by the dashed line at $K = 10$ percent in Figure 10-1. Projects A, B_{12}, C, and D all have rates of return in excess of 10 percent and are acceptable. Project E, with a rate of return of 5 percent, earns less than the cost of capital and should be rejected.

The point to be gained in examining Figure 10-1 is that given the investment projects available to Ross Concrete, the cost of capital determines not only which projects will be accepted but also the total scale of investment outlay undertaken by the firm. For example, if K suddenly declined in the market to 3 percent from 10 percent, Ross would be induced to obtain more funds in the marketplace and to undertake projects with a 5 percent internal rate, like E, which would otherwise have been rejected. The total scale of investment outlay would then expand. Depending on the nature of the differential cash flows between proposals B_1, B_2, and B_{12} and between proposals D_1 and D_2, the selection between these competing dependent proposals might also be changed by the lower cost of capital (see Chapter 7). Similarly, an increase in the cost of capital to, say, 30 percent from 10 percent, would cause Ross to abandon project D_1 because its rate of return is only 27 percent. Again, depending on the differential cash flows between competing proposals, the selection between B_1, B_2, and B_{12} might also change. In any case, the total scale of outlay will tend to shrink with higher costs of capital. To reiterate, the scale of total outlay (and the capital budget!) is, given available investment projects, a function of the *level* of the appropriate risk-adjusted required rate(s) used to discount expected cash flows.

Figure 10-1   *Available Investment Projects and the Cost of Capital*

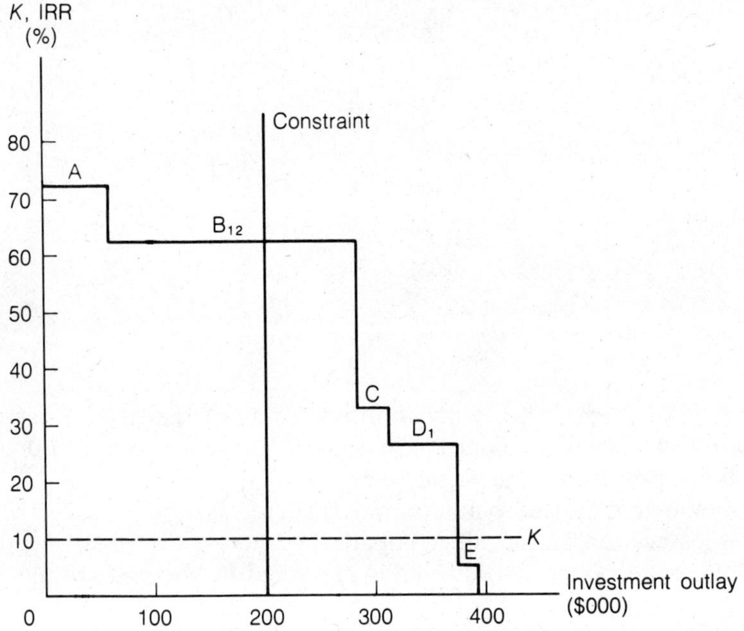

THE CAPITAL
BUDGET: A
CONSTRAINT
ON THE
AVAILABILITY
OF CAPITAL

In fact, firms sometimes do *not* accept all projects having positive net present values. At times, a constraint on the availability of funds is imposed to limit the scale of total investment outlay *below* the level that would otherwise be determined by the cost of capital. An example of such a constraint is described in Figure 10-1 for Ross Concrete by the vertical line labeled "Constraint" at a scale of total outlay of $200,000. This upper limit on total outlay for capital projects is smaller than the $375,000 outlay reached in Table 10-2 when the cost of capital, together with the given investment projects, determined the scale of total outlay. Some otherwise desirable investment projects must be forgone.

We defer, temporarily, examining the reasons for the existence of a **capital constraint** and concentrate instead on techniques for determining the capital budget *given* the capital constraint. However, it is well to state at this point that capital constraints are probably *managerially imposed*, not a reflection of limits imposed by capital markets. Moreover, there is considerable question as to whether managerially imposed capital constraints are consistent with the goal of maximizing shareholder wealth.

The approaches to capital budget determination under capital constraints analyzed here are techniques to maximize net present value and the profitability index technique. Both techniques are in use to some degree in industry. The problem of selecting investment proposals under a capital constraint is also often called the **capital rationing** problem.

Once a capital constraint has been introduced, a graph like Figure 10-1 may have particular value in illustrating the decision structure. The step diagram showing the internal rate of return on investment *projects* assumes that all projects containing economically dependent investment proposals have been narrowed to a single proposal *independent of all other projects*. Thus, in Table 10-2 and Figure 10-1, only proposal B_{12} in project B is shown because it had a higher NPV than either of proposals B_1 or B_2. Similarly, only proposal D_1 from project D is on the step diagram because it had a higher NPV than proposal D_2. However, the existence of a capital constraint means that competing and previously rejected proposals like B_1, B_2, and D_2 must be reintroduced for comparison not only to the dependent alternatives B_{12} and D_1, but to the economically independent proposals contained in projects A and C. Thus, a capital constraint requires that investment *proposals*, not projects, be evaluated.

Proposals must be reconsidered because capital constraints require that all proposals, dependent and independent, must compete for the limited funds. In that competition, smaller outlay competing proposals like B_1, B_2, or D_2 may be more desirable than larger outlay proposals like B_{12} and D_1. To see this, note in Figure 10-1 that the $200,000 capital constraint intersects the IRR step diagram at an outlay greater than the $60,000 required for project A but less than the $60,000 + $225,000 = $285,000 required to undertake *both* projects A *and* B_{12}. Best use of the

Economic Dependence Under Capital Constraints

Table 10–3   *Reduced Set of Proposals: Ross Concrete Products*

Proposal	Outlay	NPV
A	$ 60,000	$33,620
B_1	75,000	40,000
or		
B_2	150,000	55,000
C	25,000	5,000
D_1	65,000	10,000
or		
D_2	50,000	9,000

$200,000 of available funds may mean that only one of the two smaller proposals, B_1 or B_2, be undertaken.

Therefore, we cannot, if a capital constraint exists, work only with the independent projects given in Figure 10-1 and Table 10-2. Instead, we must resort to the full set of investment *proposals,* including all dependent proposals, given in Table 10-1. Reexamining Table 10-2, it is evident that in addition to undesirable project E, Ross Concrete must exclude proposal B_{12} from further consideration. The required outlay for that proposal, by itself, exceeds the $200,000 capital constraint. Eliminating project E and proposal B_{12} leaves us with the reduced set of proposals given in Table 10-3.

Techniques to Maximize Net Present Value of Proposals in the Capital Budget

Given the $200,000 capital constraint, an obvious goal in selecting among the proposals in Table 10-3 is to maximize net present value of the capital budget.

Programming Approaches   For any larger set of proposals, the most efficient way to find the optimal set of proposals that maximizes NPV is to use one of the mathematical programming approaches. Described in general terms, mathematical programming approaches establish an objective function stated in terms of the net present values of the various proposals. Independent and dependent investment proposals alike can be evaluated. Taking into account the outlays required by each proposal and the size of the capital constraint, the set of proposals that maximizes net present value but does not exceed the capital constraint is determined. Programming approaches also permit capital constraints for more than one period of time to be considered. For example, Ross Concrete has a single period constraint of $200,000. However, a constraint for a second, and succeeding, period of time could be established in the amount of, say, $100,000. Investment proposals that maximized NPV in *both* time periods could then be established—some proposals being allocated to the first period capital budget and some to the second period capital budget. It is even possible to restrict investment proposals to selected future time periods. Limitations on the use of such multiperiod constraints exist only in the ability to specify future investment opportunities and the size of capital constraints in future time periods.

Detailed consideration of mathematical programming approaches is beyond the scope of this book, our interest being primarily in introducing the reader to the basic objective of maximizing NPV under capital constraints. Other sources are readily available for more extensive study in the mathematical programming area.[3]

Evaluating Combinations of Proposals   A less technical way of maximizing NPV under a capital constraint is to evaluate various combinations of proposals—that is, to use a combinatorial approach, in which some combinations of proposals exceed the capital constraint and are declared infeasible. The combination of A and B_2 from Table 10-3, for example, represents an infeasible combination because the required outlay is \$210,000—compared to a capital constraint of \$200,000. Other combinations are feasible in that the required outlay is less than, or equal to, the capital constraint. Thus, the combination of B_1, C, and D_1 in Table 10-3 is feasible because the total outlay is \$165,000 (i.e., less than the \$200,000 capital constraint).

The central task in evaluating combinations of investment proposals is to quickly detect and discard infeasible combinations, then to evaluate feasible combinations in order to select that combination having the highest NPV. Even with a small number of proposals, the number of total combinations to be considered can be quite large. Although different ways of efficiently considering combinations exist, we use an intuitive approach suitable when the number of proposals to be considered is small.

Examination of the proposals in Table 10-3 reveals some useful ways of reducing the number of feasible combinations to consider and quickly identifying infeasible combinations. First, the six proposals contain two pairs that are mutually exclusive (B_1 and B_2, D_1 and D_2). Therefore, the maximum number of separate proposals that can be undertaken *in combination* is four. Moreover, inspection reveals that no combination of four proposals is feasible because all would require outlays in excess of the capital constraint. Second, combinations of only one proposal, though feasible, usually leave substantial unused funds within the capital constraint—enough to include additional proposals to increase NPV. Therefore, only combinations of two or three proposals need bear serious examination in this case.

Table 10-4 enumerates all feasible combinations of three proposals, their required outlays, and their NPVs.[4] Among this subset of all feasi-

---

[3]For a beginning, see Richard H. Bernhard, "Mathematical Models for Capital Budgeting—A Survey, Generalization and Critique," *Journal of Financial and Quantitative Analysis* (June 1969), pp. 111–158.

[4]No combination of three that includes proposal B_2 is feasible. For combinations of two, A and B_2 are infeasible. All other combinations of two proposals are feasible but suboptimal, since they are contained in the feasible combinations of three shown in Table 10-3. For example, combinations A and C are feasible but have a smaller NPV than A, B_1, C.

Table 10–4   *Feasible Combinations of Three Proposals: Ross Concrete Products*

Combination	Outlay	NPV
A, B_1, C	$160,000	$78,620
A, B_1, D_1	200,000	83,620[a]
A, B_1, D_2	185,000	82,620
A, C, D_1	150,000	48,620
A, C, D_2	135,000	47,620
B_1, C, D_1	165,000	55,000
B_1, C D_2	150,000	54,000

[a]Optimum combination

ble combinations of proposals, the combination consisting of A, B_1, and D_1 is optimum, since NPV is maximized at $83,620. Total outlay for that combination is $200,000—just equal to the constraint.

Evaluation of specific combinations of proposals under a capital constraint is appropriate when the number of proposals is small. Programming approaches are useful for larger numbers of proposals. In either case, the objective of maximizing NPV under the capital constraint and for the benefit of shareholders is paramount.

The Profitability Index   An alternative and often misused technique of selecting investment proposals under a capital constraint, the **profitability index** may also be employed. The profitability index, PI, is the ratio of net present value to investment outlay.

$$PI = \frac{NPV}{Outlay}$$

For any investment proposal or project to be potentially acceptable, its NPV must be positive—as must be its profitability index. If NPV is zero, the index is also zero; if NPV is negative, then so is the index.[5]

---

[5]The profitability index is also written as the ratio of the present value of future cash flows (PV rather than NPV) to the outlay, or

$$PI = \frac{PV}{Outlay}$$

It makes no difference which version is employed, but the numerical value of the index above differs from the one in the text. Using this measure, a potentially acceptable proposal must have an index greater than 1, since PV must exceed outlay. An undesirable proposal will have a PV less than outlay, or an index of less than 1.

There are four steps in the proper use of the **profitability index techniques** to select proposals under a capital constraint.

1. Compute the index for all proposals.

2. Identify all feasible combinations of projects that satisfy the capital constraint.

3. Compute the *weighted average* profitability index for each combination, calculating the weight of each proposal in the combination by dividing the outlay for each proposal by the capital constraint.

4. Select the combination with the largest weighted average profitability index.

Table 10–5   *Selecting Proposals by Profitability Index: Ross Concrete Products*

Proposal	Outlay	NPV	PI	Weight
A. Calculation of Index				
A	$60,000	$33,620	0.560	$\dfrac{\$60,000}{\$200,000} = 0.3$
B_1	75,000	40,000	0.533	$\dfrac{75,000}{200,000} = 0.375$
B_2	150,000	55,000	0.367	$\dfrac{150,000}{200,000} = 0.75$
C	25,000	5,000	0.200	$\dfrac{25,000}{200,000} = 0.125$
D_1	65,000	10,000	0.154	$\dfrac{65,000}{200,000} = 0.325$
D_2	50,000	9,000	0.180	$\dfrac{50,000}{200,000} = 0.25$

Combination	Weighted Profitability Index
B. Calculation of Weighted Index for Each Combination	
AB_1C	$(0.3)(0.56) + (0.375)(0.533) + (0.125)(0.200) = 0.393$
AB_1D_1	$(0.3)(0.56) + (0.375)(0.533) + (0.325)(0.154) = 0.418^a$
AB_1D_2	$(0.3)(0.56) + (0.375)(0.533) + (0.25)(0.180) = 0.413$
ACD_1	$(0.3)(0.56) + (0.125)(0.200) + (0.325)(0.154) = 0.243$
ACD_2	$(0.3)(0.56) + (0.125)(0.200) + (0.250)(0.180) = 0.238$
B_1CD_1	$(0.375)(0.533) + (0.125)(0.2) + (0.325)(0.154) = 0.275$
B_1CD_2	$(0.375)(0.533) + (0.125)(0.2) + (0.25)(0.180) = 0.270$

[a]Largest weighted index.

Table 10-5 shows how this procedure is applied to the reduced set of proposals facing Ross Concrete. In panel A an index for each proposal is calculated together with the weight of each proposal. Note that the weight simply reflects the *proportion* of the total budget that would be used by the specific proposal.

Panel B identifies all feasible combinations of three proposals and shows how each weighted profitability index is calculated. For instance, the first term in the calculation of the index for combination AB_1C is the weight of A (0.3) times the profitability index of A (0.56). The second term in the weight of B_1 (0.375) times the profitability index of B_1 (0.533). The third term is the product of the weight and profitability index of C. In each case, the weights and indexes were taken directly from panel A. The weighted profitability index for the entire proposal, 0.393, is the sum of these three terms.

The last step in this procedure is to identify the combination with the largest weighted index. In this instance, that combination is AB_1D_1, with an index value of 0.418. Note also that the identical combination is selected by the NPV criterion as shown in Table 10-4. This is no accident. Both methods of analysis always select the appropriate combination.[6] However, the weighted profitability index method accomplishes the task in a greater number of steps than are required when we directly maximize the NPV subject to the budget constraint.

THE CAUSES OF CAPITAL CONSTRAINTS

Techniques for selecting investment proposals under capital constraints are in fairly wide use. An important question is whether the existence of a capital constraint is legitimate. Even when the NPV of proposals is maximized under a capital constraint, the resulting NPV is less than would have occurred in the *unconstrained* case. For example, Ross Concrete's unconstrained capital budget in Table 10-2 resulted in an NPV of $148,620. Maximizing NPV under the $200,000 capital constraint in Table 10-4 resulted in an NPV of only $83,620. Through the existence of the capital constraint, shareholders give up NPV and a resulting expected increase in wealth of $148,620 − $83,620 = $65,000. Therefore, the imposition of a capital constraint is apparently inconsistent with the goal of maximizing shareholder wealth. The justifications for capital constraints deserve, as a result of this inconsistency, further inquiry.

---

[6]Since our profitability index is defined as NPV/outlay, we did not need to worry about the proportion of the budget left unused as cash because the NPV of cash is zero. However, if the index is defined as PV/outlay as shown in note 5, the profitability index of cash left unused is 1, and the weighted profitability index must include the proportion of the budget in cash times the profitability index of cash.

It seems unlikely that capital constraints of the type under examination could arise in capital markets, for these constraints imply that at the limit posed by the constraint, no additional funds are available at *any* cost of capital. To see this, refer back to Figure 10-1 for Ross Concrete. At the $200,000 capital constraint, the vertical line labeled "Constraint" intersects the line $K = 10$ percent for the cost of capital. If we viewed the capital constraints as a condition imposed by the market, it would appear that the "message" Ross Concrete is receiving from the market is that capital is available at a cost of 10 percent up to $200,000, but no additional dollars are available beyond that—in effect making the cost of one additional dollar infinitely high.

Capital Constraints Arising in the Market

It is difficult to define conditions wherein the market would limit funds to the firm in the way that capital constraints suggest; we are talking of a pure scale phenomenon *somehow* causing required rates on all of the firm's investments to become, in effect, infinitely high at the margin. One possible cause, an increase in risk premiums after the capital constraint has been reached, would seem to be ruled out. The risk-adjusted discount rate is adjudged appropriate for the risk of *all* projects (projects all of equal risk) being considered. If more projects of the *same* risk are undertaken, it is difficult to understand why, with risk thus constant, the required rate should become, in effect, infinitely high at some level. And cost of capital cannot be said to increase because of increased leverage since the target capital structure is being held constant at all scales of investment.

Assuming that additional capital *is* available, perhaps at a higher cost, what arguments exist for managerially imposed capital constraints that leave behind unexploited, desirable investment projects and fail to maximize increases in wealth for shareholders? Such arguments are made and should at least be recorded here because of their widespread existence.

Managerially Imposed Capital Constraints

Reliance on Internally Generated Funds   Some firms have a policy of financing investment projects *only* from internally generated funds. Under no circumstances will they permit debt to be employed to finance projects, nor are any new equity issues to be sold. The scale of investment is then confined to available, currently retained earnings plus accumulated cash and short-term investments not needed for operations. If more desirable projects exist than can be financed by internally generated funds, it is argued that capital constraints should be imposed.

This argument implies a blanket rule without any qualifications. It may be, for example, that a firm relies solely on internally generated funds because the shareholders are averse to the risks of debt—the tax subsidy benefits of debt to be discussed in Chapter 12 notwithstanding. No one can argue against their risk preferences. Yet, the costs in terms of forgone wealth increases caused by desirable projects being not undertaken due to a capital constraint must be measured and weighed against whatever benefit being free from debt has for these shareholders. In some years at least, the losses due to forgone wealth gains from unexploited projects may be so high that the prohibition against debt might well be voluntarily abandoned. Once that possibility has been admitted, no blanket rule for internally generated funds can be allowed. At least initially, capital budgets should be determined without managerially imposed capital constraints to measure the cost of imposing capital constraints in any given year.

A similar argument extends to another reason advanced for relying on internally generated funds—the loss of control for existing shareholders if new common stock is sold to outsiders to finance projects. Whatever value existing shareholders may place on having control of a firm must be balanced against the losses arising from projects forgone because of an imposed capital constraint. Again, no blanket rule should apply. The unconstrained capital budget must be determined to find out how costly, in any year, the imposition of a capital constraint will be. Only then can the benefits of control be compared to the costs of capital constraints.[7]

Capital Rationing for Units of an Organization   It is sometimes argued that departments or other units of a firm should use capital constraints because they are allocated a fixed quantity of capital funds from headquarters and must make the best use of them. This argument puts the cart before the horse. Assuming that additional capital is available to the firm at a price, the department or unit should be allocated the amount of capital it can profitably employ, just as in a firm in the unconstrained capital budgeting situation. To do otherwise may cause departments having many desirable projects to end up excluding some because of the managerially imposed constraint. Furthermore, departments having few desirable projects may undertake undesirable projects simply to use up their quota of capital funds. Neither action is consistent with the goal of maximizing shareholder wealth.

Organizational Limits on the Growth of the Firm   When the number of desirable investment projects is large relative to the existing size of the

---

[7]A growing body of literature addresses the problem of valuing control. At this point there is no general agreement about the value, if any, that control might convey to an investor.

firm, it is sometimes thought that the firm will be unable to exploit all the projects because of short-run constraints on the availability of managerial talent and inertia involved in changing the organization of the firm to adjust to growth. Consequently, it is argued that capital constraints are justified to prevent the firm from undertaking more activity than it can manage in a given period.

This argument is really not an argument for capital constraints as much as it is for proper specification of the costs associated with investment projects. If, as is often true, firms experience managerial difficulties with growth caused by investment projects, the costs of the growth should be estimated and the returns of all projects scaled downward accordingly. Given the cost of capital, fewer projects will then be undertaken, not because of capital constraints, but because project returns were initially overestimated.

An Unresolved Problem

The fact is that capital constraints sometimes *are* managerially imposed—even though theories predicated on the goal of maximizing shareholder wealth suggest that such actions are inconsistent with that goal. Resolution of this apparent conflict between theory and practice is not easy. Perhaps other concerns, such as preserving control of a firm by using only internal financing have overriding importance for some shareholders, in which case concentration solely on shareholder wealth maximization is not sufficient. Or, for reasons yet unknown, the market-determined cost of capital may suddenly increase greatly when a firm's demands for capital reach a certain level. Even if the cost of capital does not become infinitely high as capital constraints imply, it may become so high that the capital constraint is a reasonable approximation of market conditions. We do not have enough knowledge about this issue to rule out such a possibility.

Probably the best approach is to always start with the unconstrained capital budget. If arguments to impose a capital constraint exist, the benefits and costs (in terms of forgone desirable investment proposals) can be separately assessed before a decision is made to impose, or not to impose, the constraint.

OTHER MANAGERIAL PRACTICES THAT CREATE PROBLEMS

Much of the content of Chapters 7, 8, and 9 has been devoted to establishing better decision rules to avoid predictably suboptimal decisions. In that spirit, we examine the not-uncommon practices of the use of multiple investment selection criteria and of artificially high discount rates.

Table 10–6 *Capital Budgets Evolved from Joint Use of Net Present Value and Payback Methods*

Project	Outlay	NPV	Payback Period
A	$100,000	$10,000	2.8 years
B	50,000	7,000	2.0
C	75,000	11,000	4.0
D	120,000	−4,000	2.5
E	60,000	5,000	1.6

Capital Budgets

NPV Method Alone			NPV and Payback		
Project	Outlay	NPV	Project	Outlay	NPV
A	$100,000	$10,000	A	$100,000	$10,000
B	50,000	7,000	B	50,000	7,000
C	75,000	11,000	E	60,000	5,000
E	60,000	5,000		$210,000	$22,000
	$285,000	$33,000			

Multiple Investment Selection Criteria

Some firms select investment projects by the joint use of two separate selection criteria. Among such firms, the combination of the payback method with either the net present value or the internal rate of return method is especially prevalent. When two criteria are used, an investment project must be selected by *both* criteria if it is to be accepted. Selection by only one criterion is insufficient for project acceptance.

If the two selection criteria used by a firm always agree in selecting or rejecting projects, the practice of using joint criteria is a harmless, if redundant, action. However, if the criteria sometimes disagree and only one may be considered to be consistent with the goal of maximizing shareholder wealth, the resulting capital budget may be too small and may not contain the proper combination of projects. An example of this tendency is given in Table 10-6, which uses the NPV and payback methods to evaluate a set of available investment projects. Of the available projects shown, D is not acceptable by the NPV method computed with the prevailing cost of capital. With a maximum allowable payback period of 3 years, only project C with an estimated 4 year payback period is unacceptable by the payback method. Using the NPV method alone, the capital budget would consist of projects A, B, C, and E, with a total outlay of $285,000 and a total net present value of $33,000. Using *both* criteria, the failure of project C to pass the payback test reduces the budget to projects A, B, and E, with the smaller total outlay and net present value of $210,000 and $22,000, respectively. Shareholder wealth does not increase as much as it would if only the NPV method were followed and total capital outlay reduced. If shareholder wealth maximization is the goal, the NPV method should be used.

Still other firms use some sort of discounted cash flow method to evaluate projects but employ **artifically high discount rates** in that method. For example, suppose that a firm estimates the required rate for certain proposals to be $K = 12$ percent. However, the firm decides, arbitrarily, to inflate the required rate to 20 percent for all projects and to compute net present values on that basis. The effect of this practice will be to reject some projects that should be accepted. Table 10-7 describes such a case. If the cost of capital is $K = 12$ percent, all the projects in Table 10-7 are acceptable by the NPV method. Instead, if the firm uses a discount rate of 20 percent to evaluate projects, projects E and F will be rejected. Use of the high discount rate lowers the total size of capital budgets, favors short-lived investments, and results in foregone increases in shareholder wealth due to omitted projects.

Artificially High Discount Rates

The real question raised by the practice of artificially high discount rates is, What is the cost of capital? If $K = 12$ percent represents the *best* estimate of the risk-adjusted required rate on the firm's investment proposals, there can be no justification for using the artificially high 20 percent discount rate. To argue that the 20 percent discount rate is to allow for uncertainty concerning the cost of capital estimate is an argument for improving cost of capital estimates. If the firm really believes that the rate is more than 12 percent, it should estimate that higher rate and not arbitrarily, use some artificially higher figure such as 20 percent.

Table 10–7 *Effect of Using Artificially High Discount Rates*

Project	Outlay	NPV at 20% Discount Rate	NPV at $K = 12\%$
A	$100,000	$4000	$ 8,571
B	100,000	5000	12,500
C	40,000	1333	4,286
D	75,000	1250	6,696
E	50,000	−1667	1,786
F	85,000	−4250	1,518

SUMMARY   If capital is available to a firm in unconstrained amounts at the prevailing cost of capital, it should determine its capital budget entirely on the basis of the net present values of the investment proposals contained within projects. In effect, once the investment proposals have been given, it is the market-determined cost of capital that determines the total scale of investment outlay undertaken by the firm. However, if a capital constraint exists, the firm may not be able to undertake all investment projects having positive net present values.

Programming approaches, as well as evaluation of combinations of investment proposals, can be used to select that combination of proposals that maximizes net present value when capital is rationed. However, unlike the unconstrained capital budgeting case, the existence of a capital constraint requires that all economically dependent investment proposals contained in investment projects be considered as separate alternatives to other, economically *independent*, proposals. The profitability index technique is also used in determining the capital budget under capital constraints; however, this technique, properly used, requires additional steps in computation compared to maximization of NPV subject to a constraint.

It is doubtful that the market imposes the type of capital rationing constraint under which additional capital is not available at *any* price. Instead, capital rationing constraints are probably managerially imposed. The reasons for imposing these constraints vary, but the validity of such actions is open to question because they may require the forgoing of increases in wealth due to the improper rejection of desirable projects. Similar undesirable results tend to be produced when firms employ multiple investment selection criteria or artificially high discount rates to evaluate investment projects.

GLOSSARY OF KEY TERMS

Artificially High Discount Rate   A discount rate higher than a firm's risk-adjusted cost of capital.

Capital Constraint   A fixed upper limit on the level of funds to be provided to finance capital projects.

Capital Rationing   The practice of allocating capital within a specific dollar constraint.

Multiple Investment Selection Criteria   The simultaneous use of two or more investment selection criteria to accept or reject investment projects.

Profitability Index   The ratio of an investment proposal's net present value to the required investment outlay.

Profitability Index Technique   A way of allocating capital within a capital constraint by ranking according to the magnitude of the profitability index.

Fogler, H. Russell. "Ranking Techniques and Capital Rationing," *Accounting Review* (January 1972), pp. 134–143.

Johnson, Robert W. *Capital Budgeting.* Dubuque, IA: Kendall/Hunt Publishing Co., 1977.

Weingartner, H. Martin, "Capital Rationing: *n* Authors in Search of a Plot," *Journal of Finance* (December 1977), pp. 1403–1431.

SELECTED REFERENCES

QUESTIONS

1. What is the relation between a firm's cost of capital and the optimal scale of investment if the firm has no capital constraints and the cost of capital is the appropriate discount rate for all projects?

2. What does the imposition of a capital constraint imply about the cost of capital to the firm?

3. Why does the existence of a capital constraint mean that economically dependent investment proposals must be evaluated in different combinations?

4. What are the likely effects if a firm uses multiple investment selection criteria or artificially high discount rates in accepting or rejecting investment projects?

5. Critique the following statement. "We employ a capital constraint because our firm finances all projects internally."

6. Predict the impact of using capital constraints within departments of a firm.

7. "If we undertook every profitable project available to our firm, we'd break under the stress. An organization can absorb only so many new tasks at a time." What does this statement suggest that this firm should do in evaluating investment projects?

PROBLEMS

1. Morgan Floor Covering Company has calculated the net present value of several projects using a cost of capital of $K = 10$ percent.

Each project consist of a single economically independent invest-ment proposal. Using the profitability index technique, find the optimal set of projects under a capital constraint of $500,000.

Project	Outlay	NPV
A	$100,000	$9080
B	80,000	5810
C	70,000	3175
D	300,000	4495
E	33,000	2996
F	94,000	1700
G	5,000	1818

2. Brink Company is considering the following independent invest-ment proposals.

Project	Outlay	NPV
A	$ 2,500	$ 909
B	16,500	1498
C	35,000	1588
D	40,000	2905
E	50,000	4540

A capital constraint of $100,000 exists.

By evaluating the NPV of alternative combinations of proposals and, alternatively, using the profitability index, construct Brink Company's capital budget.

3. Peck Athletic Supply, Inc., has generated the following investment proposals.

Proposal	Outlay	NPV
A	$100,000	$15,000
B	10,000	2,000
C_1	50,000	10,000
C_2	75,000	14,000
D	40,000	4,800

Proposals A, B, and D are economically independent, whereas C_1 and C_2 are mutually exclusive. Faced with a $10,000 capital con-straint, what is the optimal set of proposals to maximize NPV?

4. Hart Clinics, Inc., confronts the following set of investment proposals.

Proposal	Outlay	NPV	Payback Period (years)
A	$ 70,000	$10,000	1
B_1	95,000	25,000	4
B_2	75,000	15,000	2
C	110,000	50,000	1
D	45,000	7,000	3
E	50,000	6,000	1.5

Proposals A, C, D, and E are economically independent. Proposals B_1 and B_2 are mutually exclusive. To be accepted by Hart, a proposal must have an NPV greater than zero and a maximum payback period of 3 years. Otherwise it is rejected. Determine, by its selection criteria, Hart's capital budget. What are the consequences of Hart's use of dual criteria for the shareholders of the firm?

5. The Smith and Wetzel Corporation is confronted with the following investment proposals.

Proposal	Outlay	PV of Cash Inflows ($K = 10\%$)
A	$30,000	$ 35,000
B	70,000	100,000
C	50,000	60,000
D	90,000	100,000

(a) If $500,000 is available to S & W at 10 percent, what proposals should the firm select if A, B, C, and D are independent? What is the resulting increase in shareholder wealth?

(b) If funds are limited to $220,000, which proposals (assume economic independence) should be accepted, and what is the increase in shareholder wealth?

(c) Now assume that B and C are mutually exclusive. Under capital constraints of $220,000, which proposals should now be accepted?

6. Magic Pan Restaurants is considering several ways of stimulating business: an advertising campaign, a sweepstakes giveaway program, and the establishment of a take-out service.

Available Investment Projects:
Magic Pan Restaurants

Economic Dependence of Underlying Proposals	Proposal or Project	Description	Initial Outlay	NPV
Complementary	A			
Complementary	A_1	Sweepstakes Giveaway	$300,000	$200,000
Complementary	A_2	Advertising Campaign	200,000	100,000
Complementary	A_{12}	Both	500,000	400,000
Independent	B	Take-out Service	300,000	210,000

Magic Pan faces a capital constraint of $600,000.

Find the optimal set of proposals for Magic Pan by evaluating the NPV of alternative combinations of proposals and by using the profitability index technique.

Valuation and Financing Decisions

Valuation

The capital budgeting decisions discussed in Chapters 6 to 10 assumed that decision makers had previously estimated the appropriate required rate of return to be employed as a discount rate in evaluation of investment prospects. It is now time to look more closely at this required rate or, as we will term it, the cost of capital. This inquiry takes us through Chapter 16. In this chapter, we consider how to value the firm, as distinguished from single investment proposals. Chapters 12 and 13 examine the financing decision, the choices between debt and equity financing a firm may make, and the possible effects of such choices on shareholder wealth. Out of those chapters comes the notion of a target capital structure, a desired mix of debt and equity, that the firm plans to employ in financing its assets and new investments. In Chapter 14, we consider the dividend decision firms make regarding their common stock. This is part of the financing decision of a firm, since whatever cash is not paid out as cash dividends to common shareholders can be retained to provide common equity financing. Chapters 15 and 16 address the problem of *estimating* the required rate of return for an investment proposal, given the firm's target capital structure.

In Chapter 11 we are interested in how the *market* values the outstanding debt and equity securities of a firm. Subsequent chapters demonstrate that it is market valuation that matters in determining a firm's cost of capital. Required rates for individual financing sources are interdependent. Therefore, financial managers must understand how both debt *and* the ownership position are valued by the market to see how the value of the ownership position is affected by various financing choices. Stated alternatively, it is the value of the firm, reflected in the value of all its securities, that is fundamental to understanding behavior of the value of the ownership.

Appendix 11A discusses issues of business failure, bankruptcy, and reorganization. Valuation of options is described in Appendix 11B.

THE J. C. LAYTON VALUATION PROBLEM

Many approaches to determining the **value of a firm** exist. To illustrate and compare them, we use the valuation problem faced by J. C. Layton, a manufacturer of sportswear.

Management of J. C. Layton, Inc. have attempted to value the firm's common stock because sale of new stock in the market is contemplated. Presently, all the firm's securities, including common stock, are closely held and not traded in the market. The current balance sheet of the firm is given in Table 11-1.

The president and chairman of the board of the firm has led a committee of board members in attempting to find a value for Layton's 1 million common shares. Considerable controversy has surrounded these attempts because the committee have been unable to agree on the proper valuation procedure. Five alternative valuation procedures have been identified so far: book value, par value, liquidating value, replacement cost, and discounted cash flow.

The wide discrepancy among preliminary valuations obtained with some of the procedures has led to the hiring of College Consultants, a firm of enterprising students putting their classroom skills to work. College Consultants is charged with evaluating the five procedures and

Table 11–1   *Balance Sheet: J. C. Layton, Inc. ($000)*

Assets			Liabilities		
Current			Current		
Cash	$123		Accounts Payable	$ 243	
Accounts Receivable	644		Wages Payable	67	
Inventories	973		Bank Note (9%)	370	
		$1740			$ 680
			Long-term Debt (7%)		3000
Noncurrent			Equity		
Equipment		2310	Preferred Stock (5%) ($50 par)	$ 500	
Plant		2450	Common Stock ($1 par)	1000	
			Paid-in Capital	200	
			Retained Earnings	1120	
					2820
Total		$6500			$6500

arriving at a best estimate of value for J. C. Layton by a fully explained procedure—one that J. C. Layton can follow in the future. Their report follows.

The word *value* has many connotations, but our interest is in the valuation of assets whose future cash flows can be directly transferred from buyer to seller. The **value of securities** depends on the size and timing of projected cash flows, the riskless rate of interest, the riskiness of the cash flows, and investor attitudes toward risk and expected return. Expected return and risk are attributable to an investment that can be transferred from one individual to another in impersonal capital markets.

VALUE

The value of a financial asset (a security) is defined as the *price* at which the asset should sell when bought and sold by well-informed investors in a market. Value need not be identical to current market price, but we would expect value to be related to a market price that could be expected to be achieved at *some* point in the future. It would seem to make little sense to say that the value of a share of common stock is $100 when it is currently trading at $10 per share and there is no information that, when presented to the market, would cause a change in value to $100. Suppose, for example, that a firm's common stock is currently selling for $7 per share. After careful investigation and analysis you find that the firm has perfected a patent that will have a substantial positive impact on earnings. Furthermore, you are confident that no one else in the capital market knows anything about this development. You feel that the value of one share is $25 rather than $7. Once you have purchased a share of stock for $7, either you must wait for the company to make an announcement or you must begin spreading the word yourself if you are to benefit from your prior knowledge. Until such an adjustment in market price occurs, the *realizable value* is the current market price of $7. No one will pay you $25 for each of your shares because they still can be purchased in the market for $7 each.

When an individual can obtain information that is not available to others in the market and knows that an adjustment in market price will occur when other investors discover the information, it makes sense to differentiate between current market price and some "true" or underlying value. But in highly competitive markets such as the major stock exchanges, where millions of individuals focus their attentions on a small proportion of the total issues available and the likelihood of discovering new information that is unknown to other market participants is small, the best estimate of value is *market price*. Such markets were earlier in the text called *efficient markets* because all currently available information is reflected in market prices.

Determining the value of an asset that is traded in such markets is easy. One need only look up the price in the financial section of the newspaper.[1] When, as in Layton's case, common shares are not publicly traded, it is not so easy to find market value at a given time. Still, market value remains the appropriate concept of valuation even for securities not publicly traded. Their owners' wealth is determined by what well-informed investors would be *willing* to pay for them.

Other concepts of value do exist and, before pursuing the process of estimating market value, these are examined.

Book Value   J. C. Layton's shares are closely held by nearly 100 individuals and there have been no trades in the past 2 years. Consequently, some might argue that **book value** is the proper basis for valuing the firm.

Book value is simply the value as recorded on the books—the balance sheet. For debt, book value is the face value, or in other words, the principal amount to be paid at maturity (its due date) by the issuer.[2] For common stock, the book value is the sum of the par value of the common stock, paid-in capital, and retained-earnings accounts.[3] The book value of the Layton long-term debt is $3 million, and common stock has a book value of $2.32 million ($1,000,000 + $1,320,000). Since there are 1 million common shares outstanding, the book value per share is $2.32.

Unfortunately the amounts that appear on the balance sheet as book

---

[1]In addition to the financial section of your daily paper, many bond and stock prices are reported in *The Wall Street Journal* (issued every business day), *Barron's* (issued weekly), and *The Commercial and Financial Chronicle*. Data on average yields and their behavior over time can be found in such publications as *The Federal Reserve Bulletin* and *Survey of Current Business*.

[2]To be more precise, book value also includes any premium or discount related to the issuance of the bonds and still on the books. Premium is the amount received by the firm in excess of face value at time of issue and is shown as an account on the books to be amortized over the life of the debt. It is an addition to the book value of debt. Alternatively, a discount is an amount deducted from book value of debt reflecting that at the time of issue, dollars received were less than the face value of debt. It too is amortized over the life of the debt.

[3]Par value is the number by which shares outstanding are multiplied to record the amount in the common stock account. "Paid-in capital" is the account reflecting the additional amount paid in by stockholders above par value. If a $1 par value stock is sold at $10, $9 is credited to paid-in capital and $1 to the common stock account. "Retained earnings" is the account reflecting the accumulation of earnings (or losses) of the corporation that have not been paid out in dividends, since the corporation began. These account definitions are somewhat simplified in the interest of brevity. Your further study should amplify and expand these brief statements.

values are simply historical recordings. They do not necessarily bear any relation to the value of future cash flows upon which market value depends. Book values are a record of the amount invested at various points in time. Though it is possible to find some situations when book values might be useful, they are unlikely to be of much help in finding the market value of a typical firm. Book value reflects past occurrences, whereas market value reflects those that are anticipated for the future.

Par Value

The use of **par value,** as it is established in Layton's corporate charter, has no implications for the value of the shares. Layton's $1 par value is simply a number by which the outstanding number of shares are multiplied to arrive at the balance sheet entry for the common stock account. The number is arbitrary. Some companies issue only "no par" stock so that the amount received by the firm from the sale of common stock can be lumped into one balance sheet account rather than two, paid-in capital and common stock. Yet, "no par" stock producing expected future cash inflows will have *market* value.

Liquidating Value

Liquidating value is the amount that would be received if Layton were to cease operations and sell all assets to the highest bidders. Automobiles, land, buildings, manufacturing equipment, and inventories could all be sold in various secondhand markets or at an auction.

Any firm always has the option of liquidation, and one would expect liquidating value to be the *lowest* price someone would pay for a firm. When economic events make selling the assets of the firm superior to continuing operations, a rational manager who works in the best interests of shareholders should recommend liquidation; unfortunately, however, few firms liquidate voluntarily to maximize the wealth of shareholders. Few managers are willing to admit that their firm is less valuable than the liquidation value of the assets, so many liquidations do not take place until the firm is forced into liquidation by financial distress, failure, or bankruptcy. (Appendix 11A describes such financial distress situations.)

Preliminary estimates of liquidating values for J. C. Layton are as follows.

Asset	Liquidating Value
Cash	$ 123,000
Accounts Receivable	627,000
Inventory	450,000
Equipment	1,250,000
Plant	3,250,000
	$5,700,000

Deducting book values of current liabilities, long-term debt, and preferred stock, the amount available for common shareholders would be $1.52 million, $1.52 per share. (Book values accurately represent the amount legally payable to debtholders and preferred stock owners before common stockholders can receive any funds.)

Liquidating value reflects the value of existing assets when used in other activities. Only by coincidence would it reflect the value of *future* cash flows to be generated by the existing firm. The real benefit of liquidating value is to provide a benchmark with which to compare the value of future cash flows from continued operations. If liquidating value is found to be greater than the value of future cash flows, the firm should cease operations and sell the assets; if not, operations should continue.

Replacement Cost (Less Depreciation)

Another method of valuation requires the estimation of **replacement cost of assets, less depreciation.** This is a method of valuation sometimes used in real estate when no comparative market data can be used to value property. For example, an insurance appraiser might estimate the cost of rebuilding or replacing an asset today, then deduct accumulated depreciation in proportion to the asset's expired life.

J. C. Layton originally paid $500,000 for one of its plants. The plant has been in operation for 15 years. Given a depreciable life of 40 years and using the straight line depreciation method (yearly depreciation equals original cost divided by the years of depreciable life), the current book value of that plant is $312,500. Using the most recent building cost data, it appears that the plant could be replaced for $1.5 million. Since the existing facility has been used for $15/40$ of its expected life, $15/40$ of $1.5 million must be deducted from the replacement cost to find replacement cost less depreciation.

$$\text{Replacement cost less depreciation} = \$1,500,000 - \frac{15}{40}(\$1,500,000)$$

$$= \$937,500$$

Applying this procedure to the rest of the firm's plants, the replacement cost less pro rata depreciation is estimated to be $7.65 million. For equipment, $2.64 million is the estimated replacement cost, and for current assets, the estimate is $1.76 million. Total assets using this method are $12.05 million. Deducting the current and long-term liabilities as well as the par value of preferred stock yields a value available to common stockholders of $7.87 million, or $7.87 per common share.

As with some of the methods already discussed, this method, too, has serious flaws. It does not focus on the value of future cash flows. It focuses on the value of a hypothetical new, and therefore fictional, building with fictional depreciation, and is of little use in valuing an operating company.

Discounted Cash Flow

Book value, par value, liquidating value, and replacement cost reflect entirely different concepts of value that may have little or no relation to the value of future cash flows. For this reason we must develop methods of valuation that include timing, size, and risk of cash flows in a systematic fashion and represent an *approximation* of the market processes that determine value in an efficient market made up of well-informed investors.

The cash flows of a firm belong to suppliers of funds who exchange money or services for a *claim* to future cash flows. In the simplest case, a laborer provides his services for 2 weeks before he is paid. Effectively, he is loaning the firm money (i.e., he supplies funds) in exchange for a promise by the firm to pay in 2 weeks. Each hour he works increases his claim on the firm's resources. Various suppliers may provide raw materials in exchange for a claim on the firm's resources to be paid in 30 days. A bank may make a short-term loan of $50,000 in exchange for a promise to repay principal plus interest in ninety days. Other individuals whom we call *investors* may provide cash on a longer term basis. Their claims on future resources are called *long-term securities*. Bondholders, as an example, might provide present dollars in exchange for a promise of periodic interest and principal payments over a specific period of time, whereas other investors may exchange similar amounts for promises of fixed-dividend payments (preferred stock) or for variable-dividend payments and the opportunity for capital growth (common stock).

For the normal operating firm, the short-term claims (current liabilities) can be valued at their book values since cash payment will occur soon. However, the same is not true of the longer term claims—debt, preferred stock, and common stock. An analyst must undertake the task of estimating future cash flows and determining their value if the analyst is to value a firm successfully.

No single valuation model is mechanically applicable to all securities. Rather there is a *family* of models, all derived from the concept of *present value*, or *discounted cash flow*, discussed in Chapter 5. The basic model

$$V = \sum_{t=1}^{n} \frac{C_t}{(1 + k)^t}$$

can be adapted to find the value V of future cash flows, provided one can estimate the size of the expected cash flow C_t, the timing t, and the risk-adjusted discount rate k.

In general, the *larger* the expected cash flow, the *longer* the flows are expected to continue, and the *lower* the risk premium included in the discount rate, the greater the value of a security.

VALUATION OF SECURITIES

In this section we develop valuation models for three types of securities—debt, preferred stock, and common stock. We do not claim that these models duplicate the process by which all investors value a security. Rather, we present a model of the valuation process that includes the basic components of value and is a *logical approximation* of the market valuation process. The fundamental interdependence of values of different financing sources (see Chapters 12 to 16) makes it desirable to consider values for all securities—including common stock, the matter of Layton's immediate interest.

A Bond Valuation Model

Our **bond valuation model** begins with a simple definition: a bond is a form of debt characterized by a series of regular interest payments and a final lump sum payment of principal at maturity.[4] The lump sum payment is called the *face value* or *maturity value* (usually $1000 per bond) and the interest payments are a fixed percent of that value. That fixed percent is called the *coupon rate*. In principle, interest payments could occur at many different intervals; however, they are usually paid semiannually. Thus, to calculate the dollars of semiannual interest payments, we multiply the coupon rate by the maturity value and divide by 2.[5] The value of the total cash flows to which the bondholder has a claim is the present value of the interest payment stream and the present value of maturity value, as follows:

---

[4]The reader may wish to refer to Appendix 3A, where debenture (unsecured) bonds such as these are distinguished from secured bonds.

[5]In many cases it is not difficult to project the cash flows for bonds or preferred stock. Both have fixed periodic payments. The bond has a fixed interest payment, maturity value, and maturity date. The only uncertainties lie in the fluctuation of future interest rates and the possibility that the firm may call (retire) the bond earlier than the projected maturity date. However, a few poor quality bonds for which there is considerable doubt about the ability of the firm to make interest and principal payments present special problems. The analyst must project the *expected* cash flows (interest and principal payments) in the future. Those expectations must be lower than the promised payments because, except for some special types of bond, the promised payments represent the *maximum* amount the bondholder will receive. We do not develop any specific methodology for projecting such cash flows, but the reader should be aware that expectations, not promises, determine cash flow projections.

$$V = \sum_{t=1}^{2n} \frac{\frac{C}{2}}{\left(1 + \frac{k_d}{2}\right)^t} + \frac{MV}{\left(1 + \frac{k_d}{2}\right)^{2n}}$$

where C is the annual interest payment, $2n$ is the number of semiannual periods, MV is the maturity value, and k_d is the appropriate annual *market rate* of interest. The rate k_d, required by the market, should not be confused with the fixed coupon rate. The latter is set when the bond is issued, whereas the former fluctuates with market conditions and attitudes of investors. The market rate is the proper discount rate to value future cash flows of a bond.

To demonstrate use of this formula, assume that a bond has 2 *remaining* years to maturity ($n = 2$), bears a 9 percent coupon rate with interest payable semiannually, and has a $1000 principal amount payable at maturity (MV). The prevailing market rate of interest for bonds of this risk and maturity is $k_d = 8$ percent (4 percent semiannually). Semiannual interest payments over 2 years means that there are $2n = 4$ compounding periods. Annual interest on the 9 percent coupon is $C = (0.09)\ \$1000 = \$90$. (The semiannual interest payment is $C/2 = \$90/2 = \$45$.) Substituting values for $2n$, C, MV and k_d into the formula, the market value of the bond is found.

$$V = \sum_{t=1}^{4} \frac{\$45}{(1.04)^t} + \frac{\$1000}{(1.04)^4} = \$163.35 + \$854.80 = \$1018.15$$

Note that the bond's market value V exceeds the maturity value MV of $1000. As long as the coupon rate exceeds the market rate k_d, the bond will be valued at such a *premium* over maturity value. If the discount rate had exceeded the coupon rate, bond value would be lower than maturity value—that is, the bone would be valued at a *discount*.

Although precise, the formula above is not convenient for future applications in the text. Therefore Equation (11-1) is used instead.

$$V = \sum_{t=1}^{n} \frac{C_t}{(1 + k_d)^t} + \frac{MV}{(1 + k_d)^n} \tag{11-1}$$

Interest payments and all compounding are in *annual* terms in Equation (11-1). However, bond values computed with this formula are very close to those obtained with the earlier formula. To see this, we can value the earlier bond.

$$V = \sum_{t=1}^{2} \frac{\$90}{(1 + 0.08)^t} + \frac{\$1000}{(1 + 0.08)^2} = \$90(1.7833) + \$1000(0.85734)$$

$$= \$1017.84$$

The difference in market price is only $0.31.

Bond Premiums, Discounts, Years Remaining to Maturity   As long as the *market* interest rate for a bond remains unchanged, the size of the premium or discount (of market value compared to maturity value) diminishes as time to maturity gets shorter. Consider, for example, the following three bonds.

Bond	Coupon Rate	Market Rate	Remaining Years to Maturity	Value
A	10%	8%	10	$1134.20
B	8	8	10	1000.00
C	6	8	10	865.80

All three bonds have 10 remaining years to maturity and have the same market rate of discount, k_d = 8 percent. Using Equation (11-1), bond A is valued at a premium over maturity value, since its coupon rate exceeds the market rate. Bond B is valued at maturity value (face value), since its coupon rate equals the market rate. Bond C is valued at a discount from maturity value since its coupon rate is less than its discount rate. [The reader should verify the bond value calculations using Equation (11-1).]

Now if the time to maturity were shorter, and the market interest rate were to stay the same, the value of bond A would fall (the premium would diminish) while the value of bond C would rise until, at maturity, their values equaled maturity value. Bond B, being valued at maturity value, would remain there until maturity. Figure 11-1 describes the behavior of the value of bonds A, B, and C as remaining time to maturity shortens. We see that as maturity shortens, the present value of the fixed principal payment (i.e., its maturity value) increases while that of the interest payments (which are diminishing in number) decreases. As time of maturity nears, maturity value increasingly dominates interest payments until, near maturity, the maturity value is the primary remaining cash flow attached to the bond and the primary source of value.

Application to J. L. Layton Bonds   The bond valuation model can be directly applied to the long-term debt of J. C. Layton, Inc. Referring to Table 11-1, we can see that this debt has a coupon rate of 7 percent and a maturity value of $3 million dollars. Interest payments are made semiannually in accordance with an agreement with the lender, and the principal must be repaid in 10 years in a lump sum. Unlike many bonds,

Figure 11-1   *Bond Values and Time to Maturity: Bond Premiums and Discounts Diminish as Years to Maturity Shorten*

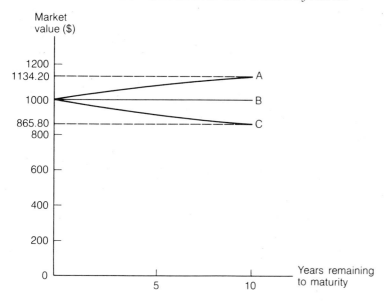

Layton's debt is not traded in the market. Rather, the whole $3 million was provided some years ago by the Fidelity Insurance Company, which continues to hold the total amount of the debt. (The bonds were *privately placed* when issued. See Appendix 3A.)

To find the value of those bonds we must determine that rate of return a lender would require to provide the same amount of funds today to J. C. Layton, Inc. That is, we must apply the *equal rate of return principle* in estimating a market value; we assess the risk of the bonds, then ask what rate of return investors require on securities of *identical* risk selling in the market. Since securities or portfolios having identical risk must sell at prices to yield the same rate of return to investors, the rate of return required by investors who buy and sell securities of identical risk must be the proper rate to use in assessing the present value of future cash flows that investors expect Layton to pay.

To find the appropriate required rate of return, one should be able to assess the risk of the bonds (beta), then determine the required rate using an estimate of the security market line. Or if that attempt is unsatisfactory, one might ask an investment banker what interest rates are currently being required on similar issues of debt. Since estimating bond betas presents both technical and conceptual problems that have not been resolved, the investment banker alternative is probably prefera-ble.[6]

In this instance, we find that similar debt has a required rate of return of 10 percent per year, a rate much higher than when Layton's debt was issued. With this information, the value of Layton's debt can be calculated. Total annual interest payments are:

$$0.07(\$3,000,000) = \$210,000$$

The maturity value is $3 million and the market rate is 10 percent. Therefore,

$$V = \$210,000 \sum_{t=1}^{10} \frac{1}{(1.10)^t} + \frac{\$3,000,000}{(1.10)^{10}}$$

$$= \$210,000(6.1446) + \$3,000,000(0.38554)$$

$$= \$1,290,366 + \$1,156,620 = \$2,446,986$$

Discount factors are taken from Appendix Tables C and D. The current market value is $553,014 below the maturity value because interest rates have risen since the debt was issued at 7 percent. If the Fidelity Insurance Company wanted to sell Layton's promise to pay annual interest of $210,000 for 10 years, with a lump sum of $3 million at maturity, it would receive $2,446,986, assuming that our assessment of the market interest rate is correct.

A Preferred Stock Valuation Model

Preferred shares offer a level dividend payment over the life of the security, making the **preferred stock valuation model** a type of annuity. In the simplest case (i.e., the security has no maturity and cannot be retired by the firm), we can write the value of preferred stock as a perpetuity:

$$V = \sum_{t=1}^{\infty} \frac{C_t}{(1 + k_p)^t} = \frac{C}{k_p} \tag{11-2}$$

where the C_t is the expected level annual dividend payment and k_p is the rate of return required by preferred shareholders.

For example, if a firm has a $100 par preferred stock with a 5 percent

---

[6]The suitability of calculating a beta and using it as the market's measure of risk in holding bonds has not been as satisfactorily accepted as in the case of stocks. Yet it seems to be a useful conceptual framework at this point. Limited studies of the values of beta for bonds so far have indicated that bond betas change over time as both years to maturity and market interest rates change.

(or \$5) yearly dividend and the current required rate is $k_p = 14$ percent, the current value *per share* is:

$$V = \frac{0.05(\$100)}{0.14} = \frac{\$5.00}{0.14} = \$35.71$$

Each share of stock sells at a price below the par value because the market rate of 14 percent is higher than the 5 percent preferred dividend.

Layton's preferred stock, having a \$50 par value and a 5 percent dividend rate, provides an annual dividend per share of $(0.05) \times \$50 = \$2.50$. The proper discount rate that reflects the risk of the preferred stock and is the required market rate on investments of identical risk is $k_p = 12$ percent. Given this information, Equation (11-2) can be applied directly to find a value per share of:

$$V = \frac{(0.05)\$50}{0.12} = \frac{2.50}{0.12} = \$20.83$$

Any investor paying this price per share expects to earn 12 percent per year on his investment.

The total value of the preferred is also easily found using Equation (11-2). The \$500,000 total par value of the preferred means that total annual preferred dividends are $(0.05) \, \$500,000 = \$25,000$. Therefore, the total value of the preferred stock is:

$$V = \frac{\$25,000}{0.12} = \$208,333$$

Valuation of bonds and preferred stock is somewhat easier than common stock valuation. Future returns to common shareholders are typically far more uncertain than returns payable to holders of bonds or preferred stock.

Common Stock Valuation Models

John Burr Williams developed an early **common stock valuation model** in which the value of a common share was the present value of all future cash dividends an owner expects to receive.[7] If all expected cash dividends per share in perpetuity are being evaluated, this valuation model is:

$$V = \sum_{t=1}^{\infty} \frac{D_t}{(1 + k_e)^t} \tag{11-3}$$

---

[7] John Burr Williams, *The Theory of Investment Value* (Cambridge, MA.: Harvard University Press, 1938), p. 56.

In this model, D_t is the dividend per share expected by *present* shareholders at each future date t. The required rate of return for equity k_e discounts these future dividends to a present value per share.

Valuation of Dividends per Share, not Total Dividends   It is important to emphasize that Equation (11-3) values dividends per share, not total dividends. From the standpoint of present shareholders, decisions leading to an increase in total dividends may not lead to proportionate increases in per share dividends because of the sale of new shares. Table 11-2 demonstrates this point. The Murdock Company is issuing new shares each year to finance expansion. Total dividends increase from $100 to $200 in 4 years. But initial shareholders, owning 1000 shares in year 0, do not similarly double their dividend receipts. The sale of 176 new shares to new owners over the 4-year period reduces dividends *per share* to $0.17 in year 4 from the level of $200/1000 = $0.20 occurring if the new shares were ignored. Initial shareholders increase by only 70 percent their dividends per share (from $0.10 to $0.17) and their total dividends to $170 from $100, as (1000) $0.10 = $100 and (1000) $0.17 = $170. The remaining $200 − $170 = $30 of total dividends is paid to owners of new shares at $t = 4$.

Insofar as present owners (at $t = 0$) of shares are concerned, increases in total dividends and dividends per share can be quite different things.

Valuation Based on Dividends, Not Earnings   A common objection to this model is that value should be based upon earnings, not dividends. Williams defended the dividend model by arguing that earnings are only a means to an end; stock must derive its value from the cash flows that shareholders expect to receive and the risk attached to those future cash flows:

Table 11–2   *Murdock Company Dividends*

	Year				
	0	1	2	3	4
Total Dividends	$ 100	$ 125	$ 150	$ 175	$ 200
Outstanding Shares	1000	1042	1071	1167	1176
Dividends per Share	$0.10	$0.12	$0.14	$0.15	$0.17
Total Dividend to Owners at Time 0	$100	$120	$140	$150	$170

If earnings not paid out in dividends are all successfully reinvested at compound interest for the benefit of the stockholder, as critics imply, then these earnings should provide dividends later; if not, then they are money lost. Furthermore, if these reinvested earnings will produce dividends, then our formula will take account of them when it takes account of all future dividends; but if they will not, then our formula will rightly refrain from including them in a discounted an- nuity of benefits.[8]

Although it is possible to properly construct a model based on the valuation of earnings that gives the same per share value as dividend valuation, we adhere to the latter model. But notice that Equation (11-3) requires that *every* cash dividend in perpetuity be estimated before per share value can be estimated. This is an impossible task if each expected future dividend is to be separately enumerated, for there are an infinite number of them! Therefore, it is convenient to use three variations of Equation (11-3) that, in compact form, can express the future dividend stream as a function of future dividend growth rates.

If all future dividends are expected to remain a constant amount D per share (the expected dividend growth rate is zero), Equation (11-3) becomes:

Zero Growth Model

$$V = \sum_{t=1}^{\infty} \frac{D}{(1 + k_e)^t} = \frac{D}{k_e} \qquad (11\text{-}4)$$

For example, Piglon Iron Works pays a current cash dividend per share of $1 and is expected to pay that amount in perpetuity. Therefore, $D = \$1$. If the required rate of return for common equity is $k_e = 9$ percent, the per share value is:

$$V = \sum_{t=1}^{\infty} \frac{\$1}{(1.09)^t} = \frac{\$1}{0.09} = \$11.11$$

Constant Growth Suppose, however, that dividends for Piglon Iron are expected to grow at some rate over time, so that investors anticipate a stream similar to that shown in the tabulation that follows. The growth rate is presumed to be 8 percent and the initial dividend payment is $1 per share. During the first year $1 grows to $1.08. During the second year $1.08 grows to $1.17. This process continues over time for as long as an 8 percent growth rate is expected. From Chapter 5 we can recognize that this sequence of dividends is growing at a constant compound rate.

---

[8]Williams, *The Theory of Investment Value* (*op. cit.*, note 7), p. 57.

Time	Dividend per Share for 8% Constant Growth Rate
0	$1.00
1	$1(1.08)^1 = $1.08
2	$1(1.08)^2 = $1.17
3	$1(1.08)^3 = $1.26
4	$1(1.08)^4 = $1.36
.	.
.	.
.	.

To obtain a formula to evaluate such a constantly growing dividend stream, we first note that the dividend at any time period t can be described as the current dividend multiplied by the appropriate compound growth factor:

$$D_t = D_0(1 + g)^t$$

where g is the periodic constant growth rate. For example, in the case of Piglon Iron the dividend at $t = 3$ is:

$$D_3 = \$1(1 + 0.08)^3 = \$1.26$$

To find the value of the constantly growing dividend stream, look back at the formula in Equation (11-3): every dividend term can be written as $D_t = D_0(1 + g)^t$ as shown above. Therefore the present value of the *growing* dividend stream over n finite intervals is:

$$V = \sum_{t=1}^{n} \frac{D_0(1 + g)^t}{(1 + k_e)^t} = D_0 \sum_{t=1}^{n} \frac{(1 + g)^t}{(1 + k_e)^t}$$

It is then possible to show[9] that this expression becomes:

---

[9]Equation (11-5) can be derived if we note that the prior expression can be written as:

$$V = D_0 \sum_{t=1}^{n} \frac{(1 + g)^t}{(1 + k_e)^t} = D_0 \sum_{t=1}^{n} a^t \qquad \text{(i)}$$

where we let $a^t = (1 + g)^t/(1 + k_e)^t$. Then, the terms $\sum_{t=1}^{n} a^t$ describe a progression having the sum:

$$\sum_{t=1}^{n} a^t = \frac{a(1 - a^n)}{(1 - a)} \qquad \text{(ii)}$$

Substituting $(1 + g)^t/(1 + k_e)^t$ for a in the right-hand side of Equation (ii),

$$V = \frac{D_0(1 + g)}{k_e - g}\left[1 - \left(\frac{1 + g}{1 + k_e} \right)^n \right] \qquad (11\text{-}5)$$

In Equation (11-5) we have the value of dividends growing at a constant rate g over n time periods. In a later section, this equation is useful, but we can also use it now to find the value of dividends *perpetually* growing at the constant rate g.

For a common stock that is expected to have a constant perpetual dividend growth (where the growth rate, g, *must be less than* k_e), the term $[(1 + g)/(1 + k_e)]^n$ approaches zero as n becomes very large.[10] In this special case, Equation (11-5) may be written:

$$V = \frac{D_0(1 + g)}{k_e - g} = \frac{D_1}{k_e - g} \qquad (11\text{-}6)$$

Equation (11-6) is a constant growth perpetual dividend valuation model. If the best prediction of a firm's future dividend payments is that they will grow at a constant rate for a long period of time, this equation provides a simple method of estimating value.

In the case of Piglon Iron, the current dividend of $D_0 = \$1$ is expected to grow at the rate $g = 5$ percent. Assuming that the required rate of return, $k_e = 9$ percent, properly reflects the risk of Piglon shares, the value per share from Equation (11-6) is:

$$V = \frac{\$1(1 + 0.05)}{0.09 - 0.05} = \$26.25$$

Naturally this value is much greater than the $11.11 value obtained earlier using Equation (11-4) with zero growth. If the same discount rate applied, but the growth rate were anticipated to be only 1 percent, the price per share would be smaller:

$$\sum_{t=1}^{n} a^t = \frac{\left(\frac{1 + g}{1 + k_e} \right)\left[1 - \left(\frac{1 + g}{1 + k_e} \right)^n \right]}{\left[1 - \frac{1 + g}{1 + k_e} \right]}$$

After simplifying,

$$\sum_{t=1}^{n} a^t = \frac{(1 + g)}{(k_e - g)}\left[1 - \left(\frac{1 + g}{1 + k_e} \right)^n \right]$$

Substituting $\Sigma\, a^t$ back into Equation (i) yields Equation (11-5).

$$V = \frac{D_0(1 + g)}{k_e - g}\left[1 - \left(\frac{1 + g}{1 + k_e} \right)^n \right]$$

[10]If $g \geq k_e$ we can see from Equation (11-5) that the value of a share would become larger and larger as the length of the growth period, n, became larger and larger. In the limit, as n approaches infinity, V_0 approaches infinity.

$$V = \frac{\$1(1.01)}{0.09 - 0.01} = \$12.63$$

Other factors being equal, the higher the growth rate, the larger the value of a share.

Variable Growth Rate   Models like Equations (11-5) and (11-6) are extremely simple to use, but they do not allow the analyst much flexibility. Not all firms conform conveniently to the zero or constant growth perpetual dividend frameworks. The range of models that one might use is limited only by the imagination. However, trying to predict the future path of dividends beyond a few years in the future is difficult—even for the most staid and conservative of firms. Consequently, intricate models that try to anticipate every possible change in future dividend growth are unlikely to be any more accurate than a much simpler model. The potential error is simply too large to allow much confidence in such a model. For this reason we will focus on a **single shift model** in which dividends grow at a rate g_1 for the first n years and at a rate g_2 for the remaining years in perpetuity.

Assume that investors expect the dividend stream of Squire Foods to grow at a rate of 15 percent for the next 4 years and, after that time, it is

Figure 11-2   *Single Shift Dividend Growth Pattern for Squire Foods*

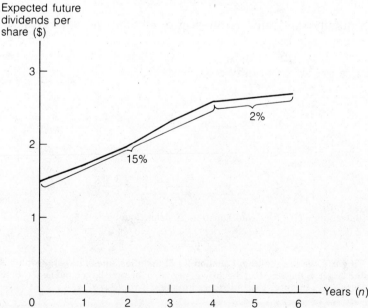

likely that dividends will grow at 2 percent per year, as shown in Figure 11-2. The current dividend is $1.50 per share and the required rate of return is $k_e = 12$ percent. Figure 11-2 portrays the single shift compounded annual growth in dividends for Squire Foods. The two growth rates separate the dividend stream into two portions—the portion growing at 15 percent and that growing at 2 percent. We will value each of the two portions of the dividend stream separately. (Remember, the present value methods assume that the cash flows take place at the end of each period.)

The first task is to predict the dividend stream for each of the next 4 years when the growth rate is 15 percent. These calculations can be made easily as in the following table.

Time	Expected Dividend Using 15% Growth Rate
0	$1.50
1	$1.50(1.15)^1 = \$1.73$
2	$1.50(1.15)^2 = \$1.98$
3	$1.50(1.15)^3 = \$2.28$
4	$1.50(1.15)^4 = \$2.62$

Given these projections, the present value of this segment of the dividend stream can easily be calculated.[11]

$$PV = \frac{\$1.73}{(1.12)^1} + \frac{\$1.98}{(1.12)^2} + \frac{\$2.28}{(1.12)^3} + \frac{\$2.62}{(1.12)^4}$$

$$= \$1.54 + \$1.58 + \$1.62 + \$1.67$$

$$= \$6.41$$

The expected dividend flows for the first 4 years have a present value of $6.41. The remaining dividends that are expected to occur in year 5 and beyond are projected to grow at a much slower rate, 2 percent. Beginning with the $2.62 dividend paid at $t = 4$, the 2 percent growth rate applies, as shown in Figure 11-2, to all future periods.

---

[11]Using Equation (11-5) we can also more directly find the present value of the growing dividend stream for 4 years by letting $n = 4$:

$$PV = \$1.50 \frac{1.15}{0.12 - 0.15}\left[1 - \left(\frac{1.15}{1.12}\right)^4\right]$$

$$= 1.50(-38.33)(-0.11152)$$

$$= \$6.41$$

Time	Dividend
4	$2.62
5	$2.62(1.02)^1 = $2.67
6	$2.62(1.02)^2 = $2.73
.	.
.	.
.	.

The present value of these flows is expressed as the summation:

$$PV = \frac{\$2.62(1.02)}{(1.12)^5} + \frac{2.62(1.02)^2}{(1.12)^6} + \cdots = \sum_{t=5}^{\infty} \frac{2.62(1.02)^{t-4}}{(1.12)^t}$$

This expression is cumbersome. An equivalent and easily evaluated expression is:

$$PV = \frac{1}{(1.12)^4}\left[\frac{\$2.62(1.02)}{0.12 - 0.02}\right] = 0.6355[\$26.72] = \$16.98$$

This expression is appropriate because all dividends *after t* = 4 grow at the constant 2 percent rate. Therefore, their value *as of t* = 4 (not at *t* = 0!) can be found by using the constant growth rate model, Equation (11-6). That value at *t* = 4 is:

$$V_4 = \frac{D_4(1 + g_2)}{k_e - g_2} = \frac{D_0(1 + g_1)^4(1 + g_2)}{k_e - g_2} = \frac{2.62(1.02)}{0.12 - 0.02} = \$26.72$$

To find the value at *t* = 0 of these dividends that begin at *t* = 5, we need only discount their value, V_4, at *t* = 4 by the appropriate present value factor $1/(1 + k_e)^4$.

Therefore the value of a Squire Foods share at *t* = 0 is the sum of the present values of the dividends growing at 15 percent and of those growing at 2 percent, or:

$$V = \sum_{t=1}^{4} \frac{1.50(1.15)^t}{(1.12)^t} + \frac{1}{(1.12)^4}\left[\frac{\$1.50(1.15)^4(1.02)}{0.12 - 0.02}\right]$$

$$= \$6.41 + \$16.98$$

$$= \$23.39$$

From this example, we can develop a general single shift growth model through use of Equations (11-5) and (11-6) that is adaptable to a wide range of growth patterns.

$$V = \sum_{t=1}^{n} \frac{D_0(1 + g_1)^t}{(1 + k_e)^t} + \frac{1}{(1 + k_e)^n} \left[\frac{D_0(1 + g_1)^n(1 + g_2)}{k_e - g_2} \right] \qquad (11\text{-}7)$$

$$= \sum_{t=1}^{n} \frac{D_0(1 + g_1)^t}{(1 + k_e)^t} + \left[\frac{1}{(1 + k_e)^t} \right] V_n$$

where V_n is the $t = n$ value of the dividends growing at a constant rate g_2, from $t = n$ to $t = \infty$.

The growth rate of dividends and the risk that shareholders must bear depend on the level of future investment, the rate of return the firm is expected to earn on that investment, and future financing policy. This implies that it may be necessary to make a product-by-product analysis of future investment opportunities. One must ask, Will product mix change in the future? Will competitive conditions change? Are there potentially major technological innovations in the industry? How are such changes likely to affect the competitive position of the firm? Will the firm use much more debt financing relative to equity in future financing? Answers to such questions must then be translated into an assessment of both the future dividend stream and risk.

Application to J. C. Layton Common Stock

Although these questions are certainly not exhaustive, they do remove some of the abstraction from the dividend valuation model. Growth and risk may be estimated only after a careful assessment of investment and financing policies.

Valuation of Layton's common shares has required considerable time spent studying financial statements, firm operations, the competitive structure of the industry, Layton's position in the industry, future investment plans, availability of financing—any information that might

Table 11–3 *Summary of Valuation Information: J. C. Layton, Inc.*

Dividend Information	
Most Recent Dividend	$0.42 per share
Anticipated Short-term Growth	22% per year for 3 years
Anticipated Long-term Growth	4% per year beyond 3 years
Risk Information	
Average Beta for Common Stock of Two Comparable Firms: 2.0	
Required Rate of Return	
Current Riskless Rate (r_f)	6%
Best Estimate of SML	$k_e = 6\% + (5\%)\beta_i$
Estimate of Required Rate from SML	$k_e = 6\% + 5\%(2) = 16\%$

have an impact on value. Since Layton's shares are not publicly traded, two comparable firms have been found whose shares are traded in an attempt to find an estimate of beta (risk) that might apply to Layton's shares. All the information gathered is summarized in Table 11-3.

Conditions appear to justify a dividend growth rate of 22 percent in each of the first 3 years and leveling off to a more modest 4 percent thereafter. This information suggests that the single shift model, Equation (11-7), should be used in valuing the shares. Analysis of two comparable firms in the same industry as Layton and traded on a stock exchange shows a beta of 2.00. This is accepted as the market's measure of risk for Layton. Finally, estimation of the security market line yields a required rate of return of 16 percent using a beta of 2.0. As with previous valuations, use of required rates of return for securities of identical risk is an application of the equal rate of return principle to find the proper share value. Dividend projection and valuations are as follows.

Time	Dividend	
0	$0.42	
1	$0.42(1.22)$	$= \$0.51$
2	$0.42(1.22)^2$	$= \$0.63$
3	$0.42(1.22)^3$	$= \$0.76$
4	$0.42(1.22)^3(1.04)$	$= \$0.79$

$$P_0 = \frac{0.51}{1.16} + \frac{0.63}{(1.16)^2} + \frac{0.76}{(1.16)^3} + \frac{0.79}{0.16 - 0.04}\left[\frac{1}{(1.16)^3}\right] = \$5.62$$

The best estimate of the value of one share is $5.62. Note that this value is substantially above the book value of $2.32 per share presented earlier.

Naturally, $5.62 is only an estimate, and some error is always possible. Nevertheless, it is the *best* estimate available given the forecasts of dividend growth. A more extensive analysis could include specifying different dividend growth rates that are to be viewed as the most likely *ranges* of growth. Using Equation (11-7), these growth rates can be translated into *ranges* of share value to view the likely span of error about the $5.62 value estimate.

THE VALUE OF THE FIRM

To this point the value of specific claims—debt, preferred stock, and common stock—that compose the firm's total capital structure has been estimated. It is a simple step from there to a derivation of the value of the entire firm. By convention this value will be the value excluding

Table 11–4   *A Comparison of Book and Market Values of J. C. Layton's Debt, Preferred Stock, and Common Stock*

	Book Value[a]	Estimated Market Value
Debt	$3,000,000	$2,446,986
Preferred Stock	500,000	208,333
Common Stock	2,320,000	5,620,000[b]
Total	$5,820,000	$8,275,319

[a]Book values taken from the balance sheet for J. C. Layton, Inc., shown in Table 11–1.
[b]The price of each share was shown to be $5.62. Since there are 1 million shares outstanding, their total value is $5.62 × 1,000,000 = $5,620,000.

current liabilities and the derivation focuses only on the value indicated for noncurrent sources of funds.

Table 11-4 summarizes book and estimated market values of J. C. Layton's securities. Because interest rates have risen since issue, the estimated market values of both debt and preferred stock, which lead holders to expect a fixed maximum dollar return, are lower than book values. No investor would pay a price equal to the book value of those securities because he or she could enter the financial markets and find securities of identical risk that promised higher rates of return. By contrast, the common shares have a market value almost 2.5 times as large as book value. The value of the future dividend stream is far greater than the amount of funds invested in the firm by shareholders. This circumstance implies that the firm has been making *profitable investments* for shareholders. We cannot, of course, determine from this information whether the firm is *maximizing* shareholder wealth, but we do know that shareholders are unlikely to be willing to sell their shares for book value.

The *total* value of the firm is obtained by adding the values of each type of security. Comparing book and estimated market totals, the market value is more than 1.4 times as large as book value.

It is possible that members of the Layton committee seeking to value common shares may object to this valuation on the basis that it contains too much "blue sky." That is, it focuses too much on the future, with all its uncertainties, rather than on objective financial records.[12] This is a

---

[12]This position is frequently taken in the nontextbook world. Public utility hearings, where the utilities' rates are established, often provide a platform for arguments about the pros and cons of book value and replacement value versus estimates of market valuation.

very perplexing objection to confront in a clear, convincing, and objective manner.

Without repeating much of what has been said earlier, the following arguments are offered in response to any such objection.

1. Investors purchase securities for the returns and risks conferred on the investors.

2. Those returns and risks are typically not immediate rewards and punishments. They occur at intervals in the future, if the firm is a going concern that will not be immediately liquidated.

3. Valuation must reflect the anticipated flows and their associated risks, otherwise it ignores the reason for purchasing securities.

4. Financial statements that reflect past actions are useful if they provide insights that will allow a view of the future, but by their very nature they are unlikely to tell analysts or investors everything they would like to know.

5. An understanding of financial statements is only the first step. The requirement that analysts project events and their economic consequences that have not yet occurred does not give the analysis less validity than if attention were confined to financial statements. In fact, it gives it more validity.

6. Just because tomorrow's events (new information) could cause the analysts to make substantial alterations in today's valuation does not invalidate that analysis unless the analyst was careless. He is not paid to be clairvoyant but to make intelligent judgments based on present information.

These points are important. Valuation is both science and art—perhaps more of the latter than we would like to admit.

SUMMARY This chapter focused on the valuation of securities. We defined *value* as the price at which a security should sell when bought and sold in a market by well-informed investors. In an *efficient market* when the analyst does not have inside information that would have a material impact on share price, the market price at any point in time is the best estimate of value. When markets are inefficient the value of the security may not correspond to existing market price, but it must be related to a market price that could be obtained at some point in the future if it is to make economic sense.

Value is a function of anticipated future events. Therefore, valuation—the process of estimating value—requires not only technical competence to use valuation models, but imagination and creativity to analyze a wide range of data and to translate that data into projections of future cash flows, risk, and required rates of return.

Several different concepts of value were discussed—book value, par value, replacement value, liquidating value, and the value of future cash flows. None of the first three concepts have any necessary relation to the value of a firm's securities because they do not focus on the cash flows that will belong to owners of those securities. Liquidating value is useful only if liquidation is considered to be a viable option for the firm. If so, liquidating value should be the minimum amount that should be paid for securities. But for most firms that will continue to be operated in the future, all securities should be valued according to the cash flow and risks that accompany an operating firm. The securities issued by the firm (debt, preferred stock, and common stock) have different risk–return characteristics, but their values are interdependent and are affected by the future performance of the firm.

GLOSSARY OF KEY TERMS

Bond Valuation Model	A representation of the market price or logical approximation to a market price that would exist if the bond price were determined in an efficient market.
Book Value	Amount(s) recorded on the books of the firm by accepted accounting practices.
Common Stock Valuation Model	A logical approximation to an efficient market price for a common stock.
Constant Growth Common Stock Model	A common stock valuation model that assumes a constant rate of growth of dividends in perpetuity.
Liquidating Value	Amount(s) expected to be received if firm operations cease and the assets of the firm were sold.
Par Value	The value assigned to each share in the common stock account on the balance sheet.
Preferred Stock Valuation Model	A representation of a preferred stock market price or a logical approximation to that price, assuming that the market price was determined in an efficient market.

Replacement Cost of Assets (Less Depreciation)	A valuation method using estimates of the replacement cost of assets, from which the depreciation proportionate to the depreciable life so far consumed is deducted.
Single Shift Growth Common Stock Valuation Model	A common stock valuation model that assumes cash dividend growth at two different rates in the future.
Value of a Firm	A logical approximation to the market price of the firm if it were to be sold in an efficient market; usually obtained by summing the market values of the securities of the company.
Value of a Security	The price at which the security would be bought and sold in an efficient market.

SELECTED REFERENCES

Bierman, Harold, Jr., and Jerome Hass. "Normative Stock Price Models." *Journal of Financial and Quantitative Analysis* (September 1971), pp. 1135–1144.

Haugen, Robert, and Prem Kumar. "The Traditional Approach to Valuing Levered-Growth Stocks: A Clarification." *Journal of Financial and Quantitative Analysis* (December 1974), pp. 1031–1044.

Holt, Charles C. "The Influence of Growth Duration on Share Prices." *Journal of Finance* (September 1962), pp. 465–475.

Mao, James C. T. "The Valuation of Growth Stocks: The Investment Opportunities Approach." *Journal of Finance* (March 1966), pp. 95–102.

Miller, Merton H., and Franco Modigliani. "Dividend Policy, Growth and the Valuation of Shares." *Journal of Business* (October 1961), pp. 411–433.

Wendt, Paul. "Current Growth Stock Valuation Methods." *Financial Analysts Journal* (March–April 1965), pp. 3–15.

QUESTIONS

1. Models of security valuation include what elements in addition to the price of time?

2. How does the determination of par value and book value of common or preferred stock differ from the determination of market price?

3. How should owners of wealth-maximizing, closely held firms make investment decisions in the absence of market-determined share prices?

4. Define cash flow in perpetuity.

5. Set up a valuation model for common stock when a current $1.00 dividend is expected to grow at 10 percent for the first five years, 7 percent for the next five years, and 5 percent thereafter.

6. What do security valuation models seek to approximate as an ideal?

7. What should be the entries in the common stock account and paid-in capital account of a new corporation that sold a hundred $10 par value common shares at $20 a share?

8. Explain how you would value the Brink Bakery if its balance sheet showed bonds and common stock outstanding, both actively traded in the market.

9. The president of Cox Company was regarded as valuable to the firm. How might the company decide how valuable he was and thus for how much to insure his life?

10. Why might a speculator wish to follow a strategy of buying bonds with low coupons when market interest rates are high and selling them later when market rates are low?

11. Use the discounted cash flow valuation model to show how the value of a bond is affected by (a) the coupon rate, (b) the time to maturity and (c) the risk premium.

12. A bond has a coupon rate of 6% and five years to maturity. For what range of market discount rates will the bond sell at a premium?

13. If a bond sells at a discount today and applicable market rates stay constant over the year, how will the value of the bond be likely to change? Explain why this change might occur.

PROBLEMS

1. If Frank promises to pay Jane $100 in one year's time and Jane requires a rate of return for this risk of 25 percent, what is the value now of Frank's promise to Jane?

2. Boase Belt Buckle Co. is expected to be liquidated in a year for one million dollars. After payment in full to all holders of debt and preferred claimholders, $500,000 are expected to be available for common shareholders. If there are 10,000 shares outstanding and the required rate of return is 8 percent, what should an investor be willing to pay now for Boase stock?

3. The Jack Bar, Inc., has the following balance sheet:

Jack Bar, Inc.

Assets		Liabilities and Equity	
Cash	$ 1,000	Wages Payable	$ 1,000
Accounts Receivable	5,000	Accounts Payable	4,000
Inventories	25,000	1990 Debentures, 8% ($1000 face value)	50,000
Furniture and Fixtures	20,000	$5 Preferred Stock ($50 par)	10,000
Building	49,000	Common Stock ($1 par)	10,000
Land	20,000	Paid-in Capital	15,000
	$120,000	Retained Earnings	30,000
			$120,000

(a) Compute the book value of all debentures.

(b) Compute the book value of all preferred shares.

(c) Compute the total and per-share book value of the common stock.

(d) What is the book value of the entire company?

(e) What is the total semiannual interest outlay on the debentures by the company? Per bond?

(f) If the assets of Jack Bar, Inc., could be liquidated for $65,000 cash (after payment of current liabilities) and if debts and preferred stock claims have to be paid before any funds are available to owners of common, what would be the per-share liquidating value of common?

4. One of the Dowdle, Inc., bottling plants was 15 years old. Dowdle, Inc., wished to sell the plant to a local bottler, but market prices were nonexistent and the company felt its worth was substantially in excess of the current book value. The plant originally cost $500,000 and had accumulated depreciation of $375,000. Dowdle called in an appraiser who felt the building had lived half its useful life of 30 years. The only way he could guess at its value (future

cash flow of data being unavailable) was to estimate what it would cost to build a new one, which was $1 million. At what price should Dowdle, Inc., offer the building for sale?

5. Suppose you wish to purchase a bond having a face value of $1000. Its coupon rate is 7 percent and the market rate on bonds of similar risk is 10 percent. It will mature in 10 years. How much should you be willing to pay for the bond? (Use semiannual compounding.)

6. A perpetual 5 percent bond ($1000 face value) requires a return in the market today of 10 percent. (a) What should it sell for? (b) If it were only a 10-year bond, what should it sell for? (c) If it were only a year to maturity what should the bond sell for? (Use annual compounding.)

7. Sid Peters was offered a new 4 percent, $1000 face value City of St. Louis bond due to mature in five years. This municipal bond required a return to investors of 6 percent. What is the maximum price he should pay if St. Louis paid interest semiannually?

8. The Lavender 15 percent preferred ($100 par) is being evaluated by an analyst at Amalgamated Insurance. Using his beta estimate of 0.85 and his estimated security market line, he calculated a risk premium of 4 percent on top of the risk-free rate of 4 percent. What value should attach to this preferred (assume preferred dividends are paid at the end of each year)?

9. What would be the value of Topaz Mining common stock, which is expected to pay a $5 dividend for 20 years (when the mine runs out and the company dissolves with no liquidating value) if the required rate of return is 10 percent?

10. If Algonquin Co. common pays $2 forever and no growth is expected, what would be its value if investors in the market require an 8 percent rate of return for this risk?

11. What is the value of Burpless Co. common if it currently pays a $4 dividend that is expected to grow at 5 percent per year for two years and then have zero growth for the remainder of its perpetual life? The required rate of return is 7 percent.

12. The cash dividends of the Ajax Co. are expected to grow at 6 percent per year forever. If it currently pays $1 per share in dividends and the return required by shareholders is 12 percent, what is the current value of an Ajax share?

13. The shares of Hibbs, Inc., are selling for $20 each. However, Sidney Sharpe feels that the shares might be undervalued. He

noted the firm currently pays a dividend of $1.50 a share. Careful analysis led Sid to believe that dividends would grow at a rate of 4 percent per year in the future. An investment having risk similar to that of Hibbs would earn investors a rate of return of about 10 percent.

(a)   What is the maximum Sid should be willing to pay for Hibbs stock?

(b)   In three months other market participants change their assessment of Hibbs to agree with Sid and the market price changes to sell at the value computed in (a). What *annual* rate of return will Sid earn if he buys the stock at $20 and sells it after the other market participants have come to agree with him (assume Sid received no dividend during the three-month period).

14.   The Rye Corp., a closely held company with 100,000 shares outstanding and 15 shareholders, has the following balance sheet and information available.

The debentures are held by Consolidated Insurance, were placed at their face value of $1000, and have a remaining maturity of eight years. Bonds of equivalent risk sell in the market to yield 8 percent.

The preferred has no call provision and has a beta of 1.0. The current riskless rate of return is 4 percent and American Investment Company estimates that the security market line is equal to r_f + (5%)β.

The common stock currently pays an annual dividend of $1 and is expected to grow over the short term (five years) at 15 percent per year and at 6 percent per year thereafter. Its beta is estimated at 1.4.

Make a comparison of the book value and the market value of the Rye Corp.

Rye Corp. Balance Sheet (000's)

Assets		Liabilities and Equity	
Cash	$ 100	Accounts Payable	$ 200
Marketable Securities	100	6% Debentures	1,000
Accounts Receivable	300	8% Preferred ($100 par)	800
Inventories	500	Common Stock ($1 par)	100
Equipment	1,000	Paid-in Capital	900
Plant	2,000	Retained Earnings	1,000
	$4,000		$4,000

15. The C.D. Electronics Company has the following items on its balance sheet.

December 31, 1982

Long-term debt 12%	$5 million
8% Preferred stock	$1 million
Common stock	$6 million

The debt matures in 10 years and the preferred is a perpetual issue. Similar risk bonds currently sell to yield 12 percent and similar risk preferred are priced to yield 14 percent. Dividends on common stock have grown during the past four years from $1.85 per share in 1978 to their current (1982) level of $2.00. This growth is expected to continue into the foreseeable future. There are 1.5 million shares of common outstanding. Stockholders require an 18 percent return on their investment.

APPENDIX 11A

FAILURE, BANKRUPTCY, AND REORGANIZATION

Although all businesses expect to be successful, many are not. Various financial indications of serious difficulty are often apparent. Cash shortages arise, borrowing may increase, accounts are overdrawn, and maintenance of plant and equipment is delayed. Careful observation of either profit or cash receipt and disbursement trends may signal pending financial discomfort. However, illiquidity (a lack of cash) makes the difficulty acute and that problem can no longer be ignored.

Inasmuch as this discussion involves liquidity, it also involves firm survival. Thus the nature, degrees, and types of business failure need to be examined briefly. We refer to **insolvency** as the inability of the firm to meet cash payments on contractual obligations. The lack of cash to meet payments of accounts payable, wages, taxes, interest, and debt retirement will constitute insolvency even though the enterprise may have a substantial and adequate dollar value of assets. When assets are plentiful in relation to liabilities, it is usually possible for the financial manager to plan ahead and arrange for sufficient cash through various sources to prevent any embarrassment. In most cases, any temporary lack of liquidity can be overcome by borrowing or through the planned liquidation of certain assets. A sound, profitable business should have no difficulty in this regard, and reasonably intelligent planning should ward off the danger. If the firm is insolvent because of successive losses, poor management, or insufficient original investment in working capital, lenders will be less willing to place funds at its disposal. The financial manager should be aware of the potential variability that exists in the availability of funds. The "willing" lender is often less willing during periods of "tight" money, great financial uncertainty, or panic.

Accounting insolvency exists when a firm's recorded assets amount to *less than its recorded liabilities*. This condition arises when successive losses create a deficit in the owner's equity account, rendering it incapable of supporting the firm's legal liabilities. The firm that is liquid and paying its current bills may nevertheless be insolvent in the accounting sense. Outsiders may not be aware of the insolvency as long as the liquidity of the firm enables it to meet its cash obligations. If protracted, such a situation usually leads to bankruptcy.

Violation of a **bond indenture agreement** will also provide a source of financial difficulty for the firm. A bond indenture is the contract between the firm and the bondholders. A trustee, a third party, acts to represent the collective interest of the bondholders. In addition to the contractual claim to interest payments, the indenture may require annual payments to a sinking fund and certain other provisions that attempt to provide for the security of the bondholders. If a firm fails in making a sinking fund payment, the trustee is responsible for undertaking appropriate action. If any other provision is not complied with, the trustee may also take action. Pressure by the trustee on the firm will usually do little to alleviate a problem already in an advanced stage. However the trustee can warn bondholders of the difficulties and help form a bondholders' committee to be activated in the event of in-court or out-of-court adjustments.

In case of financial distress marking insolvency or failure to satisfy a bond indenture, the usual alternatives are:

1. Do *nothing* but hope something will come along to save the situation.

2. Attempt to *sell out*. The firm can try to find a buyer. At such a point buyers may be few and if one can be found, the seller frequently feels fortunate if he can walk away with any portion of his original equity.

3. Go outside the judicial process to *seek adjustments* with creditors that permit the firm to keep operating, to try to work its way out. Such adjustments usually take the form of extension of time to pay and/or compositions of credit (described below).

4. *Seek court relief* in *bankruptcy* proceedings. Reorganization or liquidation will result from the bankruptcy proceedings.

5. Assign assets to a third party for liquidation.

6. Liquidate.

It is not unusual for a financially embarrassed firm to avoid bankruptcy by some sort of "workout" arrangement with its creditors. The creditors may not wish to sue for satisfaction of their claims if it appears that they would so recover a smaller proportion of these claims *and* if the financial difficulties appear to be temporary. The workout requires the agreement of almost all creditors and the loss of some or all management control by the owners. Frequently small creditors may try to hold up an agreement to a workout and thus force the major creditors to advance enough funds to pay off the recalcitrants in full or in proportions greater than those received by other creditors. If the workout is successful, in time major creditors will be able to look forward to full satisfaction of their claims and will avoid bankruptcy proceedings and the attendant court costs (including foreclosure or reorganization costs). **Out-Of-Court Adjustments**

Sometimes creditors agree to an **extension** of the maturity date of a loan for which, at the moment, the principal payment is past due. Although this does not correct a more fundamental disorder, it does give the firm more breathing room; it allows the firm to make other adjustments in its financial resources without the burden of immediate repayment of the principal of the loan. An extension is not given without cost, however. Restrictions on a firm's dividends may be imposed; major owners of small firms may be asked to put up more money; or future borrowings may be precluded except on a subordinated basis.

Composition is yet another form of adjustment of capital sources. This method involves recomposing the debt of the firm in such a way that the creditors receive partial payment for their claims—say, $.60 on $1. Creditors may find it more expedient to follow this route than to take the troubled firm to court to seek full satisfaction. Under the latter procedure they run the risk of not receiving as much as they would under the composition approach. Moreover, they would have legal costs to meet, which might more than offset any gains achieved by going to court.

A third nonbankruptcy method of adjusting capital sources involves the operation of the enterprise by a group of creditors, called a **creditors' committee,** until such time as there is sufficient liquid capital to meet the impending claims or until an acceptable composition is found.

In out-of-court adjustments, there is no legal compulsion for any creditor to accept the attempted adjustment. Any creditor not satisfied with the proposal of the majority (or minority) to relieve the financial burden of the firm can refuse the arrangement and insist that his claim be met in full; if this is not done, the creditor can take the firm to court to be liquidated or reorganized.

Bankruptcy   Court procedures may result in the firm being liquidated or financially reorganized to continue operations. A petition for bankruptcy may be volunteered by the distressed firm, or a creditor's petition may force the firm into the courts. The Bankruptcy Reform Act of 1978 sets up national judicial procedures for handling bankruptcies, replacing a 1938 Act that was confusing and sometimes conflicting in its application. The law has seven odd-numbered chapters including: Chapter 5, dealing with creditor claims; Chapter 7, dealing with liquidation procedures; Chapter 11, dealing with reorganization of firms; and Chapter 13, dealing with individuals and small business deferred payment plans.

Chapter 11 of the   Under Chapter 11 a firm is reorganized, voluntarily or involuntarily,
Bankruptcy Act   resulting in the settlement of all claims against the firm. Under *voluntary* reorganization, the firm itself may petition the bankruptcy court; but creditors including bondholders and stockholders may initiate a petition to the court as well, in which case it is termed *involuntary*. The court will follow the petition with a hearing to determine the firm's insolvency— defined in the Act as the inability of the firm to meet its contractual payments. The firm's management can then offer a plan for reorganization under voluntary bankruptcy within 120 days of petition. However, any claimant or group of claimants may submit a reorganization plan if the firm fails to do so. In any case a reorganization will involve a plan to satisfy all claimants that, once approved by the court, replaces all claims (prior to bankruptcy) on the firm. Owners of each class of claims— common stock, preferred stock, secured and unsecured debt—may seek a voice before the court. Such owners may seek approval or rejection of the plan, approval being defined as two-thirds of the amount of each class of the claims. Rejection of a plan by owners of a class of claim may not cause the court to reject the plan as long as no class more senior in priority receives more than it should under the rule of priorities. And a secured creditor must receive at least the full amount of the value of collateral used as security for that particular credit.

After consideration by all groups of claims, the court may accept or reject the plan. It *must* accept the plan if it complies to the law, all groups have approved it, and it is *fair and equitable*. A fair and equitable plan is one in which no group receives less than they would under liquidation of the business.

Once approved by the court, payments are made to the various groups in the form of securities and property, including cash. New securities are frequently issued. The allocation according to the plan is made on the basis of the *absolute priority rule* requiring that certain claims are to be satisfied in full, prior to the satisfaction of other claims. A typical ordering of claims follows:

1. *Special current debt,* such as trustee expenses, *unpaid wages* of employees earned in the last six months preceding bankruptcy but not to exceed $600 in any one case, and *taxes.*

2. *Secured creditors,* such as the holders of mortgage bonds and collateral trust bonds, but only to the extent of the liquidating value of the pledged assets.

3. *General creditors,* consisting of unsatisfied secured creditors and all unsecured creditors, but only to the extent of their proportionate interest in the aggregate claim of this class.

4. *Subordinated debt.*

5. *Preferred stockholders,* to the extent provided in their contract plus dividend arrearage.

6. *Residual claimants* (common stockholders).

Among the factors to be taken into account in a reorganization plan are the following. The capital structure must be recast to bring it in line with the projected earnings of the revamped firm. Clearly, no more senior debt should be issued than can be comfortably handled over the foreseeable future. In fact, sufficient leeway should be made for the issuance of debt securities in the future if the need arises. Because of this necessity, fixed charges are to be avoided and contingent-charge securities (such as preferred and common stock or income bonds) are used in their stead.[1] The total value of the securities to be issued is determined by capitalizing the expected future income of the firm at a rate consistent with the business risk, a statement easy to make but typically very difficult to implement. Often the recast capital structure will wipe out the junior claimants such as subordinated debt, preferred stock, and common stock.

The 1978 Act allows a breach of the *absolute priority rule.* Senior pri-

---

[1] Income bonds' interest payments are contingent on earnings.

orities, for example, may wish existing management to continue and wish to allow the firm to retain some, but reduced, shareholder interest. The court may approve this over objections of more junior claimants as long as those junior receive a *fair and equitable* payment in the plan.

In approving reorganization, the court (and SEC if asked to be involved) must decide that the reorganization value exceeds liquidation value. If such a reorganization plan does not provide an excess over liquidation value, the firm should be liquidated.

Chapter 13 of the Bankruptcy Act   For small businesses (proprietorships) with secured creditor claims of $350,000 or less and unsecured creditor claims less than $100,000, a plan can be approved allowing the firm to pay its debts over a 36-month period. The payments are made through a court-designated trustee. Such a plan is cheap to administer and if it is not successful, the firm may be liquidated under Chapter 7 or reorganized under Chapter 11.

Liquidation   Two procedures are allowable under liquidation. Under *liquidation by assignment*, the firm and creditors agree out of court to a certain distribution of assets and proceeds of sale of assets. All creditors must agree or if not, the dissenting creditor must be bought off so that an agreement must be reached.

Under Chapter 7 of the Bankruptcy Act, a court appoints a *referee* and the creditors select a *trustee* who sees to the liquidation and distribution of proceeds according to absolute priority rule allocation.

APPENDIX 11B

VALUING AN OPTION   A student searching for living accommodations at the beginning of the school year might find an apartment that seems just about right. However, wanting to explore other possibilities in the vicinity without giving up the right to this particular apartment, the student offers the manager $10 to hold the apartment for an hour. Any time during that hour the student can return and rent the specific apartment at an agreed-upon price. After the hour is up, however, the apartment can be rented to someone else.

In this situation an option has been created. The student is the purchaser of the option. He has acquired an *exclusive* right to rent an apartment for the next hour. The apartment manager sells the option. In so doing she gives up the right to rent the apartment to someone else for the next hour. Note that although the student does not have to take the apartment, the manager does have to rent it if the student decides to exercise the option.[1]

In this instance, the price of the option is $10. That price probably reflects a host of factors from the demand for housing and the arrival rate of potential renters to the probability of finding superior living arrangements through further search. This option arrangement may appear unique; however, the world is full of financial opportunities that have the characteristics of an option.

In general, an option is a contract that gives the purchaser the opportunity to buy or sell certain securities or goods at a specified price during a stipulated period. Note that the purchaser does not have to exercise that opportunity. It will be exercised only if it is advantageous to do so.

Three types of option are quite common. A call option or "call" gives the buyer the right to purchase a security at a specified price until a designated date. Since 1973 call options on many securities have traded on organized markets. A put option or "put" is an option to sell a security at a specified price until a designated date. Puts, too, are traded on organized exchanges, but the market has not been as deep or as active as the call market. Both calls and puts are purchased and sold by investors as part of their investment strategies.

A third type of option that is common is the warrant. Warrants are issued by firms raising money rather than by investors. Warrants typically have a much longer life than a put or a call, and they are often issued in conjunction with other securities such as bonds.

An example of a security that includes an option as a component of its value is a convertible bond. The value of such a bond may be divided into two parts: the value of expected interest and principal payments over the life of the bond, and the value of the option to exchange the bond for a fixed number of common shares over some designated period.

Finally, one may even view common stock of a levered firm as an option. By making contractual payments to creditors, shareholders maintain control of the firm and its assets. Those payments may be viewed as exercise prices, and the length of the option is the maturity of the debt. Shareholders will exercise their option (make payments to creditors) as long as the underlying value of the assets is greater than the exercise price. If the value of those assets is less than the exercise price,

---

[1]Please ignore all the legal problems that would accompany breach of contract. These are honest people.

shareholders will not make contractual payments and the assets of the firm will go to bondholders.[2]

We do not discuss many other unique securities that also include options. Rather, we proceed to the value of a call option. As a first step in developing an expression for the value of a call, we look at the upper and lower limits on call price. Since an option is always exercised voluntarily, it never has a price less than zero. Investors will always be willing to hold an option at a price of zero. Thus, we can write

$$CP \geq 0$$

where CP is the "call price" or the price of the option.

Also, a call must sell for a price less than the value of the underlying asset. If one call can be converted into one share of stock only upon paying the exercise price, the price of a call cannot be greater than the price of the common stock because an investor would always buy the stock rather than the option if the prices were equal. This conclusion allows us to write:

$$CP \leq P$$

where P is the price of one share of stock.

Although the price of an option can never be greater than the price of the underlying asset or less than zero, there is an additional restriction that depends on the exercise price E and the price of a share. In deriving the restriction, we assume for simplicity that the firm does not pay dividends. Consider an investor who owns one option with a current price CP and has a bank account in which he has deposited $E/(1 + r)^t$, where E is the exercise price on the option, r is the periodic rate of interest available on the deposit, and t is the number of periods until the call must be exercised.

The total value of the option plus the bank account is:

$$CP + \frac{E}{(1+r)^t}$$

In comparison with the ownership of the stock itself, this combination is superior. If it is desirable to exercise the option at expiration, there will be sufficient funds to do so. The account will be drawn down to zero, the option will have been exercised, and one share of stock will be owned.

---

[2]This description is simplified because we have not discussed the implications of multiple debt payments, but it does capture the essential elements of the option qualities of common stock.

Alternatively, if the share price is below the exercise price, the investor can purchase a share of stock in the market and still have some cash left over. Thus, the portfolio consisting of an option plus cash equal to $E/(1 + r)^t$ is as good as owning the common stock when exercise is desirable and better when it is not. In a properly functioning market, the value of that portfolio must be greater than the price of a share, so

$$CP + \frac{E}{(1+r)^t} \geq P$$

or rearranging,

$$CP \geq P - \frac{E}{(1+r)^t}$$

The value of an option must be greater than or equal to the price of a share minus the disounted value of the exercise price.

The limits on option prices are shown in Figure 11B-1, where option prices are on the vertical axis and share prices are on the horizontal axis. All option prices must be nonzero, so they lie in the first quadrant. Next, all values of the option must lie on or below the 45 degree line $CP = P$, since we know from the second restriction that the price of the call option cannot be greater than the price of the underlying common stock. Finally, CP must lie on or above the 45 degree line $CP = P - E/(1 + r)^t$ for any given number of periods to maturity as dictated by the final restriction.

Figure 11B-1   *The Limitations on Option Prices*

Option price, CP

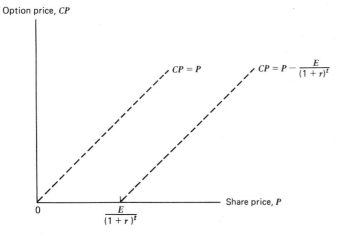

$CP = P$

$CP = P - \dfrac{E}{(1 + r)^t}$

Share price, P

0

$\dfrac{E}{(1 + r)^t}$

Figure 11B-2   *Option Price Located Within Limits of Option Value*

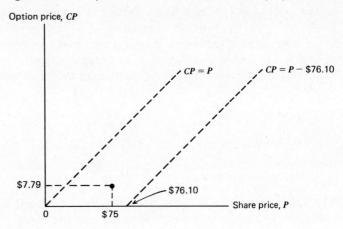

These restrictions limit the range of values that an option may have, but they do not identify the specific price at which an option should sell. To identify that price, we turn to the Black–Scholes option pricing formula.

Assuming perfect financial markets and no taxes, the valuation expression for an option is

$$CP = PN(d_1) - \frac{E}{e^{rt}} N(d_2)$$

where

$$d_1 = \frac{\ln(P/E) + (r + \frac{1}{2}\sigma^2)t}{\sigma\sqrt{t}}$$

$$d_2 = \frac{\ln(P/E) + (r - \frac{1}{2}\sigma^2)t}{\sigma\sqrt{t}}$$

In this framework,

CP = the current price of an option

P = the current price of a share of stock

E = the exercise price of an option

t = the number of years remaining before expiration

r = the continuously compounded rate of interest

e = 2.71828

$1/e^{rt}$ = the single payment, present worth factor in continuous time; recall that the single payment factor in discrete time is $1/(1 + r)^t$

σ = the standard deviation of the continuously compounded annual rate of return on the stock

$\ln(P/E)$ = the natural logarithm of the ratio of stock prices and the exercise price

$N(d)$ = the probability that a deviation less than d will occur in a normal distribution

Although much of the logic underlying this expression is rather tortuous, it can be applied relatively easily.

Assume the following values.

$P = \$75$
$E = \$80$
$t = 0.5$ (one half year or six months to expiration)
$r = 0.10$ (continuously compounded annual rate of interest)
$\sigma = 0.40$

Those values imply that

$$d_1 = \frac{\ln(75/80) + (0.10 + (0.5)(0.40)^2)0.5}{(0.40)\sqrt{0.5}} = 0.09$$

$$d_2 = \frac{\ln(75/80) + (0.10 - (0.5)(0.40)^2)0.5}{(0.40)\sqrt{0.5}} = -0.193$$

Now turning to a table of probabilities for the normal distribution as shown in Appendix E we find

$$N(d_1) = N(0.09) \qquad = 0.53$$
$$N(d_2) = N(-0.193) \qquad = 0.42$$

Substituting these values into the Black–Scholes expression for the price of a call yields

$$CP = \$75(0.53) - \frac{\$80\ (0.42)}{e^{0.1 \times 0.5}}$$

This option should sell at a price of $7.79. Note that in Figure 11B-2 the price is within the bounds discussed above.

This model is based on the assumption that no dividends are paid before the option expires. If that assumption is not correct, the call price will be *below* that predicted by the formula because share price will fall on the ex dividend date. Indeed, the larger the dividend payment, the lower the value of an option. Discussions of the option valuation problems that accompany dividend payments together with solutions to those problems have been published.[3]

---

[3]For instance, see Richard Roll, "An Analytic Valuation Formula for Unprotected American Call Options on Stocks with Known Dividends," *Journal of Financial Economics* (November 1977), pp. 251–258; John Cox, Stephen Ross, and Mark Rubinstein, "Option Pricing: A Simplified Approach," *Journal of Financial Economics* (September 1979), pp. 229–263.

CHAPTER 12

Capital Structure and the Cost of Capital

Discussions of capital budgeting and valuation in earlier chapters treated required rates of return (cost of capital) and financing decisions as
given. Whereas a **cost of capital** was used to discount future cash flows,
no attempt was made to relate that rate to the firm's financing decisions
or to discover how it might be estimated. Similarly, when the value of J.
C. Layton's securities were computed in Chapter 11, we did not ask why
the firm chose the particular mix of financial instruments and how that
choice might affect required rates on individual securities. These gaps in
our knowledge provide the focus for the next several chapters.

One question underlies much of our discussion: *How should a firm be
financed if the value of the firm and the wealth of shareholders are to be maximized?* Since in selling a security—be it common stock, one of many
forms of debt, preferred stock, or warrants—a firm sells a claim to a
portion of its future income stream, one could ask the same question in a
slightly different way. *Does it make a difference how a firm's total income
stream is divided into separate streams that are sold in the market?*

Determining the firm's financing mix or, equivalently, deciding how
its income stream should be divided among claimholders, constitutes
the capital structure decision. In making this decision managers wish to
know whether the value of the firm is increased by changing the financing mix. They might, for instance, consider whether a change in the
type, maturity, or amount of debt relative to other sources of funds
would increase the value of the firm.

To understand the impact of the mix of financing instruments used to
finance the firm, we must first understand how market forces work.
That is, we must discover how the market value of a firm changes, or if it

changes, when a form of financing other than common stock is introduced. Since an understanding of these market forces is most easily acquired in a simplified context, our initial exploration assumes that financial markets are perfect. Keep in mind, however, that the conclusions reached under perfect markets do not necessarily change when market imperfections are introduced. Indeed, the analysis presented here provides an important foundation on which more advanced analysis rests.

The **capital structure** of the firm, defined as the mix of financial instruments used to finance the firm, is simplified to include only long-term, interest-bearing debt and common stock, excluding short-term liabilities. To avoid needless complication, we assume that the firm has no growth opportunities and that all net income is paid out as dividends. The impact of dividend policy is evaluated separately in Chapter 14. Preferred stock, having a fixed dividend payment, shares some of the attributes of debt in providing **financial leverage** for the firm. Because preferred dividends are not tax deductible and interest payments on debt are, the restriction of consideration to debt allows us not only to look at the effect of financial leverage on value, but to assess the role of the tax-deductible status of interest payments as well.

Discussion of fundamental market forces and their impact on firm value with different mixes of debt and equity is divided into two parts. First, we demonstrate that when financial markets are perfect and corporate taxes are absent, firm value and shareholder wealth are unaffected by financing decisions. There is no optimal capital structure. Second, corporate taxes are introduced. Because interest is tax deductible, shareholders benefit from the reduced level of taxes paid by a levered firm. Firms should borrow as much as possible, and an optimal capital structure is virtually 100 percent debt.

This entire chapter rests on the pioneering work of Franco Modigliani and Merton Miller. The capital structure propositions developed are often called the Modigliani–Miller or MM propositions.[1]

CAPITAL STRUCTURE: PERFECT MARKETS AND NO INCOME TAXES

The debt/equity mix used by the firm will have no effect on the value of the firm if perfect markets are assumed to exist and if there are no income taxes. The fundamental concept to keep in mind is the equal rate of return principle first announced in Chapter 3: two securities of equal

---

[1]The articles in which this capital structure analysis appears are listed at the end of the chapter.

risk must be priced in the market to yield the same expected rate of return.

Two firms, Unlever, Inc., and Lever, Inc., are used to demonstrate the main points. Balance sheets and income statements, as well as other pertinent information for these two firms, are exhibited in Table 12-1. The income statements are *not* historical data but reflect investor expectations of future performance of the two firms. (Remember, valuation depends on future, *not* past performance of firms.) Unlever and Lever are identical in all ways except that Unlever uses no debt in its financing

Table 12–1   *Financial Information for Unlever, Inc., and Lever, Inc.: Perfect Markets and No Corporate Taxes*

		Unlever, Inc.	Lever, Inc.
Balance Sheets			
Current Assets		$ 2,000	$ 2,000
Fixed Assets		8,000	8,000
		$10,000	$10,000
Debt, B		0	$ 5,000
Equity, S		$10,000	5,000
		$10,000	$10,000
Expected Income Statement			
Sales		$14,000	$14,000
Cost of Goods Sold		12,200	12,200
Depreciation		800	800
Net Operating Income		$ 1,000	$ 1,000
Interest Expense		0	350
Net Income		$ 1,000	$ 650
Other Data			
Debt/Equity Ratio	B/S	0	1.0
Expected Interest Rate	k_d	—	7%
Total Dividends	$N \times D$	$ 1000	$ 650
Number of Shares	N	1000	500
Dividends per Share	D	$ 1.00	$ 1.30

mix whereas Lever uses 50 percent debt and 50 percent equity in its capital structure. Assuming no growth, both firms produce an expected net operating income stream of $1000 annually in perpetuity. It is especially important to note that the net operating income stream is a risky stream for both firms—but of identical risk for both. Finally, the $5000 of debt issued by Lever is assumed to have no maturity and to have an expected interest rate of 7 percent. It is expected to pay $350 of interest per year forever.[2]

Consider now an investment in Unlever or Lever. Suppose that an investor wanted to own 10 percent of the $1000 net operating income stream of each firm. How could that investor accomplish this feat? In the case of Unlever, Inc., it is easy. The investor need only purchase 10 percent of the 1000 outstanding shares, or 100 shares. Unlever has no debt, so the net income received and paid out as cash dividends is the same as the net operating income stream. For Unlever, the purchase of 100 shares produces an expected annual stream of $100 \times \$1 = \$100$, since cash dividends are $1 per share.

Two Identical Unlevered Streams of Income

To purchase 10 percent of the net operating income of Lever, the investor *cannot* simply purchase 10 percent of the outstanding shares. That act would entitle him to 10 percent of the net income stream but not of the net operating income stream. The interest payments on outstanding debt represent a prior claim on the stream of net operating income. That is, shareholders are paid only after bondholder claims have been satisfied. Because shareholder returns are net of interest, the net income stream is riskier than the net operating income stream—these two streams are *not* the same thing.

The investor *can* purchase 10 percent of the net operating income of Lever by buying 10 percent of the 500 outstanding common shares *and* 10 percent of the outstanding debt. The expected stream of earnings then received is $100 and consists of the following components.

---

[2]Two important points are noted here. First, the debt has an *expected* interest payment of $350. Since this is *risky* debt, the *promised* interest payment is somewhat higher. For example, the debt may actually bear a coupon interest rate of 7.2 percent and the promised interest payment will be $(0.072) \$5000 = \$360$. This amount will be paid *unless* adverse financial conditions prevent payment in some years. Bondholders, feeling that interest may not be fully paid in some years, expect, on average, to receive $350 (thus the expected interest rate of 7 percent) and not the promised $360.

Second, although perpetual debt is employed in the example, debt with any finite maturity of, say, 5, 10, or 20 years could have been used as long as this debt has the same expected interest rate of 7 percent. The critical assumptions in this section are that there are no bankruptcy costs and that the firm continues to operate even when promised interest payments are not earned in any particular year.

Expected Cash Dividends	50 shares $\times$ \$1.30 = \$ 65
Expected Interest	0.10 $\times$ \$350 = $\underline{\quad 35}$
	\$100

Ownership of 50 shares of common stock paying a \$1.30 expected cash dividend per share yields an expected dividend stream of \$65. Ownership of 10 percent of the outstanding debt entitles the investor to 10 percent of the expected annual \$350 interest payments, or \$35. The investor now owns 10 percent of the \$1000 net operating income stream of Lever, Inc. In effect, this transaction has "undone" the financial leverage used by Lever, Inc.

To be certain that the two streams of earnings from investment in both firms are of identical risk, suppose that, in some year, net operating income is only \$350 because of a fluctuation of actual net operating income below the \$1000 expected amount. The ownership of 100 shares in Unlever will provide 10 percent of that \$350 net operating income stream, or \$35. For Lever, net income will be 0 and the 50 shares the investor owns will receive no dividends. But the investor owns 10 percent of the Lever debt and will receive 0.10 $\times$ \$350 = \$35 in interest payments. In either case, his returns are the same.

Valuation of Two Identical Unlevered Streams

What will the two alternative investments in Unlever and Lever be worth? Both investments claim 10 percent of the net operating income and both are of equal risk. Since, in this case, the expected net operating income streams are of identical size (\$1000), the equal rate of return principle will require not only that both investments yield the same expected rate of return but that both have the same dollar value. If we let V_U be the total value of Unlever, Inc., and V_L the total value of Lever, Inc., it must be true that

$$V_L = V_U \qquad (12\text{-}1)$$

The value of Unlever happens to be equal to the total value of its shares S_U, which we can find if we know the rate of return required by shareholders. For Unlever, that required rate is k_u, the rate of return required for an unlevered firm. Let k_u = 10 percent. The value of Unlever is:

$$V_U = S_U = \frac{\text{Expected net operating income}}{k_u} = \frac{\text{Expected dividends}}{k_u} = \frac{\$1000}{0.10} = \$10,000$$

Since the value of the levered firm V_L must equal V_U = \$10,000, then we know that:

$$V_L = S_L + B = \$10,000$$

That is, the *sum* of the value of Lever common shares S_L, plus the value of the bonds B, must equal $10,000 as well.

If the total value of the two firms were not the same, an *arbitrage* opportunity for investors would exist. (Recall the discussion of arbitrage in Chapter 3.) Suppose, for example, that Unlever had a total value of $V_U = S_U = \$11,000$, and that Lever had a total value of $V_L = S_L + B = \$9000$. Purchase, of, say, 10 percent of Unlever would provide an expected rate of return of:

$$r_U = \frac{\text{Expected dividends}}{V_U} = \frac{\$100}{\$1100} = 0.091, \quad \text{or } 9.1\%$$

In contrast, purchase of 10 percent of the outstanding shares *and* bonds of Lever would produce an expected rate of return of:

$$r_L = \frac{\text{Expected dividends and interest}}{S_L + B} = \frac{\$100}{\$900} = 0.111, \quad \text{or } 11.1\%$$

Investors would want to sell Unlever shares and buy Lever shares *and* bonds because they represent equivalent risk investments, but yield different rates of return. The value of Unlever shares would fall and the value of Lever shares and bonds would rise until total values of $10,000 were restored for both firms and the expected rates of return were equal (i.e., $r_L = r_U = 10$ percent).

Clearly, the total values of the levered and unlevered firms are identical. Differences in capital structure appear not to make any difference to total value of the firm as long as the equal rate of return principle holds.

Unlever, Inc., and Lever, Inc., were seen to have the same total value when the investor wanted to hold *unlevered* investments. The investor had to hold bonds *and* shares of Lever, Inc., to produce such an unlevered investment in the case of the Lever investment. What if investors wanted to hold *levered* investments? How can this be done with Unlever and Lever, and what total values for the firms will result?

Two Identical Levered Streams of Income

To obtain a levered stream of income, the investor can simply purchase, say, 10 percent of the Lever, Inc., shares. This entitles the investor to 10 percent of the net income stream. Lever's outstanding debt exerts a prior claim on net operating income. The investor will own 10 percent of Lever's expected $650 income stream, or $65. But the investor cannot purchase 10 percent of Unlever, Inc.'s shares and have an investment of equal risk. Unlever has no debt and the Unlever shares have a claim on the less risky net operating income stream.

To make the investment in Unlever have the same risk as an investment in Lever shares, the investor must create "homemade leverage."

This is done by purchasing 10 percent of Unlever shares, entitling the investor to a $100 income stream by the use, in part, of personal borrowing. Assuming that the investor can borrow at the same $k_d = 7$ percent expected rate as can Lever, Inc., $500 will be borrowed. This will produce (0.07) $500 = $35 of expected annual interest charges the investor must pay. The investor's expected annual return from this holding will be $65, consisting of $100 expected to be received each year from the Unlever shares *less* the $35 expected annual interest payments on the investor's personal debt. The investor has created leverage, of the "homemade" variety, where none had existed.

The stream of cash returns from the ownership of Lever shares and from the homemade levered ownership of Unlever shares have identical risks. To see this, assume that in a future year, net operating income for both firms declines to $350. The investor owning 10 percent of the Lever shares will receive no cash dividends in that year because all earnings must be paid to owners of debt. The investors owning 10 percent of the Unlever shares and using homemade leverage will not receive anything either. The $35 received from unlevered shares (10 percent of the $350 net operating income) must be paid to the lender who provided the funds that allowed creation of the homemade leverage.[3]

Valuation of Two Identical Levered Streams

As in the case of identical unlevered streams, the valuation of identical levered streams produces the result that both streams have the same total value. The equal rate of return principle ensures this result.

The value of 10 percent of the shares of Unlever, less the amount borrowed to create homemade leverage, which is equal to 10 percent of the value of Lever's bonds, can be written $(0.10)S_U - (0.10)B = 0.10(S_U - B)$. The debt liability has the value B because investors can borrow at the same expected rate, $k_d = 7$ percent, as can Lever, Inc. Since the personal and corporate debt have the same interest payments and risk, they are worth the same to owners of such debt. The value of 10 percent of the shares of Lever, Inc., is $(0.10)S_L$. Since the levered stream obtained by owning shares in Lever is identical to the levered stream obtained by owning Unlever shares partly financed by homemade leverage, the equal rate of return principle requires that the value of the two streams be the same. That is, $0.10(S_U - B) = (0.10)S_L$, so by simplification:

---

[3]Investors creating homemade leverage must have the same limited liability provided investors in the equity of corporations. Thus, an investor in Lever shares will not, in the event of adversity for the firm, lose more than the value of his shares. Similarly, the investor purchasing Unlever shares with homemade leverage must be assumed to lose not more than the value of the unborrowed portion (his own funds) used to purchase Unlever shares if Unlever's financial fortunes are less than expected.

Value of Homemade Levered Stream		Value of Corporate Levered Stream
$S_U - B$	$=$	S_L

This expression can be rearranged as follows.

$$S_U = S_L + B$$

But what is another way of expressing the value of the Unlever shares? Since Unlever, Inc., has no debt, the total value of that firm is $V_U = S_U$. And since the total value of Lever is the sum of the value of the shares S_L and the bonds B, then $V_L = S_L + B$. Replacing S_U with V_U, and $S_L + B$ with V_L, the equality earlier stated in Equation (12-1) must hold under the equal rate of return principle. If Unlever shares are worth, as before, $10,000, then $V_U = S_U = \$10,000$. Therefore the value of Lever shares and bonds may be expressed $V_L = S_L + B = \$10,000$.

If, for some reason, the total values of the two firms were not the same, another arbitrage opportunity for investors would exist. For example, suppose that Lever had a total value of $11,000 and Unlever a total value of $9000. The expected rate of return from holding Lever shares is:

$$r_L = \frac{\text{Expected dividends}}{V_L - B} = \frac{\$650}{\$11,000 - \$5000} = \frac{\$650}{\$6000}$$

$$= 0.1083, \quad \text{or } 10.83\%$$

Owners of Lever shares receive $650 in net income and the Lever shares are worth, in total, $6000, because perpetual debt with $350 expected annual interest payments will have the value $B = \$350/0.07 = \$5000$ at the expected 7 percent interest rate. The expected rate of return of 10.83 percent from holding Lever shares is lower than could be obtained by holding Unlever shares using homemade leverage.

$$r_U = \frac{\text{Net operating income} - \text{Interest}}{V_U - B}$$

$$= \frac{\$1000 - \$350}{\$9000 - \$5000}$$

$$= \frac{\$650}{\$4000}$$

$$= 0.1625, \quad \text{or } 16.25\%$$

If Unlever stock is partly financed with homemade leverage, investors will expect net operating income of $1000 less interest on personal debt of $350 for a $650 annual return. Investors' *personal* investment is the purchase price of the shares, $V_U = S_U = \$9000$, less the value of personal debt, $\$5000$—for a $\$4000$ net investment. The resulting 16.25 percent expected rate of return is superior, for the purchase of Unlever shares with homemade leverage, to the otherwise identical investment in Lever shares. Investors will want to sell Lever shares, causing their price to *fall*, and purchase, using homemade leverage, Unlever shares—causing their price to *rise*. The price adjustment would continue until the total value of both firms is $V_U = V_L = S_L + B = \$10,000$. At that price, the value of investors' *personal* investments are equal at $V_U - B = V_L - B = \$5000$. Expected rates of return for Lever shares and Unlever shares (financed with homemade leverage) are then equal at $\$650/\$5000 = 13$ percent. This expected rate of return is greater than the rate $k_u = 10$ percent for shares of Unlever. This higher rate is required because both shares in Lever and investments in shares of Unlever using homemade leverage produce riskier streams of earnings than the stream of net operating income, for which $k_u = 10$ percent is appropriate.

Cost of Equity Capital and Share Price

Levered and unlevered firms with the same business risk and expected net operating income always have the same total value because investors can undo corporate leverage or create its duplicate, homemade leverage. These actions ensure that the equal rate of return principle will hold. What does this result mean for the cost of equity capital and the share price of the firm?

Cost of Equity Capital   Given that the total value of the firm is unchanged by financial leverage, the cost of equity capital k_e (the required rate of return) for any firm can be written as follows.

$$k_e = k_u + (k_u - k_d)\frac{B}{S} \qquad (12\text{-}2)$$

The ratio of the market value of bonds to market value of shares B/S is a measure of the degree of financial leverage—higher ratios measuring higher degrees of leverage. In Equation (12-2), higher ratios of B/S increase the required rate of return on *equity* because the term multiplied by B/S is the difference between k_u, the required rate of return on unlevered shares (or, the cost of equity capital for an unlevered firm), and k_d, the cost of debt. (This difference must be positive unless the firm is an all-debt firm. Unlevered shares receive the risky net operating income stream, while the bonds have a prior claim on income, and hence must bear lower risk than owners of an unlevered firm.) Thus, an all-equity firm will have a cost of equity capital of $k_e = k_u$ in Equation (12-2) because $B/S = 0$. When financial leverage increases, B/S becomes higher and k_e rises.

Applying Equation (12-2), recall that Unlever's cost of equity capital is $k_e = k_u = 10$ percent when no debt is utilized [i.e., $B/S = 0$ in Equation (12-2)]. But Lever has outstanding bonds worth $B = \$5000$. The total value of Lever is $V_L = \$10,000$ so that the total value of shares must be $S_L = \$5000$. For Lever the degree of leverage is $B/S = 1.0.$. Substituting $B/S = 1.0$, $k_u = 10$ percent, and $k_d = 7$ percent into Equation (12-2), Lever's cost of equity capital is $k_e = 13$ percent.

$$k_e = 10\% + (10\% - 7\%)\ 1.0 = 13\%$$

The cost of equity capital is higher for Lever than for Unlever because the stream of net income Lever shareholders receive is riskier than the stream of net operating income Unlever shareholders receive. Lever shareholders want compensation for this risk and the required rate of return, or cost of equity capital, is correspondingly greater.

Cost of Debt   The expected cost of *debt* was given as $k_d = 7$ percent for a debt/equity ratio of $B/S = 1.0$. In fact, however, the cost of debt may well rise with higher degrees of leverage. Use of more debt means greater risk for owners of debt. As the total interest payments rise with use of more debt, the interest payments come closer to the size of the expected stream of net operating income—increasing the chance that an especially low net operating income level in some future year will make the firm unable to pay interest on the debt. Bondholders will require a premium for bearing that risk and the cost of debt may be expected to rise with financial leverage. As we will see, this rising cost of debt does not change the notion that the total value of the firm is unaffected by the degree of financial leverage.

The cost of capital for the *firm* is the weighted average cost of capital computed by the following formula. **Cost of Capital for the Firm**

$$K = k_d \frac{B}{V} + k_e \frac{S}{V} \qquad (12\text{-}3)$$

This is the cost of capital used to discount the stream of *net operating income* expected to be generated by the firm. It consists of the cost of debt and equity weighted by their proportions, *at market value,* in the capital structure.

For Unlever, the cost of capital for the firm is $K = k_e = 10$ percent. This can be seen by realizing that k_e from the earlier Equation (12-2), is $k_e = k_u = 10$ percent. Then, in Equation (12-3), $S/V = 1.0$ and $B/V = 0$, because no debt is used by Unlever. Therefore the cost of capital to the firm and the cost of equity capital are the same thing for Unlever. For Lever, the fact that $B = \$5000$, $S = \$5000$, and $V = \$10,000$ means that $B/V = 50$

percent and S/V = 50 percent. With k_d = 7 percent and, from Equation (12-2), k_e = 13 percent, the cost of capital to the *firm*, K, is:

$$K = 7\% \ (0.5) + 13\% \ (0.5) = 10\%$$

Therefore, the cost of capital for the firm, K, is *identical* for all degrees of financial leverage and is equal to k_u, the cost of equity capital for an unlevered firm. Unlever and Lever have the *same* overall cost of capital of K = 10 percent. This makes sense when we note that the cost of capital for the firm is used to discount net operating income. Since the net operating income is $1000 for both firms and both firms have K = 10 percent, the total value of both firms is:

$$V_L = V_U = \frac{\$1000}{0.10} = \$10,000$$

as earlier demonstrated.

Share Price   The share price of firms is also *unaffected* by increases in financial leverage. With all net income paid out as dividends and dividends expected to be constant over time, the share price P will be:

$$P = \frac{D}{k_e} \tag{12-4}$$

where D is dividends per share. Increases in dividends per share brought about by financial leverage will be *exactly* offset by a higher cost of equity capital necessary to compensate investors for the greater risk of a levered net income stream. For example, Unlever has an unlevered net income stream of $1000 and, with N = 1000 shares outstanding, dividends per share are D = $1. With $k_e = k_u$ = 10 percent, share price for Unlever is:

$$P = \frac{\$1.00}{0.10} = \$10$$

In contrast, Lever's expected net income is $650. But that dividend is divided among 500 shares, so expected dividends per share are D = $650/500 = $1.30. From Equation (12-2), the cost of equity capital is k_e = 13 percent. Therefore, share price of Lever is:

$$P = \frac{\$1.30}{0.13} = \$10$$

Share price for Lever shares is identical to that of Unlever shares. Lever shares may have higher dividends per share but they are also riskier dividends. The resulting higher discount rate k_e ensures that share prices will not be higher for Lever shares than for Unlever shares.

Figure 12-1   *Capital Costs and Leverage: Perfect Markets and No Corporate Taxes*

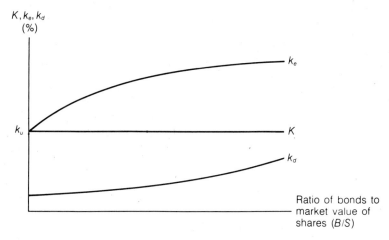

Naturally, increasing use of financial leverage will make *total* share value decline—even while share price is unchanged. More use of debt financing requires less *total* equity financing. Thus, Unlever has a total share value of $S_U = \$10,000$. Lever, because it uses $5000 of debt financing, has a total share value of $S_L = \$5000$.

The effects of finanical leverage on the cost of equity capital for the firm are graphically described in Figure 12-1. The cost of debt in Figure 12-1 rises along the curve k_d as the degree of financial leverage, measured by B/S, rises. Greater debt means greater risk for bondholders and a higher required rate of return. The cost of equity capital rises on the curve labeled k_e—according to Equation (12-2).[4] When no leverage is used, $k_e = k_u$. As leverage increases, the cost of equity capital, k_e, rises. The cost of capital for the firm, K, is the weighted average cost given in Equation (12-3). It is a *constant* for all degrees of financial leverage and is equal to the unlevered cost of equity capital k_u. Therefore, K is described by a horizontal line in Figure 12-1.

Summary of Effects of Leverage

Total value of the firm, total value of shares, and total value of the bonds of firms under different degrees of financial leverage are graphically summarized in Figure 12-2. The horizontal line V shows the total

---

[4]Equation (12-2) appears, in form, to be a straight line. This is not the case when, as in this example, the cost of debt k_d also rises with leverage.

Figure 12-2   *Value and Leverage: Perfect Markets and No Corporate Taxes*

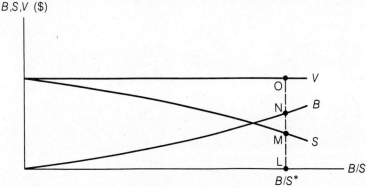

value of the firm as a *constant* for all degrees of financial leverage. The total value of bonds on the curve labeled *B* rises with greater leverage and the total value of shares on the curve labeled *S* falls with greater leverage. At any degree of financial leverage, the *sum* of the values *S* and *B* must equal *V*. For example, at *B/S** the vertical distance LM plus the vertical distance LN must equal the vertical distance LO.

Some representative effects of varying degrees of leverage on capital costs and value are presented numerically in Table 12-2, for firms having an expected net operating income of $1000 and an unlevered cost of equity capital of $k_u = 10$ percent. These effects are the same as those described graphically in Figures 12-1 and 12-2.

Table 12–2   *Leverage, Cost of Capital, and Value: Perfect Markets and No Corporate Taxes*

	Debt/Equity Ratio, *B/S*			
	0	1/3	1	3
B	0	$ 2,500	$ 5,000	$ 7,500
S	$10,000	7,500	5,000	2,500
k_d	—	0.06	0.07	0.08
k_e	0.10	0.113	0.13	0.16
K	0.10	0.10	0.10	0.10
V	$10,000	$10,000	$10,000	$10,000

Clearly, perfect markets and the absence of income taxes mean that firms cannot benefit shareholders by using financial leverage. Shareholders' wealth will not be increased. If, for example, Unlever duplicated Lever's capital structure, share price would remain at $10 per share. An investor holding 100 shares of Unlever initially worth $100 \times \$10 = \$1000$ would still have $1000 of wealth if Unlever sold $5000 of 7 percent bonds in the market and bought 500 shares of its own stock at $10 per share. The investor would receive $500 for selling 50 of his shares to the firm and would hold the remaining 50 levered shares. These levered shares are worth $10 per share or $500 for this investor. His wealth is unchanged. Thus, from the shareholder's viewpoint, *no* optimal capital structure exists.

Implications for Capital Structure Decisions

Once corporate income taxes have been introduced, financial leverage *does* affect the value of the firm. Increases in financial leverage will increase the total value of the firm and share price. The cost of equity capital does rise with greater leverage, but it does not increase as rapidly as in the case just examined (i.e., no income taxes). The firm's overall cost of capital *falls* with greater leverage.

To demonstrate these points, the firms of Unlever and Lever described in Table 12-1 are again used. However, the expected income

CAPITAL STRUCTURE: PERFECT MARKETS WITH INCOME TAXES

Table 12–3   *Financial Information for Unlever and Lever: Perfect Markets and Corporate Taxes*

	Unlever	Lever
Expected Income Statement		
Sales	$14,667	$14,667
Cost of Goods Sold	12,200	12,200
Depreciation	800	800
Net Operating Income	$ 1,667	$ 1,667
Interest	—	350
Taxable Income	$ 1,667	$ 1,317
Income Taxes (40%)	667	527
Net Income	$ 1,000	$ 790
Total Expected Payments to Investors and Government		
Interest to Bondholders	—	$ 350
Dividends to Shareholders	$ 1,000	790
	$ 1,000	$ 1,140
Taxes to Government	667	527
Net Operating Income	$ 1,667	$ 1,667

statements are changed for the purpose of this demonstration. Table 12-3 shows these revised statements.

Both firms now have identical expected net operating income before taxes of $1667—instead of $1000 as in Table 12-1. At a corporate tax rate of $\tau = 40$ percent, Unlever now has a net income after taxes of $1000. Lever has tax-deductible interest payments of $350 and net income after taxes of $790.

The Interest Tax Subsidy

The first thing to note about Unlever and Lever with corporate income taxes is that Lever pays less of its pre-tax net operating income to government than does Unlever. This beneficial result occurs because interest payments on debt are tax deductible. As a result, shareholders in Unlever receive $1000 after taxes whereas *combined* bondholders and shareholders in Lever receive $1140 after taxes. The difference in these after-tax receipts, $140, is the *expected* **interest tax subsidy.** The expected interest tax subsidy can be written as $\tau k_d B$—or the tax rate times the expected annual interest payment. Thus, with $\tau = 40$ percent and $k_d B = \$350$, the expected interest tax subsidy may be written $\tau k_d B = (0.40) \$350 = \$140$.

This interest tax subsidy is of value to shareholders because it reflects how much the government is paying to help finance assets of the firm. If interest payments were not tax deductible, tax payments would be larger. Even more important, the interest tax subsidy is a benefit enjoyed only by investors holding levered shares. Corporate leverage permits interest charges to be deducted against corporate taxable income. Investors attempting to duplicate corporate leverage with homemade leverage *cannot* deduct interest expenses on *personal* debt from *corporate* taxable income and do not enjoy the interest tax subsidy. (We consider the role of personal taxes in the next chapter.)

Assuming that the expected interest tax subsidy $\tau k_d B$ has the same risk as the stream of expected interest payments $k_d B$, the expected subsidy may be discounted at the same expected cost of debt k_d.[5] The present value of the interest tax subsidy is:

$$\frac{\tau k_d B}{k_d} = \tau B$$

This valuation of the subsidy reflects the fact that it is a much less risky stream than the stream of net income. The interest payments on bonds that give rise to the subsidy have a prior claim on net operating income over dividends to shareholders.

---

[5]That is, an investor who wanted to purchase the uncertain interest tax subsidy in the market would require a rate of return identical to that which bondholders require on debt. This assumption is restrictive but necessary to a simplified analysis of capital structure.

When the value of the interest tax subsidy, obtainable only through corporate leverage, is taken into account, the value of the levered firm V_L equals the value of the unlevered firm V_U *plus* the present value of the interest tax subsidy.

$$V_L = V_U + \tau B \tag{12-5}$$

In other words, levered firms have a greater total value than unlevered firms. We do not derive Equation (12-5), but it can be obtained by allowing for the favorable interest tax subsidy and applying the equal rate of return principle to corporate and (somewhat altered) homemade leverage ownership positions.

To value Unlever and Lever, let us suppose that k_u, the applicable *after-tax* cost of equity capital for unlevered firms, is 10 percent. The value of Unlever is then:

$$V_U = S_U = \frac{\$1000}{0.10} = \$10,000$$

as the stream of net income is appropriately discounted. Otherwise-identical Lever has a tax subsidy of $\tau k_d B = \$140$. Capitalized at $k_d = 7$ percent, the value of this subsidy is $\tau B = \$2000$. Therefore, the value of Lever is:

$$V_L = V_U + \tau B = \$10,000 + \$2000 = \$12,000$$

The *after-tax* cost of equity capital increases with the degree of financial leverage. The appropriate formula is

$$k_e = k_u + (1 - \tau)(k_u - k_d)\frac{B}{S} \tag{12-6}$$

Unlever, with no debt, has an *after-tax* cost of equity capital of $k_e = k_u = 10$ percent in Equation (12-6) because $B/S = 0$. Lever has a higher cost of equity capital for it uses $B = \$5000$ worth of debt. With Lever's total value at $V_L = \$12,000$, the total value of the shares will be $S_L = V_L - B = \$7000$. The ratio of debt to equity is $B/S = \$5000/\$7000 = 5/7$. Using this ratio along with $k_u = 10$ percent, $\tau = 40$ percent and $k_d = 7$ percent in Equation (12-6), Lever's cost of equity capital is:

$$k_e = 10\% + (1 - 0.40)(10\% - 7\%)\frac{5}{7} = 11.3\%$$

The after-tax cost of capital for the firm, K, is the weighted average after-tax cost of capital. The formula for that cost is:

$$K = (1 - \tau)k_d\frac{B}{V} + k_e\frac{S}{V} \tag{12-7}$$

Similar to Equation (12-3) in the no-tax case, the interest tax subsidy is reflected in the reduction of the cost of debt to its *after-tax cost* $(1 - \tau)k_d$.

For Unlever, Inc., application of Equation (12-7) means, with $S/V = 1.0$ and $B/V = 0$, that $K = k_e = k_u = 10$ percent. This is consistent with the earlier finding that the total value of Unlever was $10,000, since value is also found by discounting after-tax net operating income of $1000 at $K = 10$ percent. For Unlever, Inc.,

$$V_U = \frac{\text{Net operating income after taxes}}{K} = \frac{\$1000}{0.10} = \$10,000$$

In Lever, Inc., the cost of capital for the firm is found using Equation (12-7) by letting $B/V = 5/12$, $S/V = 7/12$, $\tau = 40$ percent, $k_d = 7$ percent, and $k_e = 11.3$ percent, as earlier computed using Equation (12-6).

$$K = (1 - 0.40)7\% \, \frac{5}{12} + 11.3\% \, \frac{7}{12} = 8.34\%$$

Lever's cost of capital is *less* than Unlever's cost. This is consistent with the earlier finding that Lever's total value exceeded Unlever's total value. If we capitalize the after-tax net operating income of $1000, *which Lever would have if it used no leverage*, by $K = 8.34$ percent, we find that V_L is approximately $12,000:

$$V_L = \frac{\$1000}{0.0834} = \$11,990.41 \approx \$12,000$$

Share Price   Share price will rise for shareholders as increased leverage is used. Unlever's total dividends will be paid out of net income of $1000. Dividends per share are $D = \$1$ for $N = 1000$ shares outstanding. Share price will be:

$$P = \frac{D}{k_e} = \frac{1.00}{0.10} = \$10$$

In contrast, Lever's net income and dividend stream is $790. For $N = 500$ shares, dividends per share are $1.58. Using Equation (12-6), Lever's cost of equity capital is $k_e = 11.3$ percent. Therefore, Lever's share price is:

$$P = \frac{D}{k_e} = \frac{1.58}{0.113} = \$14.00$$

Share price has increased and Lever's shareholders are better off than Unlever's shareholders. The lower risk offered by the interest tax subsidy stream means that although dividends per share are expected to be higher and riskier than for an unleveraged firm, the cost of equity capital does not rise enough to offset the expected increase in dividends.

Figure 12-3   *Leverage and the Cost of Capital: Perfect Markets and Corporate Taxes*

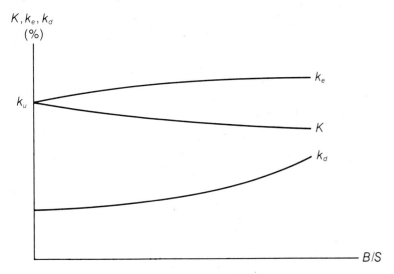

Figure 12-3 shows the effects of leverage on costs of capital for the firm. Increases in the cost of debt as leverage increases are again portrayed by the curve labeled k_d. The rising cost of equity capital produced by increased leverage is seen on the curve labeled k_e. The cost of capital to the firm, represented by K as determined in Equation (12-7), *falls* with increasing leverage.

Summary of Effects of Leverage

Figure 12-4   *Value and Leverage: Perfect Markets and Corporate Taxes*

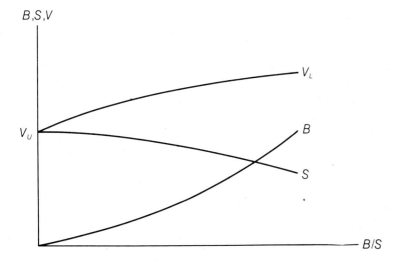

Table 12–4 *Leverage, Cost of Capital, and Value* ($k_u = 10\%$)

	Debt/Equity Ratio, B/S			
	0	0.366	5/7	1.20
B	$ 0	$ 3,000	$ 5,000	$ 7,000
S	10,000	8,200	7,000	5,800
k_d	—	6%	7%	7.5%
k_e	10%	10.9%	11.3%	11.81%
K	10%	8.9%	8.34%	7.81%
V_L	$10,000	$11,200	$12,000	$12,800

Figure 12-4 portrays the effect of leverage on value under corporate income taxes. The curve B is the market value of bonds. As leverage increases, B necessarily increases. The curve labeled S is the market value of shares. This curve falls as more debt and less equity are used in financing the firm. The beneficial effects of the interest tax subsidy on return and risk mean that total share value does not fall by an amount equal to the value of bonds issued. Consequently, the total value of the firm, shown on the curve labeled V_L, increases with leverage.

Again representative effects of varying degrees of leverage on capital cost and value are numerically displayed in Table 12-4.

Implications for Capital Structure Decisions

Shareholders *can* benefit from leverage through a higher share price, as a simple example illustrates. If Unlever decides to issue $5000 of 7 percent debt and to purchase its stock with the proceeds, investors will hear of the news. The $2000 value of the tax subsidy will be split among the existing 1000 shares and share price will rise by $2 to $12. Unlever will purchase $5000/$12 = 416.67 shares, or 41.67 percent of those outstanding. An investor owning 100 shares, 10 percent of the total outstanding, will sell 41.67 of them for (41.67) $12 = $500 but will retain 58.33 of them worth 58.33 × 12 = $700 for a total wealth level of $1200. His wealth has clearly increased by $200 since, before the decision, he owned 100 shares worth, at $10 a share, $1000. That $200 is his proportionate share of the value of the tax subsidy.[6]

---

[6]Share price would have been $14 per share just as in the case of Lever, Inc., had Unlever secretly issued debt and bought $5000/$10 = 500 shares at $10 a share. The $2000 value of

If debt is so beneficial to shareholders, why not go to even higher debt positions? Clearly, the value of the firm and share price will continue to increase. The use of virtually 100 percent debt seems to be strongly called for by the benefits of the interest tax subsidy. Chapter 13 will follow up on this question.

SUMMARY

The capital structure decision is a decision to divide the firm's income stream into streams having different risk–return characteristics, each of which is promised to a specific type of security holder. The common shareholder gets one stream, the bondholder another, and the preferred shareholder yet another. The question we asked throughout this chapter is whether dividing the income stream among various suppliers of capital has an impact on the total value of the enterprise.

When applied under conditions of perfect markets and no taxes, the equal rate of return principle implies that capital structure has no impact on the value of the firm. Dividing the income stream into elements with different risk and return characteristics leaves shareholders no better off than before the division occurred. These conclusions can be translated equally well into statements about the firm's cost of capital. The cost of capital remains unaffected by capital structure change. Any apparent advantage that seems to occur because "cheaper" debt replaces more "expensive" equity is illusory because an increase in leverage also increases the rate of return required by shareholders. That required rate k_e increases enough to exactly offset the advantage of using debt.

When corporate taxes are introduced, capital structure *does* matter. Interest payments are tax deductible. Consequently, a \$1 increase in the interest payment reduces taxes relative to an unlevered firm by an amount equal to the tax rate times \$1. In effect, the government subsidizes interest on debt and the value of a levered firm is greater than the value of an unlevered firm by the present value of the tax subsidy. This result leads to the conclusion that the firm's cost of capital is *falling* as leverage increases.

These results raise three important questions.

1. Why do corporations spend substantial sums on capital structure planning?

---

the subsidy would be spread over the remaining 500 shares in the amount of \$4 per share. Anyone selling his shares would lose the benefits of leverage. Only those retaining shares would gain. We assume that firms provide full information so that no shareholder loses his proper share of the tax subsidy.

2. Why do we observe the myriad types of securities—debt in numerous forms, common stock, preferred stock, warrants, and convertible securities—issued by corporations?

3. Why do we observe systematic differences in capital structure among firms in different industries?

Two types of answer to these questions have emerged.[7] The first explanation suggests that corporate resources are expended and different types of securities are issued to take advantage of temporary aberrations in required rates of return. Thus, the required rate on debt with a maturity of 15 years with a specific level of risk may be low relative to other types of security, so a firm issues that type of debt to take advantage of this temporary situation. Such an explanation implies the questionable presumption that corporate managers can find and act on a temporary disequilibrium in capital markets more effectively than market professionals. Also, it fails to explain capital structure differences across industries.

An alternative explanation involves systematically introducing additional elements into analysis of financing policy *and* evaluating their impact on that policy. These additional elements include personal taxes, costs of financial distress and bankruptcy, as well as conflict between shareholder and bondholder interests. We analyze each of these elements in the next chapter.

Before moving on, however, we summarize some important formulas and provide verbal explanations of each.

Perfect Markets, No Taxes

1. The value of the firm is unaffected by leverage:

$$V_L = V_U \tag{12-1}$$

2. The rate of return required by shareholders, the cost of equity capital, is equal to the required rate on unlevered shares of a firm of the same business risk plus a premium for financial leverage:

$$k_e = k_u + (k_u - k_d)\frac{B}{S} \tag{12-2}$$

3. The cost of capital for the firm is weighted average of the required rates of return on debt and equity. That cost of capital is constant.

$$K = k_d\frac{B}{V} + k_e\frac{S}{V} = k_u \tag{12-3}$$

---

[7]See A. Barnea, R. Haugen, and L. Senbet, "Market Imperfections, Agency Problems and Capital Structure: A Review," *Financial Management* (Summer 1981), p. 8.

Perfect Markets, Corporate Taxes

1. The value of a levered firm is equal to the value of an unlevered firm *plus* the value of the interest tax subsidy:

$$V_{\text{L}} = V_{\text{U}} + \tau B \qquad (12\text{-}5)$$

2. The after-tax rate of return required by shareholders, the after-tax cost of equity capital, is equal to the after-tax required rate of return on unlevered shares plus a premium for financial leverage:

$$k_e = k_u + (1 - \tau)(k_u - k_d)\frac{B}{S} \qquad (12\text{-}6)$$

3. The after-tax cost of capital for the firm is a weighted average of the after-tax required rates of return on debt and equity:

$$K = (1 - \tau)k_d\frac{B}{V} + k_e\frac{S}{V}$$

GLOSSARY OF KEY TERMS

Capital Structure	The mix of sources of financing. It traditionally excludes short-term liabilities.
Cost of Capital	The minimum rate of return that a firm must earn on new investments to maintain the value of existing shares. That rate is measured as the weighted average of the costs of each source of financing in the firm's capital structure. (In a world of corporate taxes, it is expressed on an after-tax basis.)
Debt	A liability; in this chapter, used interchangeably with long-term bonds.
Equity	Ownership capital including preferred stock, common stock, and retained earnings; in this chapter, used interchangeably with common stock.
Financial Leverage	Dividing the firm's income stream between two types of investors—bondholders who have prior claim on earnings and shareholders who receive residual earnings. The use of both sources of financing magnifies expected shareholder returns and increases their risk. Leverage is often measured by the ratio of debt to equity, *B/S*.
Interest Tax Subsidy	The annual tax saving accruing to the firm as a result of the deductibility of interest prior to computing taxes.

SELECTED REFERENCES

Fama, Eugene, and Merton H. Miller. *The Theory of Finance.* New York: Holt, Rinehart and Winston, 1972.

Haley, C. W., and Lawrence D. Schall. *The Theory of Financial Decisions.* New York: McGraw-Hill Book Co., 1973.

Lewellen, Wilbur G. *The Cost of Capital.* Dubuque, IA: Kendall/Hunt Publishing Co., 1976.

Modigliani, Franco, and Merton H. Miller. "The Cost of Capital, Corporation Finance and the Theory of Investment." *American Economic Review* (June 1958), pp. 261–297.

Modigliani, Franco, and Merton H. Miller. "Corporate Income Taxes and the Cost of Capital: A Correction." *American Economic Review* (June 1963), pp. 433–443.

Stiglitz, J. E. "A Re-Examination of the Modigliani–Miller Theorem." *American Economic Review* (December 1969), pp. 784–793.

QUESTIONS

1. Define the term "cost of capital" of the firm.

2. What is meant by an optimal capital structure?

3. The rate of return required by a firm's bondholders is generally lower than the return required by its shareholders. Explain why one would expect this relationship.

4. Does the debt policy of a firm matter if capital markets are perfect?

5. What is meant by "creating homemade leverage?"

6. In a world of perfect capital markets and no income taxes, why doesn't the firm's cost of capital change when a firm replaces equity with debt?

7. "The cost of capital is solely a function of management preferences." Discuss this statement.

8. If their firm were to issue debt and use the funds to retire some of its outstanding shares in a world of corporate taxes would the after-tax cash flow paid to investors be expected to increase? Explain.

PROBLEMS

1. The Enterprise Travel Company on Mars, where there are no corporate income taxes, has an expected net operating income of

$600, all of which is paid out as dividends, and no growth is in sight. The rate of return required on earnings streams of similar risk is 6 percent.

(a) Calculate the value of this unlevered company that has 100 shares outstanding.

(b) What is its value per share?

(c) Suppose now that Enterprise sells $5000 of 4.5 percent perpetual bonds at face value and purchases and retires 50 of its 100 shares. What are the cost of debt, cost of equity, and cost of capital, if the value of remaining shares outstanding is $5000?

2. Bobit is an unlevered firm valued at $10,000. There are no corporate taxes, 1000 shares of common stock are outstanding, and expected income is $800 per year. All income is paid out in dividends. Juliet, another firm operating in the taxless environment, is valued at $10,000, and its operating earnings have the same risk as those of Bobit. Juliet has 500 shares outstanding and $5000 of 6 percent perpetual debt. Its no-growth expected net operating income is also $800 per year. It pays out in dividends all available income after interest payments. Perfect markets exist and the equal rate of return principle applies.

(a) What is the cost of equity capital for Bobit and Juliet?

(b) Dick buys 100 shares of stock of Juliet. What is his total outlay and what is his expected rate of return?

(c) Suppose Jane buys 100 shares of Bobit, what is her total outlay and what is her expected rate of return?

(d) Why is the expected rate of return greater for Dick than for Jane?

3. The financial manager of Minot Power Company knows that his current unlevered cost of capital is 10 percent and that the required rate of return on debt if the firm were to borrow is 6 percent. Assume that there are no corporate taxes, no growth in earnings and that all earnings are paid out as dividends.

(a) What would be the cost of equity, k_e, if the company is financed with 50 percent debt at market value?

(b) What would k_e be if Minot were to finance with only one-fourth debt at market value?

(c)   Find k_e if debt financing were two-thirds of the capital structure at market value.

4.   Find the interest tax subsidy for Salem Dry Goods Store, which has $4000 of 10 percent debt and an effective corporate income tax rate of

(a)   22 percent

(b)   40 percent

(c)   48 percent

5.   Caliper Cuddle Company can issue new debt of the same risk and maturity as that of presently outstanding perpetual debt. Estimate the after-tax cost of this net debt if the current debt has a coupon rate of 8 percent, a face value of $1000, and a market value of $800. The corporate tax rate is 50 percent.

6.   If the value of the no-growth, unlevered Waller Bandit Shop is $5000, what would be the value if its tax rate were 22 percent and it issued $2000 in 7 percent perpetual debt to retire equity? (Assume that no further debt would ever be issued and that financial markets are perfect.)

7.   The Galloping Gertie Ranch has total assets valued at $500,000 and its expected pretax operating income is $100,000, implying a 14 percent after tax cost of capital for this unlevered firm. It pays an average effective federal corporate income tax of 30 percent. Mr. Dupree has asked the Purple Insurance Company what rate it would charge for a $200,000 loan that would be used to retire another shareholder's equity interest, leaving him sole owner. If Galloping Gertie could borrow at 10 percent, how would it affect

(a)   cash flow available to Mr. Dupree;

(b)   the value of Dupree's ownership; and

(c)   the firm's cost of capital?

Assume that the other shareholder knows that the firm will borrow to retire the shares.

8.   Walter's Beverage Company is a firm whose debt/equity ratio is 0.10. Charles Walter, president and chief financial officer, has talked with the Mukilteo Investment Banking Company about new financing. He learned from Mr. Mukilteo that debt up to a 1.0 debt/equity ratio would cost him the same as the current debt, 12 percent. Walter's Beverage has a tax rate of 40 percent and an esti-

mated unlevered cost of capital of 16 percent. Mr. Walter asked Mr. Mukilteo how his cost of equity would change if he financed with debt up to a 1 to 1 debt/equity ratio. Answer for Mr. Mukilteo.

9.   What is the cost of capital for Sleezy Mining Company, which has a 10 percent income tax rate, a cost of equity capital of 12 percent, and a pretax cost of debt of 8 percent? Debt is 40 percent of the capital structure.

10. Goody Raisins, Inc., is a company that has long believed in not financing with debt. Jim Goody, a recent management school graduate, has taken over the business, debt free. He learned in school that the government would share in his debt service costs so that he would enhance the value of the company ownership through the debt financing. Goody Raisins has 100,000 unlevered shares which trade on the Pullman Stock Exchange at $20 each. The firm pays out all of its earnings in dividends, expects no growth, and has a cost of equity capital of $k_e = 10$ percent. For practical purposes, perfect markets and the equal rate of return principle apply. The corporate income tax rate is 40 percent.

Jim Goody asks you as financial analyst to prepare a table for him reflecting the value of the company and the cost of capital to the firm for debt/equity ratios of 0, 0.25, 0.5 and 1.0. Assume stock is purchased and retired with debt proceeds and assume that the cost of debt will be 5.5 percent, 6.0 percent, and 6.5 percent, respectively, for debt/equity ratios of 0.25, 0.50, and 1.0. These debt/equity ratios would require $434,783, $769,230, and $1,250,000 of debt, respectively.

11. Jupiter, an all-equity financed firm operating in perfect capital markets without income taxes, has a 20 percent required rate of return. The financial manager finds that she can replace one-half of the $10,000 outstanding shares of Jupiter with debt at 10 percent. Net operating income of $20,000 would not be expected to change and earnings per share would increase substantially. Is this a good deal for shareholders?

12. The T. Mann Company, an all-equity firm, has a cost of capital of 15 percent and a current market value of $10,000. All financial markets are perfect and there are no income taxes. The costs of debt available to the firm for various debt/equity ratios are as follows:

B/S	0	$\frac{1}{4}$	$\frac{2}{3}$	$\frac{13}{16}$
k_d	$4\frac{1}{2}\%$	5%	8%	10%

(a)   Find the cost of equity capital for each debt/equity ratio and graph the relationship between capital costs and leverage.

(b)   Graph the relationship between leverage and the value of the firm.

CHAPTER 13

Additional Influences on the Capital Structure Decision

The preceding chapter left us with an understanding of how market forces affect capital structure decisions. That understanding was gained under the assumption of perfect markets, both with and without corporate taxes. In that context, the policy implications for the firm are clear. In the absence of corporate income taxes, financial leverage has no impact on firm value, investors are indifferent to the amount of borrowing undertaken by any firm, and no optimal capital structure exists. If corporate income taxes are present, firm value will be maximized with 100 percent debt, investors prefer corporate leverage, and the optimal capital structure for any firm is virtually 100 percent debt.

Although very important to understanding fundamental influences of capital structure on the value of the firm, the policy implications of Chapter 12 are not comforting when the behavior of actual firms is observed. Firms subject to corporate income taxes do not employ 100 percent debt financing. Indeed, some very well-known firms such as IBM and Xerox use very little debt. Also, evidence suggests that there are significant capital structure differences among industries. If an optimal capital structure exists, it is apparently less than 100 percent debt financing. Clearly, what has been said so far about capital structure does not tell the whole story.

While maintaining the foundation established in the previous chapter, we introduce three additional elements that may have an impact on a firm's capital structure decisions: personal income taxes, financial distress and bankruptcy, and bondholder–shareholder conflicts of interest. Each topic is discussed in turn.

PERFECT MARKETS WITH CORPORATE AND PERSONAL TAXES

The somewhat disturbing results with corporate taxes change with the introduction of a graduated personal tax structure in which interest is taxed at a higher rate than dividends and capital gains. Capital structure is once again irrelevant: $(V_U = V_L)$, but interestingly enough there will be an optimal amount of debt in the *economy*. Some firms must issue debt, though firm value will depend neither on *which* firms are levered nor on *how* much debt an individual firm issues.[1]

To illustrate the impact of personal taxes, we assume that financial markets are perfect and that the net operating income stream NOI is riskless. Therefore the rates k_u, k_d, and k_e that are applied to unlevered income, debt, and levered income, respectively, are also risk free. In the absence of personal taxes, all three rates must be equal to one another and to the riskless rate. However, when there are *personal* taxes and the tax rates on interest are different from those on dividends and capital gains to shareholders, the rates of return before personal taxes will not be the same. Expected rates of return for investors who are indifferent between purchasing debt and equity will be identical *only on an after-personal-tax basis*. We designate those after-personal-tax rates as k_{ua}, k_{da}, and k_{ea}. These assumptions are more restrictive than necessary, but they simplify the presentation considerably.[2]

Given these basic assumptions, we proceed to an analysis of the impact of personal taxes on required rates of return, development of an expression for firm value, and discussion of how managerial incentives to maximize firm value combine with a graduated personal tax structure to eliminate the advantage of debt financing. The section concludes with a brief look at some broader implications and empirical evidence.

Personal Taxes and Required Rates of Return

Two characteristics of the existing U.S. tax code are relevant when analyzing the impact of personal taxes on firm value. First, all investors do not pay the same tax rate. By law, some investors (e.g., charitable foundations and universities) are not subject to personal taxes. Other investors are taxed at much higher rates. Second, the effective tax rate on dividends and capital gains τ_s is less than the tax rate on interest payments τ_b. A significant portion of equity returns occurs as capital gains. Tax rates on those gains are lower than tax rates on interest (after exclusions allowed by law), and the actual payment of taxes can be deferred

---

[1]The ideas presented in our discussion of personal taxes come from Merton H. Miller, "Debt and Taxes," *Journal of Finance* (May 1977), pp. 261–275.

[2]Risky cash flows can be assumed, but the presentation would become more complicated without altering our fundamental conclusions.

until the securities are sold, thus driving the *effective* tax rate on equity even lower.

This section focuses on the impact of differential personal taxes on debt and equity returns on required rates of return observed in the market. The next section extends this analysis to derive an expression for the value of the firm. The progressive nature of the personal income tax structure will become important in the subsequent discussion of implications for corporate debt policy.

Assume that *all* investors are taxed at one rate on interest received and at another rate on dividends and capital gains and that the personal tax rate on debt, $\tau_b = 40$ percent, is greater than the rate on equity, $\tau_s = 20$ percent. Finally, assume that investors require a 10 percent rate of return *after personal taxes* on a risk-free investment. Investors can elect to hold either corporate debt or corporate equity. The question is, At what required rate of return, k_e and k_d, will investors be indifferent to holding debt and equity?

The equal rate of return principle tells us that securities of identical risk must sell at prices that yield identical expected rates of return. Thus, when there are personal taxes, the after-personal-tax expected rate of return on debt $k_d(1 - \tau_b)$ must equal the after-personal-tax expected rate of return on equity $k_e(1 - \tau_s)$. And, given that investors require 10 percent after personal taxes on risk-free investment, both expected rates of return must also equal 10 percent. These equalities may be written as follows.

$$k_d(1 - \tau_b) = k_e(1 - \tau_s) = 0.10$$

When $\tau_s = 0.20$, k_e may be derived by noting that

$$k_e(1 - 0.20) = 0.10$$

so

$$k_e = \frac{0.10}{1 - 0.20} = \frac{0.10}{0.80} = 0.125, \quad \text{or } 12.5\%$$

Following the same procedure to determine k_d yields:

$$k_d = \frac{0.10}{1 - 0.40} = \frac{0.10}{0.60} = 0.167, \quad \text{or } 16.7\%$$

When $k_e = 12.5$ percent and $k_d = 16.7$ percent *before* personal taxes, risk-free equity and debt yield identical expected returns after taxes. If either debt or equity had a lower expected rate of return, no investor would want to hold that security because identical investment in a security of identical risk would yield a higher expected rate of return. Similarly, if k_d exceeded 0.167 or if k_e exceeded 0.125, all investors would

Table 13–1   *Pre-tax Required Rates of Return on Debt and Equity for a Range of Personal Tax Rates on Debt and Equity*

	$\tau_s = 0$		$\tau_s = 0.1$		$\tau_s = 0.2$	
τ_b	k_d	k_e	k_d	k_e	k_d	k_e
0.2	0.125	0.10	0.125	0.111	0.125	0.125
0.3	0.143	0.10	0.143	0.111	0.143	0.125
0.4	0.167	0.10	0.167	0.111	0.167	0.125
0.5	0.200	0.10	0.200	0.111	0.200	0.125

want to purchase the security with the higher expected rate of return. Only when $k_d = 0.167$ and $k_e = 0.125$ are all investors willing to hold both debt and equity. Only at those rates can firms *sell* both debt and equity.

Table 13-1 further illustrates the impact of personal taxes on required rates using tax rates on equity from 0 to 0.2 and tax rates on debt from 0.2 to 0.5. Notice that the higher the personal tax rate, the higher the expected pre-personal-tax rate of return necessary if all securities are to have identical expected rates of return *after* personal taxes.

Values of the Firm With and Without Personal Taxes

To illustrate the implications of personal taxes for firm financing policy, we use Lewis Liquidators, a firm that is expected to generate perpetual net operating earnings (NOI) of $1000 per year. Those earnings are risk free. As in the preceding example, the required rate of return after personal taxes on a riskless security is 10 percent. All corporations are taxed at the corporate tax rate of $\tau = 40$ percent.

No Personal Taxes   First, recall the situation in which there are no personal taxes and the firm is unlevered. The value of Lewis Liquidators is:

$$V_U = \frac{\text{NOI}(1 - \tau)}{k_u} = \frac{\$1000(1 - 0.4)}{0.10} = \$6000$$

because shareholders expect to receive $600 per year after corporate taxes and require a 10 percent rate of return.

But what would happen if the firm were levered, having $1000 of perpetual debt outstanding. In the absence of personal taxes, we know that the value of the levered firm is equal to the value of the unlevered firm plus the value of the corporate interest tax subsidy. When debt is perpetual, that value may be written:

$$V_L = V_U + \tau B$$

or, in this case,

$$V_L = \$6000 + 0.4(\$1000) = \$6400$$

Leverage increases firm value by $V_L - V_U = \$6400 - \$6000 = \$400$. However, such changes in value associated with leverage will not necessarily be obtained when there are personal taxes.

With Personal Taxes   Suppose that all investors pay tax rates of $\tau_s = 0.20$ on equity returns and $\tau_b = 0.40$ on debt returns. As shown in the preceding section, those tax rates cause required rates for debt and equity to be $k_d = 16.67$ and $k_e = 12.5$ percent if 10 percent is the after-personal-tax required rate for both these riskless securities. These required rates apply to both unlevered and levered firms.

   If Lewis Liquidators were unlevered, its value would become:

$$V_U = \frac{\text{NOI}(1 - \tau)}{k_u} = \frac{\$1000(1 - 0.4)}{0.125} = \$4800$$

This is less than $V_U = \$6000$, the value for Lewis found in the absence of personal taxes, a result that should not be surprising. Investors must pay a lower price for the same flows if they expect to receive 12.5 percent rather than a 10 percent return before personal taxes. However, it is not the valuation effect of personal taxes that we wish to focus on. The question is whether the expression for the value of a levered firm will differ from that derived without personal taxes. That is, will $V_L - V_U$ still equal τB?

   If Lewis Liquidators issues $1000 of debt at 16.67 percent, the value of shares will be:

$$S = \frac{(\text{NOI} - k_d B)(1 - \tau)}{k_e} = \frac{(\$1000 - \$166.70)(1 - 0.4)}{0.125} = \$4000$$

Since bonds are worth $1000, the value of the levered firm is:

$$V_L = S + B = \$4000 + \$1000 = \$5000$$

Leverage does increase firm value with this specific set of personal tax rates, but only by $V_L - V_U = \$5000 - \$4800 = \$200$, whereas without personal taxes firm value increased by $V_L - V_U = \$6400 - \$6000 = \$400$. Why is debt less valuable in this situation than in the example without personal taxes? The answer lies in a comparison of after-tax cash flows from debt financing.

A Revised Expression for Firm Value Under Personal Taxes

Without personal taxes, the firm's after-tax cash flows increase by (0.4) (0.10) $1000 = $40, the amount of the interest tax subsidy, when a firm is levered. With personal taxes, there are three incremental cash flows resulting from use of leverage. First, the interest rate on debt is larger by $0.1667 - 0.10 = 0.0667$, so there is an *additional* interest tax subsidy of $\tau (k_d - k_{da})B = 0.4 (0.1667 - 0.10) \$1000 = \$26.68$.

At the same time, the *entire* interest tax subsidy generates a personal tax liability for shareholders. That tax liability is $\tau_s(\tau k_d B) = 0.2 ((0.4) (0.1667) (\$1000)) = \$13.34$.

Finally, note that interest represents cash payments that are shifted from shareholder to bondholder because debt rather than equity financing is employed. Since those payments are now personally taxed at 40 percent rate for bonds rather than 20 percent rate for equity, the *incremental* taxes are:

$$(\tau_b - \tau_s)k_d B = (0.40 - 0.20) (0.1667) (\$1000) = \$33.34$$

The sum of these three elements yields a net cash flow representing the personal tax consequences of the firm using corporate leverage.

$$\text{Net cash flow} = \$26.68 - \$13.34 - \$33.34 = -\$20$$

Notice that this flow is negative because the increase in personal taxes more than offsets the increase in the interest tax subsidy at the corporate level. As long as τ_b exceeds τ_s, it will remain negative, and net cash flows to investors associated with leverage will be less than they would be in the absence of personal taxes. The *value* of these flows after corporate and personal taxes, which we call the net personal tax effect (NPTE) is found by discounting the net cash flow at the after-personal-tax required rate of return.

$$\text{NPTE} = \frac{-\$20}{0.10} = -\$200$$

Deducting that amount from the value of the interest tax subsidy in the absence of personal taxes, $\tau B = \$400$, yields the incremental value of the firm due to leverage.

$$\tau B + \text{NPTE} = \$400 - \$200 = \$200$$

Note that this amount equals the increase in value of the firm with leverage earlier computed with personal taxes. The value of the levered firm with this particular set of tax rates, therefore, becomes:

$$V_L = V_U + \tau B + \text{NPTE}$$
$$= \$4800 + \$400 - \$200$$
$$= \$5000$$

which is equal to the sum of debt and equity values earlier computed.

An expression of the net personal tax effect is easily derived from the net cash flows identified.[3] That expression is:

$$\text{NPTE} = - \left[\frac{(1 - \tau)(\tau_b - \tau_s)}{1 - \tau_b} \right] B \qquad (13\text{-}1)$$

and the value of the levered firm becomes:

$$V_L = V_U + \tau B - \left[\frac{(1 - \tau)(\tau_b - \tau_s)}{1 - \tau_b} \right] B \qquad (13\text{-}2)$$

It is not the mere existence of personal taxes that invalidates the expression $V_L = V_U + \tau B$. Rather, it is the *difference* between those rates that is important. If personal tax rates are equal ($\tau_b = \tau_s$), the value of the firm is once again $V_L = V_U + \tau B$, as was true in the absence of personal taxes. Under those circumstances, debt financing and equity financing impose identical personal tax penalities on investors, so there can be no net personal tax advantage to either form of financing.

Table 13-2 illustrates further use of Equation 13-1: τ_b ranges from 20 to 52 percent, while τ_s is held constant at 20 percent.

As shown in column 2, k_e and k_u must be greater than 10 percent because, like bondholders, shareholders must expect to earn 10 percent after taxes. Thus, when τ_s is fixed at 20 percent $k_u = k_e = 0.10/(1 - 0.2) = 0.125$. Values for k_d appear in column 3. Note that as τ_b increases, k_d increases because the equal rate of return principle dictates that all risk-free investments earn 10 percent after personal taxes. Column 4 shows the after-tax cost of debt to the firm. Because interest is tax deductible, the effective cost of debt to the corporation is $k_d(1 - \tau)$, not k_d. Values of V_U and τB, which are not affected by the changing personal tax rate on interest, appear in columns 5 and 6. Column 7 shows the net personal tax effect and column 8 indicates the value of the levered firm.

Notice that when $\tau_b = 0.20$, NPTE is zero because τ_s also is 0.20. Identical payments to debt and equity are taxed at identical rates, and

---

[3]The after-tax cash flows are:

$$\tau(k_d - k_{da})B - \tau_s(\tau k_d B) - (\tau_b - \tau_s)k_d B$$

Since $k_d = k_{da}/(1 - \tau_b)$, that flow may be written:

$$\frac{\tau k_{da} B}{1 - \tau_b} - \tau k_{da} B - \frac{\tau_s(\tau k_{da} B)}{1 - \tau_b} - \frac{(\tau_b - \tau_s)k_{da} B}{1 - \tau_b}$$

Discounting this flow at the after-tax rate k_{da} yields:

$$\text{NPTE} = \frac{\tau B - \tau B(1 - \tau_b) - \tau_s \tau B - (\tau_b - \tau_s)B}{1 - \tau_b}$$

which on simplification becomes:

$$\text{NPTE} = - \left[\frac{(1 - \tau)(\tau_b - \tau_s)}{1 - \tau_b} \right] B$$

TABLE 13–2   *Firm Value with a Constant Personal Tax Rate on Equity ($\tau_s = 0.20$) for Several Tax Rates on Debt*

τ_b	$k_e = \dfrac{k_{ea}}{1 - \tau_s}$	$k_d = \dfrac{k_{da}}{1 - \tau_b}$	$k_d(1 - \tau)$	V_U	τB	NPTE	V_L
0.20	0.125	0.1250	0.0750	$4800	$400	$ 0	$5200
0.30	0.125	0.1430	0.0857	4800	400	(85.71)	5114.29
0.40	0.125	0.1670	0.1000	4800	400	(200)	5000
0.50	0.125	0.2000	0.1200	4800	400	(360)	4840
0.52	0.125	0.2083	0.1250	4800	400	(400)	4800

investors reap the entire advantage of the interest tax subsidy τB. As τ_b increases, so does NPTE, and firm value falls. Indeed, when $\tau_b = 0.52$, NPTE totally offsets τB (i.e., NPTE = τB). There are then no valuation benefits from leverage.

Another way of looking at the impact of personal taxes requires a comparison of k_e and $k_d(1 - \tau)$ in columns 2 and 4. Both k_e and $k_d(1 - \tau)$ reflect the cost of equity and debt to the firm after corporate taxes. Note that when τ_b is less than 0.52, $k_d(1 - \tau)$ is less than k_e. The cost of debt is lower than the cost of equity, so debt is the preferred form of financing. But when $\tau_b = 0.52$, $k_e = k_d(1 - \tau)$ and the firm is indifferent to the form of financing used. We conclude, therefore, that when NPTE = τB, $k_e = k_d(1 - \tau)$. One view focuses on the relative value of the tax subsidy and the personal tax effect. The other focuses on the relative cost of each source of funds. The views are equally valid.

From this point it is only a short step to develop interesting debt policy implications under a more realistic tax structure.

Corporate Debt Policy Under Personal Taxes

As we indicate earlier, two characteristics of the U.S. tax code are important. Investors face different tax rates ranging from zero to 50 percent and the effective tax rate on equity is less than the effective rate on debt for most investors. To this point we have ignored the progressive nature of income taxes and focused on the differential tax rates on debt and equity, assuming all investors paid the same tax rate on debt and the same rate on equity.

In this section we combine both characteristics of the tax code. We assume a progressive personal tax structure in which tax rates on interest vary from zero to 50 percent and the *effective* tax rate on equity is lower than the rate on debt.

If all corporations are taxed at the same rate, if personal tax rates on debt exceed those on equity ($\tau_b > \tau_s$), and if the range of personal tax rates is large enough, it can be shown that there is an optimal amount of *total* corporate debt in the economy but firm value is unaffected by debt. At equilibrium, $V_L = V_U$ for all firms. To show this, we assume for simplicity that equity returns are *not* taxed ($\tau_s = 0$), whereas debt returns are taxed at progressive rates between $\tau_b = 0$ and 50 percent. All firms are risk free and if unlevered, pay required rates on equity financing of $k_e = k_{ea}$. Firms will find it desirable to replace equity with debt financing if it has a lower after-corporate-tax cost than equity capital. Allowing for the interest deduction against corporate taxes, the after-tax cost of debt financing to firms is $(1 - \tau)k_d$. The after-tax cost of equity financing is k_e. Debt financing will be used as long as its after-tax cost to firms is less than that for equity; that is $(1 - \tau)k_d < k_e$. There will be no advantage to debt financing if required rates on debt financing rise to:

$$k_d = \frac{k_e}{1 - \tau} \qquad (13\text{-}3)$$

At that rate, the after-tax costs of debt and equity financing are the same; that is, $(1 - \tau)k_d = k_e$. In Figure 13-1, the points k_e and $k_d = k_e /(1 - \tau)$ on the vertical axis indicate the *range* of required rates for debt, $k_e \leq k_d < k_e /(1 - \tau)$ over which, taking into account the tax deductibility of interest payments, it *pays* firms to use debt instead of equity financing.

But what happens to the required rate for debt assessed by investors on firms using financial leverage? This rate depends on the tax rate

The Total Amount of Corporate Debt

Figure 13-1   *The Optimal Quantity of Total Debt in the Economy*

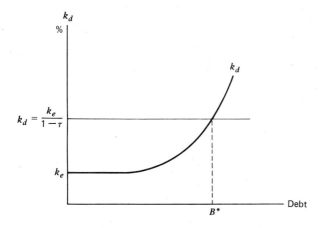

investors face for taxable debt returns. To purchase debt rather than equity, investors must receive an after-personal-tax required rate on debt at least equal to tax-free equity returns; that is, $(1 - \tau_b)k_d \geq k_e$ must prevail. The higher the personal tax rate on debt return, the higher the required rate k_d. That rate may be written:

$$k_d = \frac{k_e}{1 - \tau_b} \tag{13-4}$$

A tax-exempt investor ($\tau_b = 0$) would be willing to hold debt having a required rate equal to tax-free equity (i.e., $k_d = k_e$). Investors paying taxes on debt returns ($\tau_b > 0$) would assess required rates greater than k_e; the higher the tax rate τ_b, the greater the required rate for debt k_d. Collectively, if firms were initially unlevered and began to offer debt with the required rate $k_d = k_e$, they would attract only tax-exempt investors. To obtain still more leverage, firms would have to offer higher rates according to Equation (13-4) to lure investors in successively higher tax brackets into purchasing debt rather than tax-free equity. The curve labeled k_d in Figure 13-1 shows the maximum amount of debt that will be demanded by investors at each level of k_d. The maximum amount demanded increases as k_d rises because investors in higher tax brackets will be attracted to debt rather than equity. Note that firms will not be able to offer different debt interest rates to investors with different personal tax rates. All debt is issued at the same time and bears the required (coupon) rate offered to the last, highest tax bracket investor induced to purchase higher taxed debt rather than equity.

Bringing firms and investors together, consider the intersection of the horizontal line drawn from $k_d = k_e /(1 - \tau)$ and curve k_d. Firms will issue all of the debt that investors demand when $k_d \leq k_e /(1 - \tau)$, whereas if $k_d > k_e/(1 - \tau)$, only equity will be issued. Thus, the horizontal line can be viewed as a supply curve of debt at the highest rate firms are willing to pay. In turn, the curve k_d is, as just seen, a demand curve. The point of intersection between the supply and demand curves determines the total quantity of debt, B*, that will exist in the economy. Firms will not issue more debt in total than B* because the rate required by investors would exceed the maximum rate firms would be willing to pay. We now have an optimal *total* amount of corporate debt in the economy when corporate and personal taxes are considered. All firms will pay the same rate $k_d = k_e /(1 - \tau)$ on debt, the upper limit in Figure 13-1. But at that rate, there remains no benefit to firms from issuing debt; that is, firms are indifferent to using debt and equity financing. We will see that for each firm the value of the levered firm then equals the value of the unlevered firm (i.e., $V_L = V_U$).

To illustrate what happens at the individual firm level, assume that the corporate tax rate is $\tau = 0.40$ for all firms and that the *effective* personal tax rate on equity τ_s is one-fourth the rate on debt τ_b.

An Illustration of the Value of the Individual Firm

From Figure 13-1 we know that firms will be indifferent to debt and equity financing when:

$$k_d = \frac{k_e}{1 - \tau} = \frac{k_e}{1 - 0.4} \qquad (13\text{-}5)$$

Second, we know that the *last* investor who can be enticed to hold debt must be indifferent between debt and equity. Thus, in the absence of risk, the expected after-tax return for investors *in that tax bracket* will be the same for both debt and equity:

$$k_e(1 - \tau_s) = k_d(1 - \tau_b)$$

or

$$k_e(1 - 0.25\,\tau_b) = k_d(1 - \tau_b) \qquad (13\text{-}6)$$

Substituting Equation (13-5) into Equation (13-6) and solving for τ_b and τ_s, the personal tax rates for investors who are indifferent between debt and equity yields $\tau_b = 0.4706$ and $\tau_s = 0.25\,\tau_b = 0.1176$. Given these rates, the value of any levered firm using Equation (13-2) is:

$$V_L = V_U + \tau B - \left[\frac{(1 - \tau)(\tau_b - \tau_s)}{1 - \tau_b} \right] B$$

$$= V_U + 0.4B - \left[\frac{(1 - 0.4)(0.4706 - 0.1176)}{1 - 0.4706} \right] B$$

$$= V_U + 0.4B - 0.4B = V_U$$

Firms will have the same value regardless of the amount of debt issued. Investors in lower tax brackets ($\tau_b < 0.4706$) will hold *only* debt because the return on riskless debt is greater than the return on riskless equity. Similarly, investors for whom τ_b exceeds 0.4706 will hold *only* equity because the expected return is higher than that on debt, given identical risk.

Though individual firms are indifferent between debt and equity financing because $V_L = V_U$ in equilibrium, there is an optimal total amount of debt in the economy. Indeed, it is the issuance of that debt that forces interest rates up and mandates irrelevance at the individual firm level. This model appears to give the same results as the original tax-free model presented in Chapter 12 because debt policy for individual firms

Is Debt Policy Irrelevant?

does not matter. But in reality the depth of our understanding has increased significantly. Built into our tax structure is a mechanism that should tend to mitigate the valuation impact of the original interest tax subsidy. In combination with other considerations introduced in sections that follow, the tendency of personal taxes to reduce the advantage of debt may be important.[4]

To conclude, a look at some recent empirical evidence may be helpful. Studies have detected positive and statistically significant share price reaction to increases in leverage under controlled circumstances.[5] Consistent with Equation (13-2) and the tax rate differential $(\tau_b - \tau_s) > 0$, that reaction is smaller than would be expected if the full benefit of the interest tax subsidy τB were captured by shareholders in the absence of personal taxes. Yet, because the reaction is positive, these results suggest that *some* benefits from debt exist for at least some firms and that even if our existing tax structure does reduce the gain from debt financing, it does not eliminate it for all firms. The result where $V_L = V_U$ with personal taxes is valid under the assumptions, but it does not appear to tell the whole story.

FINANCIAL DISTRESS AND BANKRUPTCY

Unless debt is risk free, bondholders recognize that circumstances may arise in which a firm is unable to meet contractual obligations, which include timely payment of interest and principal as well as other stipulations. That is, a firm may *default* on its bonds. Default or threat of default creates financial distress and, perhaps, bankruptcy. This section identifies potential costs of financial distress and bankruptcy, then examines the impact of those costs on the capital structure decision.

Greater reliance on debt financing increases the possibility of default on debt obligations in "bad times." In the absence of any costs associated with financial distress and bankruptcy, the enhanced probability of default would be of no consequence to the value of the firm because neither liquidating value nor going concern value is affected by default. For instance, a going concern actually earning zero net operating income in a given year while having $40 million of interest payments due on outstanding debt will be in default on its debt obligations. Creditors as

---

[4]This model has many interesting implications about investor behavior. For instance, it suggests that tax-exempt institutions should never hold common stock and that high tax bracket investors will always prefer to hold unlevered shares using homemade leverage. However, we ignore these issues.

[5]See Ronald Masulis, "The Effects of Capital Structure Change on Security Prices: A Study of Exchange Offers," *Journal of Financial Economics* (June 1980), pp. 139–178.

well as shareholders may be unhappy with the year's earnings, but there is no reason for the value of the firm to change as long as expectations about the distribution of *future* cash flows remains the same. Holders of defaulted debt might take over the firm or gain other concessions in reorganization. Pieces of paper and ownership may change, but the firm's managers should continue to make the same value-maximizing decisions regardless of who controls the firm. If liquidation or continued operation is value-maximizing before default, it remains so after default and is a separate issue from default and distress.

But there are costs associated with financial distress and bankruptcy that arise when financial markets are not perfect. We need to identify these costs and study how they might affect the financing mix of the firm.

Financial distress occurs when a firm is in imminent danger of violating terms of a debt contract (i.e., of going into default). Examples of such violations include failure to maintain specific financial ratios (e.g., debt to equity), violation of restrictions on additional debt issue, and inability to make required payments on debt. When terms of debt contracts are violated, the debtor firm is in default. As a consequence of default, creditors may meet with the firm to renegotiate debt contracts while the firm continues uninterrupted operations. But if such a meeting does not satisfy creditors or if they do not anticipate a fruitful meeting, the firm may be required to file for *bankruptcy*. Under such conditions, creditors seize control of the firm, its operations, and its assets. Assuming that the firm is a going concern, bankruptcy may result in a change of ownership (creditors may become owners), but the firm will continue to operate. If the firm is worth more "dead than alive," it will cease to operate. Assets will be sold (the firm will be liquidated) to satisfy claims of creditors.

The costs of financial distress are *indirect*. They include loss of revenues from customers who decide to purchase goods from a firm more likely to offer continuity of supply, hesitancy of suppliers to sell to the firm on credit and requiring cash-in-advance payments that may interrupt the flow of production, loss of experienced labor, time associated with managerial concern over financial distress, and lost revenues from investment opportunities forgone because of distress. For firms in bankruptcy, the same indirect costs exist as well as *direct costs* of bankruptcy, namely, payments to such third parties as a bankruptcy trustee, attorneys, accountants, and other consultants who assist owners of debt claims and the firm during the travail of bankruptcy and reorganization or liquidation. All these costs, direct and indirect, *impair* the going concern value of the stream of expected net operating income of the firm.

Expected Costs of Financial Distress and Bankruptcy

**Value of the
Levered Firm
Under Costly
Financial Distress
and Bankruptcy**

The greater the degree of financial leverage, the greater the probability of financial distress and default and the greater the present value of expected cost of distress and default. The influence of these costs on the value of the levered firm are summarized in Equation (13-7).

$$V_L = V_U + \tau B + \text{NPTE} - \begin{array}{c}\text{Value of expected costs}\\\text{of financial distress and bankruptcy}\end{array} \quad (13\text{-}7)$$

The first two terms reflect the value of the unlevered firm and the interest tax subsidy in the absence of personal taxes. The net personal tax effect discussed in the preceding section appears as the third term. The last term reflects the value of expected cost of financial distress and bankruptcy. Note that personal taxes and expected costs of bankruptcy and financial distress combine to reduce the valuation benefits of leverage below that represented by τB, the value of the interest tax subsidy. To simplify the discussion, let the terms $\tau B - \text{NPTE}$ be the net interest tax subsidy after personal taxes, which we assume to be positive.

As leverage increases, the expected value of the net interest tax subsidy increases. However, since the probability of distress and default also increases, so too does the discounted value of expected costs of distress and default. Increasing leverage has both a positive and a negative impact on the value of the firm. As long as the marginal gain in net interest tax subsidy exceeds the combined marginal effects of personal taxes and expected cost of distress and bankruptcy, the value of the firm will increase with greater leverage. But it is possible that at some degree of leverage, the marginal gain will equal marginal cost and the value of the firm will be maximized; an optimal quantity of debt at *less than* 100 percent debt financing will have been reached.

Figure 13-2   *The Relation Between Firm Value and Leverage With and Without Costs of Financial Distress and Bankruptcy*

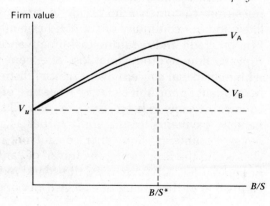

Figure 13-2 illustrates such an optimal capital structure, where the degree of leverage is measured as the ratio of debt to equity, B/S. In Figure 13-2, B/S^* represents the value-maximizing amount of debt when bankruptcy costs are introduced with personal taxes and the interest tax subsidy. Such a relationship is entirely possible if personal taxes by themselves do not offset the interest tax subsidy, so that net interest tax subsidy is positive and if expected costs of financial distress and bankruptcy increase sufficiently with leverage so that the marginal cost will offset the remaining marginal benefit of the net interest tax subsidy. These circumstances are plausible, but it is not clear whether they represent the situation facing a significant number of firms.

Arguments and Evidence on Costs of Financial Distress and Bankruptcy

Regrettably, most of the arguments and evidence on costs have centered on direct costs of bankruptcy rather than on the indirect costs of financial distress. It is easy to understand why: it is comparatively simpler to measure payments to trustees, accountants, and other third parties under bankruptcy than it is to measure lost sales to customers.

Two types of argument are used to suggest that bankruptcy costs are not large enough to create an optimal capital structure. First, if bankruptcy costs were so large, firms would seek alternative forms to conventional debt financing such as income bonds. Income bonds promise interest only if earned. Failure to earn sufficient funds to make interest payments would not precipitate bankruptcy nor necessarily cause financial distress (though failure to meet contractual principal payments could do both). Yet, comparatively rare use of income bonds could signal that bankruptcy costs are not as large as many believe.[6] A second argument supporting low direct bankruptcy costs states that for firms in financial distress, mergers or buyouts can accomplish the same result as reorganization under bankruptcy but without direct costs of bankruptcy proceedings. If merger or buyout is a cheaper way of reorganizing than bankruptcy, rational investors would undertake the former, not the latter. Value of the firm would depend on relatively small costs of merger or buyout, not direct bankruptcy costs.[7] On the empirical level, few studies of actual bankruptcy costs have been reported. But they suggest that direct costs are relatively small.[8]

---

[6]See Merton H. Miller, "Debt and Taxes," *Journal of Finance* (May 1977), pp. 261–275.

[7]See R. Haugen and L. Senbet, "The Insignificance of Bankruptcy Costs to the Theory of Optimal Capital Structure," *Journal of Finance* (May, 1978), pp. 383–393.

[8]See Jerold Warner, "Bankruptcy Costs: Some Evidence," *Journal of Finance* (May 1977), pp. 337–347, which studies railroad bankruptcies. Direct bankruptcy costs averaged only 5.3 percent of the value of the firm at the time of declaration of bankruptcy and 1.4 percent

Unless the net interest tax subsidy is small, direct bankruptcy costs are unlikely to be sufficient to create a maximum value at any but the most extreme levels of debt financing. Marginal cost of financial distress and bankruptcy will be less than marginal benefits of the net interest tax subsidy except at the extreme. But that conclusion overlooks the indirect costs of financial distress, which, when combined with direct costs could indeed be large enough to create an optimal capital structure within more conventional ranges. Unfortunately, problems of measurement make it very difficult to provide evidence on the matter. The possibility that an optimal capital structure determined *solely* by a tradeoff between net interest tax subsidy and expected costs of bankruptcy and financial distress remains open.[9]

BOND-HOLDER–SHARE-HOLDER CONFLICTS OF INTEREST

One source of costs precipitated by bankruptcy involves payments to lawyers and trustees who represent contending parties and oversee firm operations during a period of reorganization. That security holders are willing to incur such costs suggests that they do not trust one another. Perhaps there are conflicts among owners and lenders that are costly to resolve. In this section we identify potential sources of conflict that, though most apparent during periods of financial distress, are inherent in the bondholder–shareholder relationship.

Recognize first that as owners of the firm, shareholders exert some degree of control over managers. Shareholders prefer that managers make decisions that will improve the lot of owners. In most widely held firms, however, owner control is imperfect. Owners must rely on the judgment of management, hoping that proper incentives will foster a shareholder-oriented management. But how will other security holders fare if managers are shareholder oriented? What are the sources of conflict? What costs are imposed on security holders by potential or actual conflict? How do such costs affect the financing decision?

-----

of value 5 years before bankruptcy. A second smaller study of more heterogeneous firms found that bankruptcy costs averaged 7.5 percent of liquidating value: J. S. Aug, J. H. Chua, and J. J. McConnell, "The Administrative Costs of Corporate Bankruptcy," Purdue Working Paper, Revised, Purdue University, West Lafayette, IN, December 1980.

[9]Some argue that liquidation costs should be part of the discounted costs of financial distress and bankruptcy because such costs, made up of losses from distress sale of assets, are not insignificant. But this argument misses the point that bankruptcy and liquidation are separate events. A firm that is expected to remain a going concern at the time that leverage is undertaken will be expected to remain a going concern even though bankruptcy could lead to a change in ownership and control. Liquidation occurs only if the firm is worth more dead than alive, before or after bankruptcy.

Table 13–3 *Cash Inflow Payments to Bondholders and Shareholder Wealth: Dykes Sheet Metal, Inc.*

	State of Economy	
	Weak	Strong
A. Unlevered Firm		
Cash Inflow from Operations	$100	$500
B. Levered: First Bond Issue		
Cash Inflow from Operations	100	500
Promised and Expected Interest and Principal on First Bond Issue	77	77
Cash Payment to Shareholders	$ 23	$423
C. Levered: First and Second Bond Issue		
Cash Inflow from Operations	$100	$500
Expected Interest and Principal on First Bond Issue	50	77
Expected Interest and Principal on Second Bond Issue	50	77
Cash Payment to Shareholders	$ 0	$346

In the absence of restrictive agreements with bondholders, it is possible for shareholders to make use of the limited liability feature of the corporate form of organization to make themselves wealthier at the expense of some holders of bonds. Wealth is shifted from bondholders to shareholders. The possibilities are illustrated in Tables 13-3 and 13-4 for Dykes Sheet Metal, Inc. For simplicity, Dykes is assumed to exist for one period, a year. There are no corporate or personal income taxes.

The cash flow from operations 1 year hence depends on the state of the economy as panel A in Table 13-3 shows. If the economy is weak, that inflow will be $100; if strong, it will be $500. These states are equally likely, so the expected cash inflow for the unlevered firm is $300. At the

Conflicts Regarding Financing Policy

Table 13–4 *Shareholder Wealth Gains at Expense of Bondholders Through Financing Policy: Dykes Sheet Metal, Inc.*

	Value of Firm, V_U	Bond Value, B	Share Value, $V_L - B$	Bond Proceeds	Shareholder Wealth
Unlevered Firm	$250	$ 0	$250	$ 0	$250
Levered Firm					
First Bond Issue	$250	$ 70	$180	$ 70	$250
First and Second Bond Issues	$250	$110	$140	$125	$265

prevailing required rate of return for an unlevered firm, $k_u = 20.0$ percent, the value of the unlevered firm is:

$$V_U = \frac{\$300}{1 + 0.20} = \$250$$

That amount also constitutes the wealth of the Dykes shareholders as shown in Table 13-4. But, immediately after that investment, those shareholders decide to issue bonds and retire equity, distributing the proceeds to themselves. They offer bonds promising to pay a total of $77 in principal and interest 1 year hence. This is a riskless investment, as Table 13-3 shows in panel B. No matter which state of economy prevails, the cash flow from operations more than covers payments to bondholders. If the required rate for riskless bonds is 10.0 percent, bonds are worth $70. Table 13-4 indicates that shareholder wealth will remain at $250 after this initial bond transaction. The value of the firm is still $V_L = V_U = \$250$. The value of shares is $V_U - B = \$250 - \$70 = \$180$. Shareholder wealth consists of the $180 share value plus $70 of bond proceeds distributed to themselves, or, $180 + $70 = $250.

But immediately after the first bond issue, Dykes's shareholders sell a *second* debt issue of equal priority, which also promises $77 of interest and principal 1 year hence. A glance at panel C shows that *both* the second and first bond issues will now be risky, not riskless. If the economy is strong, holders of each issue will receive the promised $77. But if the economy is weak, only $100 will be available to pay both sets of bonds. Because of limited liability, bondholders cannot obtain more from shareholders in the event of a weak economy. Furthermore, since both bond issues have equal priority and both are promised identical amounts, they have equal claim on earnings and will split the $100 so that each set of bondholders receives $50. Each set of bondholders now owns risky debt offering equal chances of receiving $50 *or* $77 a year hence, so the expected dollar return is $63.50, assuming that the two states of the world are equally likely.

What are the wealth consequences of this transaction? Buyers of the second bond issue recognize that the second bonds are risky. They will require a rate of return greater than the riskless rate of 10.0 percent and will not pay $70 for the second bond issue, but somewhat less. Suppose that they pay $55 and expect to earn a required rate of return of approximately 15.5 percent to compensate for risk. This is also the new market value of the identical first bond issue because of its transition from riskless to risky status. Buyers of the first bond issue paid $70 for riskless bonds but find that additional bonds of equal claim have made their bond issue risky. The market value of the old bonds is $55, down from $70. Holders of the first bond issue lose $70 - $55 = $15 in wealth.

Buyers of the second bond perceived the risk and paid the correct market value of $55; *they* do not lose wealth. And who gains? The shareholders—at the expense of the original bondholders!

In Table 13-4, the firm is still worth $250. Both bond issues have a combined market value of $2 \times \$55 = \$110$, so that the value of the shares is $250 - \$110 = \$140$. In addition, shareholders hold proceeds from the first bond issue, sold as riskless bonds for $70, plus proceeds from the second of $55 for total wealth of $140 + \$70 + \$55 = \$265$. Compared to the prior wealth position of $250 with only the first bond issue, the additional debt issue has increased shareholder wealth by $265 - \$250 = \$15$, precisely the loss in wealth experienced by the holders of the first bond issue.[10]

Apparently, shareholders can make themselves wealthier at the expense of bondholders through financing policy by continuing to issue additional bonds having equal claim to earnings compared to previously issued bonds. A clear conflict of interest exists between wealth-maximizing shareholders and bondholders. This example assumes that bondholders are naive and easily fooled. Of course, they are not, but we defer on that point until we have considered the wealth shifts that are possible under investment policy.

Conflicts Regarding Investment Policy

Shareholders can also gain wealth at the expense of bondholders by issuing bonds with the promise to undertake investments of a given degree of risk and then undertaking investments of higher risk. Bonds become riskier than originally perceived by the market. Bondholder wealth is subsequently reduced, and the amount of the reduction is shifted to shareholders.

As an example of this type of action, consider a new firm having two mutually exclusive investment proposals, A and B. For simplicity, proposal A is assumed to be riskless and proposal B is risky. Both proposals require the same $50 outlay. When discounted at the appropriate required rates of return, the present values of the proposals are PV = $80 for A and PV = $70 for B. Given the $50 outlay for each proposal, the net present values for each proposal are NPV = $30 for A and NPV = $20 for B. Now it would appear that proposal A would be preferred to B because it has the higher NPV. But this is not necessarily the case if shareholders can deceive bondholders. Consider Table 13-5.

We suppose that shareholders announce that riskless proposal A will be undertaken and that its present value is $80. They offer a portion of

---

[10]The basic idea of wealth shift through financing policy is developed in Eugene Fama and Merton Miller, *The Theory of Finance* (New York: Holt, Rinehart and Winston, 1972).

Table 13–5   *Shareholder Wealth Gains Through Investment Policy Promising Investment Proposal A*

Investment Proposal	PV	NPV	Bond Value	Share Value	Shareholder Wealth If Take A	Shareholder Wealth If Take B
A	$80	$30	$60	$20	$80	—
B	70	20	40	30	—	$90

the riskless future returns from proposal A in the form of interest and principal payments on bonds. Because the bonds are riskless, their current value is $60 and buyers will pay that amount for them. Shareholders receive the proceeds from the riskless bond sale. Their wealth consists of the value of the shares plus the cash proceeds from the sale of bonds or ($80 − $60) + $60 = $80.

But what if shareholders promise proposal A to bondholders but instead undertake risky proposal B after bonds have been sold? If buyers of bonds *knew* that risky proposal B would be undertaken, the bonds would be perceived as risky and would be worth only $40, not the $60 for riskless bonds. As it is, bondholders believe that riskless proposal A will be undertaken and so pay $60 for the bonds. If shareholders *then* undertake B, the outstanding bonds will fall to $40 in value as their risk is correctly perceived. At the same time, wealth will increase from $80 to $90. To understand why shareholders' wealth increases by $10, recall first that the present value of B is $70. Thus, the value of shares is $70 less $40 for the value of bonds, or, $30. Shareholders' wealth consists of the $30 share value *plus* $60 of proceeds obtained from sale of bonds originally perceived as riskless but rendered risky by the deception. Stated alternatively, the $10 increase in shareholder wealth from the deception consists of the $20 wealth loss of bondholders shifted to shareholders less the difference between the net present values of proposals A and B. Shareholders have a clear incentive to deceive bondholders about the risk of investments to be undertaken because a prospective wealth gain is available.[11] A conflict of interest is again evident.

Finally, shareholders in firms having outstanding bonds have an incentive to *underinvest* because prospective wealth gains from investment would be received by bondholders, not shareholders. That is, the en-

---

[11]The same incentive to choose the riskier investment while promising a less risky investment to bondholders exists if the net present values of competing investments are the same.

hanced cash flow from a desirable investment may reduce the risk and increase the expected dollar return of outstanding bonds, thereby increasing bond value at the expense of shareholders. Bondholders would benefit from the investment while shareholders would lose.

To demonstrate this point, assume that financial markets are perfect and there are no income taxes so that the value of a levered firm is $V_L = V_U$. Suppose that a firm's existing investments generate an expected net operating income of $10 per year in perpetuity and that it has outstanding perpetual risky debt in the amount of $50 *book value* with a coupon interest rate of 8 percent. Annual *promised* interest payments are (0.08) $50 = 4 per year; but in light of the risk of the flows, bondholders expect only $3.50 per year. If the required rate for unlevered firms is $k_u = 10$ percent and the required rate for risky debt is $k_d = 7$ percent, the values of the firm, risky debt, and shares are as follows:

Value of firm: $$V_L = V_U = \frac{\text{NOI}}{k_u} = \frac{\$10}{0.10} = \$100$$

Value of debt: $$B = \frac{\text{Expected interest payments}}{k_d} = \frac{\$3.50}{0.07} = \$50$$

Value of shares: $$S = V_U - B = \$100 - \$50 = \$50$$

Now suppose the firm has an investment opportunity requiring an outlay of $10 and generating $1.50 of expected return per year in perpetuity. Discounted at the 10 percent required rate, the NPV is $1.50/ 0.10 - $10 = $5, and the investment opportunity is desirable. But if the firm undertakes the investment, improved cash flow makes the outstanding bonds less risky and increases *expected* (not promised) interest payments. Suppose that the required rate for debt would fall to $k_d = 5$ percent and expected interest payments increase to $3.95 per year if the investment is undertaken. New values for the firm, bonds, and shares are:

Value of firm: $$V_L = V_U = \frac{\$10 + \$1.50}{0.10} = \$115$$

Value of outstanding bonds: $$B = \frac{\text{Expected interest payments}}{k_d} = \frac{\$3.95}{0.05} = \$79$$

Value of shares: $$S = V_U - B = \$115 - \$79 = \$36$$

The value of the firm increases to $115 because of the investment. The lower risk for bonds increases their value to $79. Shareholders' wealth declines from $50 to $36 as a result of the decline in share value. They lose wealth even though the investment is desirable. Bondholders are made wealthier because the risky debt has become less risky and therefore worth more.[12]

Shareholders will not want to undertake an otherwise desirable investment if bondholders are the beneficiaries of the investment. Bondholders would, of course, be pleased with such an investment. A conflict of interest is present.

Managing Conflicts of Interest

We have demonstrated three sources of potential conflict of interest between shareholders and bondholders. First, financing policy can be used to shift wealth to shareholders. Second, investment policy can be used by shareholders to shift wealth by using borrowed funds to finance investments that are riskier than those originally promised to bondholders. Third, firms have an incentive to underinvest if desirable investment opportunities would benefit bondholders at the expense of shareholders.

In managing conflicts of interest, it must be recognized that bondholders are *not* naive or easily fooled. They recognize that shareholders (or financial managers acting on their behalf) will attempt to resolve conflicts in their own favor. Unless alternative ways of dealing with conflicts are found, bondholders will require higher rates of return and coupon interest rates for bonds to compensate for additional risk created by conflicts of interest. If this happens, debt financing becomes more expensive for firms, and *shareholders* bear the costs of the conflict in the form of lower prices for newly issued bonds. Therefore, shareholders may have an incentive to accept restraints on their own actions in the form of legally binding restrictive agreements made with bondholders to lower the costs to shareholders of conflict of interest.[13] Examples of such restrictions include limitations on additional debt financing (or placing additional debt issues on a lower priority of claim), limitations on dividend payments to shareholders and provision of some form of security (all to reduce increases in risk and wealth shifts to shareholders from financing policy), limitations on the uses of borrowed funds to protect

---

[12]Stewart Myers, "Determinants of Corporate Borrowing," *Journal of Financial Economics* (November 1977), pp. 147–176.

[13]An analysis of debt agreements that goes far beyond the material presented here may be found in Clifford Smith and Jerold Warner, "On Financial Contracting: An Analysis of Bond Covenants," *Journal of Financial Economics* (June 1979), pp. 117–161. Furthermore, restrictive agreements are not the only way to manage costs of conflict. Firms could issue convertible rather than ordinary debt. This would allow bondholders to convert debt securities into a specific number of shares. An attempt to shift wealth to shareholders by investment policy would be only partly successful because convertible debt would tend to rise in value, to the benefit of bondholders. Incentives to shift wealth are reduced. But as Smith and Warner point out, the underinvestment incentive increases with use of convertible debt.

against wealth shifts from investment policy, and requirements that firms maintain certain investments (such as in liquid assets) that primarily benefit bondholders rather than shareholders.

For at least smaller degrees of financial leverage, shareholders will voluntarily agree to such restrictive agreements. Although the costs of compliance are not insignificant, this method of managing conflict of interest may be cheaper for many firms than paying higher coupon interest rates on bonds. But shareholders recognize that with higher degrees of leverage, incentives for wealth transfer to themselves increase, as do the costs of complying with increasingly restrictive agreements. Interest rates too may increase because restrictive agreements cannot provide full protection for bondholders. At some point, depending on the size of debt financing benefits and the costs of compliance with restrictive agreements, shareholders will *voluntarily* limit the degree of financial leverage to less than 100 percent debt financing.

Conflicting incentives between shareholders and bondholders generate costs that affect firm value are shown in Equation (13-8). **The Impact on Firm Value**

$$V_L = V_U + \tau B + \text{NPTE} - \begin{matrix} \text{Value of} \\ \text{expected cost of} \\ \text{bankruptcy and} \\ \text{financial distress} \end{matrix} - \begin{matrix} \text{Costs associated} \\ \text{with conflicting} \\ \text{incentives} \\ \text{between share-} \\ \text{holders and} \\ \text{bondholders} \end{matrix} \quad (13\text{-}8)$$

This formula differs from Equation (13-7) only by the last term, which reflects the costs of conflicting incentives created by substituting debt for equity. Those costs, combined with the net personal tax effect and the costs of financial distress and bankruptcy, should create an optimal financing mix short of 100 percent debt. Furthermore, the appropriate financing mix is likely to vary according to the specific circumstances facing the firm.

Personal taxes that reduce the value of the corporate interest tax subsidy to shareholders, costs of financial distress and bankruptcy, and costs of mitigating shareholder–bondholder conflict all influence capital structure. Almost certainly the range of capital structures that might be considered optimal for a firm will have an upper bound considerably less than 100 percent debt financing. But finding an optimal structure or range of structures is hardly a precise process. It is unlikely that management will be able to identify the impact of each of these elements precisely. Still, an attempt must be made in the face of this uncertainty. **FINDING AN OPTIMAL CAPITAL STRUCTURE**

Since managers do not have a precise model that identifies how all factors interact through financial markets to create a range of preferred capital structures for a specific firm, they must attempt to probe the market for reaction to specific financing plans.

As a first step, management might study financing policies of various firms in its industry. *Debt/equity ratios* based on both book and market values provide information about the range of financing policies existing among those firms. Market value ratios might be particularly useful because they reflect present market conditions rather than those that existed perhaps 20 years ago when the firm originally issued debt. Both average values and a range of values of debt/equity ratios will help the firm in its initial planning phase.

The next step requires that the firm test the market by contacting lenders directly or indirectly through a financial consultant such as an investment banker (see Appendix 3B). Taking into account any restrictions stemming from existing debt financing, the firm wishes to assess the market's evaluation of a variety of financing plans. As an intermediate party between the firm and investors, an investment banker might be particularly helpful at this stage. Investment banking firms have continued contact with the market, so their judgment about an optimum capital structure and the amount of debt that can be sold at different interest rates should narrow the firm's choice of capital structure further. Most firms find that interest costs on debt will begin to increase very rapidly once market-perceived risk that may be associated with bankruptcy and adverse incentive reaches a high level. Once this information has been conveyed to the firm, an upper bound to debt financing should be apparent, provided market interest rates reflect informed assessment of the firm's prospects.

The firm can move as close to that upper bound as it desires in an attempt to achieve an optimum capital structure. However, managers will not, in general, know when an optimum capital structure is achieved. Perhaps exact solutions to the optimum capital structure problem that will make capital structure planning a trivial problem will eventually be derived. In the meantime, the model of behavior in perfect markets with corporate taxes offers considerable analytical insight. It helps, when modified by expert judgment, in assessing the factors that determine an optimum capital structure.

SUMMARY   This chapter examined three additional influences on the capital structure decision: personal income taxes, financial distress and bankruptcy, and bondholder–shareholder conflicts of interest. In exploring the impact of each factor on the policy implications obtained in the preceding chapter, we found that in the absence of corporate income taxes, capital structure is irrelevant to the value of the firm, and that with corporate income taxes, the optimal capital structure is 100 percent debt financing.

Our discussion of personal income taxes revealed that under the prevailing personal tax structure, interest receipts from debt ownership are taxed at higher rates than equity returns. The higher the tax bracket of the investor, the greater the market interest rate that investors would require to give up lower taxed equity returns in exchange for higher taxed interest receipts. For all firms considered together, increases in the total quantity of debt liabilities result in higher coupon interest rates as investors in higher tax brackets are induced to purchase debt. The last investor to purchase debt would have high enough tax rates and require a high enough rate of return to eliminate any advantage for *any* firm from debt financing. The high required rate paid to the last investor must be paid to all purchasers of debt; all debt is sold at the same time at the same required rate. For each firm, the net personal tax disadvantage of debt over equity returns reflected in the high required rate exactly offsets the corporate interest tax subsidy benefit from debt financing. For each individual firm, its levered value would equal its unlevered value: $V_L = V_U$. Capital structure would be irrelevant to the value of the firm and shareholder wealth. However, there *is* an optimum amount of debt in the economy. But it does not make any difference which firms issue that debt.

Expected costs of financial distress and bankruptcy are, in principle, capable of producing an optimal capital structure of less than 100 percent debt financing. At some degree of leverage short of that point, the value of the firm will be maximized and its cost of capital minimized. As leverage increases, the probability of financial distress and default increases, as do expected discounted costs of distress and default. Marginal costs of the latter eventually outweigh gains in net interest tax subsidy associated with increasing leverage.

But the critical question is whether bankruptcy costs in combination with the net personal tax effect (NPTE) are large enough to offset the interest tax subsidy. Two arguments are used to support the view that bankruptcy costs should not offset the tax subsidy if the net interest tax subsidy, $\tau B - \text{NPTE}$, is relatively large. First, firms would use alternative forms of financing, such as income bonds on which interest is paid only if earned. Second, since direct costs of bankruptcy could be avoided by informal rather than formal reorganization, the relevant cost is the lower of either formal or informal reorganization. Empirical evidence exists to support the view that direct bankruptcy costs are, indeed, low relative to τB. If the combined effects of the net interest tax subsidy and bankruptcy costs are to result in an optimal capital structure, either the net interest tax subsidy must be much less than τB (perhaps because personal taxes do reduce, but not eliminate the subsidy), or indirect costs of bankruptcy, which are not easily measured, must be very large. It is possible, of course, for both factors to be at work.

Finally, we examined three sources of bondholder–shareholder conflict of interest: wealth shift from bondholders through financing policy, wealth shift through investment policy, and underinvestment. Wealth can be shifted from naive bondholders to shareholders if conflicts are resolved in favor of shareholders. Since bondholders are not naive, however, they perceive these conflicts of interest and demand higher required rates of return as compensation for the risks they bear. Shareholders would find that interest costs on debt would be higher because of the conflict of interest. However, if shareholders agreed to limit the range of their own actions, bondholders would require lower rates of return because of the enhanced protection. If the cost of submitting to binding agreements and the mechanism necessary to detect violations is less than the increased interest cost in the absence of the agreement, shareholders can use this method as a lower cost means of resolving conflict. Still, as leverage increases, the costs of compliance and detecting violations also increase (as may coupon interest rates as reflecting additional compensation for risks not covered by restrictive agreements) to the point where shareholders find it in their best interest to limit the quantity of bonds issued. The optimal debt quantity is then less than 100 percent debt financing.

When personal income taxes, financial distress and bankruptcy, and bondholder–shareholder conflicts of interest are combined, there is no neat formula for finding the optimal capital structure—if such exists. The process of making the capital structure decision is filled with uncertainty and is inherently complex.

GLOSSARY OF KEY TERMS

Bankruptcy Costs   Costs of formally reorganizing the firm in the event of default on debt payments are *direct* bankruptcy costs. *Indirect* bankruptcy costs associated with financial distress may also be present during reorganization.

Bondholder-Shareholder Conflicts of Interest   Conflicts regarding financing and investment policy that lead either to higher required interest rates for borrowing or agreed upon restrictive covenants in borrowing agreements.

Financial Distress	Indirect costs to firms where default may be impending. Costs include lost sales, inability to purchase materials from suppliers on credit, and managerial preoccupation with managing financial distress.
Net Personal Tax Effect	The effect on the value of the firm of personal taxes on debt and equity returns.
Personal Taxes	Taxes applied to personal income. In this chapter, personal taxes applied to returns from owning debt and equity securities.

SELECTED REFERENCES

Ang, J., J. Chua, and J. McConnell. "The Administrative Costs of Bankruptcy," Working Paper, Purdue University, December 1980.

Barnea, A., R. Haugen, and L. Senbet. "Market Imperfections, Agency Problems, and Capital Structure: A Review," *Financial Management* (Summer 1981), pp. 7–22.

Baron, D. "Default Risk, Home-made Leverage, and the Modigliani-Miller Theorem," *American Economic Review* (March 1974), pp. 176–182.

Baron, D. "Default Risk and the Modigliani-Miller Theorem: A Synthesis," *American Economic Review* (March 1976), pp. 204–212.

DeAngelo, H., and R. Masulis. "Optimal Capital Structure Under Corporate and Personal Taxation," *Journal of Financial Economics* (March 1980), pp. 3–30.

Fama, E. "Agency Problems and the Theory of the Firm," *Journal of Political Economy* (April 1980), pp. 288–307.

Fama, E. "The Effects of a Firm's Investment and Financing Decisions on the Welfare of its Security Holders," *American Economic Review* (June 1978), pp. 272–284.

Fama, E., and M. Miller, *The Theory of Finance,* New York: Holt, Rinehart and Winston, 1972.

Haugen, R., and L. Senbet. "The Insignificance of Bankruptcy Costs to the Theory of Optimal Capital Structure," *Journal of Finance* (May 1978), pp. 383–393.

Jensen, M., and W. Meckling. "Theory of the Firm: Managerial Behavior, Agency Costs and Ownership Structure," *Journal of Financial Economics* (October 1976), pp. 305–360.

Miller, M. "Debt and Taxes," *Journal of Finance* (May 1977), pp. 261–275.

Myers, S. "Determinants of Corporate Borrowing," *Journal of Financial Economics* (November 1977), pp. 147–176.

Smith, C., and J. Warner. "On Financial Contracting: An Analysis of Bond Covenants," *Journal of Financial Economics* (June 1979), pp. 117–161.

Stiglitz, J. "On the Irrelevance of Corporate Financial Policy," *American Economic Review* (December 1974), pp. 851–866.

Warner, J. "Bankruptcy Costs: Some Evidence," *Journal of Finance* (May 1977), pp. 337–347.

QUESTIONS

1. How are the advantages of corporate debt financing reduced by the current U.S. personal tax structure? What effect might the abolition of taxes on corporate earnings have on the reduction?

2. What are the three incremental cash flows that make up the net personal tax effect (NPTE)?

3. What are the expected costs of financial distress and bankruptcy? Why is it difficult to determine the significance of these costs in an actual firm's financing decisions?

4. Suppose you discovered a firm that does not have any debt in its capital structure because the chairman of the board of directors is averse to borrowing. As its financial officer, you are asked to prepare an argument in favor of borrowing moderate amounts in the market.

5. Despite the deductibility of interest cost for corporate debt, why shouldn't the firm borrow up to 100 percent of its capital? In other words, why does the *implied* cost of capital for the firm increase, as the proportion of debt in the capital structure increases beyond some point?

6. Given the existence of adverse incentives, how might shareholders benefit at the expense of bondholders? How can bondholders protect themselves?

7. How could a profitable investment benefit bondholders at the shareholders' expense?

8. What costs are associated with shareholder-bondholder conflicts of interest? What restrictions on shareholder actions might lower these costs?

1. Jerry is considering the personal tax consequences of interest from   **PROBLEMS**
   two bonds. One bond is a municipal that pays 12 percent interest
   (nontaxable). The second bond with a 20 percent coupon and selling at par is issued by a corporation. For what range of marginal
   personal tax rates will Jerry receive a larger after-tax return from the
   corporate bond?

2. Holland Corp. has a risk-free net operating income of $2500 per
   year into the foreseeable future. Holland pays a corporate tax rate of
   45 percent. The personal tax rate for all investors is 35 percent on
   debt and 15 percent on equity returns. Investors require a 12 percent rate of return after personal taxes on riskless investments.

   (a) Find the value of Holland Corp. if Holland has no debt out-
       standing and there are no personal taxes.

   (b) What is the value of Holland (unlevered) if investors must pay
       personal taxes on their investment income?

   (c) Suppose Holland issues $1500 of perpetual debt to replace a
       like amount of equity. Find the value of the firm with and
       without personal taxes.

   (d) How much do the personal taxes reduce the advantage of debt
       financing?

3. Clark Textiles is expected to generate perpetual risk-free net operating earnings of $8000. Investors require a return after personal taxes
   of 8 percent on these earnings. The corporate tax rate is 40 percent.
   All investors are taxed at the rate of 15 percent on equity returns
   and at 25 percent on debt returns.

   (a) Find the required rates of return on Clark's debt and equity
       before personal taxes.

   (b) Find the value of Clark Textiles if Clark is unlevered.

   (c) Find the value of Clark Textiles if Clark issues $10,000 of per-
       petual debt to replace a like amount of equity.

   (d) How much does leverage increase the firm's value?

   (e) In the absence of personal taxes, how much would the use of
       leverage increase Clark's value?

   (f) What is the net personal tax effect (NPTE)? Check your answer
       using formula 13-2.

(g)   Suppose a law was passed abolishing the preferential treatment given to equity returns so that both debt and equity returns were taxed to individuals at 25 percent. Answer parts (a) through (f).

4.   Suppose the corporate tax rate is 40 percent for all firms in the economy and, under a progressive personal tax structure, the effective personal tax rate on equity, τ_s, is one-half the rate on debt, τ_B.

   (a)   Find the personal tax rates for investors who will be indifferent between debt and equity yields.

   (b)   Which investors will hold debt? Which investors will hold equity?

5.   New Horizons, a new firm with a one-year expected life, estimates that it is equally likely to have a cash flow from operations one year hence of $500 or $1000. The required rate of return for the unlevered firm is 25 percent. Immediately after the initial investment, shareholders repurchase shares using proceeds from the sale of bonds promising a *total* payment of $330 in one year. The required return on these bonds is 10 percent. A second bond issue follows the first. The second issue promises $330, but the new investors require a 20 percent return on them. Both issues are of equal priority. Ignore all taxes.

   (a)   Find the value of New Horizons before the bond issues.

   (b)   What is the value of the first bond issue at the time of issue?

   (c)   What is the value of the first bond issue after the second bond issue?

   (d)   What is the expected dollar return for each set of bondholders after the second issue?

   (e)   How much has shareholder wealth increased? Where did the gain come from?

   (f)   How might the bondholders have protected themselves from loss?

CHAPTER 14

Dividend Policy

Given a firm's capital structure decision, some portion of financing needs will be raised from common equity. Additional common equity funds may be obtained in two ways: sale of additional common stock and retention of earnings. **Dividend policy** is related to the latter. Whatever cash dividend is paid, the remaining portion of earnings is retained in the firm. Given its equity financing needs, the dividend decision specifies how much of that need can be satisfied by retention of earnings and how much must be raised by sale of common shares.

Does the dividend decision have any effect on the wealth of shareholders? We attempt to answer this question in two settings: perfect markets in the absence of personal income taxes, and *with* personal income taxes and other market imperfections. The Barfield, Inc., decision problem provides a setting for this discussion. Then we consider **stock dividends** (as distinguished from *cash* dividends) and **stock splits.** Finally, we consider **stock repurchase,** an alternative means to cash dividends for distributing cash to shareholders.

Consider the case of Barfield, Inc., a manufacturer of medical equipment, which has prepared its 1982 income statement as shown in Table 14-1. Net income and earnings per share (EPS) represent an all-time high for Barfield. New investment opportunities appear to be viable, and the firm has approved a 3-year expansion with a capital budget of $15 million. This investment is expected to allow a threefold increase in sales in the coming years. Matthew Mullet, treasurer, convinced Barfield's board of directors that a capital structure consisting of 30 percent debt and 70 percent equity is appropriate. Consequently, he announced that 30 percent of the $15 million, or $4.5 million, will be raised by selling

THE BARFIELD CASE

Table 14–1   *Income Statement: Barfield, Inc.*

January 1, 1982–December 31, 1982

Revenue	$20,000,000
Costs of Goods Sold[a]	16,000,000
	$ 4,000,000
Sales and Administrative Costs	1,500,000
Net Operating Income	$ 2,500,000
Interest	500,000
	$ 2,000,000
Taxes	960,000
Net Income	$ 1,040,000
EPS (350,000 shares)	2.97

[a]Depreciation: $2,000,000.

debt and the remaining $10.5 million will be obtained through earnings retention and sale of common stock. Top management and directors claim to be committed to the firm's objective—maximizing shareholder wealth—but there is conflict on the board of directors about which dividend policy alternative will best enhance that goal.

The higher the level of cash dividends, the larger the amount of equity financing Barfield will have to raise through the sale of new shares of common stock. A decrease in cash dividends increases retained earnings and reduces the amount that must be raised by the sale of new shares to outsiders. Once established, dividend policy will determine the mix of earnings retention and new share financing.

Two of the three members of the executive committee of the board, whose function is to recommend dividend policy and dividend declarations to the full board, are in favor of retaining all earnings and eliminating the $1.15 annual dividend that has been paid in each of the past 4 years as shown in Table 14-2. That strategy would require the sale of only a small quantity of new shares to complete the $10.5 million equity financing need. Such a policy is *residual* because it meets equity financing needs first and then pays out any residual earnings as dividends. In this example, the residual dividend is zero.

When this recommendation was presented to the entire board of directors it stirred considerable debate. One group, which included the dissenting member of the executive committee, felt that reducing dividends to zero would have an immediate and *negative* impact on the price of shares. They wanted to maintain the *fixed dividend* of $1.15 per share that had been paid over the past 4 years. This policy would involve

Table 14–2   *Record of Past Dividends and Earnings per Share: Barfield, Inc.*

	1977	1978	1979	1980	1981	1982
Dividends per share	$1.00	$1.15	$1.15	$1.15	$1.15	?
Earnings per share	$2.00	$1.25	$1.75	$2.10	$1.80	$2.97
Payout Ratio (dividends ÷ earnings)	0.5	0.92	0.66	0.55	0.64	

meeting more of the $10.5 million equity financing need from the sale of common stock than the policy advocated by a majority of the executive committee.

A third group, thought by some to be a compromise group, headed by Mullet, advocated that the firm continue paying dividends, but pay only some *constant portion* of earnings in any one year. Since total equity financing needs are substantial, Mullet's group recommended a **payout ratio** (dividends ÷ net income) of 20 to 30 percent. Given current net income of $2.97 per share, this policy would result in a dividend between $0.2 \times \$2.97 = \$0.59$ and $0.3 \times \$2.97 = \$0.89$ per share in the current year. Cash dividends would be reduced from the historical $1.15 level in the current year, but not eliminated. In future years dividends would vary with the level of net income if a constant payout ratio were maintained, resulting in a clear break with the existing fixed dividend policy. As with the other policies, remaining equity needs would be met by a sale of new shares.

The alternatives favored by each of the groups do not represent all the possible alternatives. Variations of each policy are numerous. However, only these three policy alternatives were brought to the board's attention.

Mullet was asked to summarize the board's position at this date. His summary statement concluded as follows:

Two assumptions underlie each of the three proposals. (1) Dividend policy does matter to shareholders and there is an optimum policy. (2) Barfield management will be able to identify that policy and implement it to benefit existing shareholders.

. . . various members of the board of directors are in basic disagreement about whether the payout ratio (proportion of earnings paid out as dividends) is important, whether shareholders view stability *of the dividend stream as valuable, and whether consistency of policy from period to period rather than the specific* type *of policy is a prime consideration . . . .*

. . . The recent Barfield dividend policy seems to reflect the board's past desire for a stable dollar dividend as shown in Table 14-2.

To help Barfield set its dividend policy, we must start by addressing the first two assumptions underlying the disagreement. We must ask whether dividend policy, as reflected in the payout ratio and the stability of the dividend stream, is relevant. Does it really matter? To attempt to answer this question, we temporarily depart from considering Barfield's specific decision.

THE ARGUMENT THAT DIVIDEND POLICY IS IRRELEVANT

When markets are perfect and there are no personal taxes, it can be shown that maintaining a specific payout ratio or attempting to stabilize the dividend stream by paying out a large proportion of earnings in poor years and a smaller proportion in good years will not affect shareholder wealth.[1] In this discussion, the present and future investment plans of the firm are *given* and *known* to the market. Such investment plans are also independent of dividend policy in that they will be implemented regardless of the dividend policy selected by the firm. If the chosen dividend policy happens to leave insufficient retention of earnings to meet equity financing needs of investment plans, additional common shares will be sold. Two additional assumptions will simplify the discussion: there are no corporate taxes, and the firm has no outstanding debt. As pointed out later in this chapter, these assumptions are not necessary to show dividend policy to be irrelevant. They do, however, make numerical examples easier to follow.

The irrelevance of dividend policy can be demonstrated using two companies, Maggie, Inc., and Nanny, Inc. An investor named Pike owns 10 common shares of each company. The two companies are identical in every respect. They have identical business risks and an expected net income of $1000 per year in perpetuity (remember, there are no income taxes). Each company has been paying out all net income as dividends. That is, the firms have identical payout ratios of 100 percent. Neither Maggie nor Nanny has any outstanding debt, and their cost of capital is $K = k_e = 10$ percent. The value of each company's total shares at $t = 0$ is:

$$V = \frac{\$1000}{0.10} = \$10,000$$

Each company has 1000 shares outstanding, so dividends per share are:

$$D = \frac{\$1000}{1000} = \$1$$

---

[1]See Chapter 3 for the assumptions underlying perfect markets.

The price per share for each company is:

$$P = \frac{D}{k_e} = \frac{\$1}{0.10} = \$10$$

Though investors currently expect no future investment, both Maggie and Nanny discover identical investment opportunities that are expected to earn 20 percent per year in perpetuity on a $1000 outlay. The expected annual net income for each investment is $0.20 \times \$1000 = \$200$. At this point our firms part ways. Maggie decides to finance the investment by retaining earnings, and Nanny will pay out all net income as a dividend while selling new shares to finance the investment. If we assume that both companies earned $1000 during the past year and that that amount is available either for new investment or for dividend payment, then Maggie has elected a zero percent dividend payout and Nanny has elected a 100 percent payout. The question is whether Pike should prefer one of these policies to the other or should be indifferent between them.

Consider Maggie first. By cutting the dividend at $t = 0$ to zero, the firm need sell no new common stock to finance the investment. Expected *total* annual earnings starting at $t = 1$ will be the original $1000 plus 20 percent on the new $1000 investment, or $1200 altogether. Since all earnings starting at $t = 1$ will be paid out as dividends, future dividends will be $\$1200/1000 = \$1.20$ per share, since no new shares have been issued. Because the new dividend stream has the same risk as the original dividend stream, each share will now be valued, using $k_e = 10$ percent at:

$$P = \frac{\$1.20}{0.10} = \$12$$

The price increase will occur at $t = 0$ when news of the planned investment and the dividend omission is announced.

If Pike wants a $10 total dividend at $t = 0$ from his 10 shares of Maggie, he can still obtain it even though Maggie has paid out no dividend at that time. He need only reflect that his shares are now worth $10 \times \$12 = \$120$ at $t = 0$. He can sell $10 worth of his shares by selling $^{10}\!/_{12}$ of one share at $12 per share. He is left with $110 of shares and a **"homemade" dividend** of $10 created by selling shares. The $10 homemade dividend is a realization of one half of the increase in value of his shares caused by the retention of earnings and subsequent investment in assets that are expected to earn a 20 percent rate of return. That portion of Pike's wealth associated with his investment in Maggie is the value of his shares plus his homemade dividend, or, $120.

Will that portion of Pike's wealth associated with ownership of Nanny differ from $120? As we shall see, it will not.

Instead of omitting cash dividends, the otherwise identical Nanny, Inc., financed its $1000 investment at $t = 0$ by selling shares. Before selling shares, however, Nanny announced both investment plans and financing policy to the market. Since the new investment is expected to earn 20 percent and the required rate of return is only 10 percent, the $200 income stream expected to be generated is more than sufficient to compensate new investors who require only a 10 percent rate of return. Thus, share price should increase as soon as the announcement is made.

By how much should share price increase? The "extra" return on the new investment is 10 percent (20% − 10%). That is, the firm expects to earn twice the minimum required rate. This "extra" return may be expressed in dollars by multiplying the difference between the expected rate and the required rate by the amount of the investment. That is, $(0.20 − 0.10) \times \$1000 = \$100$. The value of that extra return is $\$100/0.10 = \$1000$. If the value of shares prior to the announcement is added to the value of the extra cash flow that will accrue to original shareholders, the total value of *original* shares becomes:

$$\$10,000 + \$1000 = \$11,000$$

so the new price per share is $11,000/1000 = $11. The number of new shares that must be sold at $11 per share to raise the $1000 necessary to purchase new assets is $1000/$11 = 90.91.

Now consider Pike's position in Nanny. He owns 10 shares at $t = 0$ and, since these shares are now worth $11 each, the value of his holding is $10 \times \$11 = \$110$. In addition, since Nanny paid out dividends of $1 per share, Pike receives $10 of dividends from his 10 shares. His wealth derived from holding Nanny shares is $110 + $10 = $120. But this is exactly the same as his wealth derived from the Maggie shares, where he owns $110 of stock ($9\frac{2}{12}$ shares at $12) and the $10 "homemade" dividend. Therefore Pike should be indifferent between Maggie and Nanny shares, even though, at $t = 0$, Maggie's payout ratio is zero percent and Nanny's is 100 percent. Homemade and corporate dividends are the same. By creating a homemade dividend, Pike effectively neutralizes corporate dividend policy. The dividend policy adopted by Maggie and Nanny is irrelevant to Pike and to other investors because their wealth is unchanged and because they can obtain cash that is identical to a corporate dividend by selling shares.[2]

---

[2]Our discussion has assumed that Pike wanted $10 for some purpose regardless of the firm's dividend policy; however, it could have been assumed that he did not want $10 to

These conclusions can be generalized to include all firms. *Under the assumptions stated*, dividend policy does not matter. The decision to retain earnings and reduce dividends to finance investment projects, or to finance projects by selling new shares, has no effect on the value of ownership.

We must relax some of these assumptions to see whether the irrelevance proposition still holds and is applicable to the Barfield problem.

It turns out that two of the assumptions, no corporate income taxes and the absence of debt, do not alter the validity of the irrelevance notion when they are dropped. In the case of corporate income taxes, the dividend decision remains irrelevant because dividends are paid out of after-tax (corporate income tax) cash flows. Corporate income taxes, and thus after-tax cash flows, are not affected by decisions to raise or lower cash dividends (or lower or raise earnings retentions). Nor will the existence of corporate debt alter the irrelevance proposition as long as the desired amount of debt financing is expressed as a percentage of the *total* financing need. Once that percentage has been specified, the remaining proportion of the total financing need comes from equity sources. Given the ability to create homemade dividends (or homemade earnings retentions), the irrelevance proposition holds and earnings retentions or sale of new stock can be used to satisfy the remaining financing need.

All the analysis above assumes perfect markets and the absence of personal income taxes. The assumption of perfect markets makes it possible for the firm's investment decisions to be considered separately from the dividend decision. All profitable present and future investment opportunities will be undertaken since, if sufficient earnings are not retained to provide the equity portion of required financing, additional shares can always be sold in the market. Insofar as dividend policy is concerned, the investment *policy* is said to be *fixed*. In addition, perfect markets rule out any transaction costs, flotation costs, indivisibility problems with securities, and costs of information. When these imperfections are introduced, the irrelevance proposition may no longer hold. Similarly, when we introduce personal income taxes on dividends received and capital gains realized in the creation of homemade dividends, we may find that rational investors are not indifferent to dividend policy.

---

spend now but wanted that money immediately reinvested. In that situation either the firm could reinvest by retaining earnings or Pike could reinvest by purchasing securities of identical risk with the $10 paid out. If this line of analysis were pursued, we would find that just as homemade dividends and corporate dividends are equivalent, so are homemade retention and corporate retention of earnings.

PERSONAL TAXES, MARKET IMPER-FECTIONS, AND DIVIDEND POLICY

Personal taxes complicate matters. Dividends are taxed when received at ordinary income rates, whereas capital gains resulting from earnings retention are taxed only when realized at lower rates. This tax differential appears to create an investor preference for earnings retention; but appearances are deceiving, as our analysis will show. Likewise, market imperfections introduce many elements previously ignored. Transaction costs include the *trading* costs that investors must bear when they buy and sell securities. Flotation costs are the fees the firm must pay to sell new securities. Both costs must be reflected in the dividend policy decision. Lack of divisibility of assets will make it difficult for investors to create their homemade dividends by selling fractional shares of stock. Finally, since information is not freely available to all investors, dividend policy may affect investor assessments of the firm's profitability. In that instance the value of the firm will be related to dividend policy, not because investors worry about dividends per se, but because of the information conveyed by dividend policy. In the sections that follow, each of these factors that affect dividend policy is discussed in more detail.

Personal Income Taxes

Personal income tax provisions are alleged to create differences in investor preferences between corporate and homemade dividends. If the personal tax rate on capital gains is lower than the tax rate on income, or if capital gains taxes can be delayed for years by not selling shares while personal income taxes on dividends must be paid in the year that the dividend is received, shareholders will prefer capital gains relative to dividends. Retaining earnings then becomes the preferred method of equity financing because homemade dividends obtained by realizing capital gains through the sale of stock are taxed at lower rates than are corporate dividends.

Unfortunately, however, the complexities of U.S. tax laws do not allow us to rest our analysis here. Preferences for homemade or corporate dividends will not be the same for all investors if they differ in tax status.

Personal tax laws exempt (at this writing) up to $200 of dividend and interest income ($400 for a joint return) from taxes on ordinary income, whereas capital gains are taxed at a lower rate than that applying to ordinary income. The small investor may therefore be led by the $200 exemption to prefer corporate dividends rather than homemade dividends created by realizing capital gains. The corporate dividend will not be taxed for such investors, whereas homemade dividends will create a capital gains tax liability.

Investors who have already used their $200 exemption and are in high tax brackets may prefer either a smaller or no corporate dividend. Homemade dividends that they can create themselves will be taxed at the lower capital gains rate.

That analysis presumes that investors have no way to avoid paying taxes on dividends once those dividends are received. However, Miller and Scholes argue that provisions of the U.S. tax code allow investors to reduce and perhaps to eliminate taxes on dividends.[3] This is possible because interest payments on debt are tax deductible.

Consider the following simplified example. An investor with $1000 purchases 500 shares of stock for $2 per share. Since the dividend yield is 5 percent, he receives $50 in dividends during the year. Assuming that the dividend exclusion is used up from previous purchases of common stock, the whole $50 is taxable. But suppose the individual borrowed $1250 at 9 percent and used the proceeds to buy more shares. He would then own $2250 in shares and his dividend payment would be $0.05 \times$ $2250 = $112.50. Interest payments are identical, since $0.09 \times $1250 =$ $112.50. Since interest payments are tax deductible, the investor's income from dividends is offset by the interest expense. Taxes on dividends are reduced to zero by appropriate use of leverage.

One objection to this strategy is that it increases shareholder risk. (The example above compares pre- and postleverage positions of different risk.) Miller and Scholes circumvent that objection by introducing insurance. Instead of borrowing $1250 and investing the proceeds in common stock, the investor borrows $555.55 and uses the proceeds to buy a paid-up, tax-free insurance policy. Now he owns stock worth $1000 and receives $50 of dividends. Those payments are offset by $0.09 \times $555.55 = 50 of interest on the loan and the paid-up insurance offsets the loan liability, leaving no net leverage and no tax on the dividends.

Although this is an idealized view of the tax code and taxes are not necessarily so easy to completely avoid, the crux of the matter is that under our existing tax code the effective rate on dividends can be reduced substantially in a wide range of circumstances.[4] Appearances are, indeed, deceiving. To the extent that any tax disadvantage of dividends exists for individuals, it is much smaller than one would suspect by comparing marginal income and capital gains tax rates.

Finally, tax-exempt investment institutions that hold many billions of dollars of common stocks must be considered. These institutions, which include foundations, pension funds, and educational institutions, will

---

[3]M. H. Miller and M. S. Scholes, "Dividends and Taxes," *Journal of Financial Economics* (December 1978), pp. 333–364.

[4]Miller and Scholes, in "Dividends and Taxes," cited in note 3, summarize many of the salient features of the U.S. tax code.

not be led by their unique tax status to prefer either corporate or home-made dividends.[5]

Transaction and Flotation Costs

Flotation costs, which reduce the amount of funds received by the firm when new shares are sold to provide equity financing, are sustained indirectly by investors. Transaction costs of trading are sustained directly when investors buy or sell securities. Differences between these costs may cause investors to have definite preferences for either corporate or homemade dividends.

Suppose that shareholders of a firm uniformly prefer a 100 percent dividend payout ratio but the firm adopts a target dividend payout ratio of zero. All shareholders must sell part of their shares to realize the capital gains caused by 100 percent retention of earnings and so create the desired homemade dividends. Collectively, these shareholders would sustain a total transaction cost of selling shares T_S. Alternatively, had the firm accommodated the dividend preferences of its shareholders and paid out a 100 percent corporate dividend, the firm would have sustained flotation costs T_F of issuing new stock to finance investments. Taking both costs together, shareholders wanting the high dividend payout will be *worse* off when the target dividend payout ratio is zero if T_S exceeds T_F; collectively, shareholders sustain higher transaction costs in creating the homemade dividend than the firm would sustain flotation costs under a 100 percent payout policy with sale of shares to finance investments. In effect, if T_S exceeds T_F, corporate dividends cost less to provide than homemade dividends. If T_S is less than T_F, homemade dividends are the least costly and the firm should use retained earnings as the preferred form of equity financing. Interestingly, if flotation costs and transaction costs are identical, dividend policy is, again, irrelevant. No matter how the firm obtains equity financing, the negative impact on shareholders will be the same. Clearly, then, the existence of flotation costs and transaction costs is not sufficient to make shareholders prefer either corporate or homemade dividends. It is the relative size of these costs that is relevant in selecting the appropriate policy.

Normally, we reason that flotation costs are likely to be higher than trading costs for most firms. Therefore, investors will prefer that the firm retain earnings rather than sell new shares to finance profitable investments. This generalization is probably true for most firms. But a special set of circumstances in which new shares could be sold at a low flotation cost relative to transaction costs of trading cannot be ruled out.

---

[5]Other restrictions imposed by government may create preferences for dividends or capital gains, but we do not cover them in detail.

In addition to transaction and flotation costs, we must consider the problem of divisibility. The notion of a perfect market presumes that financial securities can be sold in any amounts. Most publicly held firms have millions of shares outstanding and one share represents a very small ownership claim, so their equity is divisible into relatively small parts. However, investors like Pike who hold a small number of shares in some firms will find difficulty in creating homemade dividends because fractional shares cannot be sold and the cost of selling a very few shares on an organized exchange is relatively large.

Divisibility of Securities

Collectively, personal taxes, transaction and flotation costs, and lack of divisibility may lead some investors to prefer a given payout ratio or payout pattern. How does this possibility affect the validity of the irrelevance notion illustrated with Pike and the Maggie and Nanny shares? Can the management of each firm really adopt any payout ratio it wishes without affecting share value and shareholder wealth? One view suggests that an *initial* choice of dividend policy is irrelevant and, to that extent, the irrelevance proposition may hold. However, it is suggested that *variations* in dividend policy may still adversely affect share value even though that effect may be only temporary.

Personal Taxes, Transaction and Flotation Costs, Divisibility, and the Clientele Effect

If investor preferences for dividend policies vary because of personal tax status, transaction and flotation costs, and other factors, investors will purchase the securities of firms that conform to their preferences. A firm with an established dividend policy attracts a specific *clientele*. Shareholders preferring capital gains will tend to hold shares with low payout ratios, whereas shareholders preferring current income will tend to hold shares with high payout ratios. This investor behavior is called a **clientele effect.**

From the firm's point of view, any one clientele is as good as another, so any dividend policy will lead to the same share value as any other policy that might have been chosen. However, a *change* in an established policy may imply a change in clientele. Both buyers and sellers of shares will incur transaction costs to adjust their security holdings. Those costs are penalties imposed on investors by management when it alters dividend policy. However, no permenant change in share price should occur with a change in clientele as long as investors can find firms with policies suitable to them.

To illustrate, suppose Cowens, Inc., has been paying out 50 percent of its earnings for a number of years and its shares currently sell for $10 each. If Cowens now changes its dividend policy, investors may wish to assess the costs and benefits of selling their Cowens shares and purchasing shares of a different firm whose dividend policy more nearly meets their needs. For example, after selling their Cowens shares, investors might purchase shares of several firms in a portfolio such that the *combination* of dividend policies was to their liking. At the same time, other new investors or shareholders of other firms will now find holding Cowens shares *more* attractive because of the change in dividend policy. After all trading of shares has been completed by those attracted to, and repelled by, Cowens' new dividend policy, there may be little change in the price of Cowens shares. For this to happen, there must be many investors who would find Cowens' new policy attractive in order to offset the actions of disaffected investors selling Cowens shares.

If Cowens should change its dividend policy frequently, causing shareholders to incur frequent transaction costs, share price is likely to be lower than it otherwise would be. How *much* lower cannot be determined on the basis of the evidence that is available. An unstable dividend policy adds transaction costs for investors, which some might like to avoid. It may be that firms will want to adopt a consistent dividend policy. Avoiding unnecessary changes in a dividend policy, once adopted, will then allow investors to avoid additional transaction costs.

At the same time, management must be willing to recognize when a significant alteration in the financial or operating position of the firm calls for a reassessment of policies. When specific reasons relating to the profitability and vitality of the firm indicate a change in policy, the change should be made. Frivolous changes should probably be avoided.

Information Costs   Shareholders always face uncertainty about the future profitability of a firm. Contrary to the assumptions of perfect markets, information that might reduce that uncertainty is not free. Indeed, some investors may incur substantial costs to obtain information about the prospects of the firm. But even those who have the resources and are willing to pay may not be able to obtain all the information they desire. They must make do with tidbits provided by management, market letters, the opinions of professional analysts, financial data in Moody's Industrial Manuals, or other less common sources, all of which are likely to have some cost in cash or in use of scarce time.

In the face of costly information, one source to which investors turn is the firm itself. However, they are likely to be wary of simply believing everything that managers say (and do not say). After all, it is in the managers' personal economic interest to make investors think that all is well with the firm and management is doing a good job. In addition, earnings, sales, and cost figures, historical or projected, are subject to various forms of manipulation—most of which are not specifically intended to deceive. In such a situation investors may look to dividends and dividend policy to provide information about the future.

The notion that dividend policy provides information to investors is reinforced by a study done some time ago concerning how firms set dividends.[6] After direct discussion with executives in charge of setting dividend policy it was found that a high proportion of firms strive to maintain a stable or slightly growing dividend stream. Dramatic changes in dividend policy were avoided where possible and management was loath to increase dividends if it did not expect the increase to be maintained in the future—that is, management appeared to be reluctant to cut dividends. If at all possible, historical dividend levels were maintained. Reluctance to reduce dividends appeared to stem from two sources. First, managers felt that investors counted on the dividend and would be upset by cuts. As a consequence, share prices would be adversely affected. Second, a cut in dividends might reflect adversely on the ability and judgment of management.

A third possible reason for managers to prefer a **stable dividend policy** stems from legal restrictions facing certain investors. Many financial institutions, trustees, and pension funds must invest in securities contained in a *legal list*. For a firm's shares to be eligible for that list, its dividend payment stream must be well established. Firms reducing or omitting a dividend payment within fairly recent history run the risk of being declared ineligible for purchase by institutional investors.

Investors who are affected by legal restrictions on their choice of common stock tend to buy and sell stock in large quantities. Consequently, their inability to buy shares with unstable dividend policies may be a potentially important factor causing the market to reward firms with stable policies. The importance of appearing on a legal list will, of course, vary among firms. If it is important, it may be so only for a very few firms. Nevertheless, if managers perceive that it is important and try to avoid drastic changes—especially cuts—investors may quite correctly view dividend declarations as providing information about management perceptions of the future.

If a firm that has historically followed a stable dividend policy raises or lowers its dividend unexpectedly, it produces an *announcement effect* on share price. Share price may rise with an increase in dividends (the future looks more promising than originally expected), and it may fall with a decrease in dividends (the future is not as promising as originally expected). An example of the effects of stable and unstable dividend streams will demonstrate this point.

Consider two new firms, Milton, Inc., and Frieda Company, alike in all respects except dividend policy. Their earnings and dividends are

---

[6]John Lintner, "Distribution of Incomes of Corporations Among Dividends, Retained Earnings and Taxes," *American Economic Review* (May 1956), pp. 97–113.

Table 14–3   *Dividends, Earnings, and Payout: Milton, Inc.*

	1977	1978	1979	1980	1981	Average
Dividends per share	$3.20	$4.80	$3.20	$4.00	$4.80	$4.00
Earnings per share	$4.00	$6.00	$4.00	$5.00	$6.00	$5.00
Payout Ratio	0.80	0.80	0.80	0.80	0.80	0.80

shown in Table 14-3 and Table 14-4. Assume that both companies have investment opportunities requiring that, on average, 20 percent of earnings be retained. Average annual earnings over the 5-year period are $5 per share for both companies, and average dividends per share are $4. As of 1981, both managements believe that $5 per share represents the level of expected annual earnings per share in future years.

Suppose that investors of both firms view dividends as an indicator of the future profitability of those firms. Neither set of shareholders knows what management's expectations of the future are. With its stable dividend of $4 per year, Frieda Company might convey management expectations of future profitability more effectively through dividend policy than can Milton, Inc. Milton's dividend fluctuates with earnings from period to period. Even though dividends are always 80 percent of realized earnings, it would be difficult for investors to discern, after observing a particular 80 percent payout, whether management's expectations of the future had changed. Frieda's management could, because dividends have been historically stable, signal its expectations by raising or lowering the $4 dividend.

To the extent that dividends are viewed as an important source of information by both investors and managers, those policies that convey information easily should be preferred. Such policies may reduce both the perceived risk and costs of obtaining information. If so, they should increase the price that investors are willing to pay for the firm's shares. That is, one might expect common stock of Frieda Company to sell at slightly higher prices than that of Milton, Inc.

Table 14–4   *Dividends, Earnings, and Payout: Frieda Company*

	1977	1978	1979	1980	1981	Average
Dividends per share	$4.00	$4.00	$4.00	$4.00	$4.00	$4.00
Earnings per share	$4.00	$6.00	$4.00	$5.00	$6.00	$5.00
Payout Ratio	1.00	0.67	1.00	0.80	0.67	0.80

From the discussion above it is possible to discover how a firm wishing to convey maximum information to the market might set dividend policy. First management would assess future profitability and form expectations about future earnings levels. These expectations might be called *permanent* earnings. With these expectations in mind, management might set a target payout ratio. That target ratio is the proportion of permanent earnings that will be paid out, regardless of fluctuations in actual earnings. If dividend policy is set in this way, there are two reasons for altering dividends per share. First, expectations about permanent earnings might change. Second, even though permanent earnings were unchanged, the target payout might be altered by changes in the financial and operating environment of the firm.

As a practical matter it may still be difficult for investors to determine the real reason for a change in dividends. They can never be certain why dividends increased or decreased; but given the company history and management practices of a specific firm that constitute generally available information, a reasonable assessment should be possible.

The **information content** of dividend policy varies from firm to firm. Availability of alternative sources of information as well as specific circumstances facing a firm may make dividend policy an inefficient and highly ambiguous source of information. Also, we should recognize that managerial attempts to fool the market and maintain dividends when their expectations of permanent earnings are falling may only create future problems for management. Maintaining dividends when earnings decline might convey a temporary sense of security regarding the profitability of the firm. However, as actual earnings continue to decline, perhaps irregularly, shareholders will realize that the current dividend cannot be maintained and will expect a decline in future dividends. When that expectation commonly held, share price will fall even if high dividends are temporarily maintained.

Finally, we should note that the possibility of information content in dividends reinforces the argument made in discussing the *clientele effect* about the value of a stable dividend policy. Not only may such a policy reduce trading costs, it should also reduce shareholder uncertainty about the prospects of the firm. When a firm suddenly changes policies, investors may feel that a careful reevaluation of the firm is in order. That reevaluation may take time as the investors reassess existing information. As a result, the value of shares may be more unstable and shareholder wealth may decline.

A View of Some Evidence

Even the most appealing argument must be rejected if it remains unsupported by careful data analysis. The arguments that payout policy is a matter of indifference to the firm and that dividends convey information to investors are no exception.

Several studies have attempted to identify any relation between dividend policy amd share value.[7] In 1974 Black and Scholes attempted to identify the impact of dividend yield on value. They were unable to find any advantage to either a relatively high or a relatively low dividend payout. A more recent study conducted by Gordon and Bradford in 1980 reaches a similar conclusion. These investigators found that the value of an extra dollar of dividends is roughly equivalent to an extra dollar of capital gains.

These results are consistent with the view that payout policy is irrelevant because one clientele is as good as another. Unfortunately, they are also consistent with the view that each firm has an optimum dividend policy that maximizes shareholder wealth and that each firm has found that wealth-maximizing policy. Whatever the real explanation, it is comforting to note that there is no evidence that firms are paying out either too much or too little to the detriment of shareholders.

Controversy characterized several early attempts to identify the information content of dividends. However, there appears to be general agreement now that an unanticipated increase in the regular dividend is viewed as positive information by shareholders, and an unanticipated cut in regular dividends is viewed negatively. These conclusions rest on an analysis of share price changes around quarterly dividend announcements. One of the most recent of such studies found "that changes in quarterly dividends provide useful information beyond that provided by quarterly earnings numbers."[8]

The Dividend Extra

Firms sometimes separate their cash dividends into two components—a "regular" dividend and an **"extra" dividend**. Since both components are taxed the same and a dollar in regular dividends will purchase the same amount of goods and services as a dollar of extra dividends, why do some firms bother to identify a component of the total dividend payment as an "extra"?

One explanation of extras rests on an information content argument.

---

[7]See, for example, I. Friend and M. Puckett, "Dividends and Stock Prices," *American Economic Review* (September 1964), pp. 656–682; F. Black and M. Scholes, "The Effects of Dividend Yield and Dividend Policy on Common Stock Prices and Returns," *Journal of Financial Economics* (May 1974), pp. 1–22; R. Gordon and D. Bradford, "Taxation and the Stock Market Valuation of Capital Gains and Dividends: Theory and Empirical Results," *Journal of Public Economics* (October, 1980), pp. 109–136.

[8]J. Aharony and I. Swary, "Quarterly Dividend and Earnings Announcements and Shareholder Returns: An Empirical Analysis," *Journal of Finance* (March 1980), pp. 1–12.

If many firms prefer a stable dividend policy and if managers are reluctant to cut the level of regular dividends, an extra may be viewed as an attempt to avoid sending false signals to the market when management perceives earnings as temporarily high and wishes to pay higher dividends in the short run. Rather than send a strong, positive signal by increasing regular dividends, then risk having to send a subsequent, negative signal by cutting that regular dividend in the future, management can try to indicate that part of the payment is temporary. As a device to avoid false signals, the extra will accompany high, but unstable earnings. Recent work by Brickley suggests that many firms do use extras as if they are trying to avoid false signals.[9] The market appears to respond positively to dividend extras, but the response is less than if the regular dividend had been increased by the same amount.

Unfortunately, still other firms appear to pay a dividend extra so regularly that it is difficult to believe that shareholders view the extra as different from the regular dividend. In such instances, omission of an extra may be interpreted as bad news by the market just as if a regular dividend were cut. Persistent repetition of dividend extras is puzzling because it does not appear to fit nicely into the view that an extra is a special signal. Only further analysis will help solve this puzzle.

THE BARFIELD PROBLEM

Given the range of issues from dividend irrelevance with perfect markets to the complex issues raised by market imperfections and personal taxes, how should Barfield solve its problem? Mullet, the treasurer, knew that he had to consider all those issues before reporting to the board of directors.

Existing Dividend Policy

In reviewing Table 14.2, Mullet recalled the rationale underlying previous dividend decisions. Barfield decided in the early 1970s that a policy of stable cash dividends, which were periodically increased when the board felt a higher dividend could be maintained, would be most appropriate. At that time the level of profitable new investment opportunities appeared to be minimal. The board of directors felt that any new opportunities could be financed with debt and retained earnings without disrupting the stable dividend policy.

In assessing that policy over the past few years, Mullet believed that Barfield had attracted a loyal group of shareholders who had come to

[9] J. Brickley, *Shareholder Wealth, Information Signalling* and the *Specially Designated Dividend*, Unpublished PhD Dissertation, University of Oregon, Eugene, Or., 1982.

expect and rely on the dividend. He felt that a new earnings report that indicated no dividend payment would cause genuine concern, if not anger, among those shareholders. Although he was not sure what would happen to share price, he reasoned that the necessary sale of new shares to *complete* equity financing needs would, after chopping the dividend, yield relatively low prices per share to the firm. Also he noted that even complete elimination of the $1.15 cash dividend over the next 3 years would not provide all funds necessary to avoid selling new shares.

In spite of these misgivings about disrupting existing policy, Mr. Mullet knew that only a carefully reasoned analysis would sway members of the board of directors whose views were different from his. As a consequence, he began his analysis by evaluating each policy that had been proposed.

Analysis of the Amount of External Financing Required by Three Dividend Policies

Recall that three policies were proposed by the various groups in the board of directors.

1. Eliminate dividends entirely through 1985.

2. Pay out 20 to 30 percent of earnings as dividends until 1985.

3. Maintain the $1.15 dividend.

Regardless of which policy was selected, funds would still have to be raised by selling new shares. However none of the members of the board had yet assessed either the amount of new money to be obtained by selling new shares or the number of shares to be issued. That knowledge appeared to be a prerequisite for an intelligent decision.

Mullet's first task was to project earnings for each of the next 3 years. The future earnings projection had to reflect not only earnings from existing assets but those resulting from the new investments as well. Annual projections are summarized as follows.

	1983	1984	1985
Projected Earnings (000,000)	$1.1	$1.6	$2.2

Given projected earnings, Mullet prepared Tables 14-5A, 14-5B, and 14-5C for the board of directors to indicate, respectively, the total amount of earnings to be retained, the total amount raised through the sale of new shares, and the total number of shares issued. In all cases he assumed that new shares would be issued in early 1983 (the next few months).

Table 14–5A *Internal and External Financing When No Dividends Are Paid: Barfield, Inc.*

	1982	1983	1984	1985
Earnings (000)	$1040	$1100	$1600	$2200
Dividends (000)	0	0	0	0
Dividends per share	0	0	0	0
Earnings Retained (000)	1040	1100	1600	2200
Cumulative Retentions (000)	1040	2140	3740	5940

Total Amount of New Share Financing:	$10,500,000 − $5,940,000 = $4,560,000
Price at Which New Shares Are Sold:	$15
Number of New Shares:	$4,560,000/$15 = 304,000

Table 14-5A considers a policy of omitting dividends entirely for 1982 as well as for each of the next 3 years. Total retentions over that period would be $5.94 million. Since total needs are $10.5 million, the remaining $4.56 million must be raised by selling new shares.

Before computing the number of shares to be sold, Mr. Mullet had to estimate the price at which new shares would sell under this policy. Shares are currently selling for $20 each. However, the combination of cutting dividends to zero and flotation costs probably would result in proceeds to the firm of not more than $15 per share. Even that figure

Table 14–5B *Internal and External Financing When Payout Ratio Is 20 Percent: Barfield, Inc.*

	1982	1983	1984	1985
Earnings (000)	$1040	$1100	$1600	$2200
Dividends (000)	208	220	320	440
Dividends per share	$0.59	$0.32	$0.46	$0.64
Earnings Retained (000)	832	880	1280	1760
Cumulative Retentions (000)	832	1712	2992	4752

Total Amount of New Share Financing:	$10,500,000 − $4,752,000 = $5,748,000
Price at Which New Shares Are Sold:	$17
Number of New Shares:	$5,748,000/$17 = 338,118

Table 14–5C   *Internal and External Financing When Dividends of $1.15 per Share Are Maintained: Barfield, Inc.*

	1982	1983	1984	1985
Earnings (000)	$1040	$1100	$1600	$2200
Dividends (000)	402.5	890.2	890.2	890.2
Dividends per share	$1.15	$1.15	$1.15	$1.15
Earnings Retained (000)	637.5	209.8	709.8	1309.8
Cumulative Retentions (000)	637.5	847.3	1557.1	2867.9

Total Amount of New Share Financing:	$10,500,000 − $2,866,900 = $7,633,100
Price at Which New Shares Are Sold:	$18
Number of New Shares:	$7,633,100/$18 = 424,061

seemed high because an investment banker who was consulted did not think that Barfield could sell additional stock at any reasonable price if it omitted dividends. He cautioned against this plan and admitted that his firm might be reluctant to help Barfield sell such an issue. Still, Mullet felt that the board should know the number of shares that would have to be sold at $15 each. As shown, he found that number to be 304,000.

Table 14-5B indicates the impact of maintaining a payout ratio of 20 percent over the period. Note that total retentions would be $4.752 million by 1985. Therefore $5.748 million would have to be obtained in the market. Again Mullet tried to assess the proceeds per share that Barfield would obtain from such an issue. The investment banker was much more positive about this policy. He still felt that share price would be affected adversely, although that impact might be minimized if management were careful to prepare investors for the new policy. He concluded that a price of $17 per share might be a reasonable estimate, but cautioned Mullet to be aware that shares, when sold, might yield lower proceeds to the firm.

Note that even though the net proceeds per share that accrue to the firm are higher under the second policy, the total number of shares that must be issued is larger by 338,118 − 304,000 = 34,118 shares. The reason lies in the larger amount that must be raised by selling shares when dividends are paid. Also note the projected pattern of dividends. In 1982 original shareholders would receive $208,000/350,000 = $0.59 per share, since no new shares would be outstanding when those dividends were paid. In 1983, however, there would be the original 350,000 shares plus 338,118 new shares for a total of 688,118 shares outstanding. The anticipated total dividend of $220,000 must be divided among all share-holders, so the dividend per share would fall to $220,000/688,118 = $0.32. Investor reaction to another decrease in dividends per share is unknown but it may be cause for concern. In 1984 and 1985 growth in dividends per share is large, but Barfield management might well be concerned about share price until that growth is actually realized.

Table 14-5C considers a policy of keeping dividends at $1.15 per share. That strategy would result in total retentions of only $2,866,900 over the period, so $7,633,100 would be needed from new share financing. That is substantially more than either of the other policies would require. However, the reaction of the investment banker to this policy was a bit more enthusiastic. He felt that because of the stable dividend, future share price might be less volatile than with either of the other policies and that proceeds of $18 per share might be obtained by the firm. He noted that the larger number of new shares (424,061) that would be required might be even easier to sell than the small number of shares required under the previous policy. However, when questioned more carefully, he admitted that he might be overstating the importance of a stable dividend policy when such a large expansion in the size of the firm is contemplated.

With this information at hand, Mullet began preparing his report.

In his report Mullet discussed past dividend policy, the projections he made, and comments received by the investment banker. He concluded that report with the following paragraphs:

Mullet's Report to the Board of Directors

To the extent that the firm has acquired a clientele that prefers a relatively high payout ratio and a stable dividend, a drastic change in dividend policy may upset some of these shareholders. They may dispose of their shares and write nasty letters accusing us of 'stealing' their dividends and other forms of morally reprehensible behavior.

This storm could very well be small if we have generally had good relations with our investors and respect by the market. If the reason for a reduction in dividend is made clear and if the market has confidence in the ability of our management to use funds to select investments that will benefit shareholders, unhappy investors should be able to sell their shares to investors attracted to the new dividend policy without suffering large capital losses.

If, on the other hand, the market does not have confidence in Barfield management, the reaction could be far more adverse. Investors who rely on historical trends to provide information about future growth and profitability may be unwilling to believe that opportunities are as good as Barfield anticipates. Dissatisfied shareholders will be able to sell their shares only at prices below current levels, and the firm may acquire an unsavory reputation. That is, new investors could only be attracted if current shareholders were willing to sell at a discount.

Barfield is not a particularly large firm. It has only $20 million in sales and is unlikely to be held by institutional investors. Floating new stock is likely to be extremely expensive. Every dollar that the firm must pay out in dividends represents another dollar that must be raised by selling shares. Therefore, shareholders could fare worse in the long run if the firm does not cut dividends.

There are both short- and long-run consequences of dividend policy that might concern management. If the current funds requirements are viewed as 'one-shot' needs that will not be repeated in the foreseeable future, Barfield should be very reluctant to take any action that would disturb investors. Even if all earnings were retained, new share financing will be necessary. If at about the same time that reduced dividends were announced, the firm tried to sell a relatively large issue of new shares, the subsequent price obtained might be far less favorable to original shareholders than if dividends were maintained and a larger amount of equity were issued in a more stable market.

If many more profitable investment opportunities are likely to appear, the best policy might be to announce a change and stand by it. Any adverse impact on share price that occurs on the announcement of dividend reductions may be more than offset by the fact that the firm will lay the basic groundwork for future financing with a higher proportion of retentions. The point we must always remember when considering a complete elimination of the dividend just before selling new shares is the potential adverse reaction of the market. Investment bankers might refuse to sell the issue under such circumstances, and without their help, obtaining equity funds would be virtually impossible.

In making its final decision, Barfield's board of directors should consider (1) the personal tax position of existing shareholders, (2) dividend expectations of existing shareholders, (3) the necessity and likelihood of attracting new shareholders, (4) potential disruption of the market caused by unanticipated dividend reductions, (5) the cost of new equity financing, and (6) the duration of the change in dividend policy. Above all, the firm should recognize that flotation costs are likely to make retained earnings cheaper in the long run, that there may be some advantage to a stable and well-articulated long-run dividend policy, and, that the market does not like surprises. Credibility with the investment community is hard won and easily lost!

Mullet then recommended, to the surprise of several members of the board, that the current dividend of $1.15 per share be maintained.[10]

---

[10]After considerable discussion of Mullet's points, the board voted 8 to 1 to maintain the dividend for 1982 at $1.15, with a message to shareholders regarding the need for retention in the face of very profitable investment opportunities.

Many of the key considerations in formulating dividend policy have been introduced and discussed, but although the accompanying analysis is extremely important, it is also useful to understand the mechanics of declaring and paying a dividend.

DIVIDEND MECHANICS

A dividend is a cash payment from the firm to shareholders. Although specific legal requirements must be met, the firm's board of directors has the ultimate authority in the declaration of dividends.[11] When a cash dividend is declared, a *date of record* is fixed. Investors having title to shares on that date are entitled to the declared dividend. Because payment settlement for stock transactions requires four business days, the *ex-dividend* date is 4 days before the date of record. Shares purchased by an investor after the ex-dividend date do not receive the dividend even though the purchase may have taken place before the date of record.

Suppose Barfield declared a quarterly dividend on December 21 of $1.15/4 = $0.2875 per share to stockholders of record as of January 17.[12] Someone who bought shares on January 13 would receive the dividend, but shares bought *ex dividend* on January 14 would not provide the dividend. This would be of little consequence to investors purchasing ex dividend because the market price usually drops by the amount of the dividend on the ex-dividend date.

Inflation has the effect of lowering the *real* value of accounting depreciation charges deducted from the revenue of the firm. Consequently, net income as reported by the firm is frequently overstated. If the firm plans to replace worn-out equipment or buildings at higher prices, true net income will be lower than reported net income. As a result, the true dividend payout ratio is higher than it appears from the reported data, which do not reflect the impact of inflation on replacement cost.

INFLATION AND DIVIDEND POLICY

Assume, for example, that Breighthaupt, Inc., generates $3 earnings per share before the deduction of book depreciation charges of $1 per share that are based on historical costs of depreciable assets. Reported

---

[11]See George N. Engler, *Business Financial Management* (Dallas, Texas: Business Publication, Inc., 1975), p. 278. He indicates that state laws emphasize three rules: "(1) the *net profit rule* that states dividends must be paid from past or current earnings; (2) the *capital impairment rule* prohibits payment of dividends from the capital account so that the shareholders and creditors are protected and (3) the *insolvency rule* states that the corporation may not pay dividends when insolvent."

[12]In our previous discussion of dividend policy we assumed annual payment for the sake of simplicity.

net income per share is thus $2 per share and, with an *apparent* 50 percent dividend payout ratio, the resulting dividend is $1 per share, ignoring corporate income taxes. However, the true depreciation charge per share to replace worn-out equipment or buildings at current prices is $1.50 rather than $1. Consequently, true net income is $1.50 per share rather than $2 per share. With a $1 dividend, the *true* payout ratio is 66⅔ percent rather than 50 percent. An overstatement of earnings where depreciation is not adjusted for inflation creates a downward bias in reported payout ratios.

STOCK DIVIDENDS AND STOCK SPLITS

At times, firms may act to increase the number of common shares outstanding *without* selling new shares for cash. Either the declaration of a stock dividend or the splitting of stock will accomplish this objective. No payment of cash is involved in a stock dividend, and a stock dividend is not to be confused with a cash dividend. We first show how stock dividends and stock splits are accomplished and then evaluate their significance for the value of the firm.

Mechanics

A *stock dividend* is a stated percentage increase in the number of shares outstanding. Additional shares are allocated based on a fixed proportion of shares owned by each investor prior to the declaration of the stock dividend. Thus a 50 percent stock dividend gives an additional share for every two shares of stock held by a shareholder. A *stock split* simply involves an exchange of a larger number of *new* shares for a smaller number of *old* shares, with a corresponding reduction in par value. For example, a 3-for-2 stock split gives three new shares for two old shares held by shareholders. In terms of proportionate claim in the firm's earnings, neither a stock dividend nor a stock split gives an individual shareholder something he doesn't already have. If a firm has 100 shares outstanding and an investor holds 10 shares, his 10 percent ownership position is unchanged if a 50 percent stock dividend is declared or a 3-for-2 stock split is carried out. In either case, 150 total shares will be outstanding and the investor will own 15 shares, for the same 10 percent ownership position.

Other effects of stock dividends and splits on investors are shown in Table 14-6. We observe that King Radiator Company has 100,000 shares of $30 par value common stock recorded on the books at a $3 million total par value. Retained earnings are $10.5 million, and paid-in capital totals $1.5 million. The market value of King common stock is $180 per share, or $18 million in total.

If King declares and pays a 50 percent stock dividend, 50,000 new

Table 14–6   *Effects of Stock Dividends and Stock Splits: King Radiator Company*

	Original Position	50% Stock Dividend	3/2 Stock Split
Capital Position			
Par Value of Stock	$30	$30	$20
Common Stock (at par)	$ 3,000,000	$ 4,500,000	$ 3,000,000
Paid-in Capital	1,500,000	9,000,000	1,500,000
Retained Earnings	10,500,000	1,500,000	10,500,000
Total	$15,000,000	$15,000,000	$15,000,000
Share Data			
Number of Shares	100,000	150,000	150,000
Earnings and Dividend Data			
Total Earnings	$ 900,000	$ 900,000	$ 900,000
Earnings per Share	9.00	6.00	6.00
Dividends per Share	3.00	2.00	2.00
Price Data			
Total Value of Shares	$18,000,000	$18,000,000	$18,000,000
Price per Share	180	120	120

shares will be issued to shareholders. An amount equal to $30, the par value, times 50,000 shares, or $1.5 million, is transferred from retained earnings to the common stock account. In addition, an amount equal to the *difference* between market price and par value, ($180 − $30) = $150, times the number of new shares, 50,000, is transferred from retained earnings to the paid-in capital account; this amounts to $150 × 50,000 = $7.5 million.

Alternatively, if a 3-for-2 stock split occurs, the par value is reduced from $30 to $20; in effect 150,000 shares with $20 par value replace 100,000 shares with $30 par value. When the new shares are issued, total earnings are divided among more shares, and earnings per share would be $6 rather than $9. If the firm does not increase total dividends, dividends per share would drop to $2 from $3.

If an investor held 100 shares of King Radiator before the stock split or stock dividend, his total share value would be $18,000 and dividends would total $300. After the split or dividend he would have 150 shares, valued at $120 × 150 = $18,000. Assuming that total dividends do not increase, his dividend payment is still $300. From all appearances he is no better off after a stock split or stock dividend than before.

One alleged justification for stock dividends and stock splits is that such moves improve the attractiveness of shares to investors and anything that contributes to that objective should contribute to maximization of

A Rationale for Dividends and Splits

share price. When King Radiator shares are priced at $180 each, an investor must pay $18,000 to buy 100 shares—the traditional "round lot." Although transaction costs would be expected to decline with larger trades, the transaction costs brokers and dealers charge increase considerably for small lots. Therefore smaller investors tend to avoid high price per share issues in favor of lower priced stock.[13] King might be advised to take a 10-for-1 stock split, reducing the price to $18, if it wished to attract smaller investors who could then trade in round lots of 100 shares costing $1800 rather than $18,000.

Some firms annually declare a very small stock dividend within the range of 1 to 10 percent, to keep the price per share in the desired range. Some managements encourage the view that such a dividend is a substitute for a cash dividend when the need to retain cash within the firm is important. It is doubtful that the average investor is that easily fooled, however.

Sometimes stock dividends or splits are accompanied by a dividend increase. If King Radiator maintained a $3 dividend after a 50 percent stock dividend or a 3-for-2 split, shareholders who held 100 shares before the split (150 after the split) would receive $450 a year in dividends instead of $300. If the value of those shares rises above $18,000 in such a case, it is probably because of the *information* content of the dividend increase. The preponderance of evidence suggests that stock splits and stock dividends do not, by themselves, create value, except in extreme cases. If a market price of a share rises in anticipation of a split or stock dividend, it is probably because of anticipation of payout increases— reflecting management information about earnings prospects.

STOCK REPURCHASE AS A METHOD OF DISTRIBUTING CASH AND INFORMATION

At times, some companies accumulate large quantities of cash in excess of amounts required to finance internal investment opportunities over the foreseeable future. As we know, one response to this situation is to declare an extra dividend. An alternative action is to repurchase and retire some of the firm's own stock. When a firm repurchases stock, the effect is to create a capital gain for remaining shareholders—a capital gain that can be realized by shareholders who wish to do so. All they need do is sell some portion of their existing shares to realize the gain. Equally important and disconcerting, repurchase appears to convey favorable information about the firm to investors.

---

[13]Investment firms generally suggest that the optimal price for the broadest stock distribution is between $10 and $30 a share. Lower prices are avoided primarily because of traditional connotations of "cheap" stocks.

Firms can reacquire their shares in one of three ways. First, they can purchase shares directly in the market at prevailing prices. Such purchases are regulated and must conform to SEC rules. Second, firms can extend **tender offers** in which they announce their willingness to purchase a given number of shares at a specified price within a certain period.[14] Substantial premiums above existing market prices are generally offered to entice shareholders to tender their shares. Third, repurchases may be privately negotiated with large shareholders.[15]

To illustrate, we devise a simple example of an open market repurchase in which the firm provides a mechanism for excess cash to be converted into capital gains for shareholders. Then we summarize several studies of share repurchase.

Jones Pipefitting Company has a net income of $5 million and a total market value of $50 million, or, $50 per share on 1 million outstanding shares. Normally, the firm would pay out $1.25 million in dividends, or $1.25 per share. However, the alternative of repurchasing stock is also available to the company.

In the absence of any stock repurchase, the firm's shares sell for about $50 per share. Once dividends have been declared but not yet paid, the share price will be $51.25 to reflect the dividend to be paid. As soon as the shares sell ex dividend, share price drops back to $50. An investor who owns 100 shares will receive 100 × $1.25 = $125 in dividends. In addition, his shares will be worth $50 × 100 = $5000.

To be desirable, a stock repurchase plan must leave investors *at least* as wealthy as if dividends had been paid. Therefore, rather than offering $50 per share to purchase shares, the firm should offer $51.25 for each share. That price reflects the $1.25 per share that *could* have been paid in dividends. Assuming management uses the entire $1.25 million to repurchase common stock, a total of $1,250,000/$51.25 = 24,390 shares would be acquired. Still, the *total value* of remaining shares will remain at $50 million. This makes sense because the remaining shareholders have the same claim on total cash flows as did *all* shareholders *before* repurchase. The price of those remaining shares will be:

---

[14]Firms quite often leave some flexibility about the number of shares to be purchased and the exact price to be paid. They also reserve the right to extend the offer beyond the stated time period. For an extended discussion, see L. Dann, "Common Stock Repurchases: An Analysis of Returns to Bondholders and Stockholders," *Journal of Financial Economics* (June 1981), pp. 113–138; T. Vermaelen, "Common Stock Repurchases and Market Signalling: An Empirical Study," *Journal of Financial Economics* (June 1981), pp. 139–183.

[15]An analysis of a sample of privately negotiated purchases appears in L. Dann and H. DeAngelo, "Standstill Agreements, Privately Negotiated Stock Repurchases, and the Market for Corporate Control," forthcoming, *Journal of Financial Economics*.

$$\frac{\$50,000,000}{975,610} = \$51.25$$

An investor who sold 100 shares to the firm would have $5125 in cash, and one who did not sell would have shares worth $5125. In the absence of personal taxes and market imperfections, both these individuals would be as well off as if the firm had paid a $1.25 per share dividend. However, when capital gains are taxed at a lower rate than ordinary income, creation of homemade dividends for remaining shareholders is less costly. Jones Pipefitting not only creates for remaining shareholders gains that are taxable at a lower capital gains rate, but allows such shareholders to postpone the tax to a date of sale for shares of their choice.

Stock repurchase plans are thus a way of providing an opportunity for shareholders to create homemade dividends that are taxed at *lower rates than* corporate dividends. However, the Internal Revenue Service is not unaware of this feature. Firms using a stock repurchase plan as a way of distributing excess cash can do so only on an irregular basis. If a firm systematically purchased stock in this way, the IRS could interpret this as a procedure for avoiding the ordinary personal income tax and, as a result, would exact a penalty on the offending firm. Thus share repurchase offers an alternative to the payment of cash dividends primarily on a supplemental basis.

In the example above, the decision to repurchase has no impact on investor's perceptions about the future. That is, investors did not view share repurchase as conveying either good or bad news. In examining both open market purchases and tender offers, Dann has found significant price reaction around the time of the announcement that the firm wishes to acquire its own shares.[16] Share price jumped an average of 3 percent for a sample of 121 companies upon announcement of an open market purchase plan. For a sample of 143 firms that made tender offers for their shares (at an average premium of 22.46 percent above the market price prevailing one day before the announcement), share price increased by an average of 15.4 percent *upon* announcement. The most puzzling aspect of this analysis is that share price did not return to former levels after completion of the repurchase plan. Such a permanent increase in share price deserves an explanation. Possibly, an announcement to repurchase (at least through tender offer) conveys new, highly favorable information about the prospects of the firm. However, we do not know what that information is, and we do not know why it would be conveyed in a repurchase announcement rather than by some other mechanism.

---

[16]See Dann, "Common Stock Repurchases," cited in note 14.

Clearly, repurchase involves more than just a distribution of excess cash. It also appears to involve distribution of information. Finding out exactly what that information is remains an important task for the future.

SUMMARY

Selecting a dividend policy requires that management consider a wide range of factors that may cause investors to prefer either a direct cash dividend paid by the corporation or a homemade dividend. To proceed systematically with a discussion of these factors, we first considered the conditions under which dividend policy would be irrelevant.

Given the firm's investment policy, the returns from existing and future investments, perfect markets, and no personal taxes, dividend policy does not matter. Regardless of the policy chosen, shareholder wealth will be unaffected, because perfect markets and the absence of personal taxes make shareholder indifferent between making their own dividends by realizing capital gains created by earnings retention (homemade dividends) and receiving cash dividends from the corporation while new shares are sold to finance new investment.

When these assumptions are relaxed, dividend policy may no longer be irrelevant. In the face of market imperfections and personal income taxes, shareholders may have preferences for specific dividend policies. Investors with similar preferences will prefer similar policies. Some investors will prefer firms with high payout ratios. Others will prefer low payout ratios. Still others may pay more attention to the stability of the dividend stream than to the particular payout ratio. In essence, firms with particular policies will attract particular types of investors. These investors are called a clientele. The *clientele effect* suggests that for a firm, one clientele is as good as any other, and therefore the initial choice of dividend policy is not critical. Maintaining a policy once it has been established is important, however, because a change in policy may cause some investors to sell their shares. The firm then would have to attract a new clientele. Given transaction costs, investors may be unwilling to hold the shares of firms that do not have stable or well-articulated dividend policies, except at reduced prices. The additional perceived risk and cost imparted by an unstable dividend policy may adversely affect share price.

An additional argument for maintaining a stable dividend policy, or, at a minimum, providing investors with logical reasons for changes, arises when we introduce costly information. If managers set dividend policy according to their long-term expectations about earnings and if they are reluctant to cut the level of the dividend, a stable dollar dividend with occasional increases to reflect expectations of higher earnings may be preferred. Shareholders may pay a premium for stability because they can rely on management to signal (willingly or not) the future prospects of the firm. In the absence of such a policy, information might be far more difficult and costly to obtain.

Stock dividends and stock splits can have an impact on share price if they reduce the impact of market imperfections—transaction costs and lack of divisibility. Without such imperfections, splits and stock dividends usually imply no increase in the total value of shares to the shareholders. A stock split or stock dividend may, however, provide information to the market if an increase in dividends will accompany such action. If so, it is important to separate the announcement effect of possible higher cash dividends that may accompany a split or stock dividend from the act of creating more shares. The former may logically affect value, but the latter normally will not.

A stock repurchase plan is a way of paying out cash to shareholders in the form of capital gains. In addition, information appears to be conveyed to the market, and the effect on share price is especially dramatic when shares are acquired through a tender offer.

GLOSSARY OF KEY TERMS

Clientele Effect
Investors with similar preferences for dividend policy tend to purchase securities of firms with dividend policies that conform to their preferences.

Constant Payout Dividend Policy
A dividend policy that pays a constant percent of earnings in the form of cash dividends, allowing the cash dividend to vary as earnings vary.

Dividend Policy
A corporate decision to provide some pattern of dividends to security holders.

Extra Dividend
A cash dividend in excess of the regular dividend that is not intended to be viewed as an increase in the regular dividend.

Homemade Dividend
The sale of stock holdings by an investor to obtain cash as a substitute for payment of a cash dividend by the corporation.

Information Content
Dividend declarations providing information concerning management's view of permanent earnings levels.

Payout Ratio
Common stock cash dividends divided by earnings available for common stock, usually on a per annum basis.

Stable Dividend Policy
An even payment of cash dividends policy with upward adjustments as "permanent" earnings levels increase.

Stock Dividend	A dividend paid in stock of the declaring corporation that reduces retained earnings on the books of, but not cash held by, the corporation.
Stock Repurchase	The purchase and retirement of the company's own shares with excess cash.
Stock Split	Exchange of new, lower par shares for old, higher par shares, to increase the number of shares outstanding.
Tender Offer	An offer directly to shareholders to purchase stock they hold.

SELECTED REFERENCES

Archer, S. H., and C. A. D'Ambrosio. *The Theory of Business Finance: A Book of Readings,* 3rd ed. New York: Macmillan, 1983.

Arditti, F. D., H. Levy, and M. Sarnat. "Taxes, Uncertainty and Optimal Dividend Policy." *Financial Management* (Spring 1976), pp. 46–52.

Brittain, J. A. *Corporate Dividend Policy.* Washington, D.C.: Brookings Institute, 1966.

Lintner, J. "Dividends, Earnings, Leverage, Stock Prices, and the Supply of Capital to Corporations." *Review of Economics and Statistics* (August 1962), pp. 243–269.

Millar J. A., and B. D. Fielitz. "Stock-Split and Stock-Dividend Decisions." *Financial Management* (Winter 1973), pp. 35–46.

Miller, M. H., and F. Modigliani. "Dividend Policy, Growth, and the Valuation of Shares." *Journal of Business* (October 1961), pp. 411–433.

Norgaard R., and C. Norgaard. "A Critical Examination of Share Repurchase." *Financial Management* (Spring 1974), pp. 44–51.

Pettway R. H., and R. P. Malone. "Automatic Dividend Reinvestment Plans of Nonfinancial Corporations." *Financial Management* (Winter 1973), pp. 11–18.

Walter, J. E. *Dividend Policy and Enterprise Valuation.* Belmont, CA.: Wadsworth Publishing Co., 1967.

QUESTIONS

1. What is meant by the "information content" of a dividend policy?

2. Does a dividend policy have to be stated explicitly to have information content? Explain.

3. How does the constant percentage payout policy differ from the regular-plus-extras policy from the view of shareholders?

4. How would you expect dividend policies of United States corporations to change if the dividend exemption provision of personal income taxes were eliminated?

5. How would the complete elimination of the preferential tax treatment of capital gains tend to affect corporate dividend policy?

6. Is the clientele effect inconsistent with the abstract concept of the irrelevance of a dividend policy? Explain.

7. How might the lack of a consistent dividend policy of a firm tend to reduce share price when market imperfections exist?

8. How might a conventionally computed payout ratio understate "true" payout when there is inflation?

9. How can share repurchase and retirement substitute for a dividend for shareholders?

10. Electric utility firms typically pay out a high percentage of their net income in cash dividends. The 1981 Economic Recovery Tax Act allows an investor in an electric utility to have cash dividends (up to $750 each year) automatically reinvested in the utility stock. If the stock purchased with the cash dividend is held over one year before it is sold, the profit is treated as a long-term capital gain. How does this provision benefit both the utility firm and the investor?

PROBLEMS   1. For the following data, calculate the payout ratio:

(a) Total earnings of $750,000 and total cash dividends of $150,000.

(b) Earnings per share of $5.00 and cash dividends per share of $2.00.

(c) Earnings per share of $3.00, a stock dividend of 20 percent, and cash dividends of zero.

2. The Porkie Pie Baking Company is an unlevered company with expected earnings per share of $1.50 in perpetuity, regular expected dividends of $1.50, and a share price of $15. Assume that there are no taxes, investment policy is fixed, and shares are traded in perfect markets. If the firm has an investment that is expected to generate a 10 percent perpetual rate of return and that investment requires that the firm reinvest all earnings for one year,

how many shares would make up a homemade dividend for Mrs. McNerney, owner of 100 shares of Porkie Pie, and what is the share price?

3. John Chambeau is the sole stockholder of his firm, which produces sweat suits. He has some inheritance income that makes his marginal personal income tax rate equal to 40 percent. His corporation earns $20,000 on which a 22 percent corporate income tax is applied.

    (a) If he retains all the income possible in the firm, what is the total government tax bill (corporate and personal)?

    (b) If it does not affect his personal marginal tax *rate* and he pays all earnings to himself in the form of dividends, what is the total government tax bill (corporate and personal) assuming his $100 dividend exemption is already used up?

4. Calculate the *residual* dividend per share of Tortise Company, which has 100,000 shares outstanding, $300,000 of after-tax net income, and financing needs of $220,000.

5. If Boyle Termite Company earns $3.00, $4.00, $5.00, and $3.00 per share, respectively, in four successive years,

    (a) Calculate the dividend payout ratio for each of the four years if the dividend is a stable $2.00 each year.

    (b) Calculate annual dividends per share, if the payout ratio is a constant 2/3 in every year.

6. A 2 for 1 stock split has the same *economic effect* on shareholders as what magnitude of stock dividend?

7. The Poldart Company has the following equity section in its March 31, 1981, balance sheet:

Common Stock ($10 par)	$1,000,000
Paid-in Capital	2,000,000
Retained Earnings	1,500,000

    (a) How would the above section of the balance sheet be altered with a 100 percent stock dividend if the market price per share is $11?

    (b) If the record date were Friday, April 10, when would shares trade ex- (the stock) dividend?

    (c)   How would the balance sheet above be altered with a 2 for 1 stock split?

    (d)   What do you expect to happen to the share price if the stock is split and no change in total dividends paid is to be made by the company? Why?

8.   Peck Athletic Supply Company has an excess cash balance of $1 million, equal to $1.00 a share on its one million shares. It has a net after-tax profit in 1982 of $2 million, equal to $2.00 a share, which is expected in perpetuity, and its regular annual dividend is $1.00 a share, or $.25 quarterly. The stock normally sells at $20 a share, moving from $20.25 to $20 as it goes ex-dividend.

    (a)   If Peck Athletic Supply offers to purchase $250,000 of stock, at what price should the firm offer to purchase shares from shareholders?

    (b)   How many shares would be purchased and retired with the $250,000?

    (c)   What would be the share price after the repurchase plan was carried out?

9.   Sycamore Foods, Inc., planned a major expansion that would require a total of $10 million dollars. A long-term loan of $4 million would provide part of the funds, but the remainder would have to be raised from equity. Janet Wall, a new employee in the controller's office, was asked to analyze two different dividend policies that would affect the mix of internal and external equity financing. The first policy required that Sycamore reduce its dividend payout ratio from 60 percent to 30 percent immediately. The second policy required that the firm maintain the 60 percent payout ratio the first year and then reduce it to 40 percent in the following two years. Current and projected net earnings (after all interest payments) are shown below:

Current*	Projected*	
1983	1984	1985
$1.3	$1.5	$1.9

There are currently 500,000 shares outstanding. These shares are selling for $23.50 each. However, investment bankers estimate net proceeds to the firm of $20 per share if new shares are sold and if payout is cut immediately to 30 percent. But proceeds would be

$21.50 per share if the 60 percent policy is maintained in the first year. Assume that the firm must sell any new shares by April, 1984, and that the total equity financing need must be met by the end of 1985.

(a) How much money must the firm raise internally and externally under each of the above policies?

(b) How many new shares must be issued under each policy?

(c) Why are the net proceeds per share lower under the first policy than the second?

10. A firm has after-tax earnings of $1 million for the current period and plans an investment of $600,000. The firm intends to maintain its current debt/equity ratio of 1:5.

(a) How much will be paid in dividends if the firm follows a pure residual dividend policy?

(b) How much external equity financing will be required if the firm maintains a fixed dividend payout ratio of 60%?

CHAPTER 15

Steps for Estimating the Cost of Capital of the Firm

Although perhaps it is not apparent, we have so far encountered two concepts of the cost of capital (required rate of return). The first was the **marginal cost of capital** employed in evaluating investment proposals in Chapters 6 to 10. That marginal cost is the minimum rate of return a firm must expect to earn on an investment proposal if it is to compensate investors for the risk of that proposal and at least maintain the value of existing shares of common stock. The second, the **cost of capital of the firm,** was discussed in connection with the capital structure decisions of Chapters 12 and 13. Cost of capital of the firm is applicable to the cash flows generated by the firm's *existing* investments and is applicable to valuation of the firm. It was not previously necessary to emphasize this distinction, but it now becomes important.

The necessity for the distinction hinges on the issue of business risk of investment, which includes both investment *proposals* and *existing* investments. It was asserted in Chapters 6 to 10 that the risk-adjusted marginal cost of capital used in making capital budgeting decisions must be appropriate for the business risk of each investment proposal. Since business risk may differ among investment proposals, it follows that there are as many different marginal costs of capital as there are investment proposals of differing business risk. In contrast, the business risk of the *firm* reflects the *average* business risk of all the firm's existing investments; therefore, so does the cost of capital of the firm. This means that if we use the cost of capital of the *firm* as a marginal cost, the cost of an additional dollar of financing to fund an investment proposal, we can legitimately do so *only* under *one* condition: that the business risk of the investment proposal and the *average* business risk of all the firm's existing investments be the same. Failure to observe this condition can result in using the wrong cost of capital to evaluate the investment proposal—a cost too high or too low because business risk of the proposal is lower or higher than average business risk of the firm. As will be demonstrated in Chapter 16, such errors can lead to selection of proposals that can be expected to *reduce* shareholder wealth and failure to select proposals expected to *increase* shareholder wealth.

Still, the cost of capital of the firm is a useful starting point. This chapter provides a framework for estimating the cost of capital for the firm for use as a marginal cost of capital to evaluate investment proposals. Details concerning estimates of costs of specific sources of funds are deferred to the next chapter, as are procedures for estimating the marginal cost of capital when the business risk of investment proposals differs from average business risk of the firm.

The procedures to be described are not strictly consistent with some of the issues raised in Chapter 13 concerning debt and personal taxes, costs of financial distress and bankruptcy, and costs of resolving bond-holder–shareholder conflicts. The cost of capital as presented here can be thought of as a *heuristic* tool, one that is not without problems that must be resolved. In spite of these problems, it remains a useful, widely used tool that will not be easily supplanted.

INTRO-DUCTION TO THE ISSUES: ZUBER MILLING CASE

To integrate discussion of issues to be settled in estimating the cost of capital of the firm as well as prepare for estimating the marginal cost of capital, we introduce the Zuber Milling case. Terri Zuber, president of Zuber Milling Company, returned from a finance seminar at a local university concerned about her company's procedures for selecting investment proposals. She felt that the starting point in any attempt to revise company procedures, was the estimation of the cost of capital of the firm. Until now, the company had estimated a single cost of capital that was meant to reflect the average business risk of the firm. Although the goal of reflecting that average risk was consistent with the concept of the cost of capital of the firm, Zuber wondered whether the *estimation procedure* was, itself, correct. She asked her financial staff to prepare a cost of capital exhibit to aid her inquiry. They used Equation (15-1) in developing Table 15-1 and the accompanying explanation.

$$K = (1 - \tau)k_d W_d + k_e W_e \qquad (15\text{-}1)$$

Zuber's staff reported:

We first compute weights, reflecting proportions of various financing sources in the current balance sheet. At present, debt has the proportion $W_d = 30$ percent.

Table 15–1   *Cost of Capital Computation:*
Zuber Milling Company ($000)

1. Computation of Weights

	Current Book Value	Proportion of Total Capital Structure
Bonds	$ 3,000	$\dfrac{\$\ 3,000}{\$10,000} = 0.3\ (W_d)$
Common Stock and Paid-in Capital	2,000	
Retained Earnings	5,000	$\dfrac{\$\ 7,000}{\$10,000} = 0.7\ (W_e)$
	$10,000	

2. Estimate the Cost of Each Source of Funds
    Pre-tax Cost of Debt, k_d: 9%
    After-tax Cost of Common Equity, k_e: 14%

3. Computation of the Weighted Cost of Capital
    $$K = (1 - \tau)k_d W_d + k_e W_e$$
    $$= (1 - 0.4)9\%(0.3) + 14\%(0.7)$$
    $$= 11.42\%$$

Common equity, the combined common stock and paid-in capital plus retained earnings accounts totaling $7000, has the proportion W_e = 70 percent. Then, costs of the two capital sources are estimated. Our present estimates of the debt cost reflects our outstanding 9 percent coupon rate debt issue; thus, the cost of debt is k_d = 9 percent. By dividing our last year's net income of $980,000 by the common equity account ($7 million), we obtain the cost of equity capital of k_e = 14 percent. Finally, since our financing comes from the two sources, we average them in Equation (15-1) by applying the weights to the cost of each capital source to find the cost of capital K. [That formula is of equivalent form to Equation (12-7).[1]] The formula adjusts the cost of debt downward by the factor $(1 - \tau)$ to place that cost on an after-tax basis. The cost of common equity is already stated on an after-tax basis because returns to common equity are paid with after-tax dollars. The current tax rate is τ = 40 percent, and, at that rate, we estimate the current cost of capital to be K = 11.42 percent. This cost is used to evaluate investment proposals requiring additional funds—that is, it is a marginal cost of capital.

Zuber immediately realized that judged by the standards set at the seminar, her firm's procedures for estimating the cost of capital of the firm were inappropriate. She decided to write a critique of present pro-

---

[1]The weight W_d is of the same form as the ratio of bonds to total value, B/V. The weight W_e is of the same form as the ratio S/V, the value of equity relative to total value in Equation (12-7).

cedures and ultimately, to derive a new estimate using improved procedures. Zuber's critique centered on the three steps she learned at the seminar.

Step	Procedure

1. Identify the *future* capital structure at market value that will minimize the cost of capital K for a given level of business risk of the firm. This step requires finding the optimal mix of debt and equity.

2. Estimate the cost of each source of funds. These costs will reflect the average business risk of all existing investments as well as financial risk posed by the selected capital structure.

3. Compute the weighted cost of capital using the weights and costs for each financing source in steps 1 and 2.

STEP 1: CAPITAL STRUCTURE AND THE COST OF CAPITAL

The cost of capital of the firm must reflect several elements. First, it must be appropriate for the average business risk of all investments. When firms are levered, some portion of that risk will be borne by risky debt and some by equity. In a world of perfect markets and no corporate taxes, the combined risk of debt and equity is constant, as is the cost of capital. Second, the cost of capital will reflect the tax deductibility of interest when there are corporate taxes. The interest tax subsidy will have a positive effect on the value of the firm because it will tend to reduce the cost of capital relative to that of an unlevered firm. Third, differential personal income taxes will tend to diminish the impact of the interest tax subsidy while increasing the relative cost of capital. A fourth element, costs of financial distress and bankruptcy, should also tend to increase the cost of capital. The higher the leverage, the higher the expected costs and the greater the impact on the cost of capital. Finally, costs of potential conflicts of interest between bondholders and shareholders should increase with leverage. These costs, too, should tend to raise the cost of capital. Since only the required rates of the securities that are traded can be estimated directly, properly estimated k_e and k_d must reflect all five elements. Through k_e and k_d those elements are eventually reflected in the cost of capital.

If firms are to use leverage at all, the positive effects should dominate for smaller amounts of debt. Negative elements, however, will eventually dominate if firms are to have an optimal capital structure that is less than 100 percent debt. Under these circumstances, there is likely to be a range of debt/equity mixes that have lower costs of capital than would be associated with either an unlevered capital structure or ex-

Figure 15-1   *The Range of "Optimum" Debt/Equity Ratios for a Given Level of Business Risk*

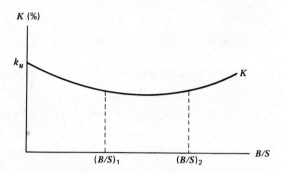

treme leveraged positions. Such a range is illustrated in Figure 15-1 by the traditional saucer-shaped cost of capital.

The Optimal Debt/Equity Mix

In the financial environment in which Zuber Milling operates, a curve such as portrayed in Figure 15-1 may describe the costs of capital prevailing under alternative capital structures reflecting market values of debt and equity. But it is difficult to know whether the saucer is relatively "flat" (implying modest reductions in cost of capital from that of an unlevered firm at the lowest point on the curve) or "deep dished" (implying substantial reductions in cost of capital). Nevertheless, Figure 15-1 implies an optimal capital structure at which the cost of capital for a *given* level of business risk is minimized and, *approximately*, both the value of the firm and shareholder wealth *are maximized*. However, that optimal position is difficult to detect with any precision. Perhaps the only concrete types of information available are debt/equity ratios of firms having similar degrees of business risk. If such firms can be identified, a range of commonly employed debt/equity mixes, such as that between $(B/S)_1$ and $(B/S)_2$ in Figure 15-1, can be found. The costs of capital for these firms may be difficult to estimate, but at least a starting point has been identified.

An investment banker might be used to further define a suitable ratio within the range of prevailing debt/equity ratios. An investment banker might assess the cost of debt financing at various debt/equity mixes and describe lower cost combinations based on knowledge of market conditions and the firm's reputation with the market.

Finally, historical experience with past financing may be useful. For example, a firm that has had difficulty in selling securities and finding ready market acceptance in the past might expect more such difficulty in the future unless issues are attractively priced to yield relatively high required rates of return.

The point is that no matter how crude the process, some attempt to find an optimal debt/equity mix for future financing should be made. Once identified, this optimal mix becomes the *target* mix. The latter affects subsequent estimates of the cost of capital.

The Target Debt/ Equity Mix

As indicated in step 1, the costs of various financing sources are interdependent and are affected by the degree of financial leverage. Therefore, estimation of the costs of financing sources must be preceded by the specification of the target debt/equity mix to be employed by the firm in the future. Thus, the required rate of return for debt k_d must be determined at the **target capital structure,** as must the required rate of return for equity k_e. The required rate of return for debt may be estimated by the investment banker or, in the case of a direct loan, by the lending institution. The investment banker can also provide useful estimates of the required rate of return for equity. But the necessity of specifying the target capital structure before determining required rates of return can be demonstrated by restating the formula for the required rate of return for equity capital k_e, given earlier in Equation (12-6):

$$k_e = k_u + (1 - \tau)(k_u - k_d)\frac{B}{S} \tag{15-2}$$

The degree of financial leverage, given by B/S, the ratio of debt to equity, is clearly required to compute the proper risk premium for k_e to reflect the risk of financial leverage.

Failure to account for the effect of the target capital structure on costs of financing sources will cause the resulting cost of capital to be in error—a result leading to incorrect selection among investment proposals having business risks equal to the average business risk of the firm.

Discrepancies Between Present and Future Debt/ Equity Mixes

When a firm has detected what appears to be an "optimal" capital structure within the range $(B/S)_1-(B/S)_2$ in Figure 15-1, this optimal mix becomes the *target* capital structure. This target can then be compared to the existing mix. Discrepancies between existing and target mixes can be identified, and management can plan future financing strategies accordingly.

In general, there are two financing strategies that management might employ to reach the target capital structure in the event of a serious discrepancy. First, the firm might decide on **recapitalization.** For a firm that was substantially below its target debt/equity ratio, management could recapitalize by issuing new debt and purchasing its own common shares with the proceeds to achieve the target mix. Note that business risk is unchanged by this transaction, since the firm retains the same assets. Only the cost of capital falls if the firm has been correct in identifying an optimal target capital structure. Second, and more typically, management would finance new, profitable investment proposals, in a gradual approach to the target over time. For instance, in the previous example, management might finance new investments exclusively or primarily with debt until the target capital is achieved.[2]

With either strategy, the appropriate weights to use in computing a marginal cost of capital for average risk investments are the *target* weights.

The Mix of Newly Issued Common Stock and Retention of Earnings in the Target Capital Structure

Notice that the mix of common stock and retention of earnings was *not* part of the discussion of the optimal capital structure. At a point in time, the mix of common stock plus paid-in capital and retained earnings on a firm's balance sheet is merely a historical record of how equity financing needs have been met by sale of new common stock or retention of earnings. It has no relevance to current and future market conditions applicable to the cost of capital of the firm.

But the mix of internally generated funds and newly issued common stock used in financing investments may matter in that it may affect k_e. We assume that the firm has identified an appropriate dividend policy (Chapter 14) and thereby an appropriate mix of internal and external equity, given the investment proposals of the firm. The "cost" of that mix is k_e, the rate of return required by shareholders.

Critique of Present Procedures for Selecting the Target Debt/Equity Mix

Compared to desired procedures under step 1, Zuber noted two errors in current procedures. From Table 15-1, it is evident that no attempt has been made to find an optimal debt/equity mix. Instead, the financial staff used book values of debt and equity to compute the proportion of debt W_d and common equity W_e. The procedure is defective in that it *avoids* seeking the optimal debt/equity mix. Furthermore, it utilizes weights dependent on book, not market, values of various financing sources. It is the market that determines the current and future costs of various sources of capital and their dollar value. Historical data on book values are useful for some purposes but not for assessing costs of present and future financing and, ultimately, for valuing present assets and invest-

---

[2]If the firm were abandoning undesirable investments over time, it might retire common equity with proceeds from abandonment until the higher target debt/equity mix is achieved.

ment proposals. To see this, note that the ratio of debt to equity in Chapter 12 was always computed using market values of B and S (e.g., see Table 12-4). Book values, in reflecting the past, bear only a complicated relation to present and future market value.

Estimation of the cost of each financing source is not pursued in detail now (see Chapter 16). Nevertheless, the main issues surrounding the estimation process can be described at this point.

STEP 2: ESTIMATING THE COST OF EACH SOURCE OF FUNDS

In estimating the cost of capital for the firm, the objective is to find the cost, the rate of return required by investors for each financing source having a claim on the cash flows generated by the investment. Meeting this objective requires that the cost of each financing source reflect the target debt/equity mix selected by the firm. And of course, business risk is held constant and equal to the average business risk of all existing investments held by the firm.

The Objective

The financial staff of Zuber is estimating costs of capital by using, in the case of debt, the *historical* coupon rate for existing debt rather than the *current* required rate for debt as established in the market. Recall from Chapter 11 that the value of existing debt is determined by the current required rate for debt, not the coupon rate. And when the cost of capital of the firm is used as a marginal cost, it is obvious that the cost of newly issued debt under current market conditions is relevant for financing investment opportunities. Also defective is Zuber Milling's procedure for estimating the cost of equity financing. It too is based on historical financial statement data rather than information gained in the market. Given that the target debt/equity mix in step 1 has not been properly established by using market rather than book values of debt and equity, we do not know *what* debt/equity mix the existing estimates of the cost of capital are consistent with.

Critique of Present Procedures for Estimating Costs of Financing Sources

Once costs of each financing source have been estimated, based on the target capital structure, computation of the cost of capital is straightforward. The goal is to compute an after-tax cost of capital that reflects the cost and weight of each source of funds. The appropriate formula is:

STEP 3: COMPUTING THE COST OF CAPITAL OF THE FIRM

$$K = (1 - \tau)k_d W_d + k_e W_e \qquad (15\text{-}3)$$

The costs k_d and k_e are determined in the market, and the weights W_d and W_e are based on market values of debt and equity.

ZUBER MILLING'S REVISED COST OF CAPITAL PROCEDURES

With the three steps in mind, Zuber was ready to alter procedures for determining the cost of capital for the firm. With the aid of her financial staff, Zuber planned to estimate the cost of capital for her firm for the ensuing year.

Step 1: Capital Structure

After consultation with her financial staff and two investment bankers, Zuber determined that the target capital structure should be 40 percent debt, 60 percent equity—that is, a target debt/equity ratio of 40 percent/60 percent = 0.6667. She had concluded that this target structure would not produce sufficient concern among bondholders to significantly raise the required rate of return for debt. This was considerably more debt than the firm had carried historically, but it was consistent with practices of similar firms. She was not sure that this was an optimal debt/equity mix but felt it to be superior to a present policy that did not make enough use of debt financing. Recall from Table 15-1 that 30 percent debt, 70 percent equity at *book* value previously had been employed by the financial staff in Table 15-1; and of course the weights W_d and W_e Zuber used were based on market values, not book values. [Note that the formula used by the financial staff in Equation (15-1) is identical in form to the one Zuber used in (Equation 15-3). But the proper inputs and those used by the staff are very different. The lesson is unavoidable: although a correct formula is important, it is no more important than the values used in the formula. Mathematical expression cannot make sense out of nonsense.]

Zuber decided not to recapitalize the firm in accordance with the target capital structure. Instead, she would reach the target capital structure over time as investment proposals requiring additional funds were financed.

Step 2: Estimating the Cost of Each Financing Source

Given the level of average business risk of Zuber's existing investments and the target capital structure, Zuber estimated the cost of debt financing to be $k_d = 0.11$ or 11 percent. This is the required rate of return for the prevailing level of business risk and a target capital structure of 40 percent debt, 60 percent equity. Additional analysis of Zuber and similar firms indicated a required rate of return on equity for this capital structure of about 18 percent ($k_e = 0.18$).[3] That rate also reflects business risk as well as each of the other leverage-related elements discussed earlier.

Given the estimated costs k_d and k_e and the target capital structure weights W_d and W_e, Zuber computed her estimated cost of capital using Equation (15-3):

Step 3: Computing the Cost of Capital of the Firm

$$K = (1 - \tau)k_dW_d + k_eW_e$$

$$= (1 - 0.40)\ (11\%)\ (0.40) + [18\%\ (0.60)]$$

$$= 2.64\% + 10.80\%$$

$$= 13.44\%$$

This rate is nearly 2 percent greater than the cost of capital earlier estimated by the financial staff in Table 15-1. Because Zuber's staff used the 9 percent coupon rate for the cost of debt rather than the higher $k_d = 11$ percent based on the market, they underestimated the cost of debt. The cost of equity was grossly underestimated by the staff because a *market-oriented* estimate was not employed. Finally, the staff used book rather than target market weights, a procedure that gave too little weight to debt (viz., 30 percent debt rather than 40 percent debt in the capital structure).

It is necessary to distinguish between the marginal cost of capital for evaluating investment proposals and the cost of capital of the firm. The cost of capital for the firm reflects the average business risk of the firm's existing investments. It may be employed as a marginal cost of capital only for investment proposals having business risk equivalent to the *average* business risk of the firm's existing investments. Both the marginal cost of capital and the cost of capital of the firm should reflect the firm's target capital structure and the degree of financial risk it poses.

SUMMARY

[3]We are simplifying the problem of income taxes in the distinction between cost of capital of the firm and the use of that cost as a marginal cost. With marginal cost, the applicable tax rate is the marginal corporate income tax rate. For cost of capital of the firm, the tax rate is the average tax rate that applies to the existing level of taxable income. For firms with large taxable income, the marginal and average tax rates will be very close to the maximum marginal value of $\tau = 46$ percent. For firms with small taxable incomes, the marginal tax rate may well exceed the average rate. We ignore this problem to simplify the presentation. Thus Zuber's marginal *and* average tax rates equal the assumed value of $\tau = 40$ percent.

Estimating the cost of capital of the firm requires three steps:

1. Designating the target capital structure to be used in future financing.

2. Estimating the cost of individual sources of financing at the target capital structure.

3. Computing the cost of capital by weighting the costs of individual financing sources by their proportions in the target capital structure.

The goal in establishing a target capital structure is to minimize the cost of capital *holding the level of business risk constant*. The process of finding that optimal structure is hardly precise. The firm will generally not know whether it has accomplished that goal. The existence of such an optimum is implied if personal income taxes do not substantially diminish the benefits of the favorable corporate interest tax subsidy afforded by use of financial leverage. Increases in debt relative to equity financing will then act to lower the cost of capital. But costs of financial distress and bankruptcy and conflicts of interest between bondholders and shareholders limit the use of debt, ultimately raising the cost of capital with still higher leverage positions. A saucer-shaped cost of capital schedule as a function of increasing financial leverage and a minimum cost of capital are implied.

Costs of each financing source must reflect the firm's target capital structure based on market values of financing sources. When combined into an estimate of the cost of capital of the firm, each cost is weighted according to the target capital structure using market weights. All costs are expressed on an after-corporate-income tax basis. Since cost of equity financing is based on after-tax returns, only cost of debt financing must be explicitly converted to an after-tax basis to reflect the tax deductibility of interest payments.

GLOSSARY OF KEY TERMS

Cost of Capital of the Firm
The required rate of return reflecting existing business risk and financing policy of the firm. It may be computed as the weighted average required rate of individual sources of funds.

Marginal Cost of Capital
The weighted after-tax cost of each financing source of an additional dollar of new financing. It must reflect the business risk of the particular investment proposal. The cost of capital of the firm can be a marginal cost only if the proposal has a business risk level equal to that of the firm.

Recapitalization   The change in a firm's capital structure brought about by selling one type of security to replace another.

Target Capital Structure   The designated proportions of debt and equity, at market value, that the firm wishes to employ in financing investments.

See Chapter 16.   **SELECTED REFERENCES**

QUESTIONS

1. "The cost of capital relevant for any given investment is the cost of the particular source of funds raised to make the investment possible." Do you agree or disagree? Why?

2. Identify the steps for the correct estimation of the firm's cost of capital.

3. Why is it necessary to specify the firm's target capital structure before estimating its cost of capital?

4. What argument can be made for using market rather than book values of outstanding securities in determining the weights for various sources of capital?

5. What characteristics must a new investment project have to be properly evaluated by using the firm's average cost of capital as the discount rate?

6. Is the cost of capital to the firm the same as the expected rate of return to the investor?

7. What methods are typically used to alter a firm's capital structure?

8. Should the firm use the average cost or marginal cost of capital to determine the rate that must be used to evaluate new investments?

PROBLEMS

1. The Rocky Beach Boat Company has the following balance sheet:

December 31, 1982

Long-term debt 12% due 2002	$5 million
Common Stock and Paid in Capital	6 million
Retained Earnings	1 million

The financial staff has determined that the above book values reflect the firm's target capital structure. The marginal corporate tax rate is 40 percent. k_e and k_d are estimated to be 20 and 14 percent, respectively. Find the firm's cost of capital.

2. Calculate the cost of capital, K, for Belicose Manufacturing, given market value weights of the future financing mix of 0.5 debt and 0.5 common stock if the marginal corporate income tax rate is 48 percent, the cost of debt is 6 percent, and the cost of equity is 12 percent.

3. Shapely Market is an unlevered firm with a cost of capital of 20 percent. The firm is considering the issue of debt that would bring its debt/equity ratio to 0.5. At that level of leverage, debt would require a 10 percent rate of return. If the corporate tax rate were 30 percent at the margin, estimate the *change* in the cost of capital of the firm.

4. Iochief Distributing Company has a target debt/equity ratio of 1.0. The marginal corporate income tax rate is 48 percent. Find the cost of capital if the firm can sell debt at a cost of 12 percent and equity at a cost of 18 percent.

5. The Gaston and Hopewell Company has a target debt/equity ratio of 0.33 and a marginal corporate income tax of 48 percent. Management plans to have an expected $8 million in retained earnings available for next year's investments.

   (a) Compute the weights (W_e, W_d) for calculating the average cost of capital.

   (b) Calculate the cost of new financing when the cost of new debt would be 8 percent and the cost of new shares is 14 percent. Does that cost depend upon the amount of investment?

Estimating the Marginal Cost of Capital

In Chapter 15, we illustrated steps for estimating the cost of capital of the firm. To simplify matters, required rates of individual financing sources were given. In this chapter we concentrate on estimating the marginal cost of capital to be used in evaluating investment proposals. Our initial task is to estimate required rates for securities that have claim to the cash flows from a proposal. Procedures for this are extremely important because the marginal cost of capital is merely the weighted average of these individual rates. To emphasize these procedures, we simplify the situation by assuming at first that the correct risk level consistent with the required rate for each financing source has been identified. For example, when we estimate the cost of common equity financing, we assume that both business risk and financial risk have been correctly identified before beginning the estimation procedure.

Once procedures for estimating costs of each individual financing source have been examined, we go on to estimate the marginal cost of capital in two ways. The first utilizes the cost of capital of the firm as a marginal cost of capital. Chapter 15 showed that such a marginal cost is appropriate *only* for investment proposals having the same level of business risk as the average business risk of all existing investments held by the firm. Moreover, a target capital structure—a given degree of financial leverage to accompany that business risk such that the marginal cost reflects business and financial risk—is assumed. The second version is the marginal cost of capital when the business risk of investment proposals *differs* from the average business risk of investments held by the firm. In this context, the cost of capital of the firm is no longer applicable. The marginal cost must then reflect the business and financial risk associated with the particular investment proposal.

Table 16–1 *Valuation Models for Securities*
[Expected Annual Cash Flows Given]

Debt

$$(11\text{-}1) \quad V = \sum_{t=1}^{n} \frac{C_t}{(1 + k_d)^t} + \frac{MV}{(1 + k_d)^n}$$

Preferred Stock

$$(11\text{-}2) \quad V = \sum_{t=1}^{\infty} \frac{C}{(1 + k_p)^t} = \frac{C}{k_p}$$

Common Stock

1. No Growth

$$(11\text{-}4) \quad V = \sum_{t=1}^{\infty} \frac{D}{(1 + k_e)^t} = \frac{D}{k_e}$$

2. Constant Growth

$$(11\text{-}6) \quad V = D_0 \sum_{t=1}^{\infty} \frac{(1 + g)^t}{(1 + k_e)^t} = \frac{D_0(1 + g)}{k_e - g} = \frac{D_1}{k_e - g}$$

3. Single Shift Growth (two growth rates)

$$(11\text{-}7) \quad V = \sum_{t=1}^{n} \frac{D_0(1 + g_1)^t}{(1 + k_e)^t} + \frac{1}{(1 + k_e)^n} \cdot \frac{D_0(1 + g_1)^n(1 + g_2)}{k_e - g_2}$$

VALUATION AND RISK–RETURN METHODS FOR ESTIMATING COSTS OF INDIVIDUAL FINANCING SOURCES

Two approaches to estimating costs of financing sources are demonstrated. One, the **valuation method,** works by finding the rate of return required by investors through the use of expected future cash flows and the present market price of a security. Chapter 3 showed that under efficient markets, these prices should reflect the value the market places on the security. This method relies on valuation formulas presented in Chapter 11; for convenience these formulas are restated in Table 16-1. The second approach, to be applied here only in the case of common equity financing, is the **risk–return method**—an approach making use of the security market line of Chapter 4.

COST OF DEBT FINANCING

The after-tax cost of long-term debt depends on the current required rate of return for newly issued bonds of a maturity equal to that which the firm intends to issue. That required rate must reflect the business risk of the firm and the financial risk associated with its target capital structure. We can estimate this cost in two steps:

1. Estimate the rate of return required on debt of similar risk and maturity to the debt the firm wishes to issue.

2. Adjust the required rate for the effects of corporate income taxes.

To illustrate the procedure, suppose that Moore, Inc., wants to issue 20-year debt in a quantity consistent with its target capital structure. The firm is able to find a bond of similar risk to that which it would issue. That bond has a current market price of $830, a coupon rate of 8 percent, and a *remaining* maturity of 20 years.

Using the valuation method, we use the equation for bond value [Equation (11-1), repeated in Table 16-1], setting the discounted value of the future interest and principal payments equal to the current market price of the bond.

$$\$830 = \sum_{t=1}^{20} \frac{\$80}{(1 + k_d)^t} + \frac{\$1000}{(1 + k_d)^{20}}$$

There are 20 annual interest payments of $80 each. The unknown of this annual compounding model is k_d, the required return by bond-holders.[1] We can solve for k_d by a trial and error procedure (however, specially prepared bond tables or a reasonably sophisticated calculator would speed the process considerably). The trial and error procedure requires that we select a value for k_d to see if we can equate, or approximately equate, both sides of the equation. (This method is identical to that of finding the internal rate of return shown in Chapter 5.) The correct rate will be that which equates the present value of future cash flows to the market value of the bond. Suppose we try 9 percent for k_d.

$$\sum_{t=1}^{20} \frac{\$80}{(1 + 0.09)^t} + \frac{\$1000}{(1 + 0.09)^{20}} = \$80(9.1285) + \$1000(0.1784)$$

$$= \$730 + \$178 = \$908$$

Clearly, we must try a higher rate than 9 percent, since the present value of the future cash flows is greater than $830. Suppose we try 11 percent. Then:

$$\sum_{t=1}^{20} \frac{\$80}{(1 + 0.11)^t} + \frac{\$1000}{(1 + 0.11)^{20}} = \$80(7.9633) + \$1000(0.1240)$$

$$= \$637 + \$124 = \$761$$

---

[1]Throughout this chapter *annual* compounding is assumed for simplicity. Although most bonds pay interest semiannually, our simplifying assumption will have very little impact on the interest cost computed.

That present value is too low. Consequently, k_d must be somewhere between 9 percent and 11 percent. Trying 10 percent, we find:

$$\sum_{t=1}^{20} \frac{\$80}{(1 + 0.10)^t} + \frac{\$1000}{(1 + 0.10)^{20}} = \$80(8.5136) + \$1000(0.1486)$$

$$= \$681 + \$149 = \$830$$

At a discount rate of 10 percent, the present value of the future cash flows of the bond just equals the current price. Therefore, the required rate of return is $k_d = 10$ percent.

The required rate of return found in this way is the **yield to maturity** received by the investor if the bond is purchased at the current price and held until maturity so that the investor receives all future interest payments plus the maturity value. We assume that k_d so found is also the *expected* rate of return. This assumption is not consistent with proper valuation theory. We *should* find the required rate for debt that makes the present value of *expected* future interest and principal payments equal the current market price. Instead, we found it by discounting the *promised* coupon interest payments and principal payment. With risky corporate debt, promised payments *exceed* expected payments because of the possibility of default. Therefore, given the price of the bond, finding the discount rate for higher *promised* rather than *expected* payments results in an estimate of the required rate that is biased upward.[2] A required rate estimated from expected cash payments would be preferable, but is extremely difficult to obtain. Consequently, we use the required rate k_d based on promised payments *as if* it were an expected rate—knowing that it is biased upward compared to the true expected rate.

Once a required rate k_d has been estimated, it must be adjusted for the tax-deductible character of interest payments. If τ is the corporate income tax, the after-tax cost of debt is[3]:

$$(1 - \tau)k_d \tag{16-1}$$

---

[2]If the true expected cash payments for the bond in question were $76.51 for expected annual interest over 20 years and $956.43 for the expected principal payment, the discount rate making the present value of these expected payments equal the $830 market price would be $k_d = 9.5$ percent, lower than the 10 percent rate obtained with promised payments.

[3]Instead of the valuation method, we could employ the risk–return method, applied later to the case of common equity. Based on the security market line of Chapter 4, the required rate would consist of the risk-free rate plus a risk premium. That risk premium should reflect the market risk of a bond in the same way that the risk of common stock would be represented. Unfortunately, the problems of estimating market risk for bonds are not easily surmounted. We therefore rely on the valuation approach of Equation (11-1).

The cost of preferred stock financing is relatively easy to compute. From Table 16-1, the valuation equation is:

$$V = \frac{C}{k_p}$$

where C is the expected dividend and k_p the rate of return required by preferred shareholders given the risk associated with investing in such shares. Solving the equation for k_p, we find:

$$k_p = \frac{C}{V} \tag{16-2}$$

Illustrating, suppose that Bley Company happened to have a previously issued and outstanding preferred stock issue. Assume further that Bley's actual capital structure is, at market value, identical to its target capital structure. Given the level of average business risk at hand, any new preferred stock Bley might issue in accordance with its target capital structure would have the same business and financial risk as Bley's outstanding issue. Therefore, the outstanding issue can be used to estimate the cost of *additional* preferred stock financing. [If the target and actual capital structures were not identical, Bley would have to estimate k_p for the target structure and could not use its outstanding issue. Preferred shares of appropriate risk of other firms could then be used with Equation (16-2).] Bley's outstanding issue pays a 7 percent rate and has a par value of $5 million and a market value of $3.375 million. The *total* annual dividend is $0.07 \times \$5,000,000$, or $350,000. Given this payment and the market value of $3.375 million, the required rate for preferred share financing is:

$$k_p = \frac{\$350,000}{\$3,375,000} = 0.1037, \quad \text{or } 10.37\%$$

Since preferred stock dividends are not tax deductible for the issuing firm, no tax adjustment is made. The after-tax cost of preferred stock financing equals its required rate of return.

Since the estimate of k_p is based on promised rather than expected dividend payments, the resulting estimate is biased upward from the true expected rate. This bias was explained earlier for the case of the cost of debt. Again, we ignore the bias to avoid undue complexity.

Although calculating the cost of common stock financing is conceptually identical to calculating the cost of any source of funds, the actual process creates greater problems for the analyst. Firms issuing debt and preferred stock create a promise to pay specific amounts at regular intervals. Expected payments are usually only slightly less than promised payments for firms having no serious prospect of default. But similar promises are not made when common stock is issued. Future dividends, on which the value of common shares is based, are subject to considerable uncertainty.[4] Consequently, estimates of the magnitude and risk of future dividend streams are important elements in any assessment of the cost of common stock financing.

Two approaches to measuring the cost of common stock financing are illustrated in this section. In the first approach, the valuation method using models from Table 16-1, adapted for the purpose, is chosen to estimate the required rate of return for equity capital. In the second approach, the risk–return model presented in Chapter 4 is used to estimate that required rate. Neither approach requires adjustment for corporate taxes because returns to common shareholders are paid from *after-tax earnings*.

Estimates Using Valuation Models   Table 16-2 summarizes the common stock valuation equations from Table 16-1 and pairs them with the corresponding equations to estimate k_e. Equations (16-3) to (16-5) can be derived from each of the models shown in Table 16-2.

$$k_e = \frac{D}{V} \tag{16-3}$$

$$k_e = \frac{D_1}{V} + g \tag{16-4}$$

$$k_e = \frac{D_0}{V}[n(g_1 - g_2) + (1 + g_2)] + g_2 \tag{16-5}$$

Since the analyst must choose among three models, it is important to build a logical argument to support the use of one model rather than another in a particular instance. The question one must answer is quite

---

[4]Future payments for preferred stock and debt are also subject to uncertainty. Firms may decide to suspend dividend payments on preferred stock or may end up, through adversity, in default on their outstanding debt. In a similar manner, earnings and dividends on common shares can disappear. Thus, the differences between all these financing forms may be more in degree than in kind. Debt and preferred stock differ in this area of uncertainty from common stock in that payments to holders of these claims have an upper bound. Earnings permitting, dividends on common shares are not so limited and, compared to debt and preferred stock, the *range* of possible outcomes is much greater. So, reflect that when someone criticizes someone else's financial knowledge and acumen by saying "He does not know a stock from a bond," the criticism is not as scathing as it might appear.

Table 16–2 *Models to Estimate the Cost of Equity Capital*

Valuation Model	Model to Estimate k_e	
No Growth		
$V = \dfrac{D}{k_e}$	$k_e = \dfrac{D}{V}$	(16-3)
Constant Perpetual Growth		
$V = \dfrac{D_1}{k_e - g}$	$k_e = \dfrac{D_1}{V} + g$	(16-4)
Single Shift Model		
$V = \displaystyle\sum_{t=1}^{n} \dfrac{D_0(1 + g_1)^t}{(1 + k_e)^t} + \dfrac{D_0(1 + g_1)^n(1 + g_2)}{k_e - g_2} \cdot \dfrac{1}{(1 + k_e)^n}$	$k_e = \dfrac{D_0}{V}[n(g_1 - g_2) + (1 + g_2)] + g_2$	(16-5)

simple. Given a future capital structure and anticipated cash flows, which model conforms most closely to the pattern of dividend growth anticipated for the firm? In demonstrating each of these models, the examples all assume that the common equity issues employed reflect the appropriate levels of business and financial risk for the firms *and* their target capital structures.

Zero Growth   When the market does not expect the dividend stream to grow, the proper valuation model from Table 16-2 is:

$$V = \frac{D}{k_e}$$

such that, using Equation (16-4)

$$k_e = \frac{D}{V}$$

Assuming that the zero growth assumption is appropriate for Livesay, Inc., let $D = \$1.20$, and $V = \$10$. The cost of new share financing is, using Equation (16-3),

$$k_{ef} = \frac{\$1.20}{\$10}$$

$$= 0.10, \quad \text{or } 10\%$$

where V is the market price of the share used to solve for the cost of capital.

Constant Growth   When the market assesses that the dividend stream will grow over time, the analyst must be able to *identify* that anticipated growth pattern. If there is evidence that the constant growth model is a good approximation of market anticipation, then from Table 16-2.

$$V = \frac{D_1}{k_e - g}$$

and the required rate of return is obtained from Equation (16-4)

$$k_e = \frac{D_1}{V} + g$$

The best approximation of the rate of return required by shareholders is the *dividend yield*, D_1/V plus the anticipated growth rate of dividends.

To apply this formula, suppose that Loring Company's common stock has a current price per share of $V = \$30$, the next year's expected dividend is $D_1 = \$2.10$, and that the constant growth rate is $g = 6$ percent. Then, using Equation (16-4):

$$k_e = \frac{\$2.10}{\$30} + 0.06$$

$$= 0.13, \quad \text{or } 13\%$$

Single Shift Model   To apply the single shift model, assume that Sungro Foods has the following expected future dividend growth rate pattern.

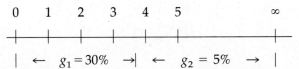

The dividend stream is expected to grow at a very rapid rate of $g_1 = 30$ percent in *each* of the next 4 years and to grow at the much slower annual rate, $g_2 = 5$ percent, thereafter. This pattern is an *approximation* of what the market appears to expect, given the current information available at $t = 0$. Using Equation (16-5) with a current dividend of $1 per share and a share price of $20, the cost of equity capital is:

$$k_e = \frac{D_0}{V} [n(g_1 - g_2) + (1 + g_2)] + g_2$$

$$= \frac{\$1}{\$20} [4(0.30 - 0.05) + (1.05)] + 0.05$$

$$= 0.1525, \quad \text{or } 15.25\%$$

Although this formula produces an approximation of k_e, it is very close to the rate that would be obtained if Equation (11-7) in Table 16-1 were solved directly for the internal rate of return.[5] The size of the estimating error depends on the size of n and the difference between g_1 and g_2. In general, the closer g_1 and g_2 are and the smaller n is, the better the approximation. For an easy approximation of k_e in a world of uncertainty, this model offers considerable flexibility.

An alternative method of estimating the cost of equity capital, or the cost of other security sources, is to estimate the risk-free rate r_f and the risk premium ϕ independently. Then by using the security market line (SML) relationship derived in Chapter 4, we can find the required rate of return for equity capital. This approach is called the *risk–return method*.

Estimates Using a Risk–Return Model

The security market line developed in Chapter 4 gave the relation between the equilibrium required rate of return on an individual security and the risk of that security. The proper measure of risk for that security is beta, which is a relative measure of market risk, the portion of the variability in the security returns that cannot be diversified away. The required return may be written, in the formula for the security market line, as:

$$k_e = r_f + (k_m - r_f)\beta_i \qquad (16\text{-}6)$$

where k_m is the required return on a portfolio consisting of all risky securities in the market and r_f is the risk-free rate.[6]

A security market line is portrayed graphically in Figure 16-1. The vertical intercept is r_f, the risk-free rate—a rate applying only for securities having no market risk, that is, for $\beta = 0$. If beta is greater than zero, a return higher than the riskless rate will be required because of the presence of market risk. How much higher the return must be depends on the degree of investor risk aversion and the size of the risk

---

[5] Given the information about Sungro, we can write:

$$\$20 = \frac{\$1(1.3)^1}{(1 + k_e)} + \frac{\$1(1.3)^2}{(1 + k_e)^2} + \frac{\$1(1.3)^3}{(1 + k_e)^3} + \frac{\$1(1.3)^4}{(1 + k_e)^4} + \frac{\$1(1.3)^4(1.05)}{k_e - 0.05} \cdot \frac{1}{(1 + k_e)^4}$$

When we solve this equation by trial and error for the internal rate of return, we find that $k_e \approx 16$ percent.

[6] Although the SML model was developed as a single time period model, it is frequently applied to a multiperiod setting, under certain assumptions. See E. F. Fama, "Multiperiod Consumption-Investment Decisions," *American Economic Review* (March 1970), pp. 163–174, and "Risk-Adjusted Discount Rates and Capital Budgeting Under Uncertainty," *Journal of Financial Economics* (August 1977), pp. 3–24.

Figure 16-1   *The Security Market Line*

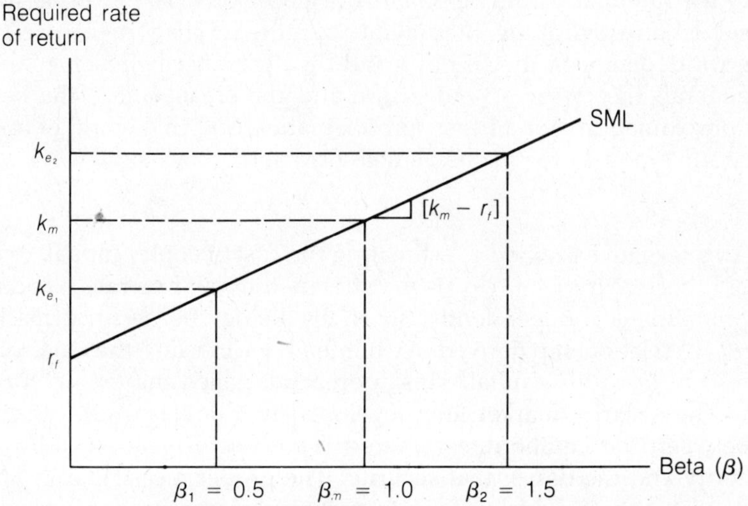

premium required by investors to hold the market portfolio. This risk premium for any asset i is $(k_m - r_f)\beta_i$. Holding constant $(k_m - r_f)$, the slope of the SML, higher risk premiums imply higher market risk, since β_i must be greater.

As shown in Figure 16-1, when $\beta = 1$ as is true for β_m, the required return on the security will equal the required return on the market portfolio, k_m. However, if $\beta_2 = 1.5$ the required return will be k_{e2}, which is greater than k_m, because more market risk is present. By the same reasoning, a lesser degree of market risk measured by $\beta_1 = 0.50$ means that the required return for the security will be less than that of the market portfolio, or k_{e1}.

Since the market risk for the market portfolio is $\beta = 1.0$, the **market risk premium** is $(k_m - r_f)$. Figure 16-2 shows how different market risk premiums affect the SML. In general, the greater that premium, the higher the required rate of return for any given β. Note as $(k_m - r_f)$ increases in Figure 16-2, the required rate for any beta β^* increases—first from k_{e1} to k_{e2}, then from k_{e2} to k_{e3}.

To use the SML to determine the cost of equity capital for a firm, three values must be estimated—the beta of the shares involved, the required rate of return for the market portfolio, and the risk-free rate. Examining Equation (16-6), we can see that k_e will then be determined.

Estimates of beta for an individual firm may be found in a number of ways. When a firm's shares are traded in a security market, beta can be estimated directly, using a procedure illustrated in Appendix 16A. In

Figure 16-2   *Impact of Changes in Market Risk Premiums*

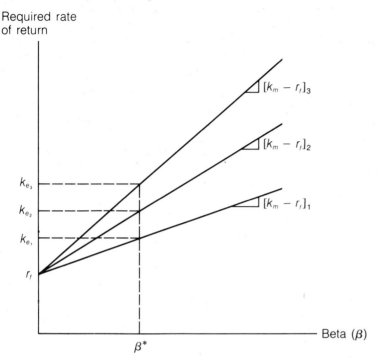

some instances, investment advisory services such as *Value Line*, with access to large amounts of data, have publicly available estimates made by their own research staffs. If a firm's shares are not traded publicly, an analyst might try to find shares of a publicly traded firm thought to be comparable in risk to those of the untraded firm. The beta of the traded shares can then be used in the approximation of k_e for shares of the untraded firm. Appendix 16B illustrates a sample application.

After computing beta for the firm's common stock, an estimate of the SML [Equation (16-6)] is required. That estimate may be obtained in several ways; however we proceed by estimating (1) the risk-free rate r_f and (2) the *market* risk premium. Guidance in this effort is provided by a series of studies of inflation and historical rates of return on stocks, bonds, and U.S. Treasury bills by Roger Ibbotson and Rex Sinquefield. The latest of the studies covers the period from 1926–1981.[7]

---

[7]R. Ibbotson and R. Sinquefield, *Stocks, Bonds, Bills and Inflation: Year by Year Historical Returns (1926–1974),"* *The Journal of Business*, Vol. 49, No. 1, January 1976, pp. 11–47.
_____ and _____ , *Stocks, Bonds, Bills and Inflation: The Past (1926–1976) and the*

We first consider the problem of estimating the risk-free rate of return. The historical study found that the **real risk-free rate** (computed after deducting purchasing power losses due to inflation) on bills was a very small positive number (about 0.1–0.2 percent). Historically, the major component of the risk-free rate consisted of compensation for purchasing power losses. If we translate this result into expectations of the future, the market risk-free rate can be approximated by the following formula:

$$r_f = r_f' + \dot{p}^e$$

where r_f' is the expected real required rate of return for risk-free investments and $\dot{p}^e$ is the **expected rate of inflation.** (This approximation formula is explained in more detail in Chapter 19, when the topic of inflation is addressed.)

Since the average historical *real* risk-free rate of return has been close to zero over a very long period, it is not unreasonable to assume that future expected real rates will also be close to zero, so $r_f' = 0.0$. Clearly, then, the expected rate of inflation is the key determinant of the risk-free rate. That rate might be approximated by the expected rate of price increase for consumption goods and services as represented in, say, the Consumer Price Index. Suppose the estimate of $\dot{p}^e$ is 8.0 percent. The risk-free rate is, therefore,

$$r_f = r_f' + \dot{p}^e = 0.0 + 8.0 = 8.0$$

A higher estimate of the inflation rate, $\dot{p}^e = 10.0$ percent, would result in a higher estimate of the risk-free rate of $r_f = 10.0$ percent.

There are alternative ways of estimating the risk-free rate. For example, one can estimate r_f using recent Treasury bill rates. However, such rates fluctuate widely, sometimes even over a brief interval. This instability can result in widely divergent estimates of the intercept of the SML. Perhaps in a period of extreme variation, one might compute an average rate over an appropriate time span to improve the stability of the estimate. Even so, the resulting estimate of the risk-free rate would reflect historical rates of inflation, not necessarily the rate felt appropriate for the future.

In measuring the market risk premium, Ibbotson and Sinquefeld cal-

Future (1977–2000) Charlottesville, Va: Financial Analysts Research Foundation, 1977. _____ and _____, *Stocks, Bonds, Bills and Inflation; Historical Returns (1926–1978),* Charlottesville, Va: Financial Analysts Research Foundation, 1979. _____ and _____, *Stocks, Bonds, Bills, and Inflation; The Past and Future,* Charlottesville, Va: Financial Analysts Research Foundation, 1982.

culated the average *difference* between stock market returns, as reflected in the Standard and Poor index, and U.S. Treasury bill returns. That difference has varied between 8.3 and 9.2 percent, depending on the period studied. These historical average differences provide useful estimates of *future* risk premiums, $(k_m - r_f)$, when the primary source of variation in *both* market return, k_m, and risk-free rate, r_f, is the expected rate of inflation. In such a case, $(k_m - r_f)$ is independent of the level of expected inflation. A historical average of the difference between stock and Treasury bill returns may then be a reasonable approximation of the risk premium to be expected in the future.

Under these circumstances, an estimate of $(k_m - r_f)$ in the 8–9 percent range seems justified. However, it is difficult to make a strong argument for selection of a specific number within that range. In the examples to follow, we use $(k_m - r_f) = 8.8$ percent as an estimate of the market risk premium. That estimate represents an average of the range of estimates by Ibbotson and Sinquefield.

Combining estimates of the risk-free rate of $r_f = 8$ percent and the market risk premium of $k_m - r_f = 8.8$ percent, the estimated security market line based on Equation (16-6) is:

$$k_e = r_f + (k_m - r_f)\beta_i$$
$$= 8.0\% + (8.8\%)\beta_i$$

Armed with the estimated SML, suppose that Darras Amusement Company has estimated the appropriate beta for its shares as $\beta_i = 0.7$. This beta estimate reflects the business and financial risk of Darras, given its target capital structure. Using the estimated SML, the required rate is:

$$k_e = 8.0\% + (8.8\%)(0.7)$$
$$= 8.0\% + 6.2\%$$
$$= 14.2\%$$

The risk premium for Darras common stock is 6.2 percent. Because Darras's beta is less than 1.0, its risk premium is less than the 8.8 percent premium attributed to the market.

COST OF RETAINING EARNINGS

Retention of earnings out of the current flow of earnings for reinvestment within the firm (rather than paying out all earnings as dividends) is an extremely important source of equity financing for many firms.

In the preceding chapter, we asserted that retention of earnings had a cost equal to the required rate of return for common equity financing, or

k_e.[8] That is, retention of earnings is not a "free" source of funds. That assertion can be justified in straightforward fashion.

If a firm decides to retain earnings rather than pay them out as dividends, shareholders are prevented from investing these funds themselves. They no longer have the opportunity to earn a competitive rate of return on amounts retained within the firm. The firm must earn that return for them. If all earnings were paid out as dividends, *shareholders* could reinvest these dividends at the same level of risk present with their common shares and earn an expected rate of return k_e. Therefore, the firm must also expect to earn k_e on earnings retained if shareholders are to be at least as well off with earnings retention as with payment of cash dividends. In short, retention of earnings imposes an opportunity cost equal to the required rate k_e.

Summary of Methods

The valuation method of estimation and the risk–return method offer viable procedures for estimating the cost of equity capital. Both provide an *approximation* of the true cost. The accuracy of these approximations depends, in part, on the skill of the analyst.

The key to a satisfactory multiperiod valuation estimate lies in identification of the proper model and one's ability to assess the growth rates anticipated by the market. These are extremely difficult tasks because there are no well-defined standards by which an estimate may be compared. Alternatively, the risk–return framework requires a correct assessment of market risk and the security market line. Neither task is easy, and there is ample opportunity to introduce error.

We recognize these problems not to indicate that estimates of k_e using either method are useless, but to emphasize the care that is required in the estimation process. Perfect estimates do not exist in a world of uncertainty. Depending on the quality of information available to the analyst, confidence held in the estimate by the analyst will vary.

ESTIMATING THE MARGINAL COST OF CAPITAL FOR THE FIRM

Suppose that a firm wishes to estimate a marginal cost of capital applicable to investment proposals having business risk equal to the average business risk of all existing investments. That is, the firm plans to use the cost of capital for the firm as a marginal cost of capital. We illustrate this estimation process using the case of Petty Aluminum Fabrication

[8]The reader may note that the combination of flotation costs and relatively low capital gains taxes should make retained earnings a cheaper form of equity financing. However, most firms pay dividends and issue new shares. Such actions would not make sense unless the marginal costs of both sources of funds are approximately equal.

Table 16–3 *Book and Market Values of Long-term Financing: Petty Aluminum Fabrication*

	Book Value	Percent	Market Value	Percent
6% Long-term Debt	$18,000,000	45.0	$14,914,000	27.0
7% Preferred Stock	7,000,000	17.5	4,900,000	9.0
Common Equity	15,000,000	37.5	35,225,000	64.0
Total	$40,000,000	100.0%	$55,039,000	100.0%

Company. This case also serves to summarize the procedures for estimating costs of individual financing sources.

Petty Aluminum is a fabricator of window frames. Its president, Mr. Petty, is relatively inexperienced in financial matters and has hired two students from a local university to help him estimate his cost of capital. The students, Davis and Hawver, asked Petty for some up-to-date financial information. He responded with Table 16-3.

Davis and Hawver explained that the cost of capital for the firm is the weighted (at market value) after-tax cost of each financing source. This cost reflects the average business risk of all Petty's existing investments and the financial risk posed by the firm's target capial structure. The formula for computing the marginal cost of capital of the firm is:

$$K = (1 - \tau)k_d W_d + k_p W_p + k_e W_e \qquad (16\text{-}7)$$

[This is a version of Equation (15-3) extended to include the cost of preferred stock financing.] Davis and Hawver said that (for a fee) they would (1) help determine Petty's optimal capital structure to serve as a target, (2) estimate costs of each financing source, (3) adjust the cost of debt for corporate income taxes, and (4) substitute these into Equation (16-7).

Beginning with the problem of capital structure, Davis noted that the book and market values in Table 16-3 were quite different. Obviously, the decline in market value of bonds from book value meant that current market interest rates for bonds were higher than the 6 percent coupon rate at which the outstanding bonds were issued. A similar conclusion was drawn concerning preferred stock: the current cost must be higher than the 7 percent rate at which the existing issue was sold. In contrast, the market value of common stock was a good deal higher than book value. Davis concluded that book value weights would be *especially* inappropriate in this case because they would vastly overweight debt and preferred stock relative to common equity compared to weights based on market value.

After a long discussion with investment bankers, the executive committee of the board of directors, and Petty, Davis concluded that the firm felt that the *existing capital market value* weights would be "optimal" in their future financing. That is, he arrived at 27 percent for W_d, 9 percent for W_p, and 64 percent for W_e. These weights were equal to the proportions of the current capital structure at market in Table 16-3. Davis pointed out that if a target capital structure different from the current structure had been selected, the weights of the target, not current, structure would have been relevant for costs of financing investment proposals.

Davis also noted that the firm was expected, after payment of cash dividends to preferred and common shareholders, to have about $2. million of earnings retained out of current earnings. Depending on the total outlay for investment proposals actually selected, earnings retention might or might not fully meet equity financing needs given the target capital structure. But even if new common shares had to be issued, the cost of common equity financing would be approximately the same for retention of earnings and sale of new common shares—ignoring the minor effect of flotation costs. *Together,* common equity financing through retention of earnings and sale of new common shares would equal the target W_e = 64 percent for common equity.

Meanwhile, Hawver was estimating costs of individual financing sources given the target (and actual) capital structure. He began with the cost of debt financing. The investment bankers predicted that new debt could be issued at the same rate as the yield to maturity now existing in the market for outstanding bonds of risk similar to Petty's bonds. Using the trial and error procedure to equate the present value of future cash flows from the bonds to the market value of the bonds, Hawver's goal was to find that k_d that satisfied the following equality.

$$\$14,914,000 = \sum_{t=1}^{15} \frac{\$1,080,000}{(1 + k_d)^t} + \frac{\$18,000,000}{(1 + k_d)^{15}}$$

The annual total interest rate on existing bonds is (0.06) $18,000,000 = $1,080,000. Discounting these annual payments and the $18 million maturity value, Hawver arrived at an estimated required rate of return for debt of k_d = 8 percent. Converting this to an after-tax basis using Equation (16-1) and a corporate income tax rate of τ = 40 percent, the after-tax cost of debt was estimated to be:

$$(1 - \tau)k_d = (1 - 0.40)8\% = 4.8\%$$

Hawver estimated the required rate of return k_p for preferred stock investors by first multiplying the 7 percent rate on the existing stock times the $7 million outstanding to produce an annual dividend of

$490,000. Then, using Equation (16-2) to divide $490,000 by the $4.9 million market value, the cost of preferred stock financing was found.

$$k_p = \frac{\$490,000}{\$4,900,000} = 0.10, \quad \text{or } 10\%$$

After investigating Petty's historical earnings record and the potential future investments, Hawver concluded that the company could reasonably be called a *constant* growth firm. His best estimate for the dividend growth rate was $g = 6$ percent. The annual dividend the next year was expected to be $2.76 per share, according to the executive committee of the board. The price per share was $34.50 and, using Equation (16-4), the required rate of return for common equity was:

$$k_e = \frac{D_1}{V} + g = \frac{\$2.76}{\$34.50} + 0.06 = 14\%$$

This is the cost of common equity financing, whether obtained by retention of earnings or sale of new common stock.

Together, Davis and Hawver had determined the costs of each financing source given the target capital structure. Using Equation (16-7) the estimated cost of capital for the firm was:

$$K = (1 - \tau)k_d W_d + k_p W_p + k_e W_e$$

$$= (4.8\%)(0.27) + (10\%)(0.09) + (14\%)(0.64)$$

$$= 1.296\% + 0.9\% + 8.96\%$$

$$= 11.156\% \sim 11.2\%$$

This rate was accepted by management as a marginal cost to evaluate all investment proposals having the same business risk as the average business risk of the firm's existing investments.[9]

---

[9]It would not be practical to maintain the actual capital structure at target levels at all points in time. In a year when internal capital outlays are somewhat smaller than usual, strict adherence to the target structure might require that small quantities of less important financing forms be issued with high flotation costs. For example, Petty uses relatively little preferred stock. Strict adherence to the target structure might, in a year of small capital outlays, cause Petty to issue, say, 300 shares of preferred stock as part of the overall financing. Flotation costs would then be too high to make such financing practical. The target capital structure is a desired average structure over time. Year-to-year variation can be allowed to reduce flotation costs. For example, if financing at the target structure requirements called for a small (and expensive) preferred stock issue, it would be cheaper to obtain the equivalent dollar amount of financing by increasing the quantity of, say, debt in that year. Over time, the actual preferred stock position would grow increasingly smaller than the target position for a growing firm. Ultimately, it would pay the firm to issue a relatively larger quantity of preferred stock at a lower average flotation cost to restore the actual capital structure to the target capital structure.

ESTIMATING MARGINAL COSTS OF CAPITAL FOR INVESTMENT PROPOSALS OF DIFFERING BUSINESS RISK

More generally, a firm represents a collection of many investments with perhaps quite different degrees of business risk. To illustrate the point, consider a firm having only two existing investments, Able and Baker. For simplicity, each investment has the same market value and the firm happens to be unlevered. The risk of Able is measured by a beta of 0.5, and Baker's risk is represented by a beta of 1.5. Since the firm is unlevered, the respective betas measure only business risk. And because the betas differ, Able and Baker investments have different costs of capital. Assuming that the estimated SML from Equation (16-6) is the same as earlier used in the Darras Amusement Company example, the respective costs of capital for Able and Baker investments are:

Able

$$k_{eA} = r_f + (k_m - r_f)\beta_A = 8\% + (8.8\%)(0.5) = 12.4\%$$

Baker

$$k_{eB} = r_f + (k_m - r_f)\beta_B = 8\% + (8.8\%)(1.5) = 21.2\%$$

These costs are represented by points A and B on the security market line in Figure 16-3. As for the firm, its business risk is measured by the weighted average of the individual betas. Since both investments have equal market value, the weights used are also equal. The weighted average of the business risks of the two existing investments, the busi-

Figure 16-3   *Multiple Discount Rates*

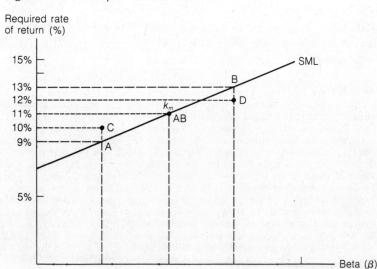

ness risk of the *firm*, is $\beta_{AB} = (0.5)\ (0.5) + (0.5)1.5 = 1.0$. The cost of capital of the unlevered firm, using the estimated SML is:

$$k_{eAB} = 8\% + (8.8\%)\ (1.0) = 16.8\%$$

which, by coincidence, equals the required rate of return on the market portfolio.

Now if the firm considers investment proposals, management must first determine the appropriate risk and applicable cost of capital for each proposal before it can be evaluated. Proposals having a risk equal to $\beta_B = 1.5$ must be evaluated using the Baker cost of capital. It would never be appropriate to evaluate proposals of these disparate risks with k_{eAB}, the cost of capital for the firm. The business risk of the firm is $\beta_{AB} = 1.0$, different from that of each proposal.

To illustrate potential consequence of inappropriate use of the cost of capital of the firm, suppose that the firm confronts two economically independent proposals: 1 and 2. Proposal 1 has a risk of $\beta_A = 0.5$, identical to existing investment Able, and proposal 2 has a risk of $\beta_B = 1.5$, equivalent to the risk of Baker. Proposal 1 has an expected rate of return equal to $r_1^* = 14$ percent, whereas proposal 2 has an expected rate of return of $r_2^* = 20$ percent. If the firm improperly uses the cost of capital of the firm, $k_{eAB} = 16.8$ percent, to evaluate each proposal, it would *reject* proposal 1 ($r_1^* = 14$ percent $< k_{eAB} = 16.8$ percent) and *accept* proposal 2 ($r_2^* = 20$ percent $> k_{eAB} = 16.8$ percent). But this is contrary to the accept/reject decisions that should have been made to maximize shareholder wealth. As Figure 16-3 indicates, the $r_1^* = 14.0$ percent expected rate of return for proposal 1 is *above* the appropriate cost of capital of 12.4 percent for the risk of $\beta_A = 0.5$. Acceptance of this proposal would be expected to increase shareholder wealth and it should have been accepted. Its erroneous rejection has caused shareholders to forgo an expected wealth increase. At the same time, proposal 2 has an expected rate of return of $r_2^* = 20$ percent, *below* the appropriate cost of capital of $k_{eB} = 21.2$ percent for business risk of $\beta_B = 1.5$. Undertaking this undesirable proposal would result in a decrease in shareholder wealth. The cost of capital of the firm would be appropriate only for an investment proposal having risk of $\beta = 1.0$, the average business risk of the two existing investments held by the firm.

The case for estimating different costs of capital for investment proposals of differing risk is compelling; the problems in actually making reliable distinctions in risk and reasonable estimates of alternative costs of capital are formidable. We illustrate a desirable course for firms to follow, acknowledging the difficulties as they appear.

Estimating Alternative Costs of Capital for Investment Proposals

Suppose that Borg Industries has estimated its cost of capital for the firm based on its target capital structure of W_d = 40 percent debt and W_e = 60 percent equity. Given the average level of business risk of Borg's existing investments and the target capital structure, the estimated cost of debt was k_d = 11 percent, which, with a corporate tax rate of τ = 40 percent, indicated an after-tax cost of debt of:

$$(1 - \tau)k_d = (1 - 0.4)11\% = 6.6\%$$

The estimated beta for common equity was β = 1.25. With an estimated security market line of k_e = 8 percent + 8.8 percent β, the estimated cost of equity capital was:

$$k_e = 8\% + 8.8\%(1.25) = 19\%$$

Using Equation (16-7), the estimated cost of capital of the *firm* was:

$$K = 6.6\%(0.40) + 19\%(0.60)$$

$$= 2.64 + 11.40$$

$$= 14.04\% \sim 14\%$$

However, investment proposals like Borg's are often thought to have different business risks from each other and from the average business risk of existing investments held by the firm. The problem is to measure these differences in risk. But how? Borg's existing debt and equity issues are traded in the market and reflect average business risk of the firm. Existing investments of differing risk owned by Borg are not separately traded in the market. It is not possible to obtain market values at each separate existing investment to estimate different costs of capital for investments of different risk. In other words, the market gives us information about the existing investment "omelette" for Borg but not for the separate "eggs."

An imprecise but at least tractable approach to this difficulty is to estimate betas for *other* firms whose securities are traded in the market—firms thought to have levels of business risk similar to the risk of investment proposals in the firm. For example, suppose that Borg has investment proposal A, having a risk thought similar to another firm, Ajax, Inc. Ajax common shares have a beta of 0.85. (Such a beta could be accepted from a source such as *Value Line*, or Borg could compute Ajax's beta following procedures shown in Appendix 16A.) A cost of capital utilizing Ajax's beta of 0.85 rather than Borg's cost of capital for the firm (based on a beta of 1.25) would be used to evaluate proposal A. Other investment proposals thought to have risk similar to still other comparable firms could be similarly evaluated using still other costs of capital.

There are several difficulties in the process of using data from comparable firms to estimate distinct costs of capital. First, and most obvious, the declaration that a given investment proposal has a risk similar to that of some comparable firm is largely based on intuition. Such a matching up may, in fact, be inappropriate. But even if the matching *is* correct, there are additional difficulties. The matching is based on comparable *business risk*. Yet, the comparable firm may have a quite different capital structure from that of Borg. Consequently, the beta of the comparable firm may reflect the same business risk but a different level of *financial* risk because of differences in leverage. In such cases, it is necessary to adjust the beta of the comparable firm to reflect the target capital structure of Borg. (Appendix 16B describes such adjustments.)

We assume a simpler case with Borg. It has identified three distinct *risk* classes for investment proposals: A, B, and C. It has also been fortunate in identifying three firms, Ajax, Bellerophon, and Castor, thought to have levels of business risk respectively equivalent to risk classes A, B, and C. Furthermore, the three firms have capital structures *identical* to Borg's target capital structure. Consequently, the estimated betas for the three comparable firms correctly discern differences in business risk but have the *same* financial risk as that of Borg.[10]

Under these assumptions, Borg has estimated the betas for the comparable firms as follows.

$$\text{Ajax} \quad \beta_A = 0.85$$

$$\text{Bellerophon} \quad \beta_B = 1.35$$

$$\text{Castor} \quad \beta_C = 1.90$$

With the estimated SML, these differences in risk imply three different costs of equity capital.

Risk class A $\quad k_{e_A} = 8\% + 8.8\%(0.85) = 15.48\%$

Risk class B $\quad k_{e_B} = 8\% + 8.8\%(1.35) = 19.88\%$

Risk class C $\quad k_{e_C} = 8\% + 8.8\%(1.90) = 24.72\%$

Given Borg's target capital structure of $W_d = 40$ percent, $W_e = 60$ percent, and the after-tax cost of debt of $(1 - \tau)k_d = 6.6$ percent, Borg has three different marginal costs of capital when Equation (16-7) is used.

---

[10]Even here, we are in muddy waters. Little is known about debt capacity and costs of debt for firms of differing business risk. We cannot know whether Borg, upon undertaking investment proposals of different business risk, would change the average business risk of the firm such that the cost of debt (and preferred stock were any outstanding) *changed* for Borg's target capital structure. The change in the firm's business risk might cause an alteration in Borg's target capital structure. In the remainder of this discussion, we assume that Borg's target structure and the cost of debt are *unchanged* by the business risk of whatever investment proposals are undertaken.

Risk class A $K = 6.6\%(0.4) + 15.48\%(0.6) = 11.928\%$, or 11.9%

Risk class B $K = 6.6\%(0.4) + 19.88\%(0.6) = 14.568\%$, or 14.6%

Risk class C $K = 6.6\%(0.4) + 24.72\%(0.6) = 17.472\%$, or 17.5%

In practice, reliable estimates of different costs of capital for proposals of different business risk are difficult to achieve. Yet the effort must be made if it is thought that business risk of proposals differs significantly from the average business risk of existing investments held by the firm. The potential unfavorable consequences of using the cost of capital of the firm in this situation are evident and provide the motivation to form alternative costs of capital, however imprecise estimates of these may be.

SUMMARY

To develop estimates of the marginal cost of capital, it is necessary to estimate costs of individual sources of funds. Assessing these costs requires both technical competence in working with valuation models and the risk–return model plus sound judgment. Estimating the cost of debt and preferred stock financing is at least technically easier than estimating the cost of common equity financing. Cash payments promised to bondholders and preferred shareholders are clearly specified before these securities are sold. However, as residual claimants, holders of common shares have no upper bound to future dividends if investments held and undertaken produce gains for shareholders. The analyst can choose a common stock valuation model assuming zero growth, constant growth, or multiple growth rates for expected future cash dividends *or* a risk–return model. The risk–return model requires an estimate of beta as well as an estimate of the security market line. Both approaches require considerable judgment and provide ample opportunity for error. The cost of retaining earnings is equal to the cost of issuing new common shares. It is an opportunity cost to shareholders who must give up dividend payments as an alternative to earnings retention.

When the firm is estimating the cost of capital of the firm, that cost will reflect two conditions: the average business risk of all investments in the firm, and the target capital structure of the firm. When used as a marginal cost of capital, the cost of capital of the firm is applicable only to investment proposals having a degree of business risk equal to the average business risk of all existing investments held by the firm. If a firm uses the cost of capital of the firm to evaluate investment proposals having higher or lower levels of business risk than the firm, it may reject desirable investment proposals and accept undesirable ones.

When business risks of investment proposals differ from the business risk of the firm, the firm should estimate alternative costs of capital, each reflecting the level of business risk of each proposal as well as the firm's target capital structure. This is a difficult task to carry out with precision.

GLOSSARY OF KEY TERMS

Expected Rate of Inflation	The expected future rate of change in prices of consumption goods and services; as used here, a forecast used to estimate the risk-free rate component of the security market line.
Market Risk Premium	The difference between the required rate of return on the market portfolio and the risk-free rate. The increment in required rate of return established in the market for an increment in market risk (beta) of the security.
Real Risk-Free Rate	The expected rate of return from riskless investment after taking account of expected future inflation of prices of consumption goods and services.
Retention of Earnings	Income of the firm retained for reinvestment and not paid out as cash dividends to common shareholders.
Risk–Return Method	Determining the cost of capital by estimating market risk and using the security market line.
Valuation Method	Determining the cost of capital by using the future expected cash flows and the present price of a security.
Yield to Maturity	The rate of return, usually on bonds, that equates the present value of promised interest and principal payments with the current market value of a bond.

SELECTED REFERENCES

Lawrence, David W. "The Effects of Corporate Taxation on the Cost of Equity Capital." *Financial Management* (Spring 1976), pp. 52–57.

Lewellen, Wilbur G. *The Cost of Capital.* Dubuque, IA.: Kendall/Hunt, 1976.

Nantell, Timothy, and R. Carlson. "The Cost of Retained Earnings." In *Issues in Managerial Finance*, E. Brigham and R. Johnson, Eds. Hinsdale, Ill.: Dryden Press, 1976.

Petry, Glenn H. "Empirical Evidence on the Cost of Capital Weights." Financial Management (Winter 1975), pp. 58–65.

Scott, David F., Jr., and John D. Martin. "Industry Influence on Financial Structure." *Financial Management* (Spring 1975), pp. 67–73.

QUESTIONS

1. Distinguish between the cost of capital for a specific investment and the cost of capital for a firm.

2. What does the slope of the security market line measure?

3. What factors might determine whether a firm used a valuation model to calculate the cost of equity capital instead of the security market line?

4. What does it mean to say a stock is a high beta stock?

5. Which stocks are likely to have low betas?

6. If an investment project is not of equivalent risk to the existing operations of the firm, what adjustments are necessary to determine an appropriate discount rate?

PROBLEMS

1. If a bond carries a 10 percent coupon and has 10 years to maturity, find the before-tax yield to maturity if the price is (a) $79.14, (b) $100, and (c) $113.42.
   Note: Bond prices are often quoted for $100 maturity value.

2. Calculate the after-tax cost of debt for Bowles Inc. if more debt can be sold at the yield to maturity of the current debt. The current face value, 20-year, 6 percent bond sells at $900. Bowles' marginal tax rate is 40 percent.

3. What is the cost of the Erls Eggplant Company preferred stock if $100 par 6 percent preferred can be sold at (a) par value? (b) At $60? (c) At $120?

4. Calculate the cost of the sale of Overton common shares where the growth in dividends is expected to be 15 percent for five years and 5 percent thereafter. The common shares can be sold for $20 given the current dividend of $1.

5. Calculate the cost of the sale of Overton common shares described in Problem 4 if (a) dividends are expected to grow at the rate of 1 percent forever and (b) if no dividend growth is expected.

6. Calculate k_e when the riskfree rate is 5 percent, the return on the

market portfolio is expected to be 10 percent and the beta for a comparable company is 1.5.

7. Calculate the cost of equity for Thuringer Meat Company if it has a beta of 0.8 and the security market line is $0.06 + 0.08\beta$.

8. Ellerbee Manufacturing expects to pay 8 percent to investors for any new debt it issues. The cost of equity is 15 percent. If it raises 30 percent of its funds from debt and 70 percent from common equity, what are the marginal costs of capital for Ellerbee? Ellerbee has a corporate tax rate of 40 percent.

9. The anticipated cost of new debt financing for Ultra, Inc., is 7 percent. The cost of equity capital is 15 percent. All investments are financed with equal proportions of debt and common equity. What is the firm's marginal cost of capital if the corporate tax rate is 40 percent?

10. The Strong Corporation has the following capital structure which it wishes to maintain, at market value in the future:

Bonds (9% coupon)	6,000,000
Preferred Stock (11%)	2,000,000
Common Equity (320,000 shares)	12,000,000
	20,000,000

The common stock sells for $25 per share and is expected to pay a $1.50 dividend next year. Bonds have a market price of $900 each. They have 10 years to maturity. Even though the new bonds have a maturity of 20 years, they will have the same cost as the old bonds. Preferred shares are selling at par value. Anticipated dividend growth into the foreseeable future is 10 percent annually. The firm has a marginal tax rate of 50 percent. Compute the marginal cost of capital.

11. The Tiger Paw Company has no debt and a one year life. Currently it is valued at $100 and has a required rate of return of 10 percent with a beta of 1.5. If the expected risk-free rate is 6 percent and the expected return on the market portfolio is 8.67 percent, (a) what discount rate should the firm use on a project requiring a $100 investment if the project has a beta of 2.0? (b) Should the business firm accept the project if the expected return is 14 percent? (c) What happens to the value of the firm, assuming a one-year project life, if this project with a 14 percent expected rate of return is accepted?

12. You are given the following information about Moonstone Corporation:

Senior Mortgage Bonds (12%)	$4 million maturity value
Preferred Stock (8%)	$1 million maturity value
Common Stock (6 million shares)	$6 million maturity value
Retained Earnings	$1 million maturity value
Bond Price	$95 per $100 maturity value
Preferred Stock Price	$100 per $100 par value
Common Stock Price	$7 per share
Dividends	$1 per share

The firm considers current market values to be within the range of its optimal capital structure. Dividend growth rate is expected to continue at 2 percent indefinitely. Moonstone's tax rate is 40 percent. (a) Find the cost of capital for the firm. (b) For what projects is Moonstone's cost of capital the appropriate discount rate?

13. Westcoast Laboratories has discovered a new substance with the properties of a vegetable cooking oil with almost no calories. They estimate that it will take them three years to develop this product. At that time they think they will be able to sell the product specifications to a marketing firm for about three times the amount of the investment required today to set up the test laboratory. Westcoast is an all-equity firm. They estimate the project has a beta of 2.5. The security market line is $k = 10\% + 8\%\beta$. Should Westcoast go ahead with the development?

APPENDIX 16A

COMPUTING BETA AND k_e FOR A FIRM

Oakway Company wants to estimate its cost of equity capital using the security market line. The first task is to estimate the beta associated with the firm's common stock. In simplest terms, β is an indication of the sensitivity of the rate of return on Oakway's common stock to changes in the rate of return on the whole market. Since Oakway shares are traded on an exchange, the rate of return for each period may be computed using the formula

$$r_t = \frac{D_{t+1} + P_{t+1} - P_t}{P_t}$$

where r_t is the actual rate of return over some period, say 1 month or 1 year, D_{t+1} is the dividend paid at the end of the period, and $P_{t+1} - P_t$ is the capital gain or loss from share price change over the period. The rate of return on the market may be calculated in the same way, using a market index such as the Standard and Poor's Index of 500 stocks. Once these returns have been computed, they can be plotted on a graph such as Figure 16A-1 and a regression line can be calculated. The slope of that line is the beta (β) for common stock. That slope is a relative measure of the *sensitivity* of movements in common stock rate of return to the market rate of return. The steeper the slope, the riskier the security, because it is then more sensitive to movements of returns in the whole market.

In Table 16A-1 we show the actual calculation of beta for Oakway shares. Those who have had a basic statistics course may want to follow the calculation. However, this is not essential. It is important to know what beta represents and how it might be used to compute k_e, but the essentials of risk–return analysis will not be lost if the calculations are not readily understood.

Figure 16A-1   *The Relation Between Firm and Market Returns*

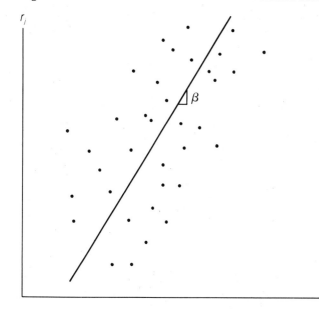

Table 16A–1 *Calculation of Beta for Oakway Company*

Time	1 Rate of Return on Common Stock Index, r_{mt}	2 Difference, $r_{mt} - \bar{r}_m$	3 $(r_{mt} - \bar{r}_m)^2$	4 Rate of Return on Oakway Common Stock, r_{jt}	5 Difference, $r_{jt} - \bar{r}_j$	6 Product of Deviations, $(r_{mt} - \bar{r}_m)(r_{jt} - \bar{r}_j)$
19×2	0%	-8.7%	75.69	-1.25%	-10.87	94.57
19×3	25%	16.3%	265.69	30.00%	20.38	332.19
19×4	-8%	-16.7%	278.89	-11.25%	-20.87	348.53
19×5	22%	13.3%	176.89	26.25%	16.63	221.18
19×6	16%	7.3%	53.29	18.75%	9.13	66.65
19×7	12%	3.3%	10.89	13.75%	4.13	13.63
19×8	-10%	-18.7%	349.69	-13.75%	-23.37	437.02
19×9	23%	14.3%	204.49	27.50%	17.88	255.68
19×0	11%	2.3%	5.29	12.48%	2.86	6.58
19×1	-4%	-12.7%	161.29	-6.25%	-15.87	201.55
Sum	87	0.0	1582.10	96.23	0.00	1977.58

Average Return on Stock Index, $\bar{r}_m = \dfrac{\Sigma \bar{r}_{mt}}{n} = \dfrac{87}{10} = 8.7\%$

Variance of Stock Index, $\sigma_m^2 = \dfrac{\Sigma(r_{mt} - \bar{r}_m)^2}{n} = \dfrac{1582.1}{10} = 158.21$

Average Return on Oakway Common, $\bar{r}_j = \dfrac{\Sigma r_{jt}}{n} = \dfrac{96.23}{10} = 9.62\%$

Covariance of Rate of Return Between Stock Index and Oakway Shares, $\text{cov}(r_j r_m) = \dfrac{\Sigma(r_{mt} - \bar{r}_m)(r_{jt} - \bar{r}_j)}{n} = \dfrac{1977.58}{10} = 197.76$

Calculated Beta for Oakway, $\beta_i = \dfrac{\text{cov}(r_j r_m)}{\sigma_m^2} = \dfrac{197.76}{158.21} = 1.25$

Column 1 of Table 16A-1 is the 10-year time series of annual rates of return r_{mt}, from a stock index representative of the market portfolio.[1] From this series, we can find the average rate of return $\bar{r}_m$ over the 10 years. Then, by finding the annual differences between the actual returns for the stock index and the average return in column 2, we can determine the squared differences in column 3 and the resulting variance of the rate of return of the market portfolio σ_m^2.

The Beta for Oakway Shores

Then, columns 4 and 5 permit us to determine the average returns from Oakway common stock, $\bar{r}_j$ and the annual deviations from that average. In column 6, the product of the respective deviations of actual returns from average returns for the stock index and Oakway common shares is formed. From this product the covariance of the two rates of return can be estimated. It remains only to estimate beta for Oakway by dividing the covariance estimate by the variance of the return on the stock index to form the estimated beta.

The estimated beta for Oakway is 1.25. To complete our estimate of the cost of equity capital k_e, we must estimate the security market line. Following the procedures used with Darras Amusement Company in the chapter, the estimated security market line is:

The Cost of Equity for Oakway

$$k_e = 8\% + (8.8\%)\beta$$

with $\beta = 1.25$, the cost of equity for Oakway is:

$$k_e = 8\% + (8.8\%)1.25 = 19\%$$

APPENDIX 16B

Assume that Company A wants to estimate the marginal cost of capital for an investment proposal having business risk different from the business risk of Company A. It identifies another firm, Company B, which is thought to have a level of business risk comparable to that of the investment proposal. The estimated beta for common shares of Company B is 1.5. The problem is that Company B has a capital structure different from that of Company A's target capital structure.

ESTIMATING k_e FROM A COMPARABLE FIRM

---

[1]The Standard and Poor's 500 stock average and the New York Stock Exchange Index are among the indexes commonly used to estimate betas.

Company A's Target Capital Structure

$$W_d = 0.20 \text{ , } W_e = 0.80$$

$$B/S = \frac{0.20}{0.80} = 0.25$$

Company B's Target Capital Structure

$$W_d = 0.40 \text{ , } W_e = 0.60$$

$$B/S = \frac{0.40}{0.60} = 0.6667$$

Company B is more highly levered, and its estimated 1.5 beta value includes a larger premium for financial risk. Company B's beta is a *levered* beta.

It is necessary to first find Company B's unlevered beta, which reflects the common degree of business risk. A formula for *approximating* an unlevered beta from a levered beta is:

$$\beta_u = \frac{\beta_l}{1 + (1 - \tau)\dfrac{B}{S}} \qquad (16B\text{-}1)$$

where β_u and β_l are unlevered and levered betas, τ is the corporate tax rate, and B/S is the debt/equity ratio. For Company B, the levered beta was $\beta_l = 1.5$. Company B's tax rate is $\tau = 0.46$ and, as just seen, the ratio of debt to equity is $B/S = 0.6667$. Using Equation (16B-1), Company B's unlevered beta, the estimated level of business risk, is:

$$\beta_u = \frac{1.5}{1 + (1 - 0.46)(0.6667)} = \frac{1.5}{1.36} = 1.103$$

Given the unlevered beta, Company A can then *relever* it to be consistent with Company A's target capital structure. The formula for relevering beta is a rearrangement of Equation (16B-1).

$$\beta_l = \beta_u \left[1 + (1 - \tau)\frac{B}{S} \right] \qquad (16B\text{-}2)$$

Company A's target capital structure has a debt/equity ratio of $B/S = 0.25$ and the applicable corporate tax rate is $\tau = 0.35$. The proper levered beta for Company A is:

$$\beta_l = 1.103[1 + (1 - 0.35)\,(0.25)] = 1.103(1.1625) = 1.282$$

This relevered beta reflects the business risk of the investment proposal to be evaluated *and* the financial risk of Company A's target capital structure.

It remains to estimate k_e for the investment proposal. If the estimated security market line is $k_e = 8\% + 8.8\%\ \beta$, the cost of equity capital for the investment proposal is:

$$k_e = 8\% + 8.8\%(1.282) = 19.3\%$$

If Company A had used Company B's levered beta of 1.5 without correction, it would have estimated a cost of equity capital of:

$$k_e = 8\% + 8.8\%(1.5) = 21.2\%$$

Failure to adjust for differences in financial leverage would have resulted, in this case, in an excessively high cost of equity capital.

SECTION V

Leasing, Combining Firms, and Inflation

CHAPTER 17

Leasing

Firms need not purchase an asset to acquire its services. The alternative of renting or leasing exists for a wide range of assets—from copying machines, typewriters, and wedding gowns to automobiles, freight cars, computers, office buildings, and manufacturing plants. Indeed, it would be hard to imagine an asset that could not be acquired through a leasing arrangement.

In its simplest form a lease involves periodic payments from one firm (the **lessee**) to another firm (the **lessor**) in exchange for the use of an asset owned by the lessor. For example, suppose that a chemical firm needs to obtain laboratory equipment having a $100,000 purchase price. The firm could raise the necessary financing and purchase the asset, or it could negotiate a **lease agreement** in which another firm (the lessor) purchases the equipment and leases it to the chemical firm (the lessee) in exchange for payments of $25,000 per year over 6 years. Such arrangements are quite common.[1]

Many firms act as lessors. Some manufacturing firms such as IBM routinely lease rather than sell their equipment to customers. Banks, too, through wholly owned subsidiaries, are heavily involved in leasing. A bank may own an asset directly and provide all the necessary funds for acquisition, or it may purchase the asset, then sell claims to lease payments to other institutions. A third group of companies specialize in leasing. They may purchase anything from computers and airplanes to machinery, then lease the assets to firms that use them in their business operations. Finally, some firms specialize in setting up leasing arrangements. They earn a fee for bringing together potential lessees and lessors and for helping to negotiate the terms of such arrangements.

The leasing industry is not a small, obscure segment of the economy.

---

[1]As a matter of convention, such arrangements lasting less than a year are called rental agreements rather than leases.

Over the past 20 years it has become a multibillion dollar industry. With the added impetus of the Tax Reform Act of 1981, which liberalizes leasing laws, the industry should continue to grow.

Whether the primary purpose of a leasing arrangement is to acquire the use of assets or to sell tax credits, the arrangement must meet Internal Revenue Service standards for the lease payment to be fully tax deductible. In the past certain rules of thumb were identified to distinguish between a leasing arrangement and a lending agreement. If the IRS found that the arrangement did not satisfy those rules, the lease payment was declared nondeductible except for a portion identified as interest on a loan and depreciation on the asset. Given the current uncertainty about the characteristics of a valid leasing arrangement, we do not pursue these rules further. Rather, we assume throughout our discussion that the full lease payment is tax deductible. The reader should recognize, however, that tax regulations must be consulted to determine how the IRS will view any proposed leasing arrangement.

This chapter discusses the more common types of leasing arrangements, together with alleged advantages and disadvantages of leasing compared to purchasing. Then a model for evaluating lease and purchase alternatives is developed and demonstrated. Most of our discussion proceeds from the view of the lessee, but we recognize that our model could be used by either lessee or lessor. Although a discussion of leasing from the view of a lessor is an important topic, it is too specialized to be covered in an introductory text.

TYPES OF LEASE ARRANGEMENT

The types of leasing arrangement that are possible seem to be limited in number only by the creativity of the lessor and lessee. However, from the view of the lessee, there are three general classes of leases.

Financial Leases

With a **financial lease** the lessee does more than undertake a contractual arrangement with the lessor for the use of the asset in exchange for a fixed set of future lease payments. The lessee is also obligated to maintain the asset in a satisfactory state of repair even though the lessee has no ownership rights. Lessors are frequently subsidiaries of financial intermediaries and have little interest in undertaking maintenance and repair activities.

Financial leases are typically not cancelable by the lessee. Therefore, the future lease payments are fixed in both annual and total amounts—even though the lessee may later have no use for the asset. Failure to make lease payments subjects the lessee to adverse consequences because the lessor can sue the lessee for default on the lease obligations.

In a **sale and leaseback arrangement,** a firm desiring the use of an asset first purchases it, then sells it to a lessor while agreeing to lease the asset it has just sold. It is a well-known form of financial lease. A **leveraged lease** typically is arranged through a financial intermediary. It is a financial lease in which debt and equity claims on the future lease payments are sold by the intermediary to outside parties.

Operating Leases

A second major form of leasing arrangement is the **operating lease.** Two characteristics differentiate an operating lease from a financial lease. First, an operating lease can usually be canceled by the lessee. The lessee has an obligation to make payments while using the asset, and he may be required to give notice of termination a specified amount of time before that obligation dissolves, but he is not automatically obligated for the duration of the original lease agreement. Second, the lessor typically maintains the asset. Any repairs or other expenses associated with maintaining the asset at a prescribed quality or level of efficiency are the obligation of the lessor or, in some cases, his specified agent. Automobile leasing and apartment leasing often fall into this category.

Tax Credit Leases

A **tax credit lease** is a means of buying and selling certain tax benefits associated with asset purchase in the guise of a lease agreement. The lessor is typically the owner of the asset *for tax purposes only;* the lessee retains title to the asset. In contrast to financial leases, in which cash lease payments pass between lessee and lessor, only cash payments for tax benefits occur in a tax credit lease. Since the unique benefits of such arrangements created by the Tax Reform Act of 1981 have generated considerable controversy, it is unclear whether Congress and the IRS will allow these opportunities to continue in their present form. See note 2, below, for more details.

ALLEGED ADVANTAGES OF LEASING OR BUYING

Many advantages of leasing over buying (or the other way around) are alleged to exist; some of these are presented and evaluated below.

Greater Flexibility of Leasing

It is sometimes claimed that leasing is superior to buying because the lessee can, in the event of a change in future needs, escape the lease by canceling it. This argument clearly applies to operating leases, since, typically, financial leases are not cancelable.

The opposing argument is that a cancelable lease agreement raises the risk to the lessor that future lease receipts will stop and that a delay will ensue while a new lessee for the asset can be found on future, as yet undefined, terms. This contingency is potentially costly for the lessor. Following the dictum "There's no such thing as a free lunch," the lessor can be expected to charge a higher lease payment in order to be compensated for that potential cost. Therefore, the lessee must pay for the right to cancel and it is always possible to pay too much. In any case, the right to cancel is never free.

Escaping Risks of Technological Obsolescence

Sometimes assets are rapidly outmoded and replacement is desirable because of a fast rate of change in technology. Some have claimed that leasing is ideal in this situation because the lessor can avoid bearing the risk of significant declines in the market value of obsolete assets.

In opposition, it is argued that *someone* must bear the costs of such risks. Risk of technological obsolescence does not disappear simply because an asset is leased. The lessor is the bearer of that risk and can be expected to require compensation for that role. If both lessor and lessee foresee the same rate of obsolescence for an asset, the costs of such obsolescence will be seen as no different between leasing and buying. The lessor will charge for that cost in the lease payment and, at least on that count, the lessee is no better or worse off than if the asset had been purchased. No "free lunch" is available through leasing.

Evading Restrictive Covenants of a Loan

Sometimes existing loan liabilities of a firm involve restrictive covenants—preventing, the firm from the use of additional debt financing to acquire additional assets, for example. In such situations, it is argued that leasing is desirable because it permits the firm to escape restrictive covenants that do not apply to new leases.

Those opposing this argument claim that new lease payments will impair the safety of payments to other creditors of the firm because a greater proportion of the assets in use by the firm require the payment of fixed periodic cash sums in the form of interest and principal payments on debt and lease payments. The increased risk to debtholders will cause the cost of debt for the firm to rise in the market as the financial risk premium increases. Thus, the firm may make a *one-time* gain by the use of leasing to escape restrictive covenants of debt, but there will be *future* costs of the deceit. Either future debt financing will contain restrictive covenants against additional leasing or there will be higher costs of debt caused by compensation to debtholders for risk posed by future leasing. In both cases, the firm will eventually pay for the *one-time* gain: this advantage of leasing is not free.

Some assets purchased by the firm, such as land, are not normally depreciable for tax purposes. Such nondepreciable assets, when leased, are alleged to improve after-tax earnings because the full lease payment is tax deductible.

Improvement of After-tax Earnings

This argument ignores the possibility that the lessee must pay for the implied ability to charge off the nondepreciable asset for tax purposes through the vehicle of the leasing arrangement. For if the *lessor* cannot depreciate the asset owned and leased out, the lease payment must be higher than would be charged if the asset could be depreciated for tax purposes. Leasing nondepreciable assets must be as attractive to the lessor as leasing depreciable assets, otherwise it will not pay the lessor to acquire nondepreciable assets and lease them.

Leasing is not infrequently viewed as advantageous because it permits firms to obtain the use of additional assets over and above those that can be purchased under a capital budget constraint. That is, if a firm has exhausted funds available to finance acquisition of assets under a capital constraint, leasing may be used to acquire the use of additional assets that cannot be acquired by purchase because no more funds are available.

Avoiding Capital Constraints

This alleged advantage of leasing arises because leasing is compared to a very unfavorable alternative—not having the use of desirable assets because they cannot be purchased. If the leased assets can be profitably employed, it is not surprising that leasing appears to be advantageous. But is this comparison valid? Readers of Chapter 10 will recall that capital constraints are likely to be managerially imposed. Whether leasing is desirable is a question to be answered by relaxing the managerially imposed capital constraint and comparing leasing to a properly composed purchase alternative reflecting the cost of additional funds.

A lessor having relatively high tax rates can be expected to take full advantage of depreciation tax subsidies associated with assets it owns and leases. A potential lessee having a relatively low tax rate cannot gain as much tax advantage from owning an asset *or* leasing it as can the lessor. Some of the tax savings enjoyed by the lessor may be passed on, under competitive pressure, to lessees in the form of lower lease payments. Consequently, it is argued that firms having low tax rates *may* find that leasing is preferable to asset purchase.

Utilizing Tax Rate Differentials Between Lessor and Lessee

Opposition to this argument centers on its generality—suggesting that the existence of tax rate differentials between lessor and lessee may be a real leasing advantage but is not sufficient to *guarantee* that leasing is preferable to buying. Much depends on the level of the lease payment and on the tax rates, depreciation methods, and borrowing policies of the potential lessee.

Utilization of Differences in Depreciation Method

In a competitive leasing market, lessors using accelerated depreciation for assets leased may pass on some of their high, near-term tax savings to lessees. This behavior may be of special advantage to lessees using, if assets are owned, straight line depreciation methods. Therefore, it is claimed, leasing will appear more attractive than asset purchase.

Those in opposition to this argument would ask why the potential lessee uses the less desirable straight line method for tax purposes? Failure to use an accelerated depreciation method for tax purposes is usually suboptimal behavior for a firm. If the potential lessee evaluates the asset purchase alternative using an accelerated depreciation method, it is possible that asset purchase would be more attractive than leasing. Once again, leasing can be made to appear advantageous because it is compared to an asset purchase alternative hampered by a suboptimal managerial policy.

Utilization of the Investment Tax Credit and Depreciation Tax Subsidy

Some firms have such large tax losses or tax credits that they could not use either the investment tax credit or the depreciation tax subsidy associated with purchase of a new asset. In the simplest case, the firm's tax bill remains zero regardless of whether the asset is purchased. Such a firm can purchase an asset and sell only the tax benefits to another firm that has sufficient income to enjoy the tax benefits. The vehicle used to effect such a sale is the tax credit lease.

From the standpoint of the lessee, the ability to sell tax credits is a real advantage. But this is not a true advantage of leasing. The changes in the tax law permitting this action used the form, but not the substance, of a leasing arrangement. The law could have achieved the same result without reference to leasing simply by permitting the direct sale of tax benefits by the purchaser of those assets. Benefits of selling cash flows that the firm could not otherwise obtain can be attributed to the tax law, not leasing, and in that sense such benefits are illusory advantages of leasing.[2]

---

[2]There is considerable confusion about the exact interpretation of the new tax laws as they relate to leasing. Whether the law eventually will be *interpreted* as liberally as it was thought to have been written is uncertain. It is not unlikely that the main beneficiaries of the new law will be lawyers. For additional discussion, see "Many Planned Leasing Deals May Fall Apart in Wake of the Treasury's New Regulations," *The Wall Street Journal,* October 23, 1981. Also, John E. Chapoton, "A Clarification of the New Rules for Tax

Except for tax credit leases, every alleged advantage of leasing discussed above is answered by one of three counterarguments. (1) The advantage is real, but it must be paid for by the lessee; (2) the advantage is illusory because it is compared with a purchase alternative handicapped by suboptimal managerial policies or because (as with the tax credit lease) the advantage is wrongly attributed to leasing; or (3) the advantage is real but may not be sufficient to make leasing preferable to purchasing. Valid generalizations about the superiority of either lease or purchase are not possible. Case by case evaluation of specific lease and purchase alternatives is required before conclusions about a given arrangement can be made.

Need for Specific Evaluation of Lease and Purchase Alternatives

When a levered firm purchases an asset, some portion of asset value is financed with debt. For example, a firm with a target capital structure of 30 percent debt and 70 percent equity would finance a $100,000 computer with $30,000 of debt and $70,000 of equity. Of course we do not mean that the firm literally raises those exact amounts at the time of purchase, but in the longer run it seeks to maintain that mix. Borrowing 80 percent of the purchase price today would, therefore, require larger proportions of equity financing in the future.

LEASING, BORROWING, AND CORPORATE CAPITAL STRUCTURE

If the same firm entered a financial leasing arrangement, it would agree to make a series of fixed payments over the duration of the lease. These obligations cannot easily be canceled. Financial distress and possibly even bankruptcy can accompany violation of a financial lease contract as well as with violation of a loan agreement. And like principal and interest payments on debt liabilities, lease payments are fixed and so create financial leverage. Lease obligations are very like those on a secured loan and have similar effects on the firm's capital structure. Given these similarities, leasing might be viewed as a close substitute for secured debt financing. As a *first approximation*, therefore, we assume that leases replace debt on a dollar for dollar basis.

Consider, again, the decision to acquire services of a computer costing $100,000. Assume that the firm has a preacquisition balance sheet as shown at the top of Figure 17-1. Assets are $500,000 and liabilities are divided between $150,000 of debt and $350,000 of equity. The firm has attained its target mix of 30 percent debt and 70 percent equity.

Leasing,'' *The Wall Street Journal*, December 8, 1981. Furthermore, the new tax laws are not the sole motivation for leasing to make use of investment tax credits and the depreciation tax subsidy. Before the passage of that law, financial leases were useful to some firms unable to use these benefits. See the Anaconda Aluminum example in S. C. Myers, D. A. Dill, and A. J. Bautista, ''Valuation of Financial Lease Contracts,'' *Journal of Finance* (June 1976), pp. 799–819.

Figure 17-1   *A Comparison of Lease and Purchase on the Balance Sheet of a Firm*

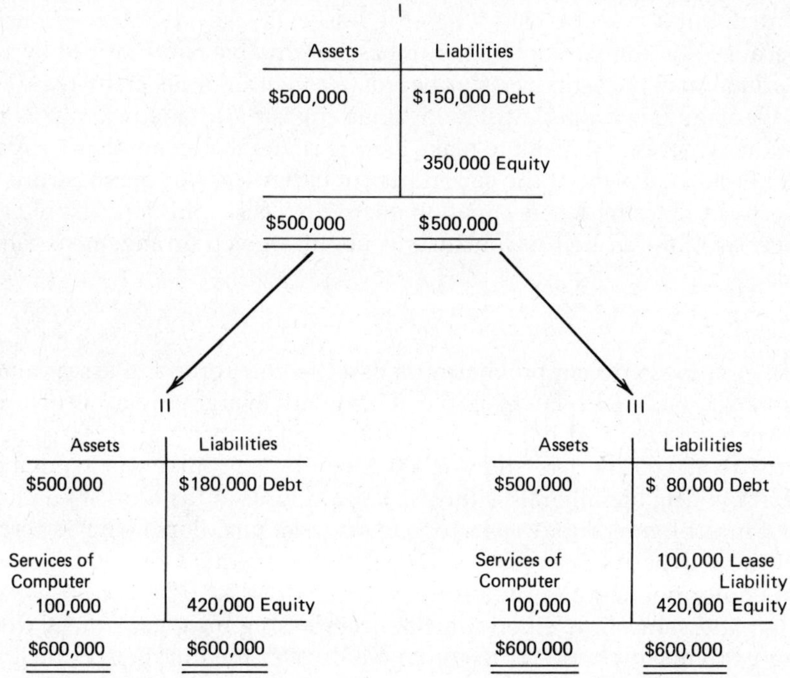

I

Assets	Liabilities
$500,000	$150,000 Debt
	350,000 Equity
$500,000	$500,000

II

Assets	Liabilities
$500,000	$180,000 Debt
Services of Computer 100,000	420,000 Equity
$600,000	$600,000

III

Assets	Liabilities
$500,000	$ 80,000 Debt
Services of Computer 100,000	100,000 Lease Liability
	420,000 Equity
$600,000	$600,000

Purchasing the new computer creates an asset of $100,000. On the liability side, debt increases by $30,000, making the total level of debt $180,000. That incremental debt will be viewed as a *secured loan*. In the event of financial distress, the lender has first claim on the proceeds generated by sale of the computer. Equity increases by $70,000 making a total of $420,000. These totals are shown in balance sheet II of Figure 17-1.

An *economically equivalent* balance sheet can be constructed if the firm leases the computer. Although the firm does not own the asset in a legal sense, computer services are acquired. Since those services cost $100,000, they are entered on balance sheet III as an asset. A lease agreement generates an obligation to make periodic lease payments. For simplicity, assume that the present value of those periodic payments is $100,000. An obligation similar to debt is created. Clearly, however, the firm is above its *target* debt ratio when a lease is viewed as debt. In addition to the $150,000 of existing debt, a new obligation of $100,000 gives $250,000 of "debt," and the debt ratio increases to ($250,000/ $600,000) = 0.417 or 41.7 percent. To maintain its target capital structure, the firm must reduce the level of existing debt and increase the level of equity. In this instance, the firm can increase its equity by

$70,000 and reduce debt by an identical amount. As shown in balance sheet III the liability structure becomes $80,000 of debt, $100,000 lease liability, and $420,000 of equity.

Note in comparing balance sheets II and III that equity is the same, but the lease liability reduces debt on a dollar for dollar basis when a firm attempts to maintain a target capital structure. For this reason, the lease/purchase decision has also been called a lease/borrow decision.[3]

Although this example highlights the role of leasing in capital structure planning, we must be careful not to take the comparison between secured debt and a leasing arrangement too far. The rights of a typical lessor *are* different from the rights of a secured lender. Lessors may have a right to the salvage value of an asset. Also, their position in the event of financial distress is typically stronger than that of a secured creditor.[4] Such differences may mean that a lease liability will not displace debt on a dollar for dollar basis as indicated in Figure 17-1; but without specific information to the contrary, the "dollar for dollar" assumption should yield a reasonable approximation.

THE CHOICE BETWEEN LEASE AND PURCHASE ALTERNATIVES

Techniques for evaluating lease/purchase alternatives depend in part on the nature of the lease arrangement. Although specific lease arrangements can vary widely, evaluation techniques can be grouped into two categories: tax credit leases and financial/operating leases. In all cases, evaluation of lease/purchase alternatives depends on *differential* cash flows between leasing and purchasing. Furthermore, all techniques require that the purchase alternative be separately evaluated as a preliminary step.

Evaluation of the Purchase Alternative

Before evaluating the lease alternative, the firm must decide whether an asset is worth purchasing. Evaluation of the purchase alternative is accomplished by discounting the incremental after-tax cash flows of the

---

[3]See Myers, Dill, and Bautista, "Valuation of Financial Lease Contracts," cited in note 2.

[4]Tax credit leases may be structured so that the lessor is an owner for tax purposes only. Since the lessee maintains actual ownership and control of the asset, the lessor may be in no better position than a secured creditor. For instance, *The Wall Street Journal* reports that ". . . the rules increase the financial risk borne by companies that buy and lease back to its original owners the equipment under lease. The regulations say that the company that buys tax credits in this manner may have to reimburse them to the government if the leased property is later sold or seized by a bankruptcy trustee or secured lender. That means the company acquiring and leasing out the equipment may have to wheedle some sort of waiver or approval from a troubled corporation's secured creditors to insure that the lease—and the acquiring company's tax credits remain valid." ("Many Planned Leasing Deals May Fall Apart in Wake of the Treasury's New Regulations," cited in note 2.)

project at the appropriate cost of capital *K*, consistent with the firm's target capital structure and the risk of the investment project. The resulting net present value indicates whether purchasing the asset will enhance shareholder wealth. If NPV exceeds 0 *and* if lease is superior to purchase, the asset should be leased. Decision rules applicable when NPV is less than 0 will be discussed at the end of the chapter. In either case, once the valuation of the purchase alternative has been completed, the firm is ready to evaluate differential cash flows between lease and purchase alternatives. Our analysis begins with a consideration of tax credit leases.

Tax Credit Leases[5]   As explained in the preceding section, a tax credit lease results in the sale of investment tax credits and the depreciation tax subsidy, which a firm could not use to its greatest advantage, in exchange for an immediate cash payment from the lessor. All other cash flows are assumed to be identical to those associated with purchase in this simple case. That is, a firm will purchase an asset using the same financing plan as if the lease alternative were not available. Then ownership of the tax benefit will be transferred via the leasing arrangement. That sale, for cash and a note, will be structured so that lease and note payments are identical and *the only cash that flows between lessor and lessee is the immediate (t = 0) cash payment for the tax benefits.* These flows are shown in Figure 17-2. When compared to purchase, the lessee gives up the right to tax benefits that could not be obtained anyway, in exchange for a cash payment from a firm that can use the benefits. No other flows will be affected by this transaction.

Evaluation of tax credit leases is demonstrated using Martin Lumber Company, a firm considering the purchase of a log loader. The loader costs $40,000, has a 6-year economic and depreciation life, and has an expected zero salvage value. A 10 percent investment tax credit amounting to $4000 would be allowed if the asset were purchased. However, Martin faces large current and expected future tax losses such that, regardless of whether the loader is purchased, current and expected future taxable income is zero. Consequently, the firm cannot offset the investment tax credit against income taxes and no future tax reduction due to the depreciation tax subsidy will be obtained. Those benefits are of no current use to Martin, but they may be valuable to another firm that has positive earnings and can use the tax credits.

---

[5]It is unclear how long this controversial arrangement will last. We include it in our analysis even though it may be eliminated or substantially altered by Congress because it illustrates the incentives that emerge from U.S. tax laws and shows how changes in contracting opportunities among firms can affect investment policy.

Figure 17-2   *The Relation Between Lessee and Lessor in a Tax Credit Lease*

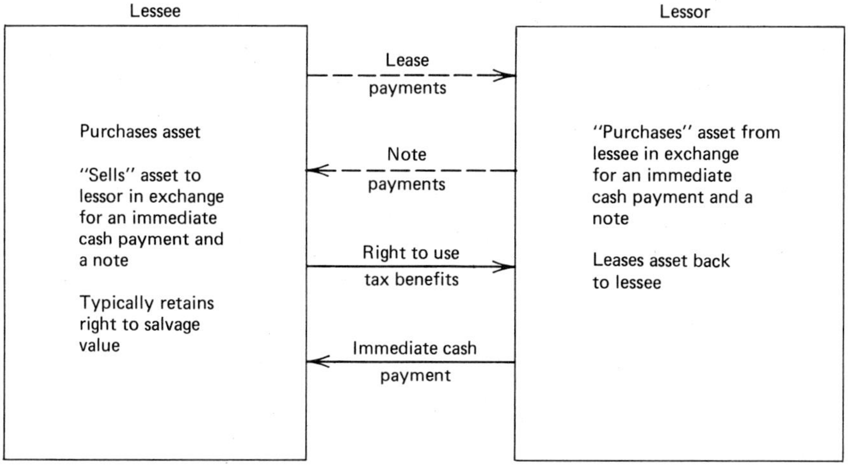

Lessee		Lessor
Purchases asset	Lease payments →	"Purchases" asset from lessee in exchange for an immediate cash payment and a note
"Sells" asset to lessor in exchange for an immediate cash payment and a note	← Note payments	
	Right to use tax benefits →	Leases asset back to lessee
Typically retains right to salvage value	← Immediate cash payment	

Since lease and note payments are set up to be identical, no lease and note payments flow between firms. Rather, both firms simply make bookkeeping entries.

In computing the NPV of purchase, Martin's management correctly ignored the unusable tax credits. But even in the absence of those benefits, the net present value was zero.

Martin's legal counsel suggested that the firm contact another company to explore the possibility of a tax credit lease. He emphasized that a prospective lessor need not be in the same industry as Martin. The key consideration is that such a firm have expected taxable income large enough to be able to use Martin's tax credits. In such an arrangement, Martin would purchase the loader for $40,000. Subsequently, the loader would be sold to the lessor, though the lessor would be the owner for tax purposes only and Martin would retain title to the equipment. In exchange for the loader, the prospective lessor would issue an interest-bearing note for $40,000 and pay Martin in cash for the tax benefits. Lease payments would be arranged to exactly equal payments on the note. Thus, the lease obligation would be exactly offset by the note obligation so that no cash changed hands for these payments. Transactions for lease and note payments would be mere offsetting bookkeeping entries. Payment for the tax benefits is the only differential cash flow between lease and purchase alternatives for this tax credit lease. Leasing is a disguised form of purchase and subsequent sale of tax benefits.[6]

---

[6]For an interesting example of a "real world" tax credit lease, see "Ford Set to Raise Up to $200 Million Via Sale to IBM," *The Wall Street Journal*, November 6, 1981.

Table 17–1 *Calculation of Depreciation Tax Subsidy for Log Loader*

Year	Total Depreciable Outlay	Depreciation Factor	Depreciation Charge, d_t	Depreciation Tax Subsidy, τd_t
$t = 1$	$40,000	6/21	$11,429	$4572
$t = 2$	40,000	5/21	9,524	3810
$t = 3$	40,000	4/21	7,619	3048
$t = 4$	40,000	3/21	5,714	2286
$t = 5$	40,000	2/21	3,809	1524
$t = 6$	40,000	1/21	1,905	762

The price paid by the lessor to Martin is a matter for negotiation. But the *range* of possible prices can be estimated.

The maximum amount that Martin should expect to receive is the present value of the tax benefits available to the lessor discounted at an appropriate risk-adjusted rate. Assume that, if sold, the investment tax credit would be of immediate use to the lessor; thus the $4000 credit has a present value of $4000. Calculation of the depreciation tax subsidy using sum-of-the-years-digits depreciation is shown in Table 17-1, assuming that the appropriate tax rate is 40 percent.[7]

Column 2 shows the depreciable outlay of $40,000. That outlay is multiplied by the sum-of-the-years-digits depreciation factors shown in column 3 to obtain the depreciation charges in column 4. Note that this accelerated method of depreciation creates a large writeoff in early years and a very small writeoff in later years. Multiplying the depreciation charges by the 40 percent corporate tax rate yields the tax subsidy in the last column.

Finding the appropriate rate at which to discount these flows is a more difficult task. The risk-adjusted rate must reflect the risk of the flows to the lessor. If the lessor has large, stable earnings relative to the tax benefits and those benefits are almost certain to be used, a low rate

---

[7]Sum-of-the-years-digits is used for illustrative purposes. The writeoff available through the tax law is more complex. See Appendix 8A for a discussion of the ACRS system. The sum-of-the-years digit depreciation factors of Table 17-1 are computed by first summing the numbers from 1 to 12, the depreciable life. That sum is given by the formula $N = n(n+1)/2$. Then, fractions are formed by dividing each year of depreciable life by N to produce depreciation factors n/N for t=1, (n−1)/N for t=2, . . ., 1/N for t = n. In the table, N = 21 for n = 6 and the resulting depreciation factors are there displayed.

may be justified. The lower the probability that the flows can be used, the greater the risk.[8] In this instance, we assume that a 12 percent rate is an appropriate required rate, which reflects the rate on secured debt financing. Thus, we can write:

$$\frac{\text{Value of}}{\text{tax benefits}} = \frac{\text{Value of investment}}{\text{tax credit}} + \frac{\text{Value of depreciation}}{\text{tax subsidy}}$$

$$= \$4000 + \sum_{\tau=1}^{N} \frac{\tau d_t}{(1.12)^\tau}$$

$$= \$4000 + \$4572(0.893) + \$3810(0.797) + \$3048(0.712)$$
$$+ \ \$2286(0.636) + \$1524(0.567) + \$762(0.507)$$

$$= \$4000 + \$11{,}993$$

$$= \$15{,}993$$

The maximum that Martin can expect to receive is $15,993, given the 12 percent discount rate. If Martin were to receive this price for the benefits, the net present value of the transaction to the lessor would be zero. To provide an incentive for another firm to act as a lessor, Martin would have to require less than the $15,993 maximum value for the benefits.

The *minimum* price that Martin should accept for the tax benefits is the amount of wealth sacrificed in the sale. In this example, Martin's evaluation of the purchase alternative produced a net present value of zero, taking into account that the tax benefits are useless under this alternative. Therefore, the minimum price for the tax benefits is zero. At some price greater than zero, but less than $15,993, sale of the tax benefits makes Martin better off leasing than purchasing. And, at the same time, the lessor will be better off because the value of the tax benefits acquired will be greater than the price paid for them. For instance, if a transaction price of $4000 is eventually negotiated, Martin will gain $4000 − $0 = $4000 and the lessor will gain $15,993 − $4000 = $11,993.[9] If Martin had found a *negative* NPV of $8000 for the loader, then $8000 would have been the minimum price of the tax benefits and the negotiating range

---

[8]See note 4, where the potential impact of financial distress in the lessee firm on the risk of the lessor's tax benefits is discussed.

[9]As might be expected, rules of thumb regarding the appropriate price for tax benefits have evolved quickly. For instance, Richard E. Rustin reports ("Small Firms Grow More Attractive to Brokers Setting Tax-Benefit Sales," *The Wall Street Journal*, November 23, 1981) that a 5-year lease generates a cash payment from the lessor of about 20 percent of the value of the assets. However, one must be wary of such rules for general application.

would have lain between $8000 and $15,993. In this instance $8000 is the minimum price because the asset will have a net present value *less than zero* and consequently should not be leased or purchased if the firm is to be paid less than $8000.

Financial Leases   A standard financial lease may be motivated, in part, by the desire to sell tax benefits that cannot be used; however, there are substantial differences of incremental cash flows between a tax credit lease and a financial lease as well as between a financial lease and purchase.

First, the initial investment is eliminated through a financial leasing arrangement. In the previous example, Martin Lumber actually purchased the log loader before transferring the assets to the lessor. That transfer of ownership for tax purposes generated a cash inflow for the tax benefits and a promissory note from the lessor. But lease payments offset the payments on the note. From the standpoint of the lessee, the only difference between purchase and a tax credit lease is the initial cash inflow for the tax benefits. A standard financial lease would normally entail no such flow. Either the asset would be purchased directly by the lessor or it could be purchased from the lessee for the full purchase price in a sale–leaseback arrangement. Since the initial outlay is avoided, it is treated as a positive cash flow to the lessee when a financial lease is compared to purchase.

Second, in a financial lease, the lessee gives up both the investment tax credit and the depreciation tax subsidy that could be used if the asset were purchased. Salvage value, as well, may be lost if the lessor rather than the lessee can dispose of the asset at the end of its economically useful life. All three of these incremental flows are negative when lease is compared to purchase.

Third, the lessee incurs lease payments. Those payments typically occur at the beginning of each period and they are tax deductible. Any lease payment is viewed here as decreasing the firm's tax liability immediately, so a firm that makes lease payments at the beginning of each period does not have to wait until the end of the period to gain a tax benefit. When compared to purchase, these after-tax flows are clearly negative.[10]

Financial Lease Evaluation Without Salvage Value   To illustrate evaluation of a financial lease, we turn again to Martin Lumber Company. In

---

[10]Depending on the specific terms of the lease, the exact timing of cash flows may differ from the sequence described in each of the paragraphs above. For instance, lease payments at the beginning of the period might be viewed as affecting tax payments at the end of the period. An analyst could easily determine the appropriate timing from a detailed study of the lease agreement and company policies.

Table 17–2   *Differential Cash Flows Associated with Leasing the Log Loader*

	Cash Flow						
	$t = 0$	$t = 1$	$t = 2$	$t = 3$	$t = 4$	$t = 5$	$t = 6$
1. Outlay if Loader Is Purchased	+$40,000						
2. Investment Tax Credit		−$4,000					
3. Depreciation Tax Subsidy		−4,572	−$3801	−$3048	−$2286	−$1524	−$762
4. After-tax Lease Payment	−5,400	−5,400	−5400	−5400	−5400	−5400	0
5. Net Cash Flows from Leasing	+$34,600	−$13,972	−$9201	−$8448	−$7686	−$6924	−$726

contrast to the preceding example, Martin Lumber is now assumed to be able to make full use of the investment tax credit and the depreciation tax subsidy if the asset is purchased. The net present value, taking into account those benefits, is positive, so purchase is an acceptable alternative. This illustration is further simplified because the log loader has no salvage value. The effect of salvage value on the analysis is deferred to a later section.

In the course of investigating methods of acquiring the use of a log loader, Martin was told that a financial lease arrangement leaving all responsibility for maintenance and repairs to Martin could be negotiated. In subsequent negotiations, the prospective lessor offered Martin a 6-year lease with annual payments of $9000 due at the beginning of each year. The question is whether lease or purchase is the preferred alternative. The first task is to identify the differential cash flows from leasing as shown in Table 17-2.

Leasing saves the $40,000 initial outlay for the loader. That positive flow is shown in line 1 at $t = 0$. But both the investment tax credit and the depreciation tax subsidy associated with ownership are lost.[11] Those outflows appear in lines 2 and 3, respectively. Calculation of the depreciation tax subsidy using sum-of-the-years-digits depreciation was shown in Table 17-1.

Lease payments (L) are $9000 per year, payable at the beginning of each year. If the firm has taxable income greater than the lease payment

---

[11]Without proper qualification, the word "lost" may be misinterpreted. Although the lessee does not obtain the benefit of these flows directly, he may still benefit in a competitive leasing market. The lessor, who does obtain the investment tax credit and the depreciation tax subsidy, may pass part or all of those benefits back to the lessor in the form of lower lease payments. The same reasoning applies to any interest tax subsidy that the firm appears to lose when leasing rather than purchasing. Lower lease payments may reflect any interest tax subsidy gained by the lessor.

in each year, after-tax cash flows become $L (1 - \tau) = \$9000 (1 - 0.4) = \$5400$ each year from $t = 0$ to $t = 5$. Those negative flows appear as item 4 in the table.

When the differential flows in each column are summed on line 5, the differential stream of net cash flows associated with leasing rather than purchasing are obtained. Those flows are, implicitly, the differential after-tax *financing* flows associated with the lease transaction. The lessor is implicitly *lending* \$34,600 to Martin at $t = 0$ in exchange for promised lease payments, the investment tax credit, and the depreciation tax subsidy. These flows must be sufficient to return that financing plus an approximate required rate of return to the lessor.

How can these differential net cash flows be used to evaluate the leasing alternative? There are a number of appropriate methods, but a simple and direct method involves computing the amount that the firm could borrow if the same set of payments were promised to a lender. That amount is called an *equivalent loan*. In this example the set of promised payments is the sequence beginning with \$13,972 at $t = 1$ and ending with \$726 at $t = 6$. The amount of the equivalent loan B_0 can be compared to C_0, the implicit loan in the lease. *If* C_0 exceeds B_0, the same future payments produce a larger implicit loan in the lease than could be provided by an equivalent loan in the marketplace. Leasing is then superior to purchase. But if C_0 is less than B_0, the implicit loan is less than the equivalent loan and purchase is preferred to leasing.

The equivalent loan approach assumes that a lease replaces debt on a dollar for dollar basis. The assumption may not be strictly true, but it is probably not an unreasonable approximation at the outset. An equivalent loan must have after-tax interest and principal payments that are identical to the differential outflows from leasing as shown on line 5 of Table 17-2. The formula for an equivalent loan (the logic for which is presented in Appendix 17A) is:

$$B_0 = \sum_{\tau=1}^{n} \frac{C_t}{[1 + (1 - \tau)k_d]^t} \tag{17-1}$$

The after-tax differential flows from leasing for $t = 1$ to $t = n$, C_t, are discounted using the after-tax, risk-adjusted rate on secured borrowing $(1 - \tau)k_d$, where k_d is the pre-tax borrowing rate.[12]

---

[12]By now many students will wonder what, if anything, happened to the interest tax subsidy in this analysis. After all, when a firm decides to lease rather than purchase, any *direct* interest tax subsidy is lost. Are we assuming a Modigliani–Miller world with corporate taxes as discussed in Chapter 12, where the value of the interest tax subsidy is τB, or are we assuming a world with both corporate and personal taxes (Chapter 13) in which individual firms are indifferent to debt and equity? The answer is that this form of analysis will yield correct results *regardless* of the world one assumes because the advantage *if any* of debt financing will be reflected in the interest rates derived from the market and in the

Since the differential cash flows of leasing have been identified, the remaining task before calculating B_0 is to estimate the appropriate risk-adjusted discount rate. That estimate requires a prior estimate of the risk associated with the combined investment tax credit, depreciation tax subsidy, and after-tax lease payments. The most frequent argument is that the discount rate appropriate for those flows is best approximated by the lessee's secured borrowing rate. That argument rests on the assumption that the risk associated with those flows is similar to the risk that an existing lender would bear. Although that assumption need not be correct, the firm's current borrowing rate does offer a convenient first approximation, which can be modified if additional information about the risk of the flows emerges from further analysis.

Martin Lumber's existing borrowing rate is 12 percent and its tax rate is 40 percent. The amount of an equivalent loan therefore can be written:

$$B_0 = \sum_{\tau=1}^{6} \frac{C_t}{[1 + (1 - 0.4)0.12]^t} = \sum_{\tau=1}^{6} \frac{C_t}{[1 + 0.072]^t}$$

$$= \$13,972(0.933) + \$9201(0.870) + \$8448(0.812) + \$7686(0.757)$$

$$+ \$6924(0.706) + \$726(0.659)$$

$$= \$39,087$$

Whereas leasing provides an implicit loan of $C_0 = \$34,600$ now in exchange for six future annual payments, Martin Lumber could borrow $39,087 for the same set of payments. Because $B_0 = \$39,087 > C_0 = \$34,600$, purchase is preferred to lease. (See Appendix 17B for a numerical example verifying that $B_0 = \$39,087$ is the correct amount for the equivalent loan.)

If Martin's management is uneasy about its use of a 12 percent discount rate, an alternative method of evaluating the lease might be useful. Using the internal rate of return method and Appendix Table C, it is possible to compute the implicit interest cost of financing implied by the differential leasing flows on line 5 of Table 17-2. The discount rate r^*, which makes the present value of differential outflows equal to the differential inflow at $t = 0$, can be found using Equation (17-2).

$$C_0 = \sum_{t=1}^{n} \frac{C_t}{[1 + (1 - \tau)r^*]^t} \tag{17-2}$$

---

lease payment required by the lessee. (See Appendix 17A) In addition, Equation 17-1 can be adapted to reflect the fact that an "equivalent loan" may actually be a composite of sources, some having tax-deductible payments and others that do not. Keep in mind, however, that it is the discount rate associated with the risk of the stream of payments C_t that underlies the derivation of Equation (17-1) in Appendix 17A, regardless of the types of claim that comprise the composite loan.

Since r^* is the rate on the implicit loan $C_0 = \$34,600$, r^* is the implicit cost of leasing. In the Martin Lumber example, $r^* = 0.209$ or 20.9 percent. Since $r^* = 0.209 > k_d = 0.12$, it is *cheaper* to purchase than to lease.[13] Indeed, even if Martin underestimated k_d by as much as 8 percent, it would still be cheaper to purchase than to lease.

The Effect of Salvage Value   Martin Lumber anticipates that the log loader will have a zero salvage value at the end of 6 years. As a consequence the firm does not expect to sacrifice any terminal cash flow by leasing. Suppose, however, that salvage value net of any taxes is anticipated to be $5000. How will that flow affect the lease/purchase decision?

First recognize that Martin Lumber (the lessee) will not enjoy cash inflows upon disposal of the asset. Therefore, salvage value is a loss (negative cash flow) at termination of the lease. To evaluate the lease, Martin must ask how much that differential outflow will add to the equivalent loan. The answer depends on the risk associated with that cash flow. Normally we anticipate the risk of cash flows from salvage value to exceed the risk associated with the combined investment tax credit, depreciation tax subsidy, and after-tax lease payment. Any lender would require a higher rate of return for that higher risk. We denote that higher rate of return by k_0.

Following the reasoning used to develop our expression for B_0 in the absence of salvage value, the *increment* to the equivalent loan B_0 associated with salvage value can be written:

$$\Delta B_0 = \frac{S_n}{(1 + k_0)^n}$$

where S_n represents the expected net of tax salvage value at termination of the lease.

Assuming that a discount rate of 25 percent is applicable to the salvage value of the log loader:

$$\Delta B_0 = \frac{\$5000}{(1.25)^6}$$

$$= \$1310$$

Adding that amount to the previous equivalent loan, we find:

---

[13]Remember the problems associated with internal rate of return when using this methodology. Net cash flows need not have the same sign over the entire lease period, so multiple internal rates are possible. Also, if NPV of purchase is negative and r^* exceeds k_d, one cannot tell whether leasing is sufficiently superior to warrant acquiring the use of the asset through lease. As will be seen, the equivalent loan approach aids analysis of the latter situation.

$$B_0 + \Delta B_0 = \$39,087 + \$1310$$

$$= \$40,397$$

Comparing $40,397 to $34,600, which was the implicit loan available from leasing, makes purchase even *more* desirable than when there was no salvage value. That outcome should be no surprise. If purchase is preferred before consideration of salvage value, it can only become better when salvage value sacrificed by leasing is included.

To summarize our analysis, leasing and purchasing may be compared in three easy steps.

1. Compute the differential cash flows from leasing in each period. Combine all flows *except* salvage value. Because the latter is likely to have different risk characteristics, it is treated separately.

2. Select the appropriate discount rates k_d and k_0 and compute the equivalent loan, where

$$\text{Equivalent loan} = B_0 + \Delta B_0 = \sum_{t=1}^{n} \frac{C_t}{[1 + (1 - \tau)k_d]^t} + \frac{S_n}{(1 + k_0)^n}$$

3. If $B_0 + \Delta B_0 > C_0$, the equivalent loan exceeds the implicit loan and purchase is superior to lease. If the inequality is reversed, lease is superior to purchase.

The Decision to Acquire the Use of Assets   Our analysis to this point focuses on the differential value of leasing. It does not reveal whether the use of the asset is desirable by either means of acquisition. That decision may be made using the following rules.

1. Acquire the asset by purchase if the NPV of purchase is greater than zero *and* $[C_0 - (B_0 + \Delta B_0)]$ is less than zero.

    Example: The net present value of purchasing an asset is $5000. The only remaining question is whether leasing is preferable. Suppose that the implicit loan on the lease is $C_0 = \$30,000$ and the equivalent loan is $B_0 + \Delta B_0 = \$40,000$. Since $C_0 - (B_0 + \Delta B_0) = \$30,000 - \$40,000 = -\$10,000$, the asset should be purchased, but not leased.

2. Acquire the asset by lease if the NPV of purchase is less than zero, but $[C_0 - (B_0 + \Delta B_0) + \text{NPV}]$ is greater than zero.

    Example: The net present value of purchasing an asset is $-\$2000$, so the asset should not be purchased. However, the implicit loan, $C_0 = \$60,000$, exceeds the equivalent loan, $(B_0 + \Delta B_0) = \$55,000$. The excess is more than enough to offset the negative NPV of purchase. Since $C_0 - (B_0 + \Delta B_0) + \text{NPV} = (\$60,000 - \$55,000 - \$2000) = \$3000$, the asset should be leased, but not purchased.

3. Do not acquire the asset by lease or purchase if the NPV of purchase is negative and $[C_0 - (B_0 + \Delta B_0) + \text{NPV}]$ is less than zero.

Example: The net present value of purchasing an asset is $-\$8000$, so the asset should not be purchased. However, C_0 and $(B_0 + \Delta B_0)$ are $\$60,000$ and $\$55,000$, respectively, as shown in the example above. The excess of the implicit loan over the equivalent loan is insufficient to offset the negative NPV of purchase. Since $C_0 - (B_0 + \Delta B_0) + \text{NPV} = (\$60,000 - \$55,000 - \$8000) = -\$3000$, use of the asset should not be obtained either by lease or by purchase even though leasing is preferred to purchase.

For the loader being considered by Martin Lumber, leasing was found to be inferior to purchase. With salvage value included, the equivalent loan was $B_0 + \Delta B_0 = \$40,397$, and the implicit loan on the lease was $C_0 = \$34,600$. Thus, we find that

$$C_0 - (B_0 + \Delta B_0) = \$34,600 - \$40,397 = -\$5797$$

The decision to acquire the asset falls under either rule 1 or rule 3 depending on the NPV estimated for the purchase alternative. If NPV exceeds zero, Martin should acquire use of the asset by purchasing. Leasing is an inferior means of acquiring a desirable asset. If NPV is less than zero, Martin should not acquire use of the asset. Purchasing is undesirable and leasing makes acquisition even more undesirable.

SUMMARY As an alternative to purchasing an asset, a firm may acquire its use by leasing from another firm. Typically, the user of the asset, the lessee, agrees to pay a series of fixed lease payments to the owner of the asset, the lessor, over a defined interval of time. The lease payments are tax deductible for the lessee. A *financial lease* arrangement requires that the lessee pay, in addition to the lease payments, for repair and maintenance expenses of the asset. In contrast, repairs and maintenance are usually the responsibility of the lessor under an *operating lease*. In addition, operating leases are cancelable by the lessee, whereas financial leases are not. Recent tax law changes eliminated many restrictions on leasing. It is now possible, under the guise of a "lease," for one firm to sell tax benefits to another. We have called such arrangements *tax credit leases*.

Many advantages of leasing over asset purchase are alleged to exist. Some may well be real advantages. Yet, their existence does not automatically mean that leasing is always preferable to buying. Only by comparing the costs of leasing under a specific lease arrangement with a properly structured purchase alternative can the decision to lease or purchase be intelligently made. No generalities concerning the superiority of leasing or buying appear to be valid.

We presented methods of evaluating both tax credit and financial lease arrangements. A lessee might approach evaluation of a tax credit lease by asking two questions, What is the minimum amount that the firm should accept in payment for tax benefits? and What is the maximum amount the firm should expect to receive for those benefits? Answers to those questions establish a range to facilitate negotiation of appropriate compensation for tax benefits.

A typical financial lease may be evaluated in three stages. First, differential flows between lease and purchase should be estimated. Those flows include saving of the initial outlay that would be required if the asset were purchased, lost investment tax credits and depreciation tax subsidy, the amount of the lease payment, and the salvage value of the asset if that value does not accrue to the lessee when the lease terminates. Typically, the resulting flows will have the appearance of an implicit loan where the lessee receives an initial cash inflow followed by a stream of cash outlays. Second, the firm should compute the value of an equivalent loan—a loan that has a set of outflows identical to those of the implicit loan for the lease. Third, management should compare the amount of the equivalent loan to the amount of the implicit loan. If the former is larger than the latter, purchase is superior to lease. But if the implicit loan is greater than the equivalent loan, leasing is superior. However, only the *relative* superiority of lease or purchase is established in this analysis. Before deciding whether to proceed with either alternative, the firm should evaluate the net present value of purchasing. If that NPV is positive, the firm should lease or purchase depending on the outcome of the leasing analysis. If the NPV of purchase is negative, the firm will lease only if leasing is sufficiently superior to offset the negative NPV of asset purchase.

GLOSSARY OF
KEY TERMS

Financial Lease   A long-term lease agreement, not cancelable by the lessee, in which the lessee has the responsibility of repairing and maintaining the leased asset.

Lease Agreement	An arrangement whereby one firm may obtain the use of an asset owned by another firm in exchange for lease payments.
Lessee	The firm paying for the use of the leased asset.
Lessor	The owner of the asset being leased.
Leveraged Lease	An instrument whereby the debt and equity claims to future lease payments from a financial lease are sold by a financial intermediary to outside parties.
Operating Lease	A lease agreement under which the lessor has responsibility for repairing and maintaining the leased asset.
Sale and Leaseback Agreement	An agreement whereby the ultimate lessee acquires the asset and sells it to the ultimate lessor, with an agreement to then lease the asset from the lessor.
Tax Credit Lease	A leasing arrangement in which the firm sells tax benefits it cannot use.

SELECTED REFERENCES

Anderson, Paul, F., and John D. Martin. "Lease *vs* Purchase Decisions: A Survey of Current Practice." *Financial Management* (Spring 1977), pp. 41–47.

Bower, Richard S. "Issues in Lease Financing." *Financial Management* (Winter 1973), pp. 25–33.

Lewellen, Wilbur G., Mike Long, and John J. McConnell." Asset Leasing in Competitive Capital Markets." *Journal of Finance* (June 1976), pp. 787–798.

Myers, Stewart, David Dill, and Alberto Bautista. "Valuation of Financial Lease Contracts." *Journal of Finance* (June 1976), pp. 799–819.

Miller, Merton, and Charles Upton. "Leasing, Buying and the Cost of Capital Services." *Journal of Finance* (June 1976), pp. 761–786.

Ofer, Aharon R. "The Evaluation of the Lease *vs* Purchase Alternatives." *Financial Management* (Summer 1976), pp. 67–74.

Schall, Lawrence D. "The Lease-or-Buy and Asset Acquisition Decision." *Journal of Finance* (September 1974), pp. 1203–1214.

Sorensen Ivar, and Ramon Johnson. "Equipment Financial Leasing Practices and Costs: An Empirical Study." *Financial Management* (Spring 1977), pp. 33–40.

Vanderwicker, P. "The Powerful Logic of the Leasing Boom." *Fortune* (November 1973), pp. 132–136.

QUESTIONS

1. If you were a lessor of an asset, would you charge a higher lease payment under a financial or an operating lease arrangement? Why?

2. Critique the notion that leasing is advantageous because additional capital for investment is very difficult for a firm to obtain.

3. Many hospitals are unable, by current regulation, to use accelerated depreciation methods to determine the costs upon which rates charged to patients are determined. In many cases, however, the full amount of lease payments can be reflected in their costs and hospital rates. Is this state of affairs an argument for leasing rather than purchasing assets by hospitals? Why?

4. "Our firm always leases computers because they become obsolete as quickly as improved computers become available." Comment on this statement.

5. Would you advise a firm to lease assets in order to preserve its borrowing capacity? Defend your answer.

6. A telephone company typically installs its own phone equipment when it provides telephone service to a home or office. What type of leasing arrangement is it?

PROBLEMS

Note: All problems in this chapter will use a five-year period and a 6 percent after-tax borrowing rate for debt. The corporate tax rate is 40 percent. Assets will be fully depreciated over five years in all problems. Lease payments are made at the beginning of each year. An investment tax credit of 10 percent is available on all assets and realized at $t = 1$. Salvage value is given net of all taxes. Use 20 percent as the appropriate risk-adjusted discount rate for salvage value.

Annual sum-of-years digits depreciation charges for a $100,000 asset is given below. The reader may obtain desired depreciation charges for any particular asset by multiplying by the appropriate multiple or fraction.

Year	Annual Depreciation for a $100,000 Asset (Sum-of-the-Year-Digits)
$t = 1$	$33,000
$t = 2$	26,667
$t = 3$	20,000
$t = 4$	13,333
$t = 5$	6,667

1. Cassandra Business Forecasting Company is evaluating the acquisition of a computer. If purchased, the computer costs $200,000 and has a five-year life. At the end of five years the computer will have no market value. The same computer can be leased under a financial lease for a five-year period for a $55,000 annual lease payment, payable at the beginning of each year. Assuming that the NPV of the computer is positive, should it be leased or purchased?

2. Jason Wunderkind, president of Argonaut Shipping, Inc., is wondering whether to lease or purchase a small cargo crane. The crane, if purchased, costs $55,000, lasts five years, and will be worth $10,000 in salvage at the end of its life. The same crane can be leased for five years for a $10,000 annual lease payment under a financial lease. Assuming that the NPV of the crane is positive, should it be leased or purchased?

3. Karl Boudreaux, president of Chicory Coffee Company, has an opportunity to obtain, by financial lease, a coffee roaster for annual payments of $18,900 over a five-year period. An identical roaster can be purchased for $75,000 and, at the end of five years, will have a salvage value of $5000. Linear Trend, the firm's accountant, has determined that, using straight line depreciation, leasing is the best course of action. The roaster has a positive NPV if purchased. Critique Linear Trend's conclusion.

4. The Ryan Brewery buys an asset for $300,000. The asset has a five-year life and the expected salvage value is $40,000. What is the maximum annual lease payment the firm should be willing to make if it sold the asset for $300,000 to a leasing company and leased it back under a five-year financial lease? (*Hint:* Find the present value of the differential value of leasing, ignoring the capitalized after tax lease payments. Set this amount equal to the expression for the present value of after-tax lease payments, and solve.)

5. Martin Maxwell is considering the lease or purchase of an asset that costs $100,000 and is expected to have no salvage value at the end of its five-year life. The firm's current and expected future taxable income is zero. Their accountant is investigating the possibility of a tax credit lease. Suppose that, if sold, the Investment Tax Credit would be usable immediately. What is the maximum payment the firm can expect to receive as payment for the tax benefits? Use 15 percent as the required rate to discount the tax subsidies.

APPENDIX 17A

This appendix develops the logic underlying the expression used to compute the value of an equivalent loan, Equation (17-1).

Table 17A-1 illustrates the underlying structure of the problem. Since an equivalent loan must have cash payments after taxes that are identical to the differential cash flows from leasing, we begin in panel A by equating the after-tax cash flow from leasing C_t with after-tax principal and interest payments from the equivalent loan. Differential cash flows from leasing include any investment tax credit, the depreciation tax subsidy, and after-tax lease payments. Salvage value is not included in these flows. As in the chapter text, it is valued separately. Two reasons underlie this decision. First, salvage value would appear to have a magnitude of risk entirely different from the other differential flows. Second, we assume that normally salvage value will not support a debt contract with tax deductible interest payments.

Cash flows from the equivalent loan are easily described. At $t = 1$, interest payments are computed as the appropriate borrowing rate k_d times the total amount of the equivalent loan outstanding at $t = 0$, B_0. Since those payments are tax deductible, the pre-tax cost is multiplied by $(1 - \tau)$. In addition, the firm pays part of the principal. That payment is B_0, the equivalent loan at $t = 0$, minus the equivalent loan at $t = 1$, B_1. Note that after-tax principal and interest are equated to differential lease flows at each time t. The only expression in panel A that has a slightly different form is the expression at $t = n$, the termination of the lease. After that last payment is made, there will be no further debt outstanding. All the equivalent loan at $t = n - 1$ is repaid at the end of the last period, so the principal payment is simply B_{n-1}.

Turning to panel B, we compute the amount of borrowing at any time t by solving the cash flow equality shown in panel A for the equivalent loan at the beginning of the period. For instance, the cash flow equality at $t = 1$ from panel A is:

$$C_1 = (1 - \tau)k_d B_0 + (B_0 - B_1)$$

which implies that:

$$C_1 + B_1 = B_0 [1 + (1 - \tau)k_d]$$

so:

$$B_0 = \frac{C_1 + B_1}{1 + (1 - \tau)k_d}$$

DERIVATION OF THE LEASING MODEL

Table 17A–1   *Deriving Equivalent Loans for Lease Cash Flows*

A. Setting Up the Cash Flows

	Differential After-tax Cash Flow from Leasing		Differential After-tax Cash Flow from Borrowing
$t = 1$	C_1	$=$	$(1 - \tau)k_d B_0 + (B_0 - B_1)$
$t = 2$	C_2	$=$	$(1 - \tau)k_d B_1 + (B_1 - B_2)$
$t = 3$	C_3	$=$	$(1 - \tau)k_d B_2 + (B_2 - B_3)$
.	.	.	.
.	.	.	.
.	.	.	.
$t = n - 1$	C_{n-1}	$=$	$(1 - \tau)k_d B_{n-2} + (B_{n-2} - B_{n-3})$
$t = n$	C_n	$=$	$(1 - \tau)k_d B_{n-1} + B_{n-1}$

B. Amount of Borrowing at Time t C. General Formula for Borrowing at $t = 0$

$$t = 0 \qquad B_0 = \frac{C_1 + \boxed{B_1}}{1 + (1 - \tau)k_d}$$

$$t = 1 \qquad \boxed{B_1} = \frac{C_2 + \boxed{B_2}}{1 + (1 - \tau)k_d} \qquad B_0 = \sum_{t=1}^{n} \frac{C_t}{[1 + (1 - \tau)k_d]^t}$$

$$t = 2 \qquad \boxed{B_2} = \frac{C_3 + B_3}{1 + (1 - \tau)k_d}$$

.

.

.

$$t = n - 2 \qquad B_{n-2} = \frac{C_{n-1} + \boxed{B_{n-1}}}{1 + (1 - \tau)k_d}$$

$$t = n - 1 \qquad \boxed{B_{n-1}} = \frac{C_n}{1 + (1 - \tau)k_d}$$

as shown in panel B. Borrowing at each point in time is derived in exactly the same way.

The amount of borrowing that could be obtained at $t = 0$ can be computed in two ways. Starting with the last period, we can solve for the amount of borrowing at $t = n - 1$ because the cash flows from leasing at $t = n$ are known. Then we could substitute that amount of borrowing into the expression above to find the appropriate amount of borrowing at $t = n - 2$. Continuing in that fashion we would eventually get to B_0. Alternatively, we can recognize that through simple substitution as shown by the arrows in panel B,

$$B_0 = \sum_{t=1}^{n} \frac{C_t}{[1 + (1 - \tau)k_d]^t}$$

That formula is shown in panel C. We interpret B_0 as the amount the firm could borrow at rate k_d by making payments equivalent to the net cash flow from leasing. Clearly, if that amount is greater than the net cash inflow from leasing at $t = 0$, the firm should purchase the asset. If B_0 is less than the net cash inflow from leasing, the firm should lease.

In the text, Equation (17-1) was used to compute the equivalent loan at $t = 0$. Now each of the expressions in panel B is used to illustrate how the equivalent loan at each time t can be computed.

First calculate the loan outstanding at the end of the fifth year, which will yield an after-tax outflow of $726 at the end of the sixth year.

$$B_5 = \frac{C_6}{1 + (1 - \tau)k_d} = \frac{\$726}{1 + (1 - 0.04)0.12} = \$677$$

To see that $677 is, indeed, the appropriate loan to generate that outflow, calculate the interest payment by multiplying the interest rate times the amount of the loan. That payment is $0.12 \times 677 = \$81$. Because that payment is tax deductible, the after-tax outflow is only $(1 - 0.4) \times 81 = \$49$. Adding the principal payment to $677 to the after-tax cost of interest gives $677 + \$49 = \$726$. Cash outflows from leasing are identical to cash outflows from lending.

Using the same formulas the amount of borrowing for each year can be computed.

$$B_4 = \frac{C_5 + B_5}{1 + (1 - \tau)k_d} = \frac{6924 + 677}{1.072} = \boxed{7091}$$

$$B_3 = \frac{C_4 + B_4}{1 + (1 - \tau)k_d} = \frac{7686 + \boxed{7091}}{1.072} = \boxed{13,784}$$

$$B_2 = \frac{C_3 + B_3}{1 + (1 - \tau)k_d} = \frac{8448 + \boxed{13,784}}{1.072} = \boxed{20,739}$$

$$B_1 = \frac{C_2 + B_2}{1 + (1 - \tau)k_d} = \frac{9201 + \boxed{20,739}}{1.072} = \boxed{27,929}$$

$$B_0 = \frac{C_1 + B_1}{1 + (1 - \tau)k_d} = \frac{13,972 + \boxed{27,929}}{1.072} = 39,087$$

Each amount of borrowing appears in the second row of Table 17B-1.

Having shown all these calculations, which yield equivalent loans at each time t, we hasten to add that those calculations are not necessary to evaluate a prospective leasing arrangement. In the case of Martin Lumber, an analyst need only compare the implicit loan associated with leasing—$34,600—with the amount of the equivalent loan at the same time—$39,087. For the same set of payments, one would always choose the alternative that would provide the largest immediate cash inflow.

APPENDIX 17B

**VERIFI-
CATION OF
THE
EQUIVALENT
LOAN**

The Martin Logging example in Table 17-2 of the text resulted in an equivalent loan of $B_0 = \$39,087$. This loan was the maximum amount that could be borrowed at a 12 percent interest rate by promising the after-tax future cash flows on line 5 of Table 17-2.

Table 17B-1 provides a numerical example verifying that a truly equivalent loan has been created. Line 1 identifies each of the cash flows associated with leasing that is to be used as a reference. Principal balances of the equivalent loan outstanding appear in line 2. Starting with $39,087 and a 12 percent rate of interest, the interest payment on the equivalent loan in the first year would be $0.12 \times \$39,087 = \$4690$. That amount is shown in line 3. After taxes, the effective interest payment appearing in line 4 is $(1 - 0.4) \times \$4690 = \$2814$. But to have an equivalent loan outflow identical to that implicit in the lease, the firm must reduce principal on the equivalent loan so that the total outflow at the end of the first year ($t = 1$) is $13,972, which is equal to the lease payment at $t = 1$. Principal must be reduced by $\$13,972 - \$2814 = \$11,158$. That principal payment appears in line 5. Given that payment, the amount of the loan outstanding at the end of the first year is $\$39,087 - \$11,158 = \$27,929$, the same as the original amount of the loan; that amount appears in line 2.

Now the whole process begins anew as the interest expense at the end of the second year ($t = 2$) is calculated using the principal balance at the end of the first year. If these calculations are repeated each year, a series of principal and interest payments as shown in line 6 will be created. If the amount of the loan has been correctly calculated, that series of payments will be identical to the differential flows from leasing. At termination of the lease the loan would be retired and there will be no further payments.

This example shows that $39,087 is, indeed, the equivalent loan.

Table 17B–1   *An Analysis to ShowThat $39,087 Is the Equivalent Loan*

	Cash Flows						
	$t = 0$	$t = 1$	$t = 2$	$t = 3$	$t = 4$	$t = 5$	$t = 6$
1. Differential Cash Flows from Leasing	+$34,600	−$13,972	−$9,201	−$8,448	−$7686	−$6924	−$726
2. Equivalent Loan	39,087	27,929	20,739	13,784	7091	677	
3. Interest Payment		−4,690	−3,351	−2,489	−1654	−851	−81
4. After-tax Interest Payment		−2,814	−2,011	−1,493	−993	−510	−49
5. Principal Payment		−11,158	−7,190	−6,955	−6693	−6414	−677
6. Total Debt Payment After Taxes		−13,972	−9,201	−8,448	−7686	−6924	−726

<u>Comparison of Lease and Purchase</u>

Since the implicit loan generated by the lease at $t = 0$ is less than the cash flow that would be generated by an equivalent loan at $t = 0$, the asset should be purchased. For the same set of future payments, one would always choose to receive $39,087 rather than $34,600 at $t = 0$.

CHAPTER 18

Combining Firms and Internal Expansion

Earlier chapters on capital budgeting focused on internal expansion, however, firms can also expand by acquiring other companies. Such opportunities, which are often joined under the category of mergers and acquisitions, are **external expansion** opportunities. Conceptually, at least, acquiring or combining with an existing firm presents no unique analytical problems. As with internal expansion, the goal of the purchaser or *acquiring firm* is to evaluate the impact of external expansion on shareholder wealth. This goal remains paramount—the romantic folklore, regulatory restrictions, charismatic personalities that have come to be associated with acquisitions, and numerous articles on "merger movements" notwithstanding.

Mergers, especially among large firms whose shares are widely traded, generate considerable interest in the financial press. That interest stems not only from the large size of many such transactions but from the economic and public policy issues raised when large economic units combine resources. Many questions might be asked about these business combinations. (1) Why do firms combine? (2) Who gains when two firms combine? Shareholders of the buying firm? Shareholders of the selling firm? Both? Debtholders of one or both firms? (3) How competitive is the market for acquisitions? (4) Why do many acquisition attempts fail? (5) Why would the management of a firm fight acquisition by another firm when the price being offered is far above current market prices? (6) Do firms pay premium prices to acquire other firms and, if so, how large are the premiums? (7) How might an acquisition be valued?

All these questions could not be answered in one chapter even if all the answers were known; they do provide, however, some flavor of the enduring interest many people have in mergers and acquisitions. They should alert the reader to the breadth of the topic. In the following pages, we focus on the relation between internal and external expansion, the valuation of a potential acquisition, and the process of setting a range of prices for an acquisition. These topics provide a foundation from which many of the questions above may be intelligently addressed.

TYPES OF EXTERNAL EXPANSION

Expansion, internal or external, may also be classified according to whether it is vertical, horizontal, or conglomerate. A **vertical expansion** is one in which the firm expands into its supplier's business or into its customer's business. When a steel producer purchases a coal-producing firm or purchases land from which it will mine coal, it is engaging in vertical expansion. **Horizontal expansion** occurs when a firm expands its present line of operations. A food chain purchasing another food chain illustrates this form of growth. Finally, a firm might consider **conglomerate expansion,** which entails entry into an unrelated industry. If a meat packer enters the toy industry by purchasing an existing toy company or constructing its own toy division, it would be engaging in conglomerate expansion.

The various legal forms of combination are described in Appendix 18A, which also contains a brief description of the accounting treatment of mergers. For our purposes, although there exist several alternative legal forms of combination, we shall use only one—*merger*—to represent combinations generically. Furthermore, since the goal of the firm is to maximize the wealth of the owners, we must choose a perspective from which to evaluate mergers. Generally we view mergers *from the viewpoint of the buying or surviving firm*. The *buyer* is assumed to be the surviving entity and the *seller* is the firm absorbed.

In most cases internal and external expansion opportunities are mutually exclusive investment alternatives and evaluation requires selecting that alternative with the largest NPV, or in other words, the alternative that maximizes the wealth of owners. Therefore, the first task facing the manager is to compare properly all opportunities available to the firm. This process is illustrated in the next section.

COMPARISON OF INTERNAL AND EXTERNAL EXPANSION: JORGENSON COMPANY

The Jorgenson Company, a producer of sporting goods, is considering the expansion of its operations to include a line of women's athletic shoes. Two opportunities are available. First, a new plant might be constructed at a desirable site at Winona, Minnesota. Second, the firm might purchase an existing company to gain immediate entry into the market. Of the many firms producing women's athletic shoes, only Latta Shoe Company appears to fit Jorgenson's needs. Inquiry has already indicated that Latta Shoe could be purchased. Jorgenson's problem is to identify the best means of entry into the chosen market—internal or external expansion.

Internal Expansion

As with most investment opportunities, the Winona plant could be constructed in several different physical sizes, and a number of production processes are available. In the Jorgenson case, the initial technical and economic studies ruled out all but two plant scales, large and small, and two production processes, one relatively more capital intensive than the other. Thus, only four competing possibilities need to be evaluated for the internal expansion alternative.

The after-tax cash flows of each of the four alternative modes of operation are shown in Table 18-1. For simplicity, annual flows are assumed to be perpetual, and the entire outlay is assumed to occur when construction begins. Since new facilities can be constructed in a relatively short time, cash inflows begin 1 year from the present.[1] Note that the larger plant involves greater capacity and thus a greater sales potential. If the shoe is widely accepted and demand is strong, that demand can be met with the larger plant. Of course, larger capacity requires, for each corresponding type of technology, a larger initial capital outlay as well as larger *annual* capital outlays necessary to maintain productive assets. (Annual outlay replaces worn-out assets and is shown net of the annual depreciation tax subsidy. Refer to note 1 for details.)

Given the cash flows, Jorgenson must identify the appropriate risk-

---

[1]To avoid the distracting influence of tax adjustments, the cash flows in Table 18-1 are presented solely in after-tax terms. For those interested in these adjustments, a summary of such for the smaller (i.e., low capital intensive) alternative is set out for a hypothetical tax rate of $\tau = 40$ percent.

	Pre-tax Flow, C	After-tax Flow, $(1 - \tau)C$
Sales	$11,667	$7,000
Operating Cost	5,000	3,000
Annual Capital Outlay	2,500	1,500

After-tax annual capital outlays are pre-tax outlays less the annual depreciation tax subsidy. We assume that the average depreciable life of the plant and equipment is 7.4 years. Therefore, annual depreciation charges of $18,500/7.4 = $2500 per year are contemplated. Assuming that the firm must actually reinvest the same amount in capital outlays to maintain the plant and equipment, the pre-tax cash outflow is also $2500. The depreciation tax subsidy is (0.40)$2500 = $1000. Therefore, the after-tax annual capital outlays are $2500 − $1000 = $1500.

Table 18–1   *After-tax Cash Flows: Jorgenson Company, Athletic Shoe Project*

	Smaller Plant		Larger Plant	
	Low Capital Intensive	High Capital Intensive	Low Capital Intensive	High Capital Intensive
Annual Cash Receipts from Sales	$ 7,000	$ 7,000	$10,000	$10,000
Annual Cash Operating Cost	3,000	2,000	4,000	3,000
Annual Capital Outlay	1,500	2,000	2,000	2,500
Initial Capital Outlay	18,500	29,000	20,000	36,000

adjusted cost of capital to evaluate each alternative. Two steps are required. Jorgenson must first specify the appropriate capital structure to be employed in financing this and other ventures. Once that task has been completed, the appropriate risk premium, reflecting the risk of this particular venture, must be found.

After selecting the target capital structure, Jorgenson found that for the shoe industry, the relative market risk measure, beta, is higher than that for sporting goods. Therefore a cost of capital recognizing both the target capital structure and the risk of investing in the women's athletic shoe venture is estimated to be K = 10 percent.[2] That required rate exceeds the 8 percent cost of capital Jorgenson uses at the same target capital structure for evaluating opportunities in its lower risk existing sporting goods line.

Present values of projected cash flows appear in Table 18-2. To illustrate the computations necessary to derive these present values, consider the first column of present values of the smaller plant with low capital-intensive production technology. The present values of sales receipts and operating costs are computed by dividing each tax-adjusted annual cash flow by the cost of capital. This is a simple application of the formula for the present value of a level, perpetual flow. Thus,

$$\text{Present value of sales receipts} = \frac{\$7000}{0.10} = \$70,000$$

$$\text{Present value of operating costs} = \frac{\$3000}{0.10} = \$30,000$$

---

[2]We recognize that with varying degrees of capital intensity, it is highly likely that different required rates of return would apply to the different levels of capital intensity. However, we maintain the use of the same discount rate in this example to make the analysis less complex.

Table 18–2   *Present Value of Cash Flows: Jorgenson Company, Athletic Shoe Project*

	Smaller Plant		Larger Plant	
	Low Capital Intensive	High Capital Intensive	Low Capital Intensive	High Capital Intensive
Present Value, Sales Receipts	$70,000	$70,000	$100,000	$100,000
Present Value, Operating Costs	−30,000	−20,000	−40,000	−30,000
Present Value, All Capital Outlays	−33,500	−49,000	−40,000	−61,000
Net Present Value	$ 6,500	$ 1,000	$ 20,000	$ 9,000

The present value of capital outlays is composed of two parts, the initial outlay ($18,500) and the present value of annual after-tax outlays necessary to maintain equipment. That is,

$$\text{Present value of capital outlays} = \$18{,}500 + \frac{\$1500}{0.10} = \$33{,}500$$

To obtain the net present value, the PV of operating costs and capital outlays is subtracted from the PV of sales receipts. Entries for each column are obtained in this manner.

Now focus on the net present values. All are positive, so shareholder wealth would be expected to increase regardless of the alternative selected. The greatest increase in wealth would occur, however, when the larger plant is combined with low capital intensity. The net present value of that alternative is $20,000. Its nearest competitor, a large plant with high capital intensity, has an NPV of only $9,000. Clearly, of the two larger plant opportunities, the alternative with the higher NPV is the best internal expansion opportunity.

But can the firm rest its analysis here? No. Even though the best *internal* opportunity has been identified, the NPV from external expansion could prove to be larger. Internal expansion must compete with external expansion before management can reach an informed decision.

Latta Shoe Company   Of the many athletic shoe companies in existence, only Latta Shoe Company was a viable potential acquisition. Owner Judy Latta indicated that she would sell all the outstanding common shares for $20,000 (she refused to sell just a majority of shares). Upon purchase, Jorgenson Company would receive all the assets and assume all current liabilities plus a $10,000 long-term loan Latta Shoe has outstanding. Recognizing that some portion of acquired current assets is financed (offset) by assumed current liabilities, Jorgenson is, in effect, paying $30,000 for the firm's *net* working capital and fixed assets. Of that $30,000 total price, Jorgenson's assumption of the $10,000 long-term loan means that part of the purchase is being financed by the use of financial leverage.

Jorgenson realized that evaluating Latta Shoe required more than simply projecting future net cash inflows of that existing firm. For example, if the existing firm is not being efficiently managed, a very low cost change in managerial procedures might result in cost savings, producing even higher future net cash inflows. Also, proper evaluation would require that potentially desirable changes in the Latta Shoe technology be considered to see whether such improvements would increase net cash flow. Such potential improvements in managerial procedure and technology must be evaluated, to permit a valid comparison of internal and external expansion alternatives. Presumably, Jorgenson's internal expansion alternative reflects Jorgenson's best choice of technology and managerial procedure. To fail to identify the same for the Latta Shoe alternative would, if such improvements are worthwhile, bias the net present value of external acquisition downward.

Jorgenson estimates that without any additional investment, Latta Shoe annual sales will average $10,000. Potential improvements in managerial procedures should produce annual operating costs of only $6000, and annual capital outlays necessary to maintain the existing technology would be $1000 (all these cash flows are expressed in after-tax terms). But owner Ken Jorgenson did not stop here. He studied the possibilities of technologically improving Latta Shoe. First he recognized that without changing capacity, Latta's equipment could be modernized. That modernization would cost $5000 but would reduce operating costs by $2000 each year. Additional annual capital outlays of $200 would be required to maintain that equipment. These flows appear in the second column of Table 18-3.

Table 18–3   *Alternative Cash Flow Data: Latta Shoe Company*

	Existing Firm	Same Capacity, Modernize Equipment	Larger Capacity	
			Low Capital Intensive	High Capital Intensive
Annual Cash Receipts from Sales	$10,000	$10,000	$15,000	$15,000
Annual Cash Operating Cost and Taxes	6,000	4,000	11,000	8,500
Annual Capital Outlays	1,000	1,200	2,000	2,500
Added Initial Outlay	0	5,000	6,500	8,000
Purchase Price	30,000	30,000	30,000	30,000

Finally, capacity can be increased so that expected annual receipts from sales would be $15,000. That capacity could be obtained with low or high capital intensive processes. The latter would require an added initial outlay of $8000; the former would require $6500. Cash flows associated with these alternatives are shown in the third and fourth columns. In all cases, annual cash flows are perpetual, begin at the end of the first year, and are adjusted for income taxes.

As in the preceding case of internal expansion, the appropriate discount rate is presumed to be 10 percent. It is not unreasonable to assume that the cost of capital is independent of the *means* (internal or external) of entry into a new industry, since the relative market risk *measure*, beta, should apply to both alternatives. Even though the current financing mix of Latta Shoe may differ from the target financing mix determined by Jorgenson, future financing of Jorgenson Company will adjust for those differences, and it is the future financing mix that matters in determining the cost of capital (see Chapters 15 and 16). In short, a prospective purchaser *with access to capital markets* should evaluate a prospective acquisition as if it were financed with the target structure regardless of its current capital structure.

Present values for the four alternatives using the appropriate 10 percent discount rate appear in Table 18-4. The present values of sales receipts and operating costs were computed as shown for internal expansion. Included in the present value of all capital outlays are the purchase price, any additional initial outlays, and the present value of annual capital outlays.

Among the four alternatives, maintaining existing capacity while modernizing equipment yields the highest net present value. That NPV of $13,000 is more than six times larger than its nearest competitor. Buying Latta and making *no* improvements in equipment has an NPV of zero, whereas producing more capacity and employing a low capital-intensive technology results in a negative NPV.

Table 18–4   *Present Values of Cash Flows: Latta Shoe Company*

	Existing Firm	Same Capacity, Modernize Equipment	Larger Capacity	
			Low Capital Intensity	High Capital Intensity
Present Value of Sales Receipts	$100,000	$100,000	$150,000	$150,000
Present Value of Operating Costs	−60,000	−40,000	−110,000	−85,000
Present Value of All Capital Outlays	−40,000	−47,000	−56,500	−63,000
Net Present Value	$ 0	$ 13,000	−$ 16,500	$ 2,000

Now Jorgenson can choose between its best internal and external opportunities. Recall from Table 18-2, that the best internal expansion opportunity has an NPV of $20,000. Clearly, this alternative is superior to purchasing Latta and modernizing its equipment. Shareholder wealth should be $7000 ($20,000 − $13,000) greater if internal expansion rather than external expansion with Latta Shoe is selected.

Table 18-4 implies that management of Latta Shoe Company appears to be forgoing profitable investment opportunities. If Jorgenson can modernize Latta's equipment and reduce costs by $2000 per year, why can't Latta's management accomplish the same task? Alternatively, why doesn't Judy Latta increase the price of the firm to reflect the net benefit ($13,000) of these improvements? Assuming that other potential buyers exist in the market, someone may be willing to pay more than the $30,000 total price for the firm. By failing to modernize or make other investors pay for the privilege of buying her firm and modernizing, Latta is essentially giving away a portion of her wealth. Any time existing owners and managers are not exploiting available opportunities, profit potential exists for astute outsiders to purchase the firm and take advantage of those opportunities.

Perhaps an even broader issue deserves a more detailed discussion. Under what conditions will profit opportunities from acquisition actually be available? Will acquisition generally be a more favorable way of entering an industry than internal expansion? These questions are considered in the following section.

AN ANALYSIS OF REASONS FOR ACQUISITION

There are circumstances in which acquiring an existing firm will be the preferred means of expansion. But management can never rely on generalizations proclaiming such advantages. Only an analysis of the comparative benefits of internal expansion and external expansion in a particular situation can reveal whether a particular external expansion is preferred, or not preferred, to internal expansion. Many of the *apparent* advantages of acquisition can turn out to be illusory, as can be seen by examining the case of Silveira Construction Company.

Silveira Construction Company

Silveira Construction is a builder of freeway overpasses. Silveira has been observing the growth of McKim Homes, Inc., a builder of tract homes. Silveira claims to see great advantages in acquiring McKim. McKim's earnings have grown, and are expected to grow, at a much faster rate than Silveira's. Furthermore, McKim's management is much more capable than any Silveira could assemble to expand *internally* into the home building industry. Moreover, Silveira will be able to obtain a much larger market, and a greater share of the market more quickly, by purchasing McKim than under an internal entry alternative. Finally, since returns from building overpasses and building homes are not perfectly correlated over time, Silveira expects to obtain a favorable diversification effect to reduce business risk, and thus the cost of capital for the combined firm.

When Merger Does Not Benefit Shareholders

On the surface, Ron Silveira's reasons for purchasing McKim appear to make sense. Only one item is missing—the *price* of McKim. If the investors in financial markets were as well informed on McKim's prospects as Silveira, one would expect the current price of McKim shares to reflect all these advantages. The market, consisting of millions of investors buying and selling shares, should appraise future earnings growth, unique management, and market share in estimating future cash flows. The resulting market price that Silveira would pay for McKim shares should yield a net present value of zero. (This assumes that there are none of the unique benefits available *only* by formal merger to be discussed shortly.) Unless there are systematic pricing errors or Silveira is better informed about McKim's prospects than the rest of the market, there is no reason to believe that acquisition will provide any advantages over internal expansion—regardless of managerial or growth considerations. As long as those factors are priced correctly, the NPV of the acquisition will be zero.

But what about the diversification effect associated with combining Silveria and McKim? Recall that the relevant business risk for making financial decisions is the risk that cannot be diversified away—market risk. As measured by the beta of the entire firm, that risk reflects the sensitivity of firm returns to market returns. Though combining firms may certainly change the risk of the surviving firm, the market risk of *each* activity—heavy construction and home building—will be unaffected.[3] It is not the total risk of the surviving firm but its market risk that matters. Nonmarket risk is diversified away when investors hold the market portfolio. If shareholders of both firms are already diversified, there should be no pure diversification benefits for shareholders from combining Silveira and McKim. If those shareholders are not well diversified, the question is whether combining these particular firms is an *efficient* way to achieve diversification. Shareholders are more likely to find that they can diversify far more widely and far more efficiently by

---

[3]The combination of two assets will produce a beta that is a simple weighted average of the individual betas. See Chapter 4 for a discussion of the impact of selecting assets with different market risks (betas) on their combined beta.

Table 18–5   *Silveira–McKim Merger Conditions:*
Both Firms Properly Valued

	Silveira	McKim	Merged Firm
Annual Earnings	$ 1,000,000	$ 500,000	$ 1,500,000
Number of Shares	500,000	250,000	1,000,000
Earnings per Share	$2	$2	$1.50
Price per Share	$20	$40	$20
Price/Earnings Ratio	10–1	20–1	13.33–1
Total Share Value	$10,000,000	$10,000,000	$20,000,000

purchasing many different firms' shares in the market than by having Silveira purchase shares of just *any* firm to effect a diversification plan.

As an example of illusory benefits of mergers, consider the financial impact of combining Silveira and McKim. We examine two situations: both firms are appropriately valued by the market, and McKim is undervalued by the market. In Table 18-5, which illustrates the first case, the price/earnings ratio relates current price to current earnings. This ratio is a popular, but crude, measure of the cheapness or dearness of common stock to the investment industry.[4]

Both firms are worth $10 million dollars before the merger. In the absence of unique benefits of the form discussed later, which may make formal combination by merger desirable, the value of the merged firm will be $20 million, or the sum of the separate values of the firms. We assume that Silveira acquires McKim by trading Silveira shares for McKim shares. Since McKim shares sell for $40 each and Silveira shares sell for $20, Silveira's management must trade *two* Silveira shares for *one* McKim share. McKim has 250,000 shares outstanding, so 500,000 new Silveira shares are necessary to consummate the merger. After the firms are combined, 1 million Silveira shares will be outstanding. Note that this implies current earnings per share of $1.50 = ($1,000,000 + $500,000)/1,000,000. Although it may appear that shareholders are worse off because earnings per share are lower for both sets of shareholders, that conclusion is incorrect. It is not earnings per share that

[4]The ratio of price to earnings (P/E) is employed to simplify the valuation procedure. However, such a ratio must be used carefully. It is entirely possible for the cost of capital to change while that ratio remains constant. Also, a change in the P/E ratio does not always imply a change in the cost of capital. In this example, the P/E ratio offers a simple method of obtaining values without going through a more detailed present value analysis that would obscure the basic points.

matter but shareholder wealth. As we will now see, shareholder wealth is unchanged by this merger.

Consider the case of Chuck Gall, an investor who, before merger, owned two shares of Silveira and one share of McKim. His holdings are worth $80. These combined shares generated $6 in earnings and the *average* price/earnings ratio is $80/$6 = 13 ⅓. This "homemade" diversification yields the same benefit as does the formal combination of the two firms. After the merger, Gall holds four shares of Silveira worth $20 each. Again those shares are backed by $6 of earnings, so the price/earnings ratio is 13 ⅓. In short, the risk–return position of Gall is identical whether the two firms are formally merged or an investor simply holds them in his own portfolio.

Now suppose that a less well-informed market has undervalued McKim. Rather than $40 per share, McKim shares sell for $30 per share. Since Silveira's analysis indicates that McKim is worth $40 a share, he concludes that a quick purchase of McKim before the market (and McKim's current shareholders) recognizes its error should result in handsome gains for him and other Silveira shareholders.

Table 18-6 shows the basic financial data associated with the merger of the two firms. Silveira will trade 1.5 of its shares that sold for $20, for each of McKim's shares that have been selling for $30. A total of 375,000 new shares will be issued, so 875,000 Silveira shares will be outstanding after the merger.

To this point all shareholders are as well off as if no merger had taken place, for the market determines price and, as yet, the market has not recognized that McKim shares, or the merged Silveria–McKim shares, are undervalued. However, Silveira shareholders may consider themselves to be in a better position if the market does correct its pricing error, since they own shares in an undervalued firm with good manage-

Table 18–6   *Silveira–McKim Merger Data:*
McKim Undervalued

	Silveira	McKim	Merged Firm
Total Earnings	$ 1,000,000	$ 500,000	$ 1,500,000
Number of Shares	500,000	250,000	875,000
Earnings per Share	$2	$2	$1.71
Price per Share	$20	$30	$20
Price/Earnings Ratio	10:1	15:1	11.7:1
Total Share Value	$10,000,000	$7,500,000	$17,500,000

ment and future growth prospects. But unless the market does recognize its mistake, their wealth will be unaffected.

It is interesting to examine who gains and who loses *if* the market does recognize its error. Originally McKim had 250,000 shares outstanding. If those shares were undervalued by $40 − $30 = $10 each, the value of the merged firm should increase by $10 × 250,000 = $2.5 million. Since there are 875,000 shares outstanding after merger, the price per share should increase by

$$\frac{\$2,500,000}{875,000} = 2.857$$

or about $2.86 per share. Notice, however, that the original holders of McKim shares do not reap all the benefits of the market correction. Since they hold only 375,000 of the outstanding shares of the combined firms, their wealth increases by about 375,000 × $2.86 = $1,072,500. The remainder of the $2.5 million increase in value accrues to the original Silveira shareholders.

Unless one suggests that the very act of merger caused the market to correct its error, it is hard to argue that combining the firms produced any benefits whatsoever. Because the market made and corrected an error, and because Silveira management was able to hide the truth from McKim shareholders, there was a wealth transfer from McKim shareholders to Silveira shareholders. If no merger had occurred and the market corrected its error, each McKim shareholder would have gained $10 per McKim share. But because they traded each of their McKim shares for 1.5 Silveira shares, they gained only 1.5 × $2.86 = $4.29.

By detecting an error in the market and by being able to act *before* the market corrected its mistake, Silveira shareholders gained. Indeed, their gain is McKim's shareholders' loss.

The possibility of a firm's shares being undervalued in the market raises the question of whether the potential gain for shareholders of the acquiring firm, assuming that the market eventually corrects its error, is a unique advantage of merger. Apparently, it is not. Knowledgable investors, recognizing that the firm was undervalued, could include McKim shares in their own portfolios and await the day when the market sees the error of its ways and revises the price of McKim shares upward. No merger would be required to exploit an undervalued situation. Moreover, purchasing undervalued shares in the market may have certain advantages over actual merger. The shareholder does not have to take the chance that Silveira may have difficulty managing McKim—that is, that the two managements may not blend together well and that there will be a "falling out," with resulting internal difficulties.

This example highlights two important points. First, some apparent advantages of acquisition may prove to be illusory. If shares of the selling firm are properly priced to reflect all expected future cash flows and their risks, then its faster growth, larger market share for products sold, and unique management will be properly priced in the market. A purchaser will pay full value to the seller, and the net present value of the investment should be zero. Second, even if the purchaser's management detects that the seller is undervalued, benefits to the purchaser's shareholders will accrue only if the market corrects its error after a merger is completed. Even then, it is important to note that the purchaser's shareholders could have achieved the same result by purchasing shares for their own portfolios and not going through the merger process.

Some Possible Synergistic Benefits of Acquisition

But some real benefits of acquisition might exist to make that method of expansion equivalent or in some cases superior to internal expansion. Combining existing firms can increase net cash flows beyond what both firms could generate by themselves and it could reduce the cost of capital for both firms. These effects might occur when:

1. There are cost savings.

    Example: Some operations of the buying firm complement or duplicate operations in the selling firm such that cost savings may be achieved by combining firms.

2. The selling firm is mismanaged.

    Example: Appropriate managerial changes increase efficiency without requiring excessive cash outlays.

3. Total revenues can be increased.

    Example: Joint sale or use of the same marketing channels increases the demand for the merged firm's products.

4. The selling firm has tax losses.[5]

    Example: The selling firm may have large tax losses not usable in full by the selling firm. The combined firm may be able to lower its total tax bill.

5. There are imperfect financial markets.

---

[5]Tax laws do not permit losses of an acquired firm to be carried back to reduce the taxes of the acquiring firm. All or part of such losses may be carried forward only if specific conditions are met. Consequently, in valuing a potential acquisition that has losses, purchasers should seek expert tax advice about the impact of those losses on their cash flows.

Example. The selling firm and the buying firm have difficulty raising new capital because flotation costs are so high. Since there are economies of scale in raising funds, combining firms may make raising funds less expensive and thereby increase the value of the firm.

These five points do not represent a complete enumeration of all possible situations in which acquisition may have a positive net present value. But they do represent some of the more important sources of gain that a manager might wish to investigate. Such gains result from **synergy**—from efficiencies in production, sales or financing achieved by combining firms.

Potential benefits from merger when the combination results in either increased cash flow or a reduced cost of capital are shown in Table 18-7. There we compare a merger between Silveira and McKim (1) when there are no synergistic benefits, (2) when cash flow is *increased* but the cost of capital remains the same, and (3) when the cash flow remains the same but the cost of capital is reduced.

In the first column (no benefits to merger), all numbers are identical to those in column 3 of Table 18-5, where McKim was properly valued and Silveira traded two of its shares for one McKim share. In Table 18-7 we also assume a 2-for-1 trade of shares. But when the firms are combined and benefits to a merger exist, both sets of shareholders gain. Consider column 2; as a result of combination, earnings increase from $1.5 to $1.75 million. Since the cost of capital does not change, it is reasonable to assume that the same price/earnings ratio should apply to those earnings. Therefore, the total value of the firm increases to:

$$13\tfrac{1}{3} \times \$1,750,000 = \$23,333,333$$

Table 18–7   *Shareholder Wealth and Synergy:*
Silveira–McKim Merger

	No Benefits	Improved Cash Flow	Reduced Cost of Capital
Total Earnings	$ 1,500,000	$ 1,750,000	$ 1,500,000
Number of Shares	1,000,000	1,000,000	1,000,000
Earnings per Share	$1.50	$1.75	$1.50
Total Value of Shares	$20,000,000	$23,333,333	$22,500,000
Share Price	$20	$23.33	$22.50
Price/Earnings Ratio	$13\tfrac{1}{3}$:1	$13\tfrac{1}{3}$:1	15:1

or $23.33 per share. Unlike the gains that arose when McKim was undervalued, neither group of original shareholders gains at the expense of the other. These benefits of $23.33 − 20.00 = $3.33 per share are the direct result of combining the firms; they would not have occurred in the absence of combination. Investors could not have produced this gain on their own by diversifying to hold both McKim and Silveira shares.

Now consider the third column. Earnings remain unchanged, but merging the two firms reduces the cost of capital. Suppose that the price/earnings ratio that resulted after the adjustment in the cost of capital is higher—reflecting the increase in share value due to a lower cost of capital. In that case the total value of the firm is:

$$15 \times \$1,500,000 = \$22,500,000$$

or $22.50 per share. Again, these gains are the direct result of combining both firms, and both sets of shareholders gain because they were willing to combine.

Some Possible Pure Diversification Benefits of Diversification

In addition to increases in value due to synergistic expansion of cash inflows or reductions in cost of capital, it has been argued that a diversification effect may also increase the value of the firm. First, risk reduction attendant with diversification may increase **debt capacity** and thereby increase the value of the firm. Second, firms may provide diversification that investors cannot provide for themselves.

The idea underlying the debt capacity argument can be illustrated with a simple numerical example. Earnings of two firms, Roland Manufacturing and Stewart Dye Works, are shown in Table 18-8, which identifies three possible earnings outcomes for each firm. However, low earnings will not occur for both firms under the same conditions. Roland Manufacturing will have its lowest earnings ($500) under condition 1, whereas Stewart Dye Works generates its lowest earnings ($300) under condition 2. Both generate their largest earnings under condition 3. Both firms have promised $600 to their respective bondholders. If earnings are low and the full amount of the promise cannot be met, bankruptcy costs will be $30. Because bondholders of each firm recognize that there are bankruptcy costs, they pay a lower price for debt than they would in the absence of those costs. Payments to bondholders under each set of conditions are shown in Table 18-8.

Now suppose that the firms merge. Earnings of the merged entity are shown under each of the three conditions. The lowest possible level of earnings occuring under condition 1 is now $2500. That level of earnings is substantially greater than $1200, which is the sum of the promises to both sets of bondholders. Debt is now risk free. Combining the firms

Table 18–8   *Pre- and Post-Merger Earnings for Roland Manufacturing and Stewart Dye Works*

	Roland Manufacturing			Stewart Dye Works		
Condition	Earnings	Bankruptcy Costs	Payment to Bondholders	Earnings	Bankruptcy Costs	Payment to Bondholders
1	$ 500	(30)	$470	$2000	0	$600
2	3000	0	600	300	(30)	270
3	5000	0	600	3000	0	600

	Combined Firms		
Condition	Earnings	Bankruptcy costs	Payment to Bondholders
1	$2500	0	$1200
2	3300	0	1200
3	8000	0	1200

produces three results: the expected dollar returns to bondholders increases, the risk facing bondholders is reduced to zero, and bankruptcy costs are eliminated.

The new firm could issue up to $1300 (i.e., $2500 − $1200) in *new* promises without generating potential bankruptcy costs and making existing debt risky. More than $1300 of new debt must be issued to maintain bondholder risk at premerger levels. Debt capacity has increased. Furthermore, if there are economies of scale in bankruptcy, bankruptcy costs would be less than the sum of those costs for each of the separate firms.

Although it may appear that merger offers an advantage in this case, that advantage may be far more illusory than real from the view of shareholders. Unless new bonds are sold such that the risk and expected dollar return of existing bondholders are the same as before merger, bond value will increase and wealth will be shifted from shareholders to bondholders.[6] Substantial benefits such as an interest tax subsidy must accompany new debt financing or shareholders can easily lose when firms are combined. Risk reduction can work against rather than for shareholders.

---

[6]Complete development of this argument is beyond the scope of this book. The interested reader can examine the paper by Higgins and Schall cited at the end of this chapter.

In general there are three problems with the debt capacity argument. First, our understanding of the benefits of debt financing as discussed in Chapter 13 is limited and there is little evidence to support the existence of such an effect. Second, any gains from risk reduction are more likely to be captured by bondholders than by shareholders. Third, if combining firms does create greater debt capacity and wealth increases for shareholders, why hadn't more firms merged long ago? To argue that there are substantial gains from increases in debt capacity is to say that corporate officers have, over the years systematically acted against shareholder interest. Thus, although the debt capacity argument may have some validity *in specific circumstances*, it does not, at this time, provide a strong general argument for merger.

Equally difficult to substantiate is the argument that firm diversification provides a service that investors cannot provide for themselves. Even the sole owner of a machine shop who acts as proprietor, manager, and chief mechanic may find in the purchase of financial securities a far more effective source of diversification than could be obtained through acquiring other businesses. Certainly there may be instances in which firm diversification is valuable solely as a substitute for unavailable personal diversification, but as a general argument for acquiring other firms it is inadequate.

A Reminder   Even though our examples have focused on the benefits of diversification through acquisition, those benefits might be obtained through internal expansion as well. To the extent that firm diversification is valuable, either form of diversification may do. No *generalized* net advantage to either form of expansion emerges from our emphasis.

PRICE OF AN ACQUISITION   In most situations, the price of a business that is to be purchased is subject to negotiation. For a transaction to take place, the maximum amount a buyer would pay for a firm must be at least as great as the minimum price that a seller would accept. But if the maximum the buyer would pay is substantially larger than the seller's minimum, there is room for negotiation such that *both* groups of shareholders can benefit from the transaction. The maximum price the buyer will offer would be the market price of the seller *plus* the net present value of acquisition at that market price (reflecting the value to the buyer of increased cash flow resulting from prospective improvements) *minus* the net present value of the next best expansion alternative. In the case of Latta Shoe, the market price is $30,000. At that price the net present value from the best improvement of Latta Shoe in Table 18-4 is $13,000, so it would appear that Jorgenson would be willing to pay up to $30,000 + $13,000 = $43,000 for Latta Shoe. But this is not the case because Jorgenson already has an internal expansion opportunity with a net present value of $20,000. Since he would have no reason to take any opportunity that promised a lower NPV, the *maximum* that he should pay for Latta Shoe is $43,000 − $20,000 = $23,000, which of course is less than the $30,000 purchase price. At that price internal and external expansion are equivalent. The minimum price the seller would accept would normally be the current market value of the company *or* the best offer, if one exists higher than the current market value. In the Latta Shoe case no alternative values were given. If we assume that $30,000 reflects the current market value of the whole firm, there will be no transaction between Jorgenson Company and Latta Shoe. Latta's minimum price is greater than Jorgenson's maximum.

But this is not always the situation. Consider two firms, Reinke Asphalt, Inc., and Henick Storm Door, Inc., which have the premerger data shown in Table 18-9. Reinke wishes to acquire Henick, and the total shareholder gain Reinke expects to achieve by improvements after the merger is an estimated NPV of $1 million, denoted by ΔS. However, if Reinke were to enter the storm door business by the *internal* expansion alternative, the shareholder gain for internal expansion would be an NPV of $500,000, denoted by ΔS_A. Thus the *maximum* price Reinke should be willing to pay for Henick would be $S_H + (\Delta S - \Delta S_A) =$ $5,000,000 + ($1,000,000 − $500,000) = $5,500,000.

At the same time, Henick shareholders realize that their minimum acceptable price would be the current market value S_H or the best alternative offer—whichever is greater. If Henick also has an offer of $5.2 million, $200,000 above current market value, then Henick's *minimum* price is $5.2 million. Therefore the price *range* within which a merger could be agreed upon is between $5.5 million and $5.2 million. Henick would be interested in getting the merger price above $5.2 million and Reinke will try to buy Henick at the lowest price possible but no more

Table 18–9 *Precombination Condition*

	Reinke Asphalt, Inc.	Henick Storm Door, Inc.
Value of Shares	$S_R = \$10,000,000$	$S_H = \$5,000,000$
Outstanding Shares	1,000,000	500,000
Price per Share	$P_R = \$10$	$P_H = \$10$

than $5.5 million. Hence, negotiation enters into price determination where information is very valuable. If Henick knew Reinke's maximum price or Reinke knew Henick's minimum, that information would be advantageous in negotiations. Let us assume that the price finally negotiated is $5,333,333—or $10.67 per Henick share. Of the total gain in value (ΔS = $1,000,000) resulting from the merger, Henick shareholders would obtain one-third or $333,333 and Reinke shareholders would obtain two-thirds or $666,667.

Now assuming that Reinke agrees to pay cash and sells new shares in the market to raise that cash, the price at which they could sell stock would be the market price reflecting the premerger value for Reinke shares, S_R = $10,000,000, plus the $666,667 gain in value due Reinke's existing shareholders, or

$$\frac{\$10,000,000 + \$666,667}{1,000,000 \text{ shares}} = \$10.67$$

Reinke could sell 500,000 shares at $10.67 (ignoring flotation costs) and raise the $5,333,333. Reinke would have a total share value, after the merger, of 1,500,000 shares $\times$ $10.67 = $16,000,000. (Note that $S_R + S_H + \Delta S$ = $10,000,000 + $5,000,000 + $1,000,000 = $16,000,000.)

Reinke's original shareholders, as a result of the merger, saw their share value increase to $10.67 and the total increase in their share values was $666,667. Henick shareholders received $5,333,333 in cash, or $10.67 for each of their 500,000 shares. Thus both Henick and Reinke shareholders ended up with an equal capital gain per share.

Exchange of Stock

Rather than receive cash from the purchasing firm, the seller may accept shares of the buyer in exchange. Selling shareholders may prefer the exchange of stock to avoid having to pay capital gains taxes from their sale of shares in the year of the sale. Thus Reinke could give 500,000 shares of its stock to Henick shareholders to effect the merger. The 500,000 shares worth $5,333,333 paid to Henick shareholders would save the firm any flotation costs involved in a market sale of new stock.

The savings in capital gains taxes for Henick shareholders could be significant. Assume a 20 percent effective capital gains rate. The total capital gain depends on the original cost to the shareholder. Suppose the typical Henick shareholder paid $6 a share. If he or she received cash on the merger, a capital gain of $4.67 a share would be recognized. The 20 percent tax takes $0.934, or almost $1 per share. Capital gains tax receipts that the government would collect from Henick shareholders would be $0.934 $\times$ 500,000, or $437,000 on a sale of $5,333,333. In contrast, the exchange of shares involves no tax at present; only on the eventual sale of Reinke stock would capital gains be taxable.[7]

Instead of negotiating with the management of a company it wishes to acquire, a potential purchaser may resort to a tender offer. A **tender** is an offer by the buyer directly to the shareholders of the company it wishes to acquire. If merger negotiations with management collapse or are judged to be hopeless to begin with, the buyer can appeal directly to the shareholders with the tender. Of course, if the seller's management holds the controlling interest in the company, the tender is a useless vehicle to the prospective buyer.[8] The buyer's tender is usually set at 10 to 20 percent above the market price, to stimulate acceptance of the tender, and it is usually left outstanding for a limited period. If the seller's management wishes to resist the takeover, it must quickly undertake a campaign to encourage shareholders not to sell.[9]

Tenders

Firms may choose to expand by internal or external means. In internal expansion the firm is acquiring the tools, labor, and management that are necessary to generate enhanced future cash inflows. External expansion is the acquisition of another firm or unit of another firm to generate expanded cash inflows. Expansion, internal or external, may be vertical, horizontal, or conglomerate. Conglomerate expansion involves entry into a field unrelated to current operations. Vertical expansion involves altering operations to include some of the activities of the firm's suppliers or customers, and horizontal expansion broadens the existing type of operation.

The principal question for either internal or external expansion is whether expansion should be undertaken at all. If so, both internal and external expansion must be evaluated to determine which method maximizes shareholder wealth for the buying firm. Evaluation of internal and external alternatives requires evaluation of the scale of output and production process combinations for both types of acquisition. For *each* type

SUMMARY

---

[7]For shareholders of the acquired firm to avoid personal income taxes at time of acquisition, the IRS must rule that the share exchange is tax free.

[8]If the tender involves the issue of new shares, the stock must be registered with the SEC, negating any element of surprise.

[9]For a detailed analysis of tender offers, see the articles by Dann, Vermaelen, and Masulis listed at the end of this chapter.

of expansion, the optimal combination must be found. The wealth gains for shareholders for each type of expansion should be compared, and the alternative that maximizes the increase in shareholder wealth chosen. All opportunities are evaluated using a weighted cost of capital reflecting the business risk and target capital structure for the asset acquisition opportunity.

Many alleged advantages of external acquisition are illusory *if* the market correctly values all future cash flows and the risk associated with these cash flows. Among such illusory advantages are more rapid growth in earnings, unique managerial talent to be obtained from the selling firm, increases in market share, and benefits from diversification effects on business risk. If the market correctly values these advantages, the buying firm will pay full price for them. If the market undervalues the selling firm, the buying firm obtains real advantages because of the lower price of the selling firm. Certain real advantages of merger may stem from synergy. This results from efficiencies associated with combining firms. Such advantages can be obtained *only* if a formal combination of firms takes place. These advantages include cost savings, tax losses, increased debt capacity, and better marketability for securities of the combined firms. When the impact of diversification on debt capacity was discussed, it was argued that debt capacity may increase as a result of merger and that the ensuing interest tax subsidy could benefit shareholders. However, good evidence of this debt capacity effect does not currently exist. Above all, it is important to recognize that any improvement in debt capacity that might accompany diversification should occur whether expansion is internal or external.

Firms may combine by cash purchase or by exchange of stock. In either case, firms may be expected to agree on a purchase price that leaves neither party to the transaction worse off or, probably, both parties better off. Compared to a cash purchase, an exchange of stock usually offers shareholders of the seller an opportunity of deferring capital gains taxes.

When the buyer does not wish to enter into negotiations with the selling management, the buyer may use a tender offer to purchase shares directly from the stockholders. Selling stockholders expect a premium over market price. The use of a tender is not usually feasible if selling company management owns controlling stock and does not wish to sell.

GLOSSARY OF
KEY TERMS

Conglomerate Expansion	Combining of unrelated firms or operating units.
Debt Capacity	A concept of a limit on the amount of debt that can be sold.
External Acquisition or Expansion	Firm expansion by means of acquiring another firm or an operating unit of another firm.
Horizontal Expansion	Expansion of operations by increasing the scale of present activities.
Internal Expansion	Expansion by growth within the firm as opposed to acquiring a going concern.
Synergy	In this use, efficiencies of production, sales, or financing that occur when firms merge.
Tender	An offer directly to shareholders of a company by a prospective buying firm.
Vertical Expansion	Expansion into customer or supplier lines of activity.

SELECTED REFERENCES

Alberts, William W., and Joel Segall. *The Corporate Merger*. Chicago: University of Chicago Press, 1966.

Dann, Larry Y. "Common Stock Repurchase: An Analysis of Returns to Bondholders and Stockholders," *Journal of Financial Economics* (June 1981), pp. 113–138.

Higgins, Robert, and Lawrence Schall. "Corporate Bankruptcy and Conglomerate Merger." *Journal of Finance* (March 1975), pp. 93–113.

Lewellen, Wilbur G. "A Pure Financial Rationale for Conglomerate Merger." *Journal of Finance* (May 1971), pp. 521–537.

Masulis, Ronald. "Stock Repurchases by Tender Offer: An Analysis of the Causes of Common Stock Price Changes," *Journal of Finance* (May 1980), pp. 305–319.

Myers, Stewart. "Introduction: A Framework for Evaluating Mergers." In *Modern Developments in Financial Management*, Stewart Myers, Ed. New York: Praeger, 1976, pp. 633–645.

Shad, John S. R. "The Financial Realities of Mergers." *Harvard Business Review* (November–December 1969), pp. 133–146.

T. Vermaelen, "Common Stock Repurchases and Market Signalling: An Empirical Study" *Journal of Financial Economics* (June 1981), pp. 139–183.

QUESTIONS

1. What options within internal and external expansion alternatives should be evaluated by the NPV method?

2. How do shareholders of a buying firm obtain benefits when they merge with an undervalued firm?

3. How might a merger of leveraged companies increase the combined debt capacity of the firms?

4. How can shareholders gain as a result of added debt capacity from a merger?

5. What major factors determine the maximum price a firm will pay for another firm?

6. What advantages accrue to the buyer and/or seller when common stock is used to purchase another firm rather than cash?

7. Under what conditions is a firm likely to use a tender offer rather than negotiate the purchase of another company?

8. Why is diversification achieved through merger not likely to be of value to the shareholders of the merging firms?

PROBLEMS

1. Meyer Soap Company produced a variety of laundry soaps. Several of the firm's senior officers considered expansion into the deodorant field. They felt they could set up their own deodorant division for an initial minimum capital outlay of $1 million using a relatively low capital-intensive production process. This opportunity would yield $460,000 a year in cash sales but require $300,000 in annual cash operating costs and annual capital outlays of $50,000. A more capital-intensive operation would involve an initial capital outlay of $1.6 million, annual cash sales of $460,000, annual cash operating costs of $250,000, and annual capital outlays of $80,000. A larger-scale plant would involve an initial capital outlay of $1.4 million, cash sales of $650,000, annual cash operating costs of $360,000, and annual capital outlays of $70,000. A more capital-intensive process in the large-scale plant would cost $2 million initially, yield the same annual cash

sales, and involve only $250,000 in annual cash operating costs, but would require $100,000 in annual capital outlays. The marginal cost of capital is 10 percent for all options under evaluation. All cash flows have been expressed in after-tax terms. Which, if any, expansion alternative should Meyer Soap choose? Evaluate all alternatives. Assume all cash flows are perpetual.

2. The Birdboard Tool Company's optimal internal expansion opportunity was to construct ovens for the bakery industry. When evaluated at a 10 percent cost of capital, this internal expansion opportunity, which would cost $10 million, was expected to yield a *net* present value, after taxes, of $2 million. The company's best acquisition alternative was to purchase the Gray Baking Equipment Company. Data on the two firms are presented below:

	Birdboard	Gray
Total Earnings	$15,000,000	$5,000,000
Number of Shares	15,000,000	5,000,000
Price/Earnings Ratio	12×	10×

(a) Calculate earnings and price per share as well as total share value for the two companies.

(b) Birdboard estimates that cost savings as a result of synergism can produce an increase in value of the combined firms of $3 million. What is the maximum price Birdboard should pay for Gray and the minimum price Gray should accept if Gray has another offer of $12 a share for its stock?

3. The Mueller and Walker Timber Company is considering the purchase of the Orton Lumber Company, a smaller firm whose assets consist primarily of mills and timber holdings. Orton's balance sheet shows the following:

Orton Lumber Company Balance Sheet

Assets			Liabilities		
Current Assets			Current Liabilities		
Cash	$ 1,000		Accruals	$ 1,000	
Receivables (net)	2,000		Payables—trade	2,000	$ 3,000
Inventory	3,000	$ 6,000	Mortgage		17,000
Fixed Assets			Equity		
Mills and Equipment (net)	$25,000		Common stock	$30,000	
Timber rights	69,000	$ 94,000	Surplus	50,000	80,000
		$100,000			$100,000

The average annual earnings of Orton after taxes are $9000. Mueller and Walker are considering buying the assets of Orton and estimate the purchase of inventory, mills, equipment, and timber rights from Orton would add $18,000 to their annual cash flow for the next 15 years, at the end of which the expected cash flow would fall to zero. Mueller and Walker estimate that a 10 percent return is required for investments of this risk.

(a) If Orton common stock sells in the market at a price/earnings ratio of 10, what is your estimate of the value of Orton equity and the market value of the entire firm?

(b) According to the information available, how do you evaluate the prospects for sale to Mueller and Walker if Orton has no other offers? (Assume that internal expansion for Mueller and Walker has been ruled out as unprofitable.)

4. Hill Gasket is negotiating with McLelland Body Company on a merger. Hill Gasket will be the surviving firm. Hill Gasket has one million shares outstanding, earns an average of $1 per share, and has a current market price of $12 per share. McLelland Body has 200,000 shares outstanding, earns an average of $0.80 per share, and sells for $8.00 per share.

(a) Assuming that there are no synergistic benefits from the merger and Hill offers two-thirds of a share for each McLelland share, how will the wealth of each McLelland shareholder be affected by a merger? How will the wealth of an investor holding 100 shares of each firm be affected?

(b) Suppose that Hill expects to generate annual cash flow savings of $20,000 a year in McLelland operations if the merger takes place. These savings are worth $2 million in discounted terms. What is the maximum value Hill should attribute to the merger? If McLelland has no alternative offers, establish the range of values within which a price of the firm would be established. How does this range change if Hill has an internal expansion alternative presently worth $600,000?

(c) Assuming that the information in (b) applies, suppose that the two firms agree on a value for McLelland of $1,835,294. How many Hill shares must be issued to purchase McLelland? What will be the wealth of a person holding 100 Hill shares and 100 McLelland shares before and after the merger?

5. Mary owns a figure salon. Business is quite good in strong economic times but poor when the economy is depressed. Jane owns a

bread factory that mass-produces a basic loaf of bread at a low price. Her business is strong during recessions but poor when the economy is stronger because her customers prefer to buy fancier breads made by other firms when they can afford to. Mary and Jane are contemplating a merger.

(a) Use the pre- and post-merger earnings estimates given below to illustrate the financial results of combining their firms.

	Mary's Salon			Jane's Bakery		
Economy	Earnings	Bankruptcy Costs	Payment to Bondholders	Earnings	Bankruptcy Costs	Payment to Bondholders
Strong	$1500	0	$1000	$ 600	$100	$ 500
Weak	$ 800	$100	$ 700	$1300	0	$1000

(b) Who is most likely to benefit from the gains in risk reduction?

APPENDIX 18A

Certain legal forms of business combinations have developed that may be useful to distinguish. These, in addition to a brief description of the appropriate accounting treatment given various forms of combinations, are presented below.

BUSINESS COMBINATIONS: LEGAL AND ACCOUNTING

Forms of External Combination

A merger is the combination of two or more firms into one company; only one entity survives, any postmerger name changes notwithstanding. Only one corporate charter, that of the buying firm, remains in existence; all other corporate charters belonging to the selling firms are automatically dissolved. All assets and debts of the selling firms are absorbed by the buyer.

Merger

A consolidation of two or more companies combines them into a *new* corporate entity with a new charter. None of the old companies and charters remain, despite the particular name chosen for the new firm. All assets and liabilities are absorbed by the new firm and shares for the

Consolidation

new corporate entity are issued to shareholders in the older firms at the agreed-upon amounts in the consolidation agreement.

Purchase of Assets   In this case all or part of the assets of the selling company are purchased by the buyer. The selling company retains all debts and, upon their eventual settlement, *may* later distribute remaining cash or stock received for the sale of assets to shareholders and then dissolve. The essential difference in this method compared to merger or consolidation is that no corporate entity necessarily disappears as the result of the transaction.

Holding Company   A holding company is a firm that owns controlling interest in the common stock of other firms. Each of these firms is called a *subsidiary*. Effective control does not always require ownership of over 50 percent of outstanding shares, so a holding company may exert control, yet own considerably less than 50 percent of those shares. Also, control need not be obtained with the permission of existing management. Shares could be purchased in the open market or perhaps a tender offer might be used to obtain necessary shares. Regardless of how shares are acquired, the holding company and the subsidiary remain separate legal entities with separate charters.

Accounting Treatment of Combinations   Accountants have used two methods of recording transactions involving business combinations—the purchase method and the pooling method.

Purchase Method   If the purchase price exceeds the book value of assets acquired, the excess is first allocated to the tangible assets up to their "fair market value." This permits increased depreciation charges for the combined firms, more than the sum of depreciation charges for the separate firms. Any excess above the allocation to assets is termed *goodwill* and must be amortized (written off against earnings) within a 40-year period. The goodwill amortization is *not* a tax-allowed expense, however. Overall, reported earnings of the combined firms will appear lower due to goodwill amortization and higher depreciation charges; after-tax cash flow increases, however.

Pooling Method   Under this method the acquired assets are recorded on the books of the surviving entity at book value, regardless of the market value of stock used in the purchase. This method would produce higher reported profits than under the purchase method. Under this method, the excess price paid over the book value of assets never shows up as a cost. The after-tax cash flow does not increase, however, as it would in the purchase method.

The Accounting Principles Board in 1970 issued Opinion No. 16 restricting use of the pooling method, but requiring it when certain conditions are met.

CHAPTER 19

Inflation
and Financial Decisions

This chapter provides an introductory analysis of the impact of **inflation** on financial decisions. We begin by showing why investor expectations of inflation are a variable in financial decision making. Development of this point introduces basic concepts and terminology leading to the effect of inflation on investor wealth. Then the issue of inflation and the cost of capital is addressed, to answer the question of how inflation should be reflected in the cost of capital. Finally, capital budgeting decisions in an inflationary environment are discussed. The question there is how should inflation be reflected in the process of evaluating and selecting investment proposals.

NOMINAL DOLLARS, REAL DOLLARS, AND PURCHASING POWER LOSSES

When investors undertake investments, they sacrifice present consumption of goods and services in exchange for higher expected future consumption. Thus, present and future prices of consumption goods and services are significant. There are important difficulties in measuring prices of representative consumption goods and services over time. The well-known Consumer Price Index is only one attempt to carry out this task for the mythical "typical" consumer. Such difficulties need not trouble us. We assume that at any time t there is some price level P_t for consumption goods and services that accurately measures prices of appropriate collections of goods and services purchased by investors.

Given price level P_t, we can distinguish **nominal dollars** from **real dollars.** A nominal dollar is—a dollar. It is defined without reference to its *purchasing power*, the quantity of consumption goods and services it will buy. In contrast, a real dollar *is* expressed in terms of its purchasing power. Thus, at any point in time t, a nominal dollar is $1, whereas a real dollar is $1/P_t$. Over time, comparative streams of nominal and real dollars would appear as follows.

Nominal and Real Dollars

	Time				
	$t = 0$	$t = 1$	$t = 2$	$t = 3 \ldots$	$t = n$
Nominal Dollar	$1	$1	$1	$1 $\ldots$	$1
Real Dollar	$\dfrac{\$1}{P_0}$	$\dfrac{\$1}{P_1}$	$\dfrac{\$1}{P_2}$	$\dfrac{\$1}{P_3}$	$\dfrac{\$1}{P_n}$

Defining inflation as the increase in the price level of consumption goods and services over time, it is evident that it will *reduce* the purchasing power of nominal dollars. Such reductions are portrayed by real dollars. Since each successive price level P_t exceeds the prior price level P_{t-1}, real dollars decline over time under inflation while the nominal dollar remains unchanged. A nominal dollar purchases fewer consumption goods and services over time.

The representation above is not the most convenient for our purposes. It will be more useful to express price levels in terms of the time $t = 0$, price level P_o, and the compound percentage *rate* of inflation, $\dot{P}$—assuming, for simplicity, that this rate is constant over time. The price level at time t becomes $P_t = P_o (1 + \dot{P})^t$ and the real dollar becomes $\$1/P_0 (1 + \dot{P})^t$. Multiplying the stream of real dollars by the time $t = 0$ price level P_o leaves the following stream of real dollars.[1]

Real Dollars as a Function of the Inflation Rate

		Time				
		$t = 0$	$t = 1$	$t = 2$	$t = 3 \ldots$	$t = n$
Real Dollar	$\left[\dfrac{\$1}{(1 + \dot{P})^t} \right]$	$1	$\dfrac{\$1}{(1 + \dot{P})}$	$\dfrac{\$1}{(1 + \dot{P})^2}$	$\dfrac{\$1}{(1 + \dot{P})^3} \ldots$	$\dfrac{\$1}{(1 + \dot{P})^n}$

Note that at time $t = 0$, nominal and real dollars are the same thing. The real dollar is expressed in terms of the base period, time $t = 0$, purchas-

---

[1]It is convenient to describe $\dot{P}$ as the inflation rate. More generally, it is the percentage rate of change in the price level. Under inflation, $\dot{P}$ is positive; under deflation, prices are falling and $\dot{P}$ is negative.

ing power. This point in time is the standard of reference by which purchasing power of nominal dollars at subsequent points in time is judged. After time $t = 0$, the process of inflation ($\dot{P} > 0$) will cause real dollars to be less than nominal dollars, reflecting reduced purchasing power. For example, if inflation occurs at a $\dot{P} = 5$ percent periodic rate after $t = 0$, the resulting real dollars are:

Real Dollars at a 5 Percent Inflation Rate

		Time		
		$t = 0$	$t = 1$	$t = 2$
Real dollars	$\left[\dfrac{\$1}{(1 + \dot{P})^t}\right]$	$\$1$	$\dfrac{\$1}{(1 + 0.05)^1} = \$0.952$	$\dfrac{\$1}{(1 + 0.05)^2} = \$0.907$

At time $t = 1$, a nominal dollar has a real value of only $0.952; it will purchase what only $0.952 time $t = 0$ dollars would have purchased. Continued inflation reduces the real dollar to $0.907 at time $t = 2$.

The process of converting nominal to real dollars is known as **deflating,** a real dollar being a deflated nominal dollar. The higher the rate of inflation, the greater the loss of purchasing power of a nominal dollar.

INVESTMENT RETURNS, INFLATION, AND PURCHASING POWER RISK

Virtually all investments provide expected future cash inflows payable in nominal rather than real dollars. Consequently, the real value of each nominal dollar received is subject to reduction if there is inflation (and purchasing power loss) *after* the investment is undertaken. If the investment pays nominal dollars of a fixed amount (fixed in that nominal dollars do not vary with the future inflation rate), the real value of the investment return will be less than orginally expected—solely because of inflation.

To illustrate, assume that an investor undertakes single period default-free investment A. It required an outlay of $100 and promises to pay a default-free nominal cash amount of $110 a year hence. The investor expects no inflation, thus, at time of investment, the expected real (and nominal) return is $110 − $100 = $10. But although investment A is free of default risk, it is not free of **purchasing power risk.** Purchasing power risk is the possibility of realized real returns differing from those expected because of unanticipated inflation. For example, suppose that inflation at the rate of $\dot{P} = 5$ percent occurs over the single period interval of the investment. The realized nominal return of the default-free investment remains at $110 − $100 = $10, or 10 percent. But the realized real return will be less than the 10 percent originally expected. Deflating the $110 nominal cash inflow at the $\dot{P} = 5$ percent inflation rate results in a realized real cash inflow of $104.76, a real return of $4.76, and real rate of return of 4.76 percent:

Real Return of Investment A

$$\frac{\$110}{1 + \dot{P}} - \$100 = \frac{\$110}{1 + 0.05} - \$100 = \$104.76 - \$100 = \$4.76$$

The investor sustains a loss in real return of $10 - $4.76 = $5.24 because of unanticipated inflation.

Not all investments necessarily impose losses in real return because of unanticipated inflation. Some investments, perhaps some common stocks, provide *additional* nominal dollars in the event of unanticipated inflation, enough to compensate for the purchasing power losses and so leave real investment returns unaffected by unanticipated inflation. Such investments have no purchasing power risk and are referred to as **hedges** against inflation. We defer discussion of these and continue with fixed nominal return investments such as A above.

The purchasing power risk of fixed nominal return investments leads investors to form expectations of future inflation. Acting on them, investor expectations of inflation influence both the **nominal required rates of return** and, as we will see, the market values of investments. The nominal required rate of return is that required by investors in terms of nominal dollars; the **real required rate of return** is that required in terms of real dollars.

Investor expectations of future inflation are held at time $t = 0$, the present, and are assumed to be the same for every investor. For simplicity, we assume that the expected rate of inflation, denoted as $\dot{P}^e$, is a constant rate expected to prevail in perpetuity (e.g., $\dot{P}^e = 5$ percent per year, forever). But do not confuse a constant rate over time with the absence of *revision* of expectations due to receipt of new information. For example, if the time $t = 0$ expectation is $\dot{P}^e = 5$ percent and new information arrives leading investors to form a higher expectation of $\dot{P}^e = 7$ percent, an immediate revision will take place—a one-time increase of 2 percent in perpetuity.[2]

EXPECTED INFLATION AND REQUIRED RATES OF RETURN

---

[2]We later drop the assumption of identical expectations. The maintained assumption of a constant rate in perpetuity avoids the complexity of different presently held expectations for different future periods of time (e.g., an investor expects 5 percent inflation for the year to follow, 7 percent for the year beyond that, and 9 percent for all remaining years in perpetuity).

Armed with these expectations, investors will set the nominal required rate of return on investment, to provide compensation for expected purchasing power losses and to provide an expected real rate of return equal to the real required rate of return. Let k be the nominal required rate of return for investment and k' be the real required rate. In the absence of expected inflation, the expected real value of cash inflows from a \$1 single period investment is \$1(1 + k'). With expected inflation, the expected real value is:

$$\frac{\$1(1 + k)}{1 + \dot{P}^e} \tag{19-1}$$

Clearly, if investors expect inflation, the nominal required rate k must exceed the real required rate k' if investors expect to earn a positive real required rate. How much higher must be the nominal required rate, k? To find out, we set Equation (19-1) equal to \$1(1 + k'), the expected real value in the absence of expected inflation.

Expected Real Value of Cash Inflow with Expected Inflation	Equals	Expected Real Value of Cash Inflow without Expected Inflation
$\dfrac{\$1(1 + k)^1}{1 + \dot{P}^e}$	$=$	$\$1(1 + k')$

Solving for the nominal required rate k, we find:

$$k = k' + \dot{P}^e + (k')\,(\dot{P}^e) \tag{19-2}$$

For example, if the real required rate is $k' = 10$ percent and the expected inflation rate is $\dot{P}^e = 5$ percent, the nominal required rate from Equation (19-2) is:

$$k = 0.10 + 0.05 + (0.10)(0.05) = 0.155, \text{ or } 15.5\%$$

A nominal required rate set according to Equation (19-2) provides compensation for *expected* purchasing power losses consistent with the expected inflation rate $\dot{P}^e$. Total compensation in Equation (19-2) is $\dot{P}^e + (k')(\dot{P}^e)$, of which the portion $\dot{P}^e$ is compensation for expected purchasing power losses on the dollar amount invested and $(k')(\dot{P}^e)$ compensates for expected losses on returns from investment. The higher the expected inflation rate, the greater must be the nominal required rate of return to provide additional compensation.[3]

---

[3]Equation (19-2) was developed by Irving Fisher. (*The Theory of Interest*, New York: Augustus M. Kelley, Publishers, 1965. Reprinted from the 1930 edition). The increased nominal required rate of return associated with increased expectations of inflation is often referred to as the Fisher effect.

Let us apply Equation (19-2) to an investment A. The real required rate is $k' = 10$ percent and the expected rate of inflation is $\dot{P}^e = 5$ percent. According to Equation (19-2), investors will require a nominal rate of return of $k = 15.5$ percent under these conditions. In the case of default-free investment A, $100 invested must provide a promised *nominal* cash inflow of $100 (1 + 0.155) = $115.50 rather than $110 to induce investors to undertake it. At the $\dot{P}^e = 5$ percent **expected rate of inflation,** the *expected* real return on the investment is then:

$$\frac{\text{Expected Real Return}}{\text{on Investment A}} = \frac{\$115.50}{1 + \dot{P}^e} - \$100 = \frac{\$115.50}{1 + 0.05} - \$100$$

$$= \$110 - \$100 = \$10$$

which equals that which would prevail in the absence of inflation. Investors in A expect to be compensated for purchasing power losses *and* to earn the real dollar return of $10—a real required rate of $k' = 10$ percent.

Does the formation of an expected inflation rate and its use to determine nominal required rates of return in Equation (19-2) eliminate purchasing power risk due to the unanticipated inflation? The answer is no, unless the investor has made a perfect forecast of future inflation. We see this in Table 19-1. The columns of the table indicate alternative *actual* inflation rates of $\dot{P} = 3, 5,$ and 7 percent. The first row is the realized nominal cash inflow of $115.50, set to earn an *expected* real rate of return of 10 percent given an expected inflation rate of $\dot{P}^e = 5$ percent. The second row is the realized real cash inflow under the alternative actual inflation rates. Third and fourth rows show corresponding realized real returns and rates of return. If the actual inflation rate happens to equal that which was expected, $\dot{P} = \dot{P}^e = 5$ percent, then actual and expected

Table 19–1   *Expectation Errors and Risky Real Returns of Investment A*

		Actual Inflation Rate, $\dot{P}$		
		3%	5%	7%
Realized Nominal Cash Inflow		$115.50	$115.50	$115.50
Realized Real Cash Inflow,	$\dfrac{\$115.50}{1 + \dot{P}}$	$112.14	$110.00	$107.94
Realized Real Return,	$\dfrac{\$115.50}{1 + \dot{P}} - \$100$	$ 12.14	$ 10.00	$ 7.94
Realized Real Rate of Return, r'		12.14%	10.00%	7.94%

real values of cash inflow, return, and rate of return are exactly as expected. The investor will have successfully avoided purchasing power losses due to inflation. But if inflation is *higher* than expected, $\dot{P} = 7$ percent not $\dot{P}^e = 5$ percent, then realized real cash inflows (returns) are less than expected. A lower than expected inflation rate of $\dot{P} = 3$ percent produces higher than expected real returns. Thus, reliance on expectations of inflation may reduce purchasing power risk of fixed nominal return investments but cannot eliminate it. This means that there may be more to expected inflation and its effect on nominal required rates of return than Equation (19-2) suggests. However, we rely on it in the balance of the discussion as a description of how nominal rates of return are affected by investor expectations of inflation.[4]

Inflation and Market Value of Securities

Expected inflation can affect the market values of securities. The extent of such effects depends on whether the security is of the fixed-promise or variable cash flow variety. **Fixed-promise securities** promise nominal cash inflows that do not vary with future inflation. Bonds and preferred stock are examples of fixed-promise securities. Variable cash flow securities have expected nominal cash inflows that *may* vary directly with future inflation. Common stocks are variable cash flow securities. In general, fixed-promise securities are subject to purchasing power risk and are sensitive to revisions in investor expectations of inflation, revisions perhaps caused by unanticipated differences between actual infla-

---

[4]If we retain Equation (19-2), we are implicitly assuming that investors are indifferent to the purchasing power risk associated with errors in expectation of inflation. If investors are risk averse in this sense, Equation (19-2) is an inadequate specification. We would need a revision of this equation to include extra compensation for bearing risk of purchasing power losses occasioned by errors in expectations.

We also are ignoring any effect of personal taxes on nominal required rates. It is sad but true that when expectations of inflation are embedded in nominal required rates of return, government taxes that compensation. This has the effect of reducing the after-personal-tax real rate of return for investors compared to a world of no expected or actual inflation. If investors set nominal required rates of return to maintain the same real after-personal-tax rate of return in the presence of expected inflation, as would prevail in its absence, the required nominal rate k^T would be:

$$k^T = \frac{\dot{P}^e + (1 + \dot{P}^e)(1 - \tau_b)k'}{1 - \tau_b} \qquad \text{(i)}$$

where τ_b is the marginal personal tax rate on interest. For investment A, the revised nominal required rate k^T for a tax rate of $\tau_b = 30$ percent, expected inflation rate of $\dot{P}^e = 5$ percent, and pre-personal-tax real required rate of $k' = 10$ percent would be:

$$k^T = \frac{5\% + (1 + 0.05)(1 - 0.30)10\%}{1 - 0.30} = 17.64\%$$

instead of $k = 15.5$ percent reached with Equation (19-2).

Table 19–2 *Effects of Expected Inflation on Market Values of Securities*

	Expected Inflation Rate, $\dot{P}^e$		
	3%	5%	7%
Bond: 11% Coupon Rate, 3-Year Maturity			
Real Required Rate, k'_d	8%	8%	8%
Nominal Required Rate, $k_d = k_d' + \dot{P}^e + (k_d')(\dot{P}^e)$	11.24%	13.4%	15.56%
Market Value	$994.16	$943.71	$896.84
Preferred Stock: $3 Dividend per Share			
Real Required Rate, k'_p	10%	10%	10%
Nominal Required Rate, $k_p = k'_p + \dot{P}^e + (k'_p)(\dot{P}^e)$	13.3%	15.5%	17.7%
Market Value	$22.56	$19.35	$16.95
Common Stock: $4 Current Dividend per Share			
Real Required Rate, k'_e	12%	12%	12%
Nominal Required Rate, $k_e = k'_e + \dot{P}^e + (k'_e)(\dot{P}^e)$	15.36%	17.6%	19.84%
Acorn Shares			
Expected Nominal Dividend Growth, g	4.5%	6%	7.5%
Market Value per Share	$38.67	$36.55	$34.85
Bicorn Shares			
Expected Nominal Dividend Growth, g	3%	6%	9%
Market Value per Share	$33.33	$36.55	$40.22
Unicorn Shares			
Expected Nominal Dividend Growth, g	3.98%	6%	8.02%
Market Value per Share	$36.55	$36.55	$36.55

tion and that which had been expected. Variable cash flow securities may or may not be risky in this sense. Sensitivity of their market values to changes in inflation expectations depends on how their expected nominal cash inflows change with revisions of expectations of inflation.

Table 19-2 summarizes representative affects of expectations of inflation on nominal required rates of return and market values of fixed promise and variable cash flow securities. Although we do not review the computations of the nominal required rate and market value, we describe how the reader may verify them. It is convenient to see these effects from two standpoints: rising expectations of inflation and purchasing power risk.

Rising Expectations of Inflation

For previously issued fixed-promise securities, rising expectations of inflation produce rising nominal required rates of return and falling market values. This is evident in Table 19-2 for the bond and preferred stock issues, since the expected rate of inflation takes on the succeeding values of $\dot{P}e$ = 3, 5, and 7 percent. The bond issue has a *real* required rate of return of k_d' = 8 percent. This rate is assumed to be a constant and *independent* of the expected rate of inflation. With Equation (19-2), an expected rate of inflation of $\dot{P}e$ = 3 percent produces a nominal required rate of return for the bond of k_d = 11.24 percent. The corresponding market value of the 3-year maturity bonds having fixed-promise annual interest payments of $110 and a $1000 maturity value is $994.16. An investor purchasing one of these bonds at this market value expects to earn the real required rate of k_d' = 8 percent plus compensation for expected purchasing power losses for a $\dot{P}e$ = 3 percent expected inflation rate.[5] But at higher expected rates of inflation, greater **purchasing power losses** are envisioned by investors. Higher nominal required rates of return are necessary to provide additional compensation for expected losses. However, the promised nominal payments of the bond are fixed. With higher nominal required rates, the market price of the bond must *fall* if an investor is to be induced to purchase the bond *and* recover higher expected purchasing power losses. Thus, at higher expected inflation rates of $\dot{P}e$ = 5 and 7 percent, the higher nominal required rates of k_d = 13.4 and 15.56 percent result in lower market values of $943.71 and $896.84, respectively.

The fixed-promise security represented by the preferred stock issue exhibits similar behavior. The real required rate is k_p' = 10 percent and is constant and independent of expected inflation. With a fixed nominal cash dividend per share of $3 in perpetuity, the market value depends on the nominal required rate of return. With expected inflation of $\dot{P}e$ = 3 percent, the nominal required rate from Equation (19-2) is k_p = 13.3 percent. The market value is $22.56 per share.[6] At that price, an investor expects to earn the real required rate of k_p' = 10 percent plus compensation for purchasing power losses at the $\dot{P}e$ = 3.0 percent rate. Higher expected rates of inflation lead to higher nominal required rates of return and lower market values.

As to variable cash flow securities, it is possible for rising expectations of inflation to result in falling, rising, *or* unchanged market values. Table 19-2 illustrates these possible outcomes with three common stocks: Acorn, Bicorn, and Unicorn. Except for their sensitivity to expected inflation, these shares are assumed to be of equal risk with an appropri-

---

[5]The market value of the bond can be found using Equation (11-1). The coupon interest payment C = $110 and maturity value MV = $1000 are discounted at the appropriate nominal required rate k_d = 11.24 percent for expected inflation of $\dot{P}e$ = 3 percent. Higher expected inflation rates will lead to higher values of k_d to be used in such valuations. A calculator is necessary to find bond values because of the fractional discount rates.

[6]The valuation model to be employed is Equation (11-2), where $V = C/k_P$.

ate and unchanging real required rate of return of k'_e = 12 percent. And for all three stocks, higher expected rates of inflation produce higher and *identical* nominal required rates of return. Thus, an expected rate of inflation of $\dot{P}^e$ = 3 percent leads, with Equation (19-2), to a nominal required rate of k_e = 15.36 percent; a higher expected inflation rate of $\dot{P}^e$ = 7 percent results in a higher k_e = 19.84 percent.

By themselves, rising nominal required rates tend to reduce market values of common shares. But this effect is opposed by any favorable effects of rising expected inflation on the nominal cash dividends investors expect to receive. Many firms may be expected to benefit from inflation to the extent that rising operating costs due to inflation are countered by rising selling prices for final output of goods and services. Nominal cash flows available to pay cash dividends may well increase with inflation. If investors expect this to occur, rising expectations of inflation may lead to rising expectations of future nominal cash dividends. The net effect on market value of shares of rising expected inflation then depends on whether increases in expected nominal dividends are sufficient to offset the rising nominal required rates of return.

Acorn, Bicorn, and Unicorn shares in Table 19-2 illustrate three possibilities. For convenience, the expected nominal dividend growth rate g of a version of the constant growth model [Equation (11-6)] is used to represent the effects of rising expected inflation on the expected nominal dividend stream:

$$V = \frac{D_1}{k_e - g} = \frac{D_0(1 + g)}{k_e - g} \qquad (19\text{-}3)$$

With the same current cash dividend per share of D_o = \$4, all three common stocks also have the same nominal required rate, k_e = 15.36 percent for an expected inflation rate of $\dot{P}^e$ = 3 percent. Given that expected inflation, the corresponding expected *nominal* dividend growth rate in perpetuity is g = 4.5 percent for Acorn, g = 3 percent for Bicorn, and g = 3.98 percent for Unicorn. Corresponding share values are \$38.67 for Acorn, \$33.33 for Bicorn, and \$36.55 for Unicorn. At these prices, investors expect to earn the real required rate of k_e' = 12 percent plus receive compensation for an expected inflation rate of $\dot{P}^e$ = 3 percent. But at higher expected inflation *and* nominal required rates, Table 19-2 shows that Acorn shares fall in value, Bicorn shares rise, and Unicorn shares have an unchanged value. This occurs even though the expected nominal dividend growth rates *increase* with expected inflation for each firm. But do they increase sufficiently to offset the higher nominal required rates of return? In the case of Acorn, they do not, and market value *falls* with higher expected inflation. In contrast, Bicorn shares rise in value. As for Unicorn, market values remain unchanged at \$36.55.

Shares such as Unicorn are referred to as *hedges* against inflation. Rising expectations of inflation produce rising expected nominal streams of dividends that *exactly* offset the higher nominal required rates of return.

To summarize, rising expectations of inflation always produce rising nominal required rates of return for *all* securities. They also produce falling market values for fixed-promise securities. Variable cash flow securities may rise, fall, or remain unchanged with an increase in expected inflation.

PURCHASING POWER RISK AND MARKET VALUE

What of purchasing power risk for fixed-promise and variable cash flow securities? In general, fixed-promise securities subject investors to purchasing power risk, as do all variable cash flow securities *except* those qualifying as hedges against inflation. Purchasing power risk stems from uncertainty about future market values of all securities (save hedges against inflation).

We can observe these contentions in Table 19-2. Suppose that an investor buys each of the securities in the table at the market values prevailing with an expected inflation rate of $\dot{P}e = 5$ percent. Immediately afterward, the *actual* rate of inflation turns out to be *higher* than expected. That information caused expectations of inflation to be revised *upward* to $\dot{P}e = 7$ percent. (Even if there is no unanticipated inflation, expectations could be revised because of other new information.) Market values of the bond, preferred stock, and Acorn shares will fall; Bicorn shares will rise in value; Unicorn shares will remain constant. Gains or losses result for all investments except Unicorn.[7] Similarly, if actual inflation is lower than expected, so that expectations are revised downward to $\dot{P}e = 3$ percent, the fixed-promise securities will rise in value, Bicorn shares will fall, and Unicorn shares be unchanged. Again, gains or losses result for all investments except Unicorn.

But at time of purchase, investors act on their expectations of inflation. Under efficient markets, such expectations reflect all information relevant to forecasting inflation. Investors cannot know at time of purchase whether future unanticipated inflation or other information will lead to upward or downward revisions of expected inflation. Therefore, they recognize that fixed-promise securities and common shares such as Acorn and Bicorn shares are subject to purchasing power risk as re-

---

[7]We ignore the possibility of creating a *portfolio* consisting of Bicorn and one of the fixed-promise securities. Such a portfolio could be constructed to be a hedge against inflation, the rising value of Bicorn shares offsetting the falling value of a fixed-promise security.

flected in uncertain market values. Only Unicorn common stock, as a hedge, is free of this source of uncertainty.

Financial decision makers are presumed to maximize shareholder wealth. Wealth is defined as the current market value of assets, including securities. But we have just seen that market value of fixed-promise and many variable cash flow securities are subject to variation due to changes in the expected rate of inflation. Therefore, the expected rate of inflation is a variable in financial decision making that should not be ignored.

    We can now see how expected inflation plays a role in the firm's cost of capital and in capital budgeting decisions.

IMPLICATIONS FOR FINANCIAL DECISIONS

When estimating the marginal cost of capital for evaluating investment proposals, financial decision makers can account for expected inflation in one of two ways: estimate the nominal cost *or* estimate the real cost. These approaches are equally valid when applied on the consistent basis to be described in the discussion of capital budgeting decisions.

EXPECTED INFLATION AND THE COST OF CAPITAL

The costs of capital estimated in Chapters 15 and 16 were based on required rates of return estimated from markets. These required rates were expressed in nominal terms, although not so identified. Each resulting cost of capital estimate therefore was an estimate of the **nominal cost of capital.** As such, the nominal cost of capital has embedded in it compensation for expected purchasing power losses consistent with the prevailing expected rate of inflation. We know that this is true because each financing source relied on by the firm has a nominal required rate fashioned according to Equation (19-2) to include compensation for expected inflation.

    To demonstrate this, suppose that Roadrunner, Inc., is estimating its nominal marginal after-tax cost of capital, denoted as K. At its target capital structure, proportions of debt, preferred stock, and common equity are, respectively, $W_d = 0.25$, $W_p = 0.15$, and $W_e = 0.60$. Its marginal corporate income tax rate is $\tau = 46$ percent. Consistent with this target capital structure and the given level of business risk, Roadrunner has estimated nominal required rates of return for the three financing sources as $k_d = 11.3$ percent for debt, $k_p = 12.35$ percent for

The Nominal Cost of Capital

preferred stock, and k_e = 15.5 percent for common equity. Using Equation (16-7) for the marginal cost of capital, the estimated nominal cost is:

$$K = (1 - \tau)k_d W_d + k_p W_p + k_e W_e$$

$$= (1 - 0.46)(11.3\%)(0.25) + (12.35\%)(0.15) + (15.5\%)(0.60)$$

$$= 1.5255 + 1.8525 + 9.3$$

$$= 12.678\%, \quad \text{or } 12.7\%$$

Roadrunner's nominal cost of capital implicitly includes compensation for expected purchasing power losses, such compensation being embedded in the nominal cost of each financing source. No further action to account for expected inflation in the cost of capital is required. Whatever expected rate of inflation is held by investors is *automatically* included in nominal K. The firm need not estimate the investor-held expected inflation rate or inquire about the real required rate of return for each financing source. However, to help illustrate the effect of changing expectations of inflation, the estimated real required rates are[8]:

$$k_d' = 6.0\% \text{ for debt}$$

$$k_p' = 7.0\% \text{ for preferred stock}$$

$$k_e' = 10.0\% \text{ for common equity}$$

Changes in the expected rate of inflation produce changes in the nominal required rate of return for each financing source and in the firm's nominal cost of capital. We illustrate this with an assumed increase in the expected rate of inflation from $\dot{P}^e$ = 5 to 7 percent. Given the estimated real required rates, the revised and higher nominal required rates for each financing source using Equation (19-2) are as follows.

Debt

$$k_d' = 6\%$$

$$k_d = 0.06 + 0.07 + (0.06)(0.07) = 0.1342, \quad \text{or } 13.42\%$$

---

[8]These estimated real required rates may be estimated by first rearranging Equation (19-2) to solve for the real required rate:

$$k' = \frac{k - \dot{P}^e}{1 + \dot{P}^e} \tag{i}$$

Then the firm specifies the expected inflation rate held by investors, in this case, $\dot{P}^e$ = 5 percent. Thus, for debt with a nominal required rate of k_d = 11.3 percent, the real required rate is:

$$k' = \frac{0.113 - 0.05}{1 + 0.05} = 0.06, \quad \text{or } 6\%$$

Preferred Stock

$k'_p = 7\%$

$k_p = 0.07 + 0.07 + (0.07)(0.07) = 0.1449$,   or 14.49%

Common Equity

$k'_e = 10\%$

$k_e = 0.10 + 0.07 + (0.10)(0.07) = 0.177$,   or 17.7%

Since nominal costs of each financing source increase with expected inflation, so does the nominal cost of capital. Again using Equation (16-7), the new nominal cost is:

$$K = (1 - \tau)k_d W_d + k_p W_p + k_e W_e$$

$$= (1 - 0.46)(13.42\%)(0.25) + (14.49\%)(0.15) + (17.7\%)(0.60)$$

$$= \qquad 1.8117 \qquad + \qquad 2.1735 \qquad + \qquad 10.62$$

$$= 14.605\%, \quad \text{or } 14.6\%$$

An increase in expected inflation from 5 to 7 percent raises the nominal cost of capital from 12.7 to 14.6 percent (see note 9, below). Of course, a reduction in expectations of inflation leads to a reduction in nominal cost of capital.

Estimates of the **real cost of capital** should be based on estimates of the nominal cost of capital. Analogous to Equation (19-2), the nominal cost of capital can be expressed as a function of the real cost K' and the expected inflation rate.

The Real Cost of Capital

$$K = K' + \dot{P}e + (K')(\dot{P}e) \qquad (19\text{-}4)$$

This expression can be rearranged to solve for the real cost K'.

$$K' = \frac{K - \dot{P}e}{1 + \dot{P}e} \qquad (19\text{-}5)$$

Given some estimate of the nominal cost, it is necessary to estimate the investor-held expectation of inflation, $\dot{P}e$, to estimate real cost K'. Realistically, such estimates of $\dot{P}e$ by financial managers are subject to error. Later we show that such errors are of no consequence in properly constructed capital budgeting decisions. We are saved from that problem at present because all investors are assumed to hold the same expectation, $\dot{P}e$.

Using Roadrunner as an example, recall that when the underlying expected rate of inflation was $\dot{P}^e = 5$ percent, the estimated nominal cost of capital was $K = 12.7$ (precisely $K = 12.678$ percent). Using Equation (19-5), the estimated real cost is:

$$K' = \frac{0.12678 - 0.05}{1 + 0.05} = 0.07312 \approx 0.073, \quad \text{or } 7.3\%$$

At a higher expected inflation rate of $\dot{P}^e = 7$ percent, the estimated nominal cost of capital was $K = 14.605$ percent. The estimated real cost of capital is:

$$K = \frac{0.14605 - 0.07}{1 + 0.07} = 0.07107 \approx 0.071, \quad \text{or } 7.1\%$$

In this case, the real cost falls slightly with a higher expected rate of inflation. This may seem surprising, since real required rates of return for each financing source did *not* change as expected inflation increased. The causes of this behavior are complex and the net consequence for cost of capital estimates relatively minor.[9]

CAPITAL BUDGETING DECISIONS AND EXPECTED INFLATION

The firm can select one of two ways of evaluating investment proposals when inflation is expected: discount nominal cash flows with the nominal cost of capital (nominal to nominal) or discount real cash flows with the real discount rate (real to real). Properly carried out, these alternative methods yield identical evaluations of investment proposals. Both methods take **adjusted nominal cash flow** for investment proposals as a starting point. We begin there as well.

---

[9]An increase in the expected inflation rate of $7 - 5 = 2$ percent led to a $14.6 - 12.7 = 1.9$ percent increase in nominal cost of capital and a $7.1 - 7.3 = -0.2$ percent reduction in real cost of capital. Nominal cost does not increase by the full increase in expected inflation, and real cost falls. Given the way we have expressed nominal required rates of return in Equation (19-2) and the marginal cost of capital formulation of Equation (16-7), the cause is tax deductibility of interest payments for corporations. Just as in note 4, where investors found that government taxes compensation for purchasing power losses embedded in nominal required rates, firms using debt in their target capital structure are able to *deduct* from their tax bills such compensation embedded in nominal interest rates. The real after-tax cost of debt financing declines with higher expected inflation embedded in higher nominal required rates for debt. This is why the real after-tax cost of capital declined for Roadrunner as expected inflation increased and why the nominal after-tax cost increased by less than the increase in expected inflation.

We caution that this result holds only for levered, not unlevered firms; for example, the real cost of capital for unlevered firms is unchanged under prevailing assumptions by an increase in expected inflation.

Inflation of prices of consumption goods and services was earlier cited as relevant for investors in making the decisions to invest rather than to enjoy present consumption. This does not mean that inflation of prices of other goods and services is irrelevant. But the latter sorts of inflation are reflected, perhaps implicitly, in estimated nominal cash flows of securities rather than in nominal required rates of return. For firms evaluating investment proposals, expected inflation of prices of nonconsumption goods and services such as labor and materials should be reflected in nominal investment proposal cash flows.

Adjusted Nominal Cash Flows for Investment Proposals

Table 19-3 illustrates such adjustments for a revenue-expanding proposal. Principles of construction follow those laid down in Chapter 7. The investment proposal, one to be evaluated by Roadrunner, requires an immediate outlay of $90,000 to purchase equipment to be used and fully depreciated over 3 years. Expected salvage value is zero. Table 19-3 first shows *unadjusted* cash flows constructed by using *current* prices of final output to estimate sales revenue and *current* prices of labor, mate-

Table 19–3   *Adjusted and Unadjusted Nominal Cash Flows*

		Time		
	$t = 0$	$t = 1$	$t = 2$	$t = 3$
Unadjusted Flows				
Initial Outlay	−$90,000			
After-tax Operating Cash Flows				
Sales Revenue		$78,519	$78,519	$78,519
Operating Cash Outlay		30,000	30,000	30,000
Pre-tax Operating Flow, CF_t		$48,519	$48,519	$48,519
Depreciation Tax Subsidy, τd_t		$13,800	$13,800	$13,800
After-tax Net Operating Flow, $(1 - \tau)CF_t + \tau d_t$		$40,000	$40,000	$40,000
After-tax Incremental Flows, C_t	−$90,000	$40,000	$40,000	$40,000
Adjusted Flows				
Initial Outlay	−$90,000			
After-tax Operating Cash Flows				
Sales Revenue (4% inflation)		$81,660	$84,926	$88,323
Operating Cash Outlay (4% inflation)		31,200	32,448	33,746
Pre-tax Operating Cash Flow, CF_t		$50,460	$52,478	$54,577
Depreciation Tax Subsidy, τd_t		$13,800	$13,800	$13,800
After-tax Net Operating Flow, $(1 - \tau)CF_t + \tau d_t$		$41,048	$42,138	$43,272
After-tax Incremental Flows, C_t	−$90,000	$41,048	$42,138	$43,272

rials, maintenance, and repair to estimate operating cash outlays. Depreciation is based on the straight line method for a charge of $30,000 per year. This results in an annual depreciation tax subsidy of $13,800 at Roadrunner's marginal tax rate of $\tau = 46$ percent. The resulting unadjusted after-tax incremental flows call for a $90,000 outlay with expected incremental after-tax inflows of $40,000 per year. In the lower portion of the table, adjusted nominal flows are constructed. It is assumed that Roadrunner expects selling prices for output and prices paid for labor, materials, maintenance, and repair to increase at a 4 percent compound annual rate. The depreciation tax subsidy is not adjusted, since depreciation charges are based on the fixed $90,000 acquisition cost of the equipment.[10] The resulting adjusted incremental after-tax flows are nominal flows reflecting expected inflation of output selling price and operating cash outlays. These particular adjusted nominal inflows happen to exceed the unadjusted inflows. This is often, but not always, is the case. For example, a firm expecting to be unable to increase output selling price as it confronts expected increases in operating cash outlays could find that adjusted inflows are less than unadjusted inflows.

Once the adjusted nominal cash flows for an investment proposal have been estimated, they can be employed in the nominal-to-nominal or real-to-real evaluation methods.

The Nominal-to-Nominal Method

Adjusted nominal cash flows can be evaluated using the nominal cost of capital. Compensation for expected inflation is embedded in the nominal cost of capital and thus is accounted for when that cost is used to evaluate the proposal. Assuming that the prevailing expected rate of inflation is $\dot{P}^e = 5$ percent, we know that Roadrunner's nominal cost of capital is (with otherwise unnecessary precision to later show certain results), $K = 12.678$ percent. Using the net present value method of Chapter 7, the adjusted nominal flows of Table 19-3 are discounted with aid of an electronic calculator at the nominal cost of capital.

$$
\begin{aligned}
\text{NPV} &= -90,000 + \frac{\$41,048}{(1.12678)} + \frac{\$42,138}{(1.12678)^2} + \frac{\$43,272}{(1.12678)^3} \\
&= -90,000 + \$36,429.47 + \$33,189.11 + \$30,247.50 \\
&= -\$90,000 + 99,866.08 \\
&= \$9,866.08 > 0
\end{aligned}
$$

----

[10]Compound rate of return factors in Appendix A may be used to adjust nominal cash flows. For example, the adjusted nominal sales revenue for year 3 is the unadjusted flow $78,519, multipled by $(1 + 0.04)^3$ [i.e., $78,519 (1 + 0.04)^3 = \$78,519(1.12486) = \$88,323$].

The same proposal could have been evaluated by evaluating expected real cash flows using the real cost of capital. To do this, the firm must estimate the investor-held expected rate of inflation for prices of consumption goods and services $\dot{P}^e$ that is embedded in the nominal cost of capital [see Equation 19-4]. By assumption, Roadrunner knows that this expectation is $\dot{P}^e = 5$ percent. Then, the firm must convert adjusted nominal to expected real cash flows and discount these using the real cost of capital K' of Equation (19-5).

The Real-to-Real Method

The formula for deflating a nominal cash flow at time t is:

$$\frac{C_t}{(1 + \dot{P}^e)^t} \tag{19-6}$$

For the Roadrunner investment proposal, the expected real values of the future nominal adjusted cash flows of Table 19-3 at a $\dot{P}^e = 5$ percent expected inflation rate are:

Time	Expected Real Cash Flow for the Proposal
$t = 1$	$\dfrac{\$41,048}{(1 + 0.05)^1} = \$39,093.33$
$t = 2$	$\dfrac{\$42,138}{(1 + 0.05)^2} = \$38,220.41$
$t = 3$	$\dfrac{\$43,272}{(1 + 0.05)^3} = \$37,379.98$

As must be the case in the presence of expected inflation, expected future real cash flows are less than the nominal cash flows, reflecting expected reductions in purchasing power.

The applicable real cost of capital is found by removing the purchasing power compensation component embedded in the nominal cost of capital using Equation (19-5). With $K = 12.678$ percent and $\dot{P}^e = 5$ percent, the real cost of capital (as earlier computed) is:

$$K' = \frac{0.12678 - 0.05}{1 + 0.05} = 0.07312, \quad \text{or } 7.312\%$$

Again, using the NPV method to discount expected *real* cash flows using the *real* cost of capital, the result is:

$$\text{NPV} = -\$90,000 + \frac{\$39,093.33}{(1.07312)} + \frac{\$38,220.41}{(1.07312)^2} + \frac{\$37,379.98}{(1.07312)^3}$$

$$= -\$90,000 + \$36,429.60 + \$33,189.35 + \$30,247.82$$

$$= -\$90,000 + 99,866.77$$

$$= \$9866.77 > 0$$

As before, NPV is positive and the proposal is acceptable.

**Comparing the
Two Methods**
It will not have been lost on the reader that the NPV values estimated under the nominal-to-nominal and real-to-real methods are nearly the same. In fact, they *are* the same. The differences observed in the Road-runner example are due entirely to rounding error (which we attempted to reduce by use of absurdly precise cash flows and costs of capital).

This equivalence of outcome held under the assumption that with costless information, the firm *knew* that the investor-held expectation embedded in the nominal cost of capital was $\dot{P}^e = 5$ percent. What happens when we more realistically assume that investor expectations of inflation are diverse? The expected rate of inflation embedded in nominal costs of capital and denoted as $\dot{P}^e$ must then be treated as a *consensus* forecast. Moreover, neither $\dot{P}^e$ nor the real cost of capital can be observed by the firm. Only the nominal cost K can be estimated directly. With costly information, the *firm's* forecast of the expected rate of inflation might well differ from the consensus forecast. If it attempts to use its own forecast in the real-to-real method, it may produce estimates of investment proposal real cash flows and the real cost of capital different from those perceived by investors under the consensus forecast. This suggests that the real-to-real method might then yield an incorrect estimate of NPV.

Happily, it can be shown that even if the firm's expected rate of inflation differs from the consensus forecast embedded in the nominal cost of capital, the resulting NPV will be the *same* as that reached with the nominal-to-nominal method. Since the latter method *implicitly* reflects the embedded consensus forecast, it yields a valid estimate of NPV, *given* the adjusted nominal cash flows. And if the real-to-real method gives the same NPV as the valid nominal-to-nominal method under *any* specified expected rate of inflation, the real-to-real method is also valid under *any* expected inflation rate equal to *or* different from the consensus forecast. All that is necessary to produce this result is to start with the same adjusted nominal cash flow and base the estimated real cost of capital on the estimated nominal cost as in Equation (17-5).[11]

---

[11]To prove the result, let $\dot{P}_f^e$ be *any* expected rate of inflation held by the firm. This expectation may or may not equal the consensus forecast $\dot{P}^e$. The firm's possibly erroneous expected real discounted value for any nominal cash flow is:

$$\frac{C_t}{(1 + \dot{P}_f^e)^t} \times \frac{1}{(1 + K')^t} \tag{i}$$

Using Equation (19-5), its possibly erroneous estimate of the real cost of capital is:

To demonstrate this result, let Roadrunner estimate its nominal cost of capital to be $K = 12.678$ percent, as before. The underlying consensus forecast of inflation is $\dot{P}^e = 5$ percent. Unable to observe the consensus forecast, Roadrunner unknowingly estimates a different expected rate of inflation, $\dot{P}^e_f = 8$ percent. Using Equation (19-6) to deflate the adjusted nominal cash flows of Table 19-3, the resulting estimates of real cash flows are too low because the expected inflation rate is too high.

Time	Firm's Expected Real Cash Flow for the Investment Proposal
$t = 1$	$\dfrac{\$41,048}{(1 + 0.08)^1} = \$38,007.41$
$t = 2$	$\dfrac{\$42,138}{(1 + 0.08)^2} = \$36,126.54$
$t = 3$	$\dfrac{\$43,272}{(1 + 0.08)^3} = \$34,350.71$

But using Equation (19-5), the estimated real cost of capital is *also* too low.

$$K' = \frac{K - \dot{P}^e_f}{1 + \dot{P}^e_f} = \frac{0.12678 - 0.08}{1 + 0.08} = 0.04331, \quad \text{or } 4.331\%$$

This estimate of 4.331 percent is substantially below the real cost of 7.312 percent earlier reached with the consensus forecast of $\dot{P}^e = 5$ percent. The result is two offsetting errors: the lower estimated real cash flows are discounted using the lower estimated real cost of capital. The resulting NPV is the same (except for rounding error) as indicated earlier using the nominal-to-nominal or real-to-real method when the latter

---

$$K' = \frac{K - \dot{P}^e_f}{1 + \dot{P}^e_f} \tag{ii}$$

Substituting Equation (ii) into Equation (i) yields:

$$\frac{C_t}{(1 + \dot{P}^e_f)^t} \times \frac{1}{\left[1 + \left(\dfrac{K - \dot{P}^e_f}{1 + \dot{P}^e_f}\right)\right]^t}$$

which, upon simplification, becomes:

$$\frac{C_t}{(1 + \dot{P}^e_f)^t} \times \frac{(1 + \dot{P}^e_f)^t}{(1 + K)^t} = \frac{C_t}{(1 + K)^t} \tag{iii}$$

The result is the same as the valid approach whereby nominal cash flow C_t is discounted using the nominal cost of capital K with the consensus forecast of inflation embedded in it. As the text shows, a value of $\dot{P}^e_f$ *different* from the consensus forecast $\dot{P}^e$ leads to offsetting errors in the firm's expected real cash flows and real cost of capital.

employs the consensus forecast of $\dot{P}^e = 5$ percent. This result can be seen from a simple calculation.

$$NPV = -\$90,000 + \frac{\$38,007.41}{(1.04331)} + \frac{\$36,126.54}{(1.04331)^2} + \frac{\$34,350.71}{(1.04331)^3}$$

$$= -\$90,000 + \$36,429.64 + \$33,189.41 + \$30,247.91$$

$$= -\$90,000 + \$99,866.96$$

$$= \$9866.96 > 0$$

We conclude that firms can use either nominal-to-nominal or real-to-real methods to evaluate investment proposals with equal result. Errors made in specifying the expected inflation rate do not invalidate the real-to-real method. The choice between methods is a matter of indifference to decision makers.

The only remaining caution is to ensure adherence of the nominal-to-nominal *or* real-to-real method. If a firm erroneously discounts nominal cash flows with the real cost of capital, it will have *failed* to account for expected inflation. The resulting NPV will be biased upward, and undesirable proposals may be accepted. And if the firm erroneously discounts real cash flows with the nominal cost of capital, it will have *double-counted* for expected inflation, once by deflating nominal cash flows and once again by using a nominal cost of capital that contains compensation for expected purchasing power losses. The resulting NPV would be biased downward, perhaps causing desirable proposals to be rejected.

SUMMARY   Inflation of prices of consumption goods and services reduces the purchasing power of nominal dollars. Such losses are reflected in reductions in value of real dollars, which are nominal dollars deflated to show their purchasing power. Future nominal cash inflows from investment are therefore subject to purchasing power losses. Unanticipated inflation occurring after an investment is undertaken will reduce the purchasing power of nominal returns so that realized real returns are less than had been expected. Investors form and act on expectations of inflation to protect against expected purchasing power losses. In the presence of expected inflation, the nominal required rate of return for investment will exceed the real required rate by the amount of compensation for expected purchasing power losses. Expectations of inflation are not error free, since actual and expected inflation need not be the same. Therefore, formation of expectations of inflation may reduce but cannot eliminate purchasing power risk of investment. Fixed-promise securities have nominal cash inflows that do not vary with inflation. Increases in expected inflation reduce market values of such securities because they are subject to purchasing power risk. Many variable cash flow securities are also subject to purchasing power risk. Such securities have expected nominal cash inflows that may vary with expected inflation. Their market values may rise or fall with an increase (or decrease) in expected inflation. Only common stocks qualifying as hedges against inflation will have market values invariant to changes in expected inflation because they have no purchasing power risk. Since wealth is dependent on the market value of assets, firms seeking to maximize shareholder wealth must reflect expected inflation in financial decisions.

Expected inflation may be reflected in the cost of capital in two ways. The firm may estimate the nominal cost based on the nominal required rates of return for each financing source. Investor-held expectations of inflation are embedded in that cost of capital and are so accounted for by the firm. Alternatively, the firm may estimate the real cost of capital, which is based on the nominal cost with compensation for expected purchasing power losses being eliminated from the nominal cost.

In capital budgeting decisions, the firm can account for investor-held expectations of inflation by one of two equally valid methods: nominal to nominal and real to real. Both methods rely on the adjusted nominal cash flows of an investment proposal. Adjusted flows include the expected affects of another type of inflation, that for selling price of the firm's fixed output and for prices paid for labor, materials, maintenance, and repair or other components of operating cash outlays. With the nominal-to-nominal method, adjusted nominal cash flows are discounted using the nominal cost of capital. With the real-to-real method, the firm's expected rate of inflation for consumption goods and services is used to deflate adjusted nominal cash flows and so produce estimated real cash flows. Using a real cost of capital based on the nominal cost of the same expectation of inflation, the expected real cash flows are discounted with the real cost of capital. If the firm happens to use an expectation of inflation different from the consensus forecast embedded in the nominal cost of capital, the real-to-real method will still produce a valid estimate of the net present value of the investment proposal.

GLOSSARY OF KEY TERMS

Adjusted Nominal Cash Flow	Investment proposal cash flows adjusted to include expected inflation of selling prices of the firm's output and of prices of labor, materials, maintenance, and repair, and other components of operating cash outlay.
Deflating	The process of converting nominal to real dollars.

Expected Rate of Inflation	The expected percentage rate of increase of prices of consumption goods and services.
Fixed-Promise Securities	Securities having promised nominal cash flows that do not vary with inflation. Examples include bonds and preferred stocks.
Hedge	Consists of variable cash flow securities having no purchasing power risk.
Inflation	The increase over time in price levels.
Nominal Cost of Capital	The cost of capital determined in the market inclusive of compensation for investors' expected purchasing power losses.
Nominal Dollar	A dollar expressed without reference to its purchasing power.
Nominal Required Rate of Return	The required rate of return in terms of nominal dollars; includes compensation for expected purchasing power losses.
Purchasing Power Losses	Reductions in the quantity of goods and services a nominal dollar will purchase; measured by a decline in real dollars.
Purchasing Power Risk	The chance that unanticipated inflation will lead to a reduction in the quantity of goods and services a nominal dollar will purchase.
Real Cost of Capital	The cost of capital expressed without compensation for expected purchasing power losses.
Real Dollar	A nominal dollar converted to show its purchasing power.
Real Required Rate of Return	The rate of return required by investors in real dollars.

SELECTED REFERENCES

Bodie, Zvi. "Common Stocks as Hedges Against Inflation," *Journal of Finance* (May 1976), pp. 459–470.

Lintner, John. "Inflation and Security Returns," *Journal of Finance* (May 1975), pp. 259–280.

Modigliani, F., and R. Cohn. "Inflation, Rational Valuation and the Market," *Financial Analysts Journal* (March–April 1979), pp. 24–44.

Nelson, Charles. "Inflation and Capital Budgeting," *Journal of Finance* (June 1976), pp. 923–931.

Rappaport, A., and R. Taggart. "Evaluation of Capital Expenditure Proposals Under Inflation," *Financial Management* (Spring 1982), pp. 5–13.

Van Horne, James. "A Note on Biases in Capital Budgeting Introduced by Inflation," *Journal of Financial and Quantitative Analysis* (March 1971), pp. 653–658.

1. Why should financial managers consider the expected rate of inflation as an important variable in their decisions?

2. How does the impact of unanticipated inflation on the rate of return differ from that of expected inflation?

3. How do investor expectations of future inflation influence the market value of investments?

4. What types of investments are likely to be hedges against inflation?

5. Homebuyers in the 1950s and 1960s were able to get long-term fixed rate mortgages at interest rates as low as 5 percent. House prices and inflation have risen dramatically since then. Owners who have kept their property are said to have fared quite well. Explain.

6. Compare purchasing power risk for securities with variable cash returns with the purchasing power risk of fixed promise securities.

1. Find the price level four periods from time $t = 0$ if prices are decreasing at the compound rate of 1 percent per period. Express the price level in terms of the time $t = 0$ price level. How much is a real dollar worth four periods from now in time 0 dollars?

2. If an investor earns 20 percent return on an investment during a period when the inflation rate is 8 percent, what is the real rate of return?

3. Suppose the expected annual inflation rate is 9 percent. Find the nominal required rate of return on an investment for which the real required return is 8 percent.

4. If the expected inflation rate was 9 percent over a period when the actual inflation rate was 10 percent, what was the realized real rate of return on an investment for which the required real rate was 8 percent?

5. Find the market value of a bond that carries a 6 percent coupon and has one year to maturity if the required real rate is 8 percent and investor expects an inflation rate of 5 percent next year. The face value of the bond is $1000.

6. Find the market value of a preferred stock that pays a perpetual dividend of $4.40 if investors expect an inflation rate of 5 percent and the required real rate for the stock is 12 percent.

7. Jeremy Corporation common shareholders require a 20 percent real return on their investment and expect an inflation rate of 5 percent. The current dividend is $1 and is expected to grow at a nominal rate of 6 percent forever. Find the current market value of a share of Jeremy stock.

8. What is the real required rate on debt if the nominal cost is 16 percent, reflecting an expected inflation rate of 6 percent? How does the nominal required rate change at a later time if the expected inflation rate is revised to 8 percent?

9. A machine that costs $30,000 has an expected life of two years and will have no salvage value. Cash flows, adjusted for the impact of inflation on revenues and costs, are estimated to be $21,500 at the end of the first year and $23,000 at the end of the second year. The prevailing expected inflation is 6 percent annually. The nominal discount rate for the project is 15 percent. Find the NPV using both the nominal to nominal method and the real to real method.

SECTION VI

Financial Analysis and Working Capital

CHAPTER 20

Financial Analysis and Planning

To this point, our concern with the risk and return aspects of financial decisions has properly emphasized future events affecting shareholder wealth—events that are influenced by present and past decisions. Financial managers must analyze both the past and present to *evaluate* what has happened to the firm, to *control* what is happening, and to *assist in planning* what will happen. At the same time, external parties—customers, suppliers, short- and long-term investors, and financial analysts—whose fortunes are linked with the firm want to analyze the firm and evaluate its financial plans. The primary, and sometimes the only, data available for analysis, especially to external parties, are contained in financial statements. This chapter presents methods of analyzing these statements.

Financial analysis and planning are very general managerial activities. Managers may attempt to analyze the historical record of a firm in order to identify factors having a significant influence upon the wealth of shareholders. But various plans aimed at increasing shareholder wealth are also subject to analysis. For example, managers may subject plans to change the firm's capital structure or to invest in various capital projects to financial analysis. Financial planning itself pertains to the process of establishing courses of action for the firm to guide future activity. For example, a budget is a financial plan.

We take a more limited view of the term **financial analysis** in this chapter. In the present context, financial analysis is viewed as the pro-

FINANCIAL ANALYSIS AND PLANNING

cess of reducing a large amount of historical financial data, taken from financial accounting statements, to a smaller set of information more useful for decision making. Financial ratios comprise an important part of that smaller set of information. Ratios are divided into four categories—liquidity, financial leverage, activity, and profitability. Ratios assist the process of financial analysis and also aid efforts at financial planning.

Information Needed for Financial Analysis and Planning

Financial analysis and planning rely heavily on standard accounting information normally available to the firm. The balance sheet and income statement of the firm are paramount among the useful types of accounting information and form the basis of analysis for this chapter. Use of accounting data is both a strength and a weakness. Its strength lies in its ready availability. Its weakness is that it is sometimes very difficult to interpret. Throughout this chapter we insert reminders about

Table 20–1   *Balance Sheet and Income Statement: Winn Company*

Balance Sheet 1984			
Current Assets		Current Liabilities	
Cash and Securities	$ 50,000	Accounts Payable	$ 35,000
Receivables	250,000	Other Payables	65,000
Inventories	250,000	Short-term Debt (7%)	250,000
Total	$ 550,000		$ 350,000
Fixed Assets		Long-term Debt (9%)	250,000
Plant and Equipment (net)	550,000	Net Worth	500,000
Total Assets	$1,100,000	Total Claims on Assets	$1,100,000

Income Statement 1984	
Sales (net)	$1,200,000
Cost of Goods Sold	818,000
Administrative Costs	100,000
Depreciation	100,000
Net Operating Income	$ 182,000
Interest Expense	40,000
Net Income Before Income Tax	$ 142,000
Income Tax (approx. 48%)	68,000
Net Income	$ 74,000

Table 20–2 *Notation for Balance Sheet
and Income Statement Accounts*

Balance Sheet Notation

CA = Current Assets

FA = Fixed Assets

TA = Total Assets

LA = Liquid Assets (cash and marketable securities)

R = Receivables (net)

I = Inventories

CL = Current Liabilities

STD = Short-term Debt

LTD = Long-term Debt

NW = Net Worth

Income Statement Notation

S = Sales

NOI = Net Operating Income

INT = Interest Expense

NI = Net Income

the problems of interpretation. These reminders are not meant to discourage the use of financial analysis, but to make the reader wary of reaching quick conclusions.

We make use of balance sheets and income statements for the fictitious Winn Company, a producer of electronic calculators. Table 20-1 shows the balance sheet and income statement for the Winn Company for 1984; these constitute the initial information needed to undertake financial analysis of that firm. In addition, our process of financial analysis calls for a set of notation for some assets and liabilities on Winn Company's balance sheets and for certain items in the income statement. The reader is advised to become familiar with this notation, given in Table 20-2, before proceeding.

Financial Ratios as a Tool of Financial Analysis

An efficient and informative method of financial analysis and planning is desirable if this important managerial process is to be accomplished quickly, thoroughly, and at relatively low cost. Analysis of the firm by financial ratios enables the financial manager, as well as interested external parties, to evaluate the firm's financial performance and condition rapidly by comparing ratios obtained from the firm with ratios obtained from comparable firms. Financial ratios also permit ready comparisons of a firm's financial performance and condition over time as a way of identifying and evaluating performance trends.

THE AMBIGUITY OF FINANCIAL RATIOS

Given the mischief that can be caused by inexperienced use, one might classify ratios with guns, automobiles, lawnmowers, and kitchen knives. Like these tools, ratios are accessible to everyone, but they are often improperly used. Ratio analysis requires considerable judgment and discretion by the analyst if it is to serve as a basis for future financial and operating decisions. Rules of thumb and other mechanical interpretations may produce disastrous decisions by those who are ill informed about the ambiguity of information that may be contained in ratios.

In the sections that follow, we indicate where particular caution is warranted. At this point, we simply note specific categories of problems.

1.   Ratios are a function of accounting conventions used by firms.

2.   They are subject to manipulation by managers.

3.   They may reflect unusual conditions at isolated points in the past.

4.   Unambiguous standards of comparison for specific ratios do not exist.

Ratio analysis is an art, not a science. The truth of this assertion is readily seen as we grapple with the inherent ambiguity of ratios in the remainder of this chapter.

FINANCIAL RATIOS FOR WINN COMPANY AND THE CALCULATOR INDUSTRY

Our first use of financial ratios involves comparison of the Winn Company to the calculator industry generally. Winn Company's financial ratios are calculated from the statements in Table 20-1 and displayed, together with ratios for the industry, in Table 20-3, which contains all the financial ratios used in this chapter.

Table 20-3 shows four classes of ratios: liquidity, leverage, activity, and profitability. As the terms suggest, liquidity and leverage ratios are used, respectively, to analyze the liquidity and leverage positions of the firm. However, the level of profitability of the firm requires the use of leverage, activity, *and* profitability ratios. For Winn Company, analyses of liquidity, leverage, and levels of profitability are carried out both by

Table 20–3   *Comparative Financial Ratios: Winn Company and Industry Averages*

	Formula	Calculation	Ratio Value	Industry Ratio Average
Liquidity Ratios				
1. Current	CA/CL	$\frac{\$550,000}{\$350,000}$	1.57	2.00
2. Acid Test	(LA + R)/CL	$\frac{\$300,000}{\$350,000}$	0.86	1.14
3. Absolute Liquidity	LA/CL	$\frac{\$50,000}{\$350,000}$	0.14	0.57
Leverage Ratios				
4. Debt/Net Worth	(STD + LTD)/NW	$\frac{\$500,000}{\$500,000}$	1.00	0.33
5. Interest Coverage	NOI/INT	$\frac{\$182,000}{\$40,000}$	4.55	12.13
6. Total Assets/Net Worth	TA/NW	$\frac{\$1,100,000}{\$500,000}$	2.20	1.50
7. Fixed Assets/Net Worth	FA/NW	$\frac{\$550,000}{\$500,000}$	1.10	0.92
8. Current Assets/Net Worth	CA/NW	$\frac{\$550,000}{\$500,000}$	1.10	0.58
9. Inventory/Net Worth	I/NW	$\frac{\$250,000}{\$500,000}$	0.50	0.25
10. Receivables/Net Worth	R/NW	$\frac{\$250,000}{\$500,000}$	0.50	0.17
11. Liquid Assets/Net Worth	LA/NW	$\frac{\$50,000}{\$500,000}$	0.10	0.17
Activity Ratios				
12. Sales/Total Assets	S/TA	$\frac{\$1,200,000}{\$1,100,000}$	1.09	1.33
13. Sales/Fixed Assets	S/FA	$\frac{\$1,200,000}{\$550,000}$	2.18	2.18
14. Sales/Current Assets	S/CA	$\frac{\$1,200,000}{\$550,000}$	2.18	3.43
15. Sales/Inventories	S/I	$\frac{\$1,200,000}{\$250,000}$	4.80	8.00
16. Sales/Receivables	S/R	$\frac{\$1,200,000}{\$250,000}$	4.80	12.00
17. Sales/Liquid Assets	S/LA	$\frac{\$1,200,000}{\$50,000}$	24.00	12.00
Profitability Ratios				
18. Net Profit Margin	NI/S	$\frac{\$74,000}{\$1,200,000}$	0.062	0.072
19. Return on Total Assets	NI/TA	$\frac{\$74,000}{\$1,100,000}$	0.067	0.096
20. Return on Net Worth	NI/NW	$\frac{\$74,000}{\$500,000}$	0.148	0.143

comparing Winn with the calculator industry averages and by viewing Winn's performance over time.

LIQUIDITY ANALYSIS BY RATIOS: WINN COMPANY COMPARED TO THE INDUSTRY

Liquidity reflects both the relative ease with which an asset may be immediately converted into cash at little or no discount from full value, and the degree of certainty concerning the amount of cash to be obtained. This definition implies that liquidity has at least two dimensions: time and risk.

Cash is the ultimate liquid asset. Other assets may be relatively liquid or illiquid depending on how quickly they can be converted to cash and on the degree of certainty in the selling price. For example, a firm holding U.S. Treasury bills can be said to hold a relatively liquid asset—but it still differs from cash. If the securities were sold prior to maturity, there would be a delay of 1 business day from date of sale until receipt of proceeds. Futhermore, the price at which they can be sold in the future is uncertain because the market interest rate on Treasury bills changes daily. An increase in the market interest rate would reduce the sale price, and a decrease would increase that price. Thus, the time and risk factors apply to Treasury bills, although there is no chance that the borrower (the U.S. government) will default on payment. By selling bills prior to maturity, the firm runs the risk of obtaining a lower rate of return than would have been obtained if the bills had been held to maturity. Only by waiting until maturity to sell can the firm obtain a specific cash payment that is known in advance.

An example of an illiquid asset is land. The price received for land depends on finding the "right" buyer—one desiring the particular characteristics of a given plot of land. This task may take months, even years, depending on the property to be sold, because land differs so much in its characteristics. In the meantime, a change in economic conditions affecting the geographic area could create wide swings in land value; that is, the price of land is volatile. Under normal circumstances, quick sale brings a lower price than could be obtained if the firm took the time to search for the "right" buyer(s). For these reasons, we normally classify land as an illiquid asset.[1]

From this view, we can see that the assets held by Winn Company shown in Table 20-1 exhibit a range of liquidity. Cash and marketable securities are considered to be sufficiently close in liquidity characteris-

---

[1]As the reader will recognize, illiquidity stems in part from lack of readily available information—a market imperfection. Search for buyers requires both time and money. These costs do not exist in a perfect market framework.

tics to be grouped under Liquid Assets in Table 20-2. But other current assets are not so liquid. Receivables, such as promises to pay by customers, vary in risk and maturity according to the customer and Winn Company's credit policies. Converting those assets to cash requires finding a buyer—a buyer perhaps likely to pay less than full value for at least some of the receivables because their risk and maturity do not exactly match the preferences of that buyer. Consequently, receivables are less liquid than cash and securities because they can be converted immediately to cash only at a discount or they must be held until all receivables are paid off in the course of business. Inventories, which range from raw materials to work in process to finished goods, are likely to be even less liquid because they tend to be more specialized for certain manufacturing or retailing and wholesaling businesses. If a firm must rid itself of work-in-process inventory when faced with an emergency, it is likely to sell at little above scrap value. Raw materials may have a more active market if they are usable by a large number of manufacturers. Finished goods may be easily sold if not highly specialized but, in general, we expect them to be less liquid than raw materials. In all the cases above, the time to find the right buyer and to negotiate a satisfactory price may be quite long. For these reasons, inventories are likely to be the least liquid of current assets. Fixed assets, made up of plant and equipment, are usually very illiquid because selling price is uncertain and because a substantial amount of time may be required to find a buyer (the "right" buyer) willing to pay full value for the assets.

Why Liquidity Matters. The firm is concerned with liquidity because it possesses short-term liabilities that it must be capable of meeting at face value. If the firm cannot meet these liabilities, its existence is threatened and, along with it, the future streams of returns to shareholders. Thus, illiquidity threatens shareholder wealth.

Winn Company has, as shown in Table 20-1, several short-term liabilities that it must meet: accounts payable, other payables, and short-term debt. In the course of business operations, the sources of funds to meet these liabilities come from the current assets of the firm. It is the liquidity of these assets (as well as cash flow) that matters in measuring the ability of Winn Company to meet its short-term obligations.

The Liquidity Ratios

Table 20-3 shows three **liquidity ratios:** the current ratio, the acid test ratio, and the absolute liquidity ratio. As the table shows, the current ratio is calculated by dividing current assets by current liabilities.

$$(1) \quad \text{Current ratio} = \frac{\text{Current assets}}{\text{Current liabilities}} = \frac{CA}{CL} = 1.57$$

The acid test ratio is calculated by dividing liquid assets and receivables by current liabilities.

(2)   Acid test ratio $= \dfrac{\text{Liquid assets + Receivables}}{\text{Current liabilities}} = \dfrac{\text{LA + R}}{\text{CL}} = 0.86$

The absolute liquidity ratio is obtained by dividing liquid assets by current liabilities.

(3)   Absolute liquidity ratio $= \dfrac{\text{Liquid assets}}{\text{Current liabilities}} = \dfrac{\text{LA}}{\text{CL}} = 0.14$

Each of these ratios represents a different time perspective in measuring the ability of the firm to meet its short-term debt obligations. The current ratio relates the quantity of current assets to current liabilities to judge the extent to which the firm could meet its short-term obligations assuming all that current assets were converted to cash. The acid test ratio has an implicitly shorter time perspective than the current ratio because it excludes the least liquid current asset, inventories, as an asset subject to liquidation for purposes of meeting short-term obligations. The shortest time perspective is presented by the absolute liquidity ratio, since only liquid assets are evaluated relative to current liabilities.

Interpretation of Liquidity Ratios

In Table 20-3, all Winn Company's liqudity ratios are low when compared to calculator industry averages. This may suggest that Winn Company is less liquid than average companies in the industry. Beyond that, Winn Company's liquidity ratios do not *automatically* mean that it has a liquidity problem. Whether a liquidity problem exists depends in part on the perspective of the person evaluating the firm and in part on the magnitude and timing of *future* cash inflows and outflows. Future liquidity, not past liquidity, is, after all, the crucial matter.

If the person evaluating Winn Company's liquidity is a commercial banker considering a loan application, that person may regard existing liquidity as too low relative to the industry and the loan may be in jeopardy. However, because Winn Company's ratios imply less-than-average liquidity does not necessarily mean that a loan will not be obtained.

The financial manager of the firm might take a different perspective—recognizing that Winn Company does have less-than-average liquidity but also recognizing that Winn is different from many firms making up the industry average of ratios. Winn, for example, may have less volatile sales and, thus, more stable cash flows than most firms in the industry. Consequently, it may *require* less liquidity than many firms.

This discussion points up a problem inherent in ratio analysis: we do not know what an *optimal* ratio value is for the goal of shareholder wealth maximization. Consequently, we cannot really say that Winn Company's current ratio of 1.57 is either "good" or "bad." How can we say that the industry average current ratio of 2.00 is an optimal ratio? No two firms in an industry face identical conditions and, moreover, we have no way of knowing whether firms represented in the industry average are behaving in an optimal fashion.

We cannot resolve this problem because the state of the art does not yet permit it. Instead, we fall back on our judgment as financial managers to supplement comparison of Winn Company liquidity ratios. If Winn Company is very like average companies in the industry, it would appear that the firm has too little liquidity and may be in danger of a liquidity crisis that might render it unable to meet its bills and from which it might not survive if creditors sue for default on payments. Actions to improve liquidity would then be in order.

However, firms can also have *too much* liquidity as measured by high values of the liquidity ratios. Again, the magnitudes of liquidity ratios required to determine that excessive liquidity exists are ambiguous. Using the industry ratios as a benchmark of comparison, very high liquidity ratios, such as a current ratio of 4.00, might warrant a conclusion that excessive liquidity exists. Such excess liquidity is inconsistent with shareholder wealth maximization because current assets may yield a relatively low average rate of return compared to the cost of financing them. Furthermore, excessive liquid assets tie up scarce capital usable in long-term, profitable, capital investment, or capital that could be disbursed to shareholders. Shareholders could profitably invest such capital outside the firm to their own benefit.

Clearly, the interpretation of liquidity ratios is best done with care. As with other financial ratios, the meaning of liquidity ratios is ambiguous. These ratios must be supplemented with *cash budgets* and *sources and uses statements*.

Sources and Uses Statements: A Supplement for Liquidity Ratios

Important questions remain about Winn's liquidity. How did the firm get into its current liquidity situation? And does the firm face a genuine problem of meeting its cash payments in the near future? Since the balance sheet information reflects the firm's financial position at a single point in time, it may provide little help in foreseeing continuing demand for cash in the coming months. A *cash budget* is useful for the latter purpose. We postpone development of cash budgets until Chapter 22. But we can find out how the firm got to its present position by constructing and evaluating a sources and uses statement.

The **sources and uses statement** identifies the major sources and uses of financing that have occurred over a given period. A *source* of funds is any increase in a liability or decrease in an asset. For instance, a reduction in accounts receivable and an increase in trade payables represent sources of funds. A *use* of funds is an increase in an asset or a decrease in a liability. An increase in inventories and a decrease in bank debt are examples of uses of funds.

A major cause of a firm's liquidity problem can arise when permanent increases in the level of fixed assets are financed with short-term liabilities. The demand for cash to meet maturing short-term obligations occurs within a year, whereas the fixed assets may generate cash flows over a number of years. Suppose, for example, that a firm obtained a 90-day bank loan to finance the construction of a new plant, that will not begin to generate the first of a long series of cash flows for 18 months. When the debt becomes due, no cash will have been generated by the asset and the firm may face severe financial distress, even bankruptcy, if other financing arrangements are not made. Short-term sources of funds in combination with long-term uses can be extremely unhealthy for any firm.

Unfortunately, such situations are not as uncommon as we might wish. A firm that has not planned adequately for a proposed expansion might delay payment of trade creditors to finance expansion. Effectively, the firm is borrowing from its suppliers to finance growth. If such a financing strategy is continued, one of two outcomes may result: creditors may demand payment by threatening the firm with bankruptcy, or they may cut off future deliveries of essential supplies. Either action may put the firm in serious trouble unless some form of accommodation is reached.

The sources and uses statement can identify inappropriate financing practices that could have led to the firm's liquidity problems. Table 20-4 shows the balance sheets for Winn Company for 1981 and 1984. A simple but revealing sources and uses statement can be constructed by taking the differences between the accounts over the 4-year period. Notice that receivables went from $50,000 to $250,000, an increase of $200,000. Clearly, this is a *use* of funds. The remaining uses of funds, inventories and fixed assets, also showed substantial increases, of $175,000 and $275,000 respectively. Looking at sources of funds, we can see that all payables increased $50,000 over the period, and short-term bank debt increased by $212,500. Long-term debt and equity increased by $387,500.

Whether these changes will create liquidity problems depends on the nature of the sources and uses of funds. If the increase in current assets and receivables is a permanent rather than a temporary, seasonal phenomenon, then long-term financing is often favored for these assets as well as for fixed assets. Long-term debt and equity financing increased

Table 20–4   *Sources and Uses Statement: Winn Company, 1981–1984*

	1981	1984	Sources	Uses
Current Assets				
Cash and Marketable Securities	$ 50,000	$ 50,000		
Receivables	50,000	250,000		$200,000
Inventories	75,000	250,000		175,000
Total	$175,000	$ 550,000		
Fixed Assets	275,000	550,000		275,000
Total Assets	$450,000	$1,100,000		
Current Liabilities				
Accounts Payable	$ 17,500	$ 35,000	$ 17,500	
Other Payables	32,500	65,000	32,500	
Short-term Debt (7%)	37,500	250,000	212,500	
Total	$ 87,500	$ 350,000		
Long-term Debt (9%)	112,500	250,000	137,500	
Net Worth	250,000	500,000	250,000	
Total Liabilities	$450,000	$1,100,000	$650,000	$650,000

over the period by $387,500. Since fixed assets of $275,000 were financed, the difference of $112,500 in permanent financing was used to partially finance a $375,000 increase in permanent current assets. Clearly, the majority of the new current assets are supported by new current liabilities. This situation may be unhealthy, and changes in the current asset–current liability relationship may be appropriate.

Like the liquidity ratios already discussed, the sources and uses statement requires careful interpretation. Basically, this statement provides a partial rationale for the current liquidity situation and allows focus on specific balance sheet accounts. The general causes of liquidity problems can be identified. Other methods of identifying these causes are discussed in sections that follow.

LEVERAGE ANALYSIS BY RATIOS: WINN COMPANY COMPARED TO THE INDUSTRY

We know from earlier chapters that **financial leverage** describes the use of debt financing rather than equity to finance some portion of the firm's assets.[2] Since these payments must be made before dividends can be paid and since failure to pay interest on debt creates financial distress

---

[2]Preferred stock financing also provides financial leverage for common shareholders. Failure to pay preferred dividends does not lead to bankruptcy. We ignore preferred stock in determining financial leverage in this chapter.

that may result in bankruptcy, managers, security holders, and others with a financial stake in the firm are interested in the proportion of debt financing. The advantage associated with an interest tax subsidy and the disadvantage associated with possible financial distress must be balanced by the firm. Again using Winn Company as an example, we want to discern whether the firm is appropriately leveraged.

Leverage Ratios   Table 20-3 lists eight **financial leverage ratios,** numbered 4 through 11, for Winn Company and the industry. Only the first three are needed to evaluate our current concern with leverage and the ability of the firm to pay its bills. The other leverage ratios are covered by our discussion of leverage and profitability.

The debt to net worth ratio (4) compares the quantity of interest-bearing debt issued by the firm with the net worth of the firm.

$$(4) \quad \frac{\text{Debt}}{\text{Net worth}} = \frac{\text{Short-term and long-term debt}}{\text{Net worth}} = \frac{\text{STD + LTD}}{\text{NW}} = 1.00$$

The net worth position represents a cushion of protection for creditors because in the event of financial adversity, shareholders will lose their investment in the firm before creditors will lose theirs. Therefore, the higher the debt/net worth ratio, the higher the degree of leverage and the greater the risk to holders of debt.

A different perspective on leverage is obtained by the coverage of interest charges ratio (5).

$$(5) \quad \text{Coverage of interest charges} = \frac{\text{Net operating income}}{\text{Interest charges}} = \frac{\text{NOI}}{\text{INT}} = 4.55$$

The lower this ratio becomes, the higher the degree of financial leverage and the greater the risk to holders of debt. A low average ratio provides less protection for debtholders if operating income temporarily (or permanently) declines. The coverage ratio and the debt/net worth ratio may give different perspectives because of variations in interest rates on outstanding debt for firms being compared. For example, two firms that have identical quantities of debt and are otherwise similar might have paid different interest rates on their debt. The two firms would have *identical* debt/net worth ratios, but the firm paying the higher interest rate on outstanding debt would possess the lowest coverage ratio and would be properly interpreted as being more highly levered.

The last leverage ratio under present consideration is the ratio of total assets to net worth.

$$(6) \quad \frac{\text{Total assets}}{\text{Net worth}} = \frac{\text{TA}}{\text{NW}} = 2.20$$

This ratio takes a broader view of leverage than does the debt/net worth ratio. The latter ratio considers only the leverage stemming from interest-bearing debt, whereas total assets/net worth considers leverage from non-interest-bearing liabilities as well. This property, easily seen by noting that the difference between total assets and net worth represents all liabilities, may be especially important for firms having relatively little interest-bearing debt but substantial quantities of non-interest-bearing liabilities such as accounts payable. High values of the total assets/net worth ratio imply a high degree of leverage, a smaller net worth cushion for creditors and, therefore, more risk for creditors. In addition to providing a broader view of leverage, the total assets/net worth ratio is particularly useful in assessing the contribution of leverage to profitability later in this chapter.

Interpretation of Leverage Ratios

From the leverage ratios in Table 20-3, we can see that Winn Company uses leverage to a greater degree than do other firms in the industry. This is evidenced by higher than average debt/net worth and total asset/net worth ratios and a lower than average coverage of interest charges ratio.

Whether Winn Company's use of leverage is excessive depends on other considerations. If Winn Company is different enough from firms represented in the industry average, it may be able to operate successfully at a higher leverage position than can the average firm in the industry. This might be true if, for example, Winn's sales were less volatile than the industry average and the resulting cash flows available to meet debt obligations are more stable over time.

If we feel that Winn Company is enough like other firms in the industry in most important respects, we might conclude that the firm is too highly leveraged. Correction of this condition by moving toward the industry leverage ratios as a benchmark would require replacement of debt with additional equity financing to expand net worth. However, as was the case with liquidity, we do not know what is an optimal leverage position. When we move toward the industry ratio benchmark, we are implicitly assuming that such a benchmark is desirable.

PROFITABILITY ANALYSIS BY RATIOS: WINN

Shareholder wealth depends on the expected returns and risks of anticipated future cash flows. Valuation of those flows is fundamentally a market process. It should be obvious that financial statements, by reflecting the past, cannot adequately capture the future activity of the firm. Historical financial information cannot directly reflect the risk and

COMPANY COMPARED TO THE INDUSTRY

timing of future cash flows. Yet, on a narrower dimension, a type of profitability analysis centering on historical book value rates of return as determined from the firm's financial statements, can provide useful information for the manager and for financial analysts outside the firm.

Profitability: A Definition

It is interesting to note that even though many academicians and practitioners talk about **profitability,** very few define the concept. Measurement of *anticipated* profitability requires that an analyst compare the expected rate of return of an investment with the rate of return required by investors in capital markets. If the expected rate is greater than the required rate, an investment is said to be profitable. The absolute size of the expected rate really tells us nothing about profitability. Only when compared to a market-determined standard does the term "profitability" become meaningful.

Ratio analysis does not permit this type of profitability assessment because it relies on accounting information that can be taken from income statements and balance sheets. Indeed, the term "profitability" is probably no longer appropriate to describe analysis of book value rates of return. However, that is what profitability analysis entails in the context of ratio analysis. It relates income as measured by the income statement to a book value measure of investment, then compares the resulting number with an appropriate industry average or historical firm average. We adhere to this definition of profitability with all its ambiguities and faults because it is widely used and because it still may provide some useful input to the evaluation and planning processes.

The Return on Net Worth Ratio: A Starting Point

Profitability is measured in ratio analysis by the return on net worth ratio (20).

$$(20) \quad \text{Return on net worth} = \frac{\text{Net income}}{\text{Net worth}} = \frac{\text{NI}}{\text{NW}} = 0.148$$

The ratio tells how many dollars of net income are returned per dollar of shareholder investment in the firm. From an examination of this ratio in Table 20-3, it appears that Winn is slightly more profitable than average firms in the industry. However, we cannot stop with this apparently good news for Winn's owners. We must learn why Winn's return on net worth is higher than the industry average, for an understanding of the major causes of this result may aid the firm in improving its future performance.

There are two types of explanation for the difference in profitability between Winn and the industry average. The first type is economic and is obtained by the **du Pont system** of financial analysis. The second stems from peculiarities of accounting practice and the effects of inflation on financial statements. Differences in the age of plant and equipment, original purchase price of assets, depreciation policies, and expensing policies affect the rate of return on net worth. Even a large disparity between industry and firm profitability ratios may be attributable to such factors. In the discussion of the du Pont analysis we assume that firm and industry data have been properly adjusted so that the ratios are comparable.

We need a way of linking the return on net worth ratio to financial conditions affecting the two terms in that ratio, net income and net worth. The du Pont system, in the form presented below, provides such linkages between financial conditions subject to managerial control and financial ratios. In basic form, the du Pont system is diagrammed in Table 20-5. Use this exhibit as a map of the sequence of analysis that follows, which combines activity, leverage, and profitability ratios.
    Remaining ratios to be discussed are:

The du Pont System of Financial Analysis

Profitability Ratios

(19)   Return on total assets $= \dfrac{\text{Net income}}{\text{Total assets}} = \dfrac{NI}{TA}$

(18)   Net profit margin $= \dfrac{\text{Net income}}{\text{Sales}} = \dfrac{NI}{S}$

Leverage Ratios

(7)   Fixed assets/Net worth $= \dfrac{FA}{NW}$

(8)   Current assets/Net worth $= \dfrac{CA}{NW}$

(9)   Inventory/Net worth $= \dfrac{I}{NW}$

(10)   Receivables/Net worth $= \dfrac{R}{NW}$

(11)   Liquid assets/Net worth $= \dfrac{LA}{NW}$

Activity Ratios

(12)   Sales/Total assets $= \dfrac{S}{TA}$

(13)   Sales/Fixed assets $= \dfrac{S}{FA}$

(14)   Sales/Current assets $= \dfrac{S}{CA}$

(15)   Sales/Inventory $= \dfrac{S}{I}$

(16)   Sales/Receivables $= \dfrac{S}{R}$

(17)   Sales/Liquid assets $= \dfrac{S}{LA}$

The two profitability ratios are dimensions of profitability separate from return on net worth (20). Return on total assets (19) measures net income per dollar invested of *total assets* (as distinguished from net worth). Net profit margin (18) shows the net income earned per dollar of sales.

The five leverage ratios show the relation of various assets and asset groupings to the size of net worth. Although these are formally classed as leverage ratios, our interest in them now is primarily to complete analytical links between other ratios of greater interest for analysis of profitability. This is because the three leverage ratios discussed pre-

Table 20–5   *Profitability Analysis by the Expanded Du Pont System*

Return on Net Worth: $\dfrac{NI}{NW}$

Leverage Contribution: $= \dfrac{TA}{NW} \times \dfrac{NI}{TA}$

Profit Margin and Total Asset Utilization Contribution: $= \dfrac{TA}{NW} \times \dfrac{NI}{S} \times \dfrac{S}{TA}$

$=$

Fixed Asset Contribution: $\dfrac{NI}{S} \times \dfrac{FA}{NW} \times \dfrac{S}{FA}$

Current Asset Contribution: $\dfrac{NI}{S} \times \dfrac{CA}{NW} \times \dfrac{S}{CA}$

Inventory Contribution: $\dfrac{NI}{S} \times \dfrac{I}{NW} \times \dfrac{S}{I}$

Receivables Contribution: $\dfrac{NI}{S} \times \dfrac{R}{NW} \times \dfrac{S}{R}$

Liquid Assets Contribution: $\dfrac{NI}{S} \times \dfrac{LA}{NW} \times \dfrac{S}{LA}$

viously, debt/total assets (4), coverage of interest charges (5), and total assets, net worth (6), are adequate to evaluate the risks of leverage without the added ratios 7 through 11.

Activity ratios, 12 through 17, are used to measure the sales revenue generated per dollar investment in a particular group of assets. High values for activity ratios indicate that a high level of sales is being generated for the dollar investment in a particular asset group, low values for activity ratios, the converse.[3]

The du Pont system is a means of linking various financial ratios to explain the level of the return on net worth ratio (20). The system operates by *breaking up* the return on net worth ratio into products of *other* financial ratios. Table 20-5 identifies the links among various ratios and return on net worth. The linkages allow us to determine the contribution of leverage, profit margin, and investment in total, current, and various types of current asset to the level of return on net worth. Once these contributions have been determined, financial managers can detect problem areas in which improvements could improve return on net worth. In demonstrating the du Pont system, we make use of the ratio data for the Winn Company and the industry from Table 20-3.

Contribution of Leverage to Profitability

Favorable use of financial leverage is capable of accentuating returns to shareholders. To indicate the contribution of leverage to profitability, the return on net worth ratio (20) can be broken into two separate ratios: Return on total assets (19) and the leverage ratio, total assets to net worth (6).[4]

$$\frac{NI}{NW} = \frac{NI}{TA} \times \frac{TA}{NW}$$

Industry: $0.143 = 0.096 \times 1.50$

Winn: $0.148 = 0.067 \times 2.20$

Comparing Winn Company with the industry, we can see that Winn's return on total assets ratio (19) is substantially below that of the industry, 0.067 compared to 0.096. Per dollar of assets committed to the enter-

---

[3]Activity ratios are often called *turnover ratios* because they may be interpreted as the number of times an asset "turns over" in producing a dollar of sales. High turnover ratios mean a high degree of asset utilization.

[4]The products of separate ratios given in Table 20-3 will not always agree with the separately determined ratio that is equal to such a product. For example, the product of the industry's net profit margin and total assets to net worth is 0.144, not the separately calculated 0.143 given in Table 20-3 for return on net worth. This is discrepancy due to rounding error and occurs at times in the discussion that follows.

prise, Winn is *less* profitable than the industry average and Winn's higher return on net worth is attained *solely* by the use of greater leverage as measured by the total assets/net worth ratio (6), which more than offsets the lower return on total assets.

Our assessment of Winn's returns on net worth suggests that since leverage is an important factor in maintaining these returns at a level comparable to the industry, this firm's returns to shareholders are riskier than those of average firms in the industry. This conclusion assumes that Winn Company is otherwise very similar to other firms in the industry. It means that in spite of their higher than average rate of return, Winn shareholders could easily be worse off than shareholders of other firms in the industry. A comparison involving only rates of return on net worth hides this fact.

Contribution of Profit Margin and Total Asset Investment to Profitability

Winn Company shareholders may not now be as pleased with the profitability performance of the firm because so much of it depends on financial leverage. It is even more likely that displeasure would be voiced over the low return on total assets ratio since, if this ratio could be improved, return on net worth would also be substantially improved given the relatively high degree of leverage.

To learn *why* Winn's return on total assets ratio compares unfavorably with the industry's ratio value, we can break the return on net worth ratio (20) into *three* different ratios: total assets/net worth (6), net profit margin (18), and sales/total assets (12).

$$\frac{NI}{NW} = \frac{TA}{NW} \times \frac{NI}{S} \times \frac{S}{TA}$$

Industry: $0.143 = 1.50 \times 0.072 \times 1.33$

Winn: $0.148 = 2.20 \times 0.062 \times 1.09$

Winn's lower return on total assets ratio, 0.067, is due to lower net profit margin, 0.062, and sales/total assets, 1.09. Improvement in Winn's profitability will require improvement in one or both of the two latter ratios.

The financial manager of Winn Company might, upon evaluating the lower profit margin revealed by this analysis, conclude that expenses require greater control if profit margins are to be improved. Moreover, given that total asset activity is less than average as reflected in the relatively low sales/total assets ratio, the firm must either increase sales while holding down investment in assets committed to the enterprise or, given the level of sales, reduce the quantity of assets used by the firm in generating sales.

If it happens that sales are not likely to change in the short run, the financial manager seeking to improve total asset activity must identify the types of assets in which excessive investment has been made. If excessive funds committed to certain assets can be released from the enterprise or more profitably employed, the sales/total assets ratio can be increased and the return on net worth ratio augmented. The remaining portion of profitability analysis concerns itself with identifying areas where assets are excessive and underutilized in the Winn Company.

With Winn Company having a lower than average sales/total assets ratio, it is possible that fixed or current assets, or both, are excessive in relation to sales being generated. We can find out more about the problem of asset utilization by analzying the contribution of fixed assets to profitability. To do this we break the return on net worth ratio into three different ratios: net profit margin (18), fixed assets/net worth (7), and sales/fixed assets (13).

Contribution of Fixed and Current Asset Investments to Profitability

$$\frac{NI}{NW} = \frac{NI}{S} \times \frac{FA}{NW} \times \frac{S}{FA}$$

Industry: $0.143 = 0.072 \times 0.92 \times 2.18$

Winn: $0.148 = 0.062 \times 1.10 \times 2.18$

In this breakdown of returns to net worth, we observe that Winn's sales/fixed assets ratio is exactly the same as that of the industry. Winn's fixed assets/net worth ratio (7) is higher, but this is only corroborating evidence for Winn's earlier identified high leverage position. This means that Winn's investment in fixed assets is generating sales at exactly the same rate as in the industry, and no overinvestment on Winn's part in fixed assets is indicated.

Apparently, Winn's low sales/total assets ratio identified above is due to the relatively high investment in current assets. We can confirm this by breaking the return on net worth ratio into three different ratios in a manner analogous to our analysis of fixed assets.

$$\frac{NI}{NW} = \frac{NI}{S} \times \frac{CA}{NW} \times \frac{S}{CA}$$

Industry: $0.143 = 0.072 \times 0.58 \times 3.43$

Winn: $0.148 = 0.062 \times 1.10 \times 2.18$

Winn's sales/current assets ratio (14) is substantially lower than the industry's ratio. In other words, Winn generates fewer sales per dollar invested in current assets, and this causes lower total asset utilization and lower returns on net worth.

Having reached such a conclusion, we need to know whether all, or only part, of the current asset investment is excessive relative to sales. Fortunately, information on this issue is easily obtained by extending the method of the analysis now under discussion.

To assess the part each current asset plays in the identified overinvestment in current assets, the following breakdowns of the return on net worth ratio are used.

Inventory Contribution

$$\frac{NI}{NW} = \frac{NI}{S} \times \frac{I}{NW} \times \frac{S}{I}$$

Industry: $0.143 = 0.072 \times 0.25 \times 8.00$

Winn: $0.148 = 0.062 \times 0.50 \times 4.80$

Receivables Contribution

$$\frac{NI}{NW} = \frac{NI}{S} \times \frac{R}{NW} \times \frac{S}{R}$$

Industry: $0.143 = 0.072 \times 0.17 \times 12.00$

Winn: $0.148 = 0.062 \times 0.50 \times 4.80$

Liquid Assets Contribution

$$\frac{NI}{NW} = \frac{NI}{S} \times \frac{LA}{NW} \times \frac{S}{LA}$$

Industry: $0.143 = 0.072 \times 0.17 \times 12.00$

Winn: $0.148 = 0.062 \times 0.10 \times 24.00$

By evaluating each of these breakdowns we find that relative to the industry Winn Company has excessive investments in inventories and receivables and a deficient investment in liquid assets. This conclusion is supported by Winn Company's relatively low ratio of sales/inventories (15) and sales/receivables (16). Too much capital is invested in these assets relative to sales being generated and, as a result, profitability is lower than it would be if the quantities of these assets were trimmed. The deficiency of the liquid assets position is evidenced by the relatively high ratio of sales/liquid assets (17). This implies that overutilization of liquid assets exists with the attendant risk of sudden loss of liquidity under adversity. With the industry used as a benchmark, liquid assets should be expanded while receivables and inventories are being trimmed. On balance, current assets would then decline, but their composition would be altered in favor of liquid assets.

The rather long sequence of analysis of Winn Company through the use of financial ratios belies the brevity of the actual process when analysis is in the hands of a financial manager accustomed to its use. With ratio information at hand, the rapidity of the process can be understood if the reader examines Table 20-3 once again and follows through the recapitulation of the main events and conclusions of the analysis carried out above.

RATIO ANALYSIS OF WINN COMPANY COMPARED TO THE INDUSTRY: A RECAPITULATION

In liquidity analysis, use of the current ratio (1), acid test ratio (2), and absolute liquidity ratio (3) enabled us to discern in Table 20-3 that compared to the industry, Winn Company was relatively illiquid. If the industry ratio data are adequate to judge the Winn Company, then Winn Company's low liquidity ratios imply either that current assets must be increased against current liabilities or that current liabilities must be reduced against current assets.

Our leverage analysis of Winn Company showed that both the debt/net worth ratio (4) and the total assets/net worth ratio (6) were higher than the comparable industry ratios in Table 20-3. In addition, coverage of interest changes ratio (5) was lower than for the industry. Using the industry as a benchmark, Winn Company should expand net worth relative to debt and other creditor claims.

The important role of leverage at the Winn Company was made apparent when profitability was analyzed. When the return on net worth ratio (20) was broken into the total assets/net worth ratio (6) and the return on total assets ratio (19), we saw that much of the current return on net worth was produced by leverage and that, in fact, returns on total assets were low relative to the industry. In turn, return on total assets was low because the net profit margin ratio (18) and the sales/total assets ratio (12) were relatively low. Winn Company needed to improve both these ratios to approach industry performance. To improve asset utilization by increasing sales relative to assets, it was found that a reduction of current assets against sales was required. This conclusion was reached because the sales/fixed assets ratio (13) was comparable to the industry performance but the sales/current assets ratio (14) was relatively low—implying insufficient sales generated by current assets and, therefore, underutilization of current assets. Evaluation of the sales/inventories (15), sales/receivables (16), and sales/liquid assets (17) ratios showed that relative to sales, excess quantities of inventories and receivables were being held and that the quantity of liquid assets held was insufficient. The latter finding was consistent with the illiquidity earlier identified through liquidity analysis.

In short, Winn Company has insufficient liquidity, too much leverage, too low a profit margin, and too much invested in inventory and receivables. Corrections for these problems are part of the financial planning process described below. Before we render such assistance to Winn Company, however, we examine the firm's history by use of ratio analysis.

RATIO ANALYSIS OF WINN COMPANY OVER TIME

The current performance and condition of Winn Company probably did not happen all at once. Warnings must have occurred earlier. However, an examination in Table 20-6, of Winn Company's balance sheet and income statement over the past 4 years does not, on superficial examina-

Table 20–6   *Financial Statements: Winn Company, 1981–1984*

	1981	1982	1983	1984
Current Assets				
Cash and Securities	$ 50,000	$ 46,700	$ 50,000	$ 50,000
Receivables	50,000	110,000	175,000	250,000
Inventories	75,000	126,600	191,700	250,000
Total	$175,000	$283,300	$ 416,700	$ 550,000
Fixed Assets	275,000	366,700	458,300	550,000
Total Assets	$450,000	$650,000	$ 875,000	$1,100,000
Current Liabilities				
Accounts Payable	$ 17,500	$ 23,300	$ 29,200	$ 35,000
Other Payables	32,500	43,300	54,200	65,000
Short-term Debt (7%)	37,500	90,100	166,600	250,000
Total	$ 87,500	$156,700	$ 250,000	$ 350,000
Long-term Debt (9%)	112,500	160,000	238,000	250,000
Equity	250,000	333,300	387,000	500,000
Total Liabilities and Equity	$450,000	$650,000	$ 875,000	$1,100,000
Sales	$600,000	$800,000	$1,000,000	$1,200,000
Cost of Goods Sold	409,000	545,000	682,000	818,000
Administrative Expense	50,000	66,600	83,300	100,000
Depreciation	50,000	66,600	83,300	100,000
Operating Income	$ 91,000	$121,800	$ 151,400	$ 182,000
Interest Expense	12,750	20,707	33,082	40,000
Net Income Before Income Tax	$ 78,250	$101,093	$ 118,318	$ 142,000
Income Tax	37,560	48,525	56,793	68,000
Net Income	$ 40,690	$ 52,568	$ 61,525	$ 74,000

tion, reveal much unfavorable information. Profits have nearly doubled in 4 years!

However, when financial ratios are calculated for each of the 4 years we find that several of the unfavorable conditions identified for the most recent year, 1984, were also evident and getting worse in earlier years. Table 20-7 shows that 1981 was similar in many respects to the industry average ratio data in Table 20-3. Winn had, even at that time, greater leverage, but the liquidity position was identical. The return on total assets ratio was roughly comparable as were the net profit margin and sales/total assets ratios. Given Winn's higher leverage position, the return on net worth ratio was markedly greater.

Evaluating Winn Company ratios over time, we can see that: the liquidity ratios (1–3) all decline; the leverage ratios (4–11) all indicate higher leverage; profit margins decline (18); return on assets declines (19); and utilization of inventories and receivables in generating sales, as measured by activity ratios (15) and (16), declines.

Table 20–7   *Financial Ratios Over Time: Winn Company, 1981–1984*

	Formula	1981	1982	1983	1984
Liquidity Ratios					
1. Current	CA/CL	2.00	1.81	1.67	1.57
2. Acid Test	(LA + R)/CL	1.14	1.00	0.90	0.85
3. Absolute Liquidity	LA/CL	0.57	0.30	0.20	0.14
Leverage Ratios					
4. Debt/Net Worth	(STD + LTD)/NW	0.60	0.75	1.05	1.00
5. Interest Coverage	NOI/INT	7.14	5.88	4.58	4.55
6. Total Assets/Net Worth	TA/NW	1.80	1.95	2.26	2.20
7. Fixed Assets/Net Worth	FA/NW	1.10	1.10	1.18	1.10
8. Current Assets/Net Worth	CA/NW	0.70	0.85	1.08	1.10
9. Inventory/Net Worth	I/NW	0.30	0.38	0.50	0.50
10. Receivables/Net Worth	R/NW	0.20	0.33	0.45	0.50
11. Liquid Assets/Net Worth	LA/NW	0.20	0.14	0.13	0.10
Activity Ratios					
12. Sales/Total Assets	S/TA	1.33	1.23	1.14	1.09
13. Sales/Fixed Assets	S/FA	2.18	2.18	2.18	2.18
14. Sales/Current Assets	S/CA	3.43	2.82	2.40	2.18
15. Sales/Inventories	S/I	8.00	6.32	5.22	4.80
16. Sales/Receivables	S/R	12.00	7.27	5.71	4.80
17. Sales/Liquid Assets	S/LA	12.00	17.13	20.00	24.00
Profitability Ratios					
18. Net Profit Margin	NI/S	.068	.066	.062	0.062
19. Return on Total Assets	NI/TA	.090	.081	.070	0.067
20. Return on Net Worth	NI/NW	.163	.158	.159	0.148

Clearly the financial manager of Winn Company, by use of financial ratios with comparisons of Winn's performance and condition over time, might have identified the problems in liquidity, leverage, profit margins, and excess inventories and receivables at incipient stages. Remedial action could have been taken in a more timely fashion.

FINANCIAL PLANNING OF OPERATING PERFORMANCE AND CONDITION BY USE OF RATIOS

A firm can plan for future operating performance and financial condition by using target financial ratios. Target ratios may be independently derived or, if judged desirable to do so, averages of financial ratios for firms in an industry may be used.

To illustrate the process of financial planning by use of ratios, we assume that the Winn Company, at the end of 1984, decides to change its performance and financial condition to be identical, on a ratio basis, with the industry average. We also assume that for the foreseeable future, Winn Company's sales will remain at $1.2 million.

To quantify the changes that must occur for the firm to change its financial condition, the firm can develop pro forma financial statements. That is, the firm creates hypothetical balance sheets and income statements using the assumption that the anticipated changes in the firm's financial condition have been effected. These statements identify all major changes that must be made and provide a target toward which the firm desires to move.

Pro forma financial statements for Winn Company derived from industry financial ratios appear in Table 20-8, which shows three columns. The first indicates Winn's current financial position. The second shows each pro forma account as it would appear if all changes were accomplished. Column three presents the difference between existing statements and the pro forma statement.

Given these calculations, the major changes in Winn's financial statements are easily summarized. Better control of inventories and receivables (using procedures discussed in Chapter 23) will reduce those assets by a total of $250,000. Of this amount, $50,000 can be used to bring liquid assets to the desired level of $100,000. The net amount of $200,000 obtained by reducing current assets can be applied, in part, to reduce short-term debt by $175,000 to the desired level of $75,000. Long-term debt can be retired with the remaining $25,000. However, an additional $100,000 necessary to reduce existing long-term debt to the desired level of $125,000 should be raised, either through an infusion of new equity funds or through retention of earnings. Either outside funds obtained from investors or internally generated funds retained in the business will bring net worth to its desired level of $600,000.

Table 20–8   *Actual 1984 and Pro Forma Balance Sheets and Income Statements: Winn Company*

	1984	Pro Forma	Changes
Current Assets			
Cash and Securities	$ 50,000	$ 100,000	+$ 50,000
Receivables	250,000	100,000	− 150,000
Inventories	250,000	150,000	− 100,000
Total	$ 550,000	$ 350,000	−$200,000
Fixed Assets	$ 550,000	$ 550,000	0
Total Assets	$1,100,000	$ 900,000	−$200,000
Current Liabilities			
Accounts Payable	$ 35,000	$ 35,000	0
Other Payables	65,000	65,000	0
Short-term Debt (7%)	250,000	75,000	−$175,000
Total	$ 350,000	$ 175,000	−$175,000
Long-term Debt (9%)	$ 250,000	$ 125,000	−$125,000
Equity	500,000	600,000	+ 100,000
Total Claims	$1,100,000	$ 900,000	−$200,000
Sales	$1,200,000	$1,200,000	0
Cost of Goods Sold	718,000	718,000	0
Administrative Expense	100,000	100,000	0
Depreciation	100,000	100,000	0
Operating Income	$ 182,000	$ 182,000	0
Interest Expense	40,000	16,500	−$ 23,500
Net Income Before Tax	$ 142,000	$ 165,500	+$ 23,500
Income Tax (48%)	68,000	79,440	+ 11,440
Net Income	$ 74,000	$ 86,060	+$ 12,060

1. Determine the desired size of all asset categories by dividing Winn's pro forma sales by the industry's activity ratios relevant for each asset.

$$\text{Total assets} = S \div \frac{S}{TA} = \frac{\$1,200,000}{1.33} = \$900,000$$

$$\text{Fixed assets} = S \div \frac{S}{FA} = \frac{\$1,200,000}{2.18} = \$550,000$$

$$\text{Current assets} = S \div \frac{S}{CA} = \frac{\$1,200,000}{3.43} = \$350,000$$

$$\text{Inventories} = S \div \frac{S}{I} = \frac{\$1,200,000}{8.00} = \$150,000$$

(continued)

$$\text{Receivables} = S \div \frac{S}{R} = \frac{\$1,200,000}{12.00} = \$100,000$$

$$\text{Liquid assets} = S \div \frac{S}{LA} = \frac{\$1,200,000}{12.00} = \$100,000$$

2. Determine the desired net worth position by dividing target total assets of $900,000 by the industry ratio of total assets/net worth.

$$\text{Net worth} = TA \div \frac{TA}{NW} = \frac{\$900,000}{1.50} = \$600,000$$

3. Determine the total interest-bearing debt position by multiplying the target net worth position of $600,000 by the industry ratio of debt/net worth.

$$\text{Total debt} = NW \times \frac{STD + LTD}{NW} = \$600,000 \times 0.33 = \$200,000$$

4. Determine the target current liability position by dividing target current assets of $350,000 by the industry current ratio.

$$\text{Current liabilities} = CA \div \frac{CA}{CL} = \frac{\$350,000}{2.00} = \$175,000$$

5. Determine short-term debt by subtracting from target current liabilities of $175,000 the $100,000 level of accounts payable and other payables (the latter are assumed not to change in this problem but obviously could be changed if desired).

Short-term debt = $175,000 − $100,000 = $75,000

6. Determine long-term debt by subtracting short-term debt from total debt of $200,000.

Long-term debt = $200,000 − $75,000 = $125,000

7. Recompute interest expense at 7 percent on short-term debt and 9 percent on long-term debt (assuming that these rates have not changed).

Short-term interest = 0.07 × $75,000 = $ 5,250
Long-term interest = 0.09 × $125,000 = $\underline{\quad 11,250}$
$16,500

8. Recompute taxes at 48 percent and determine the new net income as shown in Table 20–8.

Winn Company's target financial performance and condition were determined fairly quickly by use of financial ratios. This method is very flexible, since we could have achieved alternative pro forma statements for different levels of sales than the $1.2 million assumed in Table 20-8.

The real problem is not the mechanics of the pro forma construction process but the validity of the target financial ratios used in the process. We employed industry ratios as targets for Winn Company, but the earlier comments on the ambiguity of financial ratios and the absence of definitive optimal ratio values should be important reminders that the determination of target financial ratios for planning purposes is also an imprecise selection process.

A major assumption implicit in using financial ratios to estimate pro forma operating performance and condition for the firm is that target financial ratios are invariant to the scale of the firm's activity. In other words, it is assumed that desired asset levels expand *proportionally* to sales. However, this assumption may not hold for some kinds of assets.

A Problem of Proportionality

For example, the analysis in Table 20-8 assumed that a target level of the sales/total assets ratio of 1.33 was appropriate for the existing $1.2 million level of sales. But what if pro forma sales were $5 million? Would the same target ratio have been applicable? The answer to that question may well be no because some classes of assets do not necessarily increase proportionally to increases in sales. One of these classes is fixed assets, for a given level of fixed assets may serve a wide range of sales. Liquid asset holdings, as we see in Chapter 22, also do not increase proportionally to sales; nor do inventories.

That is, for large increases in sales, the use of financial ratios to establish pro forma desired levels of assets must be carefully qualified. One way of providing more refinement to minimize the nonproportionality problem is to use industry ratio data broken down by size of firm. When substantial increases in sales are projected, a better judgment on new desired asset levels may be made in this way than when the firm's *existing* ratios are employed.

We have seen that financial ratios greatly assist financial analysis of the performance and condition of the firm and are also helpful in planning future desired asset levels and estimating working capital requirements associated with capital budgeting proposals. At the same time, certain ambiguities in the interpretation of financial ratios have been identified as well as the problem of the assumption of proportionality in using ratios to plan the future financial condition of the firm.

DISTORTING EFFECTS OF ACCOUNTING PRACTICES AND INFLATION ON FINANCIAL RATIOS

But additional qualifications remain. One relates to the general difficulty of comparing ratios of two different firms; a second relates to difficulties interjected by the presence of inflation. Both illustrate inadequacies of accounting data, which should be corrected to permit valid inferences to be drawn from ratio analysis. To identify these inadequacies and the problems they present, we have prepared an example.

Under generally accepted accounting principles, considerable variation in some accounting practices is tolerated. For example, firms may use several different methods for valuing inventory. Different degrees of conservatism in estimating and validating bad debts can be expected to prevail. Differences in methods of determining depreciation are also permitted. Finally, the valuation of fixed assets by *historical costs* rather than current market value may produce substantial differences in financial ratios when different companies are compared or the same company's performance is evaluated over time. Such differences are made worse under inflationary conditions.

We do not give a complete analysis of *why* differences in accounting treatment produce variations in financial ratios between firms. Nor do we comment on which accounting methods are "best." Rather, we simply show the range in the measured magnitudes of some financial ratios that can result from differences in accounting treatment and from the existence of inflation. In Table 20-9, two firms, Schreiber, Inc., and Opray Company, are represented. Schreiber is a newer company whose fixed assets reflect higher purchase prices because of inflation and less accumulated depreciation than does Opray. Schreiber also values in-

Table 20–9   *Effects of Differing Accounting Treatments and Inflation on Financial Ratios*

	Schreiber, Inc.	Opray Company
Current Assets		
Liquid Assets	$100	$100
Receivables	500	600
Inventories	500	450
Total	$1,100	$1,150
Fixed Assets	1,900	1,200
Total Assets	$3,000	$2,350
Current Liabilities	$550	$550
Net Worth	2,450	1,800
Total Claims	$3,000	$2,350
Net Sales	$6,000	$6,125
Cost of Goods Sold	4,000	4,050
Depreciation	200	140
Operating Income	$1,800	$1,935
Income Taxes (50%)	900	968
Net Income	$ 900	$ 968
Return on Net Worth	36.7%	53.8%
Net Profit Margin	15.0%	15.8%
Sales/Total Assets	2.0	2.6
Sales/Current Assets	5.4	5.3
Sales/Inventory	12.0	13.6
Sales/Receivables	12.0	10.2

ventories by the first-in-first-out (FIFO) method. When prices of purchased goods are rising, the FIFO method tends to show higher inventory values, lower cost of goods sold, and higher net income performance than under the last-in-first-out (LIFO) method employed by Opray. Finally, Schreiber is more conservative in allowing and validating higher bad debts than Opray. Thus, even though gross sales of the two firms are identical, net sales and reported net receivables are lower for Schreiber than for Opray.

Collectively, Opray's accounting practices lead, in the face of inflation, to lower reported levels of inventory and fixed assets than in Schreiber's case. Although Opray's practice of charging off fewer bad debts against sales does produce a larger receivables position (and higher sales), the net effect is a lower reported total assets position. Against the higher level of sales, Opray Company's performance in profitability and in asset utilization *appears* to be superior. Adjustments to give the two firms similar accounting treatments are necessary to make comparisons between their financial ratios more valid. Furthermore, valuation of fixed assets on a market value basis are also needed to form valid comparisons between the two firms.

Apart from financial ratios calculated from financial statements of individual firms, there exist several published sources of financial ratios.

SOURCES OF FINANCIAL RATIOS

A well-known collection of 14 average-valued financial ratios for 125 industries—termed *lines of business activity*—is published by Dun and Bradstreet. Not only are average ratio values in the form of the statistical median value given, but a range of ratio values including upper and lower quartile ratio values is provided. The number of ratios published is not as broad as the number used in this chapter, but missing ratios can often be estimated by manipulating those that are given.

Dun and Bradstreet

The U.S. government, jointly through the Federal Trade Commission and the Securities and Exchange Commission, provides quarterly data on income statements, balance sheets, and financial ratios for several industry groupings in the Quarterly Financial Report for Manufacturing.

Quarterly Financial Report for Manufacturing

This association comprised of commercial bank officers published 11 financial ratios annually in *Statement Studies*. Financial statements making up the data for these ratios come from loan transactions at banks.

Robert Morris Associates

Ratio data are broken down by size of firm within an industry and over 150 industries are reported on.

SUMMARY   *Financial analysis* is the process of reducing a large amount of historical financial data to a smaller set of more useful information for decision-making purposes. *Ratios* comprise part of that information. They are used to identify strengths and weaknesses of a firm and to aid in financial planning. Though there are many ratios that a financial analyst could compute, the basic purpose of all is to provide information about risk–return characteristics of the firm. Unfortunately, that information is often ambiguous. Historical orientation, accounting problems, and absence of unambiguous standards of comparison combine to cloud interpretation and to move ratio analysis toward the realm of art rather than science.

Four categories of ratios are used, to analyze *liquidity, financial leverage*, and *profitability. Liquidity* reflects the ability of the firm to meet short-term liabilities as they come due. An asset is said to be liquid if it can be easily converted to cash at a relatively certain price. Measuring the liquidity of a firm requires a comparison between current assets and current liabilities. Current, acid test, and absolute liquidity ratios are used for this purpose. *Financial leverage* arises when a firm uses fixed-payment financing (debt) rather than equity to finance some portion of its assets. Financial leverage increases the risk that shareholders must face because it increases the variability of returns and creates a greater possibility of financial distress. At the same time, debt is subsidized by the federal government (through tax deductions on interest payments), so the problem of the firm is to balance the advantages and the disadvantages of this form of financing. Firms use two ratios of two types, those that measure relative amounts of debt and equity financing and those that measure fixed financial payments on debt relative to net operating income. Though both types find wide use, the latter are probably the least ambiguous. *Profitability* analysis requires the firm to relate income to investment and to compare the resulting ratio with an appropriate industry standard or firm average. The initial ratio used is return on net worth. Once that ratio has been computed, its component parts can be examined using an expanded version of the *du Pont system*, which allows a firm to identify the source of any variation from the standard of comparison—thus assisting plans for remedial action that might be necessary.

Great care must be taken when comparing a firm's ratio with some standard. When comparing with industry averages, the analyst is assuming that industry standards are reasonable targets for the firm.

When historical firm averages are used as a standard, it is being assumed that product mix technology, demand, and accounting practices are consistent from one year to the next.

In addition to helping management identify problems that have arisen in the past, financial ratios can facilitate future financial planning. They provide targets to use in developing pro forma financial statements for projected levels of sales.

GLOSSARY OF KEY TERMS

Activity Ratios	Ratios that measure sales generated per dollar investment in assets. They are important in analyzing the components of profitability. Also known as *turnover ratios*.
du Pont System	A method of separating the rate of return on net worth into its component parts to identify specific sources of abnormal performance. Developed by the du Pont de Nemours Company.
Financial Analysis	The process of reducing a large amount of historical financial data to a smaller set of more useful information for decision-making purposes.
Financial Leverage	The use of fixed-promise financing (debt) rather than equity to finance some portion of a firm's assets.
Financial Leverage Ratios	A set of ratios used to measure the degree of financial leverage. These ratios are divided into two groups—those that measure relative amounts of debt and equity and those that measure promised financial charges relative to operating income.
Liquidity	Reflects the ability of the firm to meet short-term liabilities as they come due. An asset is said to be liquid if it can quickly be converted to cash at a relatively certain price.
Liquidity Ratios	A set of ratios used to measure the ability of the firm to meet short-term liabilities as they come due.
Profitability	A profitable investment is one that has an expected rate of return greater than the rate of return required by the market. In the context of ratio analysis, profitability is reflected by the dollar return per unit of investment. The typical *measures* of profitability are return on net worth and return on total assets.
Sources and Uses Statement	Identifies the major increases and decreases in assets and liabilities between two points in time and provides important information to explain

a firm's liquidity position. A *source* of funds is an increase in a liability or a decrease in an asset. A *use* is a decrease in a liability or an increase in an asset.

SELECTED REFERENCES

Beaver, William. "Financial Ratios as Predictors of Failure." In *Empirical Research in Accounting: Selected Studies* (Chicago: University of Chicago Press, 1966), pp. 71–127.

Edmister, Robert O. "An Empirical Test of Financial Ratio Analysis for Small Business Failure Prediction." *Journal of Financial and Quantitative Analysis* (March 1972), pp. 1477–1493.

Helfert, Erich A. *Techniques of Financial Analysis,* 4th ed. Homewood, IL: Richard D. Irwin, 1977.

Lev, Baruch. *Financial Statement Analysis: A New Approach.* Englewood Cliffs, NJ: Prentice-Hall, 1974.

Murray, Roger F. "The Penn Central Debacle: Lessons for Financial Analysis." *Journal of Finance* (May 1971), pp. 327–332.

Reiling, Henry B., and John C. Burton. "Financial Statements: Signposts as Well as Milestones." *Harvard Business Review* (November-December 1972), pp. 45–54.

QUESTIONS

1. Define the term "financial analysis." How does financial analysis differ from ratio analysis?

2. Define the terms "liquidity," "financial leverage," and "profitability."

3. Define and discuss problems of interpreting financial ratios. Why is ratio analysis often called an "art?"

4. Discuss the liquidity of the following assets: An inventory of Christmas cards in July, a used car, two tickets to the final game of the NBA championships, used office furniture, the headquarters building of a major corporation.

5. Why should a firm be concerned about its liquidity position?

6. How does a sources and uses statement supplement liquidity ratios?

7. Why should shareholders be concerned about too much liquidity?

8. How do the "profitability ratios" fall short in measuring profitability for a firm?

9. Compare the debt/equity and interest coverage ratios as measures of the impact of financial leverage.

10. Suppose a firm has a consistently high return on net worth. Does this imply that the firm does not need to worry about liquidity problems? Explain.

11. What role does the du Pont system play in ratio analysis?

12. Two firms in the same industry have identical rates of return on net worth. Can we conclude that they are equally profitable?

13. Why is it important to analyze trends in financial ratios as well as the level of ratios at a point in time?

14. Discuss the assumption underlying the use of financial ratios to construct pro forma financial statements.

1. The 1981 balance sheet and income statement for Leonard Corporation are shown below. Compute the necessary financial ratios, then analyze the performance of the firm as compared to the industry average. Use the du Pont system to explain profitability performance. **PROBLEMS**

Leonard Corporation

Balance Sheet, December 31, 1981

Assets		Liabilities	
Cash	$ 7,000	Accounts Payable	$ 50,000
Marketable Securities	10,000	Taxes Payable	18,000
Receivables	65,000	Bank Note (9%)	40,000
Inventories	70,000	Total	$108,000
Total	$152,000	Long-term Debt (7%)	55,200
Fixed Assets	120,000	Common Equity	108,800
	$272,000		$272,000

Leonard Corporation

Income Statement, December 31, 1981

Net Sales	$816,000
Cost of Goods Sold	652,800
Gross Margin on Sales	$163,200

Operating Expenses		
Selling	$42,000	
General Administrative	87,000	
Total Operating Expenses		129,000
Net Operating Income		$ 34,200
Less		
Interest on Long-term Debt	$ 3,864	
Interest on Notes Payable	3,600	
Total Interest		7,464
Income Before Taxes		$ 26,736
Federal Income Taxes (50%)		13,368
Income After Taxes		$ 13,368

Ratio:	Leonard Corporation	Industry Standard
Current		2.22
Acid Test		1.39
Absolute Liquidity		0.28
Return on Net Worth		0.124
Total Assets to Net Worth		1.61
Return on Total Assets		0.077
Net Profit Margin		0.026
Sales/Total Assets		3.00
Sales/Fixed Assets		5.00
Sales/Current Assets		7.50
Sales/Inventory		20.00
Sales/Receivables		15.00
Sales/Liquid Assets		60.00

2. Using the information below compute the balance sheet for a firm having $1.8 million in sales.

Sales/Total Assets	3.00
Sales/Fixed Assets	5.00
Sales/Current Assets	7.50
Sales/Inventories	20.00
Sales/Receivables	15.00
Sales/Liquid Assets	60.00
Current Ratio	2.00
Total Assets/Net Worth	1.40

Proceed in the order of the ratios given. (Long-term debt will be the residual item in the balance sheet.)

Assets	Liabilities and Capital
Liquid Assets	Current Liabilities
Receivables	Long-term Debt
Inventories	Net Worth
Total Current Assets	Total Liabilities and Capital
Plant and Equipment	
Total Assets	

3. Analyze the liquidity position of Sortino Ski Corporation as it changed between 1978 and 1981. Then construct a sources and uses statement to identify the source of any problem you discover. Recommend any actions that might improve Sortino's position. Note that sales increased from $1.1 million to $3 million over the period.

Assets	1978	1981	Liabilities and Capital	1978	1981
Cash	$ 13	$ 32	Accounts Payable	$ 58	$330
Accounts Receivable	60	226	Bank Loan	46	156
Inventories	147	496	Equipment Contracts	4	2
Prepayments	2	12	Salaries Payable	2	8
Total Current Assets	$222	$766	Federal Taxes Payable	4	24
			Total Current Liabilities	$114	$520
Fixed Assets	27	68	Loan from Officer	52	3
Total Assets	$249	$834	Common Stock	13	56
			Retained Earnings	70	255
			Total Liabilities	$249	$834

4. Assume that Winn Company anticipated an increase in sales from $1.2 to $1.4 million. Assuming that industry averages shown in Table 20-3 are appropriate standards, project a pro forma balance sheet (it may be helpful to follow the format developed in Table 20-8). Discuss the weaknesses associated with this method of constructing pro forma statements and suggest any alternatives that you feel might be preferable. Assume that accounts payable and other payables increase proportionately with sales. Also note that because industry ratios are rounded to two decimal places, the numbers you obtain will vary depending upon the sequence of steps used in the analysis.

5. Kramer Groceries is considering the installation of a $300,000 system of computerized checkout equipment. The manager estimates that the new machines could improve their current profit margin of 2 percent by at least $\frac{1}{2}$ percent without a change in their current level of $4.5 million sales. Kramer's sales/assets ratio is 3. What change in return on assets is expected?

6. Choose a firm and make a comprehensive financial analysis of it. Make sure to obtain necessary industry data and examine the pattern of relevant ratios over a five-year period. Be sure to comment on liquidity, financial leverage, and profitability. Do you perceive any specific problems facing this firm? Critique your own analysis. What assumptions were necessary? Do they seriously weaken your conclusions?

Working Capital Management

Working capital management is the process of planning and controlling the level and mix of the current assets of the firm as well as financing these assets. Specifically, working capital management requires financial managers to decide what quantities of cash, other liquid assets, accounts receivable, and inventories the firm will hold at any point in time. In addition, financial managers must decide how these current assets are to be financed. Financing choices include the mix of current as well as long-term liabilities.

An indication of the importance of working capital management to firms can be found in Table 21-1, which shows asset and liability mixes of four categories of firms—manufacturing, wholesaling, retailing, and services. More than 75 percent of assets in wholesaling and retailing are current assets. And even in manufacturing, where we usually think of large investments in physical facilities, more than 59 percent of assets are current assets. Service industries have the smallest investment in current assets primarily because they do not require the large investments in inventories held by firms of other types. When we consider financing of current assets, we observe that current liabilities are a smaller percentage of total assets than are current assets. For example, the service industry has current liability financing upward of 40 percent of total assets, whereas current assets are more than half of total assets. By implication, firms must employ a mix of current liabilities and long-term financing sources to finance investments in current assets. Still, the proportions of total assets financed by current liabilities are not insignificant, ranging from 33.9 to 60.7 percent of total assets for the sectors

Table 21-1 Working Capital Accounts as a Percentage [a] of Total Assets of Selected Sectors and Industries, 1978

Category	Cash and Equivalent	Accounts Receivable	Inventories	Other	Current Assets	Accounts Payable	Notes Payable	Other Accruals	Current Liabilities
Manufacturing									
Soap and Detergent	8.5%	31.0%	24.7%	2.1%	66.3%	18.9%	11.6%	9.6%	40.2%
Meat Packing	6.0	31.8	20.4	1.0	59.3	14.6	17.0	9.1	40.7
Publishing/Printing	6.9	28.9	29.7	3.2	68.7	15.0	10.7	17.0	42.7
Wholesaling									
Furniture	7.5	38.6	37.1	1.6	84.7	24.2	14.7	13.3	52.2
Jewelry	8.2	32.7	49.0	1.7	91.6	29.1	16.8	8.3	54.2
Sporting Goods	6.6	26.7	51.9	1.3	86.5	22.7	17.0	9.4	49.2
Retailing									
Office Supplies	7.3	30.8	41.0	1.1	80.2	21.1	14.1	10.7	45.8
Hardware	6.2	16.1	51.4	2.1	75.8	15.3	11.6	8.2	35.0
Department Stores	7.0	17.5	50.6	1.9	77.0	15.2	8.8	9.9	33.9
Services									
Data Processing	10.9	31.8	4.6	5.3	52.5	11.3	14.8	13.8	40.0
Legal Services	23.6	22.3	1.1	7.4	54.4	4.2	23.0	13.1	40.3
Travel Agencies	17.2	49.3	1.8	5.9	74.2	26.7	15.7	18.4	60.7

[a] Percentage values are based on total assets for the firm.
Source: Robert Morris Associates Annual Statement Studies, 1978. Taken from Keith V. Smith, Ed., Readings on the Management of Working Capital, 2nd ed. West Publishing Co., St. Paul, MN, 1980, p. 12.

shown in Table 21-1. Current liability, or short-term financing, is an important source of financing for most firms.

This chapter provides an overview of the working capital management process. After clarifying some widely used terminology, we pose and attempt to answer an important question, Why *do* firms invest in current assets? Then we describe the sources of financing for the firm's investment in current assets. At the end of the chapter, we attempt to reconcile working capital management decisions with our general goal of shareholder wealth maximization.

In practice, we hear the terms "working capital management," "working capital," and "net working capital" used in ambiguous ways. Clarification is necessary to avoid confusion.

Working capital is the current asset investment of the firm. **Net working capital** is the difference between the firm's current assets and current liabilities; it describes the part of the current asset investment financed from long-term capital financing sources. The remaining part of current asset financing is necessarily provided by current liabilities. **Working capital management** is management of the level and mix of current assets *and* their financing, which includes current liabilities and long-term sources.

Understanding of this terminology can be reinforced by looking at Table 21-2, which records information taken from the balance sheet of Logan Logging Company. Logan's working capital is the $40,000 investment in current assets. Its net working capital is $25,000—the difference

**SOME TERMI-
NOLOGY**

Table 21–2   *Working Capital and Financing Sources:*
Logan Logging Company

Current Assets		Current Liabilities	
Liquid Assets	$ 5,000	Accounts Payable	$ 5,315
Receivables	15,000	Short-term Loans	9,685
Inventory	20,000	Total	$15,000
Total	$40,000	Term Loan	10,000
Fixed Assets	40,000	Mortgage Payable	25,000
		Common Equity	30,000
Total Assets	$80,000	Total Claims	$80,000

Net working capital = Current assets − Current liabilities

= $40,000 − $15,000

= $25,000

between $40,000 of current assets and $15,000 of current liabilities. Working capital management provides the basic principles to use in determining the $40,000 investment in current assets, the mix of assets making up that total, the $15,000 of financing from current liabilities, and the $25,000 of financing from long-term sources.

WHY FIRMS INVEST IN CURRENT ASSETS

Virtually all firms invest in current assets (working capital) and therefore must finance such investments. We know that capital is scarce. It *costs* to finance investment in current assets. There had better be good reasons to justify such investment—and there are.

In general, investments in current assets are made to avoid potentially high costs of adjusting to uncertain events, (e.g., a sudden increase or decrease in a firm's sales or production, an unanticipated increase in cash expenditures). In a more positive sense, investments in some current assets may also stimulate sales and increase the stream of expected returns for shareholders.

The **cash cycle** described in Figure 21-1 is a useful way of depicting the relations among investments in various current assets. Beginning with the investment in liquid assets, purchases of raw materials and

Figure 21-1   *The Cash Cycle*

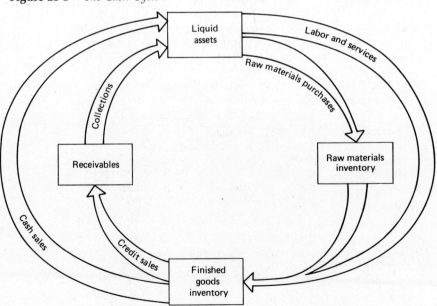

labor services are made with cash. The cash outflow associated with purchasing labor services and raw materials results in production of goods and services that, when sold, ultimately result in a stream of cash inflows returning to the liquid asset investment. The cash cycle is then complete. But there are steps along the way. Raw material purchases flow into raw materials inventory; raw materials flow out of that inventory when used in production of finished goods. The latter flow into finished goods inventory and then flow out as goods are sold. When credit sales occur, an investment in receivables is created. Upon collection, the receivable becomes cash, which flows into the liquid assets investment. *Cash* sales of finished goods flow directly to the liquid asset investment.

The investment in each type of current asset acts as a *reservoir*. When outflow exceeds inflow, the investment (the level of the reservoir) declines. When outflow is less than inflow, the investment increases. If inflow equals outflow, the investment is unchanged; that is, the level of the reservoir stays the same.

The Liquid Asset Investment

Firms invest in liquid assets held in the form of cash or other short-term marketable or nonmarketable assets. Uncertainty about the near-term rate of inflows and outflows in the cash cycle and the costs of adjusting to an unfavorable imbalance between inflow and outflow justify such a liquid asset balance.

An unfavorable imbalance of cash flows is represented in Figure 21-2, which plots the daily (it could have been weekly or monthly) cash in-

Figure 21-2   *Daily Cash Inflows and Outflows*

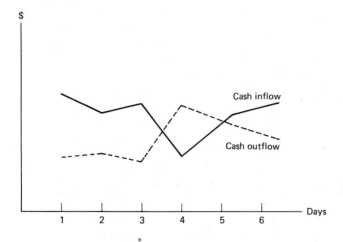

flows and outflows for a firm for a 6-day period. On days 1 to 3 and 5 and 6, cash inflows exceed cash outflows; the imbalance is favorable. But on day 4, outflow exceeds inflow. Day 4 cash inflow is insufficient to provide funds for that day's cash outflow. Now in the *absence* of a liquid asset investment, the firm would have a liquidity crisis (presumably minor in this case!). Required cash payments on day 4 could not be fully met. To meet the crisis, the firm could delay payment until cash inflow again exceeded outflow. But if abused, this alternative could create ill will on the part of the firm's creditors and could result in legal action because of default on payment terms of obligations. For example, suppose the delay in payment resulted in a missed payday for employees, a missed payment on a bank loan, or an omission of a promised payment on an account payable owed to an important supplier. Delaying payment is a potentially costly alternative!

The firm could also meet its liquidity crisis by selling some nonliquid asset—such as inventory. But this is difficult to do *quickly* while obtaining full value for the inventory (the "right" buyer cannot always be quickly located). A substantial loss on inventory could result from selecting this alternative. Finally, the firm could arrange to borrow the necessary amount to meet obligations. This too is costly, since interest must be paid.

These costs of adjusting to uncertainty about cash flows could be avoided by holding an investment in liquid assets. The unfavorable imbalance between cash inflow and outflow could be satisfied by drawing down the liquid asset reservoir by an amount necessary to fully meet day 4 cash payments. *Some* investment in liquid assets is justified by uncertainty about cash inflows and outflows and the costs of mitigating any effects of an unfavorable imbalance of flows.

The Receivables Investment

Firms invest in receivables (grant credit sales) for two reasons: to avoid high costs of adjusting to uncertainty about demand for its services and to stimulate sales.

For some kinds of service, uncertainty about the level of demand would make cash sales rather expensive. Utility services for gas, water, and electricity face an uncertain demand from a given customer. Cash sale would require someone from the utility to stand by the meter, gauge the consumption each hour or day, and collect cash from the customer. It is far cheaper to grant credit for a 1- or 2-month period and send a bill for the actual consumption of the service once the level of consumption is known.

But probably the more important reason for firms to carry receivables is to stimulate sales. Receivables perform this function in two ways: they may lower the effective price charged for the good or service to the customer, and they may provide a lower cost means of helping customers attain desired purchase patterns of goods and services. In short, the provision of credit sales *with* goods and services may provide an attractive and possibly unique bundle for potential customers of the firm.

When a firm charges the same prices for cash and credit sales, its offering of credit with no additional finance charge is, effectively, a price reduction. For example, suppose a firm grants credit sales under these circumstances and allows customers 1 month to pay. If the typical customer can earn a 12 percent annual rate by investing funds for 1 month, the present value of a $1 purchase at time of purchase is:

$$PV = \frac{\$1}{1 + \dfrac{0.12}{12}} = \frac{\$1}{1 + 0.01} = \$0.99$$

In effect, a 1 percent discount is being offered the credit customer. The effective price is lowered and, as in elementary economics, quantity demanded of a good or service increases with a lower price.

We need not seek far to find evidence of sales stimulation by granting credit sales that act to reduce effective purchase price. Gasoline credit cards have traditionally offered an average of 1-month delay between the time gasoline is purchased on credit and the time payment must be made. Furthermore, customers had to pay the same retail gasoline price whether they purchased on credit or with cash. But recently, a major oil company abandoned its credit card operation. The oil company announced that the savings from not having to carry the costs of maintaining a credit card function would be passed on to consumers in the form of lower gasoline prices for cash sales. Clearly, such a reduction in retail prices was absolutely necessary to maintain sales on a cash-only basis. In the absence of such an explicit price reduction, customers formerly using a credit card would face an effective price increase by paying cash. Some of these customers would be lost without an explicit gasoline price reduction.

The second source of sales stimulation, in which credit sales reduce the cost of attaining desired purchase patterns, rests on the notion that potential customers often confront purchasing constraints posed by immediate cash availability. For example, suppose that your cash inflow is $100 this week and $300 next week; in the absence of ability to borrow funds, your purchases cannot exceed $100 this week. If you would like to spend $200 this week and next and a firm offers you credit sales, you could purchase $100 for cash and $100 on credit this week. Next week, you could pay off the $100 owed. You can enjoy $200 of purchases each week, your preferred pattern, because credit is available. You do not have to postpone purchases.

But it is true that customers can provide their own "homemade" credit sales by borrowing from another source to finance *cash* purchases. Granting credit is not a unique way for firms to stimulate sales unless the terms offered are superior to those available from outside lenders. Terms are clearly superior if firms make no finance charge for credit sales, and prices for cash and credit sales are identical. Trade credit is less costly than borrowing from an outside lender. But even if the firm charges either a finance charge on credit sales or, equivalently, a higher price for goods sold on credit rather than for cash, credit sales by the firm may still be preferred to "homemade" credit sales. The latter alternative poses transaction costs in time and resources of arranging the loan from an outside lender that can be avoided by conveniently purchasing on credit from the firm. Broadly viewed, the total cost of "homemade" credit sales may exceed the total cost of buying on credit from the firm for some customers in some situations.

The Inventory Investment

Raw materials inventories help firms avoid costs of adjustment to uncertainty about production levels. In the absence of a raw materials inventory, an unanticipated increase in production would require hasty purchases of the needed materials. Hasty purchases are often expensive purchases because time cannot be taken to search out the least costly source of supply, one which perhaps cannot provide the necessary quick delivery. But a raw materials inventory investment can be drawn down to support the higher production level and avoid high costs of hasty purchases. (If you doubt this, consider that an unanticipated 3:00 A.M. urge for an egg sandwich is more cheaply satisfied if you carry an inventory of eggs. That inventory can be purchased with advance planning and with other goods at the lowest price at a discount supermarket. Without the inventory, your compulsion will lead you to seek out an all-night convenience store where the item will carry an outrageous price.)

Finished goods inventories help firms maintain an orderly production process without losing sales due to unanticipated increases in demand for a firm's products. In the absence of a finished goods inventory and with the firm producing goods at a given rate, an unanticipated increase in demand would lead to one of two undesirable consequences. First, if the firm maintains the prevailing production rate for the short run, some customers' demands will be unfulfilled. Customers may not be willing to wait for the firm to increase its production rate; they may turn to competitors for more ready availability of the goods. The firm loses sales. Alternatively, if the firm quickly increases its production rate so as to not lose sales, it bears the costs of hasty increases in production. Such costs may include premium pay for overtime, added costs of bringing on another shift of labor, and lower productivity from exhausted or poorly trained new employees. But the presence of finished goods inventory will make sales higher than in the absence of inventory *and* avoid costs of hasty increase in production. *Some* investment in raw materials and finished goods inventory is desirable.

Avoiding costs of adjusting to uncertainty and stimulation of sales were seen to be arguments for holding *some* investment in current assets. But how *much* investment should be made? This is an optimization question about which more is said at the end of the chapter. However, we can reason here that *excessive* investment in current assets is quite possible. To take an extreme case, imagine a manufacturing firm generating $1 million in annual sales. It holds $10 million (10 years of sales) of liquid assets to meet unanticipated daily cash outflows. It also holds $20 million (20 years of sales) in finished goods inventory on the grounds that it "always has what the customer wants." These investments are excessive for the size of the firm as measured by its sales. Excessive investments tie up scarce capital that is available only at a cost. It would appear that the firm has gone too far in attempting to realize the benefits of holding current assets.

Can Current Assets be Excessive?

Firms should hold *some*, but not too much working capital.

It follows directly that if firms choose to hold some level of current assets, the resulting investment must be financed. Before considering alternative sources of such financing, it is important to see that the firm's *desired* level of current assets is subject to perhaps considerable variation over time: equally variable is the level of financing *needed* for desired current assets. The nature of the variation in the financing need whether it is **permanent** or **temporary**, has an important influence on the choice of sources for financing current assets.

VARIATION IN THE LEVEL OF CURRENT ASSET INVESTMENT

It is possible to think of some sales and production levels that are lower limits for the firm in that demand will never (well, hardly ever!) go below these limits. We'll call such levels *permanent* production and sales level. Over time, if a firm grows, we can expect permanent production and sales also to grow. Now since the firm finds it desirable to hold some current asset investment for a given level of sales, it follows that there is a desired level of permanent current assets associated with given permanent levels of production and sales. Therefore, increases in permanent production and sales result in increases in desired permanent

Permanent Variation in Desired Current Assets

Figure 21-3   *Permanent, Temporary, and Total Desired Current Assets*

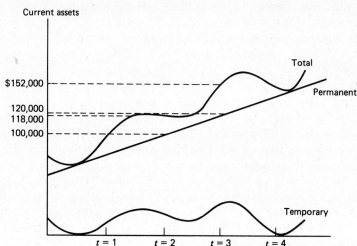

current assets—increases that will always need to be maintained because permanent production and sales will rarely fall below the new
levels.

The behavior of desired permanent current assets over time is portrayed by the straight line in Figure 21-3. At time $t = 2$, the desired
permanent current asset level is $100,000; at time $t = 3$, it is $120,000.
The $20,000 increase is permanent and reflects an underlying increase in
permanent production and sales of the firm.

**Temporary
Variation in
Desired Current
Assets**

There will also be *temporary* variation over time in the production and
sales levels of the firm. Sources of temporary variation include seasonal
influences and the effect of the business cycle. Since desired current
assets are related to sales, it can be said that the existence of temporary
variation in production and sales levels results in varying levels of *temporary* desired current assets. Temporary desired current assets are required *in addition to* permanent desired current assets. The lower limit on
temporary desired current assets is zero, since that also represents the
lower limit on temporary production and sales.

The behavior of temporary desired current assets is also shown in
Figure 21-3, by the wavy line periodically touching the horizontal axis.
At time $t = 2$, temporary desired current assets are $18,000, rising to
$32,000 at time $t = 3$.

Permanent and temporary desired current assets may be combined to obtain *total* desired current assets. The latter is shown in Figure 21-3 by the wavy line above the desired permanent current asset line. Variation in desired total current assets over time reflects variation in permanent and temporary desired current assets. For example, at time $t = 2$, permanent desired current assets of $100,000 and temporary desired current assets of $18,000 combine to make desired *total* current assets of $118,000. At time $t = 3$, permanent desired current assets are $120,000 and temporary desired current assets are $32,000; total desired current assets are $152,000. The *increase* in total desired current assets between $t = 2$ and $t = 3$ is $34,000, of which $20,000 is permanent and $14,000 is temporary.

Variation in Total Desired Current Assets

Variation over time in permanent and temporary desired current assets creates corresponding temporary and permanent financing needs to be met when financing *total* desired current assets. Not all financing sources are equally suitable for meeting these needs (see Chapter 24). For now, we describe alternative financing sources and their characteristics.

Variation in Current Asset Financing Needs

Alternative financing sources for current assets have many distinctive characteristics. At this introductory stage, we describe only three: short and long term, flexible and inflexible, spontaneous and nonspontaneous.

CURRENT ASSET FINANCING SOURCES

The distinction between **short-** and **long-term financing sources** is somewhat arbitrary. Recognizing this, it is still convenient to define short-term sources as borrowings that must be repaid within *1 year*. Short-term financing sources are thus the firm's current liabilities. Long-term sources, if they represent debt, must be repaid beyond one year.[1] Long-term equity sources of financing require, of course, no repayment, since they represent ownership claims.

Representative types of short- and long-term financing sources were

Short-term and Long-term Financing Sources

---

[1]This crude classification defines debt that is payable in only 2 or 3 years as long term. It would be more accurate to term debt with maturities in the 2–10 year range as intermediate. In fact, such terminology is often used. However, we adhere to the simple short-term/long-term description for simplicity in this introductory chapter.

shown in Table 21-2 for Logan Logging. Collectively, Logan's current liabilities provide $15,000 of the financing needed to support the $40,000 investment in current assets. These short-term sources are combined with the $25,000 of long-term financing used to finance the net working capital position of the firm. We use the Logan Logging financial information to discuss current liability financing.

Accounts Payable

Accounts payable represent amounts owed to suppliers of goods and services to the firm. They arise from the provision of credit sales by suppliers to the firm. Payment on these debts can be deferred at least for a time according to terms agreed on when trade credit is extended. (Such terms vary, but 30 days to pay is not uncommon.) Often, no explicit interest charge is assessed with such credit. And sometimes, a discount for early payment known as a cash discount is offered by suppliers. We see in a later chapter that failure to use cash discounts can be costly because, effectively, a financing charge will result. In Logan's case, the $5315 shown for accounts payable implies that monthly purchases on credit total $8084 and that Logan, on average, pays off a given bill 20 days after it is received.

Short-Term Loans Payable

The short-term loans payable of $9685 represents a loan taken out at 18 percent interest from a local bank. The loan had an original maturity of 6 months and is due 2 months from now. It is representative of the class of short-term loans, due within 1 year, available to firms. The actual instrument may be a note requiring a single payment at maturity, or an installment note requiring monthly payments. And as we shall see in later chapters, there are sources of such loans other than commercial banks.

Long-term Sources

Long-term financing sources are already familiar to the reader. In Table 21-2, Logan has a loan with a remaining maturity of 6 years plus a mortgage payable with a remaining term of 20 years. Logan has no preferred stock; but if it did, that source of funds would be considered to be long term. So too would be the firm's common equity. Note that Logan's $25,000 net working capital position is financed by a *mixture* of these long-term capital sources.

Flexibility of Short- and Long-term Financing Sources

A **flexible financing source** can be increased or decreased comparatively quickly at relatively low cost; an **inflexible financing source** cannot. The latter requires perhaps lengthy planning periods to increase *or* decrease the level of financing and may pose significant adjustment costs.

Most current liabilities of the sort described above are flexible sources. We soon see this to be true for accounts payable—a spontaneous source of financing. Financing from these sources will rise or fall quickly and at little cost as production and sales levels of the firm rise and fall. Short-term loans payable are also flexible by virtue of their short maturity (i.e., < 1 year). If financing needs increase, the firm can arrange accommodation from, for example, a commercial bank. (If the firm is creditworthy, the financing can be quickly obtained.) When financing needs decrease, the firm can pay off the short-term loan before maturity with little or no penalty. Even waiting to maturity to repay involves little cost, since the additional interest cost incurred by waiting is relatively small with the short maturity.[2]

Long-term financing sources are not as flexible as short-term sources. There are exceptions, but the differences are great enough to merit the term "inflexible sources."

To increase financing from long-term sources, a lengthy planning period may be required; additional financing cannot be quickly obtained. For example, sale of long-term debt, preferred stock, or common stock requires substantial time for an underwriter to plan and market the issue. Securing a long-term loan from a financial intermediary may be a lengthy activity, including negotiations and the loan approval process. And obtaining additional long-term financing may involve flotation cost, loan fees, or other charges. Similarly, reducing the level of long-term financing is difficult to accomplish quickly and at low cost. Debt or preferred stock issues may feature call premiums; long-term loans may have prepayment penalties that make early loan retirement expensive. Purchasing outstanding debt or equity claims involves brokerage fees for smaller purchases or even a tender offer for a large scale purchase.

The issue of flexibility is important when financing sources to support current assets are being chosen by the firm.

Spontaneous and Nonspontaneous Financing

Most financing sources are nonspontaneous in that they require a deliberate choice and subsequent action to obtain the desired financing. **Nonspontaneous sources** can be short- *or* long-term sources. They include short-term loans, long-term loans, preferred stock, and common equity. All these sources require deliberate choice and action by the firm to obtain the financing—a short-term loan must be negotiated with a bank; a long-term loan with, perhaps, an insurance company; long-term debt

---

[2]If the firm is in a position to repay a short-term loan prior to maturity, it can *effectively* do this by purchasing an interest-bearing liquid asset that can be converted to cash by sale or on maturity to pay off the loan. The liquid asset held offsets the loan liability; the loan is "paid off" for all practical purposes. Interest earned on the liquid asset can be used to offset, or partly offset, interest over the remaining term of the loan.

with an underwriter; and common stock must be issued and sold to investors, perhaps through an underwriter.

But accounts payable are a **spontaneous of financing source.** That is, when production and sales levels change for a firm, the amounts of such financing also tend to change in the same direction *without* deliberate choice or action by the firm. To see how this happens, refer to the Logan Logging balance sheet in Table 21-2. The average balance of accounts payable is $5315 for a related sales (and underlying production) level of $160,000. But suppose that sales increase to $210,000, monthly purchases from suppliers to $10,610, and average accounts payable to $6976. The increase in financing from this source is $6976 − $5315 = $1661. No deliberate action aimed at *securing* additional financing is involved. The financing spontaneously arises from purchasing more goods and services on credit to produce a higher level of output.

WORKING CAPITAL MANAGE-MENT AND SHARE-HOLDER WEALTH MAXIMI-ZATION

Throughout this book, specific financial decisions have been linked to the overall goal of shareholder wealth maximization. Subject to the ongoing hazard of predicting future consequences of financial decisions, such as cash flows for investment projects, it was often possible to establish fairly clear linkages between financial decisions and shareholder wealth. For example, we can find the net present value of an investment project and, under certain assumptions, know that this represents the expected change in shareholder wealth attributable to the project. But working capital management decisions are more difficult to link to shareholder wealth.

To clarify the problems in identifying that link, we demonstrate that working capital decisions to alter the level of current assets *and* the level of current liability financing because for current assets have a **cash flow effect,** an **investment effect,** and a **discount rate effect.** Each effect in turn influences the resulting level of shareholder wealth. Table 21-3 demonstrates cash flow, investment, and discount rate effects. Table 21-4 shows the net impact of these effects on shareholder wealth.

Table 21-3 presents alternative working capital policies for a new firm, Dahlin Enterprises. Dahlin is in the startup phase. Some decisions have already been made: the firm will invest $3 million in fixed assets and maintain that investment in perpetuity by replacing worn-out capital each year; in addition, the firms will be an *all-equity* firm except for any current liability financing sources to be employed; that is, there will be no long-term debt. (And for simplicity, Dahlin will not have income taxes.) It remains to determine the working capital policies of the firm, which are described here by two ratios: current assets to sales and the

Table 21–3   *Cash Flow, Investment and Discount Rate Effects of Alternative Working Capital Policies: Dahlin Enterprises*

	Working Capital Policy Number				
	1	2	3	4	5
Current Assets/Sales	6.00%	11.76%	17.56%	23.38%	29.20%
Current Ratio	1.5	2.0	2.5	3.0	3.5
A. Cash Flow Effects (Perpetual)					
Sales	$10,000,000	$10,200,000	$10,250,000	$10,265,000	$10,275,000
Operating Cash Outflow	8,500,000	8,300,000	8,200,000	8,190,000	8,185,000
Capital Replacement	1,000,000	1,000,000	1,000,000	1,000,000	1,000,000
Net Operating Cash Flow	$ 500,000	$ 800,000	$ 1,050,000	$ 1,075,000	$ 1,090,000
Interest on Current Liabilities	56,000	78,000	86,400	88,000	85,714
Net Cash Flow for Equity	$ 444,000	$ 722,000	$ 963,600	$ 987,000	$ 1,004,286
B. Investment Effects					
Current Assets	$ 600,000	$ 1,200,000	$ 1,800,000	$ 2,400,000	$ 3,000,000
Fixed Assets	3,000,000	3,000,000	3,000,000	3,000,000	3,000,000
Total Assets	$ 3,600,000	$ 4,200,000	$ 4,800,000	$ 5,400,000	$ 6,000,000
Current Liabilities	$ 400,000	$ 600,000	$ 720,000	$ 800,000	$ 857,143
Equity	3,200,000	3,600,000	4,080,000	4,600,000	5,142,857
Total Claims	$ 3,600,000	$ 4,200,000	$ 4,800,000	$ 5,400,000	$ 6,000,000
C. Discount Effects Cost of Capital, K	20.0%	17.0%	15.0%	14.0%	13.5%

Table 21–4   *Profitability and Shareholder Wealth Consequences of Alternative Working Capital Policies*

	Working Capital Policy Number				
	1	2	3	4	5
Current Assets/Sales	6.00%	11.76%	17.56%	23.38%	29.20%
Current Ratio	1.5	2.0	2.5	3.0	3.5
Summary of Prior Effects					
Cash Flow for Equity	$ 444,000	$ 722,000	$ 963,600	$ 987,000	$1,004,286
Equity Investment	3,200,000	3,600,000	4,080,000	4,600,000	5,142,857
Cost of Capital, K	20.0%	17.0%	15.0%	14.0%	13.5%
Profitability					
Rate of Return on Equity	13.88%	22.83%	23.62%	21.46%	19.53%
Effects on Shareholder Wealth					
Value of Firm, V	$2,220,000	$4,247,059	$6,424,000	$7,050,000	$7,439,156
Net Present Value of Alternative Policies, $NPV = V - $ Equity	− 980,000	647,059	2,344,000	2,450,000	2,296,799

current ratio (current assets to current liabilities). The former ratio measures the adequacy of the current asset investment in facilitating production and sales activities of the firm. When this ratio *increases,* more liquid assets, receivables, and inventories are being carried relative to sales. The current ratio measures the ability of the firm to meet short-term obligations as they mature.

The columns of Table 21-3 portray five working capital policies of increasing liquidity associated with successively higher ratios of current assets to sales and higher current ratios. The rows portray the cash flow, investment and discount rate effects to be described. Panel A shows that increasing liquidity results in higher sales and lower operating cash outflows. Sales are stimulated and costs reduced because of the benefits of higher current asset investment. Consequently, net operating cash flow increases with liquidity. But it does so at a diminishing rate, since the increments for each policy are positive but progressively smaller. Interest expenses for short-term borrowings included in current liabilities are deducted from net operating cash flow to obtain net cash flow available to shareholders (remember there is no long-term debt and no taxes).[3] The resulting net cash flow for equity also increases with liquidity; this is the **cash flow effect** of greater liquidity. It reflects reduced costs of operation and enhanced sales caused by larger investments in current assets.

Panel B of Table 21-3 shows the required investment in current assets for sales levels associated with each policy. Investment increases because both sales and the ratio of current assets to sales increases. This is the **investment effect** of additional liquidity. Some of the financing necessary to support current assets is provided by increases in current liabilities. These increases are modest because higher liquidity is also associated with a rising current ratio. Most of the financing for increased current assets is provided from long-term capital sources (in this case equity).

Panel C portrays the **discount rate effect.** It shows that K, the firm's cost of capital, *falls* with increased liquidity. The reason is that enhanced liquidity reduces the probability that the firm will be thrown into default and bankruptcy by its creditors. Financial crises are less likely with high liquidity.

Cash flow, investment, and discount rate effects influence the wealth of shareholders as described in Table 21-4, where the rates of return on equity for each policy are shown. These are *expected* rates computed by

----

[3]We will shortly be examining the effect of increasing liquidity on K, the cost of capital of the firm. This cost is based solely on long-term sources. Thus interest expense on short-term sources must be deducted from operating cash flows to be evaluated using K as a discount rate.

dividing expected net cash flow available to equity by the equity investment for each policy. For example, using information from Table 21-3 for policy 3, the expected rate of return on equity is:

$$\text{Expected rate of return} = \frac{\$963,600}{\$4,080,000} = 0.2362, \text{ or } 23.62\%$$

Note that the expected rate of return first increases (reaching the maximum at 23.62 percent for policy 3) and then diminishes as liquidity increases. This reflects the combined influence of the cash flow and investment effects. The former is favorable to rate of return, whereas the additional investment required by the latter is not. Initially, the cash flow effect dominates the investment effect and rate of return rises. But as increasing liquidity brings *smaller* increments to cash flow (diminishing returns!), the investment effect dominates and rate of return falls. But maximizing expected rate of return on equity investment is *not sufficient* to maximize shareholder wealth; that is, policy 3 is not *necessarily* optimal merely because it features the highest expected rate of return. We must also include the effect of alternative working capital policies on risk as reflected in the cost of capital (i.e., the discount rate effect). To do so we first value the net cash flows of the firm for each policy at the corresponding cost of capital—for example, for policy 3, $K = 15$ percent and the value of the firm is

$$V = \frac{\text{Net cash flow for equity}}{K} = \frac{\$963,600}{0.15} = \$6,424,000$$

The increasing total values of the firm shown as resulting from higher liquidity reflect the favorable cash flow and discount rate effects. However, if we compute the *net* present value of each alternative policy, we are accounting for all three influences, since the investment effect is included. For policy 3, NPV is:

$$\text{NPV} = V - \text{Equity} = \$6,424,000 - \$4,080,000 = \$2,344,000$$

As we examine each policy, we see that policy 4, with a current assets/sales ratio of 23.38 percent and a current ratio of 3.0 maximizes the increase in shareholder wealth at NPV = $2,450,000. The reduced cost of capital of $K = 14.0$ percent caused by moving to policy 4 from policy 3 offsets the necessary additional investment in total assets to produce the higher NPV. Note that this effect does not continue for higher liquidity policy 5. The small reduction in cost of capital offered by policy 5 does not offset the necessary higher investment. NPV would be lower with policy 5 than with policy 4.

In practice, it is a complex business to identify cash flow, investment and discount rate effects of alternative working capital policies on shareholder wealth. And there is an additional problem. The optimal working capital policy for Dahlin Enterprises was expressed in terms of aggregate levels of current assets and current liabilities. But it is also important to know both the optimal (wealth maximizing) *mix* of liquid assets, receivables, and inventories making up the current asset investment and optimal *mix* of individual current liabilities making up total current liabilities. The problems of linking the mix of current assets and liabilities to shareholder wealth are also complex. In Dahlin Enterprises, the wealth-maximizing working capital policy was the optimal level *and* mix of current asset investment, the optimal level *and* mix of current liabilities, that would maximize shareholder wealth. We would be fortunate in practice to duplicate this feat. But we can attempt to approximate it.

None of this discussion signals abandonment of the goal of shareholder wealth maximizing for working capital management decisions. It remains in place. But we must recognize the difficulty inherent in linking such decisions to the goal. Informed judgment and experience will continue to provide critical input into the working capital decision.

SUMMARY

Working capital management encompasses the planning and control of the level and mix of the firm's current assets and the financing of these assets. Financial managers must decide what quantities of liquid assets, accounts receivable and inventories should be held at any point in time. They must also decide what combination of long- and short-term sources will be used to finance the investment in current assets. Working capital is the firm's investment in current assets; net working capital is the difference between current assets and current liabilities.

Firms invest in current assets to avoid the costs of quickly adjusting to unanticipated changes in demand for the firm's products, its level of production, and its cash expenditures. Current assets may also stimulate the level of sales for the firm. Liquid assets in particular help the firm meet cash obligations when there is an unfavorable imbalance between cash inflow and outflow. They also help the firm avoid untimely sales of less liquid assets, supplier ill will, and the default consequences of a liquidity crisis. Investment in receivables can help reduce transaction costs associated with cash sales and may also stimulate sales by reducing effective purchase price and by helping customers attain desired purchase patterns in the face of unsuitable patterns of customer cash receipts. Finished goods inventories help avoid lost sales because goods are unavailable at the time of customer demand; they also permit a more stable flow of production, thus avoiding costs of quickly varying the level of production in response to a fluctuating demand. Raw materials inventories help avoid the excessive costs of hasty purchases made in response to unanticipated increases in the level of production.

The level of desired current assets of the firm is subject to variation over time. Some of the variation is permanent—a permanent increase in desired current assets following an upward trend in sales and production. Remaining variation in the level of desired current assets is temporary, since the underlying variation in sales and production is temporary. Not all financing sources are equally suitable for financing both types of desired current assets. Flexible financing sources, the level of which can be quickly increased or decreased at little or no cost, are suitable for financing temporary increases in desired current assets. Generally, short-term sources, current liabilities such as wages payable, accounts payable, and short-term loans, are flexible financing sources. Long-term capital sources are inflexible. Some financing sources, particularly accounts payable, are spontaneous financing sources; the levels of such financing spontaneously increase with the level of production of the firm. Nonspontaneous sources require deliberate action to obtain the desired financing. Long-term financing sources are generally nonspontaneous, as are short-term loans.

The goal of working capital decisions is shareholder wealth maximization. But it is sometimes difficult to link working capital decisions to shareholder wealth. Decisions to increase the liquidity of the firm by holding more current assets relative to sales facilitate production and sales activities of the firm; decisions to finance current assets with smaller levels of current liabilities and larger levels of long-term capital improve liquidity, by enabling the firm to better meet its short-term cash obligations out of current assets. When a firm changes its liquidity, there are three types of effect on shareholder wealth: cash flow, investment, and discount rate. Cash flow effects describe changes in the firm's net cash flow associated a change in current assets; investment effects reflect the incremental investment necessary to change liquidity; discount rate effects describe the tendency for a change of liquidity to alter default risk and, thus, the firm's cost of capital.

GLOSSARY OF KEY TERMS

Cash Cycle   The time path between the points at which cash is invested in raw materials until cash is received from customer payments on credit sales by the firm.

Cash Flow Effect	The change in operating cash flow accompanying a change in working capital management policy.
Discount Rate Effect	The change in risk and required rate of return (cost of capital) caused by a change in working capital management policy.
Flexible (Inflexible) Financing Source	A financing source, the level of which can (cannot) be quickly increased or decreased at little or no cost.
Investment Effect	The change in total investment created by a change in working capital management policy.
Liquid Asset Balance	Cash and other short-term marketable or nonmarketable assets.
Net Working Capital	Current assets less current liabilities.
Permanent (Temporary) Working Capital	The level and mix of current assets that does not (does) fluctuate on a seasonal or cyclical basis.
Short- (Long-) term Financing Source	Financing that must be repaid at or earlier than (later than) 1 year hence.
Spontaneous (Non-spontaneous) Financing Source	Financing sources, the level of which changes (does not change) without deliberate choice or action by the firm in response to changing levels of sales and production.
Working Capital	Current assets
Working Capital Management	The process of planning *and* controlling both the level and mix of the firm's current assets and liabilities.

SELECTED REFERENCES

Beranek, William. *Working Capital Management*. Belmont, CA: Wadsworth Publishing Co., 1966.

Cohn, Richard A., and John J. Pringle. "Steps Toward an Integration of Corporate Financial Theory." In *Management of Working Capital: A Reader*, Keith V. Smith, Ed. St. Paul, MN: West Publishing Co., 1974, pp. 369–375.

Knight, W. D. "Working Capital Management—Satisficing Versus Optimization." *Financial Management* (Spring 1972), pp. 33–40.

Smith, Keith V. "An Overview of Working Capital Management." In *Management of Working Capital: A Reader*, Keith V. Smith, Ed. St. Paul, MN: West Publishing Co., 1974, pp. 3–20.

Smith, Keith, V. "Profitability Versus Liquidity Tradeoffs in Working Capital Management." In *Management of Working Capital: A Reader*, Keith V. Smith, Ed. St. Paul, MN: West Publishing Co., 1974, pp. 409–422.

Van Horne, James V. "A Risk–Return Analysis of a Firm's Working Capital Position." *Engineering Economist* (Winter 1969), pp. 71–88.

1. Define working capital, net working capital, and the cash cycle.   **QUESTIONS**

2. What impact would the following changes in the cash cycle have on the level and mix of working capital?

    (a) New technology shortens a fabricating process by three days.

    (b) In anticipation of a shortage of essential raw materials, a firm triples the size of its orders of raw material.

    (c) The firm expands sales by granting more liberal credit terms.

    (d) The firm's major customers face a sudden reduction in demand that is expected to last from one to two years.

3. Differentiate between permanent working capital and temporary working capital.

4. How might a highly risk-averse manager plan his working capital requirements as opposed to a financial manager who is less risk averse? Explain.

5. Why might a firm wish to allow credit sales?

6. What role does flexibility play in the decision to hold various levels of current assets?

7. How can working capital decisions increase shareholder wealth?

8. Why might a liquidity problem arise if a firm financed a large portion of a permanent increase in working capital with short-term debt?

9. How should a manager choose a mix of short-term and long-term financing for a current assets?

10. Distinguish between a spontaneous source of funds and a flexible source of funds.

11. Describe how you think the level and mix of current assets and

liabilities of a cannery or a swimsuit manufacturer might vary over a year. Be sure to support your description.

12. Carefully define and distinguish among investment, cash flow, and discount rate effects.

13. How would unanticipated fluctuations of short-term interest rates be expected to affect the manager's preference between short- and long-term debt?

14. Mike Doughtry, the financial manager of Bilyard Enterprises, was told that the firm had an opportunity to increase sales five times in the next year—from 1000 to 5000 units. After some thought, he was not pleased about the prospect. Even though physical facilities were adequate to produce at this higher level and sufficient labor could be obtained, he worried about the working capital needs of the firm. Given that the cash cycle for this firm takes 120 days, suggest the range of problems that Mr. Doughtry must solve if production is to be able to increase five-fold.

PROBLEMS 1. A balance sheet for Purdy Goods, Inc. is shown below.

Purdy Goods, Inc. Balance Sheet, 1982

Cash	$ 10,000	Accruals	$ 10,000
Receivables (Net)	40,000	Accounts Payable	30,000
Inventory	25,000	Total Current Liabilities	$ 40,000
Total Current Assets	$ 75,000	Common Stock	20,000
Fixed Assets	25,000	Surplus	40,000
Total Assets	$100,000	Total	$100,000

(a) Determine the amount of working capital and net working capital.

(b) Suppose a permanent $100,000 increase in sales requires an additional $50,000 in working capital. Accruals should remain the same. Payables are predicted to increase by about 10 percent of the increase in sales. If the firm wishes to maintain the current proportion of short- and long-term sources of total funds, how much must be borrowed in the short term?

2. Select three firms in an industry and compute the proportion of funds invested in individual current asset and liability accounts. Do

you find great variation among these proportions? How might any variation be explained?

3. Given the following information, compute the amount of time required to complete a cash cycle for Monary Manufacturing, a producer of industrial goods.

	Average Amount of Time in a Stage of Production
Stock of raw material	4 months
Manufacture of semifinished products	1 month
Stock of semifinished products	2 months
Assembly	1 month
Stock of finished products	4 months
Accounts receivable	2 months

If $1000 per month is spent to maintain the stock of raw material, how much money will the firm have spent on raw material before cash is collected for finished goods produced by the first $1000 of raw material purchased? Suppose the whole manufacturing process can be reduced by two months. What impact should this have on the firm's working capital needs? Explain.

4. The cash flow cycle for General Manufacturing is 18 months. The cash flow forecast from the manufacturing process is given below:

Quarter	1	2	3	4	5	6
Cash Inflow (Outflow)	($1M)	($2M)	$1.5M	($0.8M)	$2M	($1M)

The firm has the minimum cash balance on hand at the beginning of Quarter 1. How much permanent financing is needed? What is the maximum temporary financing needed?

5. If Joe's Pie Company desires a liquidity policy that would provide a sales to current assets relationship of 10 to 1 and a current ratio of 3 to 1: (a) compute working capital and net working capital requirements for Joe's, if the owner projects annual sales of $50,000; (b) if for year 5 the owner predicts sales of $75,000, how much additional long-term or equity financing would he have to provide if he wished to maintain the same liquidity level as measured by S/CA and CA/CL?

6. Alice's Dress Shop estimates an initial outlay for fixtures in her new

shop of $20,000, to be depreciated over 10 years (straight line, no salvage value). Alice expects to be taxed at 25 percent of her income. She projects sales per year of $100,000 and cash operating costs, not counting depreciation, of $78,000. (a) If the $20,000 equity capital investment has a required rate of return of 20 percent, what is the net present value of the business, assuming a 10-year life? (b) Industry ratios suggest she should have a sales to current assets ratio of 5 to 1 and a current ratio of 2 to 1; how much more will Alice have to invest in the business to achieve these ratios? (c) How does working capital affect the net present value and return on total assets?

CHAPTER 22

Management
of Liquid Assets

It was established in Chapter 21 that firms are justified in holding *some* liquid assets because of the costs of adjustment to unfavorable imbalances between cash inflow and outflow. In this chapter we provide basic tools for the important task of planning and controlling the level and mix of liquid asset balances to be held by the firm.

As a preliminary step to introducing these tools, we modify our terminology and make clear the importance of uncertainty in the planning and controlling process.

It is convenient to represent imbalances between cash inflow and outflow by the phrase **net cash flow,** or cash inflow *minus* cash outflow. A favorable imbalance means that net cash flow is *positive,* whereas an unfavorable imbalance is represented by a *negative* net cash flow. A firm having only positive (or zero) net cash flows would not need to hold a liquid asset balance. But negative net cash flows require a financing source to make up the difference between cash inflow and outflow. Liquid assets are held to be drawn down in the event of negative net cash flows.

Most firms confront negative net cash flows from time to time. It would be relatively easy to determine necessary holdings of liquid assets if the timing and size of future negative net cash flows were known with certainty. Unfortunately, this is not the case. Net cash flows are subject to often considerable variation both in timing and magnitude. Given uncertainty concerning future net cash flows, the problem of determining the level and mix of liquid asset balances to be held is much more complex. It is anticipated *and* unanticipated negative net cash flows that the firm must be prepared to finance from the liquid asset balance.

Effectively using the tools for finding the desired level and mix of liquid asset balances requires an understanding of the types of variation that future net cash flows may exhibit. We turn first to the issue of variation in cash flows.

TOTAL, SEASONAL, INTRA-MONTHLY, AND RANDOM VARIATION OF NET CASH FLOW

A firm's daily net cash flow is shown in Figure 22-1a. The erratic line TV describes the **total variation** of daily *net* cash flow over 1 year. Every type of influence capable of causing variation in net cash flow is there reflected. In evaluating total variation, the financial manager has a substantial incentive to reduce his own uncertainty about future net cash flow behavior by attempting to predict *systematic* sources of the variation. Systematic sources of variation tend to produce *repetitive* patterns of net cash flow over time. Two potential sources of systematic variation are **seasonal** and **intramonthly** variation. If these sources of variation are properly estimated, the remaining variation is **random variation.**[1]

The three components of total variation, seasonal, intramonthly, and random, are graphically described in Figure 22-1b, where the smooth line SV *estimates* seasonal variation in net cash flow. Such variation can result from many causes, but suppose that in this example, the firm produces goods at a constant rate of output all year and experiences most of its sales in the winter months. Thus cash inflows exceed cash outflows from November through April but are less than cash outflows from May through October. In other words, *net* cash inflows occur only from November through April. If we subtract each point on the seasonal variation line SV from the total line TV, all the remaining variation is either intramonthly or random. These two sources of variation are expressed by lines MV and RV.

The intramonthly line MV estimates the behavior of net cash flow over a month. This smooth pattern happens to show net cash inflows in the first half of the month and net cash outflows in the latter half. Such a pattern could result from, among other things, the firm's billing practices and the timing of payments to its creditors.

The random variation line RV shows the remaining variation and by

---

[1]It is beyond the scope of this book to consider forecasting techniques for estimating seasonal and intramonthly net cash flow variation. The distinction between total, seasonal, intramonthly, and random variation is made here to provide a basis for different types of tools used in liquid asset management. In addition, seasonal and intramonthly variations do not represent the *only* sources of systematic variation in net cash flow. It may be possible to discern systematic variation within smaller periods such as every half month or every week. We do not attempt this level of precision.

Figure 22-1   *Total, Seasonal, Intermonthly, and Random Variation of Net Cash Flow*

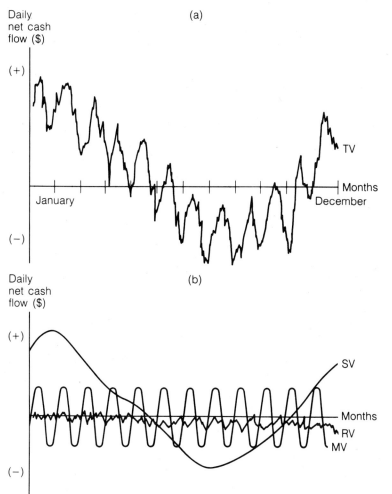

definition reveals no systematic pattern. The link between the different types of variation can be seen by noting in Figure 22-1*b* that if we *vertically* add the lines SV, MV, and RV, we obtain the line TV in Figure 22-1*a*. That is, total variation is the sum of seasonal, intramonthly, and random variation.

Different tools used in liquid asset management are best applied to different types of variation in future cash flows. In this chapter, the **cash budget** is applied to the problem of seasonal variation in net cash flows and a **minimum desired liquid asset balance model** is applied to intra-monthly and random variation of net cash flows.[2]

THE CASH BUDGET

Cash budgets are oriented toward the future, not the past. They are a useful tool in assessing the effects of seasonal variation in net cash flow on the liquid asset position of the firm. In providing this useful service, cash budgets serve both the planning and control functions. Planning is assisted because the budget permits the firm to evaluate the magnitude and timing of future net cash inflows and outflows. In helping to ascertain when predicted net cash outflows will reduce the firm's liquid asset position below desired levels, the cash budget permits the firm to make arrangements for sources of financing to meet these outflows. Sources of financing include borrowing from external parties and selling some interest-earning liquid investments. The control function is aided because the cash budget represents a standard of comparison against which actual future cash receipts and expenditures resulting from operations may be compared.

A *cash budget* is a detailed statement of anticipated cash inflows and outflows over future months. Information necessary for preparing a budget includes a sales forecast for each month and an estimate of the payment patterns exhibited by the firm's customers in response to the sales, the billing date, and the credit terms extended by the firm. Taking into account the firm's expected bad debt losses on credit sales, these two types of information permit the firm to estimate monthly cash receipts from customers. These receipts, together with other sources of cash inflow to be identified shortly, make up cash inflows to the firm. Cash outflows result from several causes. Expenditures on supplies to produce output at levels consistent with predicted sales and to change desired levels of inventories must be estimated. Payments for wages and salaries are also very important causes of cash outflows. These expenditures may occur considerably in advance of the actual time of sales because of lead time required to acquire supplies and to produce the product. Many additional causes of cash outflow can also be important for firms. Rather than enumerate all possible causes of cash inflow and outflow, we provide a representative, but not exhaustive, list of them in Table 22-1.

---

[2]A cash budget can be used to work with any kind of systematic variation in net cash flow and *could* be extended to work with intramonthly variation. Our minimum desired liquid asset balance model utilized deals with the intramonthly systematic variation; thus, in our example we can confine the cash budget to seasonal variation.

Table 22–1   *Causes of Cash Inflows and Outflows*

Cash Inflows	Cash Outflows
Cash Sales	Cash Purchases
Collection on Accounts Receivable	Payment of Accounts Payable
Sales of Securities	Wages and Salaries
Loans	Income Taxes
Sale of Assets	Insurance
Other (legal judgments, etc.)	Advertising
	Utilities
	Interest on Bonds and Notes
	Dividends and Withdrawals
	Retirement of Loans or Securities
	Capital Expenditures

To illustrate both the technique and the importance of cash budgeting, consider the Christensen Company. As of January 1, Christensen has established a 6-month sales forecast (Table 22-2) reflecting seasonal variation in demand for the firm's products—demand peaking in April. Purchases of supplies for producing output follow the seasonal pattern of sales but occur 1 month in advance of sales because it takes this long to produce the firm's products. Purchases, also shown in Table 22-2, imply the receipt of goods, but not payment for the purchases. Based on the information in Table 22-2, as well as other information, a cash budget for Christensen Company can be constructed. The construction process is in four parts: cash inflows, cash outflows, net cash flows, and scheduled borrowings and repayments of funds.

A Sample Analysis

Cash Inflows   Christensen's only sources of cash inflows are collections on sales to its customers. Christensen extends terms of net 30 days to its customers—meaning that customers are asked to pay within 30

Table 22–2   *Forecast of Sales and Purchases: Christensen Company*

	January	February	March	April	May	June
Sales	$200,000	$260,000	$350,000	$500,000	$400,000	$300,000
Purchases	130,000	175,000	250,000	200,000	150,000	150,000

days of date of the invoice. Not all customers comply, and this means that Christensen's monthly collections are not equal to the current month's sales. To establish monthly collections, Christensen must estimate the *payment pattern* of its customers—the pattern describing the percentage of a given month's sales being collected within specified time intervals after the month of sale. Christensen finds that largely because of its end-of-month billing, the pattern is such that 80 percent of a given month's sales is collected within the 30 days following that month and 18 percent is collected in the second month following the month of sale. The remaining 2 percent of sales is uncollectible and is charged off as bad debt.

The projected cash receipts from collections beginning January 1 can be estimated utilizing the payment pattern, the estimated bad debt percentage, and the magnitudes of November and December *actual* sales as well as *forecasted* sales for January through June. This is done in Table 22-3. The top row of Table 22-3 shows actual sales from November and December and forecasted sales for January through June. Collections for January are composed of $144,000 from sales made in December ($180,000 × 0.80) and $36,000 from sales made in November ($200,000 × 0.18). Thus, the payment pattern is applied to the past 2 months' sales to estimate January collections from each relevant prior month's sales. Total collections from the two months are $144,000 + $36,000 = $180,000. Since the only cash inflows for Christensen are collections on sales, January cash inflow is *also* budgeted at $180,000. (In the same month, 2 percent of November sales, or $4000, is charged off as a bad debt.) Total collections for February can be obtained in the same way. They consist of 80 percent of January sales ($200,000 × 0.80 = $160,000) plus 18 percent of December sales ($180,000 × 0.18 = $32,400), for a total of $192,400. The reader is left with the task of verifying the total collections for the remaining months. When total collections for each month have been obtained, Christensen's budgeted cash inflows can be established (row 1 of Table 22-3).

Cash Outflows   Analysis of Christensen's total cash outflows begins with a discussion of payments for purchases. The firm's suppliers all extend credit on purchases of net 30 days, and Christensen always pays approximately 30 days after receipt of items purchased. Thus, the firm purchased $100,000 worth of supplies in December. Payments for these purchases occurs 30 days later in January, as Table 22-3 reveals. All payments shown in Table 22-3 for February through June occur 1 month after the purchases listed in Table 22-2. Thus, June purchases of $150,000 in Table 22-2 do not appear in this 6-month cash budget.

All remaining payments adding to total cash outflows are identified

Table 22–3 *Cash Budget: Christensen Company*

	November	December	January	February	March	April	May	June
Sales	$200,000	$180,000	$200,000	$260,000	$350,000	$500,000	$400,000	$300,000
Collections								
1 Month Previous (80%)			144,000	160,000	208,000	280,000	400,000	320,000
2 Months Previous (18%)			36,000	32,400	36,000	46,800	63,000	90,000
(1) Total Cash Inflows			$180,000	$192,400	$244,000	$326,800	$463,000	$410,000
Cash Outflows								
Payment on Purchases			$100,000	$130,000	$175,000	$250,000	$200,000	$150,000
Wages and Salaries			30,000	35,000	50,000	40,000	30,000	30,000
Utilities			3,000	3,500	5,000	4,000	3,000	3,000
Term Loan Payments				15,000			15,000	
Other Outlays			1,000	3,900		2,000		
Income Tax Payments					50,000			40,000
Dividends			20,000			20,000		
Capital Outlays			50,000	5,000	15,000		160,000	
(2) Total Cash Outflows			$204,000	$192,400	$295,000	$316,000	$408,000	$223,000
(3) Net Cash Flow			(24,000)	(000)	(51,000)	10,800	55,000	187,000
Liquid Asset Balance at Beginning of Month			30,000	28,000	28,000	28,000	28,000	28,000
Liquid Asset Balance Assuming No Loans			6,000	28,000	(23,000)	38,800	83,000	215,000
Minimum Desirable Liquid Asset Balance			28,000	28,000	28,000	28,000	28,000	28,000
(4) Borrowing (Repayment)			22,000	0	51,000	(10,800)	(55,000)	(7,200)
Actual End-of-Month Liquid Asset Balance, Including Loans and Repayments			28,000	28,000	28,000	28,000	28,000	207,800

in Table 22-3. These payments, together with payments on purchases, are summed to obtain total budgeted cash outflows in row 2.

Net Cash Flows   Budgeted cash outflows are subtracted from budgeted cash inflows in each month to determine budgeted net cash flows in row 3. The net cash flows exhibit a marked seasonal pattern—net outflows occurring in January and March and net inflows from April through June. These net cash inflows and outflows imply a necessary schedule of financing—the last part of the construction process of a cash budget.

Scheduling Borrowings and Repayments   Christensen Company must now plan to finance the budgeted net cash outflows projected for January and March. One way of financing these is to sell excess liquid assets not needed to meet *day-to-day* net cash outflows. When positive net cash flows occur in April through June, the original levels of liquid assets held may be restored. Alternatively, the firm could borrow from an external party, such as a financial institution, and repay the loan from net cash inflows experienced in April through June. As it happens, Christensen's liquid asset balances are initially too small to meet projected net outflows. Consequently, the only relevant alternative is borrowing and repayment.

To determine desired borrowings and repayments, Christensen must compare its actual liquid asset balance on January 1 with the desired minimum liquid asset balance. (The minimum desired liquid asset balance as of the beginning of a month is aimed, in part, at dealing with the problem of intramonthly and random net operating cash flow variations.) Christensen's actual January 1 liquid asset balance is $30,000, which is $2000 in excess of the beginning-of-the-month desired cash balance of $28,000.

With this information, scheduled borrowings in January can be determined as in Table 22-3. Budgeted net cash outflows in January are $24,000. If no loans are taken out, liquid asset balances would be reduced to $30,000 − $24,000 = $6000 by these outflows. Therefore, to maintain a desired minimum liquid asset balance of $28,000, Christensen must schedule for borrowing of $22,000 by the end of January. This level of borrowing is maintained through February because net cash flow in February is zero. During March, a net cash outflow again occurs in the amount of $51,000. Liquid asset balances would, in the absence of borrowing, be drawn down to a negative balance of − $23,600. To restore minimum balances to the desired level of $28,000, the firm must borrow $51,000 more. As of the end of March, total borrowing will be $22,000 + $51,000 = $73,000. From April through June, net cash inflows permit the firm to maintain its desired minimum liquid asset balance and to repay the entire loan—leaving a projected substantial liquid asset balance of $207,800 at the end of June.

Armed with this information from the cash budget, the firm can alert its lender to the impending borrowing requirements over the next few months and show that loans can be repaid by the end of June. A pending liquidity crisis can be detected and forestalled by timely use of the cash budget.

Two important points require emphasis if we are to understand the usefulness of cash budgets. First, all the numbers are *estimates* and will have varying degrees of uncertainty. A prudent manager might examine the impact of alternative assumptions about certain revenue and expense items. In this manner he or she can assess the range of potential financing needs. In the case of Christensen Company both the financial manager and the firm's lender would like to know whether maximum potential financing needs in the next 3 months might be, say, $90,000 or $140,000, instead of $73,000. Second, it is important to remember how net cash flows fluctuate *within* a month. Even though a cash budget may indicate that the firm has sufficient cash flows to meet all needs without borrowing, if all outflows occur at the beginning of the month and all inflows at the end, the firm may run into financial difficulty *within* the month. This problem of intramonthly and random variation in net cash flows concerns the desired minimum level of liquid asset balances the firm wishes to maintain. To determine that minimum a new tool must be developed. Given the cash budget, we are now ready for that step.

Some Concluding Points on Cash Budgets

Reference to Figure 22-1 shows that even with seasonal variation in net cash flow evaluated and planned for in the cash budget, sufficient liquid asset balances must be on hand to deal with intramonthly and random variation in net cash flows. In Table 22-3, Christensen Company specified a desired minimum cash balance of $28,000 to deal with intramonthly and random net cash flow variations. Why was this amount specified, and not, say, $18,000 or $38,000?

MINIMUM LIQUID ASSET BALANCES

When dealing with intramonthly and random variation in net cash flows, it is useful to distinguish between operating and nonoperating cash flows. **Operating cash flows** include cash inflows from collections on current and past sales and cash outflows made up of operating ex-

Operating and Nonoperating Net Cash Flows

penses—wages, salaries, supplies, and purchases of services.[3] These cash flows exhibit most of the intramonthly and random variation with which the firm is concerned. In contrast, **nonoperating cash flows** are usually fairly certain in timing and magnitude. The principal problem associated with nonoperating cash flows is *not* one of uncertainty but one of timing—in particular, the storage of funds to meet known future cash outlays occurring at precise times. The problem of establishing liquid asset balances to manage nonoperating cash flows is deferred to a later part of this chapter. For now, the goal of finding the minimum desired balance refers to *operating* liquid asset balances.

Systematic and Random Variability of Operating Cash Flows

The problem of intramonthly and random variation in operating cash flows is graphically described in Figures 22-2 and 22-3. Figure 22-2 plots the *average* daily operating cash inflow, using a month having 22 business days, along the line CI for the Gould Company. This line, it must be emphasized, represents the *average* experience of the Gould Company in a typical month. The pattern of operating cash inflow reflects the level of past sales and the payment pattern of Gould's customers and is an estimate of *systematic* intramonthly variation. Operating cash inflows reach a peak in the vicinity of the ninth day because Gould offers a discount to customers paying within 10 days of the end of the month—the time when Gould bills its customers.

Average operating cash outflows are also described in Figure 22-2, by the line CO connecting daily cash outflows. The systematic variation portrayed by the line CO results from the level of purchasing and production activity of the firm as well as its own payment patterns. Peak outflows occur near the fifth and fifteenth business days because employees are paid at these times. The peak outflows occurring near the eighth and twenty-second days result from the firm's practice of paying its suppliers at these times.

The net operating cash flows are computed by subtracting operating cash outflows from inflows. For Gould Company, the net operating cash flows are described graphically by the line NOCF in Figure 22-3 and are given numerically in Table 22-4. Net cash outflows occur up to the sixth business day, net inflows extend from the seventh to the eighteenth business day, and net outflows again occur from the nineteenth day through the remainder of the month.

Now finding the desired minimum operating balance for Gould Company would be relatively easy if the net operating cash flow pattern

---

[3]Depreciation, an *allocation* of cost against revenue, is not considered here because it is not a cash outflow. (See Chapter 8).

Figure 22-2 *Operating Cash Flows for 1 Month*

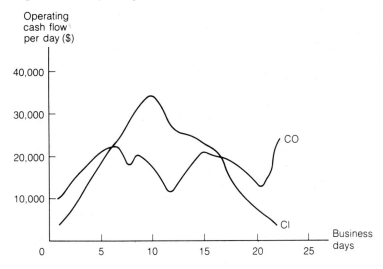

Figure 22-3 *Net Operating Cash Flows for 1 Month*

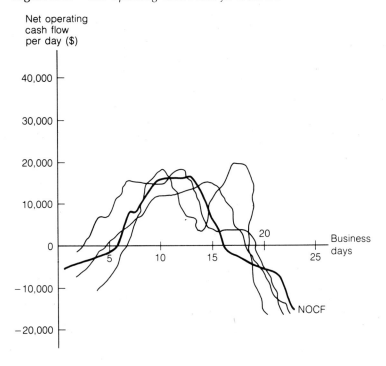

Table 22–4   *Average Daily
Net Operating Cash Flows
for a Typical Month[a]:
Gould Company*

Day	Average Cash Flow	Day	Average Cash Flow
1	−$5000	12	$6000
2	− 4000	13	5000
3	− 3000	14	4000
4	− 2000	15	3000
5	− 1000	16	2000
6	0	17	1000
7	1000	18	0
8	2000	19	− 1000
9	3000	20	− 2000
10	4000	21	− 3000
11	5000	22	− 4000

[a] We assume a 22-day operating month.

shown in Figure 22-3 and Table 22-4 never varied from month to month. Gould could merely sum up the net outflows occurring from day 19 through day 22 and from day 1 to day 6. In Table 22-4, these flows sum to $25,000. By holding $25,000 in liquid balances on day 19 of each month, the firm would always be able to meet the financing requirements posed by the ensuing days of net cash outflows. The firm would have met the problem of the intramonthly *systematic* variation in net operating cash flow described by the line NOCF in Figure 22-3.

But this is not enough. Random variation in the intramonthly cash flow pattern can still occur, and Gould must be prepared to deal with this type of variation. Graphical displays of random variation in net operating cash flow are shown in Figure 22-3 by the thin lines traced about the systematic pattern given by the line NOCF. These lines represent actual net cash flows patterns of which the line NOCF is an *average*. Since this variation is random (not systematic), it cannot be forecasted. Nevertheless, random variation must not be ignored. Creditors are not likely to be more understanding of a firm's liquidity problem simply because a given net cash outflow is attributed to random, not systematic variation in net cash flow.

Many different models that vary in sophistication and applicability might be used to find the desired minimum operating liquid asset balance in the face of intramonthly and random variation. It is not our purpose to present a wide range of such models but to illustrate the basic factors and to determine the quantity of liquid assets to be held in cash or other forms of liquid assets. Our model allows the manager to combine objective information about the probability distribution of cash outflows with managerial preferences for bearing the risk of running out of cash. The model offers a flexible way of discussing the liquidity problems faced by firms.[4]

Minimum Operating Liquid Asset Balances

The objective of Gould Company is to have a sufficient liquid asset balance on hand by the nineteenth business day of the month to withstand net cash outflows expected to last until the sixth business day of the following month. For the *average* data in Table 22-4, $25,000 in liquid asset balances held on the nineteenth business day would be sufficient to meet average *cumulative* net cash outflows of $25,000 occurring from then until the sixth business day of the following month. But we know that these cumulative net cash outflows are only an average (remember the thin net cash flow lines in Figure 22-3!). In any given month, the cumulative net cash outflow could be greater or less than $25,000. If the firm ignored the random variation in cumulative net cash outflows and always kept $25,000 in liquid asset balances on the nineteenth business day, it could expect to run out of cash 50 percent of the time in the ensuing interval of net cash outflows. Table 22-5 describes this problem by assuming that Gould has a sample taken from 48 months. Each monthly observation in the sample records the cumulative (within a portion of a 22-business-day period like the period from the nineteenth business day of one month to the sixth business day of the next month in Figure 22-3) net operating cash outflow. The *average*, or mean, cumulative net cash outflow is $25,000, but some months have greater outflows ($42,000 in month 3) and some less ($17,000 in month 48). The standard deviation of the cumulative cash outflows is $5000.[5] The standard deviation represents the random variation in net cash flow behavior, a variation that cannot easily be ignored.

To establish the minimum operating liquid asset balance, Gould assumes that the probability distribution of cumulative net cash outflows is normal and it can specify a probability (chance) it is willing to accept of

---

[4]This model appears in its original form in Stephen H. Archer, "A Model for the Determination of Firm Cash Balance," *Journal of Financial and Quantitative Analysis* (March 1966), pp. 1–11.

[5]The computation of standard deviation is skipped here to avoid duplication of material presented in earlier chapters.

Table 22–5   *Monthly Observations of Cumulative Net Operating Cash Outflows: The Gould Company*

Month	Cumulative Net Operating Cash Outflow
1	$28,000
2	19,000
3	42,000
4	21,000
.	.
.	.
.	.
48	17,000

Average Cumulative Net Operating Cash Flow: $25,000

Standard Deviation of Cumulative Net Operating Cash Flow: $5,000

running out of cash in any given month—that is, a chance of not having enough liquid assets to meet cumulative net cash outflows. Let us initially assume that the financial manager of Gould specifies a 5 percent probability of running out of cash as an acceptable risk. In the table of standard normal deviations (Z) from the mean, given in Appendix E, a 5 percent probability is equivalent to $Z = 1.645$ standard normal deviations from the mean. Multiplying the computed sample standard deviation of $5000 by $Z = 1.645$ yields a dollar amount, namely, $8225. What is this amount? It is the *extra* liquid assets Gould must hold over and above the $25,000. Figure 22-4 depicts this by plotting a normal distribution of cumulative net cash outflows with a standard deviation of $5000 and average (mean) of $25,000. Holding $25,000 of liquid asset balances exposes Gould to a 50 percent risk of running out of cash, as measured by the area under the entire right-hand half of the normal curve. However, specifying a 5 percent risk of running out of cash places the firm's desired minimum liquid asset balance 1.645 standard normal deviations to the right of $25,000, or, $25,000 + $8225 = $33,225. If the firm establishes this larger liquid asset balance, the 5 percent risk of running out of

Figure 22-4   *Normal Distribution of Cumulative Net Operating Cash Flows*

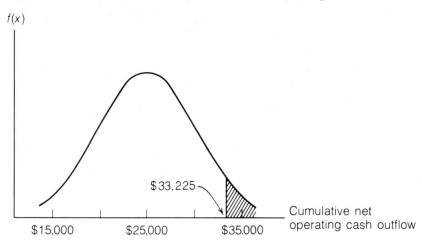

cash can be viewed graphically in the shaded area under the curve to the *right* of $33,225.

More generally, the management of Gould Company could consider many different probabilities of running out of cash. Each probability of running out of cash implies a different standard normal deviation and different quantities of additional liquid asset balances over and above the $25,000 level capable of meeting expected cumulative net cash outflows. Table 22-6 describes some of these alternatives.

If management of Gould felt that the costs of financial embarrassment were extremely high, a much smaller probability of being unable to meet cash demands might be specified. Consider two alternative proba-

Table 22–6   *Determining Minimum Operating Liquid Asset Balances: Gould Company*

1 Acceptable Probability of Running Out of Cash	2 Number of Standard Deviations	3 Average of Cumulative Net Cash Outflows	4 Additional Balances[a]	5 Total Balances
5.0%	1.645	$25,000	$ 8,225	$33,225
0.5	2.575	25,000	12,875	37,875
0.05	3.290	25,000	16,450	41,450

[a]Column 2 times the standard deviation of $5000.

bilities—0.5 and 0.05 percent. The liquid asset balance desired by the firm would increase as shown in Table 22-6. In each case the number of standard normal deviations (Z) above the average is multiplied by the computed standard deviation of $5000 to obtain the additional balances that must be added to the average. Notice that to reduce the probability of financial embarrassment from 5 to 0.5 percent the firm must increase the level of liquid assets by $8225 ($41,450 − $33,225). Whether such additional safety would be required depends on the cost of such a policy relative to the benefits. Although we cannot easily quantify these costs, we do have a model that allows management to subjectively assess the relevant tradeoffs and choose a probability commensurate with that assessment.

Let us suppose that Gould's managers choose the 5 percent probability of running out of cash and elect to hold $33,225 on the nineteenth business day of the month. Though a useful starting point, the same procedure could be applied to *any other* day in the month to establish desired liquid asset balances on that day. Thus, from the first business day until the seventh day, expected cumulative cash outflows in Table 22-4 are only $15,000 rather than the $25,000 at the nineteenth day. If the standard deviation of the cumulative cash outflow for the first 7 days of the month is correspondingly smaller than the $5000 computed for the interval beginning with the nineteenth day, the operating liquid asset balance on the first day can be smaller as well. This is because for any given probability of running out of cash, a smaller average cumulative cash outflow and standard deviation of cumulative cash outflow imply a smaller minimum balance. In short, the model is dynamic and adaptable to determining minimum liquid asset balances on *any* given day.

NON-OPERATING LIQUID ASSET BALANCE MANAGEMENT

The timing and magnitude of daily nonoperating cash flows are subject to less uncertainty than are daily operating cash flows. Nonoperating cash inflows include dividend, interest, and principal payments arising from holding equity or debt as assets. Nonoperating inflows also include all proceeds generated when the firm raises funds from outside sources including proceeds from short-term loans, bond issues, and equity issues and when funds are released from an expired investment. Primary nonoperating cash outflows are payments to creditors (principal and interest payments on outstanding debt), dividend payments on outstanding common stock, and capital expenditures. They might also include less common items such as payments on lost lawsuits.

In the short run, nonoperating cash flows may be considered to be relatively certain. For example, once the firm's own dividend payment has been declared, the precise time and magnitude of the total dividend payment is known. Furthermore, if the firm owns a U.S. Treasury bill of $10,000 face value maturing in 21 days, the firm knows that the amount of $10,000 will be received in 21 days. Even if the firm sells that bill before maturity, the transaction price will be known 1 day ahead of receipt of payment. Finally, the firm's own capital expenditures are subject to prior planning and commitments with the attendant magnitudes and timing of expenditures being, as a result, well settled.

Because the short-run magnitude and timing of nonoperating cash flows are relatively certain, **nonoperating liquid asset balances** are held principally to provide *storage* for nonoperating inflows until planned nonoperating outflows are made at future specified dates. The storage property of liquid assets is important in a number of situations. For example, the proceeds of a major bond issue might not be spent all at once on the planned expenditures for which the bonds are issued. Rather, the proceeds might be spent over time with the temporarily unused proceeds stored as interest-earning liquid investments. In addition, the portion of *net* operating cash flows needed to replace existing capital equipment, to pay dividends and interest, or to finance new capital expenditures through retention of earnings can be stored as nonoperating liquid asset balances until the time of planned expenditure. Funds to meet future tax liabilities may also be stored as liquid asset balances until payment is due.

Nonoperating Liquid Asset Balances

The problem, then, of nonoperating liquid asset management is one of *timing*. The objective of management is to schedule the maturity of investments purchased by cash inflows so as to meet planned expenditures at future dates. An example of the timing problem and its solution is given in Table 22-7 for the Luce Company. Through prior planning, Luce Company has structured its interest earning assets so that $100,000 of U.S. Treasury bills mature on day 6—the same day a $100,000 capital expenditure is to occur. On day 10, when a $200,000 dividend payment will occur, the firm has only $110,000 of U.S. Treasury bills maturing. It could, on day 10, sell prematurely $90,000 worth of bills maturing *after* day 10. However, because some present uncertainty exists as to the market price of prematurely sold bills on that future day, Luce Company finds it better to utilize the excess nonoperating cash flow occurring on day 3 to help finance the dividend payment. For on day 3, $170,000 of Treasury bills mature, out of which $80,000 in interest payments will be paid out. The excess day-3 receipts of $90,000 can be invested in bills coming due on day 10 so that, with certainty, the $200,000 outflow can be met.

Table 22–7   *Scheduling Nonoperating Cash Flows: Luce Company*

A. Nonoperating Cash Flows

Day	Outflow	Explanation	Inflow	Explanation	Net Flow
1	0	—	0	—	0
2	0	—	0	—	0
3	$ 80,000	Interest Payment	$170,000	Maturing Treasury Bill	0
	90,000	Treasury Bill Maturing in 7 Days	—	—	
4	0	—	0	—	0
5	0	—	0	—	0
6	100,000	Capital Expenditure	100,000	Maturing Treasury Bill	0
7	0	—	0	—	0
8	0	—	0	—	0
9	0	—	0	—	0
10	200,000	Dividend Payment	200,000	Maturing Treasury Bill	0

B. Maturity Schedules of Treasury Bills: End of Day

	Day 0	Day 3	Day 6	Day 10
3 days	$ 170,000	$100,000	0	0
4 days	0	0	$200,000	0
6 days	100,000	0	0	0
7 days	0	200,000	0	0
10 days	110,000	0	0	0
Over 10 days	620,000	620,000	620,000	$620,000
	$1,000,000	$920,000	$820,000	$620,000

THE BORROWING ALTERNATIVE

The decision to hold liquid assets does not preclude alternative means of financing net cash outflows. One such alternative, borrowing funds from an external source, could be used to finance cash outflows and allow the firm to reduce its holdings of liquid assets for operating and nonoperating purposes. *Provided* the firm can obtain such funds on a reliable basis, and in a timely fashion, and at an attractive cost, borrowing may offer an economical alternative to holding liquid asset balances to finance net cash outflows. Chapter 24 explores this point in more detail, but a brief example is given here.

Recall that Gould Company decided to hold a minimum operating liquid asset balance of $33,225 by the nineteenth business day of the month. This balance consisted of $25,000 to meet expected cumulative operating cash outflows (between the nineteenth day of the business month and the sixth day of the ensuing month) and $8225 to reflect the possibility that cumulative outflows may exceed the $25,000 expected amount. But Gould could have held only $25,000 (or less) in liquid assets and arranged a future loan of $8225 (or more), contingent on the needs of the firm. This loan, by providing a guaranteed source of liquidity, performs the same function as holding liquid assets.

So far, we have focused on the level of liquid asset holdings for operating and nonoperating purposes but the composition—the mix—of specific types of liquid asset remains to be determined. The array of alternative ways of holding liquid assets is large, and grows larger. Financial innovation and attendant changes in government regulation have provided new media of liquid asset investment.

THE MIX OF LIQUID ASSET HOLDINGS

Different types of liquid asset possess quite different characteristics. Without discussing each one in detail, we distinguish between cash and noncash liquid assets, then indicate (1) whether interest is paid, (2) whether there are minimum investment requirements, and (3) the extent of risk of capital loss.

Cash liquid assets are media of exchange. Without altering their form, they can be used directly in payment of cash obligations. Not many years ago, the sole media of exchange were currency, coin, and ordinary checking account balances held at commercial banks. These liquid assets have been supplemented by new forms, including negotiable order of withdrawal (NOW) accounts, combinations of ordinary checking accounts and savings accounts called telephone transfer and automatic transfer system (ATS) arrangements, and combinations of ordinary checking accounts and money market mutual funds. These liquid asset forms are listed as cash liquid assets in Table 22-8, where their other attributes are also summarized.

Cash Liquid Assets

Currency, coins, and ordinary checking accounts (insured up to $100,000 in most commercial banks) are similar in that they require no minimum investment. There is also no risk of nominal capital loss. When the funds are to be spent, the holder *always* receives the amount originally invested (e.g., a person depositing $1000 in an ordinary checking account will always receive that amount upon withdrawal). Finally, none of these forms pays interest.

NOW accounts, telephone transfer, and ATS arrangements are also

Table 22–8   *Attributes of Liquid Asset Investments*

	Minimum Investment	Risk of Capital Loss	Interest Paid
Cash Liquid Assets			
Currency and Coin	No	No	No
Ordinary Checking Accounts	No	No	No
NOW Accounts	Small	No	Yes
Telephone Transfer Arrangements	Small	No	Yes
ATS Arrangements	Small	No	Yes
Money Market Mutual Funds	Varies	Yes	Yes
Noncash Liquid Assets			
Nonnegotiable Money Market Certificates	Yes	No	Yes
U.S. Treasury Short-term Debt	Yes	Yes	Yes
Bankers' Acceptances	Yes	Yes	Yes
Commercial Paper	Yes	Yes	Yes
Negotiable Certificates of Deposit	Yes	Yes	Yes

media of exchange available through commercial banks and thrift institutions. Their most important distinction from currency, coin, and ordinary checking accounts is that they pay interest on amounts held. Interest rates paid are, however, often well below money market rates. As with currency, coin, and ordinary checking accounts, there is no risk of capital loss. Modest, but effectively zero, minimum balances are sometimes associated with these liquid asset forms. NOW accounts, which are restricted by regulation to nonbusiness uses except for sole proprietorships, are checking accounts that pay interest on the balances held. Telephone transfer and ATS arrangements make simultaneous use of a non-interest-bearing ordinary checking account and an interest-bearing savings account. The balance in the checking account is kept at zero. When checks are to be written, funds are transferred by telephone instruction to the financial institution. In the ATS arrangement, checks presented for payment at the financial institution are honored by automatically transferring necessary sums from the savings account to the checking account. The savings account acts as an interest-bearing storage for funds. Together with the ordinary checking account under the transfer arrangement, these forms *effectively* constitute interest-bearing checking accounts.

Money market mutual funds sell their own shares and invest the proceeds in money market securities such as Treasury bills, commercial paper, and bankers' acceptances. What effectively makes such an investment a medium of exchange is the possibility of simultaneous use of an ordinary checking account balance at a commercial bank. As checks are written on that account, shares in the mutual fund are liquidated to honor the checks. Depending on the particular mutual fund, a minimum investment of perhaps several thousand dollars may be required. The market value of the mutual fund depends on the level of money market interest rates. A sudden increase in the latter will *reduce* the market value of shares so that, if liquidated to honor checks, there is risk of capital loss. However, typical losses are usually not large. Interest paid on mutual fund shares is usually close to prevailing money market rates and often well above that available from NOW accounts, telephone transfer, or ATS arrangements.

Representative **noncash liquid assets** are also listed in Table 22-8. None of these are media of exchange because they cannot be spent in their immediate form in payment of cash obligations. Noncash liquid assets must be converted to one of the cash forms before they can be spent.

Noncash Liquid Assets

Financial intermediaries offer *nonnegotiable* money market certificates. These require a $10,000 minimum investment, have a 90-day maturity, and pay interest rates only slightly below money market rates. Certificates are nonnegotiable. If redeemed from the issuing institution prior to maturity, there is no risk of loss of the original amount invested, but the investor forgoes much of the interest that would otherwise be paid.

U.S. Treasury bills, bankers' acceptances, commercial paper, and negotiable certificates of deposit are all money market securities paying interest rates that differ primarily with respect to differences in risk. Minimum investment requirements range from $10,000 for bills to $100,000 for commercial paper or negotiable certificates of deposit. The latter are issued by financial intermediaries but can be sold in the market before maturity by the investor. Maturity dates at time of issue range from 90 days to 1 year. Risk of capital loss is present if money market securities are sold prior to maturity—for example, an increase in market rates after date of purchase reduces the market value of these securities. Money market securities usually offer the highest interest rates of all liquid assets.

Determining the desired liquid asset mix is a process about which generalizations are inadequate. But one general principle holds: firms should seek to minimize holdings of non-interest-bearing liquid assets such as currency, coins, and ordinary checking accounts. Such holdings must be financed at a cost while providing no interest return. Beyond this principle, the waters become muddy. Choices of particular liquid assets will be influenced by the likelihood of unanticipated use of the liquid assets

The Liquid Asset Mix

to meet cash payments. For small firms, choice may also be restricted in that the size of the liquid asset holding is below the minimum investment requirement for some assets.

Cash is suitable for the portion of desired liquid assets designated for operating purposes. The operating liquid asset balance is highly likely, at least in part, to be spent. Therefore, noncash liquid assets having risk of capital loss are not so suitable for this purpose. For example, Gould Company had a desired liquid balance for operating purposes of $33,225. It might hold all this in an interest-bearing savings account coupled with a telephone transfer or ATS arrangement. Alternatively, it could choose to hold money market mutual fund shares.

But variations on such a practice are possible, especially for firms larger than Gould Company. Suppose that Gould is 10 times larger than originally described. Its $25,000 of expected cash outflow becomes $250,000. And the $33,225 of possible outflows for which the firm was prepared to hold liquid assets becomes $332,225. Gould might decide to hold, say, $300,000 in cash liquid assets and $33,225 in noncash liquid assets. Since it expects to have $250,000 in cash outflows, the $300,000 of cash liquid assets would meet this expected need plus provide a $50,000 margin of safety. The remaining $33,225 could be invested in, say, U.S. Treasury bills, if the interest return was sufficiently greater than with cash liquid assets. (In this example, we ignore the fact that bills must be purchased in $10,000 denominations.) Gould would risk capital loss if the $33,225 were needed to meet cash outflows and the bills had to be sold prior to maturity. But it is not too likely that this will be necessary. The extra return is presumably worth the risk. Note that the original "small" Gould Company could not have done this. Proportionally, the $3322.50 amount devoted to noncash liquid assets would be too small to meet the $10,000 minimum investment required for bills.

Noncash liquid assets, while having a possible role in operating liquid asset balances, are especially well suited for nonoperating purposes. Recall from the Luce Company example that nonoperating flows are usually fairly certain, both in amount and timing. Maturities of noncash liquid assets can be scheduled to meet specific dates of payment. It is unlikely that such assets will have to be converted to cash prior to maturity. Risk of capital loss presented by marketable noncash liquid assets is rendered relatively unimportant in this case.

CASH FLOW MANAGE-MENT

Cash flow management encompasses a number of detailed arrangements for receiving and disbursing funds. A complete exposition of alternative arrangements for these activities is beyond the scope of this text. Rather, we emphasize an important principle: cash receipts should be accelerated, cash disbursements delayed. To the extent that a firm is successful in applying this principle, it can economize on its holdings of liquid assets.

The benefits of speeding cash receipts and delaying disbursements can be illustrated with the concept of **float.** Electronic funds transfer, which has implications for the ability of firms to jointly delay disbursements and speed receipts, is a potentially important future influence on cash flow management that also is discussed.

Book Versus Bank Cash Balances: The Concept of Float

In our discussions, "cash liquid assets" referred to cash held as currency or coin or held on deposit at a financial intermediary in a form usable as a medium of exchange. For simplicity, we now ignore currency and coin and refer to the financial intermediary as a bank.

It turns out that the cash balance in the bank can differ systematically from the cash balance indicated on the firm's books. The difference between bank and book balances is called *float.*

Positive float arises when checks payable to the firm are credited to its bank account more quickly than checks written by the firm are debited. Two examples of how positive float arises are shown in Table 22-9. Panel A assumes that the firm begins operation on day 1 with zero bank and book cash balances. On that day a $10 check is received and deposited in the firm's checking account and a $10 check is simultaneously written on the same checking account to pay expenditures. Before the deposit credit of $10 is released for use by the firm's bank, the check must be cleared through the bank on which the deposited check has been drawn. We assume that this deposit clearing time is 2 days, or $d = 2$. However, the firm's checks drawn on its own account take 4 days to return to the bank for payment—that is, disbursement clearing time is $c = 4$. On days 1 through 5, equal deposits and disbursements are shown on the firm's book cash balance and the book balance remains at zero. However, the firm's bank account begins to grow on day 3 as the deposit on day 1 is settled by the originating bank and because the disbursement check written on day 1 has not yet been returned to the firm's bank for payment. On day 4, the deposit from day 2 is cleared and the bank balance grows to $20. On day 5, the bank balance stabilizes at $20 because the $10 deposit made on day 3 is credited and the first $10 disbursement check drawn on day 1 finally clears such that the net change in the bank balance is zero. With $10 deposits and $10 disbursements clearing the bank account each day thereafter, the book balance will remain at zero while the bank balance is a permanent $20. This amount is positive float arising because of differences in check clearing times for deposits and

Table 22–9   *Behavior of Float: Bank Cash Balances and Book Cash Balances*

Day	Book Disbursements	Cash Withdrawal	Book Receipts	Book Cash Balance	Bank Cash Balance	Float
A. Deposit Clearing Time, $d = 2$; Disbursement Clearing Time, $c = 4$						
1	−$10	0	+$10	0	0	0
2	− 10	0	+ 10	0	0	0
3	− 10	0	+ 10	0	+$10	+$10
4	− 10	0	+ 10	0	+ 20	+ 20
5	− 10	0	+ 10	0	+ 20	+ 20
6	− 10	−$20	+ 10	−$20	0	+ 20
B. Deposit Clearing Time, $d = 1$; Disbursement Clearing Time, $c = 4$						
1	−$10	0	+$10	0	0	0
2	− 10	0	+ 10	0	$10	$10
3	− 10	0	+ 10	0	20	20
4	− 10	0	+ 10	0	30	30
5	− 10	0	+ 10	0	30	30
6	− 10	−$30	+ 10	−$30	0	30

disbursements. The existence of such float would permit the firm to withdraw $20 in cash and reduce its bank balance to zero on day 6. Book balances would then be − $20. In the absence of any changes, the firm could maintain indefinitely a *negative* book balance and a zero bank balance while investing the float to earn interest.

Panel B of Table 22-9 shows the effect of reducing the clearing time on deposited checks by 1 day. The deposit made on day 1 clears on day 2 instead of day 3. An additional day for deposit buildup is permitted by the speedier deposit clearing process and, by day 5, a larger $30 bank balance consisting entirely of float has been established. This larger amount can, as before, be withdrawn and invested and a book balance of − $30 can be maintained.

A simple estimating rule to determine float is given in the following formula:

$$\text{Float} = \text{Average daily disbursements} \times (c - d)$$

Checking the results obtained in Table 22-9, we find:

Panel A

$$\text{Float} = 10 \times (4 - 2) = \$20$$

Panel B

Float = $10 \times (4 - 1) = \$30$

Maximizing Float   It is clearly to the advantage of the firm to maximize disbursement check clearing time and minimize deposit check clearing time. Common ways of maximizing disbursement clearing time include the use of geographically distant banks for disbursement accounts including banks not part of the Federal Reserve Bank clearinghouse system. Deposit clearing times are reduced by using a field depository bank whereby checks mailed in by customers are deposited in a bank close to the customer location. The *lock box* system, whereby the customer mails his check to a post office box rented by a depository bank speeds the deposit clearing process even more because checks enter the clearing process faster than they would if mailed to a local office of the firm and then deposited in a bank for clearing. Deposits in depository banks, once the deposited checks have cleared, can be transferred to a disbursing bank on the same day by wire transfer between banks.

There is a limitation on the process of maximizing float. Suppliers and other creditors are quick to recognize that the firm is, in effect, delaying payment by using distant and slow-clearing banks for disbursements. Some ill will or even more unfavorable responses may be produced if the firm carries the process of stretching disbursement clearing time too far.

A more important factor limits the ability of the firm to withdraw its positive float from its bank balance for its own use—random cash flow variation over time. The significance of such variation can be understood by noting that the example in Table 22-9 assumed that receipts and disbursements were distributed evenly over time. The firm was able to draw down its bank balance to zero because of this condition. In fact, with cash inflows and outflows subject to variation over time, float also varies over time. Firms are likely to maintain a positive bank and book balance to meet reductions in float created when cash outflows exceed inflows. As a result, only a part of the positive float can be withdrawn. Negative book balances may still appear but not to the degree indicated in Table 22-9.

Electronic Funds Transfer (EFT)

We would be remiss if we did not warn the reader that a change in the operation of the banking system may eventually make our discussion of float obsolete. Where it is operative, the process of *electronic funds transfer* (EFT) permits virtually immediate transfer of funds from one account to another in the same bank or between banks. EFT drastically reduces both deposit and disbursement clearing times and reduces float to the point where it is no longer a matter of importance.

The centerpiece of EFT is elimination of the check as a means of funds transfer. In its place are substituted preauthorized drafts on checking accounts or immediate transfer from one account to another by electronic communication devices. For example, a firm or individual can preauthorize a creditor to put through periodic drafts against the checking account of the firm. This reduces the delays associated with writing and mailing a check to the creditor. Immediate transfer, under suitable electronic technology, involves a person or firm purchasing items or paying bills without a check. The appropriate buttons are pushed to immediately transfer funds from the account of the payor to the creditor or payee. Again, no delays for check clearing are present.

Despite its availability on a small scale in some places, EFT has not developed as quickly as its early proponents envisaged. We remain some distance from the "checkless society." The advantages of the check in terms of float, cost, provision of evidence of payment, and convenience remain important, especially to consumers. Inertia must be overcome. No doubt, EFT is the way of the future, but it may require some time to reach that future.

SUMMARY

Management of liquid assets is a continuing task of financial managers. Firms hold liquid assets because cash inflows may exceed cash outflows creating negative net cash flows, because there is uncertainty concerning the magnitude and timing of net cash flows, and because the costs of adjusting to cash deficiencies can be rather high.

Effective liquid asset management requires that the financial managers recognize that total variation in net cash flow may be of several types: seasonal, intramonthly, and random. Seasonal and intramonthly net cash flow variations are systematic in that variation tends to follow repetitive patterns. Random variation is unsystematic and lacks a repetitive pattern. Recognizing these different types of variation permits adaptation of the proper managerial tool to the particular type of cash flow.

Cash budgets provide a detailed statement of cash inflows and outflows over several future periods of time. By aiding the firm in anticipating future periods of net cash outflow, a cash budget allows time to make arrangements to finance future net cash outflows. Because a cash budget often encompasses several months, it is well adapted to analyze any systematic or seasonal variation in net cash flow.

Intramonthly and random variations in net cash flow are primarily attributable to operating cash flow variation rather than to nonoperating cash flows. The latter are known with virtual certainty within the short period of 1 month. Firms must determine a minimum level of operating liquid asset balances to finance cumulative net operating cash outflows over the month. The model developed in this chapter combines the probability distribution of net operating cash outflows with managerial preferences for bearing the risk of running out of cash. Once the probability distribution, and its mean and standard deviation have been estimated, management can specify the probability of financial embarrassment it is willing to accept and can identify a unique level of liquid assets consistent with that probability. The minimum level of liquid assets determined by this model is correct for a specific point in the month. Over the course of a month, the appropriate level of liquid assets will fluctuate according to the pattern of inflows and outflows. The important point to recognize is that minimum levels of liquid assets specified at the start of the month or the middle of the month might well be substantially different if the pattern of flows is different around each point.

Holding of liquid assets is not the only way to finance net cash outflows. Firms can arrange to borrow amounts to meet temporary net cash outflows. This course of action represents the borrowing alternative.

A wide range of alternative liquid asset forms exist from which firms can choose. These forms differ in many respects, the most important of which is the distinction between cash and noncash liquid assets. Cash liquid assets are mediums of exchange; noncash liquid assets are not. Other differences of importance include minimum required investment levels and the expected rate of interest to be received.

A critical goal of cash flow management is to speed cash receipts and delay cash disbursements. Success in following this principle can lead to reductions in the firm's liquid asset balances. If the firm can arrange matters such that deposit clearing times for receipts are shorter than disbursement clearing times, it can maximize float. The existence of float makes it possible for the firm to have a bank cash balance larger than its book cash balance. Some firms may be able to withdraw some of that float, leaving a positive bank balance but a negative book balance. Opportunities for firms to take advantage of float would disappear if electronic transfer systems came into universal use.

GLOSSARY OF KEY TERMS

Cash Budget   A detailed statement of anticipated cash inflows and outflows over a specific number of future periods. Provides a standard against which to compare actual cash positions and allows the firm to assess the amount and arrange the source of future financing as well as timing of repayment.

Cash Liquid Assets	Liquid assets usable as media of exchange without altering their form. Examples include currency, coin, ordinary checking accounts, NOW accounts, telephone transfers, and ATS arrangements, and money market mutual fund accounts.
Float	The difference between bank and book cash balances that occurs when checks payable to the firm are credited to the firm's bank account more quickly than checks written by the firm are debited.
Minimum Desired Operating Liquid Asset Balance	The minimum quantity of cash and interest-earning liquid assets the firm wishes to hold in anticipation of future operating net cash outflows.
Net Cash Flow	Cash inflow less cash outflow.
Noncash Liquid Assets	Liquid assets that cannot be used as media of exchange in their immediate form. Examples include nonnegotiable money market certificates, short-term U.S. Treasury obligations, bankers' acceptances, commercial paper, and negotiable certificates of deposit.
Nonoperating Cash Flows	Include dividend, interest, and principal payments and collections, and proceeds raised from outside sources of capital. The magnitude and timing of these flows are, in most situations, more certain than operating flows.
Nonoperating Liquid Asset Balances	Liquid assets, usually in interest-bearing form, held to meet scheduled nonoperating net cash outflows.
Operating Cash Flows	Consist of receipts from current sales, collections from past sales, and normal operating expenses such as wages, salaries, and outlays for supplies and services.
Random Variation	Variation of some variable, over time, having no identifiable repetitive pattern.
Systematic Variation	Variation, over time, having an identifiable repetitive pattern. Seasonal and intramonthly sources of systematic variation may be present in many cash flow series.
Total Variation	Variation over time that includes all systematic and random variation; the total of seasonal, intramonthly, and random variations.

SELECTED REFERENCES   Baumol, William J. "The Transactions Demand for Cash: An Inventory Theoretic Approach." *Quarterly Journal of Economics* (November 1952), pp. 545–556.

Daellenbach, Hans G. "Are Cash Management Optimization Models Worthwhile?" *Journal of Financial and Quantitative Analysis* (September 1974), pp. 607–626.

Jones, R. "Face to Face with Cash Management: How One Company Does It." *Financial Executive* (September 1969), pp. 37–39.

Orgler, Yair. *Cash Management: Models and Methods*. Belmont, CA.: Wadsworth Publishing Co., 1970.

Orr, Daniel and Merton Miller. "A Model of the Demand for Money by Firms." *Quarterly Journal of Economics* (August 1966), pp. 413–435.

Pogue, Gerald A., Russell G. Faucett, and Ralph N. Bussard. "Cash Management: A Systems Approach." *Management of Working Capital: A Reader*, Keith V. Smith, Ed. St. Paul, MN.: West Publishing Co., 1974, pp. 77–90.

Reed, Ward L., Jr. "Profits from Better Cash Management." *Financial Executive* (May 1972), pp. 40–56.

QUESTIONS

1. Why do firms hold liquid assets?

2. What are the basic functions of a cash budget?

3. In Chapter 20 liquidity ratios were developed to measure the ability of the firm to meet maturing obligations. Yet, in this chapter we suggested that cash budgets, not liquidity ratios, are a more important tool for assessing the firm's liquidity. Explain carefully why this is so.

4. Why might managers of a firm find it valuable to construct several different cash budgets by changing assumptions about the behavior of key variables?

5. Discuss the strengths and weaknesses of the model presented to assess minimum liquid asset balances.

6. What are the key factors that should be incorporated into a model for determining minimum cash balances?

7. Why might a firm hold some portion of liquid assets in the form of marketable securities?

8. Explain the meaning of the term float. How does float arise?

9. What is electronic funds transfer? Why would it make the discussion of float obsolete?

10. Why is it argued that nonoperating cash flows are more certain than operating flows in the short run?

11. Why might a firm's unused, readily available borrowing capacity affect the level of liquid assets held by the firm?

PROBLEMS

1. Alphonse House Service, Inc., projects, for April, May, and June, operating cash receipts of $300,000, $400,000, and $600,000, respectively, and operating cash outflows of $350,000, $400,000, and $400,000, respectively. Nonoperating expenditures planned for the three-month period include an income tax payment of $25,000 in June, a dividend payment of $30,000 in April, and a capital expenditure of $50,000 in May. Prepare your case to submit to the banker for possible borrowing over the three-month period, if your present liquid asset position of $20,000 contains no excess to meet any deficiency in cash flow.

2. As financial manager of Jensen Stores, you are asked to plan for the cash needs and identify any cash surpluses in the next six-month period beginning July 1. Any needs are to be provided by short-term bank loans. The sales forecast has been made by your market analyst as follows:

Month	Sales
July	$15,000
August	30,000
September	25,000
October	30,000
November	30,000
December	20,000
January	15,000
February	10,000

The following additional information may be useful. (a) This past May and June sales amounted to $10,000 per month. (b) All sales are on credit and, based upon the credit terms and previous experience, only 10 percent of each month's credit sales will be received in the month of sale, 60 percent in the following month, and the remaining 30 percent in the second month after sale. (There are no bad debt losses.) (c) Purchases are equal to 75 percent of sales. Purchases are ordered and delivered a month before sales and are paid in the same month as the purchase is made. Salaries are $1500 plus 5 percent of sales in the current month. Accruals of wages and salaries and other miscellaneous current liabilities are the same at the end of the month. (e) Rent is $400 per month, and other expenses that involve cash outlays are 2 percent of sales per month. (f) This company plans no new capital expenditures, nor will it pay dividends in this period. (g) The firm's desired beginning-of-month cash balance is $5000, but the stock of cash is expected to be $7000 on July 1. No taxes are to be paid in this period.

3. Indigo Industries anticipated cumulative cash outflows of $150,000 over the last eight days of the month. If the standard deviation of those flows was $22,000 and minimum cash balances were deemed to be $222,380, what probability of financial distress (zero cash) did Indigo bear?

4. Ellen has a cash balance decision problem. She indicates she experiences on the average a positive net cash flow during the first 10 days of the month and a negative net cash flow during the last 20 days of the month. She wants to know how much cash to have on hand at the end of day 10 if her previous experience shows that the cumulative net cash outflows during the last 20 days of the month are normally distributed with an average value of $1000 and a standard deviation of $200. Assume that she is willing to take a 5 percent chance of running out of cash.

5. Hallaq Hosiery Company faced an average cumulative cash outflow of $10,000 for the first 10 days of the month. The standard deviation of these outflows is $2000. Assuming that the distribution of outflows is normally distributed, (a) compute the cash that the firm should hold at the beginning of the month if management is willing to accept a 5 percent chance of running out of cash by the end of the tenth day. (b) Which level of cash would be chosen by a very risk-averse management wanting no more than a 0.5 percent chance of running out of cash?

6. Warehouse Lumber Company has several divisions scatt·red across the United States. The company has a long-standing policy of letting each division collect receipts for two days before forwarding them to headquarters for deposit. There are eight divisions and each collects an average of $150,000 per day. (a) If it takes an additional three days for checks to clear, how much money is tied up by the five-day delay? (b) Suppose divisions were instructed to send receipts every day (i.e., hold zero days instead of two). How much money would then be tied up?

7. Jack Armstrong is running for the State Senate. Substantial funds
    are to be raised at the beginning of his campaign and will be needed
    for expenses later. His financial manager has estimated the ex-
    penses and contributions for the six-month campaign and wishes to
    plan an investment strategy. He plans to buy T-bills in $10,000
    denominations of appropriate maturities to avoid liquidity risk. The
    remaining funds will be deposited in a checking account. Jack plans
    to contribute $70,000 of his own savings in May. Fund drives are
    expected to generate $50,000 in May, $20,000 in June, and $30,000 in
    each of the months of August and September. These contributions
    will be available at the end of the month in which they are gener-
    ated. Phone service is expected to cost $4000/month with a $1000
    installation fee in May. Office rent and staff will cost $7000/month.
    Advertising media expenses will be $10,000 for each of the first
    three months and $30,000 for each of the last three months. Signs
    will be purchased in May for $15,000. All expenses will be paid at
    the end of the month in which they are incurred. Designate the
    maturity structure of the T-bill portfolio that will optimize the use of
    excess funds without incurring liquidity risk.

CHAPTER 23

Receivables and Inventory Management

As in the case of liquid assets, receivables and inventories require alert management to ensure both efficient use of financial resources and the avoidance of financial distress. Chapter 21 laid the groundwork for the conclusion that firms are usually justified in holding *some* quantity of receivables and inventories as current assets. Receivables result from credit sales and represent an attempt to increase the level of sales and, in some cases, to lower the costs of collecting revenue from customers. Inventories of raw materials are held to prevent untimely and costly interruptions or delays of production due to temporary shortages of raw material and to avoid the payment of premium prices for hurriedly purchased material needed to keep production going. Finished goods inventories act to insulate the rate of production of goods from variation in customer demands. It is often costly to vary production levels directly in response to customer demands. Such inventories also serve to fill customer demands when additional goods cannot be produced, or otherwise obtained, immediately.

Having made a tentative case for the existence of some level of receivables and inventory, the remaining issue is how *much* of each should be held. Although too little of each may substantially diminish the marginal benefits of these assets, too much of each may impose excessive costs on the firm. Efficient use of financial resources requires that the firm attempt to find optimum levels of investment in receivables and inventories. Once the firm has estimated the optimum level of each of these classes of assets, shareholder wealth maximization requires that actual levels of the assets conform to optimum levels. Excessive levels of either receivables or inventories could tie up cash and place the firm in a liquidity crisis (remember the cash cycle in Figure 21-1). Accordingly, adequate monitoring and control mechanisms must be on hand to detect and reduce differences between optimum and actual levels of receivables and inventories.

This chapter introduces the problems associated with finding the optimum level of receivables and inventories. Means of monitoring and controlling the performance of actual levels of receivables are also evaluated.

RECEIVABLES MANAGEMENT

Firms frequently make credit sales to customers without charging them an explicit fee, or financing charge, for this service. This type of credit, called **trade credit,** arises only through the sale of goods and services—that is, it is not extended separately from the sale of goods and services.

In a positive sense, extension of credit has been seen, among other things, to be a potential stimulant to sales. Admittedly, this practice may be followed simply because the industry of which the firm is a member has established the custom and the firm cannot easily abandon the practice without a significant loss of business to its competitors. But whatever the motivation, the firm must adopt a set of credit policies.

Credit policies refer to the various policies established by the firm to guide decisions concerning: extension of credit, collection of receivables from customers, and monitoring and controlling outstanding credit. **Credit extension policies** guide financial managers in deciding which prospective customers will be granted credit, the terms of payment on such credit, and the quantity of credit to be granted the customer. **Collection policies** govern procedures followed by the firm to encourage customers to pay their bills on agreed-upon terms. **Monitoring** and **control** policies are established to help discern, and to guide corrective action, when improperly implemented credit extension or collection policies are responsible for failure of customers to pay on agreed terms or when other factors, such as business conditions facing the customer, have an important influence on customers' ability to pay. Each of these policies is examined in turn.

Credit Extension Policies

Credit extension policies comprise three types of decisions: the determination of **credit terms,** the size of the **credit line,** and the **credit standards** that a customer must meet or exceed if credit is to be granted at all. As we shall see, these important decisions have much to do with the firm's level of sales, the level of investment in receivables, the resulting cost of financing the investment in receivables, the firm's bad debt losses, and the costs of collecting payment from customers. We temporarily shrink from a simultaneous examination of these benefits and costs in an attempt to find an optimal credit policy and the level of receivables resulting from such a policy. For now, we simply concentrate on each separate decision making up credit extension policies.

Credit Terms   If a firm decides to extend credit to a customer, it normally stipulates certain credit terms. These terms include the total length of time credit will be extended, called the **credit period;** the size of the **cash discount,** if any, offered the customer for early payment of the credit extended; and the period of time within which the cash discount may be taken, the **discount period.** The customary format for stating credit terms is: percentage discount/discount period, / credit period. For example, a firm may offer customers a 2 percent cash discount on the face amount of the bill if the bill is paid within a discount period of 10 days and require that if the discount period expires without payment, payment in full be received within 30 days. These credit terms would be stated (usually on the front of the invoice) as "2%/10, net/30." A customer paying between the first and tenth day after the invoice date need pay only 98 percent of the purchase price. One paying between the tenth and thirtieth days must remit the full purchase price. Any receivable outstanding beyond 30 days is "past due."

In most cases, credit terms are applied equally to all customers. A relaxation of credit terms may be expected to increase sales to some extent because the present value of the purchase price, at time of sale, will tend to decline. For example, a more relaxed policy than the 2%/10, net/30 used above would be 2%/30, net/60. Both the discount and credit periods are lengthened, thus reducing the present value of the purchase price to the customer. But receivables will tend to increase even if no sales increase occurs, if customers, as might be expected, take the longer period to pay their bills under a more relaxed policy. To the extent that sales *do* increase, receivables will be even higher. In both cases, costs of financing the receivables position of the firm will rise as receivables increase.

Credit Lines   Individual customers, while receiving the same credit terms, may have different limits set by the firm on the amount of credit that will be extended to them. Customer firms, through their size and financial condition, vary in the amount of debt they can bear. The limit that the firm sets on the amount of credit to be extended reflects these concerns but may also be used to encourage more sales to a given customer. Thus, within limits of safety, the firm may wish to grant generous limits to a customer to encourage sales. Limits are expressed by granting the customer a line of credit of a given amount, say, $50,000. The $50,000 amount is the upper limit on the amount the customer may owe the firm at any given time. Purchases that would cause the limit to be exceeded must be paid for in cash unless the firm chooses to increase the credit line.

Credit Standards   The decision to extend *any* credit to a prospective customer, as well as the size of the credit line to be extended, depends on whether the customer can meet or exceed minimum credit standards adopted by the firm. Prospective customers failing to meet the standards will be denied credit—that is, sales will be made on a cash basis only.

From the firm's standpoint, a perfect set of credit standards would reject only the customers who ultimately would not pay their bills (their bills become bad debts), or would pay them with such prolonged delay that the collection costs would be prohibitive. Unfortunately, firms cannot know the future with such precision. With every customer granted credit by the firm, the risk exists that bills will not be collected. The problem for the firm is to utilize objective facts and subjective information to predict the bill-paying behavior of the prospective customer and to reduce the risk of nonpayment to an acceptable level. But finding that acceptable level of risk is no easy task. A stringent set of credit standards will reduce the risk of bad debt losses and lower collection expenses but will also reduce the level of credit sales because some customers who would have paid their bills will be denied credit. The objective facts and subjective information are not perfect predictors of customers' bill-paying behavior! A more relaxed set of standards will increase credit sales but produce more bad debt losses and higher collection expenses. The firm must try to find the optimum balance between benefits and costs.

It is not within our scope to discuss how firms develop a specific set of credit standards, called a *credit screen,* by which prospective customers are judged. The screen combines various objective facts and subjective information, which are given different weight by the firm according to their perceived value in predicting customer bill-paying behavior. Many firms use a formal scoring system, in which point values are assigned to both types of information, may be employed. In other cases the evaluation process is more subjective. In any event, a hypothetical, marginally acceptable credit customer is defined in terms of a minimum formal score or on minimum subjective standards. Prospective customers, evaluated on the basis of the same type of information as used in the screen, are accepted if the minimum formal score, or set of subjective criteria, is exceeded.

As indicated, the types of information used in the credit extension decision may be relatively objective or subjective. A partial listing of typical *objective data* often used in setting credit standards and evaluating prospective customers follows.

1.   Financial statements—including the use of financial ratios measuring liquidity, degree of financial leverage, and profitability.

2.   Length of time customer has been in business.

3.   Age and experience of key managerial personnel.

4.   Rate of growth of customer's business.

5.   Record of the customer's adherence to credit terms extended by other suppliers or by financial institutions.

Sources for such information are varied but much of it can be gained from institutions established to meet credit information needs. Credit reporting agencies such as Dun and Bradstreet provide useful financial and other background information about the prospective customer as well as a credit rating. Credit associations under the auspices of the National Association of Credit Management maintain regional files of credit information on many firms. Such information, which can be exchanged on a national basis, emphasizes a prospective customer's payment record with other business firms having extended credit to the customer in the past.

Examples of useful information having a more *subjective* character, and being difficult to measure, include:

1.   Honesty and integrity of the customer firm's management.

2.   Willingness of customer to put up collateral (pledge assets) to act as security for the credit.

3.   Overall economic conditions as they may affect the customer's ability, as distinguished from willingness, to pay.

4.   Importance of the firm's supply of goods and services to the customer's continued operation.

Naturally, different firms use different combinations of information they believe to be relevant as well as information not included in the partial listings above.[1]

---

[1]It is unwise to omit rules of thumb or old sayings if they help the retention of useful information. To that end, we repeat the "five C's" of credit: character, capacity, capital, collateral, and conditions. "Character" is that of the applicant; "capacity" and "capital" refer to the ability, in terms of business talent and financial support, to repay; "collateral" is self-explanatory, and "conditions" refers to the general business conditions—whether times are "good" or "bad."

Credit Collection Policies

Credit collection policies comprise all procedures followed by the firm once credit has been extended, to encourage the customer to pay its bills on agreed-upon terms. Among the decisions required under the various types of collection policies are:

1. At what point, after a customer's bill is past due, will the customer be reminded of the amount owed?

2. At what points will different reminders of varying intensity (letters, phone calls, personal visits) be used?

3. When will a professional collection agency be called in?

4. When bills are past due, at what point will a firm be refused credit on future sales until the amounts past due have been paid?

Credit collection efforts expend the firm's resources. Given the credit terms established by the firm, varying degrees of intensity of collection effort can be undertaken to induce customers to conform to the agreed-upon terms. Generally, the use of less strict credit standards will produce more sales to customers who are less likely to pay their bills on agreed terms and more likely to cause bad debt losses. Avoidance of bad debt losses from less creditworthy customers will require a more extensive and expensive collection effort.

Valuation and Credit

Viewed in terms of the framework established in Chapter 21, changes in credit policy can be seen to have an investment effect, a cash flow effect, and a discount rate effect. A relaxed credit policy that leads to an increase in receivables requires a greater investment in that type of asset—that is, an investment effect is produced. Costs of financing the larger investment in receivables increase as well. A cash flow effect is also produced by a relaxed credit policy in that sales, collection expenses, and bad debt losses all tend to increase. A stringent credit policy tends to produce investment and cash flow effects of the opposite character. Both relaxed and stringent credit policies would be expected to have discount rate effects as well, but for the moment we ignore that issue and confine our attention to the investment and cash flow effects.

Net present value analysis is a useful way of valuing alternative credit policies of the firm and selecting a policy consistent with shareholder wealth maximization. The firm would like to find the credit policy that maximizes the value of shareholder wealth. But the difficulties of obtaining necessary information to consider all possible credit policies are formidable, and a less sweeping search for the optimum credit policy is required. Typically, the firm begins with its *existing* credit policy and determines cash flows resulting from that policy. These flows can be compared to cash flows resulting from alternative credit policies to determine the incremental cash flows resulting from a change in credit policies. These incremental flows can then be evaluated at the firm's cost of capital to determine whether the net present value of the incremental flows is positive or negative. Alternative credit policies producing incremental cash flows having a negative net present value are rejected. If the alternative policy has a positive net present value, it is superior to existing policy and should be implemented. If more than one alternative policy has a positive net present value, then the policy having the highest NPV should be implemented. The example of Reese Rubber Company in Table 23-1 demonstrates an application of net present value analysis to the evaluation of alternative credit policies.

Reese Rubber Company's current credit policy is described in panel A, column 1 of Table 23-1. Reese grants terms of 2%/10, net/30 to its customers and 33 percent of its customers take advantage of the discount. Collection expenses average 0.5 percent of sales and bad debt loss is 2 percent of sales. Annual sales of $10 million are generated under the current policy. With a 40 percent gross operating profit margin (not including collection expenses), the operating results of the current credit policy produce a net operating cash flow after taxes of $1,915,333 in panel B. The ratio of sales to receivables of 10 in panel A means that in panel C, $1 million of receivables is carried under the current credit policy. Given the firm's current policies on liquid assets and inventories, total current assets are $1.8 million. Current liabilities of $430,000 produce a net working capital requirement, financed from long-term capital sources, of $1.37 million.

Reese Rubber is now considering two alternative credit policies, labeled *stringent* and *relaxed*. It wants to find out whether either of the alternative policies will produce incremental cash flows having positive net present values. To gain this information, the total cash flows resulting from each alternative policy are estimated. Then, the cash flows from the current credit policy are subtracted from those of the alternative policy to obtain the incremental cash flows gained by implementing the alternative policy.

The Stringent Policy   Column II of Table 23-1 describes the *stringent policy* under consideration by the firm. Compared to the current policy, the stringent policy in panel A allows a higher cash discount, 3 percent, but requires payment within the shorter total credit period of 20 days. Thus, earlier payment and a smaller level of receivables are implied. A larger percentage of customers, 40 percent, will decide to take the discount. The stringent policy also includes somewhat tighter credit stan-

Table 23-1 *Evaluation of Credit Policies: Reese Rubber Company*

	I Current Policy	II Stringent Policy	III Relaxed Policy	IV Incremental Flows Stringent Policy	V Incremental Flows Relaxed Policy
A. Characteristics of Policies					
1. Terms	2%/10, net/30	3%/10, net/20	1%/10, net/45	—	—
2. Percent of Customers Taking Discounts	33%	40%	25	—	—
3. Bad Debt Percentage	2%	1.5%	5%	—	—
4. Gross Operating Profit Margin	40%	40%	40%	—	—
5. Collection Expense (% of sales)	0.5%	0.25%	1.00%	—	—
6. Sales/Receivables Ratio	10.0	18.25	7.68	—	—
B. Operating Cash Flows					
1. Gross Sales	$10,000,000	$9,000,000	$11,000,000	-$1,000,000	+$1,000,000
2. Discounts	-66,667	-108,000	-27,500	-41,333	+39,167
3. Bad Debts	-200,000	-135,000	-550,000	+65,000	-350,000
4. Net Sales	$ 9,733,333	$8,757,000	$10,422,500	-$ 976,333	$ 698,167
5. Operating Expenses	-6,000,000	-5,400,000	-6,600,000	+600,000	-600,000
6. Collection Expenses	-50,000	-22,500	-110,000	+27,500	-60,000
7. Net Cash Flow	$ 3,683,333	$3,334,500	$ 3,712,500	-$ 348,833	$ 29,167
8. Income Tax (48%)	-1,768,000	-1,600,560	-1,782,000	+167,440	-14,000
9. Net Cash Flow After Taxes	$ 1,915,333	$1,733,940	$ 1,930,500	-$ 181,393	$ 15,167
C. Working Capital					
1. Liquid Assets	$ 300,000	$ 270,000	$ 1,930,500	-$ 30,000	+$ 30,000
2. Receivables (Net)	1,000,000	493,151	1,431,507	-506,849	+431,507
3. Inventories	500,000	450,000	550,000	-50,000	+50,000
4. Total Current Assets	$ 1,800,000	$1,213,151	$ 2,311,507	-$ 586,849	$ 511,507
5. Current Liabilities	-430,000	-387,000	-473,000	+43,000	-43,000
6. Net Working Capital Requirement	$ 1,370,000	$ 826,151	$ 1,838,507	-$ 543,849	$ 468,507
D.					
1. Present Value of Incremental Net Cash Flow After Taxes (K = 10%)	—	—	—	-$1,813,930	$ 151,670
2. Change in Net Working Capital Requirement	—	—	—	+543,849	-468,507
3. Net Present Value	—	—	—	-$1,279,081	-$ 316,837

664

dards, leading to lower expected bad debt losses of 1.5 percent of sales and lower collection expenses (because customers are more creditworthy) of 0.25 percent of sales. The stringent policy will have the effect of increasing the ratio of sales to receivables to 18.25 because of the shorter credit period and higher cash discount offered. In panel B, the level of sales for the stringent policy is reduced to $9 million because of the tighter credit standards. Discounts increase but bad debt expenses decline and collection expenses decrease. Net operating cash flow after taxes falls to $1,733,940 under the stringent policy. This does not automatically rule out the policy, since in panel C, the net working capital requirement *also* falls. Given the company's policies on liquid assets and inventories, both these assets will likely be reduced as a result of the reduced level of sales associated with the stringent policy. Applying the projected ratio of sales to receivables to the $9 million sales level produces a reduced receivables level of $493,151. Taken together, current assets fall to $1,213,151. The firm's current liabilities should decline to $387,000 as some of these are paid off by funds released from current assets. The *net* working capital requirement falls to $826,151.

Knowing the working capital requirements and the projected cash flow under the stringent policy, incremental cash flows are found by subtracting operating cash flows and working capital amounts in panels B and C of column I for the current policy, from those in column II for the stringent policy. The resulting *incremental* cash flows are shown in column IV of the table.[2] Summarizing, the annual net operating cash flow after taxes in row 9 of Panel B falls by $181,393 as a result of reduced sales and greater discounts—partially offset by reduced operating expenses (due to lower sales) and lower bad debt and collection expenses. The net working capital requirement falls by $543,849 in row 6 of panel C because of the decline in investment in current assets is partially offset by the reduction of current liabilities.

To evaluate the incremental cash flows (column IV), Reese finds the present value (in perpetuity) of the reduced annual net after-tax cash flows at the firm's cost of capital of $K = 10$ percent in row 1 of panel D and *subtracts* the reduction in net working capital from row 2. The resulting net present value of the incremental flows in row 3 of panel D is negative—indicating that the stringent policy is inferior to the current policy and should not be adopted. The unfavorable cash flow effect, with a present value of $-$ $1,813,930, outweighs the favorable investment effect, the reduction in net working capital of $543,849.

---

[2]Not all elements of net operating cash flow or of the balance sheet are included in panels B and C. Only the elements subject to change due to alternative credit policies are properly part of the analysis aimed at obtaining incremental cash flows.

The Relaxed Policy   Reese Rubber's alternative credit policy, the *relaxed policy*, is described in column III of Table 23-1. Credit terms, by providing a smaller cash discount and longer credit period, lend less encouragement to early payment of bills and reduce the number of customers taking the cash discount. The resulting sales/receivables ratio is expected to decline to 7.68 times—both because of the changed credit terms and because some relaxation of credit standards is permitted. Customers can be expected to take longer to pay their bills. For the same reason, bad debt expense will rise to 5 percent of sales and collection expenses will increase to 1 percent of sales.

Panel B shows that the relaxed credit policy is expected to increase sales to $11 million. Net after-tax operating cash flow will rise to $1,930,500 because of increased sales, even though bad debt and collection expenses are higher. Panel C indicates that the net working capital requirement will increase to $1,838,507 because rising current assets, especially receivables, are only partly offset by increased current liabilities.

Incremental cash flows, compared to the current policy, are shown in column V. In row 9 of panel B, annual net after-tax operating cash flow will rise by $15,167 because of higher sales, partially offset by higher bad debts and collection expenses. Net working capital requirements increase, in row 6 of panel C, by $468,507 because of higher levels of current assets.

To value the incremental cash flows of the relaxed policy, the firm's cost of capital is applied to the incremental after-tax net operating cash flow to obtain, in row 1 of panel D, a present value of $151,670. The increased net working capital requirement of $468,507 in row 2 is subtracted from this amount to obtain the negative net present value in row 3 of panel D, of − $316,837. The relaxed policy is inferior to the current policy and should not be adopted. The *favorable* cash flow effect is outweighed by the *unfavorable* investment effect.

Reese Rubber must conclude that neither the stringent nor the relaxed alternative is preferable to its current credit policy. Unless other, as yet undefined, credit policies are found to be superior, the firm should not abandon its current policy.

The Discount Rate Effect   So far, the net present value analysis of Reese Rubber Company's current, stringent, and relaxed credit policies has ignored any differences in risk, with attendant effects on the firm's cost of capital, that might result from choosing different credit policies. This issue concerns the discount rate effect of different receivables policies. We have postponed this discussion because the practical difficulties of finding the different discount rates are relatively great.

That differences in the risk of the net operating cash flow stream may result from different credit policies seems plausible. Under any given credit policy, the firm's net operating cash flow may be expected to vary with business conditions. If the firm adopts a more relaxed credit policy and sells on credit to less creditworthy customers, a downswing in business conditions may produce larger bad debt losses at a time when net operating cash flows are *already* declining because of deteriorating sales. That is, net operating cash flows may be lower during bad business conditions than they would have been if credit policy had not been relaxed, because the firm is now extending credit to less creditworthy customers who are less likely to pay in bad times. Excellent business conditions and a relaxed credit policy may accentuate peaks in net operating cash flow relative to use of the existing credit policy. This is the reverse side of the coin from what happens under poor business conditions. Less creditworthy customers prosper under good conditions but are more likely to fail under poor conditions. In any case, more relaxed credit policies tend to produce more variation in the stream of net operating cash flow after taxes. Presumably, more stringent credit policies reduce the variability of the net cash flow stream.

To the extent that greater variability of net operating cash flow after taxes produces greater variability in rates of return for investors, variability that cannot be diversified away, it is possible that beta, and the firm's cost of capital, will increase with more relaxed credit policies—that is, a discount rate effect will occur. It is difficult to estimate the change in cost of capital due to changes in credit policy alone, but we can see how the different costs of capital for credit policies offering different risks would likely be used in the case of Reese Rubber.

Table 23-1 evaluated the incremental cash flows for alternative credit policies at the firm's overall cost of capital of $K = 10$ percent. This is, in principle, incorrect if the incremental flows of these policies are of a risk character different from the overall cash flows of the firm for which $K = 10$ percent is appropriate. For example, the sales that would be lost under a more stringent credit policy are, no doubt, less creditworthy and involve greater risk of collection. These are represented by the loss of $181,393 in net operating cash flow when the stringent policy is imposed over the current policy. Therefore, a greater cost of capital should apply to these riskier *incremental* cash flows ($181,393). (In other words, a lower cost of capital should be applied to the cash flow of the more stringent credit policy, $1,733,904.) If a lower discount rate were used in the stringent policy, it would compare more favorably to the current policy. Alternatively, the use of $K = 10$ percent for the current policy *and* the relaxed policy favors the relaxed policy, whose incremental cash flows should be riskier and consequently would involve a K greater than

10 percent. Thus the incremental net present value under the relaxed policy (−$316,837) is overstated. We would regard the incremental net present value of the stringent policy using $K = 10$ percent as understated and thus the NPV of −$1,279,081 is too low.

We cannot easily find out appropriate costs of capital to evaluate incremental flows for the stringent and relaxed credit policies because such flows do not "trade," and thus are not valued separately in the market. We do not know, as a result, whether the differences in cost of capital produced by changes in credit policy are significant. Of necessity, we fall back on using the firm's overall cost of capital, in this example, to evaluate all incremental flows. In doing this, we realize that to some degree, this procedure understates the value of a stringent credit policy and overstates the value of a relaxed credit policy.

The Credit Monitoring and Control Process

Given a set of credit standards, credit terms, and credit lines established by the firm, a monitoring and control process is needed to detect when the actual level of receivables differs from the level deemed optimal by the firm's credit extension policies, and to restore the level of receivables to the optimal level.

Measures for Monitoring Receivables   It is desirable to possess **credit monitoring** measures capable of giving an *early* signal that receivables levels are getting out of control—that is, increasing above the level that is optimum consistent with the firm's credit extension and collection policies and the prevailing levels of sales. (Given these policies, variations in sales can produce variations in receivables.) One such signal that is reliable but tardy is the bad debt loss experience of the firm. A worsening bad debt trend will cause receivables to increase beyond optimum levels because a larger proportion of the receivables is constituted by potential bad debts. Earlier detection than is provided by this measure is needed. Among the measures used by firms to provide early detection of a receivables balance that differs from optimum levels are the **average collection period** and the **aging schedule of accounts receivable.**

Average Collection Period   The average collection period, in days, is found by the formula:

$$\text{Average collection period} = AR \div \frac{S}{365} = \frac{AR}{S} \times 365$$

This measure of accounts receivable activity is the number of days in the year times the reciprocal of the sales/receivables financial ratio. Increases in the average collection period (or reductions in the sales/receivables ratio) *imply* that for as yet unknown reasons, receivables are increasing because it is taking longer to collect on bills. For example, if receivables increased to a level of $1.4 million for Reese Rubber while sales increased to $12 million, the measured average collection period would be:

$$\text{Average collection period} = \frac{1,400,000}{12,000,000} \times 365 = 42.6 \text{ days}$$

However, the original collection period was:

$$\text{Average collection period} = \frac{1,000,000}{10,000,000} \times 365 = 36.5 \text{ days}$$

We infer from this that something is causing the collection period to increase and further investigation into the cause of this behavior is required.

The Aging Schedule An alternative measure of receivables activity, the aging schedule, requires that receivables be placed in age categories by dollar amount. Then the percentage of total receivables in each age category can be determined.

	Normal Schedule			Alternative Schedule	
Days Old	Dollars	Percent	Days Old	Dollars	Percent
0–30	$ 600,000	60%	0–30	$ 640,000	45.7%
31–60	300,000	30	31–60	500,000	40
61–90	100,000	10	61–90	200,000	14.3
	$1,000,000	100%		$1,400,000	100%

The normal schedule for Reese Rubber would find 60 percent of receivables less than 31 days old; 30 percent between 31 and 61 days old, and 10 percent between 61 and 91 days old. The alternative schedule, occurring when sales had increased to a $12 million annual rate and receivables increased to $1.4 million, would find the percentage of receivables less than 31 days old declining to 45.7 percent, whereas percentages in all other categories have increased. Receivables have clearly aged in the alternative schedule and, with an increased level of receivables, suggest that older receivables are not being collected.

Comparing Monitoring Measures It is difficult to choose between the two monitoring measures demonstrated here. Applied on an annual basis, each measure tends to give consistent signals of changes in the age of the receivables and speed of the collection process. When applied *monthly*, however, seasonal and random fluctuations of sales can, with no changes in credit-granting policy or collection effort, produce fluctuating values of the monitoring measures. Consequently, false signals can be given indicating that the collection period is lengthening or that the age of receivables is increasing when this is not the case. To prevent false signals, the decision maker must develop predicted seasonal behavior for any of these monitoring measures and establish allowances for random variation. Alternatively, the firm may wish to develop one of the more sophisticated monitoring devices that relate receivables back to the month in which sales actually occurred.[3]

Controlling Credit Granting and Collection Effort Processes   Suppose that the monitoring measure used by the firm to detect changes in the level of receivables signals, for example, that the level of receivables is increasing above optimum levels (given the level of sales) because the average collection period is increasing or because receivables are increasing in age. Then the control process needed to take corrective action requires that the cause of the observed trend be found. It is often difficult to determine the cause. If credit-granting decisions are made with a credit screen, records may be sampled to see whether the screening procedure is being properly administered. If no important discrepancies appear in that area then the collection effort may be at fault. Records of collection procedures may be examined to see whether normal procedures are being followed. If collection procedures are not being adhered to, enforcement of existing rules may solve the problem. If neither the credit-granting nor collection effort functions are defective, other causes, such as a slow down in economic conditions or very tight money (causing higher interest rates) may be to blame. Under these circumstances, the firm must decide whether to continue to press customers for payment and perhaps lose some of them to more lenient competitors, or to adjust policies to the temporary business conditions. The latter reaction is typical when recession strikes otherwise good customers particularly hard. Such customers often remember the lenience of the firm when economic conditions are better. The difficult problem facing a

---

[3]A distributed lag approach views any given billing by the firm as being paid over time with certain fractions of the bill being paid in given time periods after billing (e.g., for $1 of billing, 20 percent might be paid one period later, 60 percent two periods later, 10 percent three periods later, etc.). Firms would monitor the percentages of a billing received in subsequent time periods to determine whether remedial action is required. See Wilbur G. Lewellen and Robert W. Johnson, "Better Way to Monitor Accounts Receivable," *Harvard Business Review* (May–June 1972), pp. 101–109.

creditor is to know when and with whom credit policies should be enforced strictly and when and with whom they should be relaxed. Solution of this problem requires keen business insight.

Inventories of raw materials, work in process, and finished goods are typically carried by manufacturing firms. For wholesalers and retailers, the only inventories are finished goods that such firms buy and resell. For manufacturers, work-in-process inventories necessarily result because production of goods takes time to complete. (Production and operations research texts fully cover the important areas of work-in-process inventories, and we say nothing further about them.) Raw materials inventories aid the production process by preventing costly variations or shutdowns because raw materials are in limited supply or temporarily not available. Finished goods inventories fulfill customer demands when they exceed the rate of production and so avoid possible losses of sales. They also make it *less* necessary to vary the rate of production to accommodate sudden changes in customer demand. Wholesalers and retailers apply the same rationale for holding finished goods inventory as do manufacturers. However, for the former, finished goods and raw materials are the same thing and no work-in-process inventory exists.

INVENTORY MANAGE-MENT

The advantages of carrying inventories must be weighed against the costs of storing, financing, and potential obsolescence, to find an optimal inventory level. This important issue is given far more detailed treatment in texts devoted to production and operations research than we can present here. We confine our attention to a simple model of **economic order quantity** to illustrate the considerations underlying the optimum inventory level. Our example deals with raw material inventory, but the model is equally applicable to finished goods inventory whether finished goods are purchased from an outside firm or manufactured in the production process of the firm itself.

The simple economic order quantity model assumes that the level of inventory behaves in the regular time pattern shown in Figure 23-1, where inventories are instantaneously replenished in the amount of the economic order quantity Q and depleted at a uniform rate over time until exhausted. Then, inventories are restored in the amount Q and the pattern continues. The average inventory is therefore $Q/2$ for this model.

The Economic Order Quantity Model

Two classes of costs are considered in the economic order quantity

Figure 23-1   *Inventory Behavior: Economic Order Quantity*

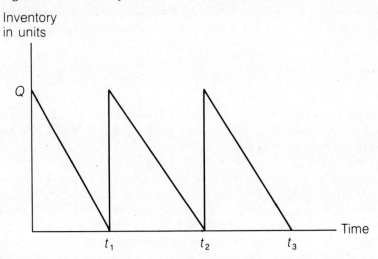

model: **order costs** and **carrying costs.** Total order costs per year O are specified as:

$$O = (o_1 + o_2 Q)\frac{D}{Q} \qquad (23\text{-}1)$$

where

o_1 = the fixed cost of placing an order of any size

o_2 = the variable cost of placing an order per unit ordered

D = annual demand by the firm for the product

D/Q = the number of orders placed in a year

Fixed order costs o_1 are independent of the size of the order. Examples of fixed costs are telephone costs, preparation of purchase orders, bill payment, and production setup charges passed on by the seller. Variable order costs depend on the size (number of units) of the order and include shipping charges and shipping insurance. Thus, dollar variable costs for a given order are $o_2 Q$—or variable cost per unit ordered times the number of units in the order. Total costs *per order* equal the sum of fixed and variable costs per order, or $o_1 + o_2 Q$. This expression is part of the total order cost expression in Equation (23-1). The other part of total order cost is D/Q, the number of orders placed per year if annual demand is D and the order size is Q. Consequently, total order cost per year is the product in Equation (23-1) of total costs per order, $o_1 + o_2Q$, and number of orders per year, D/Q.

Carrying costs include costs of storing inventories such as heat and electricity for the storage space, depreciation of storage facilities, property tax on storage facilities, any taxes on inventory, insurance for the inventory, and costs of financing the inventory. Total carrying costs per year C are expressed as a percentage a of the unit purchase price of the goods P multiplied times the average inventory level $Q/2$, or:

$$C = aP\frac{Q}{2} \qquad (23\text{-}2)$$

The firm wishes to select an order quantity Q that will minimize the total cost of ordering and holding inventory. Using Equations (23-1) and (23-2) for total order cost and total carrying cost, the total annual cost of ordering and carrying inventory, for any Q, is TC.

$$TC = O + C$$

$$= (o_1 + o_2Q)\frac{D}{Q} + aP\frac{Q}{2} \qquad (23\text{-}3)$$

If we graph order costs, carrying costs, and total costs as reflected in Equations (23-1), (23-2), and (23-3), the cost behavior as a function of order quantity is represented by the curves in Figure 23-2. Because order costs have a fixed component, they decline as order quantity increases. Carrying costs increase with order quantity. Accordingly, a minimum total cost order quantity at Q^* is implied. The order quantity Q^* minimizing total cost is expressed as:

$$Q^* = \sqrt{\frac{2o_1D}{aP}}$$

The resulting economic order quantity increases with the size of fixed order costs and annual demand and decreases as carrying cost per unit increases. The average inventory level is, of course, $Q^*/2$.[4]

As an example of the usage of the economic order quantity model, consider the inventory problem of Shiffer Farm Tools Company. A critical component of one of Shiffer's major products must be acquired from one supplier, who custom manufactures it for Shiffer alone. Shiffer has an annual demand of $D = 40,000$ units for the part and the price per unit paid to the supplier is $P = \$50$. However, the supplier has a setup cost of $o_1 = \$75,000$ to produce the parts each time an order is placed by Shiffer.

---

[4]Q^* is found by differentiating the total cost Equation (23-3) with respect to Q, setting the derivative equal to zero, and solving for Q^*.

Figure 23-2 *Economic Order Quantity to Minimize Total Cost*

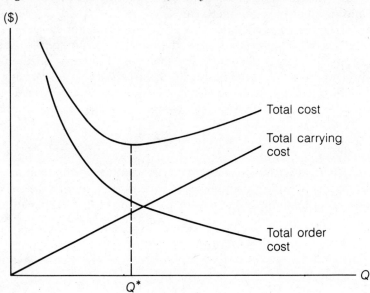

This setup charge is a cost passed on to Shiffer *in addition* to the $50 per unit price and is of the same magnitude regardless of the size of the order. Carrying costs are estimated to be $a = 30$ percent of the unit purchase price, and variable order costs, o_2, are $0.40 per unit.

Using the economic order quantity formulation, Shiffer's optimum Q^* is:

$$Q^* = \sqrt{\frac{2o_1 D}{aP}} = \sqrt{\frac{2(75,000)(40,000)}{(0.30)(50)}} = 20,000 \text{ units}$$

and the *average* inventory level is 10,000 units. Total costs under the economic order quantity of 20,000 units are, substituting Q^* and the other values into Equation (23-3),

$$TC = (75,000 + 0.40 \times 20,000)\frac{40,000}{20,000} + 0.30(50)\frac{20,000}{2} = \$316,000$$

The reader may verify that any other order quantity will produce total inventory costs exceeding those for Q^*.

A Safety Stock The economic order quantity model assumes a stable and known demand or usage for the product stocked in inventory as well as a predictable lag between order and delivery. In fact, this is hardly likely to be the case. Inventories are not drawn down to zero, nor

Figure 23-3   *Economic Order Quantity Inventory Model Modified by a Safety Block*

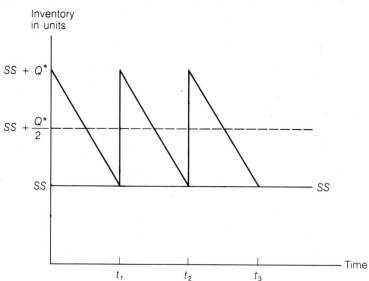

are lags between order and delivery stable. Therefore, under usual circumstances minimum, nonzero, levels of inventory are maintained in the face of uncertainty. Although we do not consider more general models capable of incorporating such complications, the concept of a **safety stock** (*SS*) to accomodate uncertainty about the behavior of demand and the rate of inventory replenishment is illustrated in Figure 23-3, where the horizontal line represents the level of the safety stock *SS*. When the economic order quantity Q^* is initially received, the inventory level will be $SS + Q^*$ and the average level of inventory is $(SS + Q^*)/2$. Higher degrees of uncertainty about the behavior of demand and the rate of inventory replenishment will lead to higher safety stock and average inventory levels. However, the optimum safety stock is subjectively established in our simple economic order quantity model.

Decisions about the desired level of inventory are difficult to relate to the goal of shareholder wealth maximization. Presumably, maintenance of inadequate inventories could reduce profitability and create additional uncertainty about shareholder returns. Whether such added risk can be diversified away is open to question, but some tendency to raise risk premiums contained in the cost of capital and to reduce the value of common shares may be present. In the other direction, excessive in-

Inventory Management and Valuation

ventory levels may reduce risk of production disruptions as well as risk premiums in the cost of capital but may also raise carrying costs more than enough to offset such gains. The precise optimum point in a *valuation* sense is by no means clear.

SUMMARY   Receivables management requires the determination of credit policies regarding credit extension and collections, and monitoring and controlling the level of receivables. Credit extension policies require decisions concerning credit terms, the size of the credit line, and the stringency of credit standards. In implementing credit standards, firms develop a credit screen that is used to identify prospective customers having a too high likelihood of not paying their bills. Credit collection policies govern the nature and intensity of the effort the firm makes to "encourage" customers to pay their bills on agreed-upon terms. It is possible to evaluate alternative more relaxed or more stringent credit policies. More relaxed credit policies produce an unfavorable investment effect because more capital must be invested to sustain a higher receivables level. But a relaxed policy tends to produce a favorable cash flow effect because of higher sales only partly offset by higher bad debt losses, collection expenses, and financing costs. A stringent policy has the reverse effect—producing a favorable investment effect by lowering the level of working capital needed to facilitate lower sales, but causing an unfavorable cash flow effect because the lower sales are only partly offset by lower bad debt losses, collection expenses, and financing costs. Whether the investment effect or cash flow effect dominates in a particular case is revealed by the use of net present value analysis. A difficulty in employing that analysis is identifying the proper cost of capital. Substantial changes in risk stemming from a change in credit policy would require a new cost of capital. However, lacking information about the risk of the incremental cash flows produced by credit policy changes, the firm's overall cost of capital must be employed. The monitoring process for receivables attempts to detect, in timely fashion, when the actual level of receivables is deviating from the optimal level. Common monitoring measures include the average collection period and the aging schedule of accounts receivable. Detected deviations from the optimal level of receivables require that the cause of deviation be identified and controlled. Excessive receivables may result from a breakdown in the application of credit extension policies or collection policies or from a deterioration in business conditions facing customers.

The main focus of inventory management centers on minimizing the total cost of an inventory policy to the firm. A simple inventory model was used to find the economic order quantity that would minimize the sum of ordering costs and carrying costs for items to be carried in inventory. However, the inventory model presented ignored uncertainty of the usage rate and delivery time, along with the potential costs of lost sales and/or interrupted production. To reflect these costs, we introduced a safety stock—a minimum level of inventory above zero that would trigger a new order.

GLOSSARY OF KEY TERMS

Aging Schedule of Accounts Receivable	A schedule that separates receivables into age categories. By examining the proportion of receivables in each age category, a manager tries to assess the *quality* of receivables and the effectiveness of collection policies.
Average Collection Period	The number of days' sales represented by total accounts receivable, or, the average number of days required to collect a bill.
Carrying Costs	All costs associated with storing, insuring, and financing inventory.
Cash Discount	A percentage discount offered credit customers if a bill is paid within a specified period, the discount period.
Collection Policies	Policies governing procedures used to encourage customers to pay their bills on agreed-on terms.
Credit Extension Policies	Policies of the firm as established in the firm's procedures used to set credit terms, credit lines, and credit standards.
Credit Line	The maximum amount a customer is permitted to owe a firm at any time.
Credit Monitoring	The process of detecting when actual receivables differ from the optimum level of receivables.
Credit Period	The total length of time given a customer to pay a bill and not be considered late in payment.
Credit Standards	The standards, high or low, set by the firm to accept or reject prospective customers. Standards, when specified in terms of specific kinds of information about customers, are referred to as a **credit screen.**
Credit Terms	The firm's set of terms describing the cash discount, the discount period, and the credit period.
Discount Period	The time given a customer to pay a bill and still receive a cash discount.

Economic Order Quantity	The order size that minimizes the total ordering and carrying costs of inventory.
Order Cost	Costs of ordering items from suppliers or from the production line.
Safety Stock	Additional inventories held by the firm in response to the existence of uncertainty and the costs of having insufficient inventory to meet demand and maintain production.
Trade Credit	Credit extended to customers when they purchase goods and services.

SELECTED REFERENCES

Benishay, Haskel. "Managerial Controls of Accounts Receivable: A Deterministic Approach," *Journal of Accounting Research* (Spring 1965), pp. 114–133.

Beranek, William. "Financial Implications of Lot-Size Inventory Models," *Management Science* (April 1967), pp. B401–B408.

Boggess, William P. "Screen-Test Your Credit Risks," *Harvard Business Review* (November-December, 1967), pp. 113–122.

Khoury, Nabil T. "The Optimal Level of Safety Stocks." In *Management of Working Capital: A Reader*, Keith V. Smith, Ed. St. Paul, MN: West Publishing Co., 1974, pp. 209–215.

Lewellen, Wilbur G., and Robert O. Edmister. "A General Model for Accounts-Receivable Analysis and Control," *Journal of Financial and Quantitative Analysis* (March 1973), pp. 195–206.

Lewellen, Wilbur G., and Robert W. Johnson. "Better Way to Monitor Accounts Receivable," *Harvard Business Review* (May–June, 1972), pp. 101–109.

Mehta, Dileep. "The Formulation of Credit Policy Models," *Management Science* (October 1968), pp. B30–B50.

Schiff, Michael. "Credit and Inventory Management—Separate or Together," *Financial Executive* (November 1972), pp. 28–33.

Snyder, Arthur. "Principles of Inventory Management," *Financial Executive* (April 1964), pp. 13–21.

QUESTIONS

1. What functions do receivables and inventories perform? Explain carefully.

2. One of your customers has gotten into a financial bind. He ap-

proaches your company for an extension of credit until his problems can be worked out. As financial manager, what course of action would you pursue? This customer is a long-time purchaser; he has consistently taken cash discounts; until this time he has been a good credit risk. Consider these factors in light of the financial manager's responsibilities to shareholders.

3. Explain how you would evaluate a proposal to alter credit terms. Set up your explanation in a logical, step-by-step fashion. Use numerical examples where relevant and identify necessary assumptions.

4. As head of the credit department of a retail store, discuss the subjective and objective qualifications you would note in making decisions to grant credit.

5. Discuss the potential impact of both easing and tightening credit terms on the risk facing shareholders. Be specific.

6. What are the primary problems in using average collection period and aging schedules to control receivables? What characteristics should a good control mechanism have?

7. Why should a financial manager be concerned with inventory management?

8. Discuss the strengths and weaknesses of the inventory model presented in this chapter.

9. If the cost of carrying inventory declines, will the optimal economic order quantity increase? Why?

1. Joe's Pie Company desires a credit policy that would provide a sales **PROBLEMS** to current asset ratio of 10 to 1 and a current ratio of 3 to 1. (a) Compute the working capital and net working capital requirements if Joe predicts an annual sales level of $500,000. (b) If Joe were considering an alternative, easier credit policy that would produce estimated sales of $750,000, compute the financing requirements for Joe if the current ratio alone changed—to 2.9 to 1.

2. Faced with considerable excess capacity, Martin Manufacturing Company decided that it would be appropriate to consider easing credit terms to stimulate sales. After considerable effort, necessary data were collected. Management was careful to remove all fixed costs (and thus no depreciation is included) in estimating the gross operating profit margin for the new policy. If the appropriate dis-

count rate is 20 percent, the tax rate is 50 percent on net cash flow, and it is assumed that the incremental flow is perpetual, what is the net present value of the new policy? Should the new policy be undertaken? (Hint: Use Table 23-1 as a guide in setting up the problem.)

	Current Policy	New Policy
Sales	$2,000,000	$2,200,000
Credit terms	2/10, net/30	2/15, net/60
Percent of Gross Sales Discounted	40%	35%
Bad Debt Percentage	1%	3%
Gross Operating Profit Margin (excluding collection expenses) on net sales	20%	25%
Collection Expenses (% of Gross Sales)	0.5%	1.1%
Sales/Receivable Ratio (Gross Sales)	11.25	7.50
Current Ratio (to be maintained)	3:1	2.7:1
Inventory Position	$170,000	$250,000
Liquid Assets	$50,000	$75,000

3. Would your answer to Martin Manufacturing's problem change if the Sales/Receivables ratio for the new policy was 6.0 times rather than 7.5 times and bad debts were 8 percent rather than 3 percent? Assume that the same discount rate applies.

4. To compute the net present value in both of the previous problems, one had to assume that the increment of investment in net working capital is constant over time. Assume that the firm has highly seasonal sales and the financial information was gathered from financial statements that were computed when accounts receivable were at a seasonal low point for the year. What type of bias would this create in your analysis? How might you avoid that bias?

5. Lawrence Earmuff Company has hired you to, among other things, evaluate their management of receivables. Given the following information, compute the end-of-year aging schedule and average collection period (assume a 360-day year for that computation) for Lawrence's operating history. Evaluate the firm's performance in this area. Are improvements possible?

	Year				
	19×1	19×2	19×3	19×4	19×5
Sales	$2400	$3600	$6000	$9600	$7200
Receivables					
Days Outstanding					
0–30	$ 180	$ 270	$ 500	$1040	$1000
31–60	30	42	100	192	125
61–90	5	10	67	368	75
End of Year Total	$ 215	$ 322	$ 667	$1600	$1200

6. Given the following information, compute the optimum order quantity, the average inventory, the number of orders per year, and the total inventory cost per year.

Annual demand	10,000 units
Purchase price per unit	$10
Fixed cost per order	$1000
Variable costs of placing an order are 40 percent of order size	
Carrying cost percentage of purchase price, 10 percent	

Financing Current Assets

Current assets are financed by a wide variety of sources of funds. For instance, on November 16, 1983, Creswell Electric Appliances (CEA) has a 60-day loan for $83,000 from a local bank and a 3-year loan for $168,000 from the same institution, secured by inventory. Both loans were negotiated at about the same time, but, according to CEA management, they were obtained for different reasons. The 60-day loan was negotiated to support increased inventory for seasonal appliance sales, whereas the $168,000 loan was used, in part, to acquire a permanent level of inventory for a new line of appliances that CEA had agreed to distribute. In addition to the 60-day loan, CEA has trade accounts payable of $120,000 and other short-term liabilities of $42,000.

Notice that CEA uses different types of borrowing for different purposes. A temporary increase in inventory is financed with a short-term loan, and a permanent increase in inventory is financed, in part, by a loan with a longer maturity. In addition to borrowing from the bank, CEA borrows from suppliers and others on a short-term basis. In this chapter we examine the types of financing arrangement available to firms and explain why the financing arrangements illustrated by CEA might be in the best interest of owners.

Given the desired investment in current assets, the firm has two financing decisions to make. First, the desired proportion of short- and long-term financing sources used to support the level of current assets must be selected. Given this decision, the second task is to determine the mix of short-term sources.

We simplify the choice of short- and long-term financing for current assets by assuming that the firm has already determined total investment in current *and* fixed assets as well as the total equity investment. It remains to select the maturity and other characteristics of the firm's debt financing, including short-term debt qualifying as current liabilities. Since the firm's total debt may provide financing for more than just

THE PROPORTION OF SHORT- AND LONG-TERM FINANCING

current assets, we further restrict the decision to debt financing of current assets.[1]

Financial Folklore   Financial folklore provides a generalization stating that the firm should match the maturity of its debt with the length of the financing need. In the case of current assets, this implies that temporary investments in current assets should be financed by short-term temporary financing and permanent investments require long-term financing. The rationale for this folklore is that short-term financing for permanent investment in current assets leaves the firm exposed to two dangers: a liquidity crisis produced by inability to *renew* short-term financing in the event of a bad year in the firm's operations, and the risk that interest rates, upon renewal of short-term loans, might be higher in the future. In addition, short-term financing imposes costs of frequent loan renegotiation on the firm.

As with much folklore, there is substantial truth in this sample. But it does not tell the whole story. First of all, it concentrates on formal debt maturity and does not account for the length of the financing relationship with a particular lender to the firm. For example, a supplier providing trade credit may grant 30 days to pay for purchases. This is indeed short-term credit. Yet a long-standing buyer–seller relationship will provide a permanent component of financing for the firm that is consistent with the normal level of purchases. The *effective* maturity of the continuously received loan is indefinitely long. The formal short maturity of such loans can often be informally extended in a bad year as the financial relationship between the firm and its creditor works to support the firm and preserve sales to the firm for its creditor. The same holds true for short-term loans granted by a bank to a firm. Formal loan maturity may be, say, 90 days, yet the financial relationship between the firm and bank may be perceived as indefinitely long. Such short-term loans are often granted with the mutual expectation between the firm and the bank that the loan *will* be renewed.

Consistent with folklore, mismanagement of the firm or severe economic conditions could lead to a severing of financial relations, with predictable consequences. Yet outstanding loans with longer maturity can also be jeopardized under the same circumstances. In short, there are strong similarities between a lengthy financing relationship involv-

---

[1]This restriction is useful but artificial. The total of the firm's debt and equity financing supports *all* the firm's assets (i.e. some of the firm's equity supports current and fixed assets).

ing a sequence of short-term loans and loans with a long formal maturity.

Folklore also ignores the role of repayment patterns of promised payments to lenders as a variable affecting the cost of borrowing and its availability. Such patterns, along with other characteristics of debt, make the emphasis on formal debt maturity contained in folklore too restricted a view. While retaining folklore as a point of departure, we show how deviations from that folklore can be justified. We see that conflicts of interest between lenders and borrowers provide adverse incentives for shareholders of the borrower to divert funds from lenders to themselves. Such incentives threaten the availability of funds in a financial relationship and, by posing enhanced default risk, increase interest rates on loans extended. Loan maturity and the structure of debt repayment patterns become variables capable of eliminating these adverse incentives and the risk for lenders posed by them. We show that matching loan maturity with length of financing need as posed by folklore is not necessarily optimal for the firm. Then ignoring conflicts of interest, we see how temporary departures from matching debt maturity with length of financing need may be justified by speculation aimed at achieving lower interest rates on borrowing and by uncertainty about the duration of financing need. To develop these points, it is useful to introduce the term structure of interest rates.

The *term structure of interest rates* depicts the relation between yield to maturity (internal rate of return) of debt and the maturity of that debt, holding default risk constant. From the standpoint of the firm, it indicates interest costs of issuing debt of alternative loan maturities. Figure 24-1 illustrates representative term structures that may confront a firm. Note that the term structures, also known as *yield curves*, portray interest costs as higher, unchanged, or lower as debt maturity increases. It is beyond our scope to explain why these different shapes can exist. We assert only that a yield curve with a positive slope does not necessarily mean that short-term debt financing is cheaper than long-term financing, nor does a negative slope necessarily mean that long-term debt financing is cheaper than short-term financing.[2] To avoid these difficulties, we assume that the yield curve confronting a firm is *horizontal*, such as curve *E* in Figure 24-1. Interest rates of alternative debt maturities are the *same*. This leaves only one important caution: the yield curve con-

The Term Structure of Interest Rates

---

[2]For a good discussion of yield curve determination, see James C. Van Horne, *The Function and Analysis of Capital Market Rates* (Englewood Cliffs, NJ: Prentice-Hall, 1970).

Figure 24-1   *Alternative Term Structures of Interest Rates*

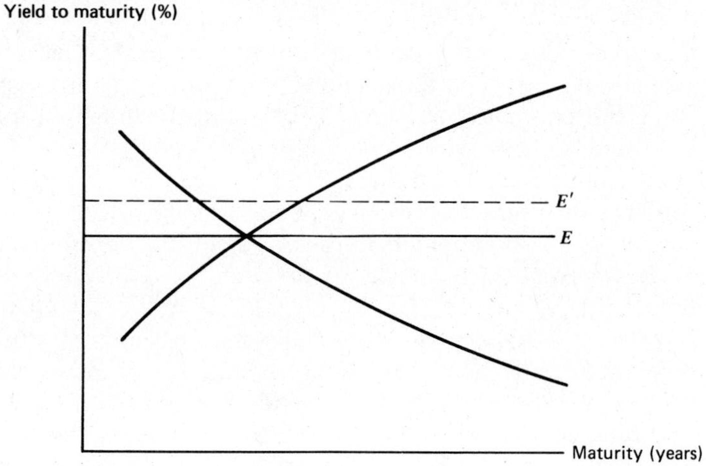

Yield to maturity (%)

fronting a firm must be of *constant default risk.* It cannot be used to compare interest costs for debt maturities of different degrees of leverage. If a firm chose to use more total financial leverage, thus increasing default risk, a new higher yield curve would be confronted as in *E'* in Figure 24-1.

The Effect of Conflicting Interests Between Borrowers and Lenders

Given that interest rates for loans of differing maturities are the same, conflicting interests between borrowers and lenders tend to make the chosen debt maturity equal to or shorter than the duration of the financing need of the firm. Loans with maturities longer than the duration of need create adverse incentives for shareholders to benefit themselves at the expense of lenders. To eliminate such incentives, firms agree to loan maturities equal to or less than the length of financing need. They also agree to repayment patterns that eliminate adverse incentives. Such compliance by the firm is in its interest because interest rates may be reduced, and loan availability increased, by eliminating conflicts of interest.

To illustrate, consider a firm needing to raise $100 of debt financing to support current assets. Assume that the firm will exist for 3 years and that funds are immediately invested. The expected cash inflows from the investment are illustrated in panel A of Table 24-1. Given these inflows, we can illustrate interest and principal payments for a 10 percent interest rate for three alternative loans with differing maturities and

Table 24-1 *An Example of Adverse Incentives That May Be Created When Debt Maturity and Loan Payment Patterns Do Not Reflect a Firm's Financing Needs*

		$t = 0$	$t = 1$	$t = 2$	$t = 3$
A.	Initial Conditions				
	Debt	($100)			
	Equity	($100)			
	Expected Cash Flow		$50	$150	$50
B.	3-Year Debt with $100 of Principal Paid in Year 3				
	Promised Debt Payments		10	10	110
	Expected Cash Flow		50	150	50
	Debt Payments		10	10	50
	Equity Payments		40	140	0
C.	2-Year Debt with $100 of Principal Paid in Year 2				
	Promised Debt Payments		10	110	0
	Expected Cash Flow		50	150	50
	Debt Payments		10	110	0
	Equity Payments		40	40	50
D.	2-Year Debt with $60 of Principal Paid in Year 2 and $40 in Year 3				
	Promised Debt Payments		10	70	44
	Expected Cash Flow		50	150	50
	Debt Payments		10	70	44
	Equity Payments		40	80	6

repayment of principal patterns. The first loan (panel B) has a 3-year maturity and promises $10 annual interest payments with a single $100 principal payment at end of year 3. The second loan (panel C) has a 2-year maturity, promising $10 in annual interest and a single $100 principal payment at end of year 2. The third loan (panel D) provides a principal payment of $60 at end of year 2 with a concluding principal payment of $40 at the end of the third year. Interest charges are then $10 for the first 2 years and $4 for the third.

It turns out that the 3-year loan in panel B provides adverse incentives to shareholders that increase risk to the lender. To see these incentives, note that during the first year, expected cash inflows are $50, with $10 paid to the lender and the remaining $40 to shareholders. In the second year, the firm expects to earn $150. If, after paying $10 to the lender, the firm pays out the remaining $140 to shareholders, the $50 expected to be generated in the third year will be insufficient to make the $110 promised debt payment. Shareholders have an incentive to pay out all earnings after the interest payment in the second year. In effect, they *then* receive the $110 − $50 = $60 remaining to be paid to the lender in the third year.

A lender aware of the expected cash inflow pattern and the adverse incentives created by this 3-year loan would view the decision to grant the loan with great caution. Protection must be afforded against actions that benefit shareholders at the expense of the lender. Note that there were two conditions creating the adverse incentive with the loan in panel B. First, the firm had sufficient expected cash inflow in the first and second years to repay a $100 loan at 10 percent interest in 2, not 3 years. It did not "need" a 3-year loan. Second, expected cash inflows in year 3 were insufficient to meet promised payments on debt.

One way of eliminating conflicting incentives in this case would, consistent with folklore, be to reduce the loan maturity to 2 years as in panel C. In this case, promised debt payments can be met from expected cash inflows in the first 2 years. Conflicting incentives are not created. Commitments to lenders are paid as soon as possible, leaving no opportunity for shareholders to drain funds from the firm. In short, debt maturity is restricted to the length of the financing "need," the minimum amount of time needed to repay a loan out of expected cash inflows.

A second way of eliminating conflicting incentives focuses not on debt maturity but on the repayment pattern. In panel D, the 3-year loan maturity is longer than financing "need." But the $60 principal payment at end of year 2 increases debt payments in the second year where expected cash inflows are relatively higher. That principal payment in the second year also eliminates the opportunity for shareholders to direct funds to themselves at the expense of debt holders.

Still another method for eliminating conflicting incentives is to make the loan maturity less than the duration of financing "need." For example, a 1-year loan with single promised payment of $110 at end of year 1 could not fully repaid out of expected cash inflow by the firm in Table 24-1. But at the time the 1-year loan matures, the lender could agree to renegotiate the unpaid balance. A financial relationship then exists for the length of financing need as distinguished from formal loan maturity. For example, the firm in Table 24-1 could pay $10 interest and $40 principal from the $50 expected cash inflow for year 1 and renegotiate a new 1-year loan for $60 at the end of year 1. As in the previous case, there remains no opportunity for shareholders to divert funds to themselves.

Selection of repayment patterns and restricting debt maturity to be equal or shorter than the duration of financing need do not exhaust the means of eliminating conflicting incentives. Lenders can also require loan agreements restricting firms from diverting funds from lenders to shareholders. In addition, lenders may charge higher interest rates in

Figure 24-2 *Effect of Creating Adverse Incentives by Lengthening Loan Maturity*

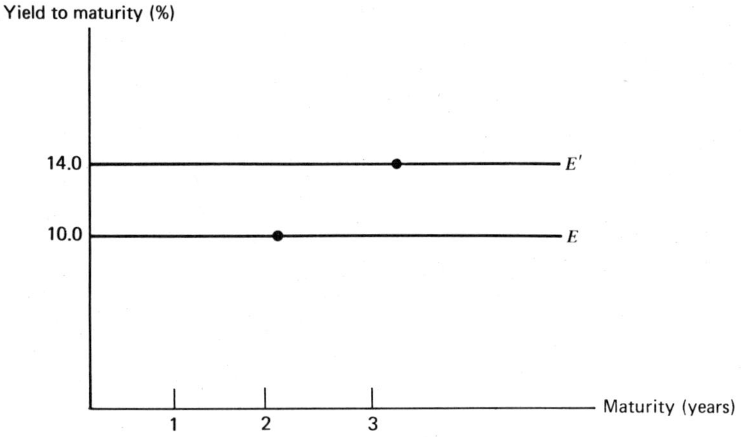

the presence of conflicting incentives, unlike the case in Table 24-1 where all loans had the same 10 percent interest rate. The latter case is illustrated in Figure 24-2.

With a 2-year financing need, the firm can borrow at the 10 percent rate indicated by the flat yield curve labeled *E*. This loan poses no conflicting incentives for lenders because maturity matches financing need. In the absence of a protective repayment pattern or restrictive loan agreement, a 3-year loan maturity would present such conflicting incentives. If made at all, such a loan would require a higher interest rate, say 14 percent, as indicated by the higher yield curve labeled *E'*. The firm ends up paying a higher interest cost because of the increased default risk posed by conflicting incentives and "jumps" to a higher yield curve.

Although constructed in a simplified environment, this example does illustrate some of the hazards of actual borrower–lender relationships. Lenders are not naive, and they recognize conflicting incentives. They want to protect themselves from situations like that shown in panel B of Table 24-1 by lending less money, restructuring payment schedules, shortening debt maturity, writing a loan agreement that imposes penalties if firms divert funds from lenders to owners, and charging higher rates of interest. Any costs of these actions are borne by owners, so it is in their interest to structure a loan in cooperation with lenders that reduces such costs. As a result, we might expect to observe the following lending practices.

1. When debt is risky, the maturity of the loan should not greatly exceed the length of time the funds are expected to be needed.

2.   When the maturity of a loan does exceed the expected length of time funds are needed, principal payments are likely to be spread over the life of the loan rather than occurring in one lump sum at maturity.

3.   Since loans having maturities less than the length of time funds are needed do not create adverse incentives, borrowers who are extremely uncertain about the amount and time pattern of financing needs may reduce costs by keeping maturities short to avoid or reduce adverse incentives.

Since financial folklore suggests that firms that borrow for periods shorter than the duration of their financial needs are at a disadvantage, it is perhaps surprising to conclude the shareholders' interests *may* be better served by borrowing for a shorter time than needs dictate. Renegotiating a loan that is of shorter duration than a firm's needs does impose risk of higher future interest rates and explicit costs of renegotiations; however, the resulting opportunity for the lender to reassess financial risk and monitor firm performance through renegotiation may also act to reduce interest cost on the initial loan. We do not yet know the extent, if any, of lender risk reduction with more frequent negotiation or the point at which higher negotiation costs might overwhelm any favorable effect of risk reduction with shorter loan maturities.

The rationale underlying the folklore was that firms that borrow for a period shorter than their needs may have trouble renegotiating a loan and may have to pay interest rates that are much higher than the rates that could have been negotiated a year earlier. That reasoning has a critical fallacy. It treats lenders as naive parties who do not recognize that a firm's fortunes may change. When borrowing for 2 years rather than 1, firms will pay an interest rate that reflects the possibility that adverse conditions may arise. If that were not the case, longer term lenders would always be losers in the market, and no rational financial institution would lend for any but the shortest of periods.

Speculation and Uncertain Length of Financing Need

Let us now ignore conflicting interests between lenders and borrowers and concentrate on two other issues affecting choice of formal debt maturity in financing current assets: the desire to speculate on future interest rates, and uncertainty concerning the length of financing need. These are influences that may also act to make debt maturity unequal to length of financing need.

Speculation   Suppose the firm in the preceding example will exist indefinitely and has a permanent need for $100 of debt financing for current assets. As in Figure 24-2, all debt maturities have interest rates of 10 percent. The longest debt maturity the firm can obtain is 20 years and the shortest 1 year. The permanent need would suggest use of the 20-year maturity. However, the financial manager expects interest rates on 20-year loans to decline *next year* to only 7 percent. The manager could initially obtain temporary financing with a 1-year loan at 10 percent and plan to obtain long-term financing by borrowing next year at 7 percent. Proceeds from next year's loan could then be used to repay the temporary 1-year loan. Over the long term, this transaction would reduce expected borrowing costs.

But interest rates increase as well as decrease. Many other long-term borrowers must not expect interest rates to drop. Otherwise, they would not borrow at 10 percent and lenders would have to reduce long-term rates relative to short-term rates to attract customers. From the discussion of *efficient markets* in Chapter 3, recall that competition among capital market participants is very keen and that in such markets it is very difficult to earn abnormal rates of return persistently. By using short-term borrowing now in anticipation of lower future rates, the manager is betting that he or she has superior information and that all other investors who borrow *now* at 10 percent are wrong.

Such temporary uses of short-term debt for long-term needs based on forecasts of lower future long-term borrowing costs are speculations. There is no shortage of cases of firms that have lost such gambles and have been forced to continue to renew short-term financing while waiting for long-term rates to decline.

Uncertain Length of Financing Need   Firms do not always *know* whether a financing need for current assets is permanent or temporary. Such uncertainty may cause the firm to initially finance a permanent increase in current assets with temporary, short-term financing, later reverting to long-term financing as the need is seen to be permanent. In short, firms can be *adaptive* in their initial use of short-term and subsequent use of long-term debt financing.

An Illustrative Case   We can illustrate folklore, conflicts of interest between lender and borrower, speculation, and uncertainty of length of financing need in a single example: Yamamoto Shipbuilding, Inc. In Table 24-2, the firm's initial balance sheet appears in the first column in addition to other relevant financial information, as well. That initial state reflects normal rates of production and sales. The desired current asset investment of $10 million poses a financing need met with both long- and short-term financing sources. Yet while $4 million of current liability financing is employed, the formal short maturity of these liabilities be-

Table 24–2   *Employment of Long- and Short-term Financing Sources: Yamamoto Shipbuilding, Inc. ($000)*

	Initial State	Temporary State	New Permanent State
Current Assets	$10,000	$12,000	$12,000
Fixed Assets	20,000	20,000	20,000
Total	$30,000	$32,000	$32,000
Current Liabilities	$ 4,000	$ 6,000	$ 4,800
Long-term capital	26,000	26,000	27,200
Total	$30,000	$32,000	$32,000
Net Working Capital	$ 6,000	$ 6,000	$ 7,200
Current Ratio	2.5	2.0	2.5

lies the lengthy financial relationship between the firm and its lenders. Most of the current liabilities reflect trade credit granted by suppliers and short-term loans extended by a bank. Both types of loan are maintained at existing levels, by payment for prior credit purchases and credit purchase of additional supplies in the case of trade credit, and by periodic renewal with renegotiation for short-term bank loans. The latter, by permitting the bank to periodically review Yamamoto's financial condition and prospects and by eliminating adverse incentives, provides short-term financing at a lower interest cost than would otherwise be possible. The remaining $6 million of financing is provided from long-term sources. Liquidity, as reflected by a current ratio of 2.5, is judged to be adequate with this proportion of short- and long-term financing.

In the second column, an unanticipated increase in demand increases sales, production, and current assets necessary to support the new level of activity. That new level of current assets is $12 million. Initially, Yamamoto's management anticipates that the higher level of activity will be temporary. Under these circumstances, the firm obtains all financing from short-term sources. Thus, $2 million of additional current assets is financed from an additional $2 million of current liabilities. Part of the increase occurs spontaneously in the financing relationship with trade creditors, since the underlying temporary increase in production generates larger accounts payable. The remaining portion is financed from temporary additional short-term bank borrowing under that financing relationship. Long-term financing is not increased to meet the temporary need, so net working capital remains unchanged at $6 million. Note that liquidity is temporarily reduced and the current ratio falls from 2.5 to 2.0.

In contrast, the third column illustrates the impact of increased activity that is assumed to be permanent. Now the $2 million increment in working capital is financed with the mixture of short- and long-term sources deemed appropriate in the initial state. Assuming that the original current ratio of 2.5 is appropriate for the new level of activity, Yamamoto increases current liabilities by $0.8 million and long-term sources by $1.2 million. Thus, net working capital increases from $6 million to $7.2 million.

Adaptive behavior exhibited by many firms when they are uncertain whether an increase in desired current assets is temporary or permanent can also be illustrated using Table 24-2. Initially, Yamamoto might choose to use short-term financing as shown in the second column. Then, if the need turns out to be permanent, the firm can adopt the financing plan shown in the third column. That strategy involves obtaining $1.2 million of long-term capital to retire a like amount of current liabilities. Such behavior may also be essential when long-term capital cannot be negotiated immediately even though the firm anticipates that the new level of activity will be permanent.

Finally, choice as governed by speculation on financing costs can also be demonstrated using the table. Suppose that the increase in desired current assets is thought to be permanent, thus posing a long-term financing need. However, Yamamoto views current costs of long-term borrowing as higher than they will be next year and satisfies financing needs with short-term sources as shown in the second column. Next year, if long-term rates fall as expected, the firm will obtain lower cost long-term financing as shown in the third column. Of course, if Yamamoto's expectations about future interest rates are wrong and long-term rates rise, either the existing term loan will be retired with even more expensive long-term debt or the firm will have to repeat its short-term borrowing.

Clearly, the choice between short- and long-term financing of working capital requirements is important. However, once the proportion of long- and short-term sources is established, equal effort is required to establish the appropriate mix of short-term sources. That task is discussed in following sections.

UNSECURED FORMS OF SHORT-TERM FINANCING

Sources of short-term financing may be divided into secured and unsecured forms. A **secured loan** entitles the lender to claim certain assets, pledged by the borrower, if the borrower fails to repay the loan under agreed-upon terms. Assets pledged to secure a loan are called **collateral.** When a loan is *unsecured*, no physical collateral exists that the lender can seize in the event of failure to pay. **Unsecured loans** are extended on the basis of the general creditworthiness of the firm—with the presumption that cash flows from operations will enable the borrower to repay the loan. Secured loans also rely on the same assumption but are made safer for the lender by the existence of collateral for additional protection. We begin with a discussion of unsecured loans.

Trade Credit   As a matter of routine, many suppliers extend trade credit on customer purchases up to the credit limit established by the supplier for the customer. Some trade credit may be extended only if assets are provided as collateral by the customer firm, but virtually all is unsecured and is treated here under that category.

Cost of Trade Credit Within Agreed-on Terms   When the customer firm (the buyer) repays trade credit within the terms agreed upon with the supplier, the cost of trade credit can be clearly determined. Within agreed-upon terms, the cost of trade credit is equal to the explicit, or measurable, cost of trade credit. For example, trade credit bearing the terms "net 30" has an explicit cost of zero (exclusive of transaction costs) if the customer firm pays within 30 days. Trade credit offering the terms "2%/10, net/30" also has an explicit cost of zero if the bill is paid within the 10-day discount period. A positive explicit cost of trade credit exists when trade credit offers a discount and the firm does not pay within the discount period. By delaying payment beyond the discount period, the customer firm forgoes the discount.

For the customer firm, the annual percentage cost of forgoing cash discounts by delaying payment is called the *explicit cost of trade credit*. That cost may be determined from the following formula.

$$k_T = \frac{d}{100 - d} \times \frac{365}{e} \tag{24-1}$$

where

k_T = the explicit cost of trade credit

d = the percentage cash discount

e = number of days payment is extended *beyond* the discount period

For credit terms of 2%/10, net/30, the customer firm's explicit cost of trade credit, if the firm pays within agreed-upon terms on the thirtieth day, is 37.2 percent using Equation (24-1).

$$k_T = \frac{2\%}{100\% - 2\%} \times \frac{365}{20} = 0.372$$

The firm is extending payment for $e = 20$ days beyond the end of the discount period. Explicit costs for other percentage discounts when 30 days is taken to pay are shown in the first row of Table 24-3. The reader may wish to verify these costs by using the formula in Equation (24-1).

Cost and Availability of Trade Credit When Agreed-on Terms Are Violated Trade credit is a financing source to the customer firm when bills are paid within agreed-upon terms. But additional trade credit may be available if the customer firm continues to charge new purchases from suppliers but delays payment to them beyond the full credit period. When this practice is followed, the *explicit* cost of trade credit declines, as examination of Table 24-3 reveals. For each percentage discount in Table 24-3, the costs of paying within agreed-upon terms at 30 days (with discount forgone) are shown in the first row. When the fixed discount forgone is spread over a longer period, as payment is delayed until 60, 90, or 120 days, the explicit cost of trade credit declines.

The reduced explicit cost of trade credit achieved by delaying payment to suppliers beyond the end of the credit period may significantly understate the true cost of trade credit under such a practice. When a firm becomes a "slow payer," the risk of extending credit to that firm may be perceived by all creditors as having increased. Financial institutions, to the extent that they will loan funds to the slow-paying firm, may charge a higher interest rate than they otherwise would, or they may request that the firm undertake risk-reducing actions such as putting up collateral. Suppliers may react by assessing an additional financing charge for late payment. In any case, the firm's cost of trade credit is not as low as the explicit costs appear when, in Table 24-3, payment is delayed. Trade credit, then, is said to have *implicit costs*—costs that raise the cost of trade credit above the explicit cost.

Even more seriously, delaying the payment of bills to increase trade

Table 24-3 *Explicit Cost of Trade Credit for 10-Day Discount Period and 30-Day Credit Period*

Total Days Taken to Pay	Days Extended Beyond Discount Period, e	Discount, d		
		1%	2%	3%
30	20	18.4%	37.2%	56.4%
60	50	7.4	14.9	22.6
90	80	4.6	9.3	14.1
120	110	3.4	6.8	10.3

696 Financial Analysis and Working Capital

credit financing may result in counteractions by suppliers that negate the increase in financing obtained. For example, suppliers may react to delayed payment by refusing to make further credit sales to the firm until the past due portion of amounts owed is fully paid. In effect, the customer firm is placed on a "cash sales only" basis. Any additional trade credit gained by delaying of payment will be eliminated fairly quickly. Even more important, chronic tardy payment by a customer firm may result in the denial of trade credit for an indefinite period by suppliers. In short, the customer firm may, by its actions, *eliminate* one of its sources of financing. To the extent that financial institutions are aware of the situation (and they usually are), the customer firm may also be unable to obtain short-term financing from this other important source as well. Altogether, the customer firm may substantially reduce the availability of all short-term financing sources by chronically delaying payment of bills beyond the full credit period.

We do not mean to paint too dark a picture of the practice of delaying payment beyond the full credit period. Some suppliers are relatively lenient on this issue because they are eager for business even if customers pay slowly. For such firms, the reduced explicit costs of trade credit portrayed in Table 24-3 may, within a range, give a reasonably accurate estimate of the true cost of trade credit *for that supplier*. A customer firm aware of such lenient policies may be able to reduce costs of trade credit by delaying payment to such suppliers without seriously damaging the availability of credit from them. Moreover, under poor economic conditions, some suppliers are disposed to be lenient to assist otherwise good customers through a difficult time. What is clear, however, is that decisions to expand trade credit by delaying payment must be carefully considered and applied on a case-by-case basis to each supplier. No generalization is adequate.

Spontaneous and Discretionary Trade Credit The *decision* to repay trade credit a given number of days *following* the receipt of the invoice creates *discretionary* trade credit, since it results from an action by the customer firm. Within the limits allowed by suppliers, increasing the number of days taken to repay provides a discretionary increase in trade credit. Similarly, a reduction in the number of days taken to repay results in a discretionary decrease in trade credit.

Once the customer firm has established a policy on trade payables further changes in trade credit financing levels that occur *spontaneously* as the level of operations of the customer firm changes. For example, if a firm's daily credit purchases are $10,000 and bills are paid 10 days after receipt, accounts payable will average $10,000 × 10 = $100,000. Furthermore, if the level of operations of the firm increases by 20 percent so that average daily credit purchases increase to $12,000, trade accounts payable will increase to $12,000 × 10 = $120,000. The additional financing of $20,000 occurs spontaneously to help finance the increased level of current assets required by a higher level of operations.

Many firms obtain unsecured financing from commercial banks to meet short-term financing needs. The terms of such credit are varied and affect both the *cost* and *availability* of the credit.

Unsecured Bank Credit

Costs of bank credit vary with the way in which interest is charged to the borrower by the bank and on the number of payments made over the life of the loan. At one time, it was necessary to distinguish between the *simple* interest rate quoted on a loan and the *effective*, or true, interest rate. Customers were quoted a simple interest rate but, in many cases, the effective interest rate was much higher. We maintain the distinction between simple and effective interest rates even though commercial banks and other lenders are now required by "truth in lending" laws to state the effective interest rate. Formulas for approximating effective interest rates are used in the body of the text because more precise computations would require present value tables of greater precision than those offered in Appendix Tables C and D. However, with powerful hand-held calculators, exact costs can be calculated with little computational effort. Note 4 illustrates the appropriate procedure.

Two types of bank loans are discussed below: the **commercial note** and the **installment loan.** Commercial notes require only a single payment by the borrower to repay the loan when the note matures. In contrast, an installment loan requires a series of periodic payments over the life of the loan to repay the amount borrowed plus interest. In both types of loan, the dollars the borrowing firm receives at the time the loan is made are called the **loan proceeds.**

Cost of a Commercial Note   Commercial notes may be either of discounted or *nondiscounted* form. In the case of a **discounted note,** *dollar* interest is computed by applying the simple interest rate to the face amount of the note, or the amount to be *repaid* by the borrower. In contrast, a nondiscounted note computes dollar interest by applying the simple interest rate to the *loan proceeds,* which in this case equal the face amount of the note. Not surprisingly, since the loan proceeds are always less than the amount repaid, given the same simple interest rate, discounted notes feature higher effective interest rates than do nondiscounted notes.

To demonstrate the calculation of effective interest rates for discounted and nondiscounted notes, consider the problem faced by Buntin Ceramics, Inc. Buntin wishes to borrow $1000 for a year. The simple interest rate is 12 percent.

To find the effective interest rate for a nondiscounted note, the formula and computations for the Buntin terms are:

$$\frac{\text{Interest payment}}{\text{Loan proceeds}} = \frac{(0.12)(\$1000)}{\$1000} = \frac{\$120}{\$1000} = 0.12, \quad \text{or } 12\%$$

The 12 percent simple interest rate is applied to the $1000 loan proceeds to determine a dollar interest payment of $120. The 12 percent effective interest rate is, in this case, exactly the same as the simple interest rate. If the note is for less than 1 year the rate must, of course, be annualized for effective comparison to other annual rates.

If the note is of discounted form, then the $120 of annual interest is subtracted from the amount borrowed of $1000 (the loan is discounted) to leave loan proceeds of $880. For this particular simple interest rate, loan proceeds are only 88 percent of the amount repaid. Since Buntin wants loan proceeds of $1000, the amount it needs to borrow in this case may be found by dividing the $1000 desired proceeds by 88 percent. The resulting amount to be repaid is $1000 ÷ 0.88 = $1136.36. Total interest will be $136.36 and the effective interest rate is:

$$\text{Effective interest rate} = \frac{\text{Interest}}{\text{Loan proceeds}} = \frac{\$136.36}{\$1000} = 0.136, \quad \text{or } 13.6\%$$

The effective interest rate is higher for discounted notes than for nondiscounted notes because interest is subtracted from the face amount of the note at the time the loan is made. Thus, actual interest to be paid is computed on the amount repaid rather than on the loan proceeds.

These conclusions are not altered if Buntin wants to borrow for a period shorter than a year—say 3 months. The simple quarterly interest rate equivalent of 12 percent annually is 3 percent. On a $1000 loan, a nondiscounted note will produce an effective *quarterly* interest rate of 3 percent:

$$\frac{\text{Effective}}{\text{interest rate}} = \frac{\text{Interest}}{\text{Loan proceeds}} = \frac{(0.03)\$1000}{\$1000} = \frac{\$30}{\$1000} = 0.03, \quad \text{or } 3\%$$

A discounted note, by subtracting the $30 of interest from the loan amount of $1000, would leave only $970 of loan proceeds. Loan proceeds are 97 percent of the amount borrowed. To obtain $1000 of loan proceeds, the firm must agree to borrow $1000/0.97 = $1030.93. With dollar interest cost of $30.93, the effective quarterly interest cost is:

$$\text{Effective rate} = \frac{\text{Interest}}{\text{Loan proceeds}} = \frac{\$30.93}{\$1000} = 0.0309, \quad \text{or } 3.09\%$$

As before, both quarterly dollar interest cost and the effective quarterly interest rate are higher for the discounted note compared to the nondiscounted note.[3]

Cost of an Installment Loan   Buntin might decide to repay the $1000 over 1 year on an installment basis with 12 equal monthly payments. Dollar interest cost for this type of loan is determined by applying the simple interest rate to the amount borrowed; in this case, $(0.12)\$1000 = \$120$. The total amount to be repaid is $1120 which, when divided into 12 equal payments, results in a monthly payment of $\$1120 \div 12 = \$93.33$.

The *approximate* effective annual interest rate for an installment loan can be obtained from the following formula.[4]

$$\text{Effective interest rate} = \frac{2 \cdot n(\text{Total interest cost})}{(\text{Loan proceeds})(m + 1)}$$

where n is the number of payments per year and m is the total number of payments. For Buntin, the effective rate is:

$$\text{Effective interest rate} = \frac{2 \cdot 12(\$120)}{\$1000(12 + 1)} = \frac{\$2880}{\$13,000} = 0.2215, \quad \text{or } 22.15\%$$

Note that this interest rate is nearly twice the simple interest rate. It is easy to see why. Dollar interest cost is based on the total amount borrowed of $1000. Yet monthly installment payments progressively reduce the amount owed each month. The borrower pays interest on the full amount borrowed for the full duration of the loan but, because of installment payments, has the effective use of a smaller average amount of funds over the life of the loan; he does not have the use of the $1000 for a full year.

Cost of Bank Credit with Compensating Balances   Some banks require, as a condition of the loan, that a borrowing firm maintain a stipu-

---

[3]For *successive* 3 month notes, the true annual rate of interest for both discounted and nondiscounted notes is greater than 4×3 percent = 12 percent for the nondiscounted note and 4×3.093 percent = 12.372 percent for the discounted note. Using quarterly compounding, the true annual rate is $(1 + 0.03)^4 - 1 = 12.55$ percent for the nondiscounted notes, and $(1 + 0.03093)^4 - 1 = 12.96$ percent for the discounted notes.

[4]Using the internal rate of return relationships, the effective interest rate i could be found by solving:

$$\$1000 = \$93.33 \sum_{t=1}^{12} \left(\frac{1}{1 + \frac{i}{12}}\right)^t$$

The effective rate so obtained is 21.5 percent. The approximation formula overestimates the true effective rate by about 1 percent in this case.

lated dollar amount on deposit in a checking account while the loan is outstanding. This deposit is called a **compensating balance.** Such balances range from 10 to 15 percent of the amount borrowed. In some loan arrangements, the borrowing firm must maintain the *average* checking account balance at the required level. In other cases, the firm must maintain the *minimum* required deposit level at all times. The latter type of requirement is much more restrictive on the borrowing firm in managing its daily cash balance. In yet other cases, a compensating balance may not be a specific requirement.

If the borrowing firm would not otherwise have maintained checking account deposits equal to the compensating balance requirement, such a requirement raises the effective interest cost of the loan. To show how this happens, we calculate the cost of the Buntin Ceramics $1000 1-year note—assuming that the note is not discounted and that the simple interest rate is 12 percent. In the absence of a compensating balance requirement, we have already seen that the effective interest rate of the note is 12 percent. However, if the loan is granted, assume that Buntin must maintain a compensating balance equal to 10 percent of the loan. If Buntin Ceramics normally keeps a minimum balance of zero, the bank, in effect, actually lends only $900. Dollar interest cost is .12 × $1000 = $120, so the effective annual interest rate becomes $120/$900 = 0.1333, or 13.33 percent. If Buntin normally keeps a $100 minimum balance in its checking account in any case, the bank is effectively loaning Buntin $1000 and the annual effective interest cost is $120/$1000 = 0.12, or 12 percent, and the effective rate equals the quoted rate. Thus, in this case, no *incremental* increase in the effective interest rate occurs because of the compensating balance requirement.

Availability of Bank Credit

The cost of bank credit for any given loan is an important issue. Even more important may be the issue of *availability*. It is in the firm's interest that bank credit be readily available when needed in the future. One way of enhancing the availability of bank credit is to obtain either a **line of credit** or a **credit agreement** (sometimes referred to as a **loan commitment**) from a bank. In addition, a long-standing banking relationship in which the firm keeps the bank fully informed of its status generally enhances the availability of bank credit.

The Line of Credit and the Credit Agreement   Firms anticipating the need for future bank financing may desire to reduce any uncertainty about future availability of such financing by obtaining either a line of credit or a credit agreement from a commercial bank. Such arrangements are especially useful when the precise amounts and future dates of financing needs are not yet exactly specified.

A *line of credit* extended to a firm by a commercial bank specifies a maximum amount of credit that the bank will extend, the conditions under which the line will be honored, the length of the loan maturity to be extended, and the interest rate the borrower must pay. Since the bank cannot know the level of future interest rates, interest rates on the loan will be stated in terms of an addition to the **prime rate of interest.** For example, a line of credit may indicate that the interest rate charged will be the prime rate plus 1 percent. The *prime rate* is the interest rate charged by the bank to its most creditworthy loan customers—usually, larger firms. As the level of open market interest rates varies, the bank will tend to change the prime rate. Thus, a firm having a line of credit will know what its interest costs will be *relative* to the prime rate.[5] However, the actual interest rate to be charged on loans taken out under the line of credit depends on the prime rate prevailing at the time bank credit is used by the firm.

A line of credit, though helping the firm to reduce uncertainty about the availability and cost of future bank credit, is not a legal commitment on the part of the bank. A reduction in the borrowing firm's credit-worthiness would permit the bank to refuse loans under a line of credit previously extended. However, the bank would be unlikely to do this unless the reduction in creditworthiness is severe. Otherwise, a line of credit would become a meaningless gesture as an arrangement for reducing uncertainty about future financing availability.

The firm can further reduce uncertainty about the future availability and cost of bank credit by negotiating a credit agreement with a commercial bank. Sometimes called a *revolving credit agreement,* this arrangement is similar to a line of credit in that the agreement specifies a maximum credit limit, up to which the firm may borrow over a specified time, and an interest rate expressed in terms of a differential from the prime rate. The credit agreement (or loan commitment) differs from a line of credit in that the arrangement is a legal commitment by the bank to the firm. In addition, a credit agreement requires the firm to pay a commitment fee, expressed as a percentage of the *unborrowed* balance under the credit agreement.

From the view of the firm, the choice between a line of credit and a credit agreement depends on the perceived likelihood of not being able

---

[5]To avoid confusion (and legal problems), it might be best to think of the prime rate as the rate charged the most creditworthy customers for loans of given maturity or range of maturities. For instance, a bank might *quote* a prime rate of 16 percent for loans of 30 to 120 days, then quite legitimately lend to a low risk customer at a lower 12 percent for *two* days if short-term money market conditions dictated such a rate. Unless maturity differences are recognized, a customer who must pay the announced prime rate plus 2 percent, or 18 percent, for a 120-day loan might argue strongly that the appropriate rate should be 14 percent (12 percent + 2 percent).

to obtain required financing when needed. As credit conditions become tighter, banks may be inclined to ration credit to their customers by limiting amounts borrowed. The credit agreement though more costly than a line of credit, does offer enhanced availability of credit in the future. Still, in a great many situations, a line of credit is entirely satisfactory to provide future availability of credit.

The Personal Nature of Bank Credit and the Value of Information   A bank must obtain information about the potential borrowing firm to determine whether a loan will be granted. Two kinds of information assist the bank in making this decision. First, information about objective economic characteristics of the borrowing firm and its industry indicate to the bank how the firm's performance has behaved over time as economic conditions have varied. Using the borrowing firm's financial statements, the bank can analyze the firm's sales, profit margin, profits, and liquidity over time and in comparison to the borrowing firm's industry. Financial ratio analysis may be an important tool in this process. Based on the bank's assessment of future economic conditions, the ability of the firm to repay a loan under these conditions can be estimated.

The second kind of information important to banks is the quality and integrity of the borrowing firm's management. Objective facts *other* than the firm's operating performance are difficult to obtain in evaluating management. As a result, it is the personal nature of the lender–borrower relationship that is important in subjectively assessing the management of the borrowing firm. When a bank has loaned money to a firm, the bank's loan officer must be in periodic contact with the borrowing firm's management and is, through this personal contact, able to make assessments of managerial quality and integrity—assessments not as readily available to other parties. This information, by allowing the bank to be better informed than other lenders about the borrowing firm, works to the benefit of both the bank and the borrowing firm.

A long-standing lender–borrower relationship, by providing valuable subjective information, benefits the bank because it enables it to develop more refined perceptions of the risk of lending to the firm. The borrowing firm is benefited because, compared to a new loan customer about which the bank has the same *objective* data, it may receive lower interest rates because the bank has better information about the quality of management. Moreover, the established loan customer is more likely to enjoy greater availability of bank credit over time. The bank simply knows more about the established customer.[6]

---

[6]When credit conditions tighten, banks respond by raising interest rates on loans and by using certain *nonprice* mechanisms to ration scarce credit—including restricting the quan-

For very large, well-established companies, an alternative source of short-term financing arises through the sale of **commercial paper,** that is, short-term, unsecured notes issued by a borrowing firm. Such notes either are sold in the open market through commercial paper dealers or are sold directly (privately placed) to individual buyers. The small number of commercial paper dealers in the United States purchase commercial paper in denominations of $25,000 or more from issuing firms. Maturities of commercial paper usually range from 1 to 6 months. Commercial paper dealers resell newly issued paper to various customers in the open market. Furthermore, by offering to buy and sell previously issued and outstanding paper, commercial paper dealers make a market that improves the liquidity of commercial paper. In contrast, commercial paper *directly placed* by the issuing firm with a particular buyer is not easily marketable. Firms that purchase privately placed paper typically hold it to maturity.

Commercial paper has come into increasing use as a source of financing. The growth in popularity of commercial paper is attributable in part to its relatively low cost compared to the cost of bank credit. Commercial paper interest rates are typically less than the prime rate of interest charged by banks to large, creditworthy customers. Commercial paper also helps firms seeking very large loans get around a technical difficulty: banks are limited by law in the magnitude of loans they can extend to a single borrower—such loans are not to exceed 10 percent of the paid-in equity capital of the bank. Consequently, large firms find it easier to obtain very large quantities of short-term financing through issuing commercial paper than by negotiating with a consortium of several banks banding together to make a loan too large for any single bank.

Commercial paper has its disadvantages as well. Smaller borrowers are effectively eliminated from the market because they are not well enough known for the market at large to sell commercial paper at low interest rates to the borrower. In addition, transaction costs of issuing paper in small quantities would be relatively large. Even for large issues, the impersonal nature of the commercial paper market, compared to a banking relationship, can have undesirable results for the continued availability of financing through this source. For example, Penn Central had large quantities of commercial paper outstanding when it became bankrupt in 1970. That firm's default on its outstanding paper made the usual buyers of commercial paper rather reluctant to buy *any* paper.

---

tity of credit extended to borrowers. Evidence exists that established bank customers pay less for loans and face fewer restrictions on the quantity of credit extended at such times. See, for example, Duane G. Harris, "Credit Rationing at Commercial Banks: Some Empirical Evidence," *Journal of Money, Credit and Banking* (May 1974), pp. 222–240.

Other firms relying on commercial paper as a source of short term-financing had to find alternative sources of financing quickly as the availability of funds from issuing commercial paper was sharply curtailed. Consequently, it is prudent for issuers of commercial paper to arrange supplementary sources of funds from banks, to enhance the availability of short-term financing in the event of a serious disruption of the commercial paper market. While such a disruption is not likely, it is only wise to obtain whatever protection the personal nature of an established banking relationship affords the firm.

SECURED FORMS OF SHORT-TERM FINANCING

Many firms find that to obtain short-term finacing in sufficient quantities, a pledge of some of its assets as collateral is necessary to secure the loan. Even though the interest rates on such secured loans are relatively high, they are *lower* than the rate that would be available on *otherwise identical* secured loan.[7] Collateral does reduce the risk that lenders must bear and shareholders agree to secured loan agreements, given additional expenses associated with such arrangements, only if there is a net advantage over unsecured borrowing.[8]

The benefit of collateral can be viewed in the context of adverse incentives associated with debt financing discussed in Chapter 13. Recall the notion of wealth shift—that is, a firm alters the risk facing investors by shifting funds from lower to higher risk investments. In a world of imperfect information, where the integrity of borrowers may be subject to question, a lender will want to ensure that assets are used to maintain and enhance the profitability of the firm. To find, unexpectedly, that an electronic calculator manufacturer to which loans were made has decided to make rocking chairs, or even worse, to find that all assets have been converted to cash to provide funds for a foreign excursion, leaving neither assets nor earning power, is more than most lenders want to risk. Collateral, *properly watched*, provides some protection against such

---

[7]Often it is noted that secured loans have higher rates than unsecured loans. There are two reasons for this apparently perverse observation. First, borrowers who are involved with secured financing tend to be seen by the lending institutions as higher risks. Thus, even though they have collateral, the added default risk of this group of borrowers is not offset fully. Second, the cost to the lending institution of making a secured loan is higher than that of an unsecured loan, because the lending institution must incur added expenses to set up the security and administer the pledged assets during the loan period.

[8]Good collateral does not necessarily make a good loan. A lender must incur costs to seize and dispose of collateral. Months, even years, of legal proceedings may precede the final sale of collateral. Loans are made on the expectation that operating earnings will be adequate to repay the loan. Profitability is the prerequisite of the loan. Collateral is only additional protection.

unfortunate occurrences because the assets cannot be legally sold without the consent of the lender. It can give the lender control over certain assets that are liquidated only under carefully specified circumstances. Lenders may be willing to bear some risk due to unfavorable effects on the firm from economic fluctuation, but they would like to reduce opportunities for unauthorized asset shift. We do not suggest that a security interest will prevent forms of asset shift. Rather, it is one method of gaining better control of the borrower and thereby reducing the probability of such occurrences. That is, a secured loan arrangement provides for the lender an additional monitoring device that is advantageous to an *honest* borrower.

Finally, collateral may impose a discipline on the firm with respect to this particular secured loan. If the firm has important operating assets pledged as collateral, the firm has a great incentive to meet all the terms of the secured loan. It may "let go" commitments on unsecured loans if necessary to meet its commitments on secured loans because of the threat of the loss of assets pledged. This incentive provides added confidence in the loan repayment for the financial institution.

Sources of secured short-term financing include commercial banks and commercial finance companies.[9] The type of secured loan obtained from any of these sources is usually described in terms of the class of assets used as collateral for the loan. We discuss two general sources of collateral for short-term financing—receivables and inventories.

Both types of asset, when used as collateral by the borrower, usually require that procedures under the Uniform Commercial Code (UCC) be followed if the lender is to have protection under the law provided by assets pledged as collateral. The UCC requires that the lender and borrower execute a *security agreement* describing the assets used as collateral. The lender must then file this agreement with the state government, to give notice to others that the assets described in the agreement are pledged as collateral. Lenders thus insure their prior claim on the assets in the event of default on the loan.

Receivables Financing

Firms having a subtantial investment in accounts receivable (outstanding credit sales) relative to other types of current assets in the normal course of operations are likely to use receivables as collateral for a short-term loan when collateral is required. Two ways of securing financing by use of receivables are discussed here: assignment of accounts receivable and factoring.

---

[9]Examples of large commercial finance companies are Commercial Credit Company and CIT Financial Corporation.

Assignment of Receivables   When all receivables are used as collateral for a loan under a *general lien*, the lender assesses both the general quality and the average size of the borrowing firm's receivables. From this assessment, a maximum borrowing limit, expressed as a percentage of the face value of accounts receivable, is stipulated. For example, a firm having receivables totaling $1 million might be permitted to borrow up to 75 percent of that amount, or $750,000, from the lending in-stituion.[10] In some instances the borrower's credit customers are informed that their receivables are being used as collateral and that payments should be made directly to the lender. In other cases, the borrower's credit customers are not informed. Rather, as the borrowing firm receives payments on its own receivables, it remits these payments to the lender. The former loan is made on a *notifcation* basis, the latter on a *nonnotification* basis.

Accounts receivable financing under a general lien can provide both *permanent* and *temporary* short-term financing for the firm. A firm having receivables with a face value of $1 million and able to borrow 75 percent of that face value from a lender could obtain a permanent level of financing of $750,000 as long as credit sales are maintained at current levels. As payment is received on existing receivables, new credit sales will generate new receivables. A single receivable of $1000 will, when paid by the customer, yield the borrowing firm $250 and the lender $750. At the same time, new credit sales of $1000 will allow the borrowing firm to obtain a replacement loan of $750 such that total borrowings remain at $750,000. Since lenders typically do not require a periodic "cleanup" of the loan balance for this type of loan, the $750,000 is permanent financing. However, a temporary increase in sales permits a temporary increase in receivables financing to accommodate increased financing needs. If receivables temporarily double to $2 million due to a doubling of credit sales, the firm could secure temporary *total* financing of $1.5 million—of which only $750,000 is permanent.

The interest cost of loans when accounts receivable are assigned is typically more than the prime rate, even for a large borrower, because of higher transaction costs to the lender in assessing, monitoring, and processing the flow of new receivables and payments on old receivables. Yet, the overall interest rate may still be lower than the cost of financing on the unsecured basis to the same firm, with the greater risk imposed on the lender.

---

[10]Instead of using a general lien, the borrower may pledge specific receivables. Upon examination, the lender might reject some of them because of excessive risk. When lenders so exert direct control over the quality of receivables, they usually are willing to lend a higher percent of their face value—say 90 percent.

The quality and the average size of receivables affect both the interest cost and amount of financing available from a lender. If a borrower has customers with high credit ratings, the maximum amount of financing available to the firm as a percentage of the face value of receivables will be relatively high—but never 100 percent! Lenders always wish to leave a margin of safety. Predictably, interest costs tend to be lower as the quality of receivables pledged as collateral is higher. If the average size of the borrowing firm's receivables is relatively large, lenders may be willing to loan a larger percentage of the face value of receivables at a lower interest cost. A smaller number of *individual* receivables reduces both the costs of managing the collateral and the opportunities of the borrowing firm to fraudulently hide payments from the lender.

Factoring Receivables   A firm can also raise funds by selling its accounts receivable to a factor—either a specialized factoring firm, a commercial finance company, or a subsidiary of a commercial bank engaging in **factoring.**

A factor purchases receivables from the firm at a discount from face value. Typical discounts are about 1 percent. For example, a firm might sell $1 million of receivables to a factor at a 1 percent discount and pay $10,000 as a factoring fee. This factoring fee is deducted from the payment by the factor to the firm. The firm does not receive immediate payment for receivables sold to the factor. The firm receives its money on the maturity dates of the invoices whether collected or not by the factor.

A factoring arrangement is usually made *without recourse* to the firm selling receivables to the factor. In such an arrangement, the factor bears all the risk of default by the firm's customers. However, the factor maintains its own credit department and must approve credit extended to the firm's customers. As a result of its analysis, the factor may refuse to approve credit sales to some customers of the firm. A factoring arrangement with recourse means that the firm bears the risk of default.

Firms wishing *immediate* payment when receivables are sold to a factor must obtain a loan from the factor, secured by the future proceeds from the receivables, and pay, in addition to the factor fee, an interest charge. If 1.5 percent per month on the net proceeds to the firm is the factor's lending rate, our firm expecting to receive a $990,000 payment in one month, would receive an immediate payment of $990,000 less interest of $0.015 \times \$990,000 = \$14,850$, or $975,150.[11]

---

[11]This represents an annual percentage cost for interest *alone* of:

$$\frac{\text{Annual interest charge}}{\text{Loan proceeds}} = \frac{\$14,850}{\$975,150} \times 12 \text{ months} = 0.1827, \text{ or } 18.27\%$$

Factor arrangements are considered to be relatively expensive ways of obtaining financing. This is especially true when the factor arrangement is without recourse such that the factor bears the risk of default by the firm's customers. The factor must take a higher discount to compensate for this risk. But as compared to other forms of financing available to a *specific firm*, factoring may be the best financing alternative. Net costs of factoring may actually be below explicit interest rates because the firm avoids the costs of servicing its own accounts receivable and, if conducted without recourse, shifts the risk of carrying accounts receivable as well as the costs of credit investigation to the factor. For a small firm, when the *fixed* costs of managing accounts receivable with a separate credit department may be high relative to the level of sales, the relatively high cost of a factoring arrangement may be worth the price.

As was the case with assignment of receivables to secure short-term loans, factoring provides both permanent and temporary financing. Credit sales of $1 million per month did, in the earlier example, sustain a 1-month loan of $975,150 when the $1 million of receivables was sold to the factor and the firm borrowed immediately on the net proceeds of $990,000 due the firm in 1 month. If the firm maintains credit sales of $1 million per month, it also maintains $975,150 of permanent financing. Furthermore, a temporary doubling of credit sales would produce a total temporary financing level of 2 × $975,150 = $1,950,030,—of which $975,150 is permanent.

Credit Card Financing   Even though major retail firms had established credit procedures for their customers, it was not until the arrival of the bank credit cards in the 1960s that retail credit sales could be efficiently introduced for smaller firms. Not only did it provide an easy system to provide credit sales, it also provided an automatic method of receivables financing. When the retailer presents the credit invoice to the bank, the retailer is paid the face amount less a percentage service fee of, say, 3 percent. Thus the retailer has little investment in receivables. This arrangement has the appearance of factoring, but in effect the bank extends credit to the consumer and the retailer becomes an intermediary.

Inventory Financing   Firms having substantial inventories relative to other current assets may tend to use such inventories as collateral when the decision to obtain a secured loan has been made. Alternative ways of controlling the collateral provided by inventories have evolved to meet the diverse needs of borrowers having different types of inventories. Among the types of security arrangement available, we consider *general liens, trust receipts,* and *warehouse receipts*.

General Lien   A firm may provide collateral for a loan by giving the lender a *general lien* over all inventories without identifying specific items included in the inventory. Such liens do not provide as much protection to the lender as the more restrictive arrangements described below because opportunities for fraudulent behavior by the borrower are greater. Specific items in inventory can be sold off by the borrower and the proceeds *not used* to satisfy the loan. Consequently, loans advanced under a general lien will be a smaller percentage of the value of the inventory.

Trust Receipt   A firm can provide security for a loan by holding specifically identified inventories in trust for the lender. When new inventory is acquired by the borrowing firm, the lender provides financing in some fraction of the purchase price and the inventory item securing the loan is specifically identified by number and/or unique description. A *trust receipt* agreement setting forth the obligations of the borrower and the specific inventory pledged as security is executed by the lender and the borrowing firm. The borrowing firm holds the specific inventory item and, when it is sold, informs the lender of the sale and pay the amount owed from the proceeds of the sale. Lenders periodically inspect the inventory records or actual inventory of the borrower to help ensure that inventory pledged as collateral has not been fraudulently sold by the borrower without notifying the lender.

Warehouse Receipt   When a firm provides inventories as security for loans, the lender may require that the inventory be controlled to an even greater extent than the trust receipt allows. In such circumstances, the lender and the borrowing firm may agree that loans will be secured by either *public warehouse* or *field warehouse receipts*. Under a public warehouse arrangement, the borrowing firm stores inventories in a public warehouse and the warehousing firm issues a receipt giving the lender formal claim on the inventory as collateral. The lender extends the agreed loan amount on the inventory and exerts strict control over the collateral. Inventory cannot be sold by the borrower and taken from the warehouse without the permission of the lender. In a field warehousing arrangement, a field warehousing firm erects a storage facility on the premises of the borrower and controls access to the inventory just as when goods are stored in a public warehouse. Again, a field warehousing receipt is issued by the warehousing firm when inventory is acquired with borrowed funds and inventory cannot be released without the lender's permission.

Characteristics of Inventory Loans   In general, inventories are not considered to be liquid assets like cash, marketable securities, or receivables. Still, some inventories are more liquid than others if economic diaster overtakes the borrowing firm and the lender must sell inventory pledged as collateral. Lenders prefer inventories consisting of items for which it is easy to find a ready market. More marketable inventories tend to consist of less specialized goods such as raw materials or finished goods of a type enjoying general use. Goods not subject to quick obsolescence are also more desirable as collateral. Thus, items such as pig iron, coal, or current models of name brand TV sets are more desirable as collateral than specialized parts for fishing reels, high fashion shoes, or hula hoops. Generally, the amount that a lender will loan using inventory as collateral depends on the liquidity of the inventory. The more liquid the inventory, the higher the percentage of inventory value that the lender will loan out.

Inventory loans can provide both permanent and temporary financing. An inventory having a stable value of $1 million could support continued financing in the amount of, say, $600,000. As the inventory is sold and loans are repaid, replacement inventory is acquired to support the loan. In contrast, increases in inventory to support temporarily higher sales will support a temporary loan that is liquidated as the inventory is sold. These so-called *self-liquidating* loans are a common form of borrowing for merchandisers.

Loans secured by inventories tend to be expensive because of the higher costs of administering the loan that must be borne by the lender. Yet, the overall interest cost may be less to the borrower than for an unsecured loan if, indeed, such a loan is available at all for the borrowing firm. The financial position of the firm could easily be such that no loan may be available to a firm without collateral.

Both commercial banks and commercial finance companies engage in inventory financing. However, many suppliers to firms offer either trade credit or other supplementary financing secured by inventories sold to the firm. Because suppliers may use such financing terms as an inducement to generate sales, it is possible that more attractive financing costs are available from suppliers offering financing assistance than from either commercial banks or commercial finance companies.

CHOOSING AMONG SHORT-TERM FINANCING SOURCES

To choose a combination of trade credit, unsecured loans, and secured loans designed to minimize costs of financing and to maintain continued availability of future financing, the financial manager must take a subjective approach. We have no decision rules to offer that simultaneously optimize all these variables to maximize shareholder wealth. The financial manager must assess the costs of each form of financing and determine its implications for future financing availability. Although the manager cannot know whether the ultimate combination of short-term financing sources is optimal, at least the more extreme cases that are likely to be suboptimal can be avoided.

As an example of the subjective process whereby short-term financing sources are selected, we consider the situation for Canty Marine Company shown in Table 24-4. Canty, a retailer of small pleasure boats and accessories, is undergoing a seasonal expansion of sales of 20 percent over normal levels. Canty's purchases on credit are allowed terms of 1%/10, net/30, and Canty has always paid bills on the tenth day after the invoice date to obtain the discount. The current situation for Canty is reflected in column 1. The difference between current assets and current liabilities of $468,100 represents the remaining financing required to support the firm's working capital position. At present this amount corresponds to the firm's net working capital position and is financed by $468,100 of long-term debt and equity capital. The pro forma position under the temporary seasonal expansion is indicated in column 2; column 3 shows the changes in current assets, current liabilities, and remaining financing required caused by the seasonal expansion. All current assets are assumed to expand by 20 percent, or a $130,000 total increase in column 2. Some of this increase will be spontaneously financed by a 20 percent, or $4400, increase in accounts payable if Canty maintains its present policy of taking discounts by paying bills in 10 days. This leaves $125,600 of remaining required financing to be obtained. Because this financing need is temporary, the firm will not raise $125,600 additional net working capital from long-term or permanent sources. Instead, it will increase current liabilities by that amount from short-term financing sources. The only remaining question is, which sources should be used?

Canty Marine is evaluating three alternative ways to meet the temporary financing need of $125,600. Assuming that the funds are required for 6 months, Canty can obtain an unsecured loan of $100,000 from a commercial bank at an interest rate of 11 percent. Alternatively, it can borrow all it needs from a commercial finance company with a general lien on *all* inventory at an interest rate of 12 percent. Finally, it can delay payment on trade credit payables to generate the required funds. The calculations at the bottom of Table 24-4 show that Canty must stretch trade credit payables by nearly 48 days to generate $125,600 and payments will be delayed 4 weeks beyond the due date of 30 days after billing. The calculated explicit cost of trade credit would then be $k_T = 7.68$ percent.

What should Canty Marine do? The choice is not obvious, and the advantages and disadvantages of all alternatives must be examined.

Stretching trade credit payables appears to have the lowest cost of all

Table 24–4   *Working Capital Needs and Cost of Financing: Canty Marine Company*

	1 Current	2 Pro Forma	3 Change
Current Assets			
Cash	$ 50,000	$ 60,000	$ 10,000
Receivables	200,000	240,000	40,000
Inventory	400,000	480,000	80,000
	$ 650,000	$ 780,000	$130,000
Current Liabilities			
Wages Payable	$ 10,000	$ 10,000	0
Trade Accounts Payable	21,900	26,300	$ 4,400
Other Payables	50,000	50,000	0
Current Portion of Long-term Debt	100,000	100,000	0
	$ 181,900	$ 186,300	$ 4,400
Remaining Financing Required	468,100	593,700	125,600
Annual Sales Rate	$2,000,000	$2,400,000	$400,000
Average Annual Trade Purchases	800,000	960,000	160,000
Average Daily Trade Purchases	2,190	2,630	440

Number of Days Trade Credit Must Be Stretched to Meet Need

$$\frac{\text{Temporary financing need}}{\text{Average daily trade purchases}} = \frac{\$125,600}{\$2,360} = 47.76 \text{ days}$$

Explicit Cost of Stretching Trade Credit by 48 Days: Terms 1%/10, net/30 days

$$k_T = \frac{1\%}{99\%} \frac{365}{48} = 0.0768, \quad \text{or } 7.68\%$$

alternatives. However, the explicit cost of 7.68 percent ignores any effects on the cost and availability of credit due to adverse supplier reaction to delayed payment. Suppliers can perform important services for Canty. Filling rush orders, ensuring prompt delivery of goods, helping maintain proper inventories, providing hard-to-obtain inventory in times of economic stress, all are valuable services that should be cultivated. Businesses that do not have cooperative suppliers often find it hard to survive. If suppliers are in a strong position with little competition, they may simply refuse to ship further inventory until past-due debts are paid. They may even ask for return of items that have not been paid for. In short, changing from a policy of taking discounts within 10 days to paying almost 30 days late is likely to cause great consternation among suppliers. Such actions are associated with sick, not healthy, firms. This is an alternative of last resort when a firm faces severe financial distress.

On the surface, the 11 percent unsecured bank loan is cheaper than the 12 percent secured loan offered by the finance company. And the latter will tie up all Canty's inventory as collateral and reduce the availability of future financing on a secured or unsecured basis. But only $100,000 unsecured credit is available. Therefore, these loans may not be comparable on interest rates alone. We need to look deeper. What services will each lender provide for the company? Are the percentage rates quoted by both institutions properly computed to reflect the terms of payment? Does either institution offer more experienced personnel who are knowledgeable about Canty's business and will provide informal advice about financial matters? Can we combine sources of funds? Which institution is the more likely to support Canty with continued financing in the event of economic problems? All these questions should be asked before final decisions are made.

We would not advocate that Canty ignore the interest rate charged by either financial institution. But in most cases, there is more to borrowing money than making prompt principal and interest payments for a single loan. Canty may need funds at regular intervals and would like to develop a continuing relationship with a particular institution as long as management feels that it is obtaining the best service for the cost. Small firms may be particularly dependent on a very limited number of lenders, and the total servicing package may be much more important to them. The very largest firms may have less use for some of the expertise offered by either type of financial institution and so may be more apt to simply compare rates between lenders. The important point is that a firm should consider its total financing needs, present and future, when selecting a financial institution with which to work.

SUMMARY

In financing desired levels of current assets, the firm must decide on the combination of short- and long-term financing sources to be employed. Financial folklore suggests that firms should finance permanent needs with long-term sources and temporary needs with short-term sources. But folklore overemphasizes formal debt maturity as distinguished from a sequence of short-maturity loans taken out and renewed under a financial relationship with a creditor. In addition, folklore ignores the structure of repayment patterns of principal on loans as an important variable. Both formal debt maturity and repayment patterns are variables that are used in several ways to reduce or eliminate adverse incentives for shareholders in the firm. For example, the following statements are likely to be true: loan maturity will not greatly exceed the length of financing need; if loan maturity does exceed length of financing need, principal payments are likely to be spread over the life of the loan; loan maturity may well be less than length of financing need, reducing risk for lenders and interest cost for borrowers.

Thus, departures from folklore are quite possible in the context of conflicts of interest between borrowers and lenders. An additional departure from folklore may be caused by speculating on the possibility of lower future interest rates. Uncertainty about the duration of financing needs may also cause firms to exhibit adaptive behavior. Management might initially borrow short term, then replace that initial financing with long-term debt if the need appears permanent.

Once the mix of short- and long-term sources has been identified, the firm can construct the short-term portion of financing from a range of financial instruments.

Short-term financing consists of loans having a maturity of up to 1 year. Loans may be either secured or unsecured. Both types rely on the future profitability of the borrowing firm to repay the loan, but secured loans provide an additional margin of protection for the lender through the existence of collateral.

Unsecured forms of short-term financing include trade credit, loans from commercial banks, and commercial paper. Trade credit is widely used by most firms as a source of short-term financing. By discretionary variations in the speed with which bills are paid, the customer firm can alter the level of trade credit financing it receives. But the level of trade credit financing also varies spontaneously as the level of economic activity of the firm changes. Attempts to increase trade credit financing by delaying payment of bills beyond the full credit period allowed by the supplier will reduce the explicit cost of trade credit. However, implicit costs may be expected to increase through this practice. More important, excessive delay of payment may sharply curtail the availability of trade credit—a factor of great importance. Unsecured bank credit, either in the form of commercial notes or installment loans, is a major source of short-term financing for firms. A central feature of such credit is its availability for established customers of a bank. Lines of credit and credit agreements are more formal ways of ensuring this availability. Commercial paper is available only to the largest, most creditworthy firms. Sold in impersonal financial markets, commercial paper is of lower cost than bank credit.

Secured forms of short-term financing discussed here include two categories—loans secured by receivables and loans secured by inventory. In general, the availability of loans using either receivables or inventory as security depends on the characteristics of these assets. Large, high quality receivables make good security for a loan. Alternatively, receivables may be sold to a factor. The latter alternative will be more costly than direct loans when a firm already has an established credit department. However, some firms may find factoring cheaper when both the cost of a loan and the expense of operating a credit department are considered. Inventory financing may include the use of a general lien, a trust receipt, or a warehouse receipt as techniques for controlling collateral.

In determining the mix of short-term financing sources, the firm must take account of the financing costs of each short-term source. But such cost comparisons are insufficient to dictate the choice of mix. Availability of future short-term financing is also an important. A lower cost, secured loan that ties up all a firm's collateral and threatens future availability of additional borrowed funds may be inferior to a higher cost, unsecured loan that does not impair availability of additional future loans. Moreover, there are many qualitative issues affecting the choice, as illustrated with Canty Marine.

GLOSSARY OF KEY TERMS

Collateral	Assets pledged as security for a loan.
Commercial Note	A loan repaid with a single payment.
Commercial Paper	Short-term, negotiable unsecured notes sold through the marketplace.
Compensating Balance	A deposit to be maintained in the borrower's checking account as a condition of obtaining a loan.
Credit Agreement	An agreement between a bank and a potential borrower whereby the bank formally guarantees that credit of a specified quantity and maturity will be available to the potential borrower. Also called loan commitment.
Discounted Note	Interest is deducted in advance from the face value of such a note to yield the loan proceeds.
Discretionary Financing	An increase in financing brought about by a deliberate action on the part of the firm.
Factoring	Sale of receivables as a means of generating cash.
Installment Loan	A loan repaid by making periodic payments rather than a single payment.
Line of Credit	An indication (not a commitment) by a bank to a potential borrower that credit will be available for a specified time and in a given quantity.

Loan Proceeds   The amount of cash received by the borrower when a loan is taken out.

Prime Rate   The announced rate of interest at which a bank lends to its highest grade borrowers on a short term basis—for example, 90 days.

Secured Loan   A loan backed by some form of collateral.

Spontaneous   A source of funds such as trade credit that automatically increases with
Financing   the level of operations of the firm.

Term Structure of   The relationship between yield to maturity and maturity of debt holding
Interest Rates   default risk constant.

Unsecured Loan   Loans extended on the basis of the creditworthiness of the firm. No collateral is involved.

SELECTED
REFERENCES

Abraham, Alfred B. "Factoring—The New Frontier for Commercial Banks." *Journal of Commercial Bank Lending* (April 1971), pp. 32–43.

Baxter, Nevins D. *The Commercial Paper Market.* Princeton, NJ: Princeton University Press, 1964.

Daniels, Frank, et al. "Accounts Receivable and Related Inventory Financing—Worthless Collateral?" *Journal of Commercial Bank Lending* (July 1970), pp. 38–53.

Donaldson, Gordon. "Strategy for Financial Emergencies." *Harvard Business Review* (November–December 1969), pp. 67–79.

Harris, Duane G. "Rationing Credit to Business: More Than Interest Rates." *Business Review, Federal Reserve Bank of Philadelphia* (August 1970), pp. 3–14.

Nadler, Paul S. "Compensating Balances and the Prime at Twilight." *Harvard Business Review* (January–February 1972), pp. 112–120.

Stone, Bernell K. "Allocating Credit Lines, Planned Borrowing and Tangible Services Over a Company's Banking System." *Financial Management* (Summer 1975), pp. 65–83.

QUESTIONS

1. How does a financial relationship between a firm and a financial institution blur the distinction between short- and long-term loans?

2. How do loans with maturities longer than the duration of need

create incentives for the shareholders to benefit at the expense of bondholders?

3. Name some ways a firm might plan to eliminate incentives for shareholders to benefit at the expense of bondholders.

4. How might bondholders attempt to protect themselves against possible losses to shareholders?

5. What is the pitfall for firms that speculate on interest rates?

6. Interpret a horizontal yield curve (term structure).

7. Can there exist several different yield curves at the same time? Give an example.

8. Distinguish between secured and unsecured financing.

9. Define the term collateral. What role does it play in the acquisition of short-term funds?

10. What is spontaneous financing?

11. What is the key difference between a line of credit and a credit agreement? Which offers the greatest risk reduction to the firm? Explain.

12. Distinguish between discounted and nondiscounted commercial notes.

13. Explain the term compensating balances, then discuss how they might affect the cost of borrowing.

14. Why are personal considerations important in establishing a banking relationship?

15. Discuss the role of commercial paper in providing short-term financing for large, well-established firms. Why is this source unavailable to small firms?

16. Comment on the argument underlying the statement "good collateral does not necessarily make a good loan."

17. Explain the difference between assignment of receivables and factoring receivables.

18. What receivable characteristics might a lender examine before accepting accounts receivable as collateral?

19. Snooker's Frozen Foods purchases varieties of berries, beans, and squash from local farmers in the Willamette Valley, then processes

and freezes them for sale to wholesalers. Processing begins in late May and continues through October. During this period substantial financing is required. Discuss the type of financing that might be appropriate for Snooker's.

20.   What is a self-liquidating loan?

PROBLEMS   **1.**   An all-equity firm with a three-year life must borrow $5000 to fund current assets. The funds are borrowed at 8 percent and invested immediately. Assume a horizontal yield curve. Expected cash flows are $2000, $6000, and $2000 for years 1, 2, and 3, respectively.

(a)   Show how shareholders can benefit at the expense of bondholders if the entire principal is repaid in year 3.

(b)   Show how the adverse incentive can be eliminated if the principal repayment is made in year 2 instead of year 3.

(c)   Show how the adverse incentive can be eliminated if a partial repayment of $3500 of principal is made in year 2 and the remaining $1500 is repaid in year 3.

2.   Firm A financed a 20-year loan for $10,000 at 14 percent. Firm B secured a short-term loan for the same amount at 14 percent for two years and was able to refinance the loan at 10 percent two years hence for the remaining 18 years. How much interest did Firm B save over Firm A's strategy? Assume only interest payments are made during the life of the loan. What risks was Firm B taking?

3.   Summer Products anticipates a seasonal sales increase of $1.5 million. If spontaneous sources of financing are typically 10 percent of sales, and $250,000 in short-term financing is required, how much of the $250,000 will be provided by spontaneous sources? How much should be obtained elsewhere?

4.   Alron, Inc. purchases goods on credit terms of 3%/15, net/30. What is the explicit cost of forgoing discounts and paying in 30 days? If the explicit cost of passing discounts decreases the longer the firm waits to pay trade creditors, why wouldn't Alron wait for 60 to 90 days to make payments?

5.   Hal Martin, treasurer of Behomin, Inc., projected a $2 million increase in sales during the next year. He was quite concerned that the firm plan to obtain adequate financing. To begin his analysis, he examined the latest balance sheet, shown below.

Behomin, Inc. Balance Sheet

Assets		Liabilities and Capital	
Cash	$ 150,000	Accounts Payable (Trade)	$1,200,000
Receivables	2,300,000	Bank Note	700,000
Inventories	3,950,000	Long-term Debt	3,000,000
Fixed Assets	3,500,000	Equity	5,000,000
Total Assets	$9,900,000	Total Liabilities and Capital	$9,900,000

Hal felt that there would be no changes in fixed assets but that current assets would vary in proportion to sales. Trade payables are expected to remain at their present proportion of sales. In the past year sales have been $24 million.

(a) What are total financing needs if sales increase by $2 million?

(b) How much of those needs will be met by spontaneous financing?

(c) Assuming that the remaining amount will be met by borrowing from a bank, how much should Behomin borrow on a nondiscounted commercial note?

(d) Behomin's primary business is selling lumber from logs that it buys and saws at its own mill. Sales are primarily to small retail lumber dealers. Given this additional information, discuss the type of security that Behomin might offer to secure its bank loan.

6. Case Products had $1.6 million receivables that it wanted to factor. A factor agreed to purchase those receivables for a 1 percent fee on a recourse basis. Receivables were typically paid in 60 days and the factor would loan money to Case for $1\frac{1}{4}$ percent per month for a 60-day period. Compute the effective interest cost of factoring.

7. If the terms of credit sales are 2%/20, net/45, what is the cost of not taking such cash discounts and paying the full amount of a bill at the end of the 45-day period? What would be the cost if the bill were paid at the end of 30 days from the invoice date? On the 15th day? On the 11th day?

8. The financial manager of ABC Company needs the full use of

$24,000 for six months. Her banker tells her that the bank will make the loan at 8 percent on a discounted commercial note. How much must the company borrow and what is the effective interest cost?

9. A firm needs the full use of $36,000 for three months. It usually maintains an average monthly deposit balance of $1000. The terms of the loan are a 10 percent compensating balance and 7 percent interest (per annum) on the amount borrowed. What is the effective interest cost of the $36,000 loan?

10. You need the full use of $60,000 for three months. How much would it cost (annual rate) for each of the following arrangements? (a) Borrow from a bank at 6 percent discounted and no compensating balance requirement, (b) borrow from a bank (nondiscounted) at 5 percent with a 10 percent compensating balance requirement (your normal bank balance is $4000), (c) borrow on a secured loan from a commercial finance company on inventory using a warehouse receipt with terms including a 6 percent simple interest rate, a flat service charge of $200, and an inventory service charge fee of 1 percent of the inventory pledged (you can borrow 60 percent of the inventory pledged) deducted at the date of the loan.

SECTION VII

International

CHAPTER 25

International Finance

Financial managers incur additional responsibilities when the firm is engaged in international transactions. For domestic firms having no subsidiaries abroad, those additional responsibilities are associated with imports or exports of goods and services. However, if the company is a *multinational* firm with subsidiaries abroad, those managers will also contend with special problems of making investment and/or financing decisions in foreign lands.

Because international transactions involve more than one currency, the first portion of this chapter focuses on markets for currencies and the determination of equilibrium exchange rates between currencies. At equilibrium, exchange rates should reflect two important concepts— purchasing power parity and interest rate parity, which will be discussed in detail. The latter portion of the chapter addresses specific decision-making problems facing the financial manager involved in international transactions.

When a financial transaction between parties in different countries takes place, exchange of the currency of one country for that of another is implied. That exchange may also be viewed as a *purchase* of one currency with another so that an exchange of dollars (U.S.) for pounds (U.K.) is the same as purchasing pounds with dollars. Such exchanges typically arise in the course of trade or investment.

Trade transactions arise from the import and export of goods and services across national borders. For example, an American firm importing goods from a French firm would usually be obliged to render payment in French francs, not dollars. Similarly, an American firm exporting goods to a French firm would usually require payment in dollars. In

SOME BASICS OF EXCHANGE RATES

these examples purchase of foreign exchange, francs with dollars or dollars with francs, is required to complete the transactions.

Investment transactions involve capital flows between countries. An American person or firm may choose to invest in British securities for which British pounds are required and future cash receipts from investment are payable in British pounds. Initial conversion of dollars to pounds and eventual reconversion of future receipts from pounds to dollars will take place during the course of the investment. Alternatively, an American firm might undertake a real investment in Great Britain in, say, plant and equipment. Using funds acquired in the United States, the firm could convert dollars to pounds to finance the investment. Again, a foreign exchange transaction takes place.[1]

Foreign Exchange Markets

Conversion of one currency into another takes place in foreign exchange markets. Such markets are located worldwide and consist largely of banks and specialized dealers linked together by a communication system. Banks maintain markets in various currencies, offering to buy and sell them in much the same way as markets are made in over-the-counter financial securities. Returns to the banks from making markets consist of the spread between bid and ask prices set by banks as well as any gains or losses from appreciation of some currencies relative to others. Markets in foreign exchange are made for both **spot** and **forward** exchange. These types of exchange are described below.

The Spot Exchange Market   The spot exchange market involves *immediate* conversion of one currency to another with *immediate* payment by the buyer of a currency. For example, an American firm owing a bill *now* due for 10.0 million French francs would purchase francs with dollars on the spot market. If a bank's selling price (the ask price) is $0.15 U.S. per franc, then the firm will multiply the number of francs to be purchased (10 million) times the dollar price per franc ($0.15). The product will yield the cost of the francs in dollars. In this instance the firm will require $0.15 \times 10,000,000 = $1,500,000 to purchase the needed foreign exchange.

---

[1]These descriptions are necessarily oversimplified. It is not always true that trade or investment transactions necessitate conversion of one currency into another. A French exporter might accept dollar payment from an American importer if it chooses to expand a liquid investment in U.S. dollars. And an American firm might finance investment in British plant and equipment by obtaining financing in Britain using pound-denominated financial securities. In fact, multinational firms may maintain holdings of many different currencies (and investments in securities denominated in various currencies) to support their operations. Still, the eventual conversion of one currency to another is a necessary feature of international finance.

Spot exchange rates are expressed either in units of foreign currency per dollar or dollars per unit of the foreign currency. Selling prices for selected foreign currencies as obtained from Bankers Trust Company for August 2, 1982 are listed below as representative of spot foreign exchange rates:

Country	U.S. $ Equivalent	Currency per U.S. $
Great Britain (pound)	1.7535	0.5703
France (franc)	0.1475	6.7775
Sweden (krona)	0.1652	6.0540
West Germany (mark)	0.4110	2.4330

For example, an American buyer of British pounds will pay $1.7535 per 1 pound or, for payment of $1, receive 0.5703 pound.

The Forward Exchange Market   Firms may also wish to receive or provide *future* delivery of a foreign currency. For example, suppose an American firm wants to have available 50,000 British pounds 90 days hence. It could wait 90 days and then purchase 50,000 pounds in the spot market. Alternatively, it could immediately contract to purchase 50,000 pounds of forward exchange. The firm will receive and pay for 50,000 pounds 90 days hence for a *presently* determined price. The seller of the forward exchange is obliged to make delivery of that sum at the contract price at that time. The forward exchange rate offered by banks determines the amount to be paid upon future delivery of the foreign currency.

Delivery of forward exchange can be arranged for a wide range of periods, but the most active markets exist for 30, 60, and 180-day delivery. Again, on August 2, 1982, the forward exchange rates (selling prices) quoted by Bankers Trust Company for British pounds were:

Britain	U.S. $ Equivalent	Currency per U.S. $
30-Day Forward	1.7541	.5701
90-Day Forward	1.7577	.5689
180-Day Forward	1.7689	.5653

A firm wanting 90-day delivery of 50,000 pounds would contract to pay $1.7577 per pound or a total of

$$\$1.7577 \times 50{,}000 \text{ pounds} = \$87{,}885$$

Why does a market for forward exchange exist? First, it allows firms engaging in trade or investment to reduce risk by contracting for forward exchange. To understand how risk is reduced, consider the alternatives available to the American firm having an obligation to pay 50,000 pounds 90 days hence in settlement of a trade account payable or to finance a planned investment in Britain. If it wishes, the American firm can hold dollars for 90 days and, at that future time, purchase pounds with dollars in the spot market. But there are risks to this approach. The *current* spot rate for British pounds on August 2, 1982 is $1.7535 as shown above. If that rate remains unchanged over the 90-day interval, the dollar value of the 50,000 pound obligation would be

$$\$1.7535 \times 50{,}000 \text{ pounds} = \$87{,}675$$

However, suppose that the dollar falls in value relative to the pound over the interval so that 90 days hence, the firm has to pay *more* dollars for each pound purchased, say $1.80 per 1 pound? The dollar value of the obligation would then be

$$\$1.80 \times 50{,}000 \text{ pounds} = \$90{,}000$$

In this instance the firm would end up paying more by waiting to purchase in the spot market than by making a forward contract now.

Since future spot rates are subject to uncertainty, the firm may wish to avoid risk of higher dollar payments to satisfy the obligation. It can do so by purchasing 50,000 pounds *forward* for the sum of $87,885 earlier determined. The firm has its future 50,000 pounds at a firm price and bears no risk of future declines in the value of the dollar on the spot market.[2]

The use of forward exchange to avoid risk of future changes in spot rates is also employed by people wishing to speculate on future gains and losses in the values of currency. For example, a firm that expects the dollar to rise in value relative to the pound in the next 90 days (it will take fewer dollars to buy a pound) might sell pounds forward at $1.7577. If spot rates subsequently fall to $1.65 per pound, the firm can satisfy the obligation to deliver 1 pound by then purchasing it for $1.65 in the spot

---

[2]An American firm due to *receive* 50,000 pounds in 90 days would be concerned with a *rise* in the value of the dollar against the pound. If the current spot rate for *buying* dollars with pounds (ignoring the spread between bid and ask) is also $1.7535 and remains unchanged over 90 days, the firm will receive $87,675 in 90 days. But if the dollar rises in value relative to the pound so that the firm receives fewer dollars per pound (say $1.65 per 1 pound) then the firm would receive only $1.65 × 50,000 pounds = $82,500. To avoid risk of such a loss, the firm could arrange to sell 50,000 pounds forward at the rate of $1.7577 to ensure receipt of $87,885.

market. When the forward contract comes due, the pound that cost $1.65 would be delivered for the contract price of $1.7577. Clearly such a transaction is profitable. Naturally, there is risk in this posture. A fall in the value of the dollar (increase in the dollar price per pound) to $1.85 per pound will cause the speculator to pay $1.85 for one pound in order to satisfy the obligation and receive only $1.7577 for delivery of that pound.

Some firms engaged in international trade or capital transactions may elect to hedge *or* speculate, depending on their assessment of future behavior of spot rates at a particular time. For example, a firm obliged to pay 50,000 pounds might elect not to hedge if it felt that the dollar would rise in value relative to the pound (fewer dollars would be required to satisfy the 50,000 pound obligation). Such a firm might simply retain dollars for 90 days and then buy the necessary pounds in the spot market on the hoped-for favorable terms. But this is a risk-bearing posture because the dollar may fall in value relative to the pound.

Changes in Spot and Forward Exchange Rates   As with any commodity, market prices of currencies will change as relative demands and supplies for them are altered. We illustrate such changes with British pounds and U.S. dollars.

Suppose that Britain becomes a major oil exporter to the United States, all other trade patterns remaining unchanged. Demand by Americans for British pounds will increase. More U.S. dollars would be offered for British pounds than was previously the case. The value of the dollar relative to the pound will fall in spot markets—that is, it will require more dollars to purchase a spot pound. Since this trade pattern revision is likely to persist, forward exchange value for the dollar will also fall—that is, the purchase or sale of pounds forward will involve larger amounts of dollars.

Comparative levels of interest rates between countries will also influence levels of spot and forward exchange rates. A sudden increase in U.S. interest rates relative to those in Britain for comparable investments will cause some investors holding pounds to shift to dollars in order to earn the higher returns. The dollar would then rise in value relative to the pound (fewer dollars are needed to purchase a pound) in spot markets. Forward exchange rates will also change. (See the section below on interest rate parity.)

It will help our understanding of the basic forces influencing spot and forward exchange rates if we focus attention on the equilibrium sets of these rates. First, we shall examine relationships among spot rates when **EQUILIBRIUM EXCHANGE RATES** there is purchasing power parity, then discuss the relationships between forward rates when there is interest rate parity.

Purchasing Power Parity

At equilibrium, the set of spot exchange rates determined in the marketplace should result in a condition known as purchasing power parity. *With parity, money wealth will have the same purchasing power regardless of the currency in which it is held.*

Table 25-1 will be useful in describing power parity. The upper portion of the table describes a bundle of goods capable of being purchased in each of three countries—Germany, Great Britain, and the United States. At the domestic price of each good in the bundle, the amounts required to purchase the bundle in each country are 16 DM (Deutschemarks) in Germany, £4 (British pounds) in Britain, and $8 (U.S. dollars). If we assume for simplicity that transportation costs for goods between countries are zero and that foreign exchange markets are perfect and efficient, then the equilibrium exchange rates computed in the table provide purchasing power parity. For any two currencies, the equilibrium exchange rate is the ratio of the expenditure necessary to purchase the bundle in each country—for example, if 16 DM are needed to purchase the bundle in Germany while £4 will purchase it in Britain,

Table 25–1 *Purchasing Power Parity*

Bundle	Germany	Great Britain	United States
2 liters of beer	4 DM	£1.75	$3
1 pound of wool	2	.25	1
1 pound of beef	10	2.50	4
	16 DM	£4	$8

Exchange Rates:

Marks and pounds (DM and £)

$$\text{DM per } £1 = \frac{16 \text{ DM}}{£4} = 4 \text{ DM per } £1$$

Marks and dollars (DM and $)

$$\text{DM per } \$1 = \frac{16 \text{ DM}}{\$8} = 2 \text{ DM per } \$1$$

Dollars and pounds ($ and £)

$$\$ \text{ per } £1 = \frac{\$8}{£4} = \$2 \text{ per } £1$$

then the exchange rate is 4 DM per £1 or, equivalently, £0.25 per 1 DM. A holder of 16 DM can purchase one bundle in Germany *or,* upon conversion of 16 DM to £4, the same bundle in Britain, *or* upon conversion of 16 DM to $8, the same bundle in the United States. Purchasing power is the same regardless of which currency an individual chooses to hold.

What assurance do we have that spot exchange rates reflect purchasing power parity? If they do not, then individuals can enhance their purchasing power by making appropriate shifts between currencies. As a result, undervalued currencies will rise in value and overvalued currencies will fall in value relative to other currencies until parity is restored. To demonstrate this, assume that the prices of goods in each country are as shown in Table 25-1, but the prevailing *exchange rates* are as shown below.

Marks and pounds (DM and £)

3 DM per £1

Marks and dollars (DM and $)

1.5 DM per $1

Dollars and pounds ($ and £)

$2 per £1

The dollar and pound reflect purchasing power parity as they should according to Table 25-1. No individual or firm can buy more goods by switching from pounds to dollars or vice versa. But the mark is overvalued relative to the pound and dollar (or the pound and dollar are undervalued relative to the mark). We can see this by noting that 16 DM will purchase 1 bundle in Germany. However, if converted to pounds at the rate of 3 DM per £1, a total of 16 DM ÷ 3 DM per £1 = £5.33 would be obtained. At the prevailing British price of £4 per bundle, approximately £5.33/£4 = 1.33 bundles could be purchased with British pounds. The mark has inferior purchasing power relative to the pound and is therefore overvalued (the pound is undervalued) at the rate of 3 DM per £1. Similarly conversion of 16 DM to $10.67 at the rate of 1.5 DM per $1 would also allow the purchase of $10.67/$8 = 1.33 bundles with U.S. dollars at the prevailing $8 bundle price. The mark also has inferior purchasing power compared to the dollar and is therefore overvalued relative to the dollar at 1.5 DM per $1.

In the above situation, holders of marks would benefit by selling marks to buy pounds or dollars and so gain purchasing power. And holders of dollars or pounds would certainly not wish to convert them to marks and so lose purchasing power. But at any point in time, quantities of marks, dollars, and pounds are fixed. The value of the mark must fall relative to pounds and dollars in response to attempts to convert marks to dollars and pounds in order to induce people to hold the fixed quantity of marks. If the exchange rate changes to 4 DM per £1 and 2 DM per $1, parity is restored.

Relative purchasing power of currencies is not the only influence upon spot exchange rates. Although we shall later see that spot rates respond to changes in demand for forward exchange in response to interest rate changes, purchasing power is probably a dominant influence. In addition, purchasing power parity does *not* imply the absence of trade between countries. Some of the beef in a German bundle could have been imported from the United States. And some beer in the U.S. bundle could have been imported from Germany.

If spot exchange rates reflect purchasing power parity, then *changes* in spot rates over time will be governed by differences in the rate of inflation between countries. For example, suppose the spot rate between dollars and pounds is $2 per £1. As in Table 25-1, £4 and $8 have the same purchasing power of one bundle of goods. But suppose that the annual inflation rate in Britain is 9.0 percent while in the United States it is 7.0 percent. One year hence, it will require

$$£4(1+0.09) = £4.36$$

and

$$\$8(1+0.07) = \$8.56$$

to purchase a bundle in Britain and the United States, respectively. With purchasing power parity, the spot exchange rate one year hence would be

Dollars and pounds ($ and £)

$$\$ \text{ per } £1 = \frac{\$8.56}{£4.36} = \$1.9633$$

Fewer dollars are required to purchase £1 because the purchasing power of the pound has declined faster than that of the dollar. The pound has fallen in value relative to the dollar over the one-year interval.

Interest Rate Parity   It is interesting to note in our discussion of spot and forward exchange rates between dollars and pounds that the spot equivalent of a pound is $1.7535 while the 30, 90 and 180-day forward equivalents are $1.7541, $1.7577, and $1.7689, respectively. Why might forward exchange rates for various delivery dates differ from the current spot rate as well as from each other? If, as is the case here, it costs fewer dollars to buy a pound now than it will cost for delivery in 90 days, why would a firm contract to pay the higher price? As we will show, the difference between spot and forward exchange rates between two countries will depend upon the interest rates in those countries. If interest rates are identical, spot and forward rates must be identical. However, differences in interest rates can cause forward exchange rates to be either higher or lower than current spot rates.

The relationship between exchange rates and interest rates can be developed using a simple example. Suppose an American firm is obliged to pay £1 in 90 days. It can arrange for this payment with either of two equivalent transactions. First, the firm may contract to buy £1 forward for $F_{\$}$ dollars at the current forward exchange rate. This present action will obviously meet the future obligation of £1.

Second, the firm could arrange an equivalent, risk-free transaction. That transaction can be divided into five steps.

1. Borrow dollars in the United States now at the riskless interest rate $k_{\$}$.

2. Exchange those dollars for pounds at the current spot rate $S_{\$}$.

3. Invest the pounds in Britain at the 90-day British risk-free interest rate, $k_{£}$.

4. Pay the British obligation with the principal and accumulated interest over the 90-day period.

5. Pay the principal and interest to the U.S. lender.

To implement this transaction, the firm must first determine the amount that must be borrowed. That amount in pounds is $£1/(1+k_{£})$ since $£1/(1+k_{£})$ will grow to £1 in 90 days. Given the current spot exchange rate $S_{\$}$, the amount that must be borrowed in the United States is $S_{\$}/(1+k_{£})$.

Once the dollars are borrowed and the investment made, the British obligation will be satisfied by the British investment. In 90 days all the American firm must do is pay back the principal and interest owed to the U.S. bank. Since the amount of the loan is $S_{\$}/(1+k_{£})$ and the U.S. interest rate is $k_{\$}$, the amount that must be paid back is

$$\frac{S_{\$}}{(1 + k_{£})} \cdot (1 + k_{\$})$$

Given these two methods of satisfying the British obligation, a rational firm will choose the method that is least costly. In 90 days the firm must either pay $F_{\$}$ for £1, then pay the £1 to satisfy the obligation, or it must repay a U.S. bank loan of $S_{\$}/(1+k_{£})$ $(1+k_{\$})$ and pay the obligation with the £1 accumulated in the British bank. In the first instance, the net outflow is $F_\$$, while in the second it is $S_\$(1+k_\$)/(1+k_£)$. In equilibrium, the firm must be indifferent between these two certain amounts so that

$$F_\$ = \frac{S_\$(1 + k_\$)}{(1 + k_£)} \tag{25-1}$$

The forward exchange rate ($F_\$$) must be equal to the spot exchange rate ($S_\$$) times the ratio of one plus the U.S. interest rate ($k_\$$) and one plus the British interest rate ($k_£$). Alternatively, by subtracting the spot rate from both sides of (25-1), the difference between forward and spot rates may be written

$$F_\$ - S_\$ = S_\$\left[\frac{k_\$ - k_£}{1 + k_£} \right] \tag{25-2}$$

When expressions (25-1) and (25-2) hold, we say that there is interest rate parity because *for identical risk* there is no incentive to invest in one country rather than another.

Table 25-2 illustrates both types of transactions when parity holds for different combinations of U.S. and British interest rates *given* a spot rate of S = \$2.00 per £1. The British risk-free interest rate for 90 days is assumed to be a constant $k_£$ = 0.03 while the corresponding U.S. risk-

Table 25–2   *Interest Rate Parity*

		U.S. Interest Rates		
		0.02	0.03	0.04
A.	Forward Transaction			
	Equilibrium forward rate			
	$F_\$ = S_\$\dfrac{(1 + k_\$)}{(1 + k_£)}$	\$1.9806	\$2.00	\$2.0194
	Amount to be paid for £1 in 90 days with an equilibrium forward contract	\$1.9806	\$2.00	\$2.0194
B.	Spot Transaction with Borrowing and Lending			
	Present amount to be loaned in British market at $k_£$ = 0.03 to meet £1 obligation:			
	$\dfrac{£1}{(1 + k_£)}$	£.97087	£.97087	£.97087
	Amount of U.S. loan taken out at spot rate of $S_\$$ = \$2.00			
	(\$2.00) × £.97087	\$1.94174	\$1.94174	\$1.94174
	Amount of repayment 90 days hence on U.S. loan at alternative rate $k_\$$			
	(\$1.94174)(1 + $k_\$$)	\$1.9806	\$2.00	\$2.0194

free interest rate takes on alternative values of $k_\$ = 0.02$, 0.03, and 0.04. Panel A of the table shows the equilibrium forward exchange rates at alternative U.S. interest rates and the amount to be paid for £1 in 90 days if the forward contract is set at the equilibrium rate. Panel B derives the amount needed to pay off the U.S. loan if dollars are borrowed to buy spot pounds to be invested in Britain. The payments to be made in 90 days are identical in Panel A and Panel B at each U.S. interest rate. It would make no difference to the American firm which transaction was employed to meet the future £1 payment obligation.

Note that a change in the differential between U.S. and British interest rates will lead to changes in ending payments for the borrowing/lending transaction and force changes in the forward rate. Suppose that the U.S. interest rate is $k_\$ = 0.02$ while the British interest rate is $k_£ = 0.03$. According to Table 25-2, either a forward or spot transaction with borrowing and lending result in an ending payment of $1.9806 for the firm. But now assume that the U.S. interest rate rises to $k_\$ = 0.04$. This will raise the ending payment for the spot transaction to $2.0194. If the forward rate remained at $1.9806, the firm would obviously prefer the forward transaction, as would other firms with a need to pay pound obligations in the future. There would be an increase in demand for future pounds and the dollar price would be bid up until there was once again no difference in final payments between the two transactions— that is, to $F_\$ = \$2.0194$.[3]

There are other transactions, such as the need to sell pounds in the future, that could be used to further illustrate interest rate parity. But they would all lead to the same result. Interest rate parity is central to explaining forward exchange rates.

The important role of interest rate differentials between countries in establishing the relationship between spot and forward rates raises an important question: Why do interest rates differ among countries? We

CAUSES OF INTEREST RATE DIFFERENTIALS BETWEEN COUNTRIES

---

[3]In showing how forward rates adjust to reflect the new interest rate differential between the United States and Britain, we have held the spot rate constant at $S_\$ = \$2.00$. This was done for simplicity. It is the equilibrium *difference* between spot and forward rates that matters as a consequence of interest rate parity. In the example above, the change to a higher U.S. interest rate would feature not only an increase in demand for future pounds but a reduction in demand for spot pounds needed in the temporarily less favored spot transaction with borrowing and lending. Perhaps the spot rate for pounds might fall to $S_\$ = \$1.995$ from $2.00. With the new interest rate differential, the new equilibrium forward rate using Equation (25-1) would then be

$$F_\$ = \$1.995 \ (1+0.0097) = \$2.0144$$

not $2.0194 when the spot rate was held constant at $2.00 as in Table 25-2.

can usefully approach this question by recalling from Chapter 19 that nominal required rates of return depend on real required rates and the expected rate of inflation. Both real rates and expected inflation rates may differ between countries to reflect differences in national conduct of monetary and fiscal policy as well as resource allocation and the sophistication of capital markets. If we assume for simplicity that real required rates are the same between countries and equal to k' for riskless securities, then differences in nominal rates labeled $k_\$$ and $k_£$ for the United States and Britain, respectively, will be solely attributable to differences in expected rates of inflation between the countries. Those inflation rates are denoted $\dot{P}^e{}_\$$ for the United States and $\dot{P}^e{}_£$ for Britain.

In our discussion of inflation from Chapter 19 we noted that when the nominal riskless return on a \$1 investment, \$1(1+k), is deflated using the expected inflation rate the resulting real return must be equal to the equilibrium real, riskless return. That is,

$$\frac{1 + k}{1 + \dot{P}^e} = (1 + k') \tag{25-3}$$

Solving this expression for the appropriate risk-free nominal rate yields

$$k = k' + \dot{P}^e + k' \cdot \dot{P}^e \tag{25-4}$$

When we apply this expression to find the nominal rate in different countries, we find that

$$k_\$ = k' + \dot{P}^e{}_\$ + k' \cdot \dot{P}^e{}_\$ \tag{25-4a}$$

in the United States and

$$k_£ = k' + \dot{P}^e{}_£ + k' \cdot \dot{P}^e{}_£ \tag{25-4b}$$

in Britain.

To explore the relationship between inflation and the difference between spot and forward rates, recall that

$$F_\$ - S_\$ = S \left[\frac{k_\$ - k_£}{1 + k_£} \right]$$

from expression (25-2). Substituting (25-4a) and (25-4b) into (25-2) and simplifying yields

$$F_\$ - S_\$ = S_\$ \left[\frac{\dot{P}^e_\$ - \dot{P}^e_£}{1 + \dot{P}^e_£} \right] \tag{25-5}$$

The greater the difference in the expected rate of inflation between the United States and Britain, the greater the nominal interest rate differential and the greater the difference between forward and spot exchange rates.

To illustrate, let the real riskless interest rate common to both the United States and Britain be $k' = 4$ percent. The U.S. expected inflation rate is assumed to be $\dot{P}^e_{\$} = 7$ percent while Britain's is assumed to be $\dot{P}^e_{£} = 9$ percent. Using these values in Equations (25-4a) and (25-4b), we find that the corresponding nominal riskless interest rates are

$$k_{\$} = 0.04 + 0.07 + (0.04)(0.07) = 0.1128$$

and

$$k_{£} = 0.04 + 0.09 + (0.04)(0.09) = 0.1336$$

Using these rates in expression (25-2) to compute the equilibrium difference between forward and spot exchange rates yields

$$F_{\$} - S_{\$} = S_{\$}\left[\frac{k_{\$} - k_{£}}{1 + k_{£}}\right] = \$2\left[\frac{0.1128 - 0.1336}{1.1336}\right] = \$2(-0.018349)$$

$$= -\$0.0367$$

Notice that we obtain an identical answer by substituting the expected inflation rates into (25-5).

$$F_{\$} - S_{\$} = S_{\$}\left[\frac{\dot{P}^e_{\$} - \dot{P}^e_{£}}{1 + \dot{P}^e_{£}}\right] = \$2\left[\frac{0.07 - 0.09}{1 + 0.09}\right] = \$2(-0.018349)$$

$$= -\$0.0367$$

An increase in the expected rate of inflation applicable to one country's currency compared to another will lead to an upward revision in that country's nominal interest rate, altering the interest rate differential and the parity solution. In the previous example, a spot rate of $2 per £1 would result, using Equation (25-1), in a forward rate for purchase or sale of pounds of

$$F_{\$} = \$2.00\left(\frac{1.1128}{1.1336}\right) = \$2.00(0.98165) = \$1.9633$$

But if the expected rate of inflation for the United States should fall to $\dot{P}^e_{\$} = 0.05$ from 0.07, then the exchange rate differential will become, in Equation (25-5),

$$F_{\$} - S_{\$} = S_{\$}\left[\frac{\dot{P}^e_{\$} - \dot{P}^e_{£}}{(1 + \dot{P}^e_{£})}\right] = \$2\left[\frac{0.05 - 0.09}{1 + 0.09}\right]$$

$$= \$2(-0.036697) = -\$0.0734$$

Clearly, since $F_{\$} - S_{\$} = \$0.0734$ and $S = \$2.00$ the forward rate would be[4]

---

[4]The reader can check the answer by using $\dot{P}^e_{\$}$ and $\dot{P}^e_{£}$ to solve for the nominal rates, $k_{\$}$ and $k_{£}$. Those rates can then be substituted into expression (25-1) to solve for $F_{\$}$.

$$F_\$ = S_\$ - \$0.0734 = \$2.00 - \$0.0734 = \$1.9266$$

EQUILIBRIUM EXCHANGE RATES: SOME FINAL COMMENTS

Our discussions of both types of parity took place in a world of perfectly functioning product and capital markets where there are no impediments to the flow of commodities and capital across international boundaries. In such an atmosphere there is little role for active financial management. We recognize, however, that there are impediments that can cause severe problems for the financial decision-maker. In the following section we outline some of these problems. In this discussion, the reader should not forget that while restrictions on the movement of capital and goods among countries may mute the competitive forces discussed above, they can seldom eliminate them. Thus, the existence of imperfection may cause varying deviations from parity, but few economies can really insulate themselves entirely from competitive forces at work in the international market place.

INTERNATIONAL FINANCIAL MANAGEMENT

Under a **free, floating** exchange rate system where rates are determined by the free market forces of supply and demand, (1) equilibrium spot exchange rates tend to change over time to reflect differences among inflation rates of different countries (a consequence of purchasing power parity), (2) the interest rate tends to incorporate the expected inflation rate and therefore the difference in the interest rates between two countries reflects the difference in expected inflation rates, and (3) the difference between spot and forward rates will reflect the difference between interest rates (interest rate parity). As foreign exchange and money markets are often regarded as *efficient*, a change in supply and demand conditions in one country should bring about a rapid realignment in the others; the exception appears to be the purchasing power parity relationship, which in practice does not hold very well in the short run.

However not all, or even a majority, of the exchange rates are freely floating. Most of the exchange rates in the world are either managed or fixed. Under a **managed** rate system, government central banks interfere in the marketplace to manage the rate at whatever level they choose. Under a fixed system, official published rates are maintained and used—interrupted occasionally by changes in the official rate (a devaluation or revaluation). Consequently the financial manager of a firm involved in international trade or of a multinational firm is faced with many additional challenges that impediments to competition present. The international finance manager must deal with expected changes in the exchange rates together with deviations from expectations caused by competitive forces and with additional political factors that affect exchange rates. Both competitive and noncompetitive factors combine to create **exchange risk.**

Expected and unexpected changes in the exchange rate may have widespread impact on a company involved with international commerce. We cannot attempt in this brief space to do more than highlight some of these considerations, leaving further study of the problems to courses in international business and international finance, where they may be examined in greater depth. A few illustrations suggest some of these considerations.

Exchange Risk

When the Mexican peso was allowed to float relative to the dollar in February 1982, the peso fell 30 percent from its previous fixed rate. The treasurer of Litton Industries, which has a subsidiary in Mexico, reported they were well prepared for the devaluation; since July 1981 they had been reducing peso-denominated assets. Other firms took on more peso-denominated debt, or sold pesos in the foreign exchange market. When the peso devalued again in August 1982 another 50 percent relative to the dollar, the head of a U.S. computer software company reported cancellation of contracts for sales to Mexico due to the doubling of the dollar cost of software to Mexican customers. These illustrations suggest that exchange rate changes can affect sales projections as well as cost and profit forecasts and that firms may seek to defend themselves against such events. One way to examine these problems is to group them into three components that comprise exchange risk. Those components are **transaction exposure, translation exposure,** and **economic exposure.**

Transaction Exposure   Transaction exposure is the potential for gain or loss that may result when transactions involve a foreign currency. Suppose Pirelli (Italy) has made a sale as of July 1, 1983 of 50,000 tires for £1,000,000 to a British tire dealership chain, with payment in pounds and delivery due in six months—on January 1, 1984. Pirelli expects a profit of 350,000,000 lire on the sale, because the current exchange rate is 2350 lire to the British pound and costs are expected to be 2,000,000,000 lire.

Expected Revenue	2,350,000,000 lire
Expected Cost	−2,000,000,000 lire
Expected Profit	350,000,000 lire

Unfortunately on August 1, 1983 the pound devalues 20 percent, so that the new exchange rate is 1880 lire to the pound. But Pirelli still expects £1,000,000 on January 1, which will convert to only 1,880,000,000 lire. When the 2,000,000,000 lire expenses are deducted, the expected profit of 350,000,000 lire becomes a loss of 120,000,000 lire. This deviation from expectations reflects the most common type of transaction exposure. Transactions subject to exposure include buying and selling goods or services on credit in another currency and borrowing or lending funds denominated in other currencies not covered by an offsetting transaction.

Translation Exposure   Translation exposure reflects the uncertainty about the amounts in balance sheet accounts as those values are translated from a local subsidiary currency to the currency of the parent company. When the subsidiary accounts are translated and consolidated into parent company accounts, the translated amounts are affected by exchange rate changes. Thus, losses or gains may be incurred that result in gains or losses in parent company equity accounts. Although these values are only accounting entries and may not affect cash flow, many executives are anxious to avoid such book losses.

Economic Exposure   Economic exposure is the prospect that the value of the firm can change because of unexpected changes in exchange rates. Presumably budgets already reflect information about expected changes. But unexpected changes such as the unexpected loss of sales by a U.S. computer software company to Mexican customers may affect the value of the software firm. Expected changes in the exchange rate can be reflected in the selling price for products or services in a sales contract. But *unexpected* changes create the greatest source of economic risk exposure. Many banks throughout the world who have made loans to Mexican customers were caught with unexpected changes in value because Mexico had difficulties in repayment following devaluation in August 1982.

As in the national or domestic case, we would expect the capital market theory conditions of Chapter 4 to apply. Namely, in perfect and efficient markets, investors diversify their portfolios to eliminate non-market risk so that *some portion* of exchange risk may be diversified away. Any attempts by individual firms to reduce their individual risk is duplicative and useless; let investors diversify and each firm is valued based on its market risk. But in practice, it seems that managements emphasize departures from perfect and efficient markets and focus on current reported earnings, including foreign exchange gains and losses. Consequently managers typically seek to control risk, as evidenced by Litton's actions.

Management employs several types of responses to the various types of exchange rate exposure. These responses include (1) balancing transaction cash flows, (2) minimizing translation exposure, (3) using of offsetting or hedging transactions, and (4) improving forecasts of exchange rate movements to improve pricing, cost, and profit control.

Management Responses to Exchange Risk

Balancing Cash Flows   The firm may try to adjust the leads and lags in cash flow that cause transaction exposure. In the example of the Pirelli sale of tires to England, Pirelli could have demanded payment in lire; thus the same currency is employed for cash inflows as well as cash outflows. This action shifts the exchange rate risk from the Italian to the British firm, however, and may affect the price that the British firm is willing to pay for the tires. Alternatively, Pirelli could have sought to shorten delivery and payment times to reduce the length of exposure or it could have incurred some of its costs in pounds, thereby reducing the amount of exposure.

Minimizing Translation Exposure   The approach the firm would use to minimize translation exposure involves actions that reduce the accounting balance sheet exposure. Suppose that Pear Computers (U.S.) has a subsidiary manufacturer in the United Kingdom whose balance sheet appears in Table 25-3.

Table 25–3   *Translation Exposure, Pear Computers*

Pear Computers, Ltd. (U.K.)
Balance Sheet, 12/31/82

Cash	£ 100	Accounts Payable	£ 200
Accounts Receivable	200	Long Term Debt	500
Inventory	300	Equity	300
Plant & Equipment	400		£1000
	£1000		

Pear Computers, Ltd. (U.K.)
Balance Sheet (translated), 12/31/82

Cash	$ 200	Accounts Payable	$ 400
Accounts Receivable	400	Long Term Debt	1000
Inventory	600	Equity	600
Plant & Equipment	800		$2000
	$2000		

The table shows that using a $2 to £1 exchange rate, £1000 translates to $2000 when Pear consolidates this statement with its parent U.S. company. Although there exist alternative accounting rules for translating accounts, U.S. companies are expected to follow the current rate method of translation (as per FASB, #52);[5] under this method all assets and liabilities are translated at the current exchange rate. Consequently, the net exposure is the amount of the equity or £300. If, for example, the pound devalues to £1.5 to the dollar, the assets would translate to $1500, the liabilities to $1050, and the equity would fall from $600 to $450, resulting in a loss of $150 on consolidated returns.

The strategy to minimize translation exposure is to minimize the recorded equity of the subsidiary. Management could consider having the U.K. subsidiary (1) increase or accelerate its dividends to the parent, (2) repurchase its shares from the parent, (3) alter terms on royalties, fees and loans, and materials so as to incur subsidiary losses that will reduce equity. This latter alternative takes time, however. If management forecasts a change in the exchange rate (not reflected in market interest rates) and wishes to reduce such translation exposure, increasing dividends or share repurchase are the most feasible alternatives.

Hedging Transactions   Hedging involves an offsetting transaction to eliminate or reduce exchange risk exposure—translation, transaction, or economic. If the firm has a net exposure in pounds, for example, a hedging transaction would create a negative exposure (or short position) in pounds. If management forecasts a pound devaluation and has a net exposure in its subsidiary of £300, then the parent could directly hedge by borrowing £300, selling these pounds for future delivery or by numerous other indirect methods. *Direct* hedging may be accomplished in the money market *or* the forward currency market. By borrowing locally in the *money market*, say £300, exchanging pounds for dollars in the *spot* market and investing in dollar money market securities, it costs the parent or trading company only the difference between the borrowing and the lending rates of interest. The interest rate difference between the United Kingdom and the United States is reflected in the exchange rate. If the firm's forecast agrees with the market, the firm has traded an exposed position for a nonexposed position at the market price for such trades—the interest rate differential. The important point is that management has eliminated risk in the event that the actual exchange rate deviates unfavorably from the expected exchange rate.

Alternatively, the finance manager could use the *forward* currency

---

[5]*Statement of Financial Accounting Standards, No. 52* (Financial Accounting Standards Board, Stamford, Connecticut).

market and sell £300 in the market, the pounds to be delivered in exchange for dollars. But the difference between the spot and forward rate reflects the market's expectation of expected change in the exchange rate. Consequently, unless firm forecasts are different from the market, the firm does not profit—but it does eliminate risk. It has exposure in the amount of £300 equity investment in the British subsidiary and it is negatively exposed (or short) in the forward market—it owes £300. If the change in the exchange rate is more drastic than the market expectation, the firm's additional loss in dollar value of equity in the British subsidiary is offset by a gain in the forward market when the firm buys pounds spot to exchange for dollars at the future contract date. These direct hedges are quick, easy, and cost little in terms of transactions costs, which average about 0.65%. However, because some currency markets are highly regulated, it may be easier to use the money market hedge; also, the currency involved may not have an efficient forward market.

Indirect hedging uses a variety of techniques to increase liabilities and decrease assets denominated in a currency whose exchange rate is predicted to depreciate. Suppose, for example, Pear Computers increased its accounts payable by slowing payments, reduced inventory by slowing purchases, and reduced accounts receivable by tightening credit. Not only would these actions reduce assets and increase liabilities exposed to risk of devaluation, they would also generate cash that could be invested in marketable securities denominated in a strong currency. If Pear Computers freed up an extra £300 and invested it in U.S. Treasury bills, its exposure could be substantially hedged.

Pricing and Cost Control   Management knows that the forward exchange rate premium or discount from the spot rate reflects the market's judgment of differences in inflation rates. Consequently management should adjust the pricing of sales in that currency to include these changes. Particularly where sales involve currencies that do not float freely, management needs to undertake its own forecasts of changes in the exchange rate and adjust its prices accordingly. Where great risk exists, a risk premium may be required in setting prices. Such forecasting will also be necessary where costs involve such currencies. Where raw materials or parts are imported, for example, cost estimates may require adjustment for projected exchange rate changes or for uncertainty.

Management may choose among several alternative approaches to reducing losses from exchange rate changes. Few firms hedge all transactions but more firms find themselves forced to make some exchange rate forecasts and, at least selectively, hedge exposures that are large and uncertain. Few industrial firms actively seek to gain from exchange rate changes. Their expertise typically lies in manufacturing a product rather than in uncovering the causes of fluctuating exchange rates. Most firms tend to balance cash flows and minimize translation exposures where forecasts suggest currencies may depreciate.

The Investment Decision

The foreign investment decision requires the same procedures as domestic decisions—net cash flows must be estimated and discounted at a rate appropriate to the risk involved so that estimates of net present value are obtained. The fundamental motivation for foreign investment is the same as for domestic investment: maximize shareholder wealth. A particular project's positive net present value can result from underlying influences such as economies of scale attributable to market expansion, production efficiency due to cheaper labor, and so on. In the financial realm, diversification and financial subsidies may contribute to the attractiveness of foreign investments.

Diversified Foreign Investment   As observed in Chapter 4, risky assets are held in portfolios by investors, and the portion of risk that cannot be eliminated as a result of diversification was termed **market risk.** The portion of total risk of a risky asset that is market risk depends on the degree of correlation of returns on that risky asset with the market basket of all risky securities. In the United States the average market risk of a security was observed to be about 0.3 or 30 percent of total risk. But other countries tend to have a less diverse economy and less political stability so that average market risk is greater.[6] Also, for many countries, market returns are relatively independent of U.S. returns so that portfolio risk could be further reduced by investors through an internationally diversified portfolio, especially using risky assets of less-developed countries.[7] Without barriers to capital markets, we would expect investors to diversify internationally, thereby offering no incentive for firms to diversify by directly investing abroad. But when international capital markets display imperfections, we would expect managers to consider what investors may be unable to accomplish themselves. Whether the motive for foreign investments rests primarily on increased cash flows or the risk reduction impacts of diversification, multinational firms do, in fact, invest abroad.

---

[6]Studies by Solnik (*Financial Analysts Journal*, July–August 1974), pp. 48–54 and D. Lessard, *Financial Analysts Journal*, (January–February 1976), pp. 32–38.

[7]See D. H. Lessard, "International Portfolio Diversification: A Multivariate Analysis for a Group of Latin American Companies," *Journal of Finance*, (June 1973), pp. 619–633.

Cash Flow Estimation   Cash flow estimation for a foreign investment proceeds under the principles developed in Chapter 8, but is complicated by additional factors. Among these are (1) a different inflation rate in the host country, (2) restrictions on remittance of capital or returns to capital from the subsidiary to the parent, (3) different tax rules, tax bases, and tax rates affecting operations abroad, and (4) expected changes in the exchange rate at which funds can be remitted. If the project under consideration is a French subsidiary and the franc is expected to depreciate 10 percent per year, then expected remittances to the parent have to be adjusted for the decline in the value of the franc relative to the dollar.

Risk Assessment   The unique aspects of risk assessment involved with foreign investment include the risk associated with unexpected changes in the exchange rate and the political uncertainties involving operation as a foreign entity. The *exchange risk* must be added to business and financial risk to determine the total risk premium. The required rate of return equation as amended is

$$k = r_f + \phi_B + \phi_F + \phi_E$$

where ϕ_B = the business risk premium required, reflecting risks of domestic economic conditions, competition, and so on; ϕ_F = the financial risk premium required, reflecting incremental risk due to use of debt financing, and ϕ_E = the exchange risk premium required, reflecting uncertainties surrounding future exchange rates.

Assessment of *political risk*, which might be viewed as a component of business risk for foreign operations, is more difficult. Firms face a similar political risk when it considers location of operations within its own domestic borders, (state to state or city to city) but these have not been quantifiable and are left for subjective evaluation. However, the political risk variability from state to state or city to city in most cases are not so great as to distort conclusions based on only business and financial risk premiums. However, for most political environments outside the parent country, political risk assumes much more importance. The political climate of sovereign nations may vary considerably and political stability may be much less dependable.

Governments may employ methods of interference, some of which may be discriminatory against foreign firms. At the extreme, they can eject foreign firms entirely by *expropriation* of assets without compensation equal to full market value. Interference may also take alternative, but less drastic forms. A government could require that a portion of ownership be held by local citizen investors; mandate that firms hire a certain percentage of management locally; regulate prices (transfer prices) of materials and parts moving out of the subsidiary to other segments of the multinational firm; erect licensing barriers to business operations and limit repatriation of dividends, payments of fees and royalties to the parent company. The possibility of such adverse government actions increases the risk of foreign investment in many countries compared to domestic investment.

In most cases management cannot rely on objective measures of political risk and must resort to subjective evaluations resulting in adjustments to the required rate of return. These adjustments made in arriving at the discount rate are likely to be more significant for less developed countries where governments are generally considered less stable than for more industrially advanced countries.

Financing Abroad   A multinational firm, by definition, operates in more than one nation. As such it has access to more than one capital market, allowing it to choose between them to its advantage. If there were no capital barriers, real or perceived, then there would exist one capital market—the world market. But, at least at present, it is generally considered that the capital markets of various nations are segmented in varying degrees from each other—those of several West European nations being less so than others. In such a case, a multinational firm has a choice to finance its needs or a subsidiary's needs from the parent country, the countries in which subsidiary operations are located, or in some cases from countries in which it has no operations. As a result of such a choice, it has been suggested that multinationals have not only a greater availability of capital but should be able to achieve a lower cost than an equivalent firm restricted to its domestic capital market.

Foreign bonds are issues of the parent firm sold in another country. Foreign bonds are promises to pay in the currency of the nation in which they are sold and thus are subject to exchange rate change and exchange risk. If bonds of Royal Dutch Shell are sold in the United States, the company promises to pay in dollars. If they are sold to yield 10 percent and the Dutch gilder is expected to depreciate relative to the dollar by 2 percent per year, the effective expected cost to Royal Dutch Shell is 10 plus 2 or 12 percent. The actual cost may turn out to be more or less than 12 percent depending on actual exchange rate changes.

Eurobonds are bonds denominated in a currency other than the issuer's currency and the currency of the country in which they are sold. If Royal Dutch Shell sold bonds in the United Kingdom denominated in dollars, they would be called Eurobonds. Again, changes in the exchange rate dictate the effective cost of the source of capital.

Other securities such as convertible bonds, preference stock, and common or ordinary shares may also be sold abroad as foreign securities or Euro securities. The issues could be issues of the parent company, a subsidiary, or a subsidiary issue whose payment is guaranteed by the parent. In some countries, the government may act as a lender, directly or indirectly subsidizing the borrower who uses the funds locally.

Given capital markets segmented from each other in varying degrees, the potential for access to subsidized loans, different debt/equity ratio norms among nations, the opportunity to borrow or invest between subsidiaries in the corporate family, and the lower market risk due to international diversification, there is an opportunity for multinational firms to obtain cheaper capital.

SUMMARY

International transactions involve more than one currency. At some juncture in consumating such transactions, currency of one country must be exchanged for the currency of another. The *spot* market is the market for *immediate* currency exchange. A U.S. firm purchasing goods abroad could enter that market, purchase the appropriate foreign currency, then use that currency to pay for foreign goods. Firms can provide for *future* delivery of a foreign currency through trading in the *forward* exchange market. In that market a firm can contract to deliver or receive a currency at a specific exchange rate at a specified time in the future. Many firms use these markets to reduce **exchange risk.** Thus a U.S. firm that agrees to purchase an Italian product at a price that is set in Italian lire may find it desirable to contract now for future delivery of lire at a specified forward exchange rate between lire and dollars. By making a forward contract, the U.S. firm eliminates the risk of adverse changes in future exchange rates that could dramatically increase the *dollar* cost of the product.

Spot and forward exchange rates are influenced by competitive factors in the market place as well as by specific policies of individual governments. In free, competitive international product and currency markets there should be **purchasing power parity.** That is, money wealth should have the same purchasing power regardless of the currency in which it is held. Individuals wishing to purchase a given bundle of goods will purchase those goods using a currency that offers the greatest purchasing power. Thus the value of a weak currency should be driven down relative to the value of a stronger currency until the purchasing power of both currencies is identical. Interest rate parity means that for *identical risk investments* there is no incentive to invest in one country rather than in another. An investor cannot increase wealth simply by exchanging one currency for another and investing in another country when there is **interest rate parity** because the relative prices of spot and forward exchange adjust to reflect gains from such opportunities.

Because exchange rates fluctuate, firms involved with international commerce must address the problems that such exchange risk imposes on the firm. One can group exposures to exchange risk into transaction, translation, and economic exposure categories. Transaction exposure is the potential for gain or loss when an international transaction involves a foreign currency. Translation exposure reflects the uncertainty about the amounts in balance sheet accounts as those values are translated from the local subsidiary currency to the currency of the parent multinational company. Economic exposure is the prospect that the value of the firm can change due to unexpected changes in exchange rates—loss of sales, increased costs, and so forth. Management may employ several types of responses to exchange rate exposure. The firm may try to adjust the leads and lags in cash flows of international transactions to reduce length and degree of exposure. A multinational could attempt to reduce translation exposure to increasing liabilities in weak currencies and increasing assets in strong currencies. Firms may also use an offsetting transaction to reduce or eliminate exposure; direct hedging can take place by the appropriate buying or selling in the forward exchange market or by borrowing in a weak currency and investing it in a strong currency money market. Forecasting exchange rate changes yields opportunities for adjusting prices and for careful planning of cost changes.

Investment decisions by multinationals in foreign operations follow the same rules as domestic decisions but exchange risk and an uncertain political environment introduce added challenges in evaluation. In selecting financing sources, a multinational firm usually enjoys access to many national capital markets and an opportunity to secure less expensive capital.

GLOSSARY OF KEY TERMS

Economic Exposure	The possible variation in firm value due to unexpected changes in exchange rates.
Eurobonds	Bonds issued in one nation whose interest and principal are denominated in currency of another nation.
Exchange Rate	The price of one unit of a specific currency in terms of another currency.

Exchange Risk	The prospect that exchange rate changes will differ from the expected change. The components of this risk are transaction, translation and economic exposure.
Expropriation	The takeover of assets of foreign-owned firms by the government.
Fixed Rate System	An exchange rate officially designated as the rate for all transactions set by government.
Foreign Bonds	Bonds sold by foreign corporations with interest and principle denominated in the currency of the country in which the bonds are issued.
Foreign Exchange	Foreign currency.
Forward Exchange	An operation in which currencies are exchanged at a future date at an agreed exchange rate.
Free, Floating Rate System	An exchange rate determined by free market interaction of buyers and sellers
Hedging	Undertaking a transaction to offset an exchange risk exposure.
Interest Rate Parity	The difference between spot and forward exchange rates reflects the interest rate differential between two countries, so there is no incentives to invest in one country rather than another *for a given level of risk.*
Managed Rate System	An exchange rate managed by government intervention in the foreign exchange market.
Multinational Firm	A firm with operations in more than one nation.
Purchasing Power Parity	Money wealth will have the same purchasing power regardless of the currency in which it is held.
Spot Exchange	Immediate conversion of one currency into another.
Translation Exposure	Uncertainty about the amounts in balance sheet accounts as those values are translated from the foreign subsidiary currency to the currency of the parent company.
Transaction Exposure	Potential for gain or loss that may result when a transaction involves a foreign currency.

SELECTED REFERENCES

Dufey, G. "Corporate Finance and Exchange Rate Variations." *Financial Management*, Summer 1972, pp. 51–57.

Dufey, G. and I. H. Giddy. *The International Money Market.* Englewood Cliffs, N.J.: Prentice-Hall, 1978.

Logue, D. E. and G. S. Oldfield. "Managing Foreign Assets When Foreign Exchange Markets are Efficient." *Financial Management*, Summer 1977, pp. 16–22.

Rodriguez, R. M. and E. E. Carter, *International Financial Management*, 2nd Ed., Englewood Cliffs, N.J.: Prentice-Hall, 1979.

Shapiro, A. "Exchange Rate Changes, Inflation, and the Value of the Multinational Corporation." *Journal of Finance*, May 1975, pp. 485–502.

QUESTIONS

1. Distinguish purchasing power parity from interest rate parity.

2. If the Italian expected inflation rate was 15 percent and the U.S. expected inflation rate was 5 percent, what would you forecast in terms of change in the spot lire relative to the spot dollar over the coming year?

3. If real interest rates are identical between countries, what will be the difference between spot and forward rates for one of the currencies assuming that there is no difference between their expected inflation rates? (Assume perfect markets.)

4. If the Treasury Bill rate in Japan is 6 percent and the bill rate in United States is 10 percent, how much of a premium or discount would you expect in a 6-month forward rate for converting yen to U.S. dollars?

5. If an exporter in the United States sells calculators to a dealer in Australia on terms of 90 days from invoice date, payable in U.S. dollars, what can the Australian dealer do to avoid the risk of an increase in the price of the U.S. dollar relative to the Australian dollar over this 90-day period? What are the costs of such a risk-reducing strategy?

6. Atlas corporation (U.S.) opened a subsidiary manufacturing operation in Venezuela. All accounts were in bolivars. The Atlas Corporation's financial office forecasts a 20 percent devaluation in the Venezuelan bolivar within the coming year. What strategies can the parent company use to minimize exchange losses in its consolidated financial statements?

7. What is exchange risk? Can a firm contracting to sell products in exchange for future payment in foreign currencies at presently agreed upon prices eliminate exchange risk by predicting future

changes in the exchange rate and pricing the products accordingly?

8. Distinguish between transaction, translation, and economic risk exposure.

9. Discuss how a firm might reduce translation exposure for its own foreign subsidiary.

10. What unique features does foreign investment bring to the capital budgeting decision?

1. If the Korean won costs $0.002, what is the price of the U.S. dollar in terms of won? **PROBLEMS**

2. The following bundle of goods can be purchased at the indicated prices in each country designated below.

	Sweden		France		Ireland	
Bundle	Unit Price (k)	Expenditure (k)	Unit Price (f)	Expenditure (f)	Unit Price (£)	Expenditure (£)
1 pair of rubber boots	20	20	22	22	2	2
2 turkeys	19.5	39	30	60	2	4
8 spark plugs	2	16	2.25	18	0.5	4

If purchasing power parity holds (under perfect markets), determine equilibrium exchange rates in terms of krona per pound, krona per franc, and francs per pound (k = swedish krona, f = French francs, £ = Irish pounds).

3. Given your answer to problem 2, you observe the following *actual* exchange rates.

Sweden   6k per £1

France   .6k per f1

Ireland   10f per £1

(a) Which currency is overvalued?

(b) Describe a transaction whereby you could gain in purchasing power through sale and purchase of currencies.

    (c)   If you and others perceived the potential purchasing power gain, describe how market forces would restore purchasing power parity.

4.   The prevailing spot rate between British pounds and German marks is 4.25 DM per £1. The riskless annual rates of interest for the two countries are k_{DM} = 12 percent and $k_{£}$ = 15 percent. Assuming perfect markets, what should be the equilibrium forward exchange rate for 180-day forward exchange between the two currencies?

5.   You are a German importer with an obligation 180 days hence to pay £40,000. How would you choose to eliminate risk of exchange losses for this impending payment if annual riskless rates of interest are k_{DM} = 12 percent and $k_{£}$ = 15 percent and the spot rate is 4.25 DM per £ when (a) the forward rate for marks is 4.5 per £1 and (b) the forward rate for marks is 3.85 DM per £1.

6.   Fred Daken works at the foreign exchange trading desk of Pillar National Bank. He notes that 90-day Treasury bill rates are 8 percent in the United States and 12 percent in London for U.K. 90-day bills. He decides to borrow one million dollars in New York under a repurchase agreement at 8 percent at Big Bank, convert this to pound sterling (at $1.80/£) and invest in U.K. bills at 12 percent for 90 days. In order to eliminate the risk that pounds would convert to less dollars in 90 days, Fred buys a contract for a 90-day forward delivery of $1,000,000 at an agreed price of $1.82/£. Ignoring transactions costs is this a good trade?

7.   If the expected annual rate of inflation is 6 percent for Germany and 9 percent for Great Britain while the prevailing spot exchange rate is 4.25 DM per £1, predict the spot rate one year hence. State any assumptions necessary for you to make the above prediction.

8.   If Amalgamated International (U.S.) can sell in Germany its one year notes with a promise to pay in marks at a fixed rate of 6 percent and the rate of inflation is expected to be 3 percent in Germany and 6 percent in the United States, what is your projected effective cost of financing?

9.   Assume that the spot rate between marks and pounds is 4.25 DM per £1. Riskless real rates of interest in *both* Germany and Britain are 5 percent annually. If the expected annual inflation rate is 6 percent for Germany and 9 percent for Britain, what is the 90-day forward exchange rate for marks under interest rate parity? Explain.

Appendices

Table A   *Future Value of a Single Payment of $1 Invested for n Periods at K Percent*

n/K	0.5	1.0	1.5	2.0	2.5	3.0	3.5	4.0	4.5
1	1.00500	1.01000	1.01500	1.02000	1.02500	1.03000	1.03500	1.04000	1.04500
2	1.01003	1.02010	1.03023	1.04040	1.05063	1.06090	1.07123	1.08160	1.09203
3	1.01508	1.03030	1.04568	1.06121	1.07689	1.09273	1.10872	1.12486	1.14117
4	1.02015	1.04060	1.06136	1.08243	1.10381	1.12551	1.14752	1.16986	1.19252
5	1.02525	1.05101	1.07728	1.10408	1.13141	1.15927	1.18769	1.21665	1.24618
6	1.03038	1.06152	1.09344	1.12616	1.15969	1.19405	1.22926	1.26532	1.30226
7	1.03553	1.07213	1.10985	1.14869	1.18869	1.22987	1.27228	1.31593	1.36086
8	1.04071	1.08286	1.12649	1.17166	1.21840	1.26677	1.31681	1.36857	1.42210
9	1.04591	1.09368	1.14339	1.19509	1.24886	1.30477	1.36290	1.42331	1.48610
10	1.05114	1.10462	1.16054	1.21899	1.28009	1.34392	1.41060	1.48024	1.55297
11	1.05640	1.11567	1.17795	1.24337	1.31209	1.38423	1.45997	1.53945	1.62285
12	1.06168	1.12682	1.19562	1.26824	1.34489	1.42576	1.51107	1.60103	1.69588
13	1.06699	1.13809	1.21355	1.29361	1.37851	1.46853	1.56396	1.66507	1.77220
14	1.07232	1.14947	1.23176	1.31948	1.41298	1.51259	1.61870	1.73168	1.85195
15	1.07769	1.16097	1.25023	1.34587	1.44830	1.55797	1.67535	1.80094	1.93528
16	1.08307	1.17258	1.26899	1.37279	1.48451	1.60471	1.73399	1.87298	2.02237
17	1.08849	1.18430	1.28802	1.40024	1.52162	1.65285	1.79468	1.94790	2.11338
18	1.09393	1.19615	1.30734	1.42825	1.55966	1.70243	1.85749	2.02582	2.20848
19	1.09940	1.20811	1.32695	1.45681	1.59865	1.75351	1.92250	2.10685	2.30786
20	1.10490	1.22019	1.34686	1.48595	1.63862	1.80611	1.98979	2.19112	2.41172
21	1.11042	1.23239	1.36706	1.51567	1.67958	1.86029	2.05944	2.27877	2.52024
22	1.11598	1.24471	1.38757	1.54598	1.72157	1.91610	2.13152	2.36992	2.63365
23	1.12156	1.25716	1.40838	1.57690	1.76461	1.97359	2.20612	2.46471	2.75217
24	1.12716	1.26973	1.42951	1.60844	1.80873	2.03279	2.28333	2.56330	2.87602
25	1.13280	1.28243	1.45095	1.64061	1.85395	2.09378	2.36325	2.66584	3.00544
30	1.16141	1.34785	1.56309	1.81136	2.09757	2.42726	2.80680	3.24340	3.74532
35	1.19073	1.41660	1.68389	1.99989	2.37321	2.81386	3.33360	3.94609	4.66735
40	1.22080	1.48886	1.81403	2.20804	2.68507	3.26204	3.95927	4.80102	5.81637
45	1.25163	1.56481	1.95423	2.43786	3.03791	3.78160	4.70238	5.84117	7.24826
50	1.28324	1.64463	2.10526	2.69159	3.43712	4.38391	5.58495	7.10668	9.03265

n/K	5.0	5.5	6.0	6.5	7.0	7.5	8.0	8.5	9.0
1	1.05000	1.05500	1.06000	1.06500	1.07000	1.07500	1.08000	1.08500	1.09000
2	1.10250	1.11303	1.12360	1.13423	1.14490	1.15563	1.16640	1.17723	1.18810
3	1.15762	1.17424	1.19102	1.20795	1.22504	1.24230	1.25971	1.27729	1.29503
4	1.21551	1.23883	1.26248	1.28647	1.31080	1.33547	1.36049	1.38586	1.41158
5	1.27628	1.30696	1.33822	1.37009	1.40255	1.43563	1.46933	1.50366	1.53862
6	1.34010	1.37884	1.41852	1.45914	1.50073	1.54330	1.58687	1.63147	1.67710
7	1.40710	1.45468	1.50363	1.55399	1.60578	1.65905	1.71382	1.77014	1.82804
8	1.47746	1.53469	1.59385	1.65500	1.71818	1.78348	1.85093	1.92061	1.99256
9	1.55133	1.61910	1.68948	1.76257	1.83846	1.91724	1.99900	2.08386	2.17189
10	1.62889	1.70815	1.79085	1.87714	1.96715	2.06103	2.15892	2.26098	2.36736
11	1.71034	1.80209	1.89830	1.99915	2.10485	2.21561	2.33164	2.45317	2.58042
12	1.79586	1.90121	2.01219	2.12910	2.25219	2.38178	2.51817	2.66169	2.81266
13	1.88565	2.00578	2.13293	2.26749	2.40984	2.56042	2.71962	2.88793	3.06580
14	1.97993	2.11609	2.26090	2.41488	2.57853	2.75245	2.93719	3.13341	3.34172
15	2.07893	2.23248	2.39655	2.57184	2.75903	2.95888	3.17216	3.39975	3.64248
16	2.18287	2.35527	2.54035	2.73901	2.95216	3.18080	3.42594	3.68872	3.97030
17	2.29202	2.48481	2.69277	2.91705	3.15881	3.41936	3.70001	4.00227	4.32763
18	2.40662	2.62147	2.85433	3.10666	3.37993	3.67581	3.99601	4.34246	4.71712
19	2.52695	2.76565	3.02559	3.30859	3.61652	3.95149	4.31569	4.71157	5.14166
20	2.65330	2.91776	3.20713	3.52365	3.86968	4.24786	4.66095	5.11205	5.60440
21	2.78596	3.07824	3.39956	3.75269	4.14055	4.56645	5.03382	5.54658	6.10880
22	2.92526	3.24754	3.60353	3.99661	4.43039	4.90893	5.43653	6.01804	6.65859
23	3.07152	3.42616	3.81974	4.25639	4.74052	5.27710	5.87145	6.52957	7.25786
24	3.22510	3.61460	4.04892	4.53306	5.07236	5.67288	6.34117	7.08458	7.91107
25	3.38635	3.81340	4.29186	4.82771	5.42742	6.09835	6.84846	7.68677	8.62307
30	4.32194	4.98396	5.74347	6.61438	7.61223	8.75497	10.06263	11.55827	13.26766
35	5.51601	6.51384	7.68606	9.06227	10.67655	12.56890	14.78529	17.37968	20.41393
40	7.03998	8.51334	10.28568	12.41610	14.97440	18.04429	21.72443	26.13307	31.40936
45	8.98500	11.12659	13.76455	17.01114	21.00236	25.90492	31.92031	39.29510	48.32717
50	11.46738	14.54202	18.42006	23.30675	29.45689	37.18987	46.90137	59.08647	74.35733

n/K	9.5	10.0	11.0	12.0	13.0	14.0	15.0	16.0	17.0
1	1.09500	1.10000	1.11000	1.12000	1.13000	1.14000	1.15000	1.16000	1.17000
2	1.19903	1.21000	1.23210	1.25440	1.27690	1.29960	1.32250	1.34560	1.36890
3	1.31293	1.33100	1.36763	1.40493	1.44290	1.48154	1.52088	1.56090	1.60161
4	1.43766	1.46410	1.51807	1.57352	1.63047	1.68896	1.74901	1.81064	1.87389
5	1.57424	1.61051	1.68506	1.76234	1.84244	1.92542	2.01136	2.10034	2.19245
6	1.72379	1.77156	1.87041	1.97382	2.08195	2.19497	2.31306	2.43640	2.56516
7	1.88755	1.94872	2.07616	2.21068	2.35261	2.50227	2.66002	2.82622	3.00124
8	2.06687	2.14359	2.30454	2.47596	2.65845	2.85259	3.05902	3.27842	3.51145
9	2.26322	2.35795	2.55803	2.77308	3.00404	3.25195	3.51788	3.80296	4.10840
10	2.47823	2.59374	2.83942	3.10584	3.39457	3.70722	4.04556	4.41144	4.80683
11	2.71366	2.85311	3.15175	3.47855	3.83587	4.22624	4.65240	5.11727	5.62399
12	2.97146	3.13842	3.49845	3.89597	4.33453	4.81791	5.35025	5.93603	6.58007
13	3.25375	3.45227	3.88327	4.36349	4.89802	5.49242	6.15279	6.88579	7.69868
14	3.56285	3.79749	4.31043	4.88711	5.53476	6.26135	7.07571	7.98752	9.00746

Table A (*continued*)

n/K	9.5	10.0	11.0	12.0	13.0	14.0	15.0	16.0	17.0
15	3.90133	4.17724	4.78458	5.47356	6.25428	7.13794	8.13707	9.26553	10.53872
16	4.27195	4.59497	5.31089	6.13038	7.06734	8.13726	9.35763	10.74801	12.33031
17	4.67779	5.05446	5.89508	6.86603	7.98609	9.27647	10.76128	12.46769	14.42646
18	5.12218	5.55991	6.54354	7.68995	9.02428	10.57518	12.37547	14.46252	16.87896
19	5.60879	6.11590	7.26333	8.61274	10.19744	12.05571	14.23179	16.77652	19.74838
20	6.14162	6.72749	8.06229	9.64627	11.52311	13.74351	16.36657	19.46077	23.10561
21	6.72508	7.40024	8.94915	10.80383	13.02112	15.66760	18.82155	22.57450	27.03356
22	7.36396	8.14026	9.93355	12.10028	14.71386	17.86106	21.64478	26.18642	31.62926
23	8.06353	8.95428	11.02624	13.55231	16.62667	20.36161	24.89151	30.37624	37.00624
24	8.82957	9.84971	12.23913	15.17859	18.78814	23.21224	28.62523	35.23644	43.29730
25	9.66838	10.83468	13.58543	17.00002	21.23059	26.46195	32.91902	40.87428	50.65785
30	15.22034	17.44935	22.89222	29.95984	39.11602	50.95025	66.21193	85.84996	111.06470
35	23.96047	28.10234	38.57471	52.79943	72.06877	98.10037	133.17593	180.31424	243.50363
40	37.71951	45.25908	65.00059	93.05060	132.78207	188.88394	267.86444	378.72156	533.86902
45	59.37954	72.89017	109.52972	163.98685	244.64249	363.68005	538.77124	795.44482	
50	93.47761	117.39029	184.56387	289.00073	450.73822	700.23498			

n/K	18.0	19.0	20.0	21.0	22.0	23.0	24.0	25.0	30.0
1	1.18000	1.19000	1.20000	1.21000	1.22000	1.23000	1.24000	1.25000	1.30000
2	1.39240	1.41610	1.44000	1.46410	1.48840	1.51290	1.53760	1.56250	1.69000
3	1.64303	1.68516	1.72800	1.77156	1.81585	1.86087	1.90662	1.95312	2.19700
4	1.93878	2.00534	2.07360	2.14359	2.21533	2.28887	2.36421	2.44141	2.85610
5	2.28776	2.38635	2.48832	2.59374	2.70271	2.81531	2.93163	3.05176	3.71293
6	2.69956	2.83976	2.98598	3.13843	3.29730	3.46283	3.63522	3.81470	4.82681
7	3.18548	3.37932	3.58318	3.79750	4.02271	4.25928	4.50767	4.76837	6.27485
8	3.75886	4.02139	4.29982	4.59497	4.90771	5.23891	5.58951	5.96046	8.15730
9	4.43546	4.78545	5.15978	5.55992	5.98740	6.44386	6.93099	7.45058	10.60450
10	5.23384	5.69468	6.19174	6.72750	7.30463	7.92595	8.59443	9.31323	13.78584
11	6.17593	6.77667	7.43000	8.14028	8.91165	9.74891	10.65709	11.64153	17.92160
12	7.28760	8.06424	8.91610	9.84974	10.87221	11.99117	13.21479	14.55192	23.29808
13	8.59937	9.59645	10.69933	11.91818	13.26410	14.74913	16.38634	18.18990	30.28749
14	10.14725	11.41977	12.83919	14.42100	16.18220	18.14143	20.31906	22.73737	39.37374
15	11.97376	13.58953	15.40703	17.44941	19.74228	22.31396	25.19564	28.42171	51.18586
16	14.12904	16.17154	18.48843	21.11378	24.08558	27.44617	31.24259	35.52714	66.54163
17	16.67227	19.24413	22.18612	25.54768	29.38441	33.75880	38.74081	44.40892	86.50410
18	19.67328	22.90052	26.62334	30.91269	35.84898	41.52332	48.03860	55.51115	112.45534
19	23.21447	27.25162	31.94802	37.40435	43.73576	51.07368	59.56787	69.38895	146.19192
20	27.39308	32.42942	38.33762	45.25927	53.35761	62.82063	73.86417	86.73618	190.04950
21	32.32384	38.59101	46.00515	54.76372	65.09630	77.26938	91.59157	108.42023	247.06436
22	38.14213	45.92330	55.20618	66.26410	79.41746	95.04134	113.57353	135.52527	321.18365
23	45.00771	54.64874	66.24742	80.17957	96.88931	116.90085	140.83121	169.40658	417.53869
24	53.10911	65.03198	79.49690	97.01727	118.20494	143.78802	174.63068	211.75824	542.80029
25	62.66875	77.38808	95.39627	117.39090	144.21005	176.85928	216.54205	264.69781	705.64038
30	143.37097	184.67529	237.37649	304.48181	389.75757	497.91296	634.82006	807.79357	
35	327.99817	440.70062	590.66882	789.74731					
40	750.38061								
45									
50									

n/K	35.0	40.0	45.0	50.0
1	1.35000	1.40000	1.45000	1.50000
2	1.82250	1.96000	2.10250	2.25000
3	2.46038	2.74400	3.04862	3.37500
4	3.32151	3.84160	4.42051	5.06250
5	4.48404	5.37824	6.40973	7.59375
6	6.05345	7.52954	9.29412	11.39062
7	8.17216	10.54136	13.47647	17.08594
8	11.03242	14.75790	19.54088	25.62891
9	14.89376	20.66106	28.33427	38.44336
10	20.10658	28.92548	41.08469	57.66504
11	27.14389	40.49568	59.57281	86.49756
12	36.64426	56.69395	86.38058	129.74634
13	49.46975	79.37154	125.25185	194.61951
14	66.78416	111.12018	181.61517	291.92926
15	90.15863	155.56824	263.34198	437.89392
16	121.71419	217.79556	381.84594	656.84082
17	164.31418	304.91382	553.67663	985.26123
18	221.82416	426.87933	802.83105	
19	299.46264	597.63110		
20	404.27466	836.68359		
21	545.77087			
22	736.79065			
23	994.66747			
24				
25				
30				
35				

Table B   *Future Value of an Annuity of $1 Per Year Invested for n Periods at K Percent*

n/K	0.5	1.0	1.5	2.0	2.5	3.0	3.5	4.0	4.5
1	1.00002	1.00000	1.00001	1.00000	1.00000	1.00000	1.00000	1.00000	1.00000
2	2.00505	2.00999	2.01502	2.02000	2.02500	2.03000	2.03501	2.04000	2.04500
3	3.01509	3.03009	3.04526	3.06040	3.07563	3.09090	3.10623	3.12160	3.13703
4	4.03023	4.06039	4.09094	4.12161	4.15253	4.18363	4.21495	4.24646	4.27819
5	5.05042	5.10099	5.15232	5.20405	5.25635	5.30914	5.36248	5.41632	5.47072
6	6.07567	6.15199	6.22961	6.30813	6.38775	6.46841	6.55017	6.63297	6.71690
7	7.10607	7.21350	7.32307	7.43429	7.54745	7.66246	7.77943	7.89829	8.01916
8	8.14166	8.28564	8.43293	8.58298	8.73614	8.89234	9.05171	9.21422	9.38002
9	9.18241	9.36849	9.55942	9.75465	9.95455	10.15910	10.36852	10.58279	10.80212
10	10.22835	10.46217	10.70283	10.94974	11.20341	11.46388	11.73143	12.00610	12.28822
11	11.27949	11.56678	11.86339	12.16873	12.48350	12.80780	13.14203	13.48634	13.84118
12	12.33597	12.68246	13.04135	13.41212	13.79560	14.19203	14.60201	15.02579	15.46404
13	13.39769	13.80928	14.23699	14.68036	15.14050	15.61779	16.11309	16.62682	17.15993
14	14.46466	14.94737	15.45054	15.97396	16.51900	17.08632	17.67704	18.29190	18.93213
15	15.53702	16.09683	16.68232	17.29344	17.93198	18.59892	19.29574	20.02357	20.78407
16	16.61477	17.25781	17.93257	18.63933	19.38029	20.15688	20.97110	21.82452	22.71935
17	17.69786	18.43038	19.20156	20.01212	20.86480	21.76159	22.70509	23.69750	24.74172
18	18.78638	19.61467	20.48961	21.41236	22.38643	23.41444	24.49977	25.64540	26.85509
19	19.88034	20.81082	21.79697	22.84061	23.94609	25.11686	26.35727	27.67121	29.06358
20	20.97979	22.01893	23.12393	24.29742	25.54475	26.87038	28.27978	29.77806	31.37144
21	22.08476	23.23911	24.47081	25.78337	27.18338	28.67649	30.26958	31.96918	33.78317
22	23.19517	24.47150	25.83788	27.29903	28.86295	30.53678	32.32902	34.24795	36.30341
23	24.31116	25.71621	27.22548	28.84501	30.58453	32.45288	34.46053	36.61787	38.93706
24	25.43278	26.97337	28.63387	30.42194	32.34916	34.42648	36.66666	39.08259	41.68922
25	26.55997	28.24309	30.06637	32.03036	34.15790	36.45925	38.95000	41.64588	44.56524
30	32.28107	34.78477	37.53913	40.56816	43.90288	47.57542	51.62289	56.08491	61.00713
35	38.14664	41.66012	45.59267	49.99460	54.92844	60.46209	66.67429	73.65218	81.49670
40	44.16037	48.88621	54.26862	60.40215	67.40286	75.40129	84.55064	95.02545	107.03043
45	50.32597	56.48086	63.61508	71.89293	81.51654	92.71988	105.78220	121.02928	138.85013
50	56.64716	64.46292	73.68387	84.57967	97.48485	112.79690	130.99856	152.66696	178.50323

n/K	5.0	5.5	6.0	6.5	7.0	7.5	8.0	8.5	9.0
1	1.00000	1.00000	1.00000	1.00000	1.00000	1.00000	1.00000	1.00000	1.00000
2	2.05000	2.05500	2.06000	2.06500	2.07000	2.07500	2.08000	2.08500	2.09000
3	3.15250	3.16803	3.18360	3.19923	3.21490	3.23063	3.24639	3.26223	3.27810
4	4.31012	4.34227	4.37461	4.40718	4.43994	4.47293	4.50611	4.53952	4.57312
5	5.52563	5.58110	5.63709	5.69364	5.75073	5.80840	5.86655	5.92538	5.98471
6	6.80191	6.88806	6.97530	7.06373	7.15328	7.24403	7.33592	7.42904	7.52333
7	8.14200	8.26691	8.39382	8.52288	8.65401	8.78733	8.92278	9.06051	9.20042
8	9.54910	9.72159	9.89745	10.07687	10.25979	10.44638	10.63661	10.83065	11.02846
9	11.02656	11.25628	11.49129	11.73187	11.97797	12.22986	12.48754	12.75125	13.02102
10	12.57789	12.87538	13.18076	13.49444	13.81643	14.14710	14.48653	14.83511	15.19292
11	14.20678	14.58352	14.97161	15.37158	15.78358	16.20813	16.64545	17.09610	17.56028
12	15.91712	16.38562	16.86990	17.37073	17.88842	18.42375	18.97709	19.54927	20.14070
13	17.71297	18.28683	18.88209	19.49983	20.14061	20.80553	21.49525	22.21096	22.95336
14	19.59863	20.29262	21.01501	21.76732	22.55044	23.36595	24.21487	25.09890	26.01916
15	21.57855	22.40871	23.27591	24.18220	25.12897	26.11840	27.15205	28.23231	29.36087
16	23.65747	24.64119	25.67246	26.75405	27.88799	29.07729	30.32421	31.63205	33.00336
17	25.84035	26.99646	28.21280	29.49307	30.84015	32.25808	33.75014	35.32078	36.97366
18	28.13236	29.48127	30.90556	32.41012	33.99895	35.67744	37.45015	39.32304	41.30129
19	30.53898	32.10274	33.75990	35.51678	37.37888	39.35325	41.44616	43.66550	46.01839
20	33.06593	34.86841	36.78548	38.82537	40.99540	43.30476	45.76185	48.37707	51.16005
21	35.71922	37.78617	39.99266	42.34901	44.86507	47.55261	50.42280	53.48914	56.76445
22	38.50519	40.86442	43.39216	46.10171	49.00562	52.11906	55.45660	59.03572	62.87325
23	41.43045	44.11195	46.99567	50.09833	53.43601	57.02799	60.89312	65.05377	69.53183
24	44.50197	47.53812	50.81541	54.35473	58.17652	62.30511	66.76457	71.58333	76.78970
25	47.72707	51.15272	54.86433	58.88779	63.24887	67.97800	73.10573	78.66792	84.70077
30	66.43880	72.43571	79.05789	86.37503	94.46049	103.39960	113.28285	124.21497	136.30728
35	90.32021	100.25168	111.43434	124.03497	138.23642	154.25198	172.31615	192.70209	215.71033
40	120.79962	136.60611	154.76126	175.63235	199.63434	227.25717	259.05542	295.68323	337.88171
45	159.69995	184.11990	212.74246	246.32523	285.74811	332.06555	386.50384	450.53155	525.85742
50	209.34769	246.21853	290.33435	343.18072	406.52698	482.53161	573.76721	683.37036	815.08142

n/K	9.5	10.0	11.0	12.0	13.0	14.0	15.0	16.0	17.0
1	1.00000	1.00000	1.00000	1.00000	1.00000	1.00000	1.00000	1.00000	1.00000
2	2.09500	2.10000	2.11000	2.12000	2.13000	2.14000	2.15000	2.16000	2.17000
3	3.29403	3.31000	3.34210	3.37440	3.40690	3.43960	3.47250	3.50560	3.53890
4	4.60696	4.64099	4.70973	4.77932	4.84980	4.92115	4.99338	5.06650	5.14051
5	6.04462	6.10509	6.22779	6.35284	6.48028	6.61011	6.74238	6.87714	7.01440
6	7.61886	7.71560	7.91285	8.11518	8.32272	8.53553	8.75374	8.97748	9.20685
7	9.34266	9.48716	9.78326	10.08900	10.40467	10.73050	11.06681	11.41388	11.77202
8	11.23021	11.43587	11.85942	12.29968	12.75728	13.23277	13.72683	14.24010	14.77326
9	13.29709	13.57945	14.16395	14.77563	15.41573	16.08536	16.78586	17.51852	18.28471
10	15.56031	15.93740	16.72198	17.54871	18.41978	19.33731	20.30374	21.32148	22.39312
11	18.03854	18.53114	19.56140	20.65455	21.81435	23.04454	24.34931	25.73292	27.19995
12	20.75220	21.38425	22.71315	24.13309	25.65022	27.27077	29.00171	30.85019	32.82394
13	23.72367	24.52267	26.21159	28.02906	29.98474	32.08869	34.35195	36.78622	39.40400
14	26.97741	27.97493	30.09486	32.39256	34.88277	37.58111	40.50475	43.67201	47.10268

Table B (continued)

n/K	9.5	10.0	11.0	12.0	13.0	14.0	15.0	16.0	17.0
15	30.54027	31.77242	34.40530	37.27964	40.41754	43.84246	47.58047	51.65954	56.11015
16	34.44160	35.94966	39.18986	42.75320	46.67182	50.98041	55.71755	60.92506	66.64886
17	38.71355	40.54462	44.50075	48.88358	53.73917	59.11768	65.07520	71.67308	78.97919
18	43.39136	45.59908	50.39583	55.74960	61.72527	68.39415	75.83649	84.14076	93.40565
19	48.51353	51.15898	56.93937	63.43954	70.74956	78.96933	88.21196	98.60327	110.28461
20	54.12233	57.27487	64.20267	72.05228	80.94701	91.02505	102.44377	115.37981	130.03299
21	60.26395	64.00235	72.26497	81.69855	92.47012	104.76857	118.81032	134.84061	153.13858
22	66.98903	71.40257	81.21410	92.50236	105.49126	120.43616	137.63187	157.41510	180.17215
23	74.35298	79.54283	91.14766	104.60261	120.20514	138.29724	159.27670	183.60153	211.80142
24	82.41653	88.49712	102.17387	118.15494	136.83182	158.65887	184.16821	213.97778	248.80768
25	91.24614	98.34679	114.41298	133.33350	155.61996	181.87109	212.79346	249.21423	292.10504
30	149.68783	164.49353	199.02020	241.33197	293.20013	356.78753	434.74615	530.31225	647.43945
35	241.68915	271.02344	341.58832	431.66198	546.68286	693.57421	881.17285		
40	386.52118	442.59082	581.82361	767.08837					
45	614.52148	718.90173	986.63391						
50	973.44860								

n/K	18.0	19.0	20.0	21.0	22.0	23.0	24.0	25.0	30.0
1	1.00000	1.00000	1.00000	1.00000	1.00000	1.00000	1.00000	1.00000	1.00000
2	2.18000	2.19000	2.20000	2.21000	2.22000	2.23000	2.24000	2.25000	2.30000
3	3.57240	3.60610	3.64000	3.67410	3.70840	3.74290	3.77760	3.81250	3.99000
4	5.21544	5.29126	5.36800	5.44566	5.52425	5.60377	5.68423	5.76562	6.18700
5	7.15422	7.29660	7.44160	7.58925	7.73958	7.89263	8.04844	8.20703	9.04310
6	9.44197	9.68295	9.92992	10.18299	10.44229	10.70794	10.98006	11.25879	12.75603
7	12.14153	12.52271	12.91591	13.32142	13.73960	14.17077	14.61528	15.07349	17.58283
8	15.32701	15.90203	16.49909	17.11892	17.76230	18.43004	19.12295	19.84186	23.85768
9	19.08587	19.92342	20.79891	21.71390	22.67001	23.66895	24.71246	25.80232	32.01498
10	23.52133	24.70886	25.95869	27.27381	28.65741	30.11282	31.64345	33.25291	42.61948
11	28.75517	30.40355	32.15043	34.00131	35.96204	38.03876	40.23788	42.56613	56.40532
12	34.93111	37.18022	39.58052	42.14159	44.87369	47.78767	50.89497	54.20766	74.32692
13	42.21871	45.24446	48.49663	51.99133	55.74590	59.77884	64.10976	68.75958	97.62498
14	50.81808	54.84090	59.19595	63.90952	69.00999	74.52797	80.49609	86.94946	127.91246
15	60.96533	66.26070	72.03516	78.33052	85.19220	92.66942	100.81517	109.68684	167.28619
16	72.93910	79.85020	87.44217	95.77991	104.93445	114.98337	126.01079	138.10855	218.47208
17	87.06815	96.02176	105.93062	116.89369	129.02002	142.42956	157.25339	173.63568	285.01367
18	103.74043	115.26588	128.11673	142.44137	158.40445	176.18835	195.99420	218.04462	371.51776
19	123.41371	138.16641	154.74008	173.35403	194.25345	217.71167	244.03281	273.55578	483.97308
20	146.62820	165.41800	186.68814	210.75842	237.98913	268.78540	303.60071	342.94470	630.16491
21	174.02130	197.84741	225.02576	256.01770	291.34680	331.60602	377.46490	429.68091	820.21447
22	206.34515	236.43844	271.03088	310.78143	356.44305	408.87536	469.05639	538.10107	
23	244.48724	282.36181	326.23712	377.04553	435.86053	503.91674	582.63012	673.62634	
24	289.49505	337.01044	392.48456	457.22509	532.74975	620.81750	723.46118	843.03295	
25	342.60418	402.04254	471.98138	554.24231	650.95483	764.60559	898.09191		
30	790.94982	966.71203							
35									
40									
45									
50									

n/K	35.0	40.0	45.0	50.0
1	1.00000	1.00000	1.00000	1.00000
2	2.35000	2.40000	2.45000	2.50000
3	4.17250	4.36000	4.55250	4.75000
4	6.63288	7.10400	7.60113	8.12500
5	9.95439	10.94560	12.02163	13.18750
6	14.43843	16.32384	18.43137	20.78125
7	20.49187	23.85339	27.72548	32.17187
8	28.66404	34.39474	41.20195	49.25781
9	39.69646	49.15265	60.74284	74.88672
10	54.59023	69.81371	89.07710	113.33008
11	74.69681	98.73920	130.16180	170.99512
12	101.84073	139.23486	189.73465	257.49267
13	138.48498	195.92883	276.11523	387.23901
14	187.95474	275.30041	401.36706	581.85852
15	254.73892	386.42053	582.98217	873.78784
16	344.89764	541.98889	846.32433	
17	466.61187	759.78442		
18	630.92614			
19	852.75036			
20				
21				
22				
23				
24				
25				
30				
35				

Table C   *Present Value of $1 Received in n Periods of K Percent*

n/K	0.5	1.0	1.5	2.0	2.5	3.0	3.5	4.0	4.5
1	0.99502	0.99010	0.98522	0.98039	0.97561	0.97087	0.96618	0.96154	0.95694
2	0.99007	0.98030	0.97066	0.96117	0.95181	0.94260	0.93351	0.92456	0.91573
3	0.98515	0.97059	0.95632	0.94232	0.92860	0.91514	0.90194	0.88900	0.87630
4	0.98025	0.96098	0.94218	0.92385	0.90595	0.88849	0.87144	0.85480	0.83856
5	0.97537	0.95147	0.92826	0.90573	0.88385	0.86261	0.84197	0.82193	0.80245
6	0.97052	0.94205	0.91454	0.88797	0.86230	0.83748	0.81350	0.79031	0.76790
7	0.96569	0.93272	0.90103	0.87056	0.84126	0.81309	0.78599	0.75992	0.73483
8	0.96088	0.92348	0.88771	0.85349	0.82075	0.78941	0.75941	0.73069	0.70319
9	0.95610	0.91434	0.87459	0.83676	0.80073	0.76642	0.73373	0.70259	0.67290
10	0.95135	0.90529	0.86167	0.82035	0.78120	0.74409	0.70892	0.67556	0.64393
11	0.94661	0.89632	0.84893	0.80426	0.76214	0.72242	0.68495	0.64958	0.61620
12	0.94190	0.88745	0.83639	0.78849	0.74356	0.70138	0.66178	0.62460	0.58966
13	0.93722	0.87866	0.82403	0.77303	0.72542	0.68095	0.63940	0.60057	0.56427
14	0.93255	0.86996	0.81185	0.75787	0.70773	0.66112	0.61778	0.57748	0.53997
15	0.92791	0.86135	0.79985	0.74301	0.69046	0.64186	0.59689	0.55526	0.51672
16	0.92330	0.85282	0.78803	0.72845	0.67362	0.62317	0.57671	0.53391	0.49447
17	0.91870	0.84438	0.77638	0.71416	0.65719	0.60502	0.55720	0.51337	0.47318
18	0.91413	0.83602	0.76491	0.70016	0.64117	0.58739	0.53836	0.49363	0.45280
19	0.90959	0.82774	0.75361	0.68643	0.62553	0.57029	0.52015	0.47464	0.43330
20	0.90506	0.81954	0.74247	0.67297	0.61027	0.55368	0.50257	0.45639	0.41464
21	0.90056	0.81143	0.73150	0.65978	0.59539	0.53755	0.48557	0.43883	0.39679
22	0.89608	0.80340	0.72069	0.64684	0.58086	0.52189	0.46915	0.42196	0.37970
23	0.89162	0.79544	0.71003	0.63416	0.56670	0.50669	0.45328	0.40573	0.36335
24	0.88718	0.78757	0.69954	0.62172	0.55287	0.49193	0.43796	0.39012	0.34770
25	0.88277	0.77977	0.68920	0.60953	0.53939	0.47761	0.42315	0.37512	0.33273
30	0.86103	0.74192	0.63976	0.55207	0.47674	0.41199	0.35628	0.30832	0.26700
35	0.83982	0.70591	0.59386	0.50003	0.42137	0.35538	0.29998	0.25342	0.21425
40	0.81913	0.67165	0.55126	0.45289	0.37243	0.30656	0.25257	0.20829	0.17193
45	0.79896	0.63906	0.51171	0.41020	0.32917	0.26444	0.21266	0.17120	0.13796
50	0.77928	0.60804	0.47500	0.37153	0.29094	0.22811	0.17905	0.14071	0.11071

n/K	5.0	5.5	6.0	6.5	7.0	7.5	8.0	8.5	9.0
1	0.95238	0.94787	0.94340	0.93897	0.93458	0.93023	0.92593	0.92166	0.91743
2	0.90703	0.89845	0.89000	0.88166	0.87344	0.86533	0.85734	0.84946	0.84168
3	0.86384	0.85161	0.83962	0.82785	0.81630	0.80496	0.79383	0.78291	0.77218
4	0.82270	0.80722	0.79209	0.77732	0.76290	0.74880	0.73503	0.72157	0.70843
5	0.78353	0.76513	0.74726	0.72988	0.71299	0.69656	0.68058	0.66505	0.64993
6	0.74622	0.72525	0.70496	0.68533	0.66634	0.64796	0.63017	0.61294	0.59627
7	0.71068	0.68744	0.66506	0.64351	0.62275	0.60275	0.58349	0.56493	0.54703
8	0.67684	0.65160	0.62741	0.60423	0.58201	0.56070	0.54027	0.52067	0.50187
9	0.64461	0.61763	0.59190	0.56735	0.54393	0.52158	0.50025	0.47988	0.46043
10	0.61391	0.58543	0.55840	0.53273	0.50835	0.48519	0.46319	0.44229	0.42241
11	0.58468	0.55491	0.52679	0.50021	0.47509	0.45134	0.42888	0.40764	0.38753
12	0.55684	0.52598	0.49697	0.46968	0.44401	0.41985	0.39711	0.37570	0.35553
13	0.53032	0.49856	0.46884	0.44102	0.41496	0.39056	0.36770	0.34627	0.32618
14	0.50507	0.47257	0.44230	0.41410	0.38782	0.36331	0.34046	0.31914	0.29925
15	0.48102	0.44793	0.41727	0.38883	0.36245	0.33797	0.31524	0.29414	0.27454
16	0.45811	0.42458	0.39365	0.36510	0.33874	0.31439	0.29189	0.27110	0.25187
17	0.43630	0.40245	0.37137	0.34281	0.31657	0.29245	0.27027	0.24986	0.23107
18	0.41552	0.38147	0.35034	0.32189	0.29586	0.27205	0.25025	0.23028	0.21199
19	0.39573	0.36158	0.33051	0.30224	0.27651	0.25307	0.23171	0.21224	0.19449
20	0.37689	0.34273	0.31180	0.28380	0.25842	0.23541	0.21455	0.19562	0.17843
21	0.35894	0.32486	0.29416	0.26648	0.24151	0.21899	0.19866	0.18029	0.16370
22	0.34185	0.30793	0.27751	0.25021	0.22571	0.20371	0.18394	0.16617	0.15018
23	0.32557	0.29187	0.26180	0.23494	0.21095	0.18950	0.17032	0.15315	0.13778
24	0.31007	0.27666	0.24698	0.22060	0.19715	0.17628	0.15770	0.14115	0.12641
25	0.29530	0.26223	0.23300	0.20714	0.18425	0.16398	0.14602	0.13009	0.11597
30	0.23138	0.20064	0.17411	0.15119	0.13137	0.11422	0.09938	0.08652	0.07537
35	0.18129	0.15352	0.13011	0.11035	0.09366	0.07956	0.06763	0.05754	0.04899
40	0.14205	0.11746	0.09722	0.08054	0.06678	0.05542	0.04603	0.03827	0.03184
45	0.11130	0.08987	0.07265	0.05879	0.04761	0.03860	0.03133	0.02545	0.02069
50	0.08720	0.06877	0.05429	0.04291	0.03395	0.02689	0.02132	0.01692	0.01345

n/K	9.5	10.0	11.0	12.0	13.0	14.0	15.0	16.0	17.0
1	0.91324	0.90909	0.90090	0.89286	0.88496	0.87719	0.86957	0.86207	0.85470
2	0.83401	0.82645	0.81162	0.79719	0.78315	0.76947	0.75614	0.74316	0.73051
3	0.76165	0.75131	0.73119	0.71178	0.69305	0.67497	0.65752	0.64066	0.62437
4	0.69557	0.68301	0.65873	0.63552	0.61332	0.59208	0.57175	0.55229	0.53365
5	0.63523	0.62092	0.59345	0.56743	0.54276	0.51937	0.49718	0.47611	0.45611
6	0.58012	0.56447	0.53464	0.50663	0.48032	0.45559	0.43233	0.41044	0.38984
7	0.52979	0.51316	0.48166	0.45235	0.42506	0.39964	0.37594	0.35383	0.33320
8	0.48382	0.46651	0.43393	0.40388	0.37616	0.35056	0.32690	0.30503	0.28478
9	0.44185	0.42410	0.39093	0.36061	0.33288	0.30751	0.28426	0.26295	0.24340
10	0.40351	0.38554	0.35218	0.32197	0.29459	0.26974	0.24718	0.22668	0.20804
11	0.36851	0.35049	0.31728	0.28748	0.26070	0.23662	0.21494	0.19542	0.17781
12	0.33653	0.31863	0.28584	0.25668	0.23071	0.20756	0.18691	0.16846	0.15197
13	0.30734	0.28966	0.25751	0.22917	0.20416	0.18207	0.16253	0.14523	0.12989
14	0.28067	0.26333	0.23200	0.20462	0.18068	0.15971	0.14133	0.12520	0.11102
15	0.25632	0.23939	0.20900	0.18270	0.15989	0.14010	0.12289	0.10793	0.09489
16	0.23408	0.21763	0.18829	0.16312	0.14150	0.12289	0.10686	0.09304	0.08110

Table C (*continued*)

n/K	9.5	10.0	11.0	12.0	13.0	14.0	15.0	16.0	17.0
17	0.21378	0.19784	0.16963	0.14564	0.12522	0.10780	0.09293	0.08021	0.06932
18	0.19523	0.17986	0.15282	0.13004	0.11081	0.09456	0.08080	0.06914	0.05925
19	0.17829	0.16351	0.13768	0.11611	0.09806	0.08295	0.07027	0.05961	0.05064
20	0.16282	0.14864	0.12403	0.10367	0.08678	0.07276	0.06110	0.05139	0.04328
21	0.14870	0.13513	0.11174	0.09256	0.07680	0.06383	0.05313	0.04430	0.03699
22	0.13580	0.12285	0.10067	0.08264	0.06796	0.05599	0.04620	0.03819	0.03162
23	0.12402	0.11168	0.09069	0.07379	0.06014	0.04911	0.04017	0.03292	0.02702
24	0.11326	0.10153	0.08171	0.06588	0.05323	0.04308	0.03493	0.02838	0.02310
25	0.10343	0.09230	0.07361	0.05882	0.04710	0.03779	0.03038	0.02447	0.01974
30	0.06570	0.05731	0.04368	0.03338	0.02556	0.01963	0.01510	0.01165	0.00900
35	0.04174	0.03558	0.02592	0.01894	0.01388	0.01019	0.00751	0.00555	0.00411
40	0.02651	0.02210	0.01538	0.01075	0.00753	0.00529	0.00373	0.00264	0.00187
45	0.01684	0.01372	0.00913	0.00610	0.00409	0.00275	0.00186	0.00126	0.00085
50	0.01070	0.00852	0.00542	0.00346	0.00222	0.00143	0.00092	0.00060	0.00039

n/K	18.0	19.0	20.0	21.0	22.0	23.0	24.0	25.0	30.0
1	0.84746	0.84034	0.83333	0.82645	0.81967	0.81301	0.80645	0.80000	0.76923
2	0.71818	0.70616	0.69444	0.68301	0.67186	0.66098	0.65036	0.64000	0.59172
3	0.60863	0.59342	0.57870	0.56447	0.55071	0.53738	0.52449	0.51200	0.45517
4	0.51579	0.49867	0.48225	0.46651	0.45140	0.43690	0.42297	0.40960	0.35013
5	0.43711	0.41905	0.40188	0.38554	0.37000	0.35520	0.34111	0.32768	0.26933
6	0.37043	0.35214	0.33490	0.31863	0.30328	0.28878	0.27509	0.26214	0.20718
7	0.31392	0.29592	0.27908	0.26333	0.24859	0.23478	0.22184	0.20972	0.15937
8	0.26604	0.24867	0.23257	0.21763	0.20376	0.19088	0.17891	0.16777	0.12259
9	0.22546	0.20897	0.19381	0.17986	0.16702	0.15519	0.14428	0.13422	0.09430
10	0.19106	0.17560	0.16151	0.14864	0.13690	0.12617	0.11635	0.10737	0.07254
11	0.16192	0.14757	0.13459	0.12285	0.11221	0.10258	0.09383	0.08590	0.05580
12	0.13722	0.12400	0.11216	0.10153	0.09198	0.08339	0.07567	0.06872	0.04292
13	0.11629	0.10421	0.09346	0.08391	0.07539	0.06780	0.06103	0.05498	0.03302
14	0.09855	0.08757	0.07789	0.06934	0.06180	0.05512	0.04921	0.04398	0.02540
15	0.08352	0.07359	0.06491	0.05731	0.05065	0.04481	0.03969	0.03518	0.01954
16	0.07078	0.06184	0.05409	0.04736	0.04152	0.03643	0.03201	0.02815	0.01503
17	0.05998	0.05196	0.04507	0.03914	0.03403	0.02962	0.02581	0.02252	0.01156
18	0.05083	0.04367	0.03756	0.03235	0.02789	0.02408	0.02082	0.01801	0.00889
19	0.04308	0.03670	0.03130	0.02673	0.02286	0.01958	0.01679	0.01441	0.00684
20	0.03651	0.03084	0.02608	0.02209	0.01874	0.01592	0.01354	0.01153	0.00526
21	0.03094	0.02591	0.02174	0.01826	0.01536	0.01294	0.01092	0.00922	0.00405
22	0.02622	0.02178	0.01811	0.01509	0.01259	0.01052	0.00880	0.00738	0.00311
23	0.02222	0.01830	0.01509	0.01247	0.01032	0.00855	0.00710	0.00590	0.00239
24	0.01883	0.01538	0.01258	0.01031	0.00846	0.00695	0.00573	0.00472	0.00184
25	0.01596	0.01292	0.01048	0.00852	0.00693	0.00565	0.00462	0.00378	0.00142
30	0.00697	0.00541	0.00421	0.00328	0.00257	0.00201	0.00158	0.00124	0.00038
35	0.00305	0.00227	0.00169	0.00127	0.00095	0.00071	0.00054	0.00041	0.00010
40	0.00133	0.00095	0.00068	0.00049	0.00035	0.00025	0.00018	0.00013	
45	0.00058	0.00040	0.00027	0.00019	0.00013				
50	0.00025	0.00017	0.00011						

n/K	35.0	40.0	45.0	50.0
1	0.74074	0.71429	0.68966	0.66667
2	0.54870	0.51020	0.47562	0.44444
3	0.40644	0.36443	0.32802	0.29630
4	0.30107	0.26031	0.22622	0.19753
5	0.22301	0.18593	0.15601	0.13169
6	0.16520	0.13281	0.10759	0.08779
7	0.12237	0.09486	0.07420	0.05853
8	0.09064	0.06776	0.05117	0.03902
9	0.06714	0.04840	0.03529	0.02601
10	0.04973	0.03457	0.02434	0.01734
11	0.03684	0.02469	0.01679	0.01156
12	0.02729	0.01764	0.01158	0.00771
13	0.02021	0.01260	0.00798	0.00514
14	0.01497	0.00900	0.00551	0.00343
15	0.01109	0.00643	0.00380	0.00228
16	0.00822	0.00459	0.00262	0.00152
17	0.00609	0.00328	0.00181	0.00101
18	0.00451	0.00234	0.00125	0.00068
19	0.00334	0.00167	0.00086	0.00045
20	0.00247	0.00120	0.00059	0.00030
21	0.00183	0.00085	0.00041	0.00020
22	0.00136	0.00061	0.00028	0.00013
23	0.00101	0.00044	0.00019	
24	0.00074	0.00031	0.00013	
25	0.00055	0.00022		
30	0.00012			
35				
40				
45				
50				

Table D   *Present Value of an Annuity of $1 Received Each Year for n Periods at K Percent*

n/K	0.5	1.0	1.5	2.0	2.5	3.0	3.5	4.0	4.5
1	0.99505	0.99010	0.98523	0.98039	0.97561	0.97087	0.96619	0.96154	0.95694
2	1.98515	1.97038	1.95590	1.94156	1.92743	1.91347	1.89970	1.88609	1.87267
3	2.97031	2.94097	2.91223	2.88388	2.85603	2.82861	2.80164	2.77509	2.74897
4	3.95062	3.90195	3.85442	3.80773	3.76198	3.71710	3.67309	3.62989	3.58753
5	4.92603	4.85342	4.78269	4.71346	4.64584	4.57971	4.51507	4.45182	4.38998
6	5.89654	5.79545	5.69723	5.60144	5.50813	5.41719	5.32856	5.24213	5.15788
7	6.86225	6.72816	6.59828	6.47199	6.34940	6.23028	6.11456	6.00205	5.89270
8	7.82319	7.65165	7.48600	7.32549	7.17016	7.01969	6.87397	6.73274	6.59589
9	8.77933	8.56599	8.36059	8.16225	7.97088	7.78611	7.60770	7.43533	7.26879
10	9.73070	9.47127	9.22227	8.98260	8.75208	8.53020	8.31662	8.11089	7.91272
11	10.67731	10.36759	10.07121	9.78686	9.51423	9.25263	9.00157	8.76047	8.52892
12	11.61929	11.25504	10.90760	10.57536	10.25779	9.95400	9.66335	9.38507	9.11858
13	12.55655	12.13370	11.73164	11.34839	10.98321	10.63495	10.30276	9.98564	9.68286
14	13.48909	13.00366	12.54349	12.10626	11.69094	11.29607	10.92054	10.56312	10.22283
15	14.41703	13.86501	13.34335	12.84928	12.38140	11.93793	11.51743	11.11838	10.73955
16	15.34039	14.71783	14.13139	13.57773	13.05503	12.56110	12.09414	11.65229	11.23402
17	16.25911	15.56220	14.90778	14.29189	13.71223	13.16612	12.65134	12.16567	11.70720
18	17.17327	16.39822	15.67270	14.99206	14.35340	13.75351	13.18971	12.65929	12.15999
19	18.08287	17.22596	16.42632	15.67848	14.97892	14.32380	13.70986	13.13393	12.59330
20	18.98797	18.04551	17.16878	16.35146	15.58920	14.87748	14.21243	13.59032	13.00794
21	19.88859	18.85693	17.90029	17.01123	16.18459	15.41502	14.69800	14.02916	13.40473
22	20.78465	19.66032	18.62098	17.65807	16.76545	15.93692	15.16715	14.45111	13.78443
23	21.67628	20.45576	19.33103	18.29222	17.33214	16.44361	15.62044	14.85684	14.14778
24	22.56351	21.24332	20.03057	18.91396	17.88502	16.93555	16.05839	15.24696	14.49548
25	23.44631	22.02309	20.71978	19.52348	18.42442	17.41314	16.48154	15.62208	14.82821
30	27.79483	25.80764	24.01602	22.39648	20.93033	19.60044	18.39207	17.29203	16.28889
35	32.03626	29.40850	27.07580	24.99865	23.14520	21.48722	20.00069	18.66461	17.46102
40	36.17325	32.83461	29.91607	27.35551	25.10282	23.11478	21.35509	19.79277	18.40159
45	40.20834	36.09442	32.55257	29.49020	26.83307	24.51871	22.49548	20.72004	19.15635
50	44.14400	39.19602	34.99992	31.42364	28.36235	25.72977	23.45564	21.48218	19.76201

n/K	5.0	5.5	6.0	6.5	7.0	7.5	8.0	8.5	9.0
1	0.95238	0.94787	0.94340	0.93897	0.93458	0.93023	0.92593	0.92166	0.91743
2	1.85941	1.84632	1.83339	1.82063	1.80802	1.79557	1.78326	1.77112	1.75911
3	2.72325	2.69794	2.67301	2.64848	2.62431	2.60053	2.57709	2.55402	2.53129
4	3.54595	3.50516	3.46510	3.42580	3.38721	3.34933	3.31212	3.27560	3.23972
5	4.32947	4.27029	4.21236	4.15568	4.10019	4.04589	3.99271	3.94064	3.88965
6	5.07569	4.99554	4.91732	4.84102	4.76653	4.69385	4.62288	4.55359	4.48592
7	5.78637	5.68297	5.58237	5.48452	5.38929	5.29660	5.20636	5.11852	5.03295
8	6.46321	6.33457	6.20978	6.08876	5.97129	5.85731	5.74663	5.63919	5.53482
9	7.10782	6.95220	6.80168	6.65611	6.51523	6.37889	6.24688	6.11907	5.99524
10	7.72173	7.53763	7.36008	7.18884	7.02358	6.86408	6.71008	6.56135	6.41765
11	8.30641	8.09254	7.88686	7.68905	7.49867	7.31543	7.13896	6.96899	6.80519
12	8.86325	8.61853	8.38383	8.15873	7.94268	7.73528	7.53607	7.34469	7.16072
13	9.39357	9.11709	8.85267	8.59975	8.35765	8.12584	7.90377	7.69096	7.48690
14	9.89864	9.58966	9.29497	9.01385	8.74546	8.48916	8.24423	8.01010	7.78615
15	10.37966	10.03759	9.71224	9.40267	9.10791	8.82712	8.55947	8.30424	8.06068
16	10.83777	10.46217	10.10588	9.76777	9.44664	9.14151	8.85136	8.57534	8.31256
17	11.27406	10.86462	10.47725	10.11058	9.76322	9.43396	9.12163	8.82520	8.54363
18	11.68958	11.24608	10.82759	10.43247	10.05908	9.70601	9.37188	9.05548	8.75562
19	12.08532	11.60766	11.15811	10.73472	10.33559	9.95908	9.60359	9.26772	8.95011
20	12.46221	11.95039	11.46991	11.01851	10.59401	10.19449	9.81814	9.46334	9.12854
21	12.82115	12.27525	11.76406	11.28499	10.83552	10.41348	10.01680	9.64363	9.29224
22	13.16300	12.58318	12.04157	11.53520	11.06124	10.61720	10.20074	9.80980	9.44242
23	13.48857	12.87505	12.30337	11.77014	11.27218	10.80669	10.37105	9.96295	9.58020
24	13.79864	13.15171	12.55035	11.99074	11.46933	10.98297	10.52875	10.10410	9.70661
25	14.09394	13.41394	12.78335	12.19788	11.65358	11.14695	10.67477	10.23419	9.82258
30	15.37245	14.53376	13.76482	13.05868	12.40904	11.81039	11.25778	10.74685	10.27365
35	16.37419	15.39056	14.49824	13.68696	12.94767	12.27251	11.65457	11.08778	10.56662
40	17.15908	16.04613	15.04629	14.14553	13.33171	12.59441	11.92461	11.31452	10.75736
45	17.77407	16.54773	15.45582	14.48023	13.60552	12.81863	12.10840	11.46531	10.88120
50	18.25592	16.93152	15.76185	14.72452	13.80074	12.97481	12.23348	11.56560	10.96168

n/K	9.5	10.0	11.0	12.0	13.0	14.0	15.0	16.0	17.0
1	0.91324	0.90909	0.90090	0.89286	0.88496	0.87719	0.86957	0.86207	0.85470
2	1.74725	1.73554	1.71252	1.69005	1.66810	1.64666	1.62571	1.60523	1.58521
3	2.50891	2.48685	2.44371	2.40183	2.36115	2.32163	2.28323	2.24589	2.20959
4	3.20448	3.16986	3.10244	3.03735	2.97447	2.91371	2.85498	2.79818	2.74324
5	3.83971	3.79078	3.69589	3.60477	3.51723	3.43308	3.35216	3.27429	3.19935
6	4.41993	4.35526	4.23053	4.11141	3.99755	3.88867	3.78448	3.68474	3.58919
7	4.94961	4.86842	4.71219	4.56375	4.42261	4.28831	4.16042	4.03857	3.92238
8	5.43344	5.33492	5.14612	4.96764	4.79877	4.63887	4.48732	4.34359	4.20716
9	5.87529	5.75902	5.53704	5.32825	5.13166	4.94637	4.77158	4.60654	4.45057
10	6.27880	6.14456	5.88923	5.65022	5.42625	5.21612	5.01877	4.83323	4.65860
11	6.64731	6.49506	6.20651	5.93770	5.68694	5.45273	5.23371	5.02865	4.83641
12	6.98384	6.81369	6.49235	6.19437	5.91765	5.66029	5.42062	5.19711	4.98839
13	7.29118	7.10335	6.74987	6.42355	6.12181	5.84236	5.58315	5.34233	5.11828
14	7.57185	7.36668	6.98186	6.62817	6.30249	6.00207	5.72448	5.46753	5.22930
15	7.82818	7.60608	7.19087	6.81086	6.46238	6.14217	5.84737	5.57546	5.32419
16	8.06226	7.82371	7.37916	6.97398	6.60388	6.26506	5.95424	5.66850	5.40529

Table D (*continued*)

n/K	9.5	10.0	11.0	12.0	13.0	14.0	15.0	16.0	17.0
17	8.27604	8.02155	7.54879	7.11963	6.72909	6.37286	6.04716	5.74870	5.47461
18	8.47127	8.20141	7.70161	7.24967	6.83991	6.46742	6.12797	5.81785	5.53385
19	8.64956	8.36492	7.83929	7.36578	6.93797	6.55037	6.19823	5.87746	5.58449
20	8.81238	8.51356	7.96332	7.46944	7.02475	6.62313	6.25933	5.92884	5.62777
21	8.96108	8.64869	8.07507	7.56200	7.10155	6.68696	6.31246	5.97314	5.66476
22	9.09688	8.77154	8.17574	7.64464	7.16951	6.74295	6.35866	6.01133	5.69637
23	9.22089	8.88322	8.26643	7.71843	7.22966	6.79206	6.39884	6.04425	5.72340
24	9.33415	8.98474	8.34813	7.78432	7.28288	6.83514	6.43377	6.07263	5.74649
25	9.43758	9.07704	8.42174	7.84314	7.32999	6.87293	6.46415	6.09709	5.76623
30	9.83472	9.42691	8.69379	8.05518	7.49565	7.00267	6.56598	6.17720	5.82939
35	10.08700	9.64416	8.85524	8.17550	7.58557	7.07005	6.61661	6.21534	5.85820
40	10.24725	9.77905	8.95105	8.24378	7.63438	7.10504	6.64178	6.23350	5.87134
45	10.34904	9.86281	9.00791	8.28252	7.66086	7.12322	6.65429	6.24214	5.87733
50	10.41371	9.91482	9.04165	8.30450	7.67524	7.13266	6.66051	6.24626	5.88006

n/K	18.0	19.0	20.0	21.0	22.0	23.0	24.0	25.0	30.0
1	0.84746	0.84034	0.83333	0.82645	0.81967	0.81301	0.80645	0.80000	0.76923
2	1.56564	1.54650	1.52778	1.50946	1.49153	1.47399	1.45682	1.44000	1.36095
3	2.17427	2.13992	2.10648	2.07393	2.04224	2.01137	1.98130	1.95200	1.81611
4	2.69006	2.63859	2.58874	2.54044	2.49364	2.44827	2.40428	2.36160	2.16624
5	3.12717	3.05763	2.99061	2.92598	2.86364	2.80347	2.74538	2.68928	2.43557
6	3.49760	3.40978	3.32551	3.24462	3.16692	3.09225	3.02047	2.95142	2.64275
7	3.81153	3.70570	3.60459	3.50795	3.41551	3.32704	3.24232	3.16114	2.80211
8	4.07757	3.95437	3.83716	3.72557	3.61927	3.51792	3.42122	3.32891	2.92470
9	4.30302	4.16333	4.03097	3.90543	3.78628	3.67310	3.56550	3.46313	3.01900
10	4.49409	4.33893	4.19247	4.05408	3.92318	3.79927	3.68186	3.57050	3.09154
11	4.65601	4.48650	4.32706	4.17692	4.03540	3.90185	3.77569	3.65640	3.14734
12	4.79323	4.61050	4.43922	4.27845	4.12737	3.98524	3.85136	3.72512	3.19026
13	4.90951	4.71471	4.53268	4.36236	4.20277	4.05304	3.91239	3.78010	3.22328
14	5.00806	4.80228	4.61057	4.43170	4.26456	4.10816	3.96161	3.82408	3.24867
15	5.09158	4.87586	4.67547	4.48901	4.31522	4.15298	4.00129	3.85926	3.26821
16	5.16235	4.93770	4.72956	4.53637	4.35673	4.18941	4.03330	3.88741	3.28324
17	5.22233	4.98966	4.77463	4.57551	4.39077	4.21904	4.05912	3.90993	3.29480
18	5.27316	5.03333	4.81219	4.60786	4.41866	4.24312	4.07993	3.92794	3.30369
19	5.31624	5.07003	4.84350	4.63460	4.44152	4.26270	4.09672	3.94235	3.31053
20	5.35275	5.10086	4.86958	4.65669	4.46027	4.27862	4.11026	3.95388	3.31579
21	5.38368	5.12677	4.89132	4.67495	4.47563	4.29156	4.12117	3.96311	3.31984
22	5.40990	5.14855	4.90943	4.69004	4.48822	4.30208	4.12998	3.97049	3.32296
23	5.43212	5.16685	4.92453	4.70251	4.49854	4.31063	4.13708	3.97639	3.32535
24	5.45095	5.18223	4.93711	4.71282	4.50700	4.31759	4.14281	3.98111	3.32719
25	5.46691	5.19515	4.94759	4.72134	4.51394	4.32324	4.14742	3.98489	3.32861
30	5.51681	5.23466	4.97894	4.74627	4.53379	4.33909	4.16010	3.99505	3.33206
35	5.53862	5.25121	4.99154	4.75587	4.54114	4.34472	4.16443	3.99838	3.33299
40	5.54815	5.25815	4.99660	4.75958	4.54386	4.34672	4.16590	3.99947	3.33324
45	5.55232	5.26106	4.99863	4.76101	4.54486	4.34743	4.16641	3.99983	3.33331
50	5.55414	5.26228	4.99945	4.76156	4.54524	4.34769	4.16658	3.99994	3.33333

n/K	35.0	40.0	45.0	50.0
1	0.74074	0.71429	0.68966	0.66667
2	1.28944	1.22449	1.16528	1.11111
3	1.69588	1.58892	1.49330	1.40741
4	1.99695	1.84923	1.71951	1.60494
5	2.21996	2.03516	1.87553	1.73663
6	2.38516	2.16797	1.98312	1.82442
7	2.50752	2.26284	2.05733	1.88294
8	2.59817	2.33060	2.10850	1.92196
9	2.66531	2.37900	2.14379	1.94798
10	2.71504	2.41357	2.16813	1.96532
11	2.75188	2.43826	2.18492	1.97688
12	2.77917	2.45590	2.19650	1.98459
13	2.79939	2.46850	2.20448	1.98972
14	2.81436	2.47750	2.20999	1.99315
15	2.82545	2.48393	2.21378	1.99543
16	2.83367	2.48852	2.21640	1.99696
17	2.83975	2.49180	2.21821	1.99797
18	2.84426	2.49414	2.21945	1.99865
19	2.84760	2.49582	2.22031	1.99910
20	2.85008	2.49701	2.22091	1.99940
21	2.85191	2.49787	2.22131	1.99960
22	2.85326	2.49848	2.22160	1.99973
23	2.85427	2.49891	2.22179	1.99982
24	2.85501	2.49922	2.22192	1.99988
25	2.85557	2.49944	2.22202	1.99992
30	2.85679	2.49990	2.22219	1.99999
35	2.85706	2.49998	2.22222	2.00000
40	2.85713	2.50000	2.22222	2.00000
45	2.85714	2.50000	2.22222	2.00000
50	2.85714	2.50000	2.22222	2.00000

Table E   *Area* Φ *(Z) Under the Normal Curve to the left of Z*

Z	.00	.01	.02	.03	.04	.05	.06	.07	.08	.09
.0	.5000	.5040	.5080	.5120	.5160	.5199	.5239	.5279	.5319	.5359
.1	.5398	.5438	.5478	.5517	.5557	.5596	.5636	.5675	.5714	.5753
.2	.5793	.5832	.5871	.5910	.5948	.5987	.6026	.6064	.6103	.6141
.3	.6179	.6217	.6255	.6293	.6331	.6368	.6406	.6443	.6480	.6517
.4	.6554	.6591	.6628	.6664	.6700	.6736	.6772	.6808	.6844	.6879
.5	.6915	.6950	.6985	.7019	.7054	.7088	.7123	.7157	.7190	.7224
.6	.7257	.7291	.7324	.7357	.7389	.7422	.7454	.7486	.7517	.7549
.7	.7580	.7611	.7642	.7673	.7704	.7734	.7764	.7794	.7823	.7852
.8	.7881	.7910	.7939	.7967	.7995	.8023	.8051	.8078	.8106	.8133
.9	.8159	.8186	.8212	.8238	.8264	.8289	.8315	.8340	.8365	.8389
1.0	.8413	.8438	.8461	.8485	.8508	.8531	.8554	.8577	.8599	.8621
1.1	.8643	.8665	.8686	.8708	.8729	.8749	.8770	.8790	.8810	.8830
1.2	.8849	.8869	.8888	.8907	.8925	.8944	.8962	.8980	.8997	.9015
1.3	.9032	.9049	.9066	.9082	.9099	.9115	.9131	.9147	.9162	.9177
1.4	.9192	.9207	.9222	.9236	.9251	.9265	.9279	.9292	.9306	.9319
1.5	.9332	.9345	.9357	.9370	.9382	.9394	.9406	.9418	.9429	.9441
1.6	.9452	.9463	.9474	.9484	.9495	.9505	.9515	.9525	.9535	.9545
1.7	.9554	.9564	.9573	.9582	.9591	.9599	.9608	.9616	.9625	.9633
1.8	.9641	.9649	.9656	.9664	.9671	.9678	.9686	.9693	.9699	.9706
1.9	.9713	.9719	.9726	.9732	.9738	.9744	.9750	.9756	.9761	.9767
2.0	.9772	.9778	.9783	.9788	.9793	.9798	.9803	.9808	.9812	.9817
2.1	.9821	.9826	.9830	.9834	.9838	.9842	.9846	.9850	.9854	.9857
2.2	.9861	.9864	.9868	.9871	.9875	.9878	.9881	.9884	.9887	.9890
2.3	.9893	.9896	.9898	.9901	.9904	.9906	.9909	.9911	.9913	.9916
2.4	.9918	.9920	.9922	.9925	.9927	.9929	.9931	.9932	.9934	.9936
2.5	.9938	.9940	.9941	.9943	.9945	.9946	.9948	.9949	.9951	.9952
2.6	.9953	.9955	.9956	.9957	.9959	.9960	.9961	.9962	.9963	.9964
2.7	.9965	.9966	.9967	.9968	.9969	.9970	.9971	.9972	.9973	.9974
2.8	.9974	.9975	.9976	.9977	.9977	.9978	.9979	.9979	.9980	.9981
2.9	.9981	.9982	.9982	.9983	.9984	.9984	.9985	.9985	.9986	.9986
3.0	.9987	.9987	.9987	.9988	.9988	.9989	.9989	.9989	.9990	.9990
3.1	.9990	.9991	.9991	.9991	.9992	.9992	.9992	.9992	.9993	.9993
3.2	.9993	.9993	.9994	.9994	.9994	.9994	.9994	.9995	.9995	.9995
3.3	.9995	.9995	.9995	.9996	.9996	.9996	.9996	.9996	.9996	.9997
3.4	.9997	.9997	.9997	.9997	.9997	.9997	.9997	.9997	.9997	.9998

The entries from 3.49 to 3.61 all equal .9998.
The entries from 3.62 to 3.89 all equal .9999.
All entries from 3.90 and up equal 1.0000.

Index

Entries and page numbers in **boldface** refer to glossary entries.

Abraham, Alfred B., 716*n*
Absolute liquidity ratio, 572
Accelerated Cost Recovery System
    (ACRS), 251–253
Accounting:
    insolvency, 332
    rate of return, 213–214, **216**
    ratios, 591–593
Accounts payable and working capital
    management, 612
Accounts receivable, aging schedule
    of, 669, **677.** *See also* Receivables
    management
Acid test ratio, 569, 572
Acquisitions, *see* External expansion
Activity ratios, 581, **595**
Adjusted nominal cash flow, 552, **559**
    comparing methods, 556–558
    for investment proposals, 553–554
    nominal-to-nominal method and,
      554
    real-to-real method and, 555–556
**Aging schedule of accounts receiv-
    able,** 669, **677**
Aharony, J., 414*n*
Alberts, William W., 531*n*
Anderson, Paul F., 502*n*
Annuity:
    future value of, 130–132
    present value of, 138–139
Arbitrage, 66, **74**
Archer, S. H., 70*n*, 97*n*, 429*n*, 637*n*
Arditti, F. D., 429*n*
Artificially high discount rates, 293,
    294
Assets, 4, **14**
    current, 604–612. *See also* Working
      capital management
    liquid, 605–606, **620**
    purchase of corporate, 536
Assignment of receivables, 706–707
Aug, J. S., 384*n*, 395*n*
Average collection period, 668–669,
    677

Bank credit:
    agreement, 700–702, **715**
    availability of, 700–702
    commercial note, 697–699, **715**
    commitment, 700
    compensating balance, 699–700,
      715
    cost of, 697–710
    discounted note, 697–699, **715**
    installment, 679, 699
    line of, 700–702, **715**

loan proceeds, 697–700, **715**
    nondiscounted note, 697–699
    personal nature of, 702
    secured by receivables, 706–707
    unsecured, 697–703
Bankruptcy, 334–336, 380–384
    capital structure, financial distress
      and, 380–384
    Chapter 11, 334–384
    Chapter 13, 336
    costs of, 381, 383–384, **394**
    involuntary, 334
    leverage, 382–383
    value of the levered firm under,
      382–383
    voluntary, 334
Bankruptcy Reform Act of 1978, 334
    Chapter 11 of, 334–336
    Chapter 13 of, 336
    liquidation under, 336
Barnia, A., 395*n*
Baron, D., 395*n*
Baumol, William J., 75*n*, 652*n*
Bautista, A. J., 487*n*, 489*n*, 502*n*
Baxter, Nevins D., 718*n*
Beaver, William, 596*n*
Beckwith, Richard E., 128*n*
Benishay, Haskel, 678*n*
Beranek, William, 620*n*, 678*n*
Bernhard, Richard H., 285*n*
Best efforts distribution, 84, 88
Beta coefficient, 107–111, **118**
    characteristic line, 107–108
    cost of capital, 445–457, 472–477
    required rate of return, 111–117
Bierman, Harold, Jr., 183*n*, 326*n*
Black, F., 414
Blue sky laws, 87
Boggess, William P., 678*n*
Bond, 80, 308
    after acquired clause, 80
    call, 80
    closed end, 80
    collateral trust, 80
    convertible, 80
    coupon rate of, 308
    debenture, 80
    default on, 380–384
    discount, 310
    euro, 746
    face value of, 308
    features of, 80–81
    foreign, 747
    general obligation, 81
    income, 80
    indenture, 332–333

    mortgage, 79–80
    municipal, 81
    open end, 80
    premium, 80, 310
    private placement, 80
    revenue, 81
    secured, 80
    serial, 81
    sinking fund, 81
    tax exempt, 81
    U.S. Treasury, 81
    valuation, 308–310
    valuation model, *see* Bond valuation
      model
    yield to maturity of, 450
    see also Debt; Securities
**Bondholder-shareholder conflict of
    interest,** 384–391, **394**
    financing policy and, 385–387
    impact on firm value, 391
    investment policy and, 387–390
    managing, 390–391
Bond indenture agreement, 332
Bond valuation model, 308–312, **325**
    application of, 310–312
    premiums, discounts, and years
      remaining to maturity, 310
Book value, 304–305, **325**
Borrower, 4, **14**
Bower, Richard S., 502*n*
Bradford, D., 414
Brigham, Eugene F., 183*n*
Brinkley, J., 415
Brittain, J. A., 429*n*
Broken cash flow series, 206–207, **216**
Brokers, 62, **74**
Burton, John C., 596*n*
Business organization, 18–19, 45–49
Business risk, 37–38, **39**, 116–117
    cost of capital, 464–468
Bussard, Ralph N., 653*n*

Capital:
    availability, 279–284
    budget, *see* Capital budget; Capital
      budgeting
    constraint, 282–291, **294**
    costs, 342–363. *See also* Cost of
      capital
    rationing, 290, **294**
    recovery, 139–140, **152**
    structure, 342–363, **363.** *See also*
      Capital structure
    venture, 90
Capital budget, 162, 178–179, **182,**
    194–197, 278–294

Capital budget (*Cont.*)
determining, *see* Determining the capital budget
process, *see* Capital budgeting
Capital budgeting, 146, 161–187, **182**
adjusted nominal cash flow and, 552–558
auditing phase, 163–164, 181, **182**
cash flow estimation, 169–170
control phase, 162–163, 180, **182**
creating projects from proposals, 173–175
decision process, 161–181
evaluation phase, 162, 169–178, **182**
expected inflation and, 552–558
grouping of proposals into projects, 170–172
inflation, 552–558
identification of opportunities, 165
implementation phase, 162, 179–180, **182**
independent proposals, 173
initial screening, 168–169
internal rate of return, 148–149, 198–199. *See also* Internal rate of return
net present value, 148, 194–197. *See also* Net present value
overview of, 162–164
payback method, 210–212, **217**
planning phase, 162, 164–169, **183**
preliminary analysis, 165–168
process, 162–164, **182**
profitability index, 286–288, **295**
programming approaches, 284–285
secondary screening and, 178
selection phase, 162, 178–179, **183**
statistical correlation and, 175–178
substitute proposals, 172–173, **183**
summary, 181–182
unequal lives, 255–265
Capital budgeting with capital constraints, 282–291, **294**
due to capital markets, 289
economic dependence under, 283–284
evaluating combinations of proposals, 285–286
internally generated funds and, 289–290
limits on growth of the firm and, 290–291
managerially imposed, 289–291
maximizing net present value and, 284–288
with no constraints on capital, 279–281
profitability index and, 286–288
programming approaches, 284–285
summary, 294
for units of an organization, 290

unresolved problem of, 291
Capital constraint, 282, **294**
causes of, 288–291
leasing and, 485
managerial, 282, 289–291
market, 289
Capital costs, 265, 269–272, **274**
depreciable outlay, 269
depreciation tax subsidy, 269–270
salvage value, 270–272
Capitalization rate, 152
Capitalizing, 132. *See also* Present value
Capital market line, 104–105, **118**
Capital rationing problem 283, **294.** *See also* Capital budgeting with capital constraints
Capital recovery problem, 139–140, **152**
Capital recovery rates, 203–206
Capital structure, 343–396, **363**
bondholder-shareholder conflicts, 384–391
corporate debt, taxes, and, 376–380
cost of capital and, 342–368
cost of capital for the firm and, 351–352, 358–359, 437–441
cost of equity capital and, 350–351, 357
decisions, 355, 360–361, 369–398
effects of leverage, 353–355, 359–360
financial distress and bankruptcy and, 380–384
finding an optimal, 391–392
future, 439–440
interest tax subsidy and, 356
leasing, borrowing, and, 487–490
optimal, 391–392, 438–439
perfect markets and, 343–361, 370–380
personal taxes and, 370–380
recapitalization, 445
required rates of return and, 370–372
share price and, 352–353
summary, 361–363, 392–394
target, 439, 440, **445**
two identical levered streams of income and, 347–350
two identical unlevered streams of income and, 345–347
value of the firm and, 356–357, 372–376, 379
Carlson, R., 469*n*
Carrying costs, 672–674, **677**
Carter, E. E., 748*n*
Cash, 4–5, **14**
balance, 647–648
budget, 626, 628–633, **651.** *See also* Cash budget
cycle, 604–605, **619**

discount, 659, **677**
future, 4, 5
near, 5
present, 4, 5
Cash budget, 626, 628–633, **651**
cash inflows, 629–630
cash outflows, 630, 632
example of, 631
net cash flows, 632
scheduling borrowings and repayments, 632–633
summary, 633
Cash cycle, 604–605, **619**
Cash discount, 659, **677**
Cash flow, 19, **29**
adjusted nominal, 599. *See also* Adjusted nominal cash flow
annualized, 260–265
broken pattern, 206–208, **216**
confusing depreciation expense with, 238–239
confusing the timing of net income with the timing of, 236–238
correlated, 175–178
cost-saving investment, 224–231
differential, 201–203, **216**
discounted, 146–149
effect, 614–618, **620**
estimation of, for a foreign investment, 743
estimation of, in an evaluation phase, 169–170
exchange risk and balancing, 741
failure to distinguish between incremental and nonincremental, 240–241
failure to identify proper investment alternatives and, 239–240
failure to identify the proper payment time horizon, 242–244
failure to incorporate net working capital requirements and, 241–242
incremental after-tax, 222–224, **226**
incremental after-tax operating, 227–230, 234, **246**
inflation, 552–558
intra-monthly, 626–627
for investments, *see* Cost saving investment projects, cash flows for; Revenue expaning projects, cash flows for
management, 647–650
net, 20, **40,** 625
net income, 236–238
net working capital requirement, 232–234, 241–242, **246**
non-operating, 633–636, **652**
operating, 633–636, **652**
pro forma statement of, 19–20
random, 626, 627

revenue-expanding investment, 213–236
seasonal, 626–627
specifying, over common life of project, 259–260
standard pattern, 208, **217**
sunk cost, 241, **247**
systematic, 634–637, **652**
terminal, 230–231, 234–235, **247**
time and compound returns and, 124–151
uniform annual equivalent, 145–146, **152,** 260–265
variation, 625–628
Cash flow effect, 614–618, **620**
Cash flow management, 646–650
electronic funds transfer and, 649–650
float and, 647–649
Cash flow patterns, 216
Cash flow series:
broken, 206–207, **216**
standard, 207, 208, **217**
Cash liquid assets, 643–645, **652**
Certificate of deposit, 79
Chapoton, John E., 486*n*
Characteristic line, 107–110
Chattel mortgage, 79
Chua, J. H., 384*n*, 395*n*
Cissell, H., 152*n*
Cissell, R., 152*n*
Claim(s):
absolute priority, 335–336
debt, 9, **14**
equity, 9, **14**
see also Securities
Clientele effect, 409–410, 413, **428**
Closed-end fund, 83
Cohn, Richard A., 560*n*, 620*n*
Collateral, 78–79, 695, **715**
Collateral trust bonds, 80
Collection period, average, 668–669, **677**
Collection policies, 658, 662, 677
Commercial note, 699–701, **715**
Commercial paper, 79, 703–704, **715**
Common life, 258–259, **274**
specifying cash flows over, 259–260
Common stock, 60, **74,** 82
authorization of, 47
bankruptcy and, 334–336
characteristics of, 48
cost of financing via, 451–459
dividends, 422–424, **429**
exchange, 528–529
as equity security, 82
new issues of, 63
"no par," 305
option, 82–83, 336–341
par value of, 304*n*, 305
previously issued, 61

primary market transactions in, 63
repurchase, 424–427, **429**
rights, 82, 88–89
secondary market transactions in, 61–63, 64
split, 422–424, **429**
tender, 425, **429**
valuation, 313–322
valuation model, 313–322, **326**
warrant, 82
see also Equity; Securities
Communication of financial information, 52–54
Comparing net present value with internal rate of return, 199–210
absence of a unique internal rate of return and, 206–208
differential cash flow and, 201
maximization of shareholder wealth and, 200–206
rate of capital recovery and, 203–206
reconciliation of methods, 208–209
scale of investment policy and, 201–203
summary, 209–210
Compensating balance, 699–700, **715**
Compensation, 7, **14**
Competitive sales, 86
Complementary proposals, 170, 171–172, **182**
Composition, 333–334
Compounding tables, 144–146
Compound rate of return, 124–127, 144–146, **152**
continuous, 128
formulas for, 150–151
frequency of compounding and, 128–129
future value and, 126–132
growth rates, 145
special uses, 144–146
uniform annual equivalent, 144–146
Conglomerate, 511, **531**
Consolidation, 535–536
Constant growth valuation model, 315–318, **325**
marginal cost of capital and, 454
Constant payout dividend policy, 401, **428**
Convertible bonds, 80
Corporate income tax*ex*, 54–56
perfect markets with, 370–380
Corporations, 47–49
bylaws of, 48
charter of, 47
franchise taxes of, 47
ownership of, 47–49
Correlation:
investment proposals, 175–178
returns, 96–100, **118**

Correlation coefficient, 96–97, **118**
diversification benefits under, 97–98
portfolio composition and, 99–100
Cosigner, 79
Cost:
bankruptcy, 381–384, **394**
capital, 269–272, **274,** *see also* Cost of capital
flotation, *see* Flotation costs
information, 410
operating and maintenance, 265–269, **274**
transactions, 68–69, **75**
see also Bank credit; Credit
Cost of assets, replacement, 306–307, **326**
Cost of capital, 342–363, **363,** 447–469
beta, 472–477
capital structure and, 342–368
common stock, 440, 451–459
debt, 351, 448–450
debt-equity mix, 350–360, 438–441
effect on net present value, 190–191
equity, 350–351, 357, 440
expected inflation and, 549–552
for the firm, *see* Cost of capital for the firm
measurement, 441–443, 460–468, 472–477
marginal, *see* Marginal cost of capital
nominal, 549–551, **560**
preferred stock, 451
real, 551–552
retained earnings, 459–460
risk, 464–468
risk-return estimation, 455–459, **469**
share price, 352–353
valuation estimation, 448, 452–455, **469**
see also Required rate of return
Cost of capital of the firm, 434–446, **444**
capital structure and, 437–441
computation of, 441–442
estimating the cost of each source of funds, 441
optimal debt/equity mix and, 438–439
in perfect markets with income taxes 358–359
in perfect markets without income taxes, 351–352
recapitalization and, 439–440
summary, 443–444
target debt/equity mix and, 439, 440
Zuber Milling case, 435–437, 442–443
Cost of debt, 351

Cost of equity captial:
  in a perfect market with income
    taxes, 357
  in a perfect market with no income
    taxes, 350–351
**Cost-reduction investment opportu-
  nity, 165, 182**
Costs:
  capital, 265, 269–272, 274
  carrying, 672–674, 677
  of financial distress and bankruptcy,
    381, 383–384
  **operating and maintenance, 265,
    268–269, 274**
  order, 672–674, 678
  of sources of funds, 441
Cost saving investment projects, cash
    flows for, 224–231
  cash inflow on disposal of an old
    asset and, 226–227
  depreciable cash outlays and, 225
  depreciation tax subsidy and, 230
  important cash flow errors and,
    236–244
  incremental after-tax operating cash
    flow and, 227–230
  initial investment outlays and,
    224–225, 227
  summary and evaluation of, 231
  terminal cash flows and, 230–231
  total outlays and, 225–227
Covariance, 96–97, 119
Cox, John, 341n
Credit:
  agreement, 702–704, 715
  card financing, 710
  collection policies, 658, 662, 677
  control, 658, 668–671
  cost, 692–708
  discount period, 659, 677
  extension policies, 658–661, 677
    credit lines and, 659–660
    credit standards and, 660–661
    credit terms and, 659
  line, 658, 659–660, 677
  line of, 700–702, 715
  monitoring, 658, 668–670, 677
    aging schedule and, 669
    average collection period and,
      668–669
    comparing measures, 669–670
  period, 659, 677
  policy, 658–671
  screen, 660, 677
  standards, 658, 660–661, 677
  terms, 658, 659, 677
  trade, see Trade credit
  valuation, 662–668
    discount rate effect, 666–668
    relaxed policy, 666
    stringent policy, 663–665

see also Debt
Creditors' committee, 334
Curley, Anthony J., 75n
Current assets, financing, 685–722
  availability of bank credit and,
    700–702
  choosing among short-term
    financing sources, 710–713
  commercial note and, 697–699
  commercial paper and, 703–704
  compensating balance and, 699–700
  conflicting interests between bor-
    rowers and lenders and, 688–692
  credit agreement and, 702–704
  financial folklore and, 686–687
  illustrative case, 693–695
  installment loan and, 699
  inventory financing, 708–710
  line of credit and, 700–702
  receivables financing, 705–708
  secured forms of short-term
    financing, 704–710
  speculation on interest rates and,
    692–693
  summary, 713–715
  term structure of interest rates and,
    687–688
  trade credit and, 696–697
  uncertain length of financing need
    and, 693
  unsecured bank credit and, 697–700
  unsecured forms of short-term
    financing, 695–704
Current asset investment, see Working
    capital management
Current assets, permanent, 609–610
Current assets, temporary, 610–611
Current ratio, 571

Daellenbach, Hans G., 653n
D'Ambroiso, C. A., 429n
Daniels, Frank, 718n
Dann, Larry, 425n, 426, 531n
Dealer, 61, 72, 74
DeAngelo, H., 395n, 425n
Debentures, 80
Debt, 60, 351, 363
  capacity, 524–526, 531
  convertible, 80
  corporate, under personal taxes,
    376–378
  costs of, 351. See also Cost of Capital
  debenture, 80
  is debt policy irrelevant?, 379–380
  equity ratio, 350–360, 438–441
  financing mix, 448–450
  long term, 80
  maturity, 683–693
  perpetual, 30
  private placement, 80
  restrictive covenants of, 484

  secured, 80, 704–710
  self-liquidating, 710
  short term, 78–79, 683–713
  subordinated, 80
  tax anticipation note, 79
  taxes, 376–378, 379–380, see also
    Taxes
  unsecured, 693–704
  see also Bank credit; Bond; Credit
Debt capacity, 524–526, 531
Debt claims, 9, 14
Debt-equity mix:
  discrepancies between present and
    future, 439–440
  optimal, 438–439
  present procedures for selecting,
    440–441
  ratio, 350–360, 438–441
  target, 439, 440
  see also Capital structure
Debt maturity, 683–693
Debt securities, 78–81
  certificates of deposit, 79
  commercial paper, 79
  convertible bonds, 80
  cost of financing via, 448–450
  debentures, 80
  federal agency bonds, 81
  federal agency notes, 80
  income bonds, 80
  installment loans, 79
  intermediate-term, 79–80
  long-term, 80
  notes payable, 78–79
  other features of, 80–81
  secured bonds, 80
  short-term, 78–79
  tax anticipation notes, 79
  tax exempt bonds, 81
  Treasury bills, 79
  Treasury bonds, 81
  Treasury notes, 80
Debt-to-net-worth ratio, 576
Decision rule, 147–149
Default, 380–384
  risk, 686
Deflating, 540, 559
Depreciable life, 229n, 246
Depreciable outlay, 225–226, 246
  as capital cost, 269
Depreciation:
  cash flow, 225–226, 229–232,
    238–240
  incremental, 227–230
  leasing and, 486
  life, 244, 246
  methods, 229–230, 251–253, 486
  outlay, 225, 246
  present value, 251–253
  tax subsidy, 230, 246 486, 492–493
Depreciaton tax subsidy, 230, 246, 486

as capital cost, 269–270
leasing, 480, 492–493
Determining the capital budget,
  278–298
  artificially high discount rates and,
    293
  with capital constraints, *see* Capital
    budgeting with capital constraints
  multiple investment selection of
    criteria and, 292–293
  with no constraints on capital,
    279–281
Differential cash flow, 201–203, **216**
Differential rate of return, 202–203,
  208–209, **216**
Dill, D. A., 487*n*, 489*n*, 502*n*
Direct transactions, 60, **74**
Discounted cash flow methods,
  146–149, **152**
  internal rate of return, 148–149
  net present value, 147–148
  valuation and, 307–308
Discounted note, 699–701, **715**
Discounting, 132. *See also* Present
  value
Discount period, 659, **677**
Discount rate, 458–464
  artificial, 293, **294**
  effect, 614–618, **620**
  present value, 136–138
Discretionary trade credit, 698, **715**
Diversification, 94, **119**
  correlation coefficients and, 96–99
  of foreign investments, 744
  with many risky securities, 101–102
  portfolios and, *see* Portfolios
  as reason for acquisition, 524–526
Dividend:
  announcement effect, 411
  date of record, 421
  ex, 421
  extra, 414, **428**
  homemade, 403–404, **428**
  information content, 411–414, **428**
  irrelevance, 402–405
  payout, 401–402
  policy, *see* Dividend Policy
  regular, 414
  repurchase, 424–427, **429**
  stability, 411
  stock, 422–424, **429**
Dividend account, 85
Dividend policy, 399–433, **428**
  announcement effect and, 411
  Barfield case, 399–402, 415–420
  capital improvement rule and, 421*n*
  clientele effect and, 409–410
  constant payout, 401
  date of record and, 421
  divisibility of securities and, 409
  ex-dividend date and, 421

"extra" dividend and, 414–415
fixed, 400
flotation costs, 408
"homemade" dividend and, 403,
  404
inflation and, 421–422
information content and, 411–414
information costs and, 410
insolvency rule and, 421*n*
irrelevance, 402–405
mechanics of, 421
net profit rule and, 421*n*
payout ratio and, 401
personal taxes, market imperfections and, 406–415
residual, 400
stable, 411–413
stock dividends, 422–424
stock repurchase, 424–427
stock split, 422–424
summary, 427–428
taxes, 405–410
tender offers, 425
transaction and flotation costs and,
  406, 408
Dominance principle, 92–94, 97–100
  119
Donaldson, Gordon, 716*n*
Dufey, G., 747*n*
Dun and Bradstreet, 593, 661
du Pont system of financial analysis,
  579–581, **595**

Economic dependence, 170–171, **182**
  under capital constraints, 283–284
Economic exposure, 738, **746**
Economic independence, 173–175,
  182
Economic life, 234–244, **246**
  capital costs and, 265, 269–272
  determining, 272–273
  operating and maintenance costs
    and, 265, 268–269
  problem of, 267
  summary, 273–274
Economic order quantity model,
  671–675, **678**
  carrying costs and, 672–674
  order costs and, 672–674
  safety stock and, 674–675
Edmister, Robert O., 596*n*, 678*n*
Effective annual rate of return, 129,
  152
Efficient frontier, 101
Efficient markets, 60, 72–73, **74**
Efficient portfolios, 101–102, **119**
Electronic funds transfer (EFT),
  649–650
Engler, George N., 421*n*
Equal rate of return principle, 59,
  65–72, **74**

availability of information and,
  70–71
divisibility and, 71–72
floatation costs and, 69–70
market imperfections and, 67–68
size of transaction and, 71
transaction costs and, 68–69
Equilibrium exchange rates, 727–733
  interest rate parity and, 730–733
  purchasing power parity and,
    727–730
  summary, 736
Equity, 21, **39**, 350, **363**
  cost of capital, 350–351, 357
  claim, 9, **14**
Equity securities, 81–83
  common stock, 82
  options, 82–83
  investment company shares, 83
  preferred stock, 81–82
  proprietors and partnerships, 81
  warrants, 82
Eurobonds, 744, **746**
Exchange rates, **746**
  basics of, 723–727
  equilibrium, 727–733, 736
  see also International finance;
    Foreign exchange
Exchange risk, 737–742, 745, **747**
  balancing cash flows and, 739
  economic exposure and, 738
  hedging transactions and, 740–741
  minimizing translation exposure
    and, 739–740
  pricing and cost control and,
    741–742
  transaction exposure and, 737–738
  translation exposure and, 738
Expansion:
  conglomerate, 511, **531**
  external, 510–531, **531**, 535–536
  horizontal, 511, **531**
  internal, 510–517, **531**
  vertical, 511, **531**
Expected rate of inflation, 458–459,
  469, 541–558, **560**
  adjusted nominal cash flows and,
    552–554
  capital budgeting decisions and,
    552–558
  cost of capital and, 549–552
  nominal-to-nominal method and,
    554, 556–558
  real-to-real method and,
    555–558
  required rates of return and,
    541–548
Expected rate of return, 22, **39**
  dominance principle and, 92–94
  financial leverage and, 32–35
  risk and, 7–9, 22–26, 95–97

Expected rate of return (*Cont.*)
single period, and standard deviation, 92
two-security portfolios and, 95–97
Expected return, 7–9, **14**
Expenditure:
fixed, 24, **40**
variable, 24, **40**
Expropriation, 743, **747**
Extention of maturity date, 333
External expansion, 510–537, **531**
consolidation, 535–536
diversification effect and, 524–526
exchange of stock and, 528–529
forms of, 535–536
holding company, 536
internal expansion compared to, 511–517
merger, 510, 535
pooling method of accounting and, 537
price of, 526–529
purchase method of accounting and, 536
purchase of assets, 536
Silveira case, 517–518
summary, 529–530
synergism and, 522–524
tenders and, 529
types of, 511
when merger does not benefit shareholders, 518–522
"**Extra" dividend,** 414–415, **428**

Factoring, 707–708, **715**
Faerber, L. G., 70*n*
Fama, Eugene F., 113*n*, 387*n*, 395*n*, 455*n*
Faucett, Russell G., 653*n*
Federal agency bonds, 81
Federal agency notes, 80
Federal Trade Commission, 593
Fielitz, B. D., 429*n*
Finance, 3, **14**
elements of, 4–9
international, 723–746
Financial analysis, 565–566, **595**
du Pont, 579–584, **595**
financial ratios as a tool of, 567–568
information needed for, 566–567
see also Ratios
Financial control, 51–52
Financial decisions, 3, 9–10, 12, **14,** 18–56
inflation, 538–559
Financial distress 332–334
and bankruptcy, 380–385, **395**
composition, 333–334
creditor's committee, 334
default, 380

extension, 333
Financial information, communication of, 52–54
Financial intermediaries, 63
Financial leases, 482, **501**
acquisition *vs.*, 499–500
evaluation of, 494–500
without salvage value, 494–498
with salvage value, 498–499
Financial leverage, 21, 30–36, **39,** 103, 343, **363,** 575–576, **595**
capital structure and, 342–368
expected rate of return, risk, and, 32–35
financial distress and bankruptcy and, 382–383
homemade, 348–350
interest tax subsidy and, 31–32
levered firm, 30, **40,** 344–363
preferred stock and, 343
profitability ratios and, 581–582
ratios, 575–577, **595**
required rate of return, wealth, and, 36
summary of effects of, 353–355, 359–360
unlevered firm, 21, **40,** 344–363
Financial leverage ratios, 576–577, **595**
debt to net worth, 576
interest coverage, 576
interpretation of, 577
total assets to net worth, 576–577
Financial manager, 1, 13, **14**
Financial markets, 10–11, **15,** 59–90
debt securities and, 78–81
efficient markets and, 72–73
equal rate of return principle and, 65–72
equity securities and, 81–83
financial securities and, 77–78
imperfections in, *see* Market imperfections
investor wealth and, 11, 59
investment banking and, 83–90
perfect, 64–65
primary, 63
regulation of, 86–87
secondary, 61–63, 64
securities traded in, 60–65
summary, 73–74
types of, 60
Financial organization, 49–51
Financial planning, 565–568, 588–591
Financial ratios, 567–594. *See also* Ratios
Financial risk, 37–38, **39–40**
Financial securities, 59, **74,** 77–78. *See also* Securities
Financing:
credit card, 708

cost of sources, 692–708
current asset, 611–614, 683–715
decisions, 9–10, **15**
discretionary, 696–697, **715**
flexibility, 612–613, **620**
foreign, 744
inventory, 708–710
long term, 611–613, 683–693
maturity, 683–693
receivables, 705–708
secured, 704–710
short term, 611–614, 683–713
source, 620
spontaneous, 613–614, **620**
unsecured, 693–704
First mortgage bonds, 80
Fisher, Irving, 542*n*
Fixed expenditures, 24, **40**
Fixed-promise securities, 544–545, **560**
Fixed rate system, 736, **747**
Fleischer, Gerald a., 275*n*
Flexible financing sources, 612–613, **620**
Float, 647–649, **652**
maximizing, 649
Flotation costs, 63, 69–70, **74**
dividend policy and, 406, 408
Fogler, H. Russell, 295*n*
Foreign bonds, 744, **747**
Foreign exchange, 724–727, 747
floating rates, 736, **747**
equilibrium rates, 727–733, 736
fixed rates, 736, **747**
interest rate parity, 730–733, **747**
managed rates, 736, **747**
markets, 724–727
forward, 725–727, **747**
spot, 724–725, **747**
purchasing power parity, 728–730, **747**
risk, 737–742, **747**
Foreign investment decision, 742–745
cash flow estimation and, 743
diversification and, 742
financing abroad and, 744–745
risk assessment and, 743–744
Forms of organization, 18–19, 45–49
corporation, 47–49
partnership, 46–47
proprietorship, 45–46
Forward exchange market, 725–727, **747**
changes in, 727
Francis, J. C., 97*n*
Free, floating exchange rate system, 736, **747**
Friend, Irwin, 75*n*, 414*n*
Furst, Richard W., 75*n*
Future cash, 4, 5
Future value, 126–132, **152**

annuity, 130–132
compounding, 125–132
equations, 127, 131, 151–152
factor, 126, 131
frequency of compounding and,
128–129
present value and, 134–137
sinking fund problems and,
131–132
on a time line, 127–128
of an uneven stream of cash flows,
129–130
of a uniform stream of payments,
130–131

General lien, 709
General obligation bonds, 81
General partnership, 46–47
Giddy, I. H., 747n
Gordon, R., 414
Grant, Eugene L., 152n, 183n, 272n

Haley, C. W., 175n, 364n
Harris, Duane G., 716n
Hass, Jerome, 326n
Hastie, K. Larry, 183n
Haugen, Robert, 326n, 383n, 395n
Hayes, Samuel L., III, 75n
Hedge, 541, **560**
   exchange risk, 740–741, **747**
   inflation, 541, **560**
Helfert, Erich A., 596n
Hess, Arleigh R., Jr., 75n
Higgins, Robert, 525n, 531n
Holding company, 536
Holt, Charles C., 326n
"Homemade" dividend, 403, 404, **428**
   taxes and, 426
Horizontal expansion, 511, **531**

Ibbotson, Roger, 457, 458–459
Imperfect markets, *see* Market
   imperfections
Income bonds, 80
Income taxes:
   corporate, 54–56
   personal, *see* Personal income taxes
Incremental after-tax cash flows,
   222–224, **246**
**Incremental after-tax operating cash
   flows, 246**
   cost saving investment projects and,
   227–230
   revenue-expanding projects and, 234
Independent proposals, 170, 173, **182**
Indirect transactions, 60, **74**
Inflation, 538–562, **560**
   adjusted nominal cash flows and,
   552–554
   capital budgeting decisions and,
   552–558

cost of capital and, 549–552
deflating and, 540
dividend policy and, 421–422
expected rate of, 458–459, **469,**
   541–558, **560**
financial decisions and, 538–559
financial ratios and, 591–593
fixed-promise securities, 544
hedges against, 541
investment returns, purchasing
   power risk, and, 540–541
market value of securities and,
   544–545
nominal dollars and, 538–540
purchasing power losses and,
   538–540, 546
purchasing power risk and market
   value, 548–549
ratios, 591–593
real dollars and, 538–540
required rates of return and,
   541–548
rising expectations of, 545–548
summary, 558–559
Inflexible financing sources, 612–613,
   620
Information:
   availability, 70–71
   bank credit, 702
   communication, 52–54
   costs, 410
   dividend content, 411–414, **428**
   financial analysis, 566–567
   stock repurchase, 424–427
Insolvency, 332
   alternatives to, 332–333
   bankruptcy, 334–336
   out of court adjustments, 333–334
Installment loans, 79, 699, **715**
   cost of, 699
Interest, 9, **15**
   differences in international rates of,
   733–736
   parity of rate of, 730–733, 746, **747**
   prime rate of, 701, **716**
   term structure of rates of, 687–688,
   718
   see also Rate of interest
Interest coverage ratio, 576
Interest tax subsidy, 31–32, **40,** 356,
   363
Intermediate-term debt, 79–80
Internal expansion, 531
   external expansion compared to,
   511–517
   types of, 511
Internal rate of return, 140–144, **152,**
   197–210, **217**
   capital budgeting and, 148–149,
   198–199
   differential, 202–206, **216**

equations, 140–144, 151
method, 140–144, **152,** 197–210
   multiple, 206–208
   net present value, 199–210
   perpetual cash flows and, 144
   rule, 148–149
   selection of investment projects
   and, 197–199
   single payment, 140–141
   uneven streams of payments and,
   141–143
   uniform stream of payments and,
   143–144
   unique, 206–208
   see also Comparing net present value
   with internal rate of return
International finance, 723–750
   causes of interest rate differentials,
   733–736
   equilibrium exchange rates and,
   727–733, 736
   exchange risk and, 737–742. *See also*
   Exchange risk
   foreign exchange markets and,
   724–727
   free, floating rate system and, 736
   hedge, 740–741
   investment decision and, 742–745
   managed rate system and, 736
   management of, 736–745
   multinational firm, 747
   summary, 745–746
Interstate Commerce Commission
   (ICC), 86
Intervals of time, 5, **15**
Intramonthly variation of net cash
   flow, 626–627
Inventory financing, 708–710
   characteristics of, 709–710
   general lien, 709
   trust receipt, 709
   warehouse receipt, 709
Inventory investment, 608–609
Inventory management, 671–676
   carrying cost, 672–674, **677**
   economic order quantity model
   and, 671–675
   order cost, 672–674, **678**
   safety stock and, 674–675
   summary, 676–677
   valuation and, 675–676
Investment, 4–5
   banker, 63–63, **74.** *See also* Investment banker
   complementary, 170–172, **182**
   cost of capital, 460–468
   cost reduction, 165, **182**
   criteria, 188–215
   decisions, 9, **15,** 116–117
   depreciable life, 244, **246**
   discount rates, 460–468

Investment (*Cont.*)
  economic dependence, 170,
    182, 283–284
  economic independence, 170,
    173–175, 182
  economic life, 243–244, 246
  effect, 614–618, 620
  independent proposal, 173, 182
  inflation, 553–558
  multiple criteria, 292–293, 294
  mutually exclusive, 173, 183
  opportunity, 165–168, 183
  project, 169–178, 183
  proposal, 169–175, 183
  revenue-expanding, 165, 183
  risk free, 6, 15
  selection criteria, 189–216
  single period, 5–6, 15
  statistical correlation, 175–178
  substitute, 170, 172–173, 183
  tax credit, 253–254
  unequal lives, 255–256
Investment banker, 63, 74, 83–90
  advising and, 84
  analysis and, 84
  best efforts and, 84, 88
  competitive sales and, 86
  description of activity of, 84–86
  functions of, 83–84
  negotiated sales and, 85–86
  private placement and, 89–90
  privileged subscription and, 88–89
  prospectus, 87
  regular underwritings and, 87–88
  regulation and, 86–87
  syndicate, 84–86
  underwriting and, 84
  venture capital and, 90
Investment company, 83
Investment decisions, 9–10, 15
Investment effect, 614–618, 620
Investment opportunities, 165–168,
  183
  cost-reduction, 165
  failure to identify proper, 239–240
  revenue-expanding, 165
Investment opportunity set, 102–104
Investment projects, 169, 183
  creating, from proposals, 173–175
  economically independent, 173–175
  grouping of proposals into, 170–172
  selection of, *see* Selection of invest-
    ment projects
Investment proposals, 169, 183
  complementary, 170, 171–172
  creating projects from, 173–175
  economic dependence of, 170–171
  economic independence of, 173–175
  grouping of, into projects, 170–172
  independent, 170, 173
  mutually exclusive, 173

  substitute, 170, 172–173
Investment tax credit, 253–254
  leasing and, 486
Investor, 4

Jensen, M., 395n
Johnson, Ramon, 502n
Johnson, Robert W., 183n, 295n, 670n,
  678n
Jones, R., 653n

Khoury, Nabil T., 678n
Klammer, Thomas, 215n
Knight, W. D., 620n
Kumar, Prem, 326n

Lanser, Howard P., 183n
Lawrence, David W., 469n
Lease, 481–501
  agreement, 481, 502
  equivalent loan, 496–500, 508–509
  financial, 482–483, 494–500, 501
  lessee, 481, 502
  lessor, 481, 502
  leveraged, 502
  model, 505–507
  operating, 483, 502
  sale and leaseback, 483, 502
  tax credit, 483, 490–494, 502
Leasing, 481–509
  after-tax earnings and, 485
  borrowing, capital structure, and,
    487–490
  capital constraints and, 485
  choice between lease and purchase
    alternatives, 490–500
  depreciation tax subsidy and, 486
  depreciation method and, 486
  derivation of the leasing model,
    505–508
  evaluation of lease and purchase
    alternatives, 487, 490
  financial lease, 482, 494–500, 501
  flexibility of, 483–484
  investment tax credit and, 486
  leveraged lease, 483, 502
  operating lease, 483, 502
  restrictive covenants of a loan and,
    484
  sale leaseback, 484, 502
  summary, 500–501
  tax credit lease, 483, 490–494, 502
  tax rate differentials and, 485–486
  technological obsolescence and, 484
  verification of the equivalent loan,
    508–509
Lee, Sang M., 183n
Legal list, 411
Legal forms of organization, 18–19,
  45–49
Lerro, A. J., 183n

Lessard, D. H., 744n
Lessee, 481, 502
  taxes and, 485–486
Lessor, 481, 502
  taxes and, 485–486
Lev, Baruch, 596n
Leverage:
  financial, 21, 30–38, 39, 343–363,
    595
  homemade, 348–350
  lease, 502
  ratios, 575–577, 595
Leveraged lease, 483, 502
Leverage ratios, *see* Financial leverage
  ratios
Levered firm, 30, 40
  total risk and, 37–38
Levy, H., 429n
Lewellen, Wilbur G., 183n, 364n, 469n,
  502n, 531n, 607n, 678n
Liability:
  of corporations, 48
  of partnerships, 47
  of proprietorships, 46
Life of investments:
  common, 258–259, 274
  depreciable, 229n, 246
  economic, 243–244, 246
  physical, 243, 247
  unequal, 255–265
Limited liability, 47
Limited partnership, 47
Line of credit, 700–702, 715
Lintner, John, 411n, 429n, 560n
Liquid asset investment, 605–606, 620
Liquid assets, 625–656
  balance, 605–606, 620, 637–642
  borrowing alternative and, 642–643
  cash, 643–645
  cash budget and, 628–645
  cash flow management, 646–650
  minimum blances, 633–640
  mix of, 645–646
  noncash, 645
  nonoperating balances and, 640–642
  operating balance and, 640–642,
    652
  summary, 650–651
  variation of net cash flow and,
    625–628
Liquidating value, 305–306, 325
Liquidation, 336
Liquidity, 570–571, 595
  analysis, 570–575
Liquidity ratios, 571–575, 595
  absolute, 572
  acid test ratio, 572
  current ratio, 571
  interpretation of, 572–573
  sources and uses statement and,
    573–575

Loan, 6
  commitment, 700
  installment, 79, 697, 699, **715**
  maturity, 683–693
  proceeds, 697–699, **716**
  secured, 704–710
  self-liquidating, 710
  unsecured, 693–704, **716**
Logue, D. E., 750n
Long, Mike, 502n
Longstreet, James R., 75n
Long-term debt, 80
Long-term financing sources,
    611–612, **620**
Long-term securities, 307
Lutz, F., 152n
Lutz, V., 152n

McConnell, John J., 183n, 384n, 395n,
    502n
Malone, R. P., 429n
Managed rate system, 738, **749**
Mao, James C. T., 326n
Marginal cost of capital, 434, **444,**
    447–477
  common stock financing, 451–459
  computing beta and cost of equity
    for a firm, 472–475
  constant growth model and, 454
  debt financing, 448–450
  estimating cost of equity from a
    comparable firm, 475–477
  expected rate of inflation and,
    458–459
  for the firm, 460–463
  market risk premium and, 456–459
  preferred stock financing, 451
  for proposals of differing business
    risk, 463–468
  real risk-free rate, 458, 459
  retention of earnings and, 459–460
  risk-return method of estimating,
    448, 455–459
  single shift model and, 454–455
  summary, 468–469
  valuation method of estimating,
    448, 452–455
  yield to maturity and, 450
  zero growth model and, 453
Market, 10–11, 60–73
  efficient, 60, 72–73, **74**
  financial, 10, **15**
  foreign exchange, *see* Foreign
    exchange
  perfect, 59, 64–65, **74**
  portfolio, 104–105, **119**
  price, 303–304
  primary, 60, 62, **75,** 83–90
  risk, *see* Market
  secondary, 60–64, **75**
  values, 10–11, **15**

see also Financial markets
Market imperfections, 59–60, 67–68,
    74, 400–410
  divisibility and, 71–72
  floatation costs, 69–70
  investor information, 70–71
  personal taxes, dividend policy,
    and, 406–415
  size of transaction and, 71
  transaction costs, 68–69
Market line:
  capital, 104–105
  security, 111–113
Market price, 303–304
Market risk, 106–111, **119**
  foreign investment and, 742
Market risk premium, 456–459, **469**
Martin, John D., 470n, 502n
Masulis, Ronald, 380n, 395n, 529n,
    531n
Meckling, W., 395n
Mehta, Dileep, 678n
Mendelson, Morris, 75n
Mergers, 510–531, 535
  accounting treatment of, 536–537
  advantages, 517–526
  conglomerate, 511, **531**
  diversification, 524–526
  price, 526–529
  reasons, 517–526
  synergy, 522–524, 531
  tender, 529
  when they do not benefit
    shareholders, 518–522
  see also Expansion; External
    expansion
Millar, J. A., 429n
Miller, Ervin, 75n
Miller, Merton H., 326n, 343, 364n,
    370n, 383n, 387n, 395n, 407, 429n,
    502n, 653n
Minimum operating liquid asset
    balances, 637–640, **652**
Modigliani, Franco, 119n, 326n, 343,
    364n, 429n, 560n
Morris Associates, Robert, 593–594
Mortgage:
  bond, 79–80
  chattel, 79
Multinational firm, 742–745, **747**
Multiperiod investment, 6, **15**
Mulitple investment selection
    criteria, 292–293, **294**
Murray, Roger F., 596n
Mutual funds, 83
Mutually exclusive investment
    proposals, 173, **183**
Myers, Stewart, 184n, 390n, 396n,
    487n, 489n, 502n, 531n

Nadler, Paul S., 718n

Nantell, Timothy, 469n
National Association of Credit
    Management, 661
Near cash, 5
Negotiated sales, 85–86
Nelson, Charles, 560n
Net cash flow, 20, **40,** 625, **652**
  intramonthly variation of, 626–627
  nonoperating, 634, **652**
  operating, 633–636
  random variation of, 626–627
  seasonal variation of, 626–627
  total variation of, 626–627
Net income, confusing the timing of
    cash flows with the timing of,
    236–238
Net personal tax effect, 374–376, **395**
Net present value, 147–148, **152,**
    188–197, **217**
  assumptions of, 192
  effect of cost of capital on, 190–191
  establishing a capital budget with,
    194–197
  internal rate of return, 199–210
  maximizing, and capital budgeting,
    284–288
  meaning of, for any project,
    192–194
  rule, 147–148
  see also Comparing net present value
    with internal rate of return
Net working capital, 21, **40,** 603, **620**
  released, 242, **246**
  requirement, 233–234, 241–242, **246**
Net worth ratios:
  debt to, 576
  return on, 578–579
  total assets to, 576–577
New York Bond Exchange, 63
New York Stock Exchange, 62
Nominal cost of capital, 549–551, **560**
Nominal dollars, 538–540, **560**
  deflating and, 540
Nominal required rates of return,
    541–544, **560**
Nominal-to-nominal method, 554,
    556–558
Noncash liqid assets, 645, **652**
Nondiscounted note, 699–701
Nonmarket risk, 106–111, **119**
Nonoperating liquid asset balances,
    640–641, **652**
Nonoperating net cash flow, 634, **652**
Nonspontaneous financing sources,
    613–614, **620**
Norgaard, C., 429n
Norgaard, R., 429n
Notes, discounted, 697–699, **715**
Notes payable, 78–79

Ofer, Aharon R., 502n

Oldfield, G. S., 750n
Open-end fund, 83
Operating and maintenance costs, 265, 268–269, **274**
Operating lease, 483, **502**
Operating net cash flow, 633–634, **652**
  systematic and random variability of, 634–636
Operating performance and condition ratios, 588–591
Options, 82–83
  valuing, 336–341
Order costs, 672–674, **678**
Organization chart, 50
Orgler, Yair, 653n
Orr, Daniel, 653n
Osborn, R., 153n
Outlays:
  cash, expensed for tax purposes, 234
  depreciable cash, 225–226, **246,** 269
  initial investment, 224–225, 227, **246**
  total, 225–226, **247**
  total initial, 234
Out-of-court adjustments, 333–334

Paid-n capital, 304n
Partnership, 46–47
Par value, 304n, 305, **325**
Payback method, 210–213, **217**
Payout ratio, 401, **428**
  target, 413
Perfect market, 59, 64–65, **74–75**
  capital structure, 343–363
  with corporate and personal taxes, 370–380
  cost of capital, 343–363
  with income taxes, 355–361
  without income taxes, 343–355
Permanent working capital, 609, **620**
Perpetual debt, 30
Personal income taxes, 56, **395**
  imperfect markets, dividend policy, and, 406–415
  net personal tax effect, 374–376
  perfect markets with, 370–380
Petry, Glenn H., 469n
Pettway, Richard H., 183n, 429n
Physical life, 243, **247**
Pogue, Gerald, 119n, 653n
Points in time, 5, **15**
Pooling accounting method, 537
Portfolios, 94–95, **119**
  compostion of, 99–100
  correlation coeffecients and, 96–99
  diversification, 94–104, **119.** See also Diversification
  efficient, 101–102
  expected rate of return and risk, 95–97

  implications of formation of, 100
  including a risk-free security, 102–104
  with many risky securities, 101–102
  market, 104–105
  required rate of retrun and, 111–117
  risk and, 91–117
  security market line and, 111–117
  single-security, 104–111
  two-security, 95–101
Preferred stock, 60, **75,** 81–82
  bankruptcy and, 334–336
  characteristics of, 48
  cost of, 451
  as equity security, 81–82
  valuation, 312–313, **325**
  see also Equities; Securities
Present cash, 4, 5
Present value, 132–140, **152**
  annuity, 138–139
  capital recovery problems and, 139–140
  discount rate, 132, 136–138
  equations, 133–139, 151
  factors, 134, 137
  future value and, 134–137
  impact of depreciation methods on, 251–253
  net, 147–148, **152,** 189–197, 199–210
  of a perpetuity, 139
  single payment, 132–134
  of an uneven stream of payments, 137–138
  of a uniform stream of payments, 138–139
Primary distributions, 84–85
Primary market, 60, **75**
  direct transactions in, 63
  indirect transactions in, 63
Prime rate of interest, 701, **716**
Pringle, John J., 620n
Private placement, 79–80, 89–90
  investment bankers and, 89–90
Privileged subscription, 88–89
Probability distribution of rates of return, 24, **40**
Profitability, 578, **595**
Profitability index, 286–288, **295**
  techniques, 287–288, **295**
Profitability ratios, 577–584
  activity ratios and, 581
  du Pont system and, 579–581
  fixed and current asset investments and, 583–584
  leverage and, 581–582
  profit margin and, 582–583
  return on net worth, 578–579
  total asset investment and, 582–583
Pro forma statements, 19–20, 31, **40**
Projected time horizon, 243, **247**
Promised return, 8, **15**

Proprietorship, 45–46
Puckett, M., 414n
Purchase accounting method, 536
Purchasing power losses, 538–540, **560**
  rising expectations of inflation and, 546
Purchasing power parity, 728–730, 745, **747**
Purchasing power risk, 540, **560**
  investment returns, inflation, and, 540–541
  market value of securities and, 548–549

Quarterly Financial Report for manufacturing, 593

Rakich, Johnathan S., 184n
Random variability of operating cash flows, 634–636, **652**
Random variation of net cash flow, 626–627
Rappaport, A., 560n
Rate of interest:
  effective, 698–699
  international differentials, 733–735
  prime, 701, **716**
  term structure, 687–688, **716**
Rate of return:
  accounting, 213–214
  compound, see Compound rate of return
  differential, 202–203
  effective annual, 129
  equal, see Equal rate of return principle
  expected, see Expected rate of return
  internal, see Internal rate of return
  nominal, 560
  probability distribution, 24, **40**
  real, 560
  required, see Required rate of return
  risk-free, 26–28
  rule, 197
  simple, 125–126
  standard deviation of, 25–26, **40**
  unique, 206–208
  variance, 25–26, **40**
Ratio(s), 565–600
  absolute liquidity, 572
  acid test, 572
  activity, 581, **595**
  ambiguity of, 568
  analysis, 565–595, **595**
  balance sheet and, 566–567
  company compared to industry by, 585–586
  coverage, 576
  current, 571
  distorting effects of accounting

practices and inflation on,
591–593
du Pont system and, 579–581
financial leverage, 575–577, **595**
financial planning, 565–568,
588–591
income statement and, 566–567
industry comparison, 585–586
leverage, 575–577
limitations, 568, 591–593
liquidity, 570–575, **595**
operating performance and condition analysis by, 588–591
payout, 401–402, 428
profitability analysis by, 577–584
sources and uses statement and,
573–575
sources of, 593–594
summary, 594–595
table of, 569
time comparison, 586–588
as tools of financial analysis,
567–568
Real cost of capital, 551–552, **560**
Real dollars, 538–540, **560**
deflating and, 540
Realizable value, 303
Realized return, 8–9, **15**
Real required rate of return, 541–544,
560
Real risk-free rate, 458, 459, **469**
Real-to-real method, 555–558
Recapitalization, 439–440, **445**
Receipt:
trust, 708–709
warehouse, 708–709
Receivables financing, 705–708
assignment of receivables,
706–707
credit card financing, 708
factoring receivables, 707–708
Receivables investment, 606–608
Receivables management, 658–671
aging schedule and, 669
average collection period and,
668–669
collection policies, 658, 662
control policies, 658, 670–671
credit extension policies, 658–661
discount period, 659
monitoring policies, 658, 668–670
summary, 676
trade credit and, 658
valuation and credit, 662–668
Reed, Ward L., Jr., 653n
Reiling, Henry B., 596n
Reilly, Frank K., 75n
Reinhardt, V. E., 184n
Reorganization, 334–336
absolute priority, 335–336
see also Bankruptcy

**Replacement cost of assets, less
depreciation,** 306–307, **326**
Replacement cycle, 258–259
Required rate of return, 26, **40, 152**
financial leverage and, 36
internal rate of return *vs.,*
148–149
nominal, 541–544, **560**
personal taxes and, 370–372
portfolio, 114–115
real, 541–544, **560**
risk and, 26–28, 111–117
single-security, 113–114
see also Cost of captial
Retained earnings, 304n, 469
cost, 456–460
Retention of earnings, 459–460, **469**
Return on net worth ratio, 578–579
Returns:
expected, 7–9
promised, 8
rate of, *see* Rate of return
realized, 8–9
Revenue bonds, 81
**Revenue-expanding investment
opportunities,** 165, **183**
Revenue-expanding projects, cash
flows for, 231–236
cash outlays expensed for tax
purposes, 234
depreciable cash outlays and, 232
evlauation of, 235–236
important cash flow errors and,
236–244
incremental after-tax operating cash
flows, 234
initial outlay and, 232–234
net working capital requirement
and, 232–234
terminal cash flow, 234–235
Rights, 82, 88–89
Risk, 6–7, **15**
aversion, 23, **40**
beta, *see* Beta
business, 37–38
cash shortage, 637–640
cost of capital, 464–468
default, 686
diversification and, 94–104
exchange, *see* Exchange risk
expected rate of return and, 7–9,
22–26, 32–55, 95–97
financial, 37–38
foreign investment and assessment
of, 743–744
leverage, 32–35
market, 106–111
nonmarket, 106–111
portfolio composition and, 99
premium, 26–28, 37–38, **40,** 456–459
promised return and, 8

realized return and, 8–9
required rate of return and, 26–28,
111–117
of a single security, 104–111
standard deviation, 25–26, **40**
total, 109–111, **119**
Risk-adjusted discount rate, 152
Risk averse, 23, **40**
Risk-free investments, 6, **15**
Risk-free rate, 22–23, 26–28, **40**
real, 458, 459, **469**
Risk premium, 26–28, **40**
**Risk-return method of estimating
financing sources,** 448, 455–459,
469
expected rate of inflation and,
458–459
market risk premium and, 456–459
real risk-free rate and, 458, 459
summary of, 460
Robicheck, Alexander A., 184n
Rodriguez, R. M., 750n
Roll, Richard, 341n
Ross, Stephen, 341n
Rubinstein, Mark, 341n
Rustin, Richard E., 493n

Safety stock, 674–675, **678**
Sale and leaseback arrangement, 483,
502
Salvage value, 229, **247**
after-tax, 230–231
as capital cost, 270–272
financial leases and, 498–499
Sarnat, M., 429n
Schall, Lawrence D., 175n, 364n, 502n,
525n, 531n
Schiff, Michael, 678n
Scholes, M. S., 407, 414
Scott, David F., Jr., 470n
Sears, Gerald A., 75n
Seasonal variation of net cash flow,
626–627
Secondary markets, 60, **75**
direct transactions in, 61
indirect transactions in, 61–63
role of, 64
Secured bonds, 80
Secured loan, 695, **716**
Secured notes, 78–79
Securities, 60–65, **74,** 77–78
bankruptcy and, 334–336
broker, 62–63, **74**
classes of, 60
common stock, *see* Common stock
convertible, 80
dealer, 61–62, **74**
debenture, 80
debt, *see* Debt securities
diversification of, *see* Diversification
dividends, *see* Dividend policy

Securities (*Cont.*)
  equal rate of return principle and,
    see Equal rate of return principle
  equity, *see* Equity securities
  financial, 59, **74**
  fixed-promise, 544–545
  inflation and market value of,
    544–545
  investment bankers and, *see*
    Investment bankers
  negotiable, 78
  nonnegotiable, 78
  notes, 78–79
  perfect markets and, 64–65
  preferred stock, 60, **75,** 81–82
  primary markets and, 63
  purchasing power risk and market
    value of, 548–549
  risk free, 102–104
  secondary markets and, 61–63, 64
  share price and leverage, 352–353
  valuation of, *see* Value of securities
  see also Common stock; Preferred
    stock
Securities Act of 1933, 86
Securities and Exchange Commission,
  U.S. (SEC), 69–71, 86–87, 593
Securities Exchange Act of 1934, 86
Security market line, 111–113, **119**
  cost of capital, 455–459
  investment decisions by the firm
    and, 116–117
  portfolio required rates of return
    and, 114–115
  security pricing on the, 115–116
  single-security required rate of
    return and, 113–114
Segall, Joel, 531n
Selection of investment projects,
  188–221
  accounting rate of return and,
    213–214
  comparing NPV and IRR, 199–210
  internal rate of return and,
    197–199
  investment criteria and, 214–215
  net present value and, 189–197
  payback method and, 210–213
  summary, 215–216
Senbet, L., 383n, 395n
Serial bonds, 81
Shad, John S. R., 532n
Shapiro, A., 750n
Shareholder wealth maximization,
  11–13
  capital structure, 384–391
  comparing NPV with IRR, 200–206
  as goal of financial decisions, 11–13
  internal rate of return, 200–206
  mergers and, 518–522
  net present value, 200–206

  working capital management and,
    614–618
Sharpe, William F., 109n, 111n, 119n
Short-term debt, 78–79
Short-term financing sources,
  611–612, **620.** *See also* Current
  assets, financing
Single period expected rate of return,
  92
Single period investment, 5–6, **15**
Single security, risk of, 104–111
  capital market line and, 104–105
  market and nonmarket, 105–111
  market portfolio and, 104–105
  security market line and, 113–114
Single shift valuation model, 318–321,
  326
  marginal cost of capital and,
    454–455
Sinking fund, 131–132, **152**
Sinking fund bonds, 81
Sinquefield, Rex, 457, 458–459
Small Business Administration (SBA),
  90
Small Business Investment Corpora-
  tion (SBIC), 90
Smidt, Seymour, 183n
Smith, Clifford, 390n, 396n
Smith, Keith V., 620n, 621n
Snyder, Arthur, 678n
Solnik, 742n
Sorensen, Ivar, 502n
Sources and uses statement, 573–575,
  595–596
  liquidity, 573–575
Spontaneous financing sources, 614,
  620
Spontaneous trade credit, 698–699,
  716
Spot exchange market, 724–725, **747**
  changes in, 727
Stable dividend policy, 411, **428**
Standard cash flow series, 207, 208,
  217
**Standard deviation of the rate of
  return,** 25–26, **40**
Statement Studies, 593–594
Stiglitz, J. E., 364n, 396n
Stock:
  common, *see* Common stock
  exchange of, 528–529
  preferred, *see* Preferred stock
  tender offers, 425, 429, 529, 531
  see also Securities
Stock dividend, 422–424, **429**
Stockholders, 47–49
  bondholders and, *see* Bondholder-
    stockholder conflict of interest
Stock repurchase, 424–427, **429**
Stock split, 422–424, **429**
Stoll, Hans R., 75n

Stone, Bernell K., 718n
Structure of firms, 49–51
Substitute proposals, 170, 172–173
Sunk cost, 241, **247**
Swary, I., 414n
Synergy, 522–524, **531**
**Systematic variability of operating
  cash flows,** 634–636, **652**

Taggart, R., 560n
Target capital structure, 439, **445**
  mix of common stock and retained
    earnings and, 440
Tax anticipation notes, 79
Tax credit lease, 483, **502**
  evaluation of, 490–494
Tax-exempt bonds, 81
Taxes:
  cash outlays expensed for purposes
    of, 234
  corporate debt policy and, 376–378
  corporate income, 54–56
  cost of retained earnings, 459–460
  credit lease, 483, 490–494, **502**
  debt policy and, 379–380
  depreciation subsidy, 230, **246,**
    269–270, 486
  dividend policy, 405–410
  form of organization, 45–49
  franchise, 47
  homemade dividends and, 426
  imperfect markets, dividend policy
    and, 406–415
  incremental after-tax operating cash
    flow, 227–230, 234
  interest tax subsidy, 31–32, 356
  investment tax credit, 253–254
  leasing and, 483, 485–486, 490–494
  net personal tax effect, 374–376, **395**
  perfect markets and, 343–361,
    370–380
  personal income, *see* Personal
    income taxes
  required rates of return and,
    370–372
  values of the firm and, 372–376, 379
Taylor, G. A., 153n
Temporary working capital, 609, **620**
Tender offers, 425, **429,** 529, **531**
Terminal cash flow, 247
  cost saving investment projects and,
    230–231
  revenue-expanding projects and,
    234–235
Term loans, 79
Term structure of interest rates,
  687–688, **716**
Time, 5–6
  intervals of, 5
  multiperiod investment, 6
  points in, 5

single period investment, 5–6
Time and compound returns, 124–158
  compound rate of return and future
    value, 125–132
  internal rate of return, 140–144,
    148–149
  net present value, 146–148
  present value, 132–140
  special uses of compounding tables,
    144–146
  summary, 149–151
Time horizon, 242–244
Total assets to net worth ratio,
  576–577
Total risk, 109–111, **119**
Total variation of net cash flow,
  626–627, **652**
Trade credit, 658–671, **678,** 696–698
  availability, 695–697
  cash discount, 659
  collection policies, 658, 662
  cost of, with agreed-on terms,
    696–697
  discretionary, 698, **715**
  explicit cost of, 696–697
  extension policies, 658–659
  line, 658–660
  period, 659
  spontaneous, 698, **716**
  standards, 658, 660–661
  terms, 658–659
  see also Credit; Receivables
Transaction costs, 68–69, **75**
  dividend policy and, 406, 408
Transaction exposure, 737–738,
  747
Translation exposure, 738, **747**
  minimizing, 739–740
Transactions, 60–65
  direct, 60–61, 63, **74**
  indirect, 60–63, **74**
Treasury bills, 79
Treasury bonds, 81
Treasury notes, 80
Trust receipt, 709
Turnover ratios, 581*n*, **595**

Underwriting, 84
  regular, 87–88
  syndicate, 85
Undivided account, 85
Unequal lives, problem of, 255–265
  common life and, 258–259
  comparison of investment
    proposals, 257–258
  equalizing, 259–265
  replacement cycles and, 258–259
  specifying cash flows and, 259–260
  summary, 273–274
  uniform annual equivalents and,
    260–265

**Uniform annual equivalent cash
  flow,** 145–146, **152**
Uniform annual equivalent (UAE)
  cash flow for the proposal,
    260–263, **274**
  economic life of an investment and,
    265–273
  problems with, 263–265
Uniform Commercial Code (UCC),
  705
Unlevered firm, 21, **40**
  total risk and, 37–38
Unlimited liability, 46
Unsecured bank credit, 697–700
  commercial note, 697–699
  compensating balances and,
    699–700
  installment loan, 699
Unsecured loans, 695–696, **716**
Unsecured notes, 79
Upton, Charles, 502*n*

Valuation:
  bond, 308–312
  common stock, 313–322, 452–455
  credit and, 662–668
  firm, 302–303, 322–324, **326**
  inventory management and,
    675–676
  model, 64–65, **75,** 308–310, 312–313,
    325, 452–455
  options, 336–341
  preferred st ock, 312–313
  replacement cost, 306–307, **326**
  securities, 303–305, 308–322, **326**
**Valuation method of estimating
  financing sources,** 448, 452–455,
  469
  constant growth model, 454
  single shift model, 454–455
  summary of, 460
  zero growth model, 453
Valuation model, 64, **75**
Value, 303–308
  book, 304–305
  constant growth, 315–318, **325,**
    454
  firm, 302–303, 322–324, **326,**
    372–376
  future, *see* Future value
  discounted cash flow and, 307–308
  liquidating, 305–306
  market price and, 303–304
  net present, *see* Net present value
  par, 304*n*, 305
  present, 132–140, **152,** 307–308
  purchasing power risk, 548–549,
    560
  realizable, 303
  replacement cost of assets, less
    depreciation, 306–307

  salvage, 230–231, 247
  security, 303–322, **326**
  single-shift model, 318–321, **326,**
    454–455
  Value Line, 457
  Value of a firm, 302, 322–324, **326**
    bondholder-stockholder conflict of
      interest and, 391
    illustration of, 379
    under financial distress and bank-
      ruptcy, 382–383
    without personal taxes, 372–373
    with personal taxes, 373–376
  Value of securities, 303–304, 308–322,
    326
    application of, 321–322
    bond valuation model, 308–312
    common stock valuation model,
      313–315
    discounted cash flow and, 307–308
    options and, 336–341
    preferred stock valuation model,
      312–313
    zero growth model, 315–321
  Vanderwicker, P., 502*n*
  Van Horne, James C., 184*n*, 561*n*, 621*n*
  Variable expenditures, 24, **40**
  Variation:
    cash flow, 626–628
    intra-monthly cash flow, 626–627
    random cash flow, 626–627,
      634–637, **652**
    rate of return, 22–26, 34–35
    seasonal cash flow, 626–627
    systematic cash flow, 634–637, **652**
    total cash flow, 626–627
  Variance of the rate of return, 25–26,
    40
  Venture capital, 90
  Vermaelen, T., 425*n*, 529*n*, 532*n*
  Vertical expansion, 511, **531**

  Wall Street Journal, The, 12, 489*n*
  Walter, J. E., 429*n*
  Warehouse receipt, 709
  Warner, Jerold, 383*n*, 390*n*, 396*n*
  Warrants, 82
  Wealth, 11, **15,** 16–30, 36
    financial leverage and, 36
    investor, 11, 59
    market value and, 28–30
    maximization, 11–13. *See also*
      Shareholder wealth maximization
    required rate of return, risk, and,
      26–28, 36
  Weingartner, H. Martin, 184*n*, 212*n*,
    295*n*
  Wendt, Paul, 326*n*
  Weston, J. Fred, 184*n*
  Williams, John D., 184*n*, 313, 315*n*
  Working capital, 20–21, **40,** 603, **620**

Working capital (*Cont.*)
  net, 21, **40,** 233–234, 242, **246,** 603, **620**
  permanent, 609–610
  temporary, 610–611
Working capital management, 601–624, **620**
  accounts payable and, 612
  cash cycle and, 604–605
  cash flow effect and, 614–618
  discount rate effect and, 614–618
  excessive assets, 609
  flexible financing sources, 612–613
  inflexible financing sources, 612–613

inventory investment, 608–609
investment effect and, 614–618
liquid asset investment, 605–606
long-term financing sources, 611–612
nonspontaneous financing sources, 613–614
receivables investment, 606–608
shareholder wealth maximization and, 614–618
short-term financing sources, 611–612
short-term loans payable and, 612

spontaneous financing sources, 614
summary, 618–619
terminology, 603–604
variation in current assets and, 609–611
why firms invest in current assets, 604–609
Workout, 333–334

Yield to maturity, 450, **469**

Zero growth valuation model, 315
  marginal of cost of capital and, 453
Zvi, Bodie, 560n